STUDIES IN PUBLIC COMMUNICATION

A. William Bluem, General Editor

PERSUASION

The Theory and Practice of Manipulative Communication

STUDIES IN PUBLIC COMMUNICATION

MASS MEDIA AND COMMUNICATION

Edited by Charles S. Steinberg

THE LANGUAGES OF COMMUNICATION

A Logical and Psychological Examination
by George N. Gordon

TO KILL A MESSENGER

Television News and the Real World
by William Small

INTERNATIONAL COMMUNICATION

Media—Channels—Functions
Edited by Heinz-Dietrich Fischer and John Calhoun Merrill

THE COMMUNICATIVE ARTS

An Introduction to Mass Media
by Charles S. Steinberg

PERSUASION

The Theory and Practice of Manipulative Communication
by George N. Gordon

MASS MEDIA AND THE SUPREME COURT

The Legacy of the Warren Years
by Kenneth S. Devol

STUDIES IN PUBLIC COMMUNICATION

PERSUASION

The Theory and Practice of Manipulative Communication

by

GEORGE N. GORDON

COMMUNICATION ARTS BOOKS

HASTINGS HOUSE, PUBLISHERS • NEW YORK

First Edition

Published simultaneously in Canada by Saunders of Toronto, Ltd., Don Mills, Ontario

Library of Congress Catalog Card Number: 78-163184

Cloth Edition ISBN: 8038-5774-8
Text Edition ISBN: 8038-5777-2

DESIGNED BY AL LICHTENBERG
PRINTED IN THE UNITED STATES OF AMERICA

This book is dedicated to the many millions of people who, throughout the ages and up to the present, have been persuaded to death.

CONTENTS

Part Three
PSYCHOLOGICAL PERSPECTIVES

Part Four
CONTEMPORARY DYNAMICS

Part Five
HUMANISTIC PERSUASION

PREFACE

AT FIRST GLANCE, this volume will probably give the reader the distinct impression that it is about everything in the world *except* persuasion. At second glance too. This is partly because persuasion is a diverting topic, and partly because persuasion often concerns matters apparently not connected with it. This is the fundamental irony of the topic to which I have set myself. Some of the most effective insights into how and why people manage to persuade one another of something—whether involving confidence-men, scientists or saints—are achieved accidentally or refracted from events that apparently have nothing to do with persuasion. Under these circumstances, therefore, much of what I (and other students of the subject) interpret as persuasion is considered by many as mere communication or the transmission of one or another insignificant aspect of culture from person to person.

This is probably the main reason that books like this one, that is, reconstructions of the entire issue of persuasion as a social activity, are so rare as almost not to exist at all. Most people interested in this phenomenon, in all probability, have displayed more intelligence but less nerve than I have, and have been wise enough to avoid so immense a subject, except in passing or in delimited contexts.

In the days of my youth, it was fashionable to associate "persuasion" with "propaganda" and analyze discrete intentional messages (usually commercial advertising, Nazi and/or Communist polemics) according to a dozen or so more-or-less semantic tricks or techniques that were, in effect, supposed to demonstrate how stupid the people were who believed such messages. The situation is entirely different today. With the passage of time, we have discovered that there are not ten or twelve rhetorical propaganda devices or techniques but, probably, many thousands of general manipulative methods of communication, of which those involving verbal communications constitute but a fraction.

The immediate impetus behind this book originates in a popular concern, expressed today across intellectual disciplinary lines, that we live at present in an "age of persuasion" in which our dispositions and actions are somehow diabolically controlled by others, and that new instruments of technology (chemical and electronic, particularly) and mass communications will, in the future, make good a science-fiction promise of mass thought control. The following chapters are a response to this concern that, the reader will note, neither confirms nor denies its pith, but hopefully shifts the argument into new, different and more productive keys—or chords.

Antecedent to the discussions that follow is a wealth of admirable groundwork laid by such social scientists as Hadley Cantril, Harold Laswell, Bernard Berelson, Leonard Doob, Carl Hovland, Paul Lazarsfeld and numerous others. In the background, also, are the interesting—and today amusing—contributions of the Institute for Propaganda Analysis, active before World War II, that, in its peculiar way, served in its time a persuasive purpose of considerable cultural importance. Influences from Europe, particularly those of various existential novelists and playwrights, and the political writings of José Ortega y Gassett have also contributed to the general configurations of this volume.

Next to these pioneers, I feel small indeed, because *en masse* they constitute an echelon of modern scholars and writers who had vision enough to pick up many loose and neglected strands of a once discredited discipline: the study of crowd behavior. Their precedents came mainly from French speculation during the nineteenth century that were dropped hastily when many new (and more attractive) topics entered the world of the behavioral sciences. They possessed both the intelligence and conviction to recognize that problems of mass persuasion were likely to be of greater immediate concern to the survival of Western civilization than other apparently pressing aspects of sociology, psychology and political science. They were, of course, dead right. And they are still right, although the issue of Nazi persuasion, and others about which they were at the time concerned, are today mostly academic. And the old notions of propaganda to which they addressed themselves have been superseded by new and more sophisticated concepts that include numerous aspects of social intercourse broadly construed as persuasive without being specifically propagandistic.

At this early point in this book, I must emphatically discourage the reader from continuing one paragraph further if he expects the slick or neat articulation of theories or laws of persuasion to emerge from the pages ahead. He is bound to be disappointed, although, if so warned and he continues reading, he will be exposed to many different kinds of social theories and even a few prospective laws. Nor should he expect to encounter a list of numbered tricks or techniques on how to improve persuasion, see through it or resist it. Many attempts at this sort of categorization have been tried, and most of them have not been saisfactory for long, except for those poor souls who teach communications theory and need lists of things for purposes of examining students—as well as theories and laws about which to lecture.

To comprehend persuasion as we are competent to describe it today, one requires a fairly wide background of interests and the innate (or cultivated) tendency to favor complexities of processes over simple provisional truths and temporarily adequate generalizations. If nothing else is demonstrated by this book, it illustrates that the history of persuasion is *all* history; the psychology of persuasion is *all* psychology; the politics of persuasion are *all* politics; and so forth into the future, as well as through the entire past of civilization.

I am calling for a tall order: the description of the *entire* elephant, not the various ropes, fans, trees and hoses of which he is fabricated. A good deal of intelligent and responsible speculation has been given every part of the beast's anatomy with different degrees of success. Some of it has led to experiment and theory in a social psychological mode concerning how and why people hold certain dispositions. Much of the best of it has related persuasion to cultural variables of special interest to sociologists. And it is sociological methods of study that are employed primarily today in the fields of advertising and public opinion research. International persuasion remains a significant, but often discrete, component of diplomatic and foreign policy studies. Broad currents of persuasion that have influenced ways of life in the past are currently the province of historians. Processes of persuasion through which individuals and culture are passing at any moment often are formulated most clearly by graphic artists, novelists, painters, playwrights and poets.

Occasionally, one also finds an awareness of these processes in the thinking of persuaders themselves: advertisers, public relations personnel, broadcasters and entertainers. But, in my opinion, this group is protected or insulated by peculiar quirks of perception (relating, I assume, to the necessity of sacrificing long visions for short term goals) from observations of more than transient interest into why and how the manipulation they they attempt does or does not work.

A voluminous literature, of coursc, is available to the student of persuasion who is interested primarily in its involvement with history, psychology, politics, sociology, international studies, psycho-biology and numerous other fields. This inquiry provides the source material for much of the content of the following pages. This literature will continue to grow in scope and sophistication, providing deeper and wider foundations for observations like those that follow, until this particular book will, hopefully, become obsolete. At that time, some other impudent observer will attempt (more successfully than I have, I imagine) to bring it all together once again into a more definitive work than both our present knowledge and my limited competences permit at his moment in history. My entry—this book—is, therefore, provisional, designed in large measure to call the attention of those who, like myself, are frequently preoccupied with trees, to the awesome presence of the forest.

In its way, this is also a book of mythology, because, as we shall shortly confirm, myths and symbols are among the most ubiquitous vehicles of persuasion. For this reason, and from the outset, I have attempted to use the term "myth" in as neutral a value sense as possible, which, incidentally, is difficult to accomplish consistently. Myths are formulated in all cultures, especially and including ours. They may or may not refer to real events and/or real people, past or present. They invariably reflect a form of cultural consensus beyond "common wisdom" and constitute the milieu for many perceptions we receive of the world around us. In the latter part of the volume, I have attempted to differentiate for purposes of clarity differences between "myths," "illusions" and "delusions." I have also, in Part Three, found it necessary to define distinctively what I have, up to that point, mainly called "dispositions" by delineating discrete concepts of "beliefs," "attitudes" and "opinions." But the reader who bears with me will, I am sure, follow these and similar methods in madness—and madness in methods.

Since I am discussing methods, let me add a word about the footnotes: they appear on the respective pages, not bunched at the ends of chapters or elsewhere, with good reason. For students, they may provide ready references to sources and topics discussed in the text, along with some guidance concerning what to look for from these materials in relevant contexts. I shall attempt, as well, to use the footnotes for the purposes of explanation, elucidation, occasional digression, and the introduction into the book of some personal matters that may interest the reader as much as they interest me. Under no circumstances do I, however, wish to divert the studious but hurried reader from the main points of discussions and arguments. For this reason, the personal pronoun "I" will drop, at the end of this Preface, from the text into the footnotes, and there it will stay to the end. Because this has been a matter of on-going (but friendly) dispute with my publisher, let no reader imagine that I am attempting to appear erudite or pseudo-scholarly (or dull) because of the relatively fine print at the bottom of the coming pages. The footnotes are intended to be read by those interested in further comments upon the matter discussed, but passed over mercilessly by those who are not.

The structure of the book reflects a methodology that I have found useful in my many years of the study of persuasion; others may not find it so. The first chapters make up a general, but vital, introduction to the study of the intentional aspects of communication and the history of persuasion. The *Logical Perspectives* are mainly historical and analytical in thrust, centering upon how and when persuasion occurs in our society, and how it is employed in our major cultural institutions. The *Psychological Perspectives* are concerned largely with discrete processes that persuade people to modify dispositions and/or change actions. In the present state of our understanding of these matters, I have also attempted to explain the reasons why these modifications may or may not occur, according to current psychological theory.

I wish that I might now affirm that Part Four, on *Contemporary Dynamics,* is a one-to-one application of the analyses of Parts Two and Three. But this is not the case. The fault lies in our stars, not in me. Our capacity for social insight has not yet reached so fine or regular a degree of development, I fear. What Part Four centers on and examines, *in reference* to Parts Two and Three, are some (certainly not all) contemporary beliefs, ideas and myths concerning persuasion relevant to matters that are of immediate social, political and cultural concern to Western civilization at the time of writing. Part Five takes us to the uncomfortable brink of the future and offers possibilities for tomorrow, one of which is that the human race may just possibly be persuaded to survive, despite evidence to the contrary.

Throughout this book, I shall not attempt to conceal my biases or pretend to a banal stereotype of the detached scholar traveling objectively through stacks of data that do not affect his life. I am convinced that all scholarship, properly so-called, may (and possibly should) affect life. The closest professional interests I presently experience are also those personally dearest to me. When, in the text to come, I feel a position of judgment or value, albeit arbitrary, must be taken, I shall take it, hoping that the reader may, if inclined, disagree with it and call me a fool. For guidance in this aspect of both my teaching and writing, I owe credit or blame to two scholars with whom *I* frequently deeply disagree but whose brave spirits I deeply admire: the late C. Wright Mills and Claude Lévi-Strauss.

I shall certainly make few friends by observing at the outset that I believe that one of today's major intellectual tragedies is our beloved, sacred and static disciplinary model of knowledge, given us by tradition, that scholars are usually frightened to modify a jot. One aspect of this state of affairs is the galloping over-specialization into which many of our potentially best minds have been rushed, minds that might have been philosophical in the sweetest sense of the word, but which have ended up merely technically agile within narrow limits.

I shall discuss this matter further subsequently. But it is important in this Preface that one assumption derived from this view be made clear, namely that the study of persuasion is *not a discipline,* and its comprehension and understanding requires more from its student than special knowledge of, say, history, social psychology and/or the political sciences. Simply because nearly all speculation about it to date—with the exception of Jacques Ellul's French volume—has been more or less uni-disciplinary and invariably specialized, this book, for better or worse, is bound, therefore, to be different.

A book is an end product of many activities, personal, intellectual and technical. I have already indicated some of the major influences upon me in the examination of persuasion in its many aspects. My former professor and colleague, Charles A. Siepmann, led me to the study of this aspect of culture about eighteen years ago and kept me at it until he knew that I could not longer run away and would remain at my own accord. At New York University, where we worked on a self-directed and abortive project, John J. Sullivan led me to refine what had been, until then, a non-productive study of social psychology. Irving A. Falk, a co-author of previous books, has allowed me to test some of my notions on his agile brain. The late John Mulholland, an unlettered but consummate expert in the field of magic, provided an example of how a free intellect may often be constricted by the academy. I must once more also express my gratitude to William Sears Jr. of NYU for his lessons in scholarly engagement and accomplishment, no matter how difficult or discouraging the task. And hundreds of anonymous teachers, whose names I cannot list, shared their experience, strength and hope with me in considering social dynamics of a kind that cannot appear in books. Russell Neale was present at both the beginning and end as always, and my gratitude to him remains a condition of the status quo.

I write in longhand by pencil, and my cats often chew up pieces of manuscript, but Mary Brophy seems invariably to come up with a creditable version of my scribbles. My gratitude goes to her and Harriet and Mary Jane Griffith for their pains in preparing the final draft of this manuscript. Most non-fiction writers thank their wives for aid and comfort. But I think I shall simply reaffirm here that, after more than twenty-one years, I love her.

I shall now, as promised, retreat to the footnotes, only to emerge occasionally at the behest of irresistible temptation. But before I go, let me affirm that everything inadequate about this volume is entirely my fault, although I am responsible for some of its better parts as well.

July, 1971
Forest Hills, New York.

GEORGE N. GORDON

INTRODUCTION

We are fairly persuaded that the technologies upon which the public media are founded are "neutral"—that they are nothing more than electrical, mechanical and/or chemical extensions of man's communicative power, and can therefore be no better or worse than the men who create the message they carry. Regrettably, the acceptance of this conventional wisdom in institutions of higher learning poses some quandaries for teachers of public communications, who are hardly encouraged by the fact that many in the university who defend freedom in their own classrooms are quite willing to proscribe what their confreres in schools or departments of communication should teach.

Captivated with the apparent logic of such pithy observations as "it's not media which matter, it is what men *do* with them," a growing number of academicians are now joining with the many zealous professionals who already are insisting that media teachers simply create future "communicators" in their own mold. What is clearly implied (where it is not forthrightly spoken) in the demands of both groups is that the teacher of communications tell students not how to use *media*, but how to use *people who attend media*. In practice, perhaps, such distinction may not seem significant, but as an educational approach this limited conception of Teacher-as-Persuader threatens grave consequences. For nowhere is the philosophical habit of thought and a spirit of fair-mindedness more urgently required than among those who will frame the nature and content of the public media in the final quarter of this century. Put simply, many assumptions now being drilled into the minds of future "communicators" could—if they become the basis of future practice—create incalculable long-range damage to the free society.

This argument in no way implies that the philosopher's concern over media purpose and direction is not an essential aspect of the quest for some deeper serenity and order in human affairs. Neither does it release the social and behavioral scientist from his continuing obligation to suggest ways in which media should help us to discover efficient and economic, but ultimately humane, ways of solving problems of the individual and of society. Nor, of course, does it remotely suggest that the artist who asks media to present some vision of the ideal and the beautiful should be slighted.

Yet once outside his own field of specialization, each of these will tend to forget the legitimate standards of inquiry and principles of creativity he would set for his own field. And since none of them holds the keys to the kingdom, their inevitable demand that media advocate special views in narrow situations at single points in history's flow is of little help to the professional communications educator.

The dilemma is thus posed. The teacher of communications dares not turn from his conviction that men can, and must, employ the media to more sensible and long-range human ends. Hence he cannot yield his prerogatives in establishing what is to be taught, and how, to the immediate requirements—however urgent—of the practitioner. Yet he can hardly allow approaches and objectives of his field to be determined by colleagues from other disciplines with limited knowledge of communications art and process, and no comprehension (let alone appreciation) of the dynamics—the forms, practices, procedures and institutions—which have grown up within our vast media system.

It is clear that any philosophical approach to higher education in the field demands an ordering which wholly will satisfy neither practitioner nor academician. Central to all thought in this matter, however, is *media-orientation*. The teacher's first intellectual commitments should be to the reality of the interlocking systems we call "public communications." He must first gain insight into the principles and pragmatics of their operation, and then turn to reflection upon how these relate to the best (and worst) that man has thought, said and done. This ordering of the significance of his knowledge and experience is not simply a preference—it is a law.

Granting this—what should a teacher of communications be able to do? Nothing more than recognize talent and encourage artfulness, or where there is potential greatness—artlessness. If he can do this, he will be useful. But if he can develop the habit of philosophical thought within himself he will achieve excellence, for this is a matter which is not so much taught as it is conveyed. In no other way can he—or any of his earnest colleagues who so sincerely want to convert him to their view—transcend the role of teacher as mere persuader.

Studies in Public Communication was designed to assist in implementation of the Communications educator's reach toward the philosopher's habit—toward the holistic view of process and system in the technological extensions of the art and science of human communication. Consonant with this aim is the work to follow—Dr. George Gordon's second contribution to the series. In setting forth essential philosophical questions regarding the communicative activity men call *persuasion*, Dr. Gordon tacitly assumes the reader's familiarity with "how to" aspects of media technics and also with those endless and often counter-productive discussions of "ethics" and "responsibilities" in public communications—where one man's piety is another man's poison. For such breadth of view we are grateful—as we might be for this book, which may serve as a manifesto for all who try to inspire by teaching.

A. Wm. Bluem, Ph.D.
Professor of Media Studies
Syracuse University

Part One

BACKGROUNDS

Wherefore, from Magic I seek assistance,
That many a secret perchance I reach
Through spirit-power and spirit-speech
And thus the bitter task forego
Of saying the things I do not know,—
That I may detect the inmost force
Which binds the world, and guides its course;
Its germs, productive powers explore,
And rummage in empty words no more.

Goethe's *Faust*, Act I, Scene I.

The beginning of wisdom is to understand reality.

Abba Eban

Chapter 1

THE NATURE OF COMMUNICATIONS

One could almost say that progress in cooperation (has) varied in inverse ratio to progress in communications.

Arthur Koestler.

WHAT are communications?

Richards' answer, given decades ago, is a convincing one, probably quite correct and useful for lecturers, professors, advertising authorities and people who specialize in entertainment and educational gadgetry. "Communications," he wrote, "take place when one mind so acts upon its environment that another mind is influenced, and in that other mind an experience occurs which is like the experience in the first mind, and is caused in part by that experience." [1] In spite of its potential utility, the psychological bias of this statement has prevented its general acceptance by communications generalists who prefer more logically oriented formulations or models.

The most popular one in use today is a direct descendant of an abstract formulation that had come into common discourse by way of the Bell Telephone Company and what seemed, in 1947, to be a highly promising approach to communications. It was in vogue during the first two decades after World War II,[2] but is now less fashionable and often discussed by contemporary thinkers with skepticism.[3] The model posited six elements involved in every act of communication—a number which might easily be doubled or halved—and was based on the six actual *physical* components used in transmitting and receiving telephone messages, or were in 1947. Because the formulation was based on tangibles, it seemed eminently rea-

[1] I. A. Richards, *Principles of Literary Criticism* (New York: Harcourt, Brace and Co., 1947), p. 177.

sonable as an abstraction that might apply to other non-telephonic communications, the components of which were not physical.

The model was comprised of 1.) a Source; 2.) an Encoder; 3.) a Message; 4.) a Channel; 5.) a Decoder; and 6.) a Receiver. This concept was modified almost immediately by a key notion in Wiener's cybernetic theories known as 7.) Feedback, familiar, these days, to most high school students and employed also in contemporary commercial jargon.[4] The major advantage of the model, beyond the obvious fact that categorization permits simple quantification, was (and is) that it yields a neat diagram of the so-called "Communication Process." (It is generally believed, by teachers in particular, that if a concept lends itself to a diagram, it is first, worth teaching and, second, probably true.) The diagram, because it contains seven elements that may be shifted around in various ways, takes many forms,[5] but in its simplest manifestation it usually looks more or less like this:

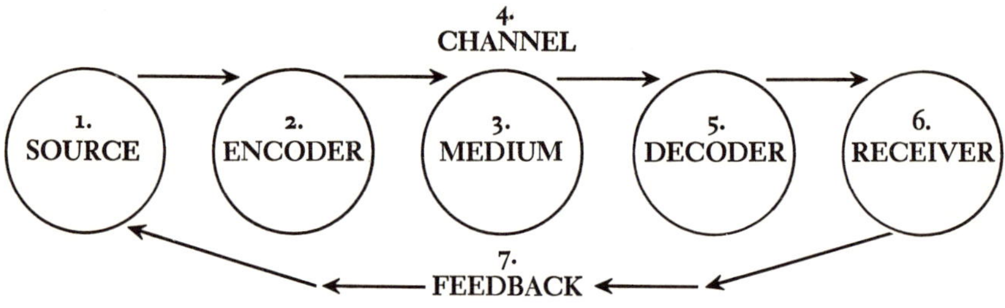

The Source is frequently pictured as a microphone; the Encoder is a telegraph key (or something); the Medium is a telegraph pole; the Decoder is a vacuum tube; and the Receiver is an ear. Significantly, few explainers of this process have found pictorial equivalents for the function of Feedback, even though it is one of the most important elements of the kind of me-

---

2 For the story of the rise of this model, see David K. Berlo, *The Process of Communication* (New York: Holt Rinehart and Winston, 1961), pp. 28–38.

3 Typical of these discontents is that of Ludwig von Bertalanffy, *General System Theory* (New York: George Braziller, 1968), pp. 100–101, which asks serious questions of all similar models of "systems" of various kinds, a problem (and thinker) to which (and whom) we shall return from time to time throughout this volume.

4 See Norbert Wiener, *Cybernetics* (Cambridge, Mass.: The MIT Press, 1965), pp. 6–8, for the seminal description of "feedback" in the days that it needed to be explained. Lest any sentimentalists or young people adhere to the belief that Wiener's concept of feedback was purely mechanical or mathematical, note that Dr. Wiener applied the concept with poetic abandon to learning theory, biology, social processes, animal and human psychology, and even discoursed in broad terms about "negative feedback" in this early volume in the library of systemization.

5 See Berlo, *op. cit.*, pp. 72, 80, 82, and 105, for some interesting examples.

chanical or electronic communications performed in calculating machines or computers.

When the communication involved, however, relates to *interpersonal* human communication (with all its intellectual and emotional impedimenta), we are obviously dealing with a complex process, so complex that it cannot be described except crudely as a "reaction." Hence, this author's suggestion that much interpersonal Feedback appears to be accomplished by Extra Sensory Perception,[6] a method of communication that most responsible adults refuse to believe exists. The concept of Feedback in this model, of course (as well as other ideas it implies), illustrates clearly the fundamental fallacy of transferring mechanical models to human affairs, a problem which will continue to arise in the pages to come and will not simply "go away" because it has been entered as a *caveat* here.

The major advantage of what we shall call the "telephone company" model of the communications process is its simplicity. No doubt, also, it displays a certain utility in describing the shared experience noted by Richards in simplistic human situations where only one or two dimensions, or types of awareness, are involved, as in the conduct of a formal gathering of corporation directors or a *pro forma* committee or faculty meeting at a decadent university. Knowledge of the categories, in these cases, may speed up procedures and limit the roles which group members play in the meeting and prevent digression, just as it stifles any form of non-conformity and the possibility of inspiration.

As an aid to understanding communications related to persuasion, it offers little except a *schema* to which to refer, *post hoc*, certain human transactions in order to clarify the same data elicited by the ancient question that men since Plato have put to each other, phrased one way or another, "Who says what to whom, with what effect and how?" [7] and presently attributed to Laswell, Cooley and others.

Vertical and Horizontal Ubiquity

Many reasons may be formulated for maintaining such constructions of the act of communication, either in a simple psychological formulation like Richards', or in the slightly more logical elaboration of the telephone company paradigm. Certain types of psychological speculations are difficult, if not impossible, to formulate unless one construes communication as shared

[6] See George N. Gordon, "What Media Am Not" in *Educational Technology*, July, 1969, p. 29, for what I thought was a little good-natured kidding of conventional communications theorists when I wrote the article. I discovered, as the result of this enterprise, that one person should not joke about another person's spiritual beliefs, and "feedback" appears to be just that to many.

[7] See George N. Gordon, *The Languages of Communication* (New York: Hastings House, Publishers, 1969), pp. 23–25. Reference to this volume will henceforth appear as G.N.G., *L C*, followed by relevant page and/or chapter numbers.

experience in a more or less mystical-causal relationship between individuals. Most responsible considerations of the phenomenon of human laughter, no matter how sophisticated, usually start with assumptions as naïve as Richards'.[8] We have noted the utilitarianism of the logically oriented model in human interactions of a mechanistic sort. It is far more useful in communications between men and machines, especially when components of the diagram are transcribed into mathematical abstractions. It may necessarily be involved in *all* communications between machine and machine, such as computers, or in relating one phase of a mechanism's activity to another.

Utility is the best defense for both of these concepts, and concepts they are. Neither has, as yet, been articulated in a general enough manner to call it a "theory," although the latter is sometimes referred to as a "communication theory." The terminology is adequate as long as the definition of the word "communications" is kept within the limits of those activities that can clearly be contained (either quantitatively or qualitatively) within the seven categories listed above. Once we run into—as we shall almost immediately—transactions which overlap these categories, or which are beside the point of them (more frequently the case), the power of the model as a theory diminishes.[9]

When we say that communications occur both *vertically* and *horizontally*, we mean, roughly, over time and through space. Probably because modern instruments of communication have achieved their most spectacular successes by conquering the limitations of space—via television, radio, jet aircraft, or some other attractive technology—most of us test our ideas of what communications are against horizontal factors within a small vertical range—for instance, the miracle of television transmission from the moon to our living room (enormously horizontal; instantaneously vertical), or pictures of the moon's surface in a color film reproduction of a weekly magazine (enormously horizontal; short-term vertical).

The vertical or time dimension of communications is, however, less insistently with us in our daily run-of-the-mill affairs. The long deceased Harpo Marx makes us chuckle at a showing of a film on television, perhaps, or we grow nostalgic as we look at a photograph of the student, soldier or gay blade we thought we once were. Time may become critical when the

[8] See G.N.G., *L C*, Chapter 15 on communicating humor, and Chapter 17 of this volume, to note how few authorities over the centuries have even attempted to answer the question of how laughter is communicated in logical terms. They prefer the easier inquiry into why men laugh, to which one can bring much colorful speculation.

[9] Were the telephone company model of communications processes merely regarded as a theory, it might be of little nuisance to contemporary discourse. It is, however, frequently also treated as a *law* (which, once again, it *may be* if our definition of "communications" is once again constricted and pruned to certain mechanisms in physics) by, of all people, social and behavioral scientists. For a sensible review of how communications relate to valid emerging concepts of information theory, see J. R. Pierce, *Symbols, Signals and Noise* (New York: Harper and Row, Publishers, 1961), particularly pp. 19–63.

impact of a classic poem or symphony reaches us. It is a *dominant* factor as we contemplate the ruins of Carthage or consider that the "New Bridge" over the Tiber was built many centuries ago. Or, at least, time in its psychological manifestation appears more critical than space in these instances. But even here, salted a bit with the existential thrust of much contemporary musing, horizontal communications more often seem important than vertical ones. One contemplates *The Last Supper now*, and, in this particular instance, time, the main channel of communications which brings the fresco to our consciousness, also assumes the mantle of an insidious *destroyer* of communication or information, as the mural almost crumbles to dust before our eyes.

Simple but accurate vertical and horizontal dimensions are possible to limn for most every manner by which man communicates. The full charting of either or both dimensions would be an endless task. But once one begins to evaluate our world from both of these perspectives, one discovers an awesome but elementary self-evident truth: little that man does (except think) as a social creature is *not* (variantly vertical and horizontal) communication, even if we exclude (gratuitously) all forms of mystical behavior, psychological and physical self-stimulation, and solitary, private actions which are never perceived by another human being.[10] What is awesome about this state of affairs is simply that the study of communications, like the study of man, *is* (in theory) the study of man himself as a social creature in all of his activities through all the span of time he has been on earth.

To categorize, therefore, the specific ways that so ubiquitous an activity occurs in civilization is in itself a major intellectual task, and for this service we are in the debt of Jurgen Ruesch upon whose analysis of the "varieties of approaches" (Ruesch's felicitous term) the list that follows is based.[11] Starting points for communications studies may include:

1. Cybernetic theory.
2. Mathematical "information" theory.
3. Computer technology.
4. Philology and historical linguistics.
5. Technology of communications instruments.

---

[10] Such an assumption is, of course, unwarranted. Much praying involves social interaction. All forms of masturbation may have eventual effects in communciation with others. The relationship of animals, wild and domestic, to men remains largely a puzzle, but a killer shark can communicate with an unwary swimmer, and my wife appears to communicate effectively with our five cats.

[11] My main source is Dr. Ruesch's article "Clinical Science and Communication Theory" in Floyd W. Matson and Ashley Montagu, *The Human Dialogue* (New York: The Free Press, 1967), pp. 51–70, in which Ruesch, one of the most astute and least recognized communications theorists in the field, lists, according to my count, forty "approaches." Ruesch, primarily a psychiatrist, has formulated them as disciplines: what we study at present. I have revised this perspective slightly and added one or two approaches implicit in Ruesch's text but not explicitly covered.

6. Epistemology of scientific inquiry.
7. Philosophy of a generalized communications theory.
8. Neuropsychology of organisms and organs.
9. Sensory process psychophysiology.
10. Psychopharmacology of drugs.
11. Normal psychological processes.
12. Complex and abnormal psychological manifestations.
13. Animal communications.
14. Small group interactions.
15. Mass (small source—large audience) communications.
16. Phonetics and structural linguistics.
17. Semantics of language.
18. Linguistic anthropology of symbols.
19. Persuasion for behavioral change.
20. Persuasion for ideational change.[12]
21. Commercial communications.
22. Family interrelationships.
23. Communications for therapy.
24. Psychoanalytic symbolism (therapeutic and critical).
25. Community relations.
26. Neurological pathology of communication organs.
27. Plastic and graphic arts.
28. Dance and pantomime.
29. Theatrical performances.
30. Music.
31. Architecture.
32. Decorative arts.
33. Handcrafts.
34. Costume design.
35. Legal manipulation.
36. Financial maneuvering.
37. Political arts.
38. Small group games.
39. Participant sport activities.
40. Observer sport activities.
41. Cooking and eating relations.
42. Sexual pleasure relationships.
43. Procreative sexual relationships.

This list may be far from all-inclusive, although it will be difficult to find any form of communication in which people indulge that could *not* be placed in one or more category. Also, the categories overlap considerably, but little more so than the gray areas that indicate the perimeters of ac-

[12] Please do not be misled by the apparent naïvete (Reusch's and mine) of limiting (for purposes of the purview) "persuasion" to two "approaches." Persuasion of one sort or another threads its way through this list, particularly as it applies to numbers 4, 5, 6, 7, 10, 12, 14, 15, 16, 17, 18, 21, 22, 23, 24, 25, 28, 29, 30, 32, 35, 36, 37, 38, and 43, as well as numbers 19 and 20.

cepted disciplines of inquiry or study in our literature, academies and professions.

A cursory study of this list demonstrates, if nothing else, both the horizontal and vertical range—and unstudied potentials—of "communications approaches" to man's intellectual life. In the light of the diversity of interests and styles of these forty-three entries, one wonders, not about the validity, but about the practicality, of Ruesch's deadpan comment, "After many years of cross-fertilization of disciplines and interdisciplinary study of communication, now we have reached the point where we need a more unitary approach to communication." [13] To achieve this end, if it is achievable, Ruesch correctly stresses the need, first, to study the *persons* communicating, next to turn to the problem of content, and lastly (and least important), to "bother with the technology of communication," [14] in his words.

Because our accepted priority of inquiry has been for the past generation exactly the inversion of the hierarchy suggested by Ruesch (technology first, content second, and people last[15]), we have, with few exceptions, learned little from the many lessons that the history of communications (the sum total of experience available in all of these categories) might have taught us concerning the connection between actions and reactions, causes and effects, and stimuli and responses fused through a span of time or space.

Duality: Logics and Psychologics

Another problem facing our best attempts to design reasonable boundaries for the study of communications (a prior condition for the treatment of persuasion) is a wonderful intellectual enigma involving all manner of human inquiry, but which is of more than ordinary interest to communications scholars, mainly because its tyranny is so rarely noticed in their considerations and does do much damage to their attempts at research of various kinds. The writer has referred to it elsewhere as "villainous," and has discoursed on it at some length.[16] Discussion here will necessarily be brief—and inconclusive.

No examination of any facet of the mind life of modern man, particu-

---

[13] Reusch, *op. cit.*, p. 58.

[14] *Ibid.*, p. 60.

[15] The priorities of neo- or popularized McLuhanism seem to run in about this order most of the time, in my opinion, especially when the popularizers are members of the communications technology fraternity or Professors of Communications Arts in college trade-oriented departments. This is probably also why fictional treatments of these technologies, like Budd Schulberg's *What Makes Sammy Run?*, Theodore White's *The View from the Fortieth Floor* or Scott Fitzgerald's novel fragment, *The Last Tycoon,* seem more relevant to important issues in mass communications than most academic books which do not concentrate on people. Exceptions, of course, are "people centered" studies like Lillian Ross' delightful book *Picture,* White's *Making of a President* series, and others.

[16] See G.N.G., *L C,* Chapter 1, "The Logics of Communications," pp. 3–18.

larly those concerned with his cultural values, can avoid confrontation with what appears to be the naturally dual nature of experience, the split that occurs in the so-called "mind-body" relationship—as manifest in "being and essence," "objective and subjective phenomena" or, as sometimes designated, "private and public data." The best characterization of the dual phenomenon is Descartes' sentence, "I think; therefore I am." The best symbol yet evolved for it is the sphinx. The problem is eternal.

It has often been solved, however, in a traditional philosophical way of solution: by ignoring it. Logical Positivists, at least from the era of Jeremy Bentham in the eighteenth century[17] to our modern scientific philosophers,[18] have excluded from their scrutiny those kinds of data that they have found (differentially in different eras), irrelevant to their specific problems —usually questions not phrased in terms amenable to available data. Contemporary British linguistic philosophers, following the stimulus of Ludwig Wittgenstein, have applied this form of self-justifying exploration to the very terms of description that man applies to his own activities.[19] But a noninvolved observer of such cerebral gymnastics immediately perceives the tautological limitations of such a method of inquiry and its result, namely that whole classes of human experience ("mind," "essence," "subjectivity," or what have you) have been excluded from its workbench. The solution to the problem is—philosophically if not practically—therefore frequently more misleading than the problem was. Considerations of this sort rarely bother positivists, because, limited as their thinking is to problems which their data can handle, they *do* indeed appear to solve them to their own satisfactions.

In order to achieve even a basic understanding of communications, however, we are left with the sphinx. The dual mode of apprehension has been described well by Susanne K. Langer as two apparent "scientific systems differently formulated, but referring to the same objects and facts, namely, mental phenomena, and equally capable of describing them . . ." "This begets," she continues, "the division of reality into thought and things," [20] seen from two simultaneous points of view as *consciousness* on one hand and *content* on the other.

Langer views this dual perspective as two facets of psychology, which, if we define psychology as the study of "mental phenomena," they indeed

[17] See J. Bronowski and Bruce Mazlish, *The Western Intellectual Tradition* (New York: Harper and Brothers, 1960), pp. 430–449, for a brilliant discussion of Bentham, particularly as a thinker in the positivistic mold.

[18] William Barrett, *Irrational Man* (New York: Doubleday and Co., 1958), pp. 18–19.

[19] For a short but neat explanation of the cleverness of the British Linguists and their pyrotechnics, see G. J. Warndck, *English Philosophy Since 1900* (London: Oxford University Press, 1958), the most important part of which is Chapter VI, pp. 62–93, devoted entirely to the work, in the first part of this century, done by Wittgenstein.

[20] Susanne K. Langer, *Mind: An Essay On Human Feeling*, Volume 1 (Baltimore: The Johns Hopkins Press, 1967), pp. 6–7.

are. One deals mainly with physical processes; the other with psychological "other forces," Langer's term, both of which are logically equivalent sources of meaningful data. If, on the other hand, one construes *logic* as a formal context of physical experiences, and *psychologic* as a matrix of "mental," "psychical," or "dispositional" states (call them what you wish), the relevance of this dualism to both the content and process of communication is clarified.

Such a construction of logics and psychologics is not merely verbal play; it is quite meaningful.[21] Logics of communications are related to content, form and aesthetics. They are amenable to positivistic analysis—in fact, to many kinds of analysis, including those evolved in the discipline of psychology. Psychologics are far more discursive, less precise, and amenable almost exclusively to those methods of analysis by which psychologists make judgments of behaviors and mental states, reflecting both their outlook's weaknesses and strengths. The greatest single problem, therefore, in most analysis of communications (and much art) is the confusion of these two perspectives and the choice of those types of judgments which are relevant to each.

The total problem in concepts of mind is summed up by Langer thus:

> All these problems spring from the desire to establish a clear and adequate concept of mind and of its relation to matter. The older ones go back to Plato in our culture and considerably further in India; but the ones here considered all bear on the actual study of mind . . . Physicalism and its opposite, the assumption of an ammaterial "psychic factor" in living structures, are attempts to define the subject matter of psychology, in the belief that if we knew exactly what we are dealing with we could apply scientific methods to this material and thus find the basic laws which govern it . . .[22]

Langer is properly skeptical about the promise of psychology to extract from a concept of mind the kinds of data that will yield "laws." (She notes that few other sciences—notably physics—started their pursuits of truth in this manner.) But she is clear about the necessity of knowing "exactly what we are dealing with," the "physical" or "psychical" in her terms; the "logical" or "psychological" in ours. The question we most profitably put to most communication in its logical phase is "*What* are we *dealing* with?" The psychological question is "*What kind of event* is *occurring* here, and how do we think it is happening?" [23] The difference between the two ques-

---

[21] See G.N.G., *L C*, Part One, pp. 3–47, for a full discussion of the summary that follows.

[22] Langer, *op. cit.*, p. 17.

[23] Langer qualifies the latter problem in the following way in its most difficult manifestation, that of human feeling: "The question is not one of how a physical process can be transformed into something non-physical in a physical system, but how the phase of being felt is attained, and how the process may pass into unfelt phases again, and

tions is critical. In our considerations to come, they will be allied both to what we consider "theory" and to the "practice" of persuasion. Because much of the latter is capable of description and analysis, it will be generally associated with logics of communications. Because "theories" are mental states of one kind or another (like generalizations and abstractions), they will be most closely related to psychologics, with the understanding that psychologics are not irrelevant to the practical history of persuasion; just as logics may refer closely to the formulation and content of theories of all kinds, not only those involved in communications.[24]

Mediums and Instruments

Another concept of significance that has become necessary equipment for any traveler into the analysis of contemporary communications is the understanding of the much-abused notion of what a *medium* of communication is and how it is likely to influence what is communicated—if indeed it does.[25] The necessity of this discussion is the direct result of the extraordinary misuse of the term "medium" in common parlance—particularly the plural "media"—to connote any device or instrument of communication, irrelevant to the content of the communication itself. In particular, McLuhan and his followers[26] have used this plural form "media" (often in a singular construction) to weld together inferences about the logical state of a communications act and also its psychological state. In fact, McLuhan's apparently absurd catch-phrase "The medium is the message" is far from meaningless; it is patently misleading, causing one to confuse a logical perspective of communications with a psychological one, at the same time that it confuses the way that experiences are mediated between people with the device that does the mediating.

Therefore, for purpose of clarity in the pages to follow, the plural form of "medium," that is "media," will be eliminated entirely from our vocabulary, except to describe the content of McLuhan-style notions of communi-

---

furthermore how an organic process in 'psychical phase' may induce others which are unfelt. Such problems, even if far from solved, are at least coherent with the rest of biological inquiry . . ." (*Ibid.*, p. 29.) As vexing as they are, we shall return to these problems in the psychologics of persuasion again and again in this volume with much the same faith that Langer displays: that if *we* cannot solve them, perhaps someone else can if we formulate them in a proper frame of reference.

24 The Part and Chapter divisions of this book have been divided (except Part One) according to the dual aspect of communications in the study of persuasion. Parts Four and Five, hopefully, will adumbrate a meeting-ground between the two, in terms of contemporary social institutions and the roles that the logics and psychologics of persuasions play in their destinies.

25 The discussion of this concept fills most of Part Three of G.N.G., *L C*, pp. 97–158, and will be reviewed in cursory terms. The reader who is puzzled or irked by this re-construction is uged to consult these chapters.

26 The title of McLuhan's *magnum opus, Understanding Media* (New York: McGraw-Hill Book Co., 1964), has done as much as any other factor to muddy these semantic waters.

cation mysticisms. When reference is made to more than one medium, we shall refer to "mediums," treating the word in much that same way that the word "auditorium" is treated in English at present.

Second, we shall limit the idea of a medium to the basic unit, at first apparently presentational, of experience that is generally transferred between people, regardless of the technology employed. Although, in some senses, the three mediums described blow (and there appear only to be *three* logically viable ones) are technologies (or techniques) of communication, they are not technologies related either to the history of mechanics, the forerunner of modern technological mastery, or science, the intellectual wellspring of technology. From a logical point of view, they are discrete, highly differentiated conduits for the transfer of thought and feeling. From the psychological perspective, they are qualities of mind. In either case, they have found innumerable instruments or devices of expression in the history of the human species. In some degree, they refer to classes of communications content—that is, one or another medium seems to handle certain kinds of contents "best," most easily, or most effectively at certain times in history. But beyond such facilitation, they relate only slightly to content.

These mediums are, in fact, a direct response to Richards' explanation of the communication process, the logical answer to the question of how experience (content) is shared between individuals in a causal relationship.

Narrative is the first medium, and it centers upon the use of language, either verbal or written, although the language employed may be either more primitive or complicated than the vocabularies to which we are accustomed in modern discourse. The function that narrative performs is that of *telling*, a mental phenomenon that it is probably philosophically impossible to describe, because one would have to *tell* what narrative is in order to describe it. Paradox or not, historical evidence and the experiences of our senses tells us that we tell, and that we do so in a great number of ways. The same evidence also differentiates telling from other mediums, although it may cooperate with them in the sharing of experience.

Picture is the second medium, and it resolves eventually to the phenomenon of sight and the picture that forms on the retinas of our eyes. Except for the blind (and, for them, who knows what compensatory factor nature has evolved?), a field of human interchange is encompassed in vision and/or "the visual," as it is called today by artists who emphasize the logic involved in this medium and often detach it from the total flux of life. Visual experiences may be employed to enhance (or even create) narratives, but the pictorial element of communication may be severed from *any* communication. All we have to do is shut our eyes.

Re-creation (or re-enactment) is the third medium, and it involves considerably different manifestations from narrative and picture. Its function, in the first place, is more socialized than the other two. And, to function best as a medium of communication, re-creation usually draws heavily both upon narrative and pictures—"telling" and "showing" in the words of the school child. Sometimes, as in the instance of dance (probably an extremely old form of re-enactment), it tells *by* showing a re-enactment. In other words, the medium of narrative is achieved by pictures (retinal in this case) achieved by re-creation.

Why, therefore, is re-enactment a medium of communication in its own class rather than a facilitation of the previous two? This question is an anthropological one, best answered by the study of primitive peoples (whose methods of communication center more upon re-enactment than upon narrative and picture), by the insistent role of the drama in recorded history, and by its ubiquity in our own culture.

These three mediums are naturally complementary in human communications. While they seem to center on the presentational aspects of interaction, this is only a first illusion. Any and all types of communication (and each of Ruesch's approaches) may be analyzed, in terms of the *experiences involved in them,* from the point of view of the degree to which they partake of narrative, picture or re-enactment, both on the part of the senders and receivers. Certainly, there exist communications that do not involve one or more of the three mediums. There is precious little re-enactment[27] in the discourse on this page. Neither are there any pictures (although printed letters *are* pictorial; they may, however, be read *to* one with little change in content). Radio drama is *only* pictorial in so far as personal images are evoked in the mind of the listener. One is hard-pressed to locate a narrative element in most of the canvases of Malevich, Mondrian, or Klee—although meaning (and therefore narrative) emerges from much supposedly abstract art, variantly, probably, for different auditors at different times. While re-enactment usually performs a narrative function, certain psychedelic theatricals and the operas of Gertrude Stein seem to offer little of it. Pornographic drawings and photographs usually emphasize re-enactment but tell us little of a narrative nature, at least in the author's opinion, when compared, as experiences in communication, even to second-rate Renaissance oils.

These have been simple illustrations of the mediums at work. They obviously operate at a basal level of human (and perhaps animal) experiential interchange. They are finite in number. They are amenable to both logical and psychological analysis. They are invariable concomitants of culture. But what of the instruments we usually call "media": TV receivers, movie film, telephones and smoke signals?

First, they are, at least, *techniques;* many of them are *technologies.* There is nothing fundamental to communicating about them, except in

27 The terms "drama" or "dramatic" will sometimes replace various forms of the words "re-creation" or "re-enactment" in the coming pages, where the major effect of a communication is theatrical.

their most simple constructions as tools. They are potentially infinite in number, limited only by circumscriptions upon man's inventive powers that have not yet been tested. With the exception of certain inevitable prototypes drawn from nature, such as spoken language (as far as we know) and "monkey-see, monkey-do" types of re-enactment, they have changed as man's social orders have changed. They operate differently in different civilizations. And the greatest number (if least significant) of them have been developed since the technological burst of the industrial evolution in England in the eighteenth century.

Second, they may most productively be considered *devices* or *instruments* for utilizing the three mediums described above. In the history of our race, they antedate what Americans call "technology" by many thousands of years. Written and oral languages are such instruments. So are clay tablets, cave drawings, primitive ceremonies, music, signs and symbols. A paint brush is also a device. So is a pencil—one of the most remarkably versatile instruments of communication available at present, far more exciting in its potential, in the opinion of many, than a motion picture camera.[28] Modern technological devices involve the gadgetry referred to today as "media," and includes a wide-ranging and heterogeneous assortment of wares, from instruments that assist in the accomplishment of ancient techniques like the typewriter to inventions that may or may not display aesthetics and grammars of their own like still and moving photographs.[29] They are directly related to the spread of communications to the masses. They expedite and accelerate the uses of the mediums discussed above, and sometimes even appear to dictate which medium should dominate in a given communication. (Re-enactment, for instance, seems particularly effective on a film or television screen.) But this is an illusion dependent upon various artistic and cultural conventions that are least noticeable to individuals who have gained expertise in the practical mastery of these instruments, for obvious reasons.

---

28 When such an observation is made to most of today's youngsters (so many of whom seem to be involved in making movies), the notion that pencil is a far more adaptable and exciting an instrument of communication than a Bolex disturbs them. Many years ago, I heard a street-hawker of cheap fountain pens pitching his wares in this fashion: "With this pen, my friends, you can write in Greek, Chinese, English, French or Spanish. You can write letters, poems, insults, short stories, novels and dramas. You can draw pictures, geometrical forms, mathematical symbols and reproductions of the greatest works of art. This pen will write letters, numbers, prayers, and protests, etc., etc., etc." I bought one of his pens, and found that his spiel was confoundingly honest.

29 Contrary to some of the best thought of our time, I do not believe that they are *art forms* (*communication forms* to some) *sui generis*. All of them are far too dependent upon aesthetic-logical factors involved in the three mediums they use (narrative, picture and/or re-enactment), despite the apparent novelty provided by an inventive technology. A discussion of this controversy (far from definitive) is taken up in Part Five of G.N.G., *L C*, pp. 237–284, but I am not satisfied with the argument there. If energies and opportunities continue, I hope to return to this problem in greater breadth and depth at some future time.

Above all, they possess, as components of culture, a symbolic attractiveness which results in a psychological disposition that impels one to simplify, exacerbate, remake or modify the powers of the three mediums, in much the manner that men have, since the onset of the technological era, accepted the assumption that the human condition will also somehow be changed at heart by the clever exploitation of technology. In this sense, all of the modern instruments of communications technology have failed to live up to their first expectations, in spite of the fact that a seemingly endless stream of visionaries are hurled into the public forum, bedazzled by their promise, to assure a gullible public that this or that variety of instrumentation portends heroic metamorphoses in culture and the subjective experiences involved in living.[30]

Qualities and Modifiers

To categorize mediums or basic forms or "thrusts" (a new but useful construction of the word) of communications, and to sever these thrusts from the technology by which they are instrumented helps to explain a good deal about why and how transfers of human experience differ from each other. What is lacking in this formulation, among other things, are the subtle, frequently subjective qualities of the processes of communications themselves. Here, one may turn profitably to a number of basic categories first described roughly by I. A. Richards in his books on literary criticism some years ago.[31] They serve essentially as modifiers of communications, again frequently interacting, one with the other, to provide an equivalent of what theatrical scholars call the "emphatic Aristotelian element" of a play—its dominant mood quality.

A clear analogy for these modifiers would be the suggestion that a different class of brain tissue is perhaps required for the perception of each, and a certain amount of rough physiological evidence gives credence to this

---

[30] They make up a formidable list of colorful characters with McLuhan, Buckminster Fuller, the late Frank Lloyd Wright, Andy Warhol, other artists, film makers, writers (including science-fiction authors), and numerous professors of communications among them, variously talented at various arts and crafts and professing various faiths. What they have in common is a proclivity to eschatology, combined with endless confidence in the protean nature of man and society. In a way, they are all optimists. Of course, some, most notably the late Aldous Huxley and George Orwell, are nay-sayers (as I suppose I am, in a minor way), but the dividing line between the merchants of joy and merchants of doom among prophets of technology is thin, because both operate on substantially the same premises concerning the trenchant effect upon the quality of life which communications technology (always) portends for the (indefinite) future. The future, however, never seems to arrive.

[31] The basic ideas for these qualifiers and their roles in communication is derived from I. A. Richards, *Practical Criticism* (New York: Harcourt, Brace and Co., 1954), pp. 181–183, although they were filtered through fifteen years of my own reflection and work, including study of discussion of these factors in Richards' other works. The result has been changes in terminology (with concurrent changes in function) for the terms, as well as the addition of one category—that of humor. A fuller discussion of these qualities appears in Part Four of G.N.G., *L C*, pp. 161–233.

concept. While numerous messages may utilize identical mediums and instruments of communication, and may be quite similar in content, they may be received by auditors in different manners, considering the effect that the communicator either wished to achieve or achieved by accident. Legends have it that certain comedians were able to read a list of names from the telephone book and elicit laughter. Many books—particularly parables and poems—may be perceived by different readers on different levels, probably meaning that different forms of cerebral stimulation occur in different people from the same communications.

These illustrations are, of course, exceptions to the way in which various factors usually qualify or modify communications. Most of the qualities of most of man's communications are pretty well controlled at the source and accurately perceived at the target. So completely do we take this function of communication for granted that we often attach great (and unnecessary) meaning to misconstructions of these qualities in trivial interactions between people.

Cognition is one quality of communications—the "sense factor." Despite the beliefs of many, cognition probably rarely travels alone through man's experiences. Computers, however, deal largely in cognitions and reject all other qualities of communication, although it is quite conceivable that other modifiers may in some manner be programmed one day into such instruments. (Qualities like humor and emotion may be programmed in certain ways if their major elements may be reduced to cognitive quantities. And, in certain instances, they may be, but such programming is extremely complicated[32]). Thinkers such as Kenneth Burke and A. N. Whitehead have justifiably warned us against placing too much faith in people whose discourse seems to deal mostly in a cognitive matrix. The charge that they are walking machines—or computers—is frequently justifiable. At any rate, they are bores.

Emotion is another quality, referred to frequently by psychologists (and others) as "affective" aspects of thought. A better word, in the opinion of many, is "feeling" when it is used as counterpoint to "thought." In a cognitive construction (paradoxically necessary to describe emotion), emotions seem to deal in metaphors and, in the process of communication, occur in three phases, 1.) an emotion intended to be communicated, 2.) an emotion perceived as communicated and 3.) an emotion felt (or unfelt) as the result of the communication. The same three phases may be related to

[32] According to Mehrabian, H. A. Simon has succeeded (or is on the brink of succeeding) in just such a task, at least theoretically. "Satisfaction," "impatience," and "discouragement" are all part of his model of cognitive functions and are capable of being handled by his information-processing system. See Albert Mahrabian, *An Analysis of Personality Theories* (Englewood Cliffs, New Jersey: Prentice-Hall Inc., 1968), pp. 171–174. The reader of this volume may judge for himself the potential of Simon's mechanistic attempt at cornering emotion by comparing it with other, similar models.

the communication of cognitions, of course, but they are much more obvious—and simple to follow—in the transfer of thought than in the transfer of feeling.

Style is another qualitative factor, intimately related to moral factors (rights and wrongs) in the content of communications. Whitehead's notion of style as "the ultimate morality of mind" [33] is central to its significance as a modifier in the interchange of experience. The origin of most style in communications is a personal matter, but style is generalized through most classes and types of shared experience, and even the absence of style (like that shown in a computer readout) *is*, oddly, a style of sorts and reflective of a *human* disposition. Stylistic considerations of communications—particularly those regarded as artistic—may be the most important qualities of the experiences. On the other hand, the style of a positive biopsy laboratory report may be irrelevant to a person who discovers that he is host to carcinoma. In this instance, a nod of a lab technician's head may be as meaningful as a ten-page report, and certainly more stylistically economical.

Humor is a delightfully enigmatic quality of communications, so delightful that we shall eventually devote a chapter to it,[34] and so baffling that it deserves a book of its own. Wellsprings of humor are well hidden—in intellect according to some analysts; in society according to others; in the unconscious of each individual according to some others; and in the feral nature of our aggressive traits according to still others. Humor as a qualifying factor in communications enhances the cognitive qualities of most interpersonal experiences, touches deeply the motive qualities, and modifies the stylistic qualities. The more objective humor is, the more cognitive and hence the more civilizing. The more subjective, the more it seems to be emotional play associated with sensual pleasure and fun. Numerous theories have been advanced concerning what purposes humor achieves in communications, and the answers given have run a range of extremes, depending on whether the theorist is logically or psychologically oriented and how well developed is his least understood sensual apparatus, his sense of humor.

Intention is the last quality of communication to be treated here, because the communication of intention is largely the subject of this volume and also the topic of detailed inquiry in Chapter 3. Suffice it to say here that all communications possess intentional aspects of one sort or another, and many of them are persuasive intentions. Intentions may, of course, be overt or covert, conscious or non-conscious, and they are frequently prone to misunderstandings that, as we shall see, are usually resolved by the per-

---

33 A. N. Whitehead, *The Aims of Education* (New York: The New American Library, 1949), p. 24.

34 See Chapter 17. Also see Chapter 15, "Communicating Humor," in G.N.G., *L C*, pp. 219–233.

ceiver in favor of his own predispositions. Problems of clarifying or hiding intentions of communications are as difficult and fascinating as any other topic of contemporary discourse as, hopefully, the subsequent chapters will reveal.[35]

Conclusion

Precise definitions of "communications" are difficult to formulate. A construction which might satisfy an information theorist would be inadequate for a poet, and vice-versa.

All communication occurs in one of two modes, however: vertically through time, or horizontally through space, or both at the same time. A startlingly large number of "approaches" to the study of communications have been evolved in our culture. Forty-three disciplines with direct application to communications are listed briefly in this chapter, and they do not, in all probability, cover the entire field.

For our impending consideration of persuasion, the dual mode of apprehending reality (a form of Cartesian dualism) became the starting point for the analysis of how and in what manner communications occur. Referring this duality to many kinds of analysis, a division into logics and psychologics is here suggested as the most immediately profitable means of severing objective from subjective factors, or "matter" from "mind."

The three basic *mediums* of communications are also freed conceptually from the currently confusing term "media" (a notion drawn from the McLuhan mystique) and used in this volume to refer to the basic ways in which experience is mediated between individuals: by narrative, by picture, and by re-enactment. Instruments or devices which are employed to effect this mediation are either techniques, like writing and drawing, or technologies, like printing and photography. The latter, while open to logical and psychological evaluation, probably do not yield to the same kind of productive aesthetic analysis that the three mediums do in their continual and inevitable interaction in human discourse. Hence they are neither "art forms" nor, as some mystics claim, "media" of human expression, but mainly intriguing facilitating devices.

All communications are also qualified or modified by certain factors, once again unquestionably interactive. These factors are cognition, emotion, style, humor and intention, all germane to how communications are first, formulated, second, transmitted and third, received. The intentional factor in communication is most intimately connected of the five to the motives, nature and effectiveness of persuasion.

---

[35] A provisional statement concerning intentions (and the motivation for the present volume) may be found in G.N.G., *L C*, pp. 204–218, containing threads of discourse that will be picked up and re-woven in Chapter 3.

Chapter 2

SYMBOLS AND SYMBOLISM

Men's symbols are a new biological way for animals to have purposes.

Weston Le Barre

Many reasons are given for the cloud of mystery that surrounds the processes involved in making and using symbols. The intellectual necessity of concentration upon symbols for psychoanalytic theory and therapy is obvious; symbolic processes are perhaps the clearest logical route we have to confirm the supposition of the unconscious. It is, however, difficult to justify a trend (now slowly passing) in which anthropologists and sociologists disregard empirical evidence in favor of symbolic speculation; but they did and do. Poets, playwrights and novelists probably cosset symbols more avidly than behavior scientists, usually resisting (like T. S. Eliot) most attempts to explain them. And literary, drama and music critics have, since the recent great revolution in symbolism brought on by house-and-garden Freudianism, frequently manufactured symbols and symbolic analyses (when all else fails) the way the magician Cardini used to produce cigarettes and billiard balls—apparently from thin air, and with much of that conjurer's insouciance.

Symbols, as states of mind, and symbolism as a socio-cultural phenomenon, must indeed seem mystical at first blush to all men everywhere and to each individual when he first learns to live in his own symbolic environment. Symbols are given factors of all cultures, powerful concepts usually associated with the important aspects of living: birth, reproduction, eating, family life, religion and death, found everywhere that man has lived. What an individual discovers—as either he or his culture matures—is that, in one degree or another and judged by certain types of evidence, symbolism appears to constitute a fraud of nature. To the degree that a person is intimately oriented to symbols, close examination reveals that there is less to them than meets the eye, quite the contrary of our first experiences with nature as we discover it in our early years. When such intimacy reaches extremes, we move, as a matter of fact, from so-called "normal" orientations to reality into the "abnormal" for reasons noted below.

Upon discovery that a symbol appears to be *less* than reality shows us (that a wedding ring does not necessarily mean a marriage has occurred; or that a dollar bill does not necessarily have an intrinsic value beyond its paper and ink), one often cannot help but to be taken back in awe at the simple raw power of symbol systems. Into the vacuum where a one-time belief in the reality of symbols turns into enlightened disillusionment (the same insights that provided wise old men in primitive cultures with their wisdom) rushes, therefore, a feeling that symbolic power is far greater and more fearful than other forces in life, and that understanding of symbols in culture and life will somehow point one's feet in the direction of the philosopher's stone.[1]

A careful study of symbols usually produces no such result.[2] It may cause one to marvel at the inventiveness of human intellect. It may cause one to diminish, in some degree, his preoccupations about man's control of his universe. It may, in freeing one from the constricting bounds of symbol worship, cause him to "take a natural delight in exercising his power with symbols," in the words of Kenneth Burke. It may also submerge him into the pedantry of symbol-hunting and simplistic symbol explaining, today's high rhetoric of psychoanalysis and literary criticism.

Little doubt exists, however, that symbols are major instruments of interpersonal or group persuasion. The major fault in many studies of persuasion is that they have not taken this fact into account and have been developed upon the assumption that clear statements concerning the functions of symbols and symbolism were unnecessary before major symbols of persuasion themselves might be discussed or analyzed. Many treatises on persuasion have centered merely on historical enunciations of what symbols have accomplished in certain contexts, with the mere notation that they were powerful (the conventional explanation for the meaning of the swastika to the Nazis, for instance) without concern for why and how these symbols obtained their power.

---

[1] A study of what personality factors are present in the personalities of people who accept the psychoanalytical concept of symbolism (the most inclusive in our culture) might shed some light on the nature of this vacuum. Freud's enthusiasm for symbols was easily understandable; they gave credence to his much-challenged assumptions about the unconscious. But as he grew into bitter (and wise) old age, he demonstrated a world-weary hyper-involvement with symbolic fallacies in such essays as *Civilization and Its Discontents* and *The Future of An Illusion* (New York: Doubleday Anchor Books).

[2] See the section *Symbols and Communication* in G.N.G., *L C*, pp. 51–94.

The Nature of Symbols

For descriptive purposes, symbols are usually first differentiated from *signs* by the observation, first, that non-human animals can respond to signs but do not appear to possess a symbol system, as far as we can tell. (K. Lorenz says that this is demonstrated by the absence of what we call "culture" among animals and, limited as our methods of observing animal behavior are, this simple explanation appears correct, and also clarifies, to a degree, our understanding of what we mean by "culture.")

J. R. Pierce's definition of a symbol is as good as any and differentiates it clearly from a sign. He describes a symbol as "(a) letter, digit, or one of a group of agreed upon marks. Linguists distinguish a symbol, whose association with meaning or objects is arbitrary, from a sign, such as a pictograph of a waterfall." [3] A more generalized, anthropological definition, like that discussed by Montagu,[4] stresses the close relationship between signs and signals. The brief denotation of a simple message like an international road sign is, of course, a sign. A symbol, on the other hand, is a more elaborate, contemplative, value-laden and ideational entity than such a road sign is to most of us.

From another perspective, one may classify symbols as components of *icons*, actually congeries of interactive symbols. Although this differentiation is employed less frequently than the one above, it is equally useful. A funeral is a ceremony or ritual—actually an organic icon—consisting of numerous symbols surrounding the burial of a corpse. The casket, individual parts of the ceremonies, the first handful of dirt thrown into the open grave ("Dust thou art . . .") are symbols. So are the black clothes, the flowers, the shroud. The expression of the bereaved, the *blackness* of their costumes, the slow pace of their movements and hushed voices are signs.

One notices, therefore, increasing complexity as one moves from sign to symbol to icon, and also the increasingly irrefutable individualistic function of each in the progression. A person may wear a black tie, suit or dress and *not* be involved in a funeral. He may also fill a hole with dirt for any number of reasons. He will not, however, be involved in the iconic occasion of a funeral unless a dead person is to be ceremoniously buried—barring his participation in a ruse or re-enactment. The concept of icons therefore hurls us into the post-graduate department of symbology, and the comprehension of iconic matters without a clear grasp of their symbolic and signal components is accordingly impossible.[5]

---

[3] J. R. Pierce, *Symbols, Signals, and Noise*, p. 293.

[4] Ashley Montagu, "Communication, Evolution, Education" in Matson and Montagu, *op. cit.*, p. 446.

[5] These differentiations and elaborations are clearly and intelligently explained in Susanne K. Langer, *Philosophy in a New Key* (New York: New American Library, 1946), pp. 20–63. In this work, Langer prefers the concept of "ritual" to the more

Many answers have been given to the question of why men create symbols, but the simplest and most convincing—after the conjecture that we create symbols because we are able to—may be that symbols are quite useful as techniques for handling our perceptions of the world around us. Discussing language, Craik observes:

> As a result of making noises in conjunction with things we build up a language, and in using language we make the discovery that this symbolical representation of events does in fact work, just as when somebody tells us that there is a train to London at a certain time we do usually find that the rest of our experiences conform with this prediction. This language is based on the assumption of external objects behaving in a certain way. The primary fact is that we have discovered something by observation and experiment—we have discovered that symbols can work and can predict our future experience. Even our use of words to express this discovery is based on the same discovery. If symbolism did not work, we could never express the fact that it failed to work; but as it does work, we can express the fact that it does, and can say a great deal more besides.[6]

A tautology? Almost, but not quite. The point is similar to Burke's delight at reducing nearly all our "notions of reality" in his words to "nothing" by symbol systems.[7] " 'Reality' could not exist for us, were it not for our profound and inveterate involvement in symbol systems . . ." he says. To mistake our immediate presence in a room for our symbolic connections with the rest of society "dissolves into a web of ideas and images that reach through our senses only insofar as the symbol systems that report them are heard or seen. To mistake this vast tangle of ideas for immediate experience is much more fallacious than to accept a dream as immediate experience. For a dream," Burke reminds us, "really is an immediate experience, but the information that we receive about today's events throughout the world most decidedly is *not*." [8]

Contrary, therefore, to accepting Burke's pseudo-alarm at the flimsiness of suppositions of reality, or Craik's almost offhand notion that symbolism expedites the catching of a train (or discovering natural laws in physics, his main point), the use of symbols not only facilitates the meaning of things (if the author interprets Burke correctly) but actually provides us with *our sole conduits as human beings to understanding certain classes of activity in the world around us.* Were we *not* surrounded by

inclusive notion of an "icon," but this is a semantic problem of little importance. The advantage of the term "icon" is that "iconic" entities may be either behavioral or material as in the preferred dictionary definition of an "icon" as "a religious picture or the corollary idea of a religious ceremony of an iconic nature."

[6] Kenneth Craik, *The Nature of Explanation* (Cambridge: The University Press, 1967), p. 27.

[7] Kenneth Burke, *Language as Symbolic Action* (Berkeley and Los Angeles: University of California Press, 1966), pp. 3–9.

[8] *Ibid.*, p. 48.

symbols and symbol systems, as Burke notes, we would *only* perceive immediate experiences, tempered, as is the case with most animals, by a certain amount of simple conditioning and flow of instinct. We would be cut off from nearly the entire series of ideas, knowledges, emotions, assumptions and dispositions that we call our "environment" in its fullest construction, above and beyond the existential world of immediate sense perceptions.

Symbol-making and using is, contrary to some beliefs, as entirely value-free an activity as mitosis or blinking one's eyes. Symbols may, of course, provide what is essentially valueless with value (the rifle that shot President Kennedy, for instance); but they may also vitiate a previous value imbued in an object (the discovery that "the pearls, my Lord, are false"). Just as symbols enrich experience by adding meaning to immediacy, they may also vitiate the meaning of immediate experience (the soap opera ingenue who discovers that her seducer is married). While, on one hand, symbols are keystones of art, drama and poetry, they are also the architects of nationalism, warfare, murder, crime and the notion of depravity itself. In this respect, symbolism is extremely similar to every other form of communication man employs with his external environment.

Origins of Symbols

But why and how? This is the problem (or set of problems) for which it may be impossible to delineate a clear set of answers because of the ancient philosophical paradox that posits that a method of reasoning (or thinking) may not itself be used to exhibit a mechanism to explain that particular method of reasoning.[9] Ensconced as we are in symbolization, we can hardly be expected to step aside from our own thinking processes in order to explain how we think. Nor do we need to. Freudian symbology has become a powerful modern symbol system *per se*, which is the explanation of much of the power and magic of psychoanalytic notions in our culture today. The value of symbols, when they are understood to be psychoanalytical, rather than merely analytical or given by culture, is enhanced for us. This is due to the enormous power of symbols in the historical trends of Freudianism in our culture.

As in most cases of hidden intellectual insights, however, merely part of the iceberg emerges above the surface (an illustration, exactly, of how symbols are used psychoanalytically), albeit a deceptively small part, but enough for clever auditors at least to hypothesize the size and shape of the total mass.

If we ask, like the biologist-philosopher von Bertalanffy,[10] what occurs, in certain cases, when the psycho-biological organism of the human being ceases to function properly, we may arrive at an hypothesis as to why sym-

---

9 "All statements written here are false" is the elementary example of this paradox given students of elementary logic.

10 See Ludwig von Bertalanffy, *General System Theory, ibid.*

bols are required by humans to function as they do in the first place.[11] After noting the reluctance of psychologists of certain schools even to discuss symbols, he quotes Allport on the puzzle that "motives in man will not be an adequate model for motives in men," a re-statement of the above paragraph and a clear explanation of why "telephone company" communications theorists have not (and may never) come to peace with the role of symbols in transfers of conceptual content.

Then, in his meticulous style, von Bertalanffy follows the well chartered path of symbols in contemporary thought and concludes:

> The distinction of *biological* and *specific human* values is that the former concerns the maintenance of the individual and the survival of the species; the latter always the concern of a symbolic universe . . . In consequence, mental disturbances of man, as a rule, involve disturbances of symbolic functions . . . Disturbances in schizophrenia are essentially also at the symbolic level and able to take many different forms: loosening of associational structure, breakdown of the ego boundary, speech and thought disturbances, concretization of ideas, desymbolization, paleologic thinking and others . . .
>
> (H)uman striving is more than self-realization; it is directed toward objective goals and realization of values . . . which means nothing less than symbolic entities which in a way become detached from their creators . . . Perhaps we may venture a definition. There may be a conflict between biological drives and a symbolic value system; this is the situation of psychoneurosis. Or there may be conflict between symbolic universes, or loss of value disorientation and experience of meaninglessness of the individual . . . Similar considerations apply to "character disorders" like juvenile delinquency that, quite apart from their psychodynamics, stem from the breakdown or erosion of the value system . . .
>
> Scientific notions such as the earth running with unimaginable speed through the universe or a solid body consisting of empty spaces interlaced with tiny energy specks at astronomical distances, contradict all every day experience and "common sense" and are more fantastic than "world designs" of schizophrenics. Nevertheless, the scientific notions happen to be "true"—i.e., they fit into an integrated scheme . . .
>
> The answer (to) whether an individual is mentally sound or not is ultimately determined by whether he has *an integrated universe consistent within the given cultural framework.*[12]

---

[11] von Bertalanffy arrives at conclusions about symbolism in mental processes not unlike those given in Otto Fenichel, *The Psychoanalytic Theory of Neurosis* (New York: W. W. Norton and Co., Inc., 1945), pp. 48–51, 442. Fenichel is operating within the more or less normal limits of the Freudian neurotic personality, while von Bertalanffy, no Freudian, assaults the symptomology of mental-behavioral breakdown directly and fully. Both conjectures are similar, however, although approached from different frames of reference.

[12] von Bertalanffy, *op. cit.*, pp. 216–219. The author notes that "existential" breakdowns that result from a sense of valuelessness or meaninglessness in life often respond well to therapy at the symbolic level, as suggested, also, by Victor Frankl's notion of logotherapy

Put another way, if human beings, during some epoch of prehistory, found it necessary to create such an "integrated universe" ("correct" or "incorrect"; "true" or "untrue") within their given cultural framework (and therefore deal sanely with reality) they *had* to exercise their (presumably given) symbol-making proclivities. What is uncomfortable about the idea of this moment of origin, of course, is the thin line that even as lucid an observer as von Bertalanffy draws between realistic conceptualization (symbol making) and utter derangement (schizophrenia at worst; neurosis at best). The difference between the two seems to depend upon the fragile boundary of an adequately "true" cultural framework, or what consensus accepts as the truth of that framework at a certain moment in history. Contemporary sociologists and anthropologists have consistently reminded us of the tenuousness and relativity of our tests for the adequacy of all of these structures, and, as they have succeeded in their mission, they have also loosened the discrete differences between symbol-making within and outside of realistic social matrices. No wonder, therefore, the feeling of discomfort that many symbol students feel toward the apparent successes in their own missions.

The barrier appears even more fragile when one considers symbols not as mysterious human "givens" but as simple metaphors, or operations of man's metaphor-making talents, an ability (usually considered linguistic) to make one thing stand for another, although the two objects have no natural connection to each other besides their common status as sense-data. To the best of the writer's knowledge, no one has ever charted this short journey in the intellectual process, except to notice that it occurs almost everywhere men are found, and that man is the only species capable of doing it—the same verities one applies to symbol making. And yet, the power of the metaphor is astounding, not only as it applies to cognitive communication, but as it relates to the substratum of emotion upon which all human experience feeds.[13]

Metaphors yield analogies which yield symbols. Once the human mind has grasped the pattern of thinking in metaphors, it is almost hurled willy-nilly into the universe of symbolic discourse. The general pattern of operation is stable, and the tools are freely available. The details now must be

---

expressed in the latter's recommended volume on symbol destruction in contemporary Western settings (including concentration camps) *Man's Search for Meaning* (New York: Washington Square Press, Inc., 1963). This latter book was originally entitled *From Death-Camp to Existentialism* and published by Beacon Press in 1959. It has become a classic, not only as an introduction to logotherapy, but as a monumental statement on the psychology of contemporary survival during what appears to me as an increasingly valueless period in history. See Frankl's epilogue added to the 1963 edition above, pp. 151–214.

[13] See G.N.G., *L C*, pp. 180–184, on the role of metaphor in symbols and emotional communications compared with one another. Also see *ibid.*, pp. 66–67.

worked out, perhaps from crude and unsophisticated vocal language to pictures to pictographs to written language, or from a primitive weapon to a lucky charm to a tribal totem to icon to a complex ritual. History and observation show no shortage of the trend towards increasingly complex utilization of symbols, a trend with unmistakable social and political ramifications, as we shall observe. But one must bear always in mind, when discussing symbols, that the same metaphor-analogue thrust that produced the arts and religion appears to lie also at the roots of our concepts of cognitive language, mathematics, scientific experimentation and technology. Simply because certain intellectual operations seem free of symbol *dominance* (physics, biology, chemistry, statistics and our modern technology, for instance), their very existence and motive concepts are rooted in metaphors, analogues, and highly stable and predictable symbols and symbol systems. It is precisely this degree of stability and predictability that give them their surface appearance of freedom from symbolic thought. This is a major central illusion in contemporary thought, possibly a form of arrogance similar to that which specialists frequently show in their disregard of the etiologies of their parochial disciplines, a mental condition similar to that which von Bertalanffy describes above as "schizophrenic." Such thinking is certainly unrealistic, if not deranged.[14]

As one observes the critical nexus between symbols and human activity —particularly higher cortical activity—one achieves insight into the highly humanoid (and social) imperatives that symbols are necessary for as conceptual tools in striving towards the increasing complexity of organizations to which we seem ever impelled. The educational psychologist Bruner records this striking facet of culture admirably when he notes, "The very essence of being human lies in the use of symbols. We do not know what the hierarchy of primacy is among speech, song, dance, and drawing, but, whichever came first, as soon as it stood for something else than the act itself, man was born; as soon as it caught on with other men, culture was born; and as soon as there were two symbols, a system was born. A dance, a song, a painting, and a narrative can all symbolize the same thing. They do so differently." [15] He goes on to say that these symbol structures (particularly clusters of them) reflect and reveal what a civilization's philosophy is, and/or what values obtain in ontology, epistemology, cosmology, law, morals, theology, "education and, even aesthetics." [16]

---

[14] Perhaps I am arrogant in implying that the lion's share of "best" scientific and technological thought in our culture is, loosely speaking, "psychotic." The line of derangement, as noted above, is frail. But the point will be picked up again in the chapters to follow, although I am mindful of the pitfalls of such blanket accusations.

[15] Jerone S. Bruner, *Toward a Theory of Instruction* (Cambridge, Mass.: Harvard University Press, 1966), p. 89.

[16] *Loc. cit.*

The Functions of Symbolism

Symbols are more or less discrete elements of culture. Symbolism is the totality of symbols which some social unit—from two to more than two billion people—employs to create and convey meaning. In other words, symbolism is the collective-cultural face of the symbolic process and is integral to the modular units of every type of social aggregation where we have discovered men, including groups of retarded children, geniuses, lunatics and concentration camp victims involved only in the passing of time until death. Unlike the symbol, symbolism appears to involve a dynamic state of affairs, internally moving without refreshment in a closed system (as in such highly stable societies of that of the Peruvian natives whose culture expired of stagnation), or continually revised and modified (as in a nation that has just passed through a military revolt).

A disorienting modern proclivity of thought is the treatment of collective psychological manifestations as mere elaborations of individual behavior, when, in fact, there seems to be a radical difference between individual and group behaviors, motivations and sensibilities. But symbolism is an exception, it appears, to this general observation. Careful observation of symbol structures in individuals and small groups does provide important data for extrapolation to a larger and more complex field, providing grounds for relevance exist. One Sioux Indian is, in some respects, all Sioux Indians, as far as symbols are concerned. One Orthodox Jew is all Orthodox Jews. One main-line Philadelphian is all main-line Philadelphians.

Writers of fiction have provided for us some of the clearest insights we possess into the group psychology of symbolism by means of carefully delineated single case studies. This, in fact, constitutes the art of such realistic authors as Sinclair Lewis, James T. Farrell, John O'Hara, Scott Fitzgerald, Saul Bellow, John Steinbeck and many, many other sensitive observers of people. Their work says far more about societal forces and counterforces than it says about man in the lonely confinement of his individual self. In effect, these writers are informal symbolic sociologists whose delineations of symbolic fibres compare favorably with results obtained by scientifically trained anthropologists and behavioral scientists.[17]

[17] We are familiar with the popularized methods of Margaret Mead, Ruth Benedict, and their students and imitators. The observational thrust that they bring to various pockets of culture resembles, in many ways, that of the novelist, and bears down hard upon the identification of symbols as they function in small social units. "Structural" anthropologists, following Claude Lévi-Strauss, appear to set themselves to a more ambitious task, that of integrating heir own (or the observer's) symbol system with that of a new culture and (based upon the premise that most primitive symbols have complex and rarely simplistic origins) construct the etiology of current symbol systems out of the interaction of man-made and natural forces that create a given social situation. This latter approach is obviously more personal, committed and involved than the older one, within the traditions of which most of us over the age of thirty studied or

With all the attention that has been given to symbols in the past fifty or more years (at least since the Freudian fad which began gaining momentum shortly after World War I), far less attention has been paid to the social role of extenuated symbolism than to individualistic symbols in the psychological life of each one of us as reservoirs of personal symbol vocabularies. The major neo-Freudian who extrapolated Freudian symbology into social symbolism was Jung, whose work was effectively promoted in the United States by the public discontents of Philip Wylie.[18] Otherwise, symbolism has been the province of psychologists who dealt mostly in discrete symbols; anthropologists, who generalized from their observations of symbols in exotic cultures; sociologists, who paid suitable obeisance to symbols as cultural forces; linguists, who were entranced with discovery that written and spoken language were themselves symbol systems, and concentrated on the symbolic elements of rhetoric; and artists and critics, who used contemporary symbols as shock treatment on their publics without much consideration either of what they were up to or how they achieved their effects.

The philosopher-mathematician A. N. Whitehead grasped the essential nature of symbolism's social function in a series of lectures delivered at the University of Virginia in 1927 that have remained, until the recent Whitehead re-discovery, comparatively unused in our contemporary archives, although frequently reprinted for small readerships.[19] Whitehead's main concern was neither with individual symbols that influence the behavior, emotions and mind-life of individuals, nor with stable symbols that appeared to recur in culture after culture.

Oddly, Whitehead's considerations seem—at first glance—to center mostly upon political and historical symbol usage, in a form of presentation that attempts to ally the psychological phenomenon of symbolism with the flow of classical philosophy. Closer observation demonstrates that this objective was merely the matrix for his insights into processes of symbolism as total cultural forces for most relatively complex recent social structures.[20]

---

read our first anthropology. See Claude Lévi-Strauss, *Structural Anthropology* (New York: Doubleday Anchor Books, 1967).

18 For Wylie's most recent revisions of Jungian psychology (and/or a look at how age and experience has tempered a young malcontent), see his *The Magic Animal* (New York: Pocket Books, 1969), a far more carefully reasoned and reflective work than one might expect (or literary critics noticed) from the man whose vitriolic *Generation of Vipers* had so cruelly kicked various American sacred cows in the early 1940's. Also see C. G. Jung, *Memories, Dreams, and Reflections* (New York: Pantheon Books, 1963), an autobiographical "collection" (assembled by Aniela Jaffe) of Jung's writing and letters, a book that clarifies a number of misconceptions both about the beginnings and development of his ideas of the collective unconscious and prototypical cultural symbols.

19 A. N. Whitehead, *Symbolism* (New York: The Macmillan Co., 1958). This small volume is now available in a paperback edition.

20 See G.N.G., *L C*, pp. 69–77.

The primary observation Whitehead makes is that, in most dynamic cultures, symbolism seems to be moving towards, but never reaches, a condition of hypothetical stasis; symbol systems are therefore always in flux. Cultures change their symbolisms slowly in their evolution. They change rapidly at times of revolution or revolt, differentially according to the cultural disorder wrought by the change. (Historians many claim that "revolts," as they define them, produce less symbolic metamorphosis than true "revolutions." They are probably correct.) Social change is also revolutionary, and phrases like "the industrial revolution" are more than rhetoric, by virtue of the large numbers of contemporary symbolisms that are upset in cultures that pass through them.[21]

Whitehead implies that periodic symbolic purges or catharses are more or less inevitable in modern life. Current symbolisms grow increasingly complex. Metaphors dominate over reality; analogies become more important than sense-data. Organizational structures dominate man-made objectives. At these times, a crisis develops, and revolutions (with or without guns), cut away much of the symbolic debris. Old symbolisms are modified or new ones encouraged in the wake of a societal holocaust. To the observer involved in the change, of course, the very foundations of his world seem to crumble when old symbolisms no longer apply to what is currently relevant in his life.[22] In volatile societies such as ours, this illusion (if it is an illusion) is always present in some degree and generally accepted as part of the individual's aging process, although some people go to great and absurd pains to resist overt displays of such disorientations.

Whitehead sees the function of symbolism in man's culture as necessary, inevitable, and beyond value judgment. Only discrete symbols themselves can be evaluated according to moral criteria, not the process of symbolism. "It seems," he says in a critical sentence, "as though mankind must always be masquerading." He continues, "This imperative impulse suggests that the notion of an idle masquerade is the wrong way of thought about the symbolic elements in life. The function of these elements . . . thereby lifts the(ir) meanings into an intensity of definite effectiveness—as elements in knowledge, emotion, and purpose—an effectiveness which the meanings may, or may not, deserve on their own account. *The object of*

---

21 Whitehead, *op. cit.*, pp. 60–67.

22 Numerous contemporary social observers think that the present symbolism of youth and worship of youthful symbolisms is responsible for today's "generation gap," and the older generations is out-of-step with changes in social symbols. They are quite wrong, because they themselves grew up in a mystique of youthful symbolism that had been becoming increasingly complex and overgrown since the nineteen-twenties. The contemporary "generation gap" is therefore a social trend hatched mostly by middle-aged free-lance intellectuals and slick magazine editors. The facts seem to point to a remarkable consonance of symbolic agreement, at present, between the over-thirty and under-thirty generations, which, by virtue of its apparent stagnation, is, in my opinion, far from healthy. The problem of young people as initiators and recipients of persuasion will be taken up in Chapter 22.

symbolism is the enhancement of the importance of what is symbolized." [23]

One may describe symbolism as the glue which individuals and groups quite conscientiously apply to the sense-data of life to provide stance and stability. Symbolism is also one of the few largely psychological operations which man performs with few stimuli, except those from his own internal drives, that yields a cool and subtle logic of a social nature. (Sexual appetites may be construed in much the same way, manifesting first, social logic in the production of the next generation, and second, the same sort of tendency as symbolism towards excess and the need for revolutionary means of limitation—warfare perhaps, and contraceptive trickery certainly). Whitehead describes the process thus: "Symbolic expression first preserves society by adding emotion to instinct, and secondly it affords a foothold for reason by its delineation of the particular instinct which it expresses." [24]

For Whitehead, symbolism occurs in two modes—one largely existential and immediate, and the other largely historical and causal, relating to how and why symbols achieved their immediate status and meaning. The terms he chooses for these modes derive from philosophy rather than psychology, and relate to phases of "presentational immediacy" (existential) and "casual efficacy" (historical).[25] The value of this extremely sophisticated binocular vision of symbolism in society can best be summed up in Whitehead's own observation that "(the) *how* of our present experience must conform to the *what* of the past in us." [26]

Symbols are therefore perceived by people in a *single* (and probably special) psychological type of perception about which little is known at present. They function, from a social viewpoint, in two modes (not unlike modes of much other, less significant, behavior): first, as immediate devices for the enhancement of meaning, significance and clarity of the thing symbolized, and second, as a manifestation of the historical flow of ideation within a given culture. To bring an example close to home, the words on this page, hopefully, constitute an immediately effective aid to perception (and communication) on the part of the reader. As a symbolism (or a symbolic system), they are also the final result of myriad causes that go back to pre-history and the evolution of spoken language, filtered through philological and historical processes, quite a remarkable record of a functional continuum and one which it is difficult for both reader and writer to begin to appreciate at *this* immediate, existential moment. Both of us, un-

---

[23] Whitehead, *op. cit.*, pp. 62–63. (Italics supplied.)

[24] *Ibid.*, p. 70. Whitehead's use of the currently unpopular word "instinct" was considered respectable in the nineteen-twenties before the nature-nurture conflict had reached its present state of confusion. His idea of instinct was, I suspect, similar to the Freudian construction today.

[25] *Ibid.*, pp. 20–59.

[26] *Ibid.*, p. 58.

like Whitehead, are probably too concerned with other, less important, matters of greater presentational immediacy than the symbols of written language.

Symbolic Meaning

Langer recognizes (after as profound a study of symbolism as has lately been attempted) that symbolic discourse must, in our time, bear a heavy onus in the intellectual life of our community. Philosophers of science—in fact, positivists of many persuasions—have created an arbitrary (and, unfortunately, probably meaningless) sharp division between propositional language, in which sense-data in its widest constructs, on the one hand, and all other kinds of experience, on the other, are regarded as totally different sorts of phenomena. The division is so extreme that the positivistic mind construes its own reality almost exclusively in a "fact" category and defends this construction by the appeal to the reasonable argument that his facts yield *results* in the laboratory, the factory, the stock market and elsewhere. What the positivist forgets (or never knew) is that yesterday's sense-data are not today's sense-data. Many of yesterday's *non*-sense-data *are* sense-data today, and vice versa. Such changes have occurred in the positivist's lifetime if he is over twenty-five, and will continue to occur in the future. The acceptance of the language of propositional sense-data is, in other words, merely a provisional expedient, because this language changes as rapidly as any other language man uses.

When the positivist lumps together, in Langer's words, "the symbolization of wishes and fears in dream or fantasy, myth and other religious beliefs and . . . all artistic expression," he is making a tragic mistake; tragic, that is, for him and his positivism, his science, his technology, and his own capacity for perception of reality.[27] First of all, his behavior is indefensible historically, as noted above, and is a symptom of a peculiar case of near-sightedness. In the second place, a less serious problem is created for the rest of us (who live, frequently, in subcultures, the terms of which are dictated by positivists) by the casual lumping together of everything that cannot be described in propositional language into *one* category of experience, the criteria of admission for which depends upon what the enterprise is *not*. These phenomena are regarded as a heap of non-cognitive garbage (serving, perhaps, psychoanalytic or therapeutic purposes) that operate on an emotional level of enterprise, irrelevant to the *testable* realities of concern for society. Langer states:

[27] Langer, *Mind*, p. 80; I am conjecturing here, but, until reading Langer's lucid analysis of this problem, I had often wondered why so many of the scientistically oriented people I know rushed off in their spare time to play violins, paint, and indulge in other "unreal" activities (by their philosophical standards), while non-positivists use their spare time to do the same kind of concrete foolish things most people do. Now I think I know.

> Like most sweeping and simple classifications, the treatment of all non-propositional symbols together as one kind with one function has thoroughly confused the study of human mentality as a whole, and especially of the crucial humanizing activity, symbolic projection. No crasser oversimplification could possibly be made than the assumpton that symbolic processes are either concerned with receiving, handling and storing information, or with externalizing and marking off emotions. The effect of symbolic expression is primarily the formulaton of perceptual experience, and the constant reformulation of the conceptual frames which the cumulative symbolizing techniques—conscious or unconscious, but rarely altogether absent—establish, one upon another, one in another, one by negation of another.[28]

One of the main intellectual mistakes of our time, according to Langer, is, therefore, *either* treating symbolism as if it were sense-data, or discarding it as unreal because it is *not* sense-data, both types of error being noticeable in present highly regarded intellectual circles, particularly at universities. Symbols have meaning, and symbolism *is* meaning, often of a nature critical to cultural life, but not the same kinds of meaning that sense-data has, nor can they or it be expected to perform in the same manner.

Ogden and Richards, in their classic taxonomy of meaning,[29] refer symbolic meaning to those types of constructions associated with psychological reactions to stimuli, and that center upon the referent of the symbol, that is, the ideas upon which symbolic analogues and metaphors are themselves based. But they add, "the reference of a symbol . . . is only one of a number of terms which are relevant to the form of a symbol." [30] They warn us away from propositional constructions of symbols—which in their day they merely called "scientific"—to which they oppose not only emotion but also other highly refined sorts of meanings. (Ogden and Richards treat literary symbols almost exclusively; and the clear differences which exist between literary and cultural symbols have yet to be given the same kind of meticulous, analytic logical-aesthetic treatment as those in literature.)

The expression of symbolic meaning is therefore almost a distinctive type of communication, at once a phase of the mediums: narrative, picture and re-enactment, and yet somehow separate from them as ever-present components of culture. In fact, no inquiry into any aspect of cultural life, in any known way, avoids the inevitable facing-up to a hard structure of predetermined symbols (or a symbolism) almost immediately upon entry into its ambit. If the first man to walk on the surface of the moon chose sym-

[28] *Loc. cit.*

[29] C. K. Ogden and I. A. Richards, *The Meaning of Meaning* (New York: Harcourt, Brace and Co., 1953), pp. 209–250. The first edition of this book was published in 1923.

[30] *Ibid.*, p. 233.

bolic actions (a poetic aphorism, a flag and a telephone call to the high priest of the tribe) before he began collecting minerals, he did just what men have been doing in all of their explorations, intellectual and physical, since pre-historic times.

The author has chosen the notion of the "symbolic umbrella" as a metaphor for the symbolic covering that, in one sense, shields man from the reality of sense-data and, in another, allows him a clearer vision (free from glare and other discomforts) of the terrain around him. In a rash moment, he even prepared a provisional model of this umbrella, bounded on one side by the contemporary institutional symbolisms of *Bureaucracy*, *Propaganda* and *Education*, and on the other by the symbolic mythologies of *Work*, *Progress* and *Happiness*.[31] There was nothing particularly wrong with the seventy-three contemporary cultural symbols the chart contained, but, looking at them in retrospect (the chart was prepared first in 1967 and revised in 1969), there was nothing entirely right about them either. What the attempt illustrates (and there is no need to reproduce it here to make the point), is the difficulty of isolating universally relevant symbols in a volatile social order, especially when one must live in and by that society's own symbolisms.

The great pity is that all of us tend to forget how we originally learned to symbolize and conceptualize symbolisms. If we did not, we might grow to have deeper and more startling insights into them than we seem capable of at present. But nature has locked this evolutionary process into the development of consciousnesses, or so Piaget, whose observations on learning are currently attracting intense interest among educational psychologists, observes. According to Flavell, Piaget tells us:

> It is not the acquisition of language that gives rise to the symbolic function. Quite the contrary, the symbolic function is a very general and basic acquisition which makes possible the acquistion of both private symbols and social signs . . . The first words the child acquires function at most as semisigns . . . (which) refer much more to idiosyncratic and ever-changing schemes of action than to fixed and stable classes of objective reality . . . (f)or a long time the child finds verbal signs as such both difficult to grasp and generally unsuitable for the representational expression of the entities with which he is preoccupied. He responds to this state of affairs by continuing to rely heavily on nonverbal symbols and by assimilating words to his symbolic orientation . . .[32]

Does the acquisition of symbol functioning therefore precede the acquisition of language? Probably.

---

[31] G.N.G., *L C*, pp. 83–87. The model was based upon suggestions from the works of Jacques Ellul and other well-known symbol hunters, particularly Max Weber, whose notions about the symbology of capitalism have often been stated and restated by numerous social thinkers.

[32] John H. Flavell, *The Developmental Psychology of Jean Piaget* (Princeton, New Jersey: D. Van Nostrand Co., 1963), p. 155.

Another significant question is why and when and if men, as individuals, unlearn this art, if they do, and if art it be. It appears that some people lose much of it in the development of conditions we regard as mental derangement. Others seem to "see through" or "see around" certain kinds of symbolism for certain periods during their lives and under severe conditions of physical stress and/or emotional pressure. Perhaps even our fear of death is signified by the dim metaphor we have made for the eventual state of non-being: the dark angel. All the rest, funerals, gravestones, monuments, are remembrances and symbols of *living*. Concepts of eternal life—heaven and hell—are symbolisms in *negation* of what sense-data tell us about mortality. And our fears of death may center on that possible instant, before we pass into oblivion, when all our carefully devised symbol structures fail, and we are faced with that *other* reality, the one that the logical positivist dares not search for and press into his practical formulae.

In the solitude of consciousness, no wonder, then, that we may inquire (of whom?) whether there are *any* truths adequate to man's state which are *not* symbolic truths, and which do not exemplify man primarily as a maker and user of symbolisms.

Conclusion

Symbols are discussed in this chapter from a number of perspectives, first as a mystical force which adds power to the essential activities of living.

Second, the relation of signs, symbols, icons and rituals—and the use of words in current discourse—are treated, as well as the need by man for symbols to interpret the massive amounts of sense-data available to him, both directly and indirectly. The value-free nature of cultural symbols is also treated from a sociological perspective.

In terms of the actual origins of symbols, a concept is advanced that man uses his symbol-making proclivities for simple biological-psychological reasons that result from specific conditions found in most human organizations and that attend, in fact, all communications. The symbol is, at root, a metaphor, and the nature of metaphorical thinking is one aspect of human behavior in his civilizations. If and when this power wanes, we are then dealing with a derangement of some sort, behavioral or mental, as one chooses.

Symbolism is a culturally determined activity, more as a totality than as the arithmetic sum of a group of symbols. Whitehead, some years ago, noted that symbolism was required inevitably in culture to give meaning to all social experience. As cultures change, so do symbols in both their phases: that of immediate experience (presentational immediacy) and as bonds to history (causal efficacy). The social viewpoint of symbolism regards the process as one of metaphorically adding or giving meaning to societal phenomena that need the sustenance of this peculiar type of power.

Symbolic meaning is another matter, frequently subsumed to one discrete category of experience by those who would rather not deal with any form of thinking or behaving that does not reflect a common-sense notion of reality. The limitations of this perspective are noted, and the ubiquity of symbolism as "the other faces" of the mediums of communication are considered in relation to contemporary values. It is noted, also, that the identification and explanation of such metaphors is a difficult task, once one travels beyond a few well circulated symbolic cliché's into the ever-changing lexicon of modern symbolism. Because symbolism appears to be prelinguistic in human experience, its sources are so deeply imbedded in consciousness that the process bespeaks a condition of humanity, and our apprehensions of it probably stop suddenly short at the same place that our awareness of life itself also ceases.

Chapter 3

COMMUNICATING INTENTION

. . . And the reply to a kick in the pants is just another kick in the pants; so pursue—but not too eagerly—injustice.

Bertolt Brecht

THE MATTER of intention was treated briefly in the last pages of Chapter 1. The author has also written elsewhere about intentions, calling them by a more general rubric, "objectives of communication." [1]

In the broad study of communications, it is, however, surprising to discover how little attention has been given intention. Much consideration has, one imagines, been euphemized away in studies of motivation in general, or subsumed into such abused terms as "propaganda," "education," "public relations," "public information," "press relations," and their kin. In the first place, a communicator is usually assumed either to *have* intentions or *not* to have them. (The wisdom of the Victorian virginal query "What are your intentions, sir?" presumes that the suitor *must* have *some sort* of intentions.) In the second place, *if* one has intentions, it is also generally understood that a communicator may (if he wishes) simply and directly articulate them. Or, if an auditor is clever or has a proper method, he may infer them backwards, from message to composer's frontal lobes.

Intention is probably a quality of all communication, just as "motivation" (as the word is usually used by psychologists) is involved with all behavior—as long as the communication and/or the behavior involves human beings.[2] This cause and effect assumption (and assumption it is) rests at the heart of our behavioral sciences, some of our philosophies, and nearly every useful generalization that has ever been offered about commu-

[1] See G.N.G., *L C*, pp. 204–218.

[2] I shall leave to Arthur C. Clarke and his colleagues in the field of technological make-believe the problem of whether computers—or similar instruments—may have

nications. Like motivations, intentions may, of course, be extremely obscure, both to persons sending or receiving a communication, and may, as in the instance of blushing or belching, function entirely beyond the control of the former. As also observed previously, many types of intention, again like motivations, may operate in that dim universe we so glibly label "the unconscious."

The qualitative question that the concept of intentions forces us to ask about human transactions is "Why?" And this question is frequently far more difficult to answer than it should be. Accordingly, we usually credit intention with a psychological power that is, on its face, unmistakable in a communication at the focus of our attention; that is, we note *overt* intention as intention.[3] *Covert* intention we often credit with nothing, or (if we are so oriented), with everything, as convention demands at the time.

The Framework of Intention

One of the few serious considerations of intention *per se* (not in a part of some other discussion) has appeared in the writings of I. A. Richards. His description of what function intention serves in poetry, in fact, is so concise that it deserves direct quotation:

> Finally . . . there is the speaker's intention, his aim, *conscious or unconscious*, the effect he is endeavoring to promote. Ordinarily he speaks for a purpose, and his purpose modifies his speech. The understanding of it is part of the whole business of apprehending his meaning. Unless we know what he is trying to do, we can hardly estimate the measure of his success. Yet the number of readers who admit such considerations might make a faint-hearted writer despair. Sometimes, of course, he will purpose no more than to state his thoughts or to express his feelings . . .
>
> Frequently his intention operates through and satisfies itself in a combination of other functions. Yet it has effects not reducible to their effects. It may govern the stress laid upon points in the argument . . . It controls the "plot" in the largest sense of the word, and is at work whenever the author is "hiding his hand." And it has especial importance in dramatic and semi-dramatic literature . . .[4]

As a quality of communication which transcends both the mediums employed (narrative, picture or drama) and the instrument chosen to dis-

---

intentions. For an amusing treatment of this notion, note the "character" of Hal in his *2001, A Space Odyssey* (New York: New American Library, 1968), or the film or both.

[3] I have previously suggested—and will not emphasize it here—that *artlessly* framed intentions in discourse are frequently all we are talking about when we refer to "objectives" or "intentions," and that artful ones—even those that are downright commercial—often slip by unnoticed. Such artlessness is, of course, frequently what commercial communicators think they are striving for, calling it "product identification," or lionizing the nuisance value of some artless advertisement. See G.N.G., *L C*, pp. 206–207.

[4] Richards, *Practical Criticism*, pp. 182–183.

tribute the communication, intention accordingly seems more vital operationally than as the critical tool Richards discussed above, an insight that he himself seems to recognize in the full course of his writings. Thanks to his acumen, the student is able to generalize the notion of intention to cover nearly the total field of human communication, no matter how expressed. The mechanistically oriented may wish to understand intention as the basic coloration of the various facets of human interactions. Merely to *state* (or *be*) is, to a degree, to imply an objective from a communications viewpoint, if one is effectively stating that he is a person and has an identity in a given culture at a certain moment.[5] This basic coloration is then overlaid with many other hues—some visible to the naked eye, some requiring special illumination—which, while they are usually in flux, signal in behavior (as audited by others) certain human objectives.

The paragraph above may sound like an excursion into ontology, but it is not. It is merely a phenomenological description of a socially observable process, and neither the state of mind or body, or the ultimate disposition of either (in the person communicating at least), are particularly important to its integrity. Nothing metaphysical is implied in such a description, nor need the observer come to any conclusions about the ultimate destiny of the person intending, or his intention.

As an example, let us note the report (selected for its specific and easily perceived objectives) in a recent best seller on how political figures are merchandised on television these days. The writer quotes an idealistic free-lance film maker who was employed to make campaign spots for a candidate and party, both of which he despised. Talking about the political specialties with whom he is forced to work, he says, "Oh, I don't know. The effect is (insidious), but I don't know what we are in our intent. If we were really being charlatans, we would give much more study to the psychological part . . . But these people aren't that smart. They're fools in fact . . . That's because they don't *know* what they're after. Their product is amorphous—it has to be amorphous—because so are they . . . I mean the Nixon people with their identical expressions and their identical dark suits . . ."[6]

The point of the book—that politicians may these days be merchandised like products sold on television—is moot and will be discussed further in Chapter 8. But the point that the film maker comes upon is equally as

---

[5] Certain analysts of interpersonal communications claim that from a metacommunications viewpoint (that is, communications about communications), it is impossible for anyone *not* to communicate, because the very act of remaining silent "says" something about the individual involved. On its own level of analysis—and delimiting its application only to certain special instruments of communications under certain conditions—this observation is certainly true and valuable, perhaps, to students of communications breakdowns in mental illness, patient-therapist relationships and human relations gambits. See Paul Watzlawick, Janet H. Beavin, Don D. Jackson, *Pragmatics of Human Communication* (New York: W. W. Norton Co., 1967), pp. 48–51.

[6] Joe McGinnis, *The Selling of the President* (New York: Trident Press, 1969), p. 116.

trenchant and important, namely, that even under conditions which ostensibly provide the clearest of objectives for communication (getting a man elected to the American presidency), the framework of intention, while ever-present, is nevertheless obscure, subject to forces and counter-forces and sometimes appears at cross purposes with itself to a knowledgeable outside observer. The speaker knows that the framework is there, in fact, what it is supposed to support, and yet the behaviors of the communicators appear to him indecisive, unclear, and, in his words, "amorphous," despite their eventual prospects of "success" in making good their intention.

From another best seller, the adulterous wife of a stuffy British foreign officer (a man she loathes) describes her husband to the hero in these terms, "Rawley's a diplomat . . . The art of the possible, that's Rawley. The limited aim, the trained mind. *Let's not get overheated. Let's not put a name to things. Let's not negotiate without knowing what we want to achieve.* He can't . . . he can't go mad: it isn't in him. He can't live for anything . . ." [7]

Here the ambiguity of intention (perceived quite correctly by his wife as the plot rolls on) provides a crisp insight into what Rawley's intentions are, or *seem* to be. In this novel, as in all of the author's spy stories (and most detective stories), the ambiguity of intention is one of the main elements of the so-called "mystery." Because the reader cannot possibly understand these objectives (unless he guesses at them or has studied the plot formulas of these novels), they are not, in a genuine sense, mysteries at all but instead deceptions. Should one reverse or modify the intentions of what the right characters say and do in contemporary espionage and mystery novels, one is well on his way to solving their puzzles. The measure of success of the fiction is how unexpected such twists in intention are. And they are cleverly handled in the works of John Le Carre, especially since his addicted readers (including the author), although they know by now what type of intentional legerdemain to expect, are still entertained by his skill.

To prove by any reliable method that the intentional framework is, indeed, omnipresent in communications is not possible. It is another assumption, based upon a faith in what observation, reason, and some psychological evidence tells us. It is (and has always been) also accepted as an assumption in most artistic criticism—once the crude notion of "art for its own sake" has been passed over by a critic, a move that he must make, unless he merely wants to repeat a phrase in Latin.

What our recognition of the framework accomplishes for us at this point may be summed up in the provisional conclusion that persuasion is not a class of human intercourse separable (in most instances) from other kinds of communication. It is instead the degree and direction of an already present quality, that of intention. Whether or not all human communica-

---

[7] John Le Carre, *A Small Town in Germany* (New York: Dell Books, 1968), p. 237.

tion may therefore fairly be termed "persuasive" is another matter, requiring a fuller knowledge of the multitude of human "plots" with their infinite number of relationships in which men are involved, a knowledge that no mind will ever contain. To guess, however, that a great percentage of it may be properly called "persuasive" is relatively safe. What we mean is simply that *the intention present in a communication is clear or potent or meaningful enough to be recognized by some auditor (if only an observer) as designed to intrude upon another person's logical or psychological processes* (not necessarily behavior, despite epistemological claims by behaviorists that such processes without "behavior"—as they define it—do not exist).

Intention and Consciousness

One might think that the separation of conscious from unconscious objectives of communication is a relatively simple matter, and so it was before the present age of psychoanalysis. This ubiquitous phenomenon of our time and place, although diminishing as a form of high fashion and cocktail party chatter, has put an enormous strain upon the whole concept of motivation and helped thoroughly to confuse the matter of intention. Those of us who have done our time (and paid our price) on the psychoanalytic couch know from personal experience how the matter of intention concerning any of our behaviors—or thoughts—may be peeled off from layer to layer to layer of interpretation when we are faced with nondirective silence of a skilled analyst or his monosyllables like "Eh?" or "So?" [8]

The *theory* of the unconscious is, of course, the primary culprit. That the concept was not born of Freud's genius is well known, and that such French neurologists and physicians as Saltpetriere, Janet, and Charcot (under whom Freud studied) had articulated notions similar to it—as well as philosophical concepts drawn from sources as different as Plato and Ernst Mach, various medieval thinkers, and a host of other precursors—now plays a potent role in the current fashion of debunking the wizard of Vienna. But Freud brought a new type of systematic thought to the concept of the unconscious, related it fundamentally to the metaphor and symbol (to what end we have noted in the previous chapter), and articulated a theory of mind that was sophisticated enough to contain the paradox of a motivational reservoir that could be neither seen, heard, felt, tasted, intuited, nor brought to consciousness directly. The Freudian contribution was heroic and formidable, no matter what the objections of his detractors,

---

[8] Let me recommend highly here (for nearly everything but its jejune, contrived ending) "Joyce MacIver's" novel, *The Frog Pond* (New York: George Braziller, 1961), that I read *before* an extensive bout with psychoanalysis and, at that time, dismissed as fanciful sensationalism. I have since re-read it and now think it is an excellent, realistic and delightfully irreverent item of cultural history.

if merely by virtue of its influence on art, literature and criticism during the first half of the current century—to say nothing of its more ambiguous function in psychotherapy.[9]

Because the ambiguities surrounding the idea of consciousness bear so critically upon intention (and therefore upon the ultimate process of persuasion), let us examine them more closely than the usual psychoanalytic perspective permits. Psychoanalysis is, after all, primarily intended to be a therapeutic device, despite other services to which it has been called. Freud wisely chose to discuss most of his insights into the unconscious in the format of the case study, and most training given psychoanalysts today centers upon processes in their own unconsciouses or those of their patients. In other words, the problem of consciousness is usually regarded as the dynamic activity of an organism or agent, not primarily as an inevitable part of human experience. Even the generalized unconscious processes identified by Freud were named after agents (or people) drawn from the drama, not identified as abstract dispositions.[10]

Kenneth Burke, however, has manfully described eight manifestations of the unconscious, heavily dependent, of course, upon Freud, and quite useful in application to the notion of intent, largely because they shade for us the usual tendency to sever strictly conscious and unconscious phenomena one from the other as if they were a totally different class of considerations in black and white, a tendency also of many psychoanalysts. Human motivations, unfortunately, admit of few simplistic formulae, particularly those relating to *genus*, for two apparent reasons: 1.) the variability of perception and feeling from individual to individual, and 2.) the interdependence of functions which entwine neurological, physical, emotional, mental and environment factors together. Only in extremely simple matters (reflex reactions, for instance) or among very simple people (some behavioral psychologists, for instance) are such complexities avoided.

Burke's categories, in essence, are:[11]

1. The unconscious processes of the body, including all the activities of growth, repair, metabolism, etc., as well as those functions involved in perception, automatic muscle activities, and certain facets of our thought processes that are probably organic but of which we are unaware.
2. Past experiences, either those that have been forgotten or repressed

[9] A good layman's approach to this topic is J. P. Chaplin, *The Unconscious* (New York: Ballantine Books, 1960). Chaplin, a non-therapeutically oriented psychologist at the University of Vermont has, in a number of books, dealt effectively with obtuse psychological matters in clear English.

[10] The most familiar are the Oedipus and Electra complexes, but by the time one finishes with Freud's followers in this labeling process, one has run through much Greek mythology, Shakespeare and the Bible. The agent is omnipresent.

[11] These categories have been modified from those of Burke, *op. cit.*, pp. 67–72.

from our own living, or those that may be vestigial in our human state and have been passed on to us by culture or hereditary factors which we cannot bring to consciousness.

3. Past experiences of which we are unaware or have been forgotten but that may be recalled to memory, given the proper association or stimulus.
4. Unconscious material which is the part of a subpersonality that we at one time assumed (or presently assume) when drugged or exposed to stress or indulging in artistic fancy.
5. The unconscious meaning and motivations intrinsic to symbols which are used consciously, the presence of which we are unaware of but, nevertheless, feel "right" in a given situation.
6. One's "societal unconscious" (the author's phrase, not Burke's), a sort of Hegelian antithesis to conscious behavior; the unnoticed generalized reaction to all intended, motivated behavior, best described by Marxian notion of class consciousness that implies, also, a concept of class unconsciousness (as in the case of the "bourgeois mind" that cannot perceive the true dynamics of social reality).
7. The unconscious manifestations we like to term "intuition," or (sometimes) "instinct," but which are probably really flashes of highly sophisticated, complex judgment (like the "stroke of genius" that revealed the unconscious to Freud) sometimes called a "creative flash."
8. We all operate, at times, on an unconscious level of sheer stupidity, more happily called "error," "ignorance," "uncertainty" and "confusion" by Burke.

How many of these categories may now be severed *absolutely* from their associations with consciousness? The reader must answer this question for himself,[12] and will naturally use himself as the agent for his conclusion. If he is not blinded by some form of doctrine, he will notice that the conscious and unconscious do not cleave from each other as neatly as he was told in psychology class, or as dramatists and writers often ask us to believe.

The Jekyll Hyde story (in which the doctor remains aware of the behavior of this bestial alter-ego) indicates how great was Robert Louis Stevenson's psychological sophistication, apparently sharper than that of his contemporary, Oscar Wilde in *The Picture of Dorian Gray,* in which the decaying portrait does not directly affect Dorian's person until he stabs it and kills himself. Or perhaps Wilde's commentary on Victorian depravity (and doubtless his own emotions) was even a little wiser than Stevenson's retelling of what is, in fact, a classical theme. Both stories, however, prod

[12] Burke's purpose in devising this list is to make a similar point, namely that the unconscious need not be invariably related to the Freudian notion of repression, as it was by Freud and so often is at present by psychoanalysts.

with considerable prescience the mutability of the conscious and non-conscious experiences of their central characters, who represent neither heroes nor villains but simply people like the authors themselves, fancifully extenuated into fascinating parables.

Unconscious intentions may be manifest in a number of ways, all relevant to communications. First, an individual (or group) may have articulated a conscious objective but actually be motivated by an unconscious one—a matter of degree rather than kind. Most professional actors, for instance, excuse their appearances in trash as the noble pursuit of pelf, while, in fact, many of them enjoy any kind of theatrical excursion. An entire nation may have articulated aims of the loftiest sort concerning the substitution, in its schools, of vocational for liberal education, and actually be responding to the pressure of labor unions to keep child labor out of the market.

Are such contradictions hypocritical or dishonest? They may be in certain instances, but, once again, we cannot judge. An advertising copywriter may consciously enjoy the breakfast cereal he is lionizing in prose and harbor unconscious resentments towards the product *only* because he has to sing its praises. On the other hand, he may receive some kind of gratification from thinking himself a prostitute, while unconsciously he loves what he is doing. Or he may, both consciously and unconsciously, enjoy or despise his work. In any case, he does it; and his finished products are likely to be similar, regardless of his intentions. The matter of conscious or unconscious intent is, from a moral point of view, irrelevant except to the man himself.

Second, an illusion of conscious intent may be employed to dissemble a *real* conscious intent that in turn articulates perfectly with an unconscious intent. Here we may list "campaign promises" intended to get a politician elected, which is exactly what he is after. Again, we are speaking of provisional matters; it is not naïve to assume that politicians frequently fool themselves consciously with their own campaign rhetoric. Self-deception is a form of intent but operates often through short periods of time.

Third, in the absence of any evidence to the contrary, a communication may have an entirely unconscious intent. The "body English" that seems mysteriously to notify a member of the opposite sex that he or she attracts one may be just this sort of communication—although the limited vocabulary of the "English" may be learned quickly and also employed consciously as a signal system.[13] Such involuntary messages (not necessarily

[13] The oddest such system (usually employed unconsciously) was pointed out to me some years ago by a Freudian psychiatrist, and both study and experience tend to confirm it. The signal of sexual excitation from certain women sitting with crossed legs is the repeated rapid swinging of the top leg creating thereby a certain amount of genital stimulation. The swinging occurs at the time the male (usually) object of attraction is *speaking*, and it stops when his voice stops. Confirmation of the validity of this neuromuscular manifestation of intention requires research more intensive than I am compe-

sexual) seem the common property of all societies, and their contents vary with the cultures no matter how simple the realm of discourse, for reasons yet to be discovered by behavioral scientists. But, once again, the margins of the unconscious in such discourse have been far from clearly drawn.

The Focus of Intent

It is difficult for many students of communications to comprehend the degree to which intention may modify the meaning of a given communication, in spite of the fact that most of us in informal situations either use statements of intention to influence our actions, or imply intentions from others that we then construe as the content of what they are trying to communicate to us. Examples include teachers who refuse, for instance, to believe that they are influenced in their grading of students (particularly on subjective tests) by what they assume a particular student's intentions to be. The home economics faculty of a major university once created a storm because an academic department was about to bestow a doctorate (in a sociologically oriented discipline) upon a man who had created a national reputation as an unorthodox nutrition expert. His intentions, they reasoned, for wanting a Ph.D. degree were bad. They assumed he merely wanted to be called "doctor," and, therefore, they also assumed that his scholarship must be faulty, his sponsor corrupt and the academic department in which he worked beneath contempt. The fact that he was an excellent student and had written a competent dissertation meant little to them in the light of what they considered the man's intentions to be.

Those of us who have tried to argue with policemen to the effect that we did not intend to light a cigarette in the subway, or drive over a speed limit know, roughly, that sometimes, under some circumstances, the intent we manage to get others to perceive in *us* may modify their behavior. To return to our Victorian virgin, there is some likelihood that she will submit to her seducer, if he can convince her that his intentions are to marry her. While intention is certainly neither a medium nor an instrument of communication, its influence on the nature of interpersonal activities is obviously critical. What is often misunderstood is where the proper focus of interest should be placed in communication and what should be at the primary attention of the observer or analyst of communications relevant to the communication process in which he is involved, as well as the reasons for the communication.

Historians, biographers, novelists, dramatists and some psychologists often lead us astray in this regard, because they are interested only in the

---

tent to give it. See the amusing article on the work (mainly) of Dr. Ray Birdwhistell on body communication in Flora Davis, "The Way We Speak 'Body Language,'" *The New York Times Magazine*, May 31, 1970, pp. 8–9, 29, 31, 32, 33, 41–42, and the more questionable propositions in the dubious book, Julius Fast, *Body Language* (New York: M. Evans and Co., Inc., 1970).

motivational factors surrounding the intention of communications and no other possibilities, conscious or unconscious, inherent in them. The intention of Edward R. Murrow's famous television broadcast in 1952 on his *See It Now* program concerning the witch hunting activities of Joseph McCarthy was obviously to discredit the junior senator from Wisconsin, as his competent biographer observes.[14] The intention of Hamlet's coaching of the players was unquestionably to "catch the conscience of the king." The intention of Franklin Roosevelt's promise in 1940 to the "mothers and fathers of America" that Americans would not die in "foreign wars" was undoubtedly to win what looked as if it might be a close presidential election.

Judging these communications (and communicators) in their perspectives above, we are led to ask two relevant questions regarding intentions: Were they conscious or unconscious? Were they true objectives—that is, honest or dishonest? In all cases, they were conscious; in all cases they were true or honest, as far as we know (granting that FDR was the political animal we have been led to believe).

Another aspect of intention concerning them, however, comes to us by way of certain experimental data from the discipline of social psychology. One must be extremely wary of such data for a number of reasons irrelevant here, but these particular studies—and others like them—are revealing both conceptually and in what they show about the behaviors of the subjects involved in them. They result largely from a number of studies performed by psychologist Carl Hovland and various associates in the 1950's.[15]

While Hovland arrived at no breath-taking conclusions, he did articulate the notion of "source credibility" which is, in effect, the force in a communication that a *perception of intent* (right, wrong or irrelevant) has upon the nature (in this case the believability) of a message at hand. While his results (and theorizing) indicate quite specifically that if the content of a message is believed for itself, its source is rarely questioned, more ambiguous communications are judged by criteria relating to the "trustworthiness" of the source. In other words, credibility depends upon the implications of intention.

In one of his experiments, Hovland exposed a group of students to a series of magazine articles on various subjects attributed to different "high credibility" and "low credibility" sources. He and Weiss report, "Under the conditions of this experiment, neither the acquisition nor the retention of *factual information* appears to be affected by the trustworthiness of the

---

[14] Alexander Kendrick, *Prime Time* (Boston: Little, Brown and Co., 1969), pp. 50–54.

[15] See Carl Hovland, Irving L. Janis, and Harold Kelley, *Communication and Persuasion* (New Haven: Yale University Press, 1953), pp. 19–55, and Carl I. Hovland and Walter Weiss, "The Influence of Source Credibility on Communications Effectiveness" in Daniel Katz (ed.), *Public Opinion and Propaganda* (New York: The Dryden Press, 1954), pp. 337–347.

source. But changes in opinion are significantly related to the trustworthiness of the source used in communications."[16] Other experimental and theoretical work has also shown that the so-called "prestige" of a communicator effects the way in which messages of various kinds are interpreted.[17]

Data such as these have been available for a considerable time and are usually construed as warnings to writers and propagandists to dress up the trustworthiness of their sources, or to cloak some devious confidence scheme in the prestige of a celebrity or status symbol. They have rarely been considered as significant statements concerning the perception of intention and its relationship to the manner in which transactions of meaning are modified by it. Nor have they been considered in anything but cursory fashion as a component of various kinds of communications under differing conditions, not merely newspaper items, magazine articles, slogans and other convenient experimental material handed to college students in test situations.

Both notions of this sort are suggested here: First, the main focus of attention to any sort of communication (on the part of the communicator or an auditor) is not the nature of the communication but usually how it is likely to be construed. Second, such constructions may attend every type of communication imaginable, although the historian, biographer, novelist, dramatist and some psychologists are then at a loss to explain how this internal process may work, except to admit that different people see things in different ways.

To many, Murrow's motives at the time of the McCarthy broadcast were self-serving and self-aggrandizing. Hamlet's motives, to King Claudius, were devilish; the Lord knows what the Players thought (although Tom Stoppard, an unusual playwright, takes a magnificent guess[18]). Roosevelt's promise (or implied promise) to keep America out of World War II was a solemn pledge to some. That *most* people believed one intent or another in each of these instances is irrelevant; observing the functions of the qualities of communications does not constitute popularity contests or political exercises decided by majority vote. The important point for the student of persuasion is the many possibilities which the focus of intention may have, *considering the nature of the perceptions of the individual who responds to the stimulus involved.*

Elsewhere the writer has considered and discussed "misread objec-

---

[16] Hovland and Weiss, *op. cit.*, p. 345.

[17] See Helen Block Lewis, "An Experiment on the Operation of Prestige Suggestion" in Guy E. Swanson, *et. al.*, *Readings in Social Psychology* (New York: Henry Holt and Co., 1952), pp. 18–29.

[18] See Tom Stoppard, *Rosencrantz and Guildenstern are Dead* (New York: The Grove Press, Inc., 1967). "We're tragedians, you see," says the Player, "We follow directions—there is no *choice* involved. The bad end unhappily, the good unluckily. That is what tragedy means," (p. 80) when the plot of Hamlet's drama is criticized by Guildenstern.

tives," [19] too facile a notion to explain the variability of the perception of intention, once the focus is turned upon the *recipient* of a communication. The process is far more subtle psychologically than the mere tendency to impose expectations (or selective critieria) upon communications and perceive them accordingly—the conventional explanations of such misreadings. This tendency, it appears on second thought, is discovered not only in so-called communications behavior, but is obviously (so obviously that it is often missed) a qualifying element of all perceptions and of all people, places and things, as well as messages, and of objects and actions and animals as well. To speak, therefore, of selective perception is to speak of *all* perception as it always functions, not to describe *one* form or peculiarity of normal or average perception, as one judges either or both.

In these terms, then, may a building have an intention? May a can of beans on a supermarket shelf? May a statue, a gerbil, a telephone, a calendar, a barometer? Of course they may, depending upon the perceptual disposition *of the individual observing them.* To a hungry man, a sandwich is to eat (a critical point in the study of persuasion to which we shall return later). To some, a cat is to stroke, as the children's book observes. To others, it is to recoil from. And to still others, it is to sneeze and break out in hives because of. Depending, therefore, upon how we direct the focus of observation, the quality of intention of any message may be relevant or irrelevant to our concerns, depending upon what we are looking at and what part of consciousness we audit it with.

Any simpler observation than this one (those, for instance, accepted in much contemporary behavioral science), are entirely inadequate for a holistic view of the communication of intention in a many-faceted cultural field including, often, situations in which vast numbers of individuals are exposed to single messages with possibly ambiguous—or hidden—intentions.[20] What is less significant about an intention than its motive, is the way in which it is perceived. And this perception is variable among different people. It may even vary for the same individual within a short period of time. Most pat psychological formulae, therefore, by which we presently judge the power of intention do not accord with empirical observation, except in limited, experimental settings that realistically describe a behavior

---

[19] See G.N.G., *L C*, pp. 215–217, and the notation there that pertinent material on the distortion of apperception can be found in Bernard Berelson and Gary Steiner, *Human Behavior* (New York: Harcourt, Brace and World, Inc., 1964), pp. 183–187, 530–532.

[20] Vance Packard, for instance, made much of the supposed intentions of advertisers and motivational researchers in *The Hidden Persuaders* (New York: David McKay, Inc., 1957), and sold a lot of books. His well-meant warnings seem today considerably overstated, not because advertisers are any less covetous than he implies, but because translating these intentional into subliminal appeals is far more difficult to accomplish than Packard was led to believe by the glib behavioral "scientists" (a word loosely used in this context) that advertising agencies consult on these arcane matters.

process *up to a point*. They are far more useful, usually, as springboards for conjecture than evidences of cause and effect.

Manifestation of Intention

Our study of persuasion is, in some respects, almost entirely an inquiry into the nature of intention and into its focus and its effects, considering particularly the multi-faceted perceptions of the attentions of others and, most important, what people in contemporary cultures are likely to *do* in response to them. This latter consideration almost constitutes a description of the process of persuasion as a form of human behavior: simply the behavioral manifestations that occur as the result of how individuals regard the intentions of others in interacting with them. Students of the process place these transactions in classes of behaviors usually called "communications," and are especially interested in them when the intentions are purveyed to large audiences by means of one of the techniques for devices associated with disseminating narratives, pictures or re-enactments.

Artists are particularly sensitive to these factors and seem often disposed to severe unilateral positions as to the nature and place of intention in art. Certain artists maintain that their art (and creative processes) have no meaning without a starting point rooted in intention. Others claim that they operate merely to satisfy themselves or certain aesthetic criteria, and vehemently deny that intention is significantly manifest in their work.[21] A smaller number take a middle position and claim to attempt to strike a balance between vague intention and the pursuit of craft or art, or search their own labors *post hoc* in order to ferret out their own intentions.

Critical criteria are influenced by the same sorts of principles. The present drama critic of *The New York Times* seems equally interested (or disinterested) in *all* intentions, and therefore writes existentially about the manifestations of theatrical art as he sees or misses them on the New York stage. A quondam drama critic for the late *Daily Worker*, when explaining his craft to the author some years ago, emphasized that intention (or degree of "social realism" the author expressed) seemed to him the most important (in fact critical) dramatic element in any play as performed on stage. Secondly, he was concerned with how well that intention (if "realistic" or "correct" enough) was communicated to the audience, and what the spectators were likely to do about it.[22] (The critic gave the play the

---

21 A novelist friend summed this viewpoint up for me a short time ago when we were discussing a possible plot for his new novel, and I noted that a particular theme would help a specific social cause considerably. "I don't write to help causes," he said, "I write to tell stories." Intentions aside, his novels have probably helped many causes anyway.

22 The reader is reminded how easily this sort of effect is achieved in certain communications. The ending of Odet's *Waiting for Lefty* saw the cast of actors (playing cab drivers) and first night audiences all yelling "Strike . . . strike . . . strike!" in unison back in the 1930's. And various rock singers and youth idols have managed to achieve

writer was associated with at the time high grades for intentions but failed it as a success in communicating them, or in its probability of evoking social action.)

Educators have recently been awakened to intentions by means of a new fashion that asks teachers to "articulate terminal behaviors" for elementary and high school children. What the phrase means, when translated from educational patois,[23] is that various educationalists (spurred on by psychologists like B. F. Skinner and educational experts like Robert F. Mager)[24] seemed recently to discover that clear, conscious, mechistic, testable and visible results were rarely articulated in modern schooling. Their obsession with objectives, the development of instruments for testing them and working out so-called "systems" to achieve them, has been the cause of considerable activity and merriment in professional educational circles. While these educators' behavioral notions of objectives sometimes sidestep the range of considerations we have made of intention in this chapter, they have indeed added to what we know about intention's manifestations a few reasonable confirmations of already verified hypotheses.

In most arts, the more obtrusive an intention, the less likely is the work of art, frequently, to first, enhance that objective and second, to communicate successfully on a cognitive or emotional level.[25] Of course, obtrusiveness and the degree to which it manifests itself anywhere is not a precise concept. It is frequently judged in reverse, from effect to cause. If a persuasive communication fails to persuade, *and* the intention seems overstated, we may assume that it was, in this instance, obtrusive. Yet, under some

---

much the same effects in their performances at festivals and other recent gatherings of their clans. Going even further back into the century one is reminded that Marcel Duchamp's "Nude Descending a Staircase" created a riot when it was first shown in New York City, and the artist probably painted it with just such an objective in mind.

23 See Benjamin S. Bloom, (ed.), *Taxonomy of Educational Objectives* (New York: Longmans, Green Co., 1956) to see how this sort of semantic nonsense gets started.

24 See B. F. Skinner's *The Technology of Teaching* (New York: Appleton-Century-Crofts, 1968), for the behavioral view of how to achieve better and clearer objectives in education by re-defining "education." See also Robert F. Mager, *Preparing Instructional Objectives* (Palo Alto, California: Fearson Publishers, 1962), for an example of what happens when you stop talking sense about the processes of education and start thinking (?) solely in terms of objectives. Both books are, in my opinion, frightening illustrations of how misconstructions of the role of intention in communication (and education) contain within themselves the potential ability to destroy or emasculate complex motivations.

25 This phenomenon is somewhat like "the law (of) Reversed Effect," which is by no means a "law" and is definitely not *regularly* applicable to any class of communications, although intentions may often "boomerang" in various ways. See J.A.C. Brown, *The Techniques of Persuasion* (Baltimore: Penguin Books, 1963), pp. 80–81. Also note the more extensive discussion of the "boomerang" of intentional communications in Robert K. Merton, *Social Theory and Society and Social Structure*, Enlarged Edition (New York: The Free Press, 1968), pp. 571–578, in Merton's discussion (written in collaboration with Paul F. Lazarsfeld) of radio and film propaganda as they appeared to the eyes of sociologists some years ago.

circumstances, judgment may be applied to this matter without reasoning backwards.

The inappropriate obtrusiveness of intention into communication may be understood as operating on a scale from "no intrusion" to "complete dominance." The objective of the communication must then be located somewhere on this scale. The famous film *Bonnie and Clyde* had intentions. They are all locatable on a continuum. So did the controversial play, *The Deputy*. Now, each of these communications must be held up to particular audiences to which they were exposed in order to judge the degree of obtrusiveness of the intentions. This will also tell us the degree to which these communications probably succeeded in "moving" their spectators.

In the case of *Bonnie and Clyde*, if we assume that the objective was to stimulate empathy by means of filmic violence (one possible objective), it succeeded admirably, considering the young, excitable, emotionally vulnerable audiences to which such types of movies appeal. *The Deputy*, on the other hand, as an anti-Catholic polemic (a fair summation, probably, of the intention of its American production), was largely an irrelevant and overly didactic intellectual exercise to most of the reasonably educated, older people who witnessed it. Its failure to carry through its intention, therefore, had to do largely with the over-emphasis, over-statement and the spurious cultural logic of that intent shown in the drama.

Most artists—even those as committed as Picasso, Shaw or Pound—recognize that didacticism (which often results from the inappropriate intrusion of intention into art) is frequently an enemy of the clear transfer of meaning, particularly emotion. For this reason, various didactic artists, overwhelmed at the necessity of communicating their intentions at any cost, have tried to write emotion out of transaction between their publics and themselves. Brecht and his idea of an "epic theatre" is one example; there are and have been others. Schoolmen who do not comprehend the enormous role of "affect" (as they call it) or emotion in education (as opposed to mere training) are equally as ready to sacrifice part of the potential communications spectrum in favor of the clear articulation and dominance of intention in schoolroom procedures. Such obsession with intent seems reasonable by virtue of its social respectability and amenability to measuring devices presently available to behavior scientists. And the trend is seen everywhere: in ninety-nine per cent of the poster art on view today; at the university; in the studios of educational and documentary movie producers (who produce the dreariest fare on today's market); in potboiler pornographic literature; in commission reports; and wherever one looks.

Nor is this merely a momentary manifestation, but a time-honored one that seems to move from communications instrument to instrument as audiences and organizations vary. The professional New York theatre was very much alive with didacticism (much of it intrusive) in the 1930's. Today, plays intended to entertain (on various themes concerning modern standards of sexuality) with intents far from didactic (like those of Neil Simon) make up much of the successful commercial fare. Many novels and films seem (to this writer), as of 1970, to have increased their didactic thrusts in the last decade. Education has been, and always is, didactic, but the present trend towards the identification of objectives is introducing to it a new and trivializing type of preoccupation with intention. It is influencing not only in classroom procedures but textbooks and the use of programmed learning devices, the latter constituting the most dreary form of educational innovation since the Palmer Handwriting System, for the simple reasons cited above.

Conclusion

Intention in communications is closely related to all forms of motivation in the flux of social life. It is a quality which, although it appears much like a medium of communication, transcends immediately perceptible characteristics of the three mediums communications and is formulated in many different ways. It is not a *class* of human transaction but an *objective*, designed to intrude upon another person's logical or psychological processes.

Unconscious intentions are frequent and are related to the numerous kinds of unconscious behavior it is possible to observe (or feel) in human transactions. Some of these are related strictly to Freudian notions of unconscious; some are not. Combinations of unconscious and conscious intentions reveal interesting insights into how and why people regard certain communications the way they do, and whether or not a communication is likely to achieve its objective. From a theoretical perspective, the problem of intent is largely psychological, centering on the way (or ways) that given audiences perceive the intentions of communicators and their communications. A good deal of experimental (and some theoretical) data exist upon the various curiosities visible in this process. What they accomplish, at present, is to force the re-evaluation of the once generally accepted concept of "selective perception" (and other theories) to explain why certain individuals do or do not respond to the intention of certain kinds of persuasive messages.

Intention also plays a critical role in artistic, affective and emotional communications, often intruding into them in such a degree that their own didactic purposes are somehow negated or reversed. Didactic trends have appeared all through the history of art and letters and are with us at present, particularly in education. In the latter field, they are currently shifting toward a naïve but positivistic (and therefore highly quantifiable) trend towards shifting the intentional aspects of all schooling towards the articulation and measurement of certain kinds of observable cognitive terminal behaviors, especially those that may most easily be graded by machines. In both art and education, evidence exists of wide misconstruction and misunderstanding of the quality of intention and of its role in communication and persuasion.

Chapter 4

HISTORY AND MYSTERY

Whatever the "ultimate" theory of communication may be, it will no doubt continue to underline the creative role of "central process" ("brain," "mind") in guiding man's impact on his cultural and biological evolution. To interpose in the sequence of perception of current events a contextual map of past, present and future aims and strategies is to open new paths of expression.

Harold Laswell

No accident locates man's first recorded—and perhaps most important—act of persuasion in Western culture in the book of *Genesis*, 3, 6. Records of intentional communications seem to pre-date most other kinds, and their origins are lost in antiquity somewhere in the quasi-feral world of man's evolving brain. This biblical sentence in comparatively recent history in the record of our race: "And when the woman saw that the tree was good for food, and that it was pleasant to the eyes, and a tree to be desired to make one wise, she took the fruit thereof, and did eat, and gave also unto her husband with her; and he did eat." [1] So began the mystery of persuasion.

Antiquity

Recent also is the relatively flimsy account of the ancient world upon which most contemporary historical scholarship stands: a handful of poets and playwrights, a few formal biographers writing about events that had ended many years before, myths retold from mouth to mouth for generations finally written down, and traces that archeology has permitted us to glean about how men once lived and died.[2] The first formal historians discovered in Greece and Rome are remarkably eloquent but no less influenced by persuasive motives than their modern counterparts are.

Both the sacred and profane drama of the Greek classical period, at least those extant,[3] were similar to "social drama" as we know it today,

[1] This is the Bible according to King James' scholars. The implications of Eve's act, although hardly described in detail, have had results that echo in every culture in the

dealing with themes of contemporary relevance and continually holding up models of how moral and legal transgressions doomed men and their societies to death and worse. In this connection, one needs only to recall the fact that *Oedipus Rex* (probably the most familiar of these plays) begins with the citizens' plea to their King to root out the evil which has brought plague and pollution upon Thebes. Even the Greek satyr-plays, of which we have only fragments, and the Roman comedies that followed them in story and style, probably functioned as more than games or sheer entertainments with their psychological commands to the audience to celebrate fruition and procreation.[4]

Philosophy was born in the matrix of intention, if only because the early thinkers set themselves, as a minimum intellectual puzzle, the definition of "the good life," either for man or his society. The early merchant-philosopher Thales, for instance and according to Durant,[5] employed his skill in physical philosophy to predict the harvests at Miletus (for his own financial profit, incidentally).

Judging from the evidence, however, one man looms above all others in antiquity for the command, vision and power of the persuasive thrusts of his thinking, the results of which are still felt by contemporary scholars and men of action in Western society. The man, of course, was Plato, and his method of discourse was roughly allegorical and vaguely dramatic, the philosopher himself weaving in and out of the *personae* of his dialogues, facing argument with argument, nuance with nuance, in illuminating his defiantly idealistic picture of man, his gods and the society in which he lives.[6]

Plato's persuasion is characterized clearly by Wells. "(He) is a land-

---

West where the custom of marriage (and the concept of sin) exists today. See Chapter 15 for discussion of what I regard as the genuine seminal error on Adam's part.

2 Some of this chronicle, as it relates specifically to propaganda, appears in George N. Gordon, Irving A. Falk, and William Hodapp, *The Idea Invaders* (New York: Hastings House, 1963), pp. 17–29. The paucity of this record is also the central theme of the remarkable mystery novel by Josephine Tey, *The Daughter of Time* (New York: Berkeley Publishing Corp., 1960).

3 The excellence of *The Complete Greek Drama* and *The Complete Roman Drama* in four volumes and published by Random House prompts their citation here as profitable excursions into the intentions of classical drama.

4 Might modern pornography and burlesque shows hide the same covert intention? Audiences for them, it is usually agreed, are made up mostly of balding (or gray-haired) men between the ages of 45 and 70, a time, in our culture, at least, when male feelings of fertility decline noticeably, especially when one does not have recourse to fantasy, particularly theatrical and/or photographic fantasy—or so I have noticed among other males my age. See John Gassner's delightfully delicate description of these early Grecian "stag shows" in *Masters of the Drama* (New York: Random House, 1940), pp. 80–82.

5 Will Durant, *The Story of Philosophy* (New York: Simon and Schuster, 1926), p. 94.

6 One of the best Plato samplers I have seen is J. D. Kaplan, *Dialogues of Plato* (New York: Pocket Books, 1950). It contains much of the pith of the *Apology, Crito, Phaedo,* and a well edited version of *The Republic.*

mark in history . . . a new thing in the development of mankind . . . Here is a man who says boldly to our race, and as if it were a quite reasonable and natural thing to say, 'Take hold of your lives. Most of the things that distress you, you can avoid; most of the things that dominate you, you can overthrow. You can do as you will with them.' " [7]

Wells is correct, regarding particularly *The Republic*, the political persuasiveness of which still remains trenchant and—sometimes to our peril—seductive. The implications behind Plato's words potentiated the extraordinary, near-perpetual motion of Platonic idealism. Until his time, man had created cultures and subsequently destroyed them, ostensibly at the whim of the gods. When man aspires to a godly state, the ancient myths tell, he is doomed, because the sin of *hubris* is the ultimate mortal crime. Neither Plato nor his teacher Socrates (and it is difficult historically to sever cleanly the characters and ideas of one from the other) directly confronted this classical truth. They provided new alternatives in place of it: Socrates (as Plato saw him), at the moment when he refuses Crito's help in escaping from his death cell and takes instead the hemlock; and Plato (as Plato perceived himself), when he dared to tamper with the psychological wellsprings of truth and beauty in *The Symposium* and of government by the gods' decree in *The Republic*.

The Origins of Argument

Persuasion, as we shall see, usually produces counter-persuasion. And Plato was answered in spirit, if not in skill, by his student Aristotle, the remains of whose writings are hardly given an opportunity, by the accidents of survival, to respond fully to the former. Aristotle was the prototypical skeptic and pragmatist; there is much to be said for the counter-force of his precept and the persuasiveness of his stance. In a way, he was history's first genuine hard-line intellectual, preferring facts to theories, knowledge to ideals. While philosophers do not enjoy placing him directly at odds with Plato, the paradigm he has handed down to men through the years has been invariably and gustily anti-Platonic, and has, perhaps, more than once saved Western man from being devoured by his own illusions, Aristotle's belief in the essential rationality of man was, even considering the standards of discourse at the time of Alexander the Great, little short of annoying, and so he himself apparently seemed to his students. His dream of an encyclopedic grasp of all knowledge was, as we know today, as fundamentally futile as Plato's notion that philosophers should be kings or that poets be exiled from the perfect state. But it is to Aristotle's credit that he was not frightened by what must have been numerous indices of his own limitations, of which he was aware in his own time.

Let Plato affirm his wisdom in the Socratic manner—by the discovery

[7] H. G. Wells, *The Outline of History* (New York: The Macmillan Co., 1921), pp. 300–301.

that ignorance is rampant in the land, and that *he who knows he does not know* is indeed the wise man. Aristotle simply wanted to *know* and directed his intellect *to find out.* According to Wells, "Plato says in effect, 'Let us take hold of life and remodel it'; and this soberer successor: 'Let us first know more of life and meanwhile serve the king.' "[8]

The modern "activist"—be he conservative or liberal, and regardless of his cause—may feel a certain chagrin, shared by the author, that the broad patterns for the major functions of political, social, religious, and almost every other type of persuasion we know at present were drawn with awesome clarity by two (or perhaps three) men 500 years before the birth of Christ. The fact remains that intellectual styles of persuasion—and even some emotionally oriented techniques—that seem peculiarly modern, because they appear in contemporary newspapers and magazines, have been open secrets for 2,500 years.

Other models and refinements were also clearly anticipated in antiquity. The oriental Sun Tzu pays deference to the possibilities of psychological warfare in *The Book of War* and anticipates contemporary Eastern "total" persuasion by today's Chinese Communists for whom, involved in a philosophical climate not unlike that of Plato's *Republic,* the source of all political, social and even personal persuasion is embodied in the mystique of the state. Nor is one encouraged to the notion of historical progress in the art of persuasion by the contemporary sounds of Cicero's attacks against Cataline,[9] or by the writings of various obscure Indian astrologers on persuasion and warfare hundreds of years before Christ.

The Roman Tradition

Persuasion today (particularly in its organized manifestation of propaganda) is associated by most writers with Mediterranean culture, particularly the "Italian hand," for more than one good historical reason. In many ways, prototypes for the development of most of the social structures in Europe which were to emerge centuries later (and continue into the present day) appear to have been first institutionalized in the Rome of the Caesars.[10] Greek notions of democracy (or the concept of the forum and the power of persuasion within the limits of the human voice), economic and cultural imperialism, as well as the distinctive genius of Roman technology were all bureaucratized in Italy by both government and convention. In a more or less organized fashion, the Roman power structure pro-

---

8 *Ibid.,* p. 302.

9 Children no longer appear to be required to suffer through Cicero's orations in the original Latin, and many educators regard this as progress. I do not. Raised as I was in a family of lawyers and jurists, it was Cicero's orations (in Latin) that convinced me to eschew, at that time, a profession so heavily dependent upon one's powers of persuasion. Little did I know what was ahead of me, and how well my enforced study of Marcus Tullius Cicero in Latin would serve.

10 The progress is well characterized in Wells, *op. cit.,* pp. 451–492.

vided the underpinnings for what, centuries later, would be considered a Latin proclivity for the manipulation of individual and collective dispositions.

Possibly no historian has understood this historical trend with quite the clarity of Shakespeare, writing about a culture which had declined and fallen a millenium and a half before he began his acting and writing career. The crux, nevertheless, of *Julius Caesar*, displays an astute insight into what made the Roman world tick: what amounts, in effect, to a contest in persuasion between Antony and Brutus concerning the benevolence of Julius Caesar in his function as, fundamentally, a politician. Whatever focus the plot of this drama (or melodrama) eventually takes in its final scenes (which should, structurally, provide the high-point of the play), the Antony-Brutus "great debate" turns out to be the psychological climax when it is produced.[11]

"Social man," in fact—the object of political persuasion—appears to have been a Roman invention, according to Hannah Arendt. "(I)t is significant . . ." she writes, "that the word 'social' is Roman in origin and has no equivalent in Greek language or thought. Yet the Latin usage of the word *societas* . . . originally had a clear, though limited, political meaning; it indicated an alliance between people for a specific purpose, as when men organize in order to rule others or commit a crime." [12] In the journey from Julius Caesar to Octavianus Augustus, one sees the refinement of this force. Caesar extended to its ultimate a Greek pattern of political and military government. He emerged as a political dictator in the modern sense combining (in a manner Hitler was to follow long afterwards) the functions of military, judicial and aristocratic leadership in the figure of one apparently highly attractive personality, who, like modern charismatic heroes, found no difficulties in attracting enemies as well as friends.

By the period of Augustus, Roman dictatorship still remained absolute, but it had been embued with the *imperia* of benevolence—what we might call today a "social conscience." How significant that the Julians preferred the title *princeps* to *imperator, dictator, perpetuus* or *tribunicia potestas,* all of which had previously fallen to Caesar. The emperors, duly deified at first and later regarded still as living gods, ruled at Rome certainly, and probably in much of the empire, at the consent of the governed,

---

[11] In his youth, Orson Welles continued the analogy into the present era by dressing his Romans in his WPA-Broadway production (in the 1930's) as modern Italians, complete with (then) contemporary Fascist uniforms. See Welles' remarkable analysis and pre-production version of the play (from his "boy genius" period) written with Roger Hill, *The Mercury Shakespeare* (New York: Harper and Brothers, 1939).

[12] Hannah Arendt, *The Human Condition* (New York: Doubleday Anchor Books, 1959), p. 24. See her full discussion on the rise of and severance, one from the other, of "social" and "political" man on pp. 23–69, for an incisive discussion of this aspect of Western tradition.

balancing a way of life, new to the world, of both "private" and "public" living that maintained a reasonable equilibrium between the two due to the persuasive influence of a sophisticated system of laws.

These edicts spelled out the proper social roles for the governors and the governed as private and public citizens, rewarding, roughly, those who obeyed them and punishing harshly those who did not. The human instruments of persuasion for the *jus publicum* throughout the empire were the echelons of *praetors*, bureaucrats of vaguely stoic persuasions, who kept the peace where possible, and achieved—considering the period—a wide margin of equality and personal freedom for those living under Roman rule, unless they presented, like the early Christians, a clear and present danger to the regime in both an attractive and persuasive context.[13]

If we allow our perspective to scan the rough contour of Rome's 590-or-so-year hegemony in the Western world, certain configurations stand out. What had been a society knit by strong militaristic and novel political forms of cultural persuasion became an empire ruled largely by law and a naïve, but deeply felt and widely understood, religious communality of agreements.[14] The latter of course, was built upon the kind of uncertain foundations on which mysticisms survive and thrive: an old pantheon of dead, foreign gods providing sanctions for the worship of a living god who, in the person of the more notorious emperors, was sometimes all too human—and frequently psychotic as well.

What mythology needed from the Romans was exactly what it got. The wages of corruption and sin in Italy itself were Rome's eventual destruction. The living god was forced to join his dead ancestors and, even better, to arise shortly from the repository of dead deities, walk for a while with mortals, and return finally to the realm of the spirit. The Western world, in short, was ripe for Christianity, with its fusion of Hebrew mysticism, Roman deification, and eschatology borrowed from the relatively liberal and sophisticated evolution of Roman law with its emphases upon society and social values.[15]

---

[13] See Erich Kahler, *Man the Measure* (New York: George Braziller Inc., 1956), pp. 97–110.

[14] In spite of the fashion of equating our culture with that of Rome (a comparison quite apt regarding technological matters, but otherwise a strained metaphor) contemporary America may be moving in quite the opposite direction from Rome, a society with a strong religious and social biases. Our culture, on the other hand, is dominated by a fusion of military and political power.

[15] The world had been waiting for this god for a long time. Hebrew tradition had predicted (and occasionally found) a savior or messiah, as the recent discovery of the Dead Sea Scrolls dramatizes for the modern theologist. The *Amphitryon* myth had also periodically appeared in Greek and Roman drama, sometimes as comedy, sometimes as tragedy, and sometimes (as in the case of Plautus' version) as both. In this story the king of the (dead) gods (Jupiter) mates with a mortal (Alcmena) in the guise of her husband (Amphitryon) and begets a strong demi-god son (Hercules) who, through

The Middle Ages

Why and how the persuasive power of Christianity which, in a remarkably short period, swept Europe and eventually located its power base, after some excursions, back in the city of Rome, cannot be discussed fully here.[16] The conversion of St. Augustine from the Manichaen to the Christian faith, however, signifies a metamorphosis in the history of the Christian persuasion comparable to the vision seen by Paul of Tarsus on the road to Damascus hundreds of years before. In his confessions, Augustine grapples with the timeless problems of meaning in life and free will to the conclusion that *faith* precedes all forms of understanding, and that all material and intellectual phenomena arise from the truth of God.

His vision reversed the Patristic philosophy of the first Church Fathers who reasoned that *knowledge* was the precondition of faith in God, quite a comfortable assumption if one looks back upon the successful experiment of Roman culture. If one, however, was able to apprehend the coming destruction (or feel it portending) of man's inventions, traditions and laws (as Augustine probably did), one tends to reject the perfectionist ideas of knowledge as the key to salvation, germane to gnostic mysticism, and choose instead the way of faith. This was largely Augustine's message to the Scholastics who were to follow him. And it relates intimately to the unsolved question of exactly what European thinkers found so attractive in the Christian faith—and to the reasons it remained repulsive as well to others, like Jews and practitioners of the Black Mass.

To ask for faith as a prior condition of consciousness is a bold step. But set in the context of the dissolving Roman Empire, barbarian wars, unrest, changing administrations of political power, anarchy, plague, corruption and the rampant mysticism of incompatible demiurges, the unity of purpose in life that the act of faith guarantees makes sense, persuasive sense—as history. Augustine asks God:

> Where did I find Thee that I might learn Thee? For in my memory, Thou wert not, before I learned Thee? Where did I find Thee that I might learn Thee, but in Thee above me? Place there is none; we go backward and forward and there is no place. Everywhere, O Truth, dost thou give audience to all who ask counsel of Thee, and at once answerest all,

---

suffering and miraculous labors, achieves immortality. (Some versions of the story are more prescient than others. One tells that Hercules *immortal* parts dwelt after death on Olympus, while his *mortal* parts descended as a spirit to the Underworld, anticipating neatly the subsequent Christian polarities of heaven and hell.)

[16] See Chapter 11 for an analysis of the power of Christian persuasion (including that which is still mediated from Rome) in contemporary society. In Anne Fremantle, *The Age of Belief* (New York: New American Library, 1955), the reader will find a lucid description of how, why and where Christianity dominated the Western mind during the Middle Ages, mostly in the selected words of its major philosophers.

> though on manifold matters they ask Thy counsel. Clearly does Thou answer, though all do not clearly hear. All consult Thee on what they will, though they hear not always what they will.[17]

Commensurate with such all-inclusive divine power, the burden of sin had somehow to be assumed into Augustine's thought and by his almost impersonal and entirely transcendent God. The result was the concept of original sin, the heritage of all humans whose destiny was finally determined only by the Grace of God alone and the instrument of his church on earth, man's one instrument of the Kingdom of God. Some of the ruthless vengeance of the Old Testament deity found its way into Augustine's tortured musings, some of the messianic teachings of Jesus, and some of the administrative *savoir faire* of the Roman bureaucracy as well. Upon its uncompromising structure was built the framework of Scholasticism and the structure which was eventually to become the Roman Catholic Church, the doctrine of which was to be exported eventually to almost every corner of the earth.

Scholasticism (which re-created, in its squabbles between Realists and Nominalists, the ancient Platonic versus Aristotelian perspectives) provided a wide range of intellectual speculation during the Middle Ages, far more filled with ferment than the rubric "Dark Ages" indicates, as long as they proceeded from Augustinian principles. Gnostic notions and devil worship, while always in evidence, were not generally considered valid intellectual fodder for too much speculation; they were earthly corruptions and treated as such. A wide range of human concerns, from science to inchoate sociology, were open, however, to free and unhampered examination, and dissents of thought were freely encouraged with more assurance in the Middle Ages than was permitted later, after the neo-classical truths of Greek and Roman were taken as dogma with the coming of the Renaissance. In the later period, many useful truths, products of the Middle Ages, were ignored by men of art, science and religion until the sixteenth century, awaiting, as it turned out, subsequent rediscovery.

In the hard-core no-nonsense intellectual combat of the second half of the first millenium of Christianity in Europe, Platonic idealism could not survive. By the thirteenth century, efforts were being made in Rome to include the antagonistic Aristotle, somehow, in the hierarchy of Christian saints. Needless to say, they failed, but they indicated how attractive the Greek encyclopedist's skeptical approach to the natural world (or medieval interpretations of that approach) were to Scholastics. By this time, Christianity was epitomized in certain figures who indicate a blooming cultural universality that would pass quickly in the next few hundred years, and leave in its wake the irrefutable challenge of the Protestant heresy. St. Francis of Assisi and Innocent III represented the culmination of the

---

[17] Quoted in *ibid.*, pp. 33–34.

Church-penitent and the Church-politic, respectively, standing for the "church as prayer and the church as power . . ."

St. Bonaventura and St. Thomas, on the other hand, epitomize the Church-pensive, the Church as thought, according to Fremantle.[18] Thomas Aquinas also represented the face of Aristotelian philosophy to Christian Europe as it had been filtered through 1,600 years of history. In the presently surviving corpus of his work (an excess of sixty books), his thinking changed—and diminished—the persuasive power of Augustinian Christianity. Set against the background of the Crusades (which introduced the pragmatic genius of the East, particularly in medicine and the occult arts, to Europe and brought to it the Averroest philosophy developed in Islam during the twelfth century), St. Thomas set the stage for the religious schism that was shortly to tear Europe apart and turn the Italian hand from matters of theology and philosophy to the manipulation of political and secular power.

Like Aristotle, St. Thomas offered a policy (called by theologists a "philosophy") of experience, slightly richer than empiricism, and far more pragmatic than the cruder "God given" speculation before it. What he accomplished for himself and countless Europeans to follow was the separation between faith, on one hand, and science or reason, on the other, anticipating Descartes' dualism and our own age of logics and psychologics. Faith and rational understanding were split at his hands, and were never to be reconciled again except by abundant exercises of *either* faith *or* reason to allow one primacy over the other in arbitrary argument. The results for the world of faith were stagnation, schism and mystical sectarianism lasting up until the present moment.[19] Reason yielded to the science, technology and neo-classicism of the Renaissance. Fremantle states that in his Aristotelian reconstruction, St. Thomas "finds the happy mean (between Democritus' reduction of thought to sense-data and Platonic idealism) by recognizing that all knowledge is derived from sense experience, but at the same time, he asserts that thought has its proper activity, by which it can draw from sense experience the materials of a knowledge which extends beyond the bounds of the world of sense." [20]

The Renaissance Church

To place the full burden of a schism (that resulted eventually in the seventeenth century College of Propagation of the Faith of the Catholic Church) upon the shoulders of St. Thomas is, of course, unjustified. Har-

---

[18] *Ibid.*, p. 147.

[19] Roots of the often heard argument that man has progressed greatly in conquering nature but has done poorly in understanding himself since the golden age of Greece were probably planted in early Thomism. See Kahler, *op. cit.*, pp. 268–294, for a resume of the immediate results of this schism.

[20] Fremantle, *op. cit.*, p. 150.

old Laswell notes[21] that the Cluniac order in France was pretty well steeped in polemical literature as early as the eleventh century. Persuasion in the Thomistic vein met the new needs, also, of a church which, by now, had fallen into corruption in political and temporal behaviors and faced the challenge of reconciling its "catholicism" with the decreasingly mystical march of science on one side, and the growth of statism, nationality and antagonism towards priests and their churches on another. If the College marks the first institutional, consciously directed agency in Western history designed to act upon the beliefs of the masses and to operate as a formal instrument of persuasion, it was well motivated by a number of natural and excellent impulses, and hardly constitutes a landmark in the history of persuasion. It did indeed provide the word "propaganda" for half-a-dozen languages, to be employed as a semantic punching bag for politicians and professors for the next 300 or more years.[22]

Most church persuasion was (and is) Thomistic, in that it has, largely, given up its medieval battle with science and reason and depends almost entirely upon both pragmatic appeals to and the emotional power of faith. The accomplishments of science, art and technology speak a persuasive language of their own, and, accordingly, even arguments within the Christian community and between sects had to confine themselves increasingly to spiritual rather than earthy matters.[23]

For spiritual and religious discontents were exactly the topics which sparked the Reformation, not a battle between faith and reason, or the defense of the spirit of science. (Most of the Protestant sects into the pres-

---

21 Harold Laswell, *Propaganda and Promotional Activities* (Chicago: The University of Chicago Press, 1969), p. 6.

22 Much has in recent years been made of the fact that the modern word "propaganda" stems from the commission of Cardinals appointed in 1622, who were subsequently known as the Sacred Congregation *de propaganda fide*, and started the linguistic beating that the word "propaganda" had taken since then. See, for instance, Michael Choukas, *Propaganda Comes of Age* (Washington, D.C.: Public Affairs Press, 1965), pp. 19–20, and William Albig, *Modern Public Opinion* (New York: McGraw Hill Book Co., 1956), pp. 291–229, both of which (following L. W. Doob) make the error of construing propaganda as a breed or strain of persuasion of a unique kind by associating it with specific techniques or certain rhetorical tricks. A more sophisticated view construes propaganda to be merely a popular euphemism for the totality of persuasive components of culture and has recently been proposed by Jacques Ellul. It will be discussed in later sections of this volume.

23 The most outstanding "cultural lag" in this regard remains the Catholic Church's present position on birth control, which may bespeak a larger logic than that presented by advocates of population control. The Church's position is not sheer dogma or merely revealed truth, as most believe. Should the Pope and his advisors eventually be shown by the judgment of history to have been acting in an ultimately (and scientifically) defensible socio-cultural manner in this age, threatened as it is by massive nuclear destruction, I should not be surprised. Neither the Pope nor I will probably be around to have the last laugh, however, if the onus of present and temporary overpopulation turns out to be the only way our race manages to survive a nuclear holocaust.

ent century were and are more frightened of the power of the scientific method than Catholicism. The Roman church, remember, had survived, had innumerable martyrs to physical rationality, and had had a good deal of experience with scientists and their advocates-men like Galileo, for instance. The thorn of protest and schism was driven into the Church's side by two major fifteenth and sixteenth century inventions: printing and nationalism, both of which resulted in the formalization of intoxicating persuasions to faith. This tendency fit perfectly the impending developments in the coming age of geographical discovery and imperialism, with its increasing demands for proselytizing the faith in the pagan world to "lead the wretched heathen to the light," in the words of Noël Coward.

The Church's persuasion (like most religious persuasion) was, at root, psychological, appealing basically to tranquillizing mysticisms in the forms of comfortable symbols by which the sense-data of life yielded neither to contemporary methods of secular philosophy nor science. As we observed in Chapter 2, symbols filled gaps in the unknown; but never entirely. Where Rome failed to square sense-data with ritual and dogma, or to reconcile profession with reality, the Protestants stepped in with their simple rituals and Christianity-by-the-book, or by and for the common man—except in England where church ritualism was transmuted by Henry VIII and his talented strategists to a remarkable royal mystique, employing not only the talents of skilled statesmen but those of historians, architects, playwrights and generals. For many years, Britain produced a distinctive road company of the Italian Renaissance, in many ways superior to its original model. Elizabeth herself was more papal (in her English way) than any of the nine Popes (with the possible exception of Gregory XIII), who dwelled in the Vatican during the years that she ruled.

For the rest, the great Protestant leaders, rising amidst the increasingly libertarian thrusts of new nationalisms, returned in differing degrees to the spare and ardent theology of the Bible itself, answering the fundamental human questions (to which Catholicism responded with iconic rituals and Romanesque bureaucracies of authority) by relatively simple metaphors and mystical symbols, nearly as parsimonious as those used by the scientists and philosophers of the later Enlightenment.

Secular Persuasion

Were the history of persuasion in Europe to be told as a drama, it would appear, at the point of the founding of the College for the Propagation of the Faith, that the Italian hand had lost its hold over German, Swiss, Dutch, French, British and (even) Italian reconstructionists. They were not only to reduce the true church to the guardian of minor territories in Europe (and larger ones in South and Central America and other colonial outposts), but to cast it into a secondary role in the exportation of

Christianity into a world that would—for the next 300 years—be largely dominated by European culture, economics, government and military power, much of it of the Protestant persuasion, if and when it looked for God's blessings.

The heritage of Greece and Rome, however, did not die this easily. Nor did it quietly relinquish its old philosophical power to northern European religious agitators, scientists, politicians or philosophers. It merely shifted locus from churchly matters to governmental issues, a self-conscious and deliberate move, achieved, of course, with the blessings of God Himself who now seemed more preoccupied with politics and statist problems than the philosophical issues that had so obsessed the giants of the Middle Ages like Augustine, Boethius, Anselm, Abeland, Bonaventura, Duns Scotus and William of Ockham.

The dramatized story at this point would also display a plot twist, so beloved of the modern scenarist, in that it swung from the hard-headed, no-nonsense, Aristotelian mode back to the idealistic notions of Plato and *The Republic* and those words-without-music that the Greek utopian had written for his philosopher-kings. The particular philosopher-king who would emerge as the particular hero of our story of persuasion would be the Florentine, Lorenzo the Magnificent (and elder), but merely because he is a better symbol of the Platonic Renaissance Italian than either Leonardo (a philosopher-artist-scientist) or Cellini (a politician-artist), or any other of the many candidates for the post, including Caesare Borgia and/or his remarkable father, Pope Alexander VI.

But Lorenzo, sadly, remains a symbol, rather than a historical or philosophical landmark, not because he lacked either profound capacities for thought or a benign program of public works—at which tourists to Italy still gawk. Florence, under his rule, was in pitiful political shape, the victim and instigator of various small wars. Lorenzo, at his death in 1492, handed over to his heir a city-state that was soon to be conquered by the French Army, although the Republic of Florence was eventually returned to the Medicis under Lorenzo's grandson. It was for this reason that an exiled functionary named Niccolo Machiavelli, in seeking the favor of Lorenzo the Younger, wrote his classic treatise on cultural, social and political persuasion that he called *The Prince.*[24]

Machiavelli's *Prince* might have been any one of three people. For political reasons, his exact character was left purposefully vague. It has often been implied that he is Lorenzo the Younger; he behaves unmistakably in many respects like Caesare Borgia, particularly in his more cold-blooded manifestations. In his benign aspects, there is something in him also of the

---

[24] See Niccolo Machiavelli, *The Prince* (New York: New Amstedram Library, 1961), for an excellent, inexpensive version of this classic with a fine introduction by Christian Gauss.

elder Lorenzo who had impressed Florence so visibly and forcefully with his personality during the years in the late fifteenth century when Machiavelli was growing up.

The stereotyped popular portrait of the black Machiavelli that has come down to us is entirely out of order, except where it fuses with notions of the Italian villain whose mischief is gratuitous—as in the case of Iago or the menaces of nineteenth century British and American dramas and later the cinema. In many ways, Machiavelli resembled the younger echelon of today's Black Hand or *Cosa Nostra* gangsters who are reputed to control much syndicated crime in the United States at present: urbane, respectable, well-schooled, highly pragmatic and resourceful enough to defend logically their extra-legalisms.

The law that Machiavelli was overstepping in his advice to the Prince was, of course, church law—and from our present perspective moral law as well—although his basic premises stand up legally remarkably well today. They imply, in effect, that the state has certain rights (or moral immunities) which individual citizens do not have. If one's family needs clothes, for instance, one has no moral right to steal from others. Should a state, however, need certain natural resources to clothe a majority of its population, the imperialist conquest of lands where these resources abound might be morally defensible. The state, in other words, demands the greatest degree of protection man can afford, and the Prince, as guardian of the state, is morally bound to be the instrument of this protection.

Where Machiavelli differed from all other persuaders before his time was in his almost total secularism, a position which must have called for considerable courage on his part. Religion, to him, meant just about as much as it means to most modern liberal politicians: another institution of the social order to be dealt with pragmatically and realistically. Priests and saints may be regarded in terms of the power they hold and use. ("How many divisions does the Pope have?") Affronts either to God's law or man's spirit are, to him, irrelevancies.

With his enormously sensitive perceptions of mob psychology and ongoing concern for the long-term welfare of the masses, Machiavelli was certainly, also, a humanist. In his skeptical but sharp analysis of the political status quo of his time, he shows evidence, as well, of a scientific bent, at least in his orderly accumulation of historical data. The manipulation of men was, to him, not only a pragmatic possibility, but quite necessary. Directed persuasion was, as Machiavelli understood it, a distinctive component of statesmanship, sometimes the soft persuasion of words, and sometimes, when necessary, the mighty persuasion of violence.

As Bronowski and Mazlish state, "(F) or Machiavelli, the existence of the state and its aquisition of power became ends in themselves. Towards these ends all other considerations must be sacrificed. One idea, which Machiavelli referred to again and again, sums this up: reason of state. A reason of state overrides everything else. It is the highest good to which Machiavelli appeals, and from which there is no appeal." [25]

Within these limits, then, the Florentine produced a relatively short masterpiece in the form of a handbook on how to use persuasive powers (and the whims of fate) of every sort for the welfare of the state. Little, perhaps, that Machiavelli suggests was entirely novel, even to its first readers. What was important was that ancient notions, many of them drawn from history, were first described in explicit fashion, and, second, they were recommended for entirely new reasons—not relating to the will of God, but rather to the welfare of man. The shift was formidable and, in its way, revolutionary. The art of persuasion was no longer the province of divine will; nor were men in their roles of persuaders necessarily instruments of salvation. They were men, and they persuaded for men's reasons that no longer needed sanctions of heaven, appeals to law, or tradition or abundant philosophical defense. The welfare of the tribe (as described by authority) became the prime moral imperative.

Nations, Politics, and Industry

Where once the church had been the main source of societal persuasion, by the eighteenth century, new demands for acculturation required that the masses of people—or at least a portion of the mass who had gained political and/or military power—assent to trust the state. The historical mold for this development had been set in pre-Elizabethan England (one of the first nations in Europe where politicians overthrew and assimilated the Roman church) by Henry VIII. He literally re-wrote the history of the conflicts between the Houses of Lancaster and York (particularly the latter) in order to gain public assent for the reign of the Tudors.[26] The movement was less blatant and daring in other countries where compromises, less dramatic than Henry's total break with Rome, took place, but the effect was much the same: the welfare and protection of the state became more important than that of the church.

Whatever part religion played in the lives of the citizens of the Enlightenment, the new state, as noted by Crane Brinton, demanded "the final earthly allegiance of all its inhabitants." [27] And with the coming of the

[25] J. Bronowski and Bruce Mazlish, *op. cit.*, p. 37. Modern syndicated gangsters do not appeal to "reasons of state" for vindication, but I have heard them defend their activities in the political sphere (and elsewhere) as realistic stabilizing counterforces in an economic community operating more by mystical sanctions than socio-economic realities. In circulating inert capital and keeping certain natural "supply and demand" markets open, they have a valid pragmatic point recognized covertly by the established powers. This establishment also is aware that such activities, although illegal, are heavily taxed by them. And when these syndicated hoods are sent to prison, it is usually for tax evasion.

[26] See Gordon, *et al.*, *The Idea Invaders*, pp. 23–24.

[27] Crane Brinton, *A History of Western Morals* (New York: Harcourt, Brace and Co., 1959), p. 270.

nineteenth century, nationalism required the increasingly sharp attention of most of the major institutions in those nations that had thrown off domination by the church and searched now among men (rather than gods) for the operative moral sanctions in life.[28] Old conflicts, of course, existed, and much of the new religious persuasion of the Protestants was distributed with an avidity that the heroes (or villains) of the Inquisition might well have envied.

Nor was religion ever to be severed entirely from its relationship to the soil—nor has it been since. Until the twentieth century, for instance, Joan of Arc (in some ways a prototypical figure of the tension between religion and nationalism) was considered by many in the Roman Catholic Church as a mortal statist. She was not canonized until the 1920's for the best of reasons: severe doubts in the Vatican and elsewhere for 500 years as to whether she was an agent of France or an agent of God. The matter was finally settled.[29]

It is even possible to defend statism's merger with the church (and its final domination of it) as the inevitable outcome of the thinking of the Enlightenment's skeptical giants—Locke, Berkeley, Hume and others—from whose thought the conceptual foundations of the dominant state were derived. This roster also includes such figures as Franklin, Jefferson and John Adams in the New World. The United States Constitution is an epitome of Enlightenment thought, not because of its democratic idealism and faith in the mystiques of parliament, collective action and the wisdom of the majority, but because, in its original state, it limited political action to the functionally persuasable part of the population: property holders, citizens, males, whites and a few others who constituted but a fraction of those dwelling in the original thirteen colonies.

Jefferson believed that widespread education would eventually increase this small percentage and that schooling would become the device by which a formidable enlightened electorate might be produced in the new, growing country. The persuasive power, therefore, of the notion of free universal education was introduced into the American national conscience at the beginning of the nineteenth century. By the end of the century (at the hands of zealous reformers), it had become an overwhelming secular moral imperative—even a potential political *right*, although the words "education" and "schools" are neither mentioned, to this day, in the corpus of our Constitution nor any of its amendments. Government by consent of the governed *demanded* a degree of indoctrination into the cultural imperatives and loyalties that the society being built in the United States in the 1800's demanded, and the pith of this notion has rarely, to the writer's knowledge, been seriously questioned, even by intelligent radicals. (They *have* ques-

[28] *Ibid.*, p. 330.

[29] See G. B. Shaw's sarcastic commentary on this problem in the Epilogue of his magnificent play *Saint Joan*.

tioned the equity of *accepted* imperatives and loyalties, however, and would substitute others for them.) To this day, for many reasons, the power of education remains, in essence and politically, what it was nearly two centuries ago: an instrument of nationalism in the operation of a state that required voters who understood their political roles.

The state is a fine cultural rallying point, and patriotism remains a powerful force, but, in Western Europe and the United States, a far more persuasive power began to percolate in the eighteenth century in the urban areas of those nations touched by the Industrial Revolution. It was a variation on the theme of nationalism that was probably encapsulated best, and in its most benign aspects, by Adam Smith. Call it "capitalism," call it "big business," call it "industrialism" (all such names are satisfactory), but it boils down to the accumulation of wealth from the proper juxtaposition of invention and labor. This accumulation of power, and the natural marketplace, having both been logically sanctified by Smith, took on the psychological dimensions of national purpose before the nineteenth century was thirty years old. Wealth trickled in numerous directions, and, while industrialism made a comparatively few people wealthy and powerful, it also blended magnificently into developing mythologies of popular government, democracy and folk tales of rags to riches—concepts which first gained popular impetus in the United States during the critical redirection of national tonus in the period of Andrew Jackson's presidency.[30]

As Heilbroner makes clear, Smith's sanctions for accumulation of wealth, while recognizing that societies evolve, could not and did not anticipate the Industrial Revolution and "see in the ugly factory system, in the newly tried corporate form of business organization, or in the weak attempts of journeymen to form protective organizations, the first appearance of new and disruptively powerful social forces." [31]

One cannot discover a particular historical point at which nationalism and industrial capitalism merged as persuasive forces—or even as critical myths of society. The mix was different in different places at different times, probably occurring in England first and most trenchantly, before the

---

30 See, of course, Arthur M. Schlesinger, Jr. *The Age of Jackson* (Boston: Little, Brown, and Co., 1945), as valuable a book as any yet written on the climate of (and for) popular persuasion in America in the first part of the last century. Covering as many facets as he does of Jackson's world, Schlesinger's volume is of utility in understanding the psychological climate in which nineteenth century capitalism (and anti-capitalism) developed ultimately into the major political, economic, social and cultural mystique in the United States and influenced so vitally its people and its value structures.

31 Robert L. Heilbroner, *The Worldly Philosophers* (New York: Time Incorporated, 1961), p. 67. Both music and economics (alone among the arts and sciences I have attempted to study) are so abstract that, in general, I think I misunderstand both in exactly the same way. I find them, in fact, quite similar. I might be persuaded to reconsider my feelings toward music (the problems is tone-deaf ears), but I stand firm on the subject of economics—except for this particular and delightful book.

two came together in the United States; although many Americans today would probably argue that the influence of capitalism on the mass mind was greater in America than in the mother country.[32] A clue to the psychological antiquity of industrialism's role in British life may be gleaned from the fact that massive amounts of gin (called by William Bolitho "the shortest way out of Manchester") became the British working classes' most potent weapon against the emotional tyrannies of the factory system as early as 1690 and shortly thereafter. In 1694, British production of gin stood at about a million gallons a year; by 1714 it had reached two million; by 1733, eleven million; and by 1742, twenty million, a progression probably closely related to the relationship of men to Britain's industrial process.[33]

What the Industrial Revolution accomplished, in part, was to change the life style of the populations of urban and semi-urban regions wherever it reached, pack people into close-living quarters, cause the birth rate to rise and motivate emigration from the land to the city—a migration which is still in progress (increased by urban opportunities for freeloading on welfare), not only in the United States but in many other countries.

Heilbroner notes that industrialism "forced a new social adaptation from the community in which it was embedded." This it did; and, along with social adaptation, psychological changes occurred also, replacing religion and nationalism with a new mystique—in turn, vaguely religious, self-serving, patriotic and mercantile—as the dominant cultural reality with which institutions of social control had to deal.[34] He continues, "The market and the factory . . . demanded a new cultural and social context to go with them. And they helped in . . . creating their own new social classes: the market created a professional merchant class and the factory a proletariat." [35] These new classes displaced old ones, just as new concepts of social

---

[32] Perhaps not. All factors are *not* equal here, but Britian certainly arrived at her period of disenchantment with myths of capitalism before we did (or will), as attested to by the socialization of much of the English economy after World War II and the step or two they remain ahead of the USA in repairing ravages of laissez-faire capitalism by means of social legislation, public works and the construction of their "welfare state," for lack of a better term.

[33] Berton Roueche, *Alcohol* (New York: Grove Press, Inc., 1960), pp. 27–28. See also pp. 47–76.

[34] Many terms have been devised for this mystique, some religious, some social and some psychological, but all add up to much the same delineation of social character. There is little difference between the imperatives of the "Protestant Ethic" as delineated by Weber (and used freely by such writers as William H. Whyte), the "acquisitive characterizations" of Erich Fromm in *The Sane Society*, David Riesman's "inner-directed" man and his world, Thornstein Veblen's cast of assorted characters and numerous other prototypes from the social psychologists' rogues galleries. What emerges is a *raison d'etre* for the no-holds-barred world of competitive capitalism that employs, one way or another, most of the viable instruments of social persuasion developed up to the nineteenth century. They demostrate that this new way of life had become a manifestation of religion, nationalism and idealism, as well as an instigator of new economic and materialistic activity.

[35] Heilbroner, *op. cit.*, p. 146.

purposes in the minds of the members of these classes displaced others. And the conflicts that inevitably arose from these changes were managed and assimilated over the passing years by persuasion mediated to the people by the managerial class (for workers dependent upon industry), the press (for those who could read), social myths (for those who could not), the opiates noted in social theory from the Comte de Saint-Simon to Fourier to Marx to Henry George (simplified and systematized into programs), the counter-force of organized labor (from its earliest days to the present, one of capitalism's most ardent allies), and educational organizations like schools and universities (such as they were, and for what they are worth).

Here and there, it appears, the persuasion did *not* work, and militant revolts, most of them minor, erupted. Marx's prediction, however, that the seeds of revolution were inherent in the capitalist factory system and capitalist market failed its tests on all counts. The proletarian revolutions of any scale during the past and present century (in places where persuasion to maintain the status quo were not heeded) flared up in countries that had not been extensively industrialized and which were overthrowing comparatively feudal aristocracies of state or religion, or both, usually in a primary effort to *achieve* the questionable benefits of the Industrial Revolution, a process still going on in countries in revolt in southeast Asia, South America and Africa.[36]

What Marx correctly anticipated was that antithesis to the abuses of capitalism, unchecked by revolution, would crystallize into potent forces that would modify severely the norms of society. That these counter-forces would be predominantly ideological rather than military, conceptual rather than activist, and legalistic rather than anarchistic, he could not possibly have forseen. Nor could he have anticipated the exact way, of which we are still uncertain, that capitalist incentives and class abrasions would become mandatory in the creation of the industrial nations of the twentieth century, including those nominally "Communist" or "Marxist" as well as those which maintain elaborate myths of free enterprise—most notably, the United States.

Our final step, therefore, in the history of persuasion, brings us to the brink of our contemporary world (and the problems and considerations of the pages to come): the persuasive force of the new social consciousness that began to surface, roughly, with the beginnings of the twentieth century in the Western World. As social organizations became increasingly complex, so did the foci of the new persuasion as it was articulated first, and

---

[36] The magnificent failure of Marxist ideology from the beginnings to 1917 (and the exposition of failures to come) may be found in Edmund Wilson, *To the Finland Station* (New York: Doubleday and Co., Inc., 1940). Wilson takes pains to discover the social and cultural origins of the Marxist illusion in European history. This is a topic which deserves equally brilliant updating to, at least, the conclusion of the Khrushchev era in the USSR, and/or the beginnings of the Castro period in Cuba, preferably at the hands of an author as polished as Wilson.

most important, in legislation, next in literature and drama, next in the intellectual development of ameliorative fashions in sociology, the development of political and social sciences, and, to a degree, in psychology as well. In education, it took the form called today "progressivism," with its equivalent concerns (also called "progressivism") in political rhetoric and behavior. In the actual economy, it was called, almost from the passage of the first income tax regulations, "creeping socialism," as realistic a name for it as any other. In the context of nationalism, it was to find its first eloquent apotheosis in the persuasion of the so-called "right thinking" community of nations in 1915 (or so) that they would "make the world safe for democracy."

The active role of persuasion had changed its form in the industrial nations. With the spread of literacy and the invention of new and ubiquitous instruments of communication like printing, the cinema, the phonograph, radio and television communication, it was expedited, spread widely and—so many believed—the intensity of its effect was also simultaneously and mysteriously changed or enhanced. Persuasion itself became industrialized in the world of commerce and called "advertising"; in the world of ideology it was known as "propaganda"; and in the world of schooling it became "citizenship education." While people, as individuals, remained in most respects much the same as they had been since antiquity, the image of their own lives and reasons for striving began changing with a rapidity hither unknown. Quite early in our present century, the contemporary age of mystery had begun.

Conclusion

From the temptation of Adam to the idealism of Woodrow Wilson is an enormous span, shorter in years than as an intellectual journey of human experience. It is no shorter a trip in the modulations of forces which have exerted their main persuasive influences on the people who lived and died in the numerous cultures which preceded this one. The main theme of the narrative is, however, disturbingly clear and uncomfortably simple, at least to this author.

A Western belief in the mystical, multi-faceted deities or single deity, and the ultimate salvation of man, either by social organization or intellectual power (the heritage of ancient Greece), yielded to other beliefs of equally persuasive force. Deities were unified or simplified into totalities, like an omnipotent gods-as-men or triadic families of more limited persuasive abilities. Complex religions were accordingly developed, whose leaders subsumed the social, intellectual and mystical tendencies of the ancients into a long and powerful hegemony over the population of most of Europe and the Near East. Differentially and at various times, the archons of religion lost power—at first, one to the other, and later to eloquent apostles of nationalism and popular governments.

The persuasion of nationalism did not die, nor was it ever replaced. It was modified by the Industrial Revolution, and a new image was formed of national welfare as a mercantile matter, a concept which still obtains in much of the world. By-products of industrialism included the invention of notions of social amelioration (contemporary versions of Plato's *Republic*) that extended to all facets of private and public life but had their greatest influence, probably, in economic affairs. The age of industrialism also produced instruments of world-wide communication, some selective and some mass. The stage was set for contemporary society in which a new vocabulary, including the words "brainwashing," "engineering of consent" and "mass persuasion," might now connote the rise of new plural deities and new mysticisms. The theatre of history has, as we shall see, not been disappointed in these expectations.

Part Two

LOGICAL PERSPECTIVES

No one seems to notice that the veneration of the word, which was necessary for a certain phase of historical development, has its perilous shadow side. That is to say, the moment the word, as a result of centuries of education, attains universal validity, it severs its original link with the divine person. There is then a personified Church, a personified State; belief in the word becomes credulity, and the word itself an infernal slogan capable of any deception. With credulity comes propaganda and advertising to dupe the citizen with political jobbery and compromises, and the lie reaches proportions never known before in the history of the world.

C. G. Jung, *The Undiscovered Self*

Chapter 5

TECHNOLOGICAL LIFE-STYLES

To be poor in order to be simple, to produce less in order that the product may be more choice and beautiful, and may leave us less burdened with unnecessary duties and useless possessions—that is an ideal not articulate in the American mind . . .

George Santayana

THE FIRST great historical thrust of persuasion as a social force in the West ended with the coming of the Industrial Revolution. Church and state both yielded power to commerce or, symbolically, to the rise of the Superman: Shaw's "good cry" by way of Nietzsche. Poets and philosophers notwithstanding, the contemporary Superman in the Western World—having been given personality by numerous legal fictions and common consents—is obviously the corporation. Whether state-owned and operated, semi-autonomous or free to pursue its own destinies, the modern corporation is an artificial, quasi-destructible (but tough), potentially immortal, human, fallible, productive, larger than life-size individual, protected by law. It was born in the period of intense mercantilism before the Industrial Revolution, but did not achieve full stature (and legal protection) until the age of mechanical technology had begun. In their diverse ways, generations of men seem to have recognized almost instinctively that technology could not, and never would, be tamed by them as mortals, and so arose the Superman, in fact, legend and story.[1]

To live in the age of the Superman is the most consistent logical challenge that a child of our times is faced with, almost from birth. Technology is a condition of modernity and, in one manifestation or another, produces a constant abrasion between itself and the human animal. Man has historically felt himself at odds—in one degree or another—with the Superman.

[1] The symbolic Superman is different in different times and places and according to the perceptions of those who enjoy the extant analogy. Mary Shelley's monster is different from Boris Karloff's, who in turn is different from King Kong, Clark Kent,

But he also came quickly to realize that his new, inchoate life-style would be increasingly dependent upon the largesse of the giant. A justifiable ambivalence (or ubiquitous schizophrenia) became, therefore, one condition of the fruits of industrialism.

Most of us have encountered the emotions felt by Thoreau that prompted his stay at Walden pond but, in balancing the risks that weigh on both sides of the scale, how many would choose to examine, at any depth, the nature of the man he himself is without the stewardship of the Superman? What manner of alien wrote:

> I went to the woods because I wished to live deliberately, to front only the essential facts of life, and see if I could not learn what it had to teach, and not, when I came to die, discover that I had not lived. I did not wish to live what was not life, living it so dear; nor did I wish to practice resignation, unless it was quite necessary. I wanted to live deep and suck out all the marrow of life, to live so sturdily and Spartan-like as to put to rout all that was not life, to cut a broad swath and shave close, to drive life into a corner, and then to get the whole and genuine meanness of it, and publish its meanness to the world; and if it were sublime, to know it by experience, and be able to give a true account of it in my next excursion.[2]

Where does man in the technological world go to achieve such confrontation? Even in warfare, invention has, by now, considerably depersonalized murder. Crime and punishment are automated. Does one take a planned "ski vacation" or a trip to "islands in the sun" on a Boeing 747? Or the other sort of "trip," on LSD, alcohol or some other sensual diversion of a technological culture? Does he buy a new automobile and drive it so fast and carelessly that his life hangs for an instant on a power-steered turn of fate? Does he "get away from it all" in his camper-trailer at a National Park to the smell of heated TV dinners and propane gas?

Satire is not required to indicate the density of the technological atmosphere in which we live and through which our impressions of reality are filtered. If one über-mass medium characterizes our time and place, it may simply be called "technology." Whether so all-encompassing a phenomenon is good or bad for individual man (or his species) is as impossible to determine as the question itself may be irrelevant to his destiny.[3] What

---

sundry interplanetary visitors and Hitler's blond élite guard. But in fundamental characteristics they are similar: strong, violent, brilliant in a pragmatic sort of way, strangely attractive to mortals, and invariably adept at metamorphosis. Similar creatures appeared, of course, before the birth of the modern corporation, but these were invariably—like Theseus—part god. The modern Superman is implicitly *man*'s creation, even if his genesis be extraterrestrial. The greatest difference is that modern Supermen are —like corporations—not *quite* immoral, and accordingly suspended in a world where the threat of oblivion is real and continuous, but unlikely.

2 Henry David Thoreau, *Walden* (New York: Time Incorporated, 1962), p. 88.

3 Broadsides against technology appear frequently, and they are refreshing reading.

concerns us here is the way in which social persuasion has accommodated the human animal to the inventions first, of science, and second, of technique, and what the results are (and are likely to become) of the companionship of two strange bedfellows.

Science Versus Technology

The metaphysic of science—that is, the spiritual wonder and amazement in the conceptual step involved in the discovery of scientific regularities by the human mind—simply cannot be intellectually degraded, either by mystics, priests or humanists, probably because its vision is so mystical, priestly, and—more than anything else—human. The unsuccessful enemies of scientific philosophy—from the time of Galileo to the present—have usually been mystics, priests and humanists—and, as we shall indicate below, even technologists and pseudo-scientists.

J. W. N. Sullivan had captured the universality of the early scientific visions of the Renaissance. "We see that the scientific outlook," he writes, ". . . constitutes a really amazing revolution in thought. The vivid world of the medievalist, a world shot through with beauty and instinct with purpose, a world having an intimate relationship to his own destiny and an intelligible reason for existing in the light of that destiny, is dismissed as an illusion. It has no objective existence. The real world, as revealed by science, is a world of material particles moving, according to mathematical laws, through space and time." [4]

Little wonder that the vision of science, thus described, so rapidly captured the imagination of the West. It was—and is—a vision of psychological beauty and asethetic (logical) perfection. Grant even that the Newtonian outlook of the mechanistic universe has, by now, passed and, in Sullivan's words, "science (now) deals with but a partial aspect of reality and . . . there is no faintest reason for supposing that everything science ignores is less real than what it accepts." [5] Grant also that there looms a steep abyss in scientific regularity, where in the behavior of particles (either macro- or microcosmic) yield not to regularities of law in nature but difficult to verify probabilities, and that a dark and frightening depth awaits the

---

Sometimes they are valuable as historical documents, and sometimes they hit a true note of insight. But, like many social manifestos, they are usually irrelevant, either from an individual or collective point of view, to what appears, at the time, to be the march of history. Reasons for this will be considered below, but this chapter will not center upon such blatant negations of technological society as, for instance, Friedrich Georg Juenger, *The Failure of Technology* (Chicago: Gateman Editions, Inc., 1956). The reason is that they shed little light upon how technology fits into contemporary persuasive practices—except as an example of the variety of totalistic negativisms that attends almost every manifestation of cultural consensus, not unlike the Black Mass in religion, for example.

[4] J. W. N. Sullivan, *The Limitations of Science* (New York: New American Library, 1949), pp. 138–139.

[5] *Ibid.*, p. 147.

inquirer who travels into this chasm. Science remains, nevertheless, one of the most vital discoveries in man's history, second, perhaps, to the discovery of individual self-consciousness, and intimately related to it.

Technology may have been an inevitable result of the growth and vigor of the period of accelerated scientific inquiry during the eighteenth century. But history provides us with numerous illustrations of various cultures with relatively elaborate technologies coexisting with the crudest scientific development. The Egyptians were masters of engineering and pharmacological technology, but apparently they utilized scientific methods of inquiry sparsely, if at all. By the period of Roman technological mastery of transportation and plumbing, the old Greek deductive genius, which had yielded (almost accidentally) the scientific thought-styles of Euclid and Archimedes, had stagnated into given principles of nature which amounted, by then, merely to spectacular techniques.

We may also discover historical moments (short ones, to be sure) when science was pursued solely as philosophy and not applied, that is, not transmuted into technique. The Golden Age of Greece contained such a brief interlude, as did the beginning of the Enlightenment in Europe until, roughly, the invention of the steam engine in the middle of the eighteenth century.

But the recent period of technological growth in the West (beginning with the nineteenth century) has been a time of rapid growth, new discovery and the avid utilization of the findings of scientists for the development of techniques. Science provided an amazing economy of method, directing the art of "know how" into matters relating to the control of the physical world, assuring almost certain success, quickly and efficiently, without the long trial-and-error periods required by other societies that had developed technological means of accomplishment without science to guide them.

The application of science to the world of reality was, of course, in itself a method, a technique *and* a technology. In the words of A. N. Whitehead, "The greatest invention of the nineteenth century was the method of invention," a phrase to ponder. In considering technology's role in modern life, he says, "We can neglect all the details of change, such as railways, telegraphs, radios, spinning machines, synthetic dyes. We must concentrate on the method itself: that is the real novelty . . . (M)an, who at times dreamt of himself as a little lower than the angels, has submitted to become the servant and the minister of nature. It still remains to be seen whether the same actor can play both parts." [6]

As amazing as the progress of science was during the nineteenth century, as Whitehead notes, particularly in mathematical physics, optics, and in the development of grand theory in chemistry and biology, the progress

---

[6] A. N. Whitehead, *Science and the Modern World* (New York: New American Library, 1953). These lectures were delivered by Whitehead in 1925. Their crisp relevance to immediately pressing problems of science in contemporary life is notable.

of technology was far more spectacular. On one hand, scientists were carrying out an intellectual revolution, and, on the other, technologists (frequently in the same person as the scientist) were in the process of modifying man's environment more extensively and rapidly than at any time in history.

This period of great technological modification slowed its pace to a creep at about the period shortly after World War I, almost as if the acceleration of the momentum that had been gathered during the preceding century began to skid into its final arc at the turn of the century.[7] *Major* technological innovations within the relatively recent past have been few but devastating: atomic weaponry, control of nucleic acids, mind-managing drugs, and one or two other inventions with lethal potentials.

Scientific inquiry, however, continued until the present moment with much the same impetus it had gathered during the nineteenth century, expanding its purview into the domains of human attitudes, thoughts and collective enterprise by means of a new phalanx of social, political and behavioral sciences. The old natural sciences reached unpredicted and challenging depths as they grappled with problems of non-determinacy and almost mystical unknowns of theoretical non-Newtonian universes. The former developed—like all primitive sciences in their earliest, fumbling stages—a rich lexicon of theories, good, bad and silly. To them have been added congeries of epicycles to correct initial theoretical defects, at which state of development we discover such disciplines as sociology, psychology, economics and others at this present moment of our ignorance.[8]

One valid historical perspective of our times is therefore an ironic one, considering the generally accepted notion that America's current materialism reflects a golden age of technological progress, while the pure sciences are neglected and stagnant in the intellectual community. This position is

---

[7] The speed of technological innovation, of course, decreased considerably during the 1920's and 1930's. Nearly all of the "modern technology" which surrounds us today made its essential inroads to our culture before World War I; its effect upon life styles and the changes it created in culture had their deepest effects, therefore, generations ago. What we have witnessed since is the refinement of this old technology, built upon inventions like radio transmission, television, automobiles, airplanes, cinema, sound recording, building techniques and mass production, all invented more than fifty years ago. (Nor should one overlook medical technology which took the physician and dentist away from barbering, and produced, among other cultural artifacts, the psychiatrist.)

[8] For a description of the function of the epicycle in inchoate science (in this case, the first and best example: Ptolemy's astronomy), see Arthur Koestler, *The Sleepwalkers* (New York: The Macmillan Company, 1959), pp. 66–69. Freudian theory, for instance, has probably developed the richest collection of corrective epicycles of all the newer sciences, provided in the works of the master's disciples like Fromm, Reik, Adler, Jung, Ferenczi, etc. But Freud is not alone. All the grand theorists in these fields have accumulated their epicyclists, especially the important ones like Marx, Keynes, Parsons, Sapir, Korzybski, Boas, *et. al.*, and we can depend on similar phenomena occurring in the future to concepts of such luminaries of the moment as Piaget, Lévi-Strauss, Chomsky and company.

not hard to understand, as scientists view the lion's share of money and attention in their culture turned to practical problem-solving by means of the therapeutic programs of psychologists and sociologists. They also witness enormous pressures placed by the federal government on university technologists to come up with solutions to medical and ecological problems that pose scientifically respectable questions only by extenuation, and which require, largely, the skills of technicians finding new applications for old technologies, not those of genuine scientists.

Their concern is a myth, however, on two specific counts. First, American (and much European) "know how" does not, as noted above, deal in technological novelty at all, but merely in innovation. Ford's belt assembly line was indeed novel; today's automated production machines carry the automobile maker's vision near to its pragmatic conclusion. The Electronic Video Recorder (like the LP Microgroove recording before it) may seem like an original triumph of technology to the CBS public relations corps, but the instrument is a sophisticated version of technological innovations well over one generation old. Other illustrations are too ubiquitous to mention, and span every aspect of contemporary culture affected by technology, from contraceptive medications to the instrumentation of space travel.

Second, our pure scientists have extended their probes, during the last twenty years, not only into the mysteries contained in atomic particles and the protein matter found in the nuclei of reproductive cells, but into the mathematical and other conceptual universes (including those within the human organism) far beyond this author's grasp but well within his capacity for appreciation. In the study of the stars (which used to be called astronomy but now deals with macrocosms unbelievably larger than the telescopic universe) scientific concepts are now emergent that promise to shake some of the prime philosophical assumptions man has made since antiquity.

The scientific community must excuse this extraordinary progress as essentially utilitarian and somehow practical. But its own diffidence does not stand in the way of the amazing purity of knowledge which it has lately produced—an open secret kept from the general public by three forces: the tendency of journalists to regard theory as unimportant and therefore to popularize only what they personally consider significant; the special languages and insular communications about science between scientists; and the displacement effect of the publicity institutions of the modern industrial world which construes scientific advancement entirely as novelty of technology, and must—for survival—pump blood into the myth of an endless arithmetical increase of technological progress.

By no means may one assume that our present culture in the West is not technological-materialist, and that instruments of technology have not so insinuated themselves into our life-styles that our dependence upon them is roughly equivalent to the way men in former times depended upon the gods of nature.[9] Technological man is as much a reality as Renaissance man was, but he is neither as novel or intimately involved in contemporary life or as progressive as he tells himself. He is an extrapolation of a vision derived from the genius of the nineteenth century, and his most vocal worshipers—followers of the Buckminster Fullers, Marshall McLuhans, Edward Bernays and other apostles of modernism—are, in fact, men and women of *yesterday* whose disengagement from their own pasts leads them to believe that (to use one of McLuhan's favorite metaphors) their rear-view mirror is their front windshield.

Techniques and Technology

The most general—and for our purposes the most useful—interpretation of technology as a cultural phenomenon is the one that, following Ellul,[10] associates the main thrust of technology with *technique*. It does not limit it either to materialistic or mechanistic devices or to specific applications of scientific theory or experiment, but includes *all varieties of the technical management of physical and social worlds*. Language, for instance, a technique of communication, is therefore a technology. So are surgery and factory management.

From this viewpoint, no period in history has developed without technology. And, in a crude way, even inventive animals, like gerbils, develop in captivity a simple technology out of the cans, spools, fabrics and bits of wood given them to play with, one of their most ingratiating and "human" characteristics. Degrees to which human societies are immersed in, or dependent upon, technology are accordingly relative matters. The history through which the reader has traveled in the previous chapter attempted to illustrate, in part, how a short period of technological inspiration (resulting largely from the developments of science) has produced the "modern industrial state," in J. K. Galbraith's term.

Ellul's *apercu* of technological culture is dim, perhaps necessarily so if in consequence of his all-encompassing construction of the technological phenomenon. His attempt is to evoke a meaningful analysis of technology's

---

[9] The first draft of this chapter is being written during the fourth day of what may or may not some day be known as "The Great Postal Strike of 1970." Already, a mild hysteria is noticeable here in New York City, because no mail has been delivered recently. As in similar situations, many of us are discovering how dependent we have become upon technology, in this case, reasonably rapid and cheap mail delivery. Our pictures of reality are presently being shifted ever-so-slightly by our new discovery. Feelings towards the striking letter carriers, union officials, and (logically or otherwise) the President of the United States seem to swing wildly between soft sympathy and righteous indignation, expressed mostly in the interests of "others": the poor who will not receive welfare checks, for example. Some of my neighbors appear strangely disassociated from the strike, their indifference indicative, I think, of their unwillingness to accept the degree that their lives have been assimilated into the technological structure of this aspect of daily life.

[10] Jacques Ellul, *The Technological Society* (New York: Alfred Knopf, 1965).

total role in contemporary persuasion. Like numerous humanistic analysts of modernity, Ellul has a well developed moral sense that does not stand up firmly against the moral neutrality of technique, or against the present tendency to deny the relevance of "goods" and "bads" to it.[11] Observers like Ellul point (with much justice) to the masterful accomplishments of technology, at the same time displaying a chilling moral straight face as they list our typical technical triumphs of the past three decades: trips to the moon, the atomic explosions at Hiroshima and Nagasaki, utilization of tranquillizing agents in treating mental illness, efficient human engineering whereby six million Jews were slaughtered in extermination camps, and similar accomplishments of technique.

Gloomy or optimistic, Ellul's analysis is also typically modern-European, reflecting characteristic contemporary continental cynicism towards the technical hegemony of the United States (and, probably, Germany as well). This is a right that, in the author's opinion, French intellectuals like Ellul have doubtless earned by virtue of their experiences during and after World War II. It is salted with envy, for all its acumen and historical and social sensitivity, and typical of much contemporary French political ideation.

Specific also to this totalistic viewpoint is a dual proposition regarding technology that postulates two principal social laws. As invariable constructs, they are "laws" merely insofar as they are contained within one given place—meaning that they are applicable to the entire world today only in those respects whereby the world manifests cultural unity, for instance in certain technical matters like standards for weights and measures, directions and dimensions of screw-threads. Ellul's laws, however, cannot apply *post hoc* to currents of technology that have been destroyed either in the eclipse of great societies or in oscillations of major cultural change. Techniques employed in building the great temples of the Indians of Peru are examples of the first exception; the technology of the magnificent Potala of Lhasa, Tibet is an instance of the second. But Ellul's observations regarding the fate of technology may be most trenchantly relevant to our own world, if, by some miracle, we survive our current plethora of military, industrial and political crises and approach, eventually, the stability of such venerable societies as the thousand-year empire of Rome.

Ellul observes, correctly in the *short* run, that systems of technique, in the first place, accelerate and tend to absorb one another. Thus, progress in technology of a given type tends to be irreversible. Having discovered and used a particularly working technique, it is practically impossible to turn

[11] *Ibid.*, p. 134. Writes Ellul (with apparent sadness) at the end of his discussion of moral and spiritual values in a technological culture, "Man alone is subject, it would seem, to moral judgment. We no longer live in that primitive epoch in which things were good or bad in themselves. Technique in itself is neither, and can do what it will. It is truly autonomous." Once again, the Superman hovers over the analogy.

back the clock of progress. Second, the developmental accumulation of technique tends to move in, roughly, a geometric progression, illustrated in our own country by the continual derivation of so many techniques from approximately 1825 to 1920, followed by the rapid development largely of *modifications* of these techniques in ever increasing clusters (sped up by the impetus of World War II) until the present day.[12]

Ellul's main argument centers on the vanity of the myth that envisions technique as acting upon a material world so as to contrive, somehow, to free man from morality in order to lead him to Paradise. This current myth of unending "progress" for mankind, historically a dubious (and unclearly articulated) proposition or cop-out or massive opiate, appears to have gathered considerable and mythologically useful power in contemporary society.[13] It also has accumulated the persuasive force of an eschatology for individuals sufficiently credulous to accept the conceit that *any* doctrine of hope is relevant to the multitude of determinisms (and accidents) involved in the unrolling of current history. That many reject it outright with nothing to put in its place (hardly an omission for which to fault them), appears to be more a sign of (frequently youthful) realism than nihilism, as frequently charged.

Ellul indicts technology for its tendencies to dehumanize living, to relegate individual man to the manipulable masses, offering him illusions of power and distracting sensation—in short, unconsciousness of his own reality—in exchange for his acquiescence to the demanding imperatives of ever-foliating new techniques.[14] His claim, of course, echoes the famous indictment of modern Europe in the 1920's by Ortega y Gasset. The latter does

---

[12] *Ibid.*, p. 89. There is no question that Ellul is describing only modern Western Europe here, not all societies that have developed and assimilated techniques. Backward nations have recently introduced derivative technologies at a stable rate—or about as fast or as slowly as they can handle them. Even the Soviet Union, emerging from economic feudalism after the October Revolution, had, in the 1920's and 1930's, to slow down the onrush of technology in order to accommodate it successfully. Ellul's principle applies, I think, to societies in which economic life and industrial growth are not strictly managed by oligarchies or a dictator. Strong central governments tend to control the fate of technique, just as they control the fate of economic, educational and political forces that result from (and are the results of) the spread of technique and the change in life-styles it usually also generates.

[13] See *ibid.*, pp. 190–193. I have also discussed the myth of progress as an American cultural symbol during the 1960's in G.N.G., *L C*, pp. 84, 91–92.

[14] *Ibid.*, pp. 402–410. I am struck here by the reaction of one drug addict—the prototypical contemporary suffered of modern *anomie* and urban technological *Weltschmerz*—who likens his heroin coma to "death without its permanence." A retreat to unconsciousness often seems a peculiarly attractive notion after reading the morning newspaper, and many people are persuaded to try it for one reason or another, some permanently. Would that it were possible to determine definitely whether this tendency is directly accelerated by technology, whether it is an invariable manifestation of a death-wish, or simply a symptom of some kind of psychopathology or partially organic disease. But neither I nor the psychiatric profession seem to know how to begin finding out.

not single out technology as the single cause of the rise of mass man, but identifies instead the triad of liberal democracy, scientific inquiry and industrialism as causes of the ruthless depersonalization in European life that was shortly to occur as the Spanish philosopher predicted.[15] Ellul's systemic fabric is woven more tightly than Ortega's and stiffened more with sociological and cultural detail, but it amounts to much the same disheartening concept. This view has never been popular with empirically oriented American social theorists. This is because it relies largely upon deductive logic and runs so palpably against the optimistic, voluntaristic orientation of American social science as auxiliary to vital persuasive forces in society. And these forces are the food upon which many of our social scientists feed: the objects of their studies and the reasons for their government and foundation research grants.

Ellul's other most trenchant observation about technique, in the writer's opinion, is one that is more comfortably acceptable to popular attitudes in the West, particularly in the light of present fashions to demonize that fraction of technology which appears to be, in common parlance, "polluting the environment" and has turned ecology into a political and economic cause.[16] But Ellul's point transcends a concern with environmental pollu-

---

15 José Ortega y Gasset, *The Revolt of the Masses* (New York: W. W. Norton and Co., 1932), pp. 54–60. Ortega had not experienced the kind of recent disenchantments we have known at the hands of technologists. Even the machine guns and poison gas of World War I that he knew were crude destructive instruments; bombs were toys; and anti-Semitism was still a "social cause" and parlor game in much of Europe. Ortega had not experienced the retreat into inventiveness and simultaneous growth in power of the new technology, nor had he reason to contemplate the numerous by-products of it discussed below. His prescient pessimism, therefore, must have seemed more disturbing to those few who listened to him in the 1920's than to the millions who read him today.

16 Presently obvious instances of pollution of air and water and the progressive ecological decline of certain parts of the world are sorry by-products of progress that admit of few detractions or arguments. The present hysteria—politically motivated in the USA in many instances and not without ideological intentions—certainly does. In the century when soft coal and other factory fuels turned Manchester, Milan and Pittsburgh into fog chambers, little outcry was heard, because the factories were perceived as sources of common welfare, and the foul air was equated with natural disasters like floods and earthquakes. The smudge-pots that warmed California's citrus trees were regarded the same way. Today, however, the internal combustion engine (which often produces a relatively less toxic stink than bituminous coal or peat) is an all-purpose villain. Also, the fact that various species of animals and marine life are reacting to man's encroachments by the threat of extinction is sad, indeed, and a moderate reason to take steps to prevent it, when possible. But nature herself, with her cruel genetic tricks, sliding polar caps and feral competition, has—at any moment of the history of life on this planet—been more ruthless in dooming wildlife to extinction than any technology—except atomic radiation—has so far. It was inevitable, perhaps, that ecological alarmists have, for years, provided grist for the persuasive mill, particularly William Vogt's twenty-year-old jeremiads and Malthusianisms and the late Rachel Carson's sophisticated prose. The talent of such essayists has centered on attacking technology for *something* heinous without actually assaulting the myth of progress or the supremacy of technique in the humane use of natural resources. While they are exciting to read, they offer us

tion and the impending extinction of various interesting forms of wild life. Its ramifications may be charted logically, and observed psychologically, in every known culture and related to all the techniques man has devised. Writes Ellul, "History shows that every technological application from its beginnings presents certain unforeseeable secondary effects which are much more disastrous than the lack of the technique would have been. These effects exist alongside those effects which were foreseen and expected and which represent something valuable and positive." [17]

In its widest ramifications, we are still trying to determine what these secondary effects from yesterday's technology are in our culture. Ellul's observations include—but extend beyond—fouled clam beds; decreasing numbers of bird species; excised lungs, gray with tar and abraded by silicones; mangled and murdered millions on super-highways and turnpikes; and the (probably) two or three generations of victims of supposedly harmless sulphur in our diets and aluminum in our numerous deodorants. These are, incidentally, all benign secondary effects, in that they are logically perceptible and psychologically containable, as well as defensible as part of the price we probably must pay for progress. Better, one may say with some logic, to be poisoned at sixty-five from an excess intake of artificial food sweeteners than to die of hyper-tension induced by obesity at fifty-five, providing the ten years of relative slimness are not spent in continual pain, hunger or tension. Better, in other words, to "see Naples and die" than to die never having seen Naples at all.

Technology's significant by-products must also be calculated in terms of new dependences and losses of individual control over the external world. Such developments may render the individual credulous, on one hand, in his acceptance of persuasion that encourages him to accept without serious question the necessity for the manipulation of his world by technique, and which requires his cooperation in that manipulation. On the other hand, each individual must be politically and tactically controllable by the power structure or "authorities" of technique for technology to work at all.

Here we came upon the ever-present threat of the breakdown of the technological system and the functional *use* of that threat as a specific social control. Because no technique is perfect, and similar technologies tend to conflict with one another, continual dysfunctions of techniques remind the individual of the chaos that the elimination of this or that aspect of technology *might* produce. Begging psychological problems (reserved for Chapter 14), what technological man faces is the continual un-

---

little advice—except to stop behaving like a technological culture. But they do not suggest that we sacrifice our philosophy of technology in the effort.

[17] *Ibid.*, p. 105. Ellul is clear that these by-products are not only the results of tactical errors and failures but attend successes as well, and frequently pass unnoticed for many years.

spoken knowledge of impotence in his dependence upon techniques of which he is not the master. A power shortage, an airplane accident, a stock market recession, an operating room death, a breakdown in law, a failure of police protection (communicated to him by the press or radio) enhances his vulnerability, so evident in his daily life. Particularly is he at the mercy of the automobile, telephone, modern plumbing and garbage disposal, four most sensitive examples, at present, for the city dweller particularly.

Against these eventualities, Ellul poses the state and its manifestations in industry, education, art, and the total sociological impact of the organizations of commercial society. They dispense the illusions of stability, encapsulated usually in assurances that they are "scientifically" oriented and "artistically" acceptable (that is, the scientific findings upon which this persuasion is based are artfully selected), mathematically precise (if possible), and previously subjected to accurate human experiment.[18]

In the world he perceives, individual technological man is therefore dehumanized by his utter dependence from birth upon techniques which he neither understands nor can master. He is, therefore, the manipulable tool of the managers of technology in the most significant aspects of his life, subject, like the narcotics addict or alcoholic, to the constant fear of withdrawal of the sustenance required to maintain his way of life or concept of his own humanity. In short, he is trapped by circumstances.

Technology and Humanity

The irony of the technological society is, therefore, the condition of sometimes involuntary, but near absolute, assent to technology that contemporary man must be persuaded—or educated—to, if Ellul's claims are justified. To accomplish this end, certain stratagems in the form of unquestionable cultural "givens" are necessary, particularly among the so-called "opinion leaders" of society.

These are propositions stating that, first, *physical* by-products of technology are inevitable and logical; *psychological* by-products are logical but not inevitable. Second, the physical by-products may be handled (or neutralized) by the application of *more* technology that will produce *no* physical by-products. Third, the psychological impact of technology, while essentially of logical origin, relates largely to communications and education. It provides a peculiar magical "hold over the mind of men" because of the special nature of technological "media," *à la* currently accepted McLuhanesque notions of "mosaic qualities" of television and similar nonsense. Fourth, technology, because it is applied science, *must* lead man forward toward the development of social techniques or systems that will solve the psychological alienation that technology itself produces. In short, applied technology will eventually yield systems which, applied to education, social

[18] *Ibid.*, pp. 341–343.

behavior, industry and economics will act as demiurges for a new utopian, quasi-Platonic, Gnostic social order.

These propositions, Ellul might insist, and the author submits, are ill conceived and partial descriptions of the role of technology in the modern state at best; and destructive, muddle-headed and obscene falsehoods at worst.

The history of these propositions, somewhat more invidiously stated (and lacking the eschatological note of the final one) appears in Ferkiss' generally sanguine analysis of the present status of technology in the West.[19] Antagonists of industrial society are followed through the *Gesell-schaft-Gemeinschaft* polarities in the social contracts of Tonnies, through Comte, Durkheim, Weber and American and German-refugee strains of anti-urban thought that wound up reducing the development of American mass culture to the currently popular German term *kitsch*.[20]

Ferkiss also relates the supposed evils of mass society to the apostles of freedom of the Enlightenment and those determinists, from Hegel onward, who equated servitude with the factory system. "Actually," writes he, "the concept of alienation is rooted in Romanticism. Alienation is man's divorce from nature, from a postulated real self . . . Certainly the huge literature on the subject bears witness to the fact that identity and its opposite, alienation, are a major theme of concern among sensitive men in Western society." [21] Ferkiss cites, in his argument, the standard Jeremiahs of non-fiction book clubs like William H. Whyte, Dwight Macdonald, Bernard Rosenberg, Gerald Sykes, Maurice R. Stein, Arthur J. Vidich, Herbert Marcuse and others.

The enemy of these critics, Ferkiss observes, is not technology itself but only one aspect of technique, the machine. They claim that "(s)ociety itself has become . . . a machine, an assemblage of standardized moving parts . . . ," and man has necessarily, in their view, become merely a cog in that machine "subject to forces beyond his control . . . Gone is freedom, gone is identity. Man is simply a machine, in a society of machines, in a physical environment of machines." [22]

---

[19] Viktor C. Ferkiss, *Technological Man* (New York: George Braziller, 1969), pp. 71–76.

[20] See G.N.G., *L C*, pp. 287–304. Ferkiss neatly blames this strain of cultural analysis upon the rural origins of many American sociologists of the '20's and '30's, and the Marxist-Freudian revulsion against capitalist industrialism (and the communications instruments that speak for them) of emigré scholars from Europe. While his observation may explain the general dispositions of the Robert Redfields and the Erich Fromms, no good reason is given for the appeal of this viewpoint for such American (and British) city-slickers as Dwight Macdonald, Gilbert Seldes, Walter Lippmann, Charles Siepmann, Louis Kronenberger, Edmund Wilson and many, many others who, at the time of their discontents, were neither Marxists nor Freudians.

[21] Ferkiss, p. 74.

[22] *Ibid.*, p. 75.

Ferkiss evades the main contentions of these social analysts not by taking issue with them, but by postulating the emergence of a new man, "different and superior," in his words, newly adapted to live in a technological world who will supersede the anomic man of the new technology. A similar new man might, of course, have overcome any debacle or destructive force that history has yet produced: *Ad absurdum,* an asbestos man might have survived Pompei; a puncture-proof man might have lived through the sack of Rome; and lead-encased man might be little bothered by the atomic flash over Hiroshima. Such Supermen (again) are no further from reality—if all science fiction is equidistant from fact—than Ferkiss' "technological man" (his term).

More germane to a realistic appraisal of the thinking of the apostles of alienation (in its various forms) is to examine its implications and logical relevance to life as we know it, and to extrapolate, if possible, present trends into the future. Here Ferkiss himself is an adequate guide. He notes[23] the blatant failures of the technique of "systems" and "systems analysis" when they are applied to social and educational matters, as well as flowering myths of technological élitism, new affluence and leisure, the deaths of our cities and the rise of suburbia. What Ferkiss, almost in despair, proposes after a view of the horizon is an Aristotelian "correction" of man's present relationship to technique, the only other progressive alternative being, he says, "to locate values in a transcendent source . . . that all men may not accept . . ."[24] and that he himself, clearly, does not find acceptable.

Begging, for this chapter at least, the question of what exactly was wrong with those historical cultures which not only "located values in transcendent sources" but lived by them (despite inevitable individual heresies), the role of persuasion in a technological society becomes once again quite clear, if that society is to survive. In essence, Ellul's view of modern propaganda as reaching into every facet of modern life, even into typical revolts *against* contemporary life styles, is justified as implied, first, in his work on technology and expanded (in a volume largely rejected in the USA) subsequently.[25]

Required for the survival of industrialism and industrial technology are

---

[23] *Ibid.*, pp. 125–153. Some of Ferkiss' observations may be more prescient than even their author appears to realize. He writes, "Systems analysis and PPBS (planning, programming, budgeting systems) are still touted as panaceas for economic and social problems . . . aerospace firms are moving into oceanography with much success (the problems and goals are not dissimilar), but their experience with urban problems has been less than happy. The technical revolutionizing of education that many electronic and related firms hoped to spearhead has not taken place." (p. 129) See also pp. 228–230.

[24] *Ibid.*, p. 248

[25] See Jacques Ellul, *Propaganda* (New York: Alfred A. Knopf, 1965). The implications of the remarkable, provocative and flawed volume will be considered in the Chapters to follow.

apparently two major changes in modern culture. First, as soon as possible after their current period of experimentation and failure ceases, current trends in the application of techniques derived from the science of nature should be discouraged from being freely and mindlessly applied to social and behavioral phenomena in schools, factories, communities at large, hospitals and, perhaps most of all, in psychiatric clinics. A technology of "man handling" may indeed exist—*has* existed, as administered by such pioneers as the brave Australians who massacred thousands of defenseless aboriginals, and by the carriers of peace to Carthage—but no rationale justifies the faith that it will be (or *must* be, as now claimed) based upon a model drawn from the technologies involving the regulatory phenomena discovered in the world of nature. Biological, chemical or physical analogies are always suspect, whether they are drawn from the behaviors of amino acids, quantum mechanics or clever apes. Behind this imperative, of course, is the implicit rejection of the suggestion that man himself may somehow be metamorphosed into a technological animal. Ferkiss' observation that "Technological man does not yet exist. His job is to invent not the future but first of all himself," asks what no human or group of humans has accomplished of all history—that is, be anything more than themselves.[26]

Second, it should also be evident that the two major extant myths of technology currently abroad in the West are equally inadequate for contemporary life. One, the myth of social perfection via technique, was adequate to maintain the class structure of the nineteenth century and to clear the tracks for the age, now finished, of great inventions. Most socialists, communists, labor leaders and intellectuals would not buy this myth in the first place. Some of them did combat themselves with the machine for a time and turned away disillusioned and sometimes rebellious. That the myth continues to exist between the covers of science-fiction volumes and in the commercials on television is amazing but indicative of the capacity of boosters on Madison Avenue to believe their own fictions. (Is anybody really listening to the words, "Progress is our most important product!" and "Better things for better living!", or have most of us learned to tune out this cant years ago?)

The other myth is more subtle and contains a grain or more truth—the absurdity of the delusion of inevitable depersonalization, dehumanization

---

[26] For those who have accepted the current rash of enthusiasm concerning "human systems" that has appeared in the educational and general press, and in various specialized journals, let me suggest the careful reading of the only study I know which realistically equates physical and social attempts at systemization in terms of both their theoretical and practical potentialities and track records, including, incidentally, "communications systems." The volume is equal to the wide-ranging intellect of the scholar who produced it, whose cross-disciplinary facility is as impressive as it is well honed. I strongly recommend (once again) Ludwig von Bertalanffy, *General Systems Theory*, to anyone who cherishes the current simplistic interpretations of physical scientific methodologies applied to human behavior.

and alienation as the price of technology that has spread from European philosophy (first) to American sociology and psychology (second) to the political and social orientations of our young people (third), as well as to dozens of neo-Marxists and amateur psychoanalysts (last).[27] Careful examination of it reveals so totally inconsistent a thesis that it is, to this writer, difficult to comprehend why (or in fact whether) the brilliant sociologists who have turned their attention to the modern industrial state (like Ellul) appear to have missed its delusive qualities entirely. Like its counterparts in the writings of Innis and McLuhan,[28] it is, in itself, destructive to individuals with distorted understanding of the wellsprings of morality.

To understand the range of inconsistency in this myth, it is first necessary to examine briefly the source of human morals. They stem, like law and all other social rules, from the communication of humans one with the other, within the confines of culture. Cross-cultural anthropologists have demonstrated that the "goods" and "bads" of any culture depend upon the peculiar relationships of the community to its physical world. Should a culture sustain itself for any length of time, should it satisfy the physical, emotional and (roughly speaking) spiritual needs of its citizens, its moral structure may be considered at least adequate—that is, the things that are good for the individual are good also for the survival of society's collective way of life. The same point, in reverse, may be made about the bads. These goods and bads, while relating invariably to certain basic matters like eating, copulating and distributing material goods, are noticeably different in different societies and at different times, their variability, one from the other, apparently unrelated to the success of cultures in maintaining and perpetuating themselves.

Although it is impossible to prove the point, history apparently teaches that, in most respects, morals are made by men, tested by men, accepted or rejected by men and passed on to the future by men.[29] True enough, man's choices are determined to some degree by his circumstances, but the circumstances themselves do not make the choices. Once again, the weight of anthropological evidence shows that environmental data alone do not reveal a tribe's roster of goods and bads. Also, two tribes living in similar (or

---

27 On the campus at which I work (and on numerous others, as reported in the press) an occasional favorite student activity is "killing" an automobile—usually justified by charging a quarter a smash at a moribund jalopy with a sledge-hammer and giving the proceeds to charity. The nature of the symbolic act is clear. The students who are most vehement in their physical attack against the car are not necessarily those associated with the New Left movements. They have, however, clearly been well indoctrinated in covert automobile-hating, either, I suppose, by their sociological or ecological studies, or both. But youth's vagaries involve many strange factors, some of which are discussed in Chapter 22.

28 See G.N.G., *L C*, pp. 240–242 on Innis. McLuhan's works need no notations here.

29 See Crane Brinton's *Introduction to A History of Western Morals*, pp. 1–29, for a discussion of what, at first, appears obvious, but is really far from a self-evident truth.

almost exactly the same) environmental surroundings may, as William James was one of the first to observe in his study of religion, evolve quite different moral schemes, one from the other.

The point of these observations is that, to the best of current knowledge, technology (or materialism in some constructions) *has no moral qualities above and beyond those that human beings choose to give it.* The assumption of the apostles of alienation—and even Ferkiss to a degree—has always been that, in some measure, socio-cultural goods and bads are inherent in technology itself—its factories, its class conflicts, its uniformity of life-style. This assumption is not unlike the old belief that books (except the Bible) were bad for man *per se;* or the newer fiction that various instruments of communications contain messages which have nothing to do with their content. Such theories are, in short, patent absurdities.

Today's mythos, however, appears to accept without question (from the rough output of advertising agencies to elegant analyses of university scholars) that a range of moral dictates, from the depths of bad to the stratosphere of good, is inherent in contemporary technology, and that, today, these moral investitures *become stronger the more the technique, technology or instrument in question resembles a human being.* Sophisticated computers, therefore, are more redolent of morality (or immorality) than the old belt system or potters wheel. In fact, the latter device is so (comparatively) virtuous today that it is used as an instrument of psychological therapy!

Men have, since antiquity, frequently looked for the sources of morality in exactly the wrong places. (Shaw, for instance, observed that an Englishman thinks he is being moral when he is merely uncomfortable). Morals begin and end in the community of men, and are communicated by all the instruments of communication available to their particular society. In our time and place, the moral nature of technology—both good and bad—is indeed a facet of persuasion, spread as broadly as Ellul claims, from schoolhouse and church to university to television station. But the dire implications derived from this fact, the author believes, are incorrect.

This conclusion rests simply upon the measure of freedom of intellect and value to which each of us, in the word of Sartre, is "condemned." Once one frees oneself from the tyranny of the myth of technological morality, sneers at it and laughs at it at the same time, he need no longer be alienated from reality by his machines (machines, after all, are a *part* of that reality) or intoxicated into unreason by their worship. Nor need he accept vague promises that he or his progeny will somehow evolve into "technological men." Nor must he even take a permanent place on the sliding scale between the absolutes of technologically oriented moral bads and goods. Let him look to humanity—its arts, its literature, its history and its gods—for morals. Let him look to technology for the advancement of that humanity and the enhancement of his self to what he decides is good. Then (and only then) will he be immune both to the ambivalent vanities of technology and its power of enslavement by persuasive myths of salvation and/or doom.

Conclusion

Technology is the super-force (personified by the notion of the Superman) of the Western world. Its myths spread far and have deep roots.

Considerable confusion exists as to how and where science and technology cleave from one another and where they overlap. This has been true since what Whitehead calls "the invention of invention," towards the end of the Enlightenment. We have observed a number of curiosities concerning technology in this respect, a major one being that the great age of new invention and techniques appears to have passed into history nearly half a century ago, while the impetus of science in Western intellectual life remains enormous. Simultaneously, the present era is one of increasing use, spread and modification of old technologies and the decreasing utilization of actual scientific accomplishment, a viewpoint rarely espoused by contemporary historians.

Arguments concerning the tyrannies of technology and the inevitable ubiquity of technological persuasion are heard on many sides and in many versions, and require careful consideration. They bespeak a broad viewpoint of societal destruction, either as the result of psychological stresses, the unintentional mismanagement of techniques, or as the results of unforeseen by-products of modern industry. A wave of naïve optimism is also apparent in the faith that our institutions may—before the hypothesized technological Armageddon—produce a species of man that will assimilate and subsequently conquer the tyrannies of life in a society as dependent as ours is upon functioning technology.

Most of these positions yield points well taken. But technology itself contains no moral values, nor is the cultural persuasion of educators, industrialists, social scientists and others accomplishing more than mediating to society arbitrary convictions that techniques, of and by themselves, are good or bad for man and society. Such fictions are extremely attractive but spun of myths. Man is the fabricator of technique, the inventor and user of atom bombs, the bestower of value upon mass uniform production, capitalist and socialist economic organizations, and the romanticist of systems engineering.

Technology's moral position depends upon the ideas that human beings convince themselves and others of, like all moral positions. In moral mobility, therefore, man—both individually and in groups—has a wider degree of latitude than he often knows. The same instruments of communications (interpersonal and electronic) that presently imbue technology with moral persuasion may be employed tomorrow (more simply than is generally realized) to break the hold of that persuasive force upon our culture. Having done this, it will release us, as individuals, from the grip of the Superman, who is, after all, neither Lucifer nor Santa Claus, but the servant of his inventor. And quite an efficient, inexpensive and loyal one he is, in the last analysis.

Chapter 6

MASS CULTURE AS PERSUASION

Specialists without spirit, sensualists without heart; this nullity imagines that it has attained a level of civilization never before achieved.

Max Weber

Most students of contemporary mass communications are aware of the various positions of the so-called authorities on mass culture in our time, and their shifting but discernably different positions.[1] Magazines, books, anthologies and texts contain the writings of such arbiters of cultural virtue as David Manning White, Ernest van den Haag, Bernard Rosenberg, Joseph Klapper, Wilbur Schramm, Marya Mannes, Leo Lowenthal, Gilbert Seldes, Dwight Macdonald and others who periodically dip into the grab bag of kitsch to come up with artistic criticism, scholarly judgments (meaning, usually, statistics), democratic optimism or aristocratic sniffing. It is possible, in one short essay, to come up with all four, in various degrees, by hedging arguments "on one hand, and on another."

The output of these analysts has remained surprisingly fresh as time has passed, and there is little need to add here to the main corpus of their observations. For a long time, mass culture was regarded as a mercurial culture trait; it seemed to change with the flighty fickleness of the public and the impress of fashion. But thanks to old movies on TV (and what must be the general acumen of both their detractors and admirers), the adage *plus ça change, plus c'est la meme chose* seems now to apply to popular culture—in the USA, at any rate.

The late comic David Burns observed a few years ago to the writer that they are still telling the same jokes in Broadway musicals that they were when Burns began his career in the early 1920's. The author's thirteen-year-

---

[1] See G.N.G., *L C*, Chapter 19, pp. 288–305.

old son's favorite film actors are Boris Karloff first, W. C. Fields second.[2] His oldest daughter has fallen under the spell of a number of color films which ape the cinematic grandeur of various movies shown at the New York World's Fair in 1939. Her favorite movie actor is a carbon copy of his father, who was her mother's favorite movie actor during World War II. Her cinematic ideal is a cliché version of a dozen old movies (most notably *The Wages of Fear*, made nearly twenty years ago), a blow-up color still from which covers an entire wall of her room. His youngest daughter has developed a passion for "TV premier films," every one of which appears to be re-make of the B movie of the '30's, in those days, sold to the public as "mid-week features."

Contrary to popular myth, mass culture does not create (or permit) much of a generation gap. Loud, way-out music is just as nerve shattering as its equivalent was a generation (or two) ago. And celebrities, from Barbra Streisand to Tiny Tim to Ringo, are as conventional—or unconventional now as then. Arlo Guthrie is as far from center (or near) as Mickey Rooney in his MGM days, and as lovable. If the Beatles are more culturally sensitive artists than the Marx Brothers were, the difference is measured by calipers. The game never ceases: Rowan and Martin for Laurel and Hardy; Jerry Lewis for Joe Penner; Pat Paulsen for Ned Sparks; James Bond for Dick Tracy; Dean Martin for James Bond *and* Bing Crosby; Jane Fonda for Marilyn Monroe; Goldie Hawn for Ann Sothern; Ruth Buzzi for Zazu Pitts. You hardly notice the changes in the cast, as the mass culture machine grinds on, speeding up here, slowing down there, sometimes more noticeably than at others, and with new instrumentation like TV, the equivalent of home-color "talkies"; all singing, all dancing, all laughing.

The reason, of course, that history repeats itself so neatly in the world of kitsch is that mass culture is a by-product of technology, and essentially obeys the same impulses it does. Like technology, its great age of investion and innovation seems to have passed. It has moved now into a period of growth, exploitation, imitation, analysis and myth. Writing about mass culture, as many have found, is presently a peculiarly discouraging occupation, because, in the long run, nothing anyone says (with exceptions) appears to

---

[2] I am myself a regular reader of the periodical *Monsters of Filmland*, testimony to the adolescent part of my nature and the scholarly (but jejune) nature of the editor of that journal, Forrest J. Ackerman. In America, it seems, no one ever really has to grow up for long. Let me add that my various other children bring into my house such gems as *Mad* and *The Rolling Stones* magazines, both of which make me nostalgic, as do the collections of yesterday's comic strips and other trivia which I run into. Even the "underground" weeklies currently available in New York City, journalistic enterprises such as *Kiss, Gay, Come, Screw, Pussy* and others (all apparently written by the same person), exude a juvenile, rebellious sort of porno-silliness that engenders in me a *dèja vu* of scatological jokes the boys used to tell in high school, little "dirty" cartoon books, much folded pornographic photographs and the local burlesque theatre. But we shall return to the plight of the middle-aged, jaded "teenager" in the chapters to come, as well as complaining Portnoys and senile teenyboppers.

have much effect either upon output, distribution or patronage.[3] It is a phenomenon somehow bigger than the scholars, journalists and historians who surround it; bigger than its own performers and writers and hangers-on; and far more powerful than its own affluent class of entrepreneurs.

Mass Culture and Technology

Mass culture, since the invention of the talking film, has created a technological backwash in our society, always in motion and sometimes labile but, overall, remarkably stagnant. The technological novelty of television, for instance, gave promise, in its earliest days, of much novelty of expression, a new juxtaposition of the mediums of narrative, picture and drama. Dave Garroway, one of the talented narrators of our time, created an image in his shows from Chicago of a fluid finger-prodding live television-eyeball, harnessed to intimate voices and subjective visions. Frenetic, under-rehearsed live drama (with soap opera accents) from the pen of Paddy Chayefsky and others also portended *something* (it was impossible to guess what); as did the documentaries, spun around that symbol of intellectualism with showman-sense, Edward R. Murrow; the nonsense of Burr Tillstrom; and the put-on infantilism of Captain Kangaroo, who, by 1968, could sadly and correctly be characterized by Charles Sopkin as owning ". . . two of the coldest, hardest, toughest-looking eyes this side of the Pecos." [4]

Whatever promise the television instrument showed in its early days, it did not live up to it. On one side (the east coast of America), it was taken over by radio broadcasting hands who, in effect, added pictures to their quiz shows, news reports, sporting events and singing commercials, and ended up where they started, but now spending and making more money. On the other side (the west coast), the film industry, with its belt-line mid-week features, horse operas and second-string Grade B, C, D, E, and F films, first

---

[3] Many of the talented analysts of mass culture (and honest critics like Dwight Macdonald, John Crosby, Renata Adler, Philip Hamberger and numerous others) gave up their mission (or aspects of it) out of boredom or frustration. Those who remain frequently are worn down by the frustrations of their positions as arbiters of culture who apparently accomplish nothing. My hat is off to Judith Crist, Pauline Kael, Michael Arlen, and a few others who stick to their guns, but they have my sympathies too. See also the delightful case studies in Gillo Dorfles, *Kitsch, The World of Bad Taste* (New York: Universe Books, 1969), to see exactly what repels the critics.

[4] Charles Sopkin, *Seven Glorious Days, Seven Fun Filled Nights* (New York: Simon and Schuster, 1968), p. 25. A sentimental encomium to the early days of television, interesting but not quite accurate, may be found in Harold Mehling, *The Great Time Killer* (New York: World Publishing Co., 1962). The tendency to lionize yesterday's mediocrity is understandable in the light of the permanent illusion that the mean of mediocrity appears to fall with the passage of time. A friend of mine is writing a doctoral dissertation on the *radio* soap opera that seems, in retrospect, a classic monument to American regional humor. In its own time, anyone indicating to his professor that he wanted to earn a Ph.D. studying such a program would have to be referred to the university psychiatrist—with justice.

unloaded the old ones on television entrepreneurs at enormous profits. When the edge had worn off the old Dorothy Lamour-Jon Hall masterpieces, they began to grind out new-old quickies and—one way or another—dumped them also onto the "boob tube," correctly named by this time. In sum, television technology had changed mass culture little. The World Series looked better than it had sounded to those who cared about baseball; but domestic dramas (or soap operas), suspense stories and much news broadcasting stayed level or ran downhill, as writers and designers added pictures to narrative and circumscribed the imaginative potential of sound broadcasting with what are now called "visuals." In fairness, they fell no flatter on television than they previously had on radio. But by 1960, mass network television was difficult to distinguish qualitatively from mass network radio two decades before.

Most analysts consider both mass culture and its purveyors highly fluid creatures, like (a better metaphor) waltzing mice. Most analysts are wrong. Mass culture is a behemoth, living, chewing and rolling in the mud every now and then, a formidable beast apparently impervious to all minor weapons used against it. It is tough, dim-witted and slow to react to anything except major environmental changes: depressions, recessions, federal legislation or rare public outcry.

That part of mass culture's output which emerges from the printing press (or similar instrument) cloaks itself in the First Amendment of the United States Constitution and resists change also, but on the grounds that it is the single main focal instrument for enlightenment in a democracy (a downright lie, in the author's opinion). Both press and broadcasters cry "censor" at anyone who squirms at their vulgarities and feeble mindedness, while the latter prattles through its loudspeakers drivel about "giving the public what it wants," "cultural democracy" and other slogans too childish to repeat, much less analyze, here. The public, as it always has and perhaps always will, takes what it gets, and learns—somewhat guiltily—either to like it or, in the enormous cultural emporium, to find something else to amuse it. Or it tunes out entirely, a recourse from mass culture that apparently more Americans take than its managers are prone to admit. "You can always turn us off," say they, and a surprising number of people from both lower and higher class strata do just that, although the captains of communications empires do not publicize the fact. People in the middle have not yet discovered that you can pull out the plug, but time may enlighten them.[5]

---

[5] While mass viewing and reading statistics are enormous (too large, often, to be meaningful) they indicate merely partial engagement, even in those cultural events that "everyone" participates in like assassinations, riots and moon shots. That *Communication News* estimates, for instance, that 59,200,000 homes in the USA are equipped with television sets, indicates little about how they are used. Trendex figures tell us that sets are *on*, but they say nothing about the perceptual state of the viewers, or how many of

As for "giving the public what it wants," Philip Abrams, from a British view, dissects the canard admirably:

> Like the belief in impartiality, the appeal to what the public wants is spurious through and through. Just as something has to be selected and something rejected whether the selecting is done consciously or not, so the highly centralized structure of broadcasting means that judgments are constantly being made about the nature of audience wants and that in practice the only test of these supposed wants is audience size. And I would suggest that to defend programs that are more "acceptable" than "authentic" on the ground that such programs having huge audiences and that these audiences show that such programs are what the public "wants" is to ignore the real relationship that exists between the broadcaster and his public and to make nonsense of the idea of want.[6]

The technological apotheosis of mass culture is, at present, television, and much general discussion of the quality and style of popular arts in America concerns video and video only, although, by extension, most social critics imply that they are also talking about other forms of mass communication and cultural interchange as well. This is not fair, on the one hand, to television, living as it does, in the USA, in a never-never land, triangulated somewhere between nineteenth-century capitalism, vague statutory notions of "the public welfare" and the old traditions of show business and journalism. Television in America is probably doing a better job of meeting the manifold objectives that the marketplace (those of law, government, the political establishments and the needs and whims of children and women of our nation—the largest segment of the present audience) demands of it than any other national video service in the world. True enough, other video services do not *try* to placate as many deities as our broadcasting nabobs do, and therefore many of them succeed better at what they do.[7]

---

them are actually watching. Estimates that 70 million newspapers are circulated in America daily are meaningless, unless you know how many people read the papers, what they read and what effect their reading has upon them. All glib purveyors of statistics about mass consumption of mass culture should bear in mind the example of the Drive-In-Cinema where, apparently, the nature of the film shown has little to do with the basic appeal of the cheap legal parking space, safety, and (in cool weather) comfort they offer today for sexually acrobatic young people and older cheaters. To return to my misspent youth, I rarely attended a movie that I really wanted to *see* with a young lady in my 'teens, unless she was enormously unattractive. Let our television nose counters also ponder the clever prostitute (about whom I was told) who, operating in a high rent and respectable apartment building (with paper thin walls), keeps her television set on and volume high to drown out the noisy antics of her playful clientele and associates.

[6] Philip Abrams, "The Nature of Radio and Television" in Allan Casty, *Mass Media and Mass Man* (New York: Holt, Rinehart and Winston, Inc., 1968), p. 85.

[7] See Walter B. Emery, *National and International Systems of Broadcasting* (East Lansing: Michigan State University Press, 1969), for a well documented picture of broadcasting around the world in the 1960's. Despite their excellence, volumes like Emery's date quickly on the heels of governmental, technological and social change, but the general spirit behind broadcasting services remains relatively constant—reflecting

Nor does this confusion of vision, on the other hand, help to clarify the full reach of technology and mass culture into our individual lives and personal constructions of reality, that is to say, describe its fullness as persuasion for cultural assent. All consumable technology is at once reflective and directive of mass culture, and no one individual's life style—from the age of about six months to death—is today immune from it. The same concatenations of social value and potential technology that give us movies, books, newspapers, magazines, radio *and* television also supply for us, in much the same manner, the homes we live in, the clothes we wear, the automobiles we drive, the cigarettes we smoke, the foods we eat, the gifts we give and receive, and, in the more intimate aspects of our lives, the technology that cleans and curries us and keeps many alive past the time nature would have had done with us. Mass culture includes the prophylaxis and contraception involved in our love making, fashions in sexual stimuli, and even influences patterns of sexual response. It dictates, in many respects, in what manner we raise our children, providing for us just as discrete and specific traditional techniques as those of the Indians and Eskimos.[8] Technology has also produced our "telephone culture," a strange form of intimacy which, combined with the jet-set mentality (more than space rocketry) has eliminated, not so much distance as the concept of terrestrial space, wideness, vastness and the slow modifications of terrain and habitat that one feels as he moves by older and slower devices across the land and water masses of the globe, and up and down its elevations.

These effects—and countless others—have both psychological significance and direct logical importance in the conduct of human life in our culture. They are psychological attitudinal ephemera, to be discussed subsequently,[9] but also, from the vantage point of this chapter, they are true conditions of living in our society. They demonstrate the ways in which the reach of mass culture is neither limited to television, radio or the printed and electronic devices of communications we know, and is in such a way related to our private and public lives that it is virtually impossible for any one of us to live beyond its reach. The man—if such there be—who

broadcasting's role in mass culture—in any one nation over many years, despite organizational and other changes. Britain is a good example where, since 1950, enormous changes have been made in the structure of broadcasting institutions, most particularly the elimination of the BBC monopoly of telecasting and the introduction of commercials on the ITA regulated stations. The basic role of broadcasting in British life, in both theory and practice, has changed little, however, since 1949. See *ibid.*, pp. 81–104.

[8] A strange device for toddlers is presently being touted on television. Called the "Jolly Jumper," it is a harness like those employed for parachutes (in miniature) that hangs from a spring contraption. The instrument evidently is supposed to pacify infants and/or take the place of a play-pen. What it also does, psychologically, in the long run to the tots trapped in it for extensive periods of time is another question, one that may never be answered. But Indians and Eskimos often swaddle their young, and their kids seem to be no more the worse for it.

[9] See Part Three.

neither watches television, goes to the movies, reads magazines, newspapers or books is still, unless he is an eremite, part of the flow and flux of the technology of mass culture, and as much a part of it as David Riesman's "inside dopester," whose bibles are *Life* and *TV Guide.* In fact, because he has spared down the multitude of impressions that the technological society is geared to provide for its citizens, he may be more sensitive to his fewer stimuli from mass culture than the individual who may have been narcotized by a larger, almost total immersion.

The only retreat from mass culture, in a technological society, is therefore not to "turn it off," because its subtle manifestations simply cannot be turned off. It may be *avoided,* at times, by the pursuit of "class" culture, but class, today, at the hands of pop satirists, and due to electronic recording, photographic reproductions of art and our general affluence, is becoming more and more difficult to sever from mass, as numerous critics have noted. At present, a great degree of cultivated sensibility differentiates this writer's reaction to the beautifully illustrated reproductions of Japanese nineteenth-century prints on his desk from that of his good friend, a press agent, who has spent his lifetime developing expertise in Oriental art. Should the writer, however, wish to believe somehow that his crude and ignorant reactions (on a child's level) to these lovely drawings is in fact as "fine" (as in the term "fine arts") as his friend's, nothing in cultural democracy or mass culture will discourage him but his own honesty. After all, a professor and writer should be "class" rather than "mass," shouldn't he?

The fact that teachers of all kinds (and most writers) are themselves instruments for *purveying* mass culture and its value system, of course, usually evades their own purview, especially those who teach undergraduates in college and believe that their disciplinary specialty somehow insulates them from the ubiquity of mass culture. Some graduate instructors are a bit more realistic, or resigned to their role as conduits of the "best ideas" of the day, in our time ideas largely derived from mass culture. One brutally true sentence emerges from Ellul's stark analysis of the role of persuasion in any state governed by the consent of its citizens; while its universality may be more circumscribed than intended by Ellul, its relationship to the spread and persuasiveness of mass culture in modern technological societies seems, to this writer, applicable almost without exception. Writes Ellul, "A thorough study of Information, Education, Human Relations, and Propaganda reveals that in practice no essential differences exist among them." [10] Once one looks beyond the distracting first glimpse of mass culture as mediated by instruments like television, movies and slick magazines, into the smaller and more serious corners of modern life, the implications of Ellul's charge reach ever closer the foundations of our illusions of modernity.

---

[10] Ellul, *Propaganda,* p. 137.

Mass Entertainment as Myth and Paradox

At the present writing, a film is on view in the author's suburban neighborhood. It is Visconti's epic, *The Damned*, a shattering, if somewhat tedious, tale, set against the period of consolidation of power by the Nazis in Germany in 1933 and 1934. It concerns a family of industrialists (Krupps?) and their intensive power struggles as they relate their destinies to Nazi strategy to control both the German army and industrialists. Performed with exhausting realism and depth, the film also contains considerable serious treatment of homosexuality, incest, greed, transvesticism, child molestation, suicide and various other aberrations. The movie is unrelieved by comic interludes, and its verisimilitude is, in its most carnal scenes, astounding. In some respects, its constant pulse resembles a Chinese water torture. Some of the audience leaving the theatre the other night were bewildered; others were drained.

In front of the playhouse, there is posted a large sign (above the self-censor's X rating) and an admonition that children under eighteen will not be admitted. Large black letters on top of the sign proclaim:

ADULT ENTERTAINMENT.
(N.B.: "Entertainment.")

This sign—and thousands of others like it—epitomizes the multitude of sins, misunderstandings, idiocies, illegalities, corruptions, banal research, stupidities, rhetoric, bogus scholarship and corrupt sociology that have occurred in the so-called "investigation" of American mass culture for decades. Nor is this merely a semantic issue. All parties involved—including the theatre manager of our local Bijou—have a reasonably clear idea of what *entertainment* is and is not. Certainly movie producers, behavioral scientists, network executives and cultural Solons should also. For the record, however, *Webster's Seventh New Collegiate Dictionary* defines "entertain" (obsolete and archaic versions eliminated) thus: ". . . to show hospitality to; to consider with favor; to provide entertainment, especially for guests."

"Entertainment" is thereafter defined in this manner: ". . . something diverting or engaging, especially a public performance."

At one stage in British history, a trip to Bedlam was unquestionably entertaining. *The Damned* may indeed be entertaining to a McLuhanite or a voyeur. Most of the people with whom I viewed it were not, in any construction of the term, even "diverted or engaged" for long. Like many good films (both serious and comic), the dramatic thrust of this one required considerable awareness of one's own presence and self-examination of individual emotions and sense-memories. The great Durante was, and is, a fine entertainer. So, to most people, is Leonard Bernstein. Pornography may be entertaining to some, repellent to others. Education, deep self-examination, spiritual experiences, vicarious pain and the tragic realities of death and destruction are, for most people most of the time, *not* entertainment.

The word "entertainment" has, however, been employed to act as a smoke screen for most serious attempts to delineate either the nature or the role of the vital elements of mass culture in the West. The Hollywood motion picture establishment, some years ago for instance, touted loud the slogan "Motion Pictures are Your Best Entertainment" in answer to some studies that indicated that crime films (and others) might conceivably have an effect of some sort upon young people which was not too healthy.[11] To this day, the public relations types who man the barricades at the Motion Picture Association of America hardly ever mention films except when coupled with the word "entertainment." Talking to them, one might think that the Hollywood studios produce nothing but laughing gas.

Most serious, perhaps, is the confusion that appears to exist—again purposely fired *on* the instruments of mass culture by its flacks—between concepts of "relaxation" and "entertainment." The present shady equation of the two stems from the "tired business man" cliché that has long been employed to defend such delights as burlesque shows that do not need defense, because they satisfy every aspect of the definition of "entertainment." That the tired businessman relaxes while being entertained is beyond dispute. That he can relax *without* being entertained, or be entertained without relaxing, is also obvious. To defend, therefore, the entire notion of mass entertainment for its anesthetic value is playing with partial truths.

Abrams notes that a claim has been made that the public may have an innate "right to triviality." [12] And it probably does. Most cultures punctuate their work periods with lazy days or weekends of one sort or another and periodic holidays. To maintain, however, that, because one has a right to relax periodically, the entire flux of a culture be turned over to inactivity is as absurd as the defense that all (or most) mass culture must be entertainment solely because it is relaxing. Granting even that entertainment is the over-riding function of mass culture (far from either apparent or true), the "entertainment as relaxation" notion denies the kind of diverting and engaging experiences which create tensions, develop conflicts, enervate and, perhaps, even exhaust one by virtue either of their extraordinary humor, intellectual stimulation or artistic brilliance. It would seem that the right to trivia, or need to relax, is a demand of culture outstandingly simple to meet in *many* ways. To find almost the entire thrust of such institutions as televi-

---

[11] These inquiries, The Payne Fund Studies of Motion Pictures and Social Values, included studies by Herbert Blumer, W. W. Charters, Edgar Dale, Henry James Forman, Charles C. Peters, Ruth Peterson and L. L. Thurstone, were made between 1933–37, and have recently been reissued (at formidible prices) by the Arno Press and *The New York Times*.

[12] Abrams, *op. cit.*, p. 84.

sion and motion pictures defending their constructions of "entertainment" under such an imperative is on its face absurd.

Most serious (and rarely entertaining) defenses of mass culture as entertainment generally begin with the articulation of various notions taken from the writings of Johan Huizinga,[13] whose not unreasonable analyses of certain aspects of society are frequently generalized into formal theory and then presented as the spine or *raison d'etre* of mass culture as we know it in the United States today. William Stephenson, using the Q-sort attitude inventory (a dubious basis for theorizing, but a basis nevertheless) is an example.[14] He articulates broad generalizations about the "real" function of mass culture, based upon specific investigations into practices that describe what is probably currently *done* by a selected populations, an activity not unlike basing school curricula upon the norms of behavior at an insane asylum. In essence, he postulates *play* as a necessary human activity of greater significance than most other common goals "realizable in the immediate future." He sees mass communications as the most viable cultural device to meet this hypothesized need, and therefore scorns the notion that mass culture is escapist or debasing in any respect, as long as it lets people play.[15]

To return to the author of the concept of *homo ludens,* Huizinga offers[16] three characteristics of play as they relate to the individual's social role. Play is, first, free, voluntary activity. Second, it involves a departure from reality and a suspension of seriousness. Third, play is distinctly separated from ordinary life "within certain limits of time and place." These observations are adequate to delimit the bounds and nature of entertain-

---

[13] See Johan Huizinga, Homo Ludens, *A Study of the Play Element in Culture* (Boston: Beacon Press, 1955).

[14] See William Stephenson, *The Play Theory of Mass Communication* (Chicago: The University of Chicago Press, 1967). In all fairness, Stephenson treads quite modestly when it comes to apply his "theory" to cultural imperatives, emphasizing the importance of play activities in life and the problem of accuracy of his analytic method in his discussion, especially pp. 190–206. In this respect, he is somewhat like Kinsey of the "first report," before the latter began deriving moral imperatives from common behaviors. I remember hearing Arthur Miller, some years ago, tell a convocation of psychologists that their search to find out what man *is* and *does* is futile, and that they should set their sights upon what man *might become.* He received a standing ovation at this point in his talk, but I have failed to notice any substantive change since then in the mere descriptive proclivites of contemporary behavioral research, especially of the kind Stephenson is doing.

[15] *Ibid.*, p. 98. Stephenson has, I think, polarized the conventional "serious" endeavors of man and the notion of "play" beyond reasonable limits. A more subtle Freudian perspective might postulate the concept of the eroticization of *work activities* to the degree that they become similar to play. A college administrator (an educational psychologist) friend of mine (a serious hard worker), showing off his experimental campus to me, once asked, "Isn't this a grand toy to play with?" For him, yes. For me, no. An anaylst might say that he has eroticized a college, while I have eroticized my favorite hobby, smoking. Versions of play, in other words, differ markedly.

[16] Huizinga, *op. cit.*, pp. 7–9.

ment, perhaps even to admit *homo ludens* into the many-faceted picture gallery of normal man as he threads his way through life. The case for the indispensibility of play, particularly for the young (but not confined to them) may also be made easily. Should one wish to dress up this notion in psychoanalytic theory, adding ornaments from the "pain-pleasure principle" (with more emphasis upon the latter than the former), one may produce a tenable defense—as if it is needed—for the ancient notion that Jack will be pretty dull company if all he does is work and, probably, a poor insurance risk as well.

To inflate this corner of the truth into a full-blown, nearly uncritical defense of the current state of mass culture in the USA is another matter. This is precisely what Harold Mendelsohn has done.[17] His book is required reading for those naïve enough to believe that modern mass culture is not a major persuasive force in the contemporary world, or that the concept of "entertainment" is more than a cruel paradoxical "cop-out" from facing implications of how technological man is shaping his culture.

Criticism of Mendelsohn's document—and the frenetic scholarship involved—must be left to the reader's own sensibilities and degree of credulity. His thesis consists of a poorly hung strand of rationalizations, strawmen (who, according to Mendelsohn, want to return to the thirteenth century), denials of self-evident propositions in the name of "rationality," issue dodging, mis-readings of cultural and theatrical history, arbitrary psychology (particularly in regard to humor), misconstructions of both the nature and function of art in history, inverse snobbism (with continual recourse to the term "cultural élite" for purposes of opprobrium) and a penultimate insulting reference to his own work as an "intellectual adventure." The saddest part of it is his final plea for a "University Institute or several University Institutes, financed and supported by the popular entertainment industries, to carry out programs of scholarly investigation into popular entertainment," [18] a magnificent suggestion, particularly if these studies are supported by the institutions that profit from modern mass culture.

There has grown a continual tendency for nearly the last fifty years to

---

[17] Harold Mendelsohn, *Mass Entertainment* (New Haven, Conn.: College and University Press, 1966). The argument of this chapter necessitates quoting Mendelsohn's acknowledgement "to the National Association of Broadcasters who made the research for this study possible . . ." For the uninitiated, the NAB is the NAM-type pressure group of the commercial broadcasting industry. Their persuasion is not restricted to the air-waves but extends to pressures upon Congressmen, Commissioners and, obviously, sociologists and psychologists as well, who, in turn, plead the industry's causes among opinion makers and the general public.

[18] *Ibid.*, p. 162. *Mass Entertainment* is a particularly discouraging work for me because of the regard I have developed for Mendelsohn on the basis of a fine reputation as a competent researcher and the excellence of much of his scholarly output prior to *Mass Entertainment*. I remember, however, Robert Service's refrain, "There are strange things done in the midnight sun by the men who moil for gold," and I make no exceptions for myself in quoting it.

lean over backwards in the defense of "entertainment," "relaxation," "play," "pleasure" or whatever one calls the "narcotizing dysfunction" (an unfortunate term describing the anesthetic effects of certain experiences) of mass culture. The illusion (or myth) that the apostles of play have created is based fundamentally upon the premise that distraction from life is a positive experiential factor rather than a negative one. While the view may have relevance to the conduct of a fraction of life in a technological society, its antithesis—at least, to this observer in the light of the history we have seen in the past two chapters—contains a more insistent message for our present culture.

It is not a myth but a paradox that so much hard work and energy and much technological expertise and financial activity attends continual efforts (of industrial proportions) to insulate the individual and the masses from the numerous tensions that complexities of modern culture have produced, both as direct and indirect by-products of our styles of public and private life.

The manufacture of cyclopropane gas is certainly a positive, contributive function in society, because it is an effective and safe general anesthetic. The gas, however, accomplishes absolutely nothing itself, except to aid in providing a field where certain skills and technical applications of knowledge may be performed efficiently, usually those of surgery. Were one to attempt to make a case that modern medicine is justified as a profession and encouraged to thrive *merely* because of its anesthetic developments, the foolishness of the notion is at once apparent. Drugs, in various forms, and alcohol, have been available for decades as pain killers of effectiveness, but capable of developing for the individual little more than individual solace against exogenic evils. Neither the Roman circuses (diversion varies as culture varies), the mystery plays of the Middle Ages, Elizabethan comedy nor Restoration satire have gained their significance in the performing arts by virtue of the manner that they removed man from the concerns of his environment (although, like scholarship, sex and song they may all have accomplished this end to some slight degree), but, instead, because of the unexpected ways they either rendered men less vulnerable to corrupt elements in culture, or provided moral insights into the great issues of their day—issues which may have lost their pith for us as we, from our twentieth century perspectives, look at them now.

All in all, *homo ludens,* while he may well exist, is a puny, insignificant manifestation of a shadow-man, mostly because the quality and nature of play—while it may energize the tired and divert the somber—is largely dissipated at the end of each day and does not renew itself in the accumulated experience either of one's individual life or the long term collection of culture traits through history, with few exceptions. The larger the conceptual edifice, therefore, built upon the vague therapy of entertainment, the more it sways on weak foundations—unless, as in the case of the Freudians, it is seen as component to an ongoing set of tensions (life and death, in their case) to be held dear, on one hand, and overcome in growth and maturity, on the other. Despite its present role in contemporary persuasion, recourse to the catch-all criterion of entertainment is an unconvincing ruse, probably rarely believed even by those who resort to it.[19]

The Cult of Corruption

We shall examine, in later chapters, specific charges leveled against various instruments of mass communication that, for certain segments of our population, they are specifically corruptive and lead to attitudes and behaviors which encourage violence, degrade values, promote moral laxity and other charges. On their faces, such postulated effects are psychological, because they are all obviously the results of the way in which reactive processes occur in the mass audience. Nor is the claim usually made that an entire audience is so affected—merely children, the poor, the impressionable, the credulous, the middle class or some other such portion of the public. In the translation of psychological effects to actual behavior, few factors from individual to individual remain constant. So it is extremely difficult—perhaps impossible—to determine exactly in what ways such causal relationships occur, although the absence of specific proof does not mean that they may not exist, especially if individual bits of evidence (some of it subjective) indicate that they do.

These individual problems await their turn for our consideration. Of importance in the present context is the assumption—shared by many fine artists, members of the academic community, some psychologists and others (but few sociologists)—that mass culture is far more than just an instrument of narcosis or entertainment; that it is not merely a "vast wasteland" (in the words of Newton Minow describing American television) or a "vast garbage dump" (a more trenchant critical comment) or a "big bowl of chop suey" [20] (in the words of another critic); that is not, in fact, the barbarian dark underside of a proliferous contemporary education, as Dwight Mcdonald and others appear to believe. This particular viewpoint sees mass culture, in all its ramifications, as instruments of the Devil,[21] as

---

[19] A better and more sophisticated defense of mass culture centers on the ways in which the individual's engagement in reality is increased by the modern instruments of communication, rather than the degree to which he is entertained or narcotized by them. One of the most lucid essays available espousing this viewpoint is Edward Shils, "Mass Society and Its Culture" in Norman Jacobs (ed.), *Culture for the Millions?* (Princeton, New Jersey: D. Van Nostrand Co., 1961), pp. 1–27.

[20] David T. Bazelon, "The Louder Reality: Behind the Busy Mirror" in David Manning White and Richard Averson (eds.), *Sight, Sound, and Society* (Boston: Beacon Press, 1968), p. 142.

[21] The Devil and his psychological hold over the minds of the contemporary public will be discussed in Part Three. Religious perspectives of persuasion as part of mass culture will also concern us in Chapter 11.

specifically corruptive of the entire population, not one part or segment of it.

Broadly speaking, little in this concept contradicts the views of exponents of mass entertainment. It merely places at odds two constructions of how entertainment, amusement and diversion (or narcosis) serve the community. The positions are not unlike those which, on one side, emphasize the enormous cultural liability that seven million alcoholics create in our nation, while, from the other, the virtues for seventy million non-alcoholic drinkers of the sedative values of alcohol are defended in cogent psychological and social terms. Neither proponent of either argument is exactly wrong; nor is he right. The justice of his position depends upon his concept of the general welfare of the commonwealth, whether the free sale of alcoholic beverages appears to be doing more harm than good to society (or vice-versa) in the long run, what legal prohibition of it might mean to our culture and the degree of alcoholic malfunction our civilization may comfortably tolerate without interfering with necessary services and functions.

Such a pragmatic outlook is neither sophistry nor muddy liberalism but a scientifically defensible suspension of judgment, necessary inevitably to discover relevant truth, like it or not, and then to re-organize institutions in such ways as to deal with it. In regard to mass culture, therefore, the view that is necessarily corruptive is as naïve (or sophisticated) as the view, begging evidence to the contrary, that it is therapeutic.

"Mass entertainment" notions are but one form of a simplistic morality from the conservative corner. "Mass corruption" is a more revolutionary idea, perhaps of greater persuasive force, because it may imply a program for change, but no less simplistic and mythological in coloration and tone.[22] These are not simple problems, and all of them are swept along by the larger tide of the technological society which invariably produces persuasion that, at a given moment, clears the way for the quantitative replacement of old technology by new technology in new areas of life. To neglect this fact is to deny a major persuasive function of mass culture in the contemporary state.

---

[22] From a common sense perspective, it is possible to agree provisionally with one or another position in regard to such sticky social problems, as long as one holds one's agreement provisionally. In the absence of evidence, however, a stand sometimes must be taken, even if it is an equivocal one. I do not believe in the legal prohibition of alcohol, for instance, although I deeply believe that all manner and means of persuasion should be employed to keep alcoholics from using this drug for suicidal purposes, because the social disorientation they create (largely at the wheels of automobiles) is a threat to me and my family. In regard to mass culture, I believe that the apostles of mass entertainment are taking greater chances with our national destiny than those who would err on the side of caution in discouraging those kinds of mass communications that might *possibly* cause social harm—mindful of the problems regarding rights of free speech that such caution generates. In my conscience, I merely ask whether *homo ludens*' need for entertainment is as great as *homo sapiens*' need for prudence and restraint.

The fundamental logistic difficulty of mass culture's function as entertainment—usually considered harmless or culturally facilitating—is that it must support the status quo by doing nothing at all, that is, merely allowing the technology of mass communications to run in a free market, at the dictates of commerce. Should elements of corruption one day be found, however, in the broad thrust of kitsch, controlling them will be difficult or impossible without damage to our beliefs in culturally democratic free expression and to the elaborate organization of technology involved, one way or another, in the mass culture industries.

One of the outstanding contemporary critics of mass culture is van den Haag, whose psychoanalytic approach to personal alienation and symptoms of disorientation are equated with life-styles associated with mass culture.[23] Van den Haag's criticism is particularly interesting, because it is almost entirely free of the artistic evaluation of those critics who are open to the charge of "cultural élitism." And almost all sharp analysts of mass culture from the late Gilbert Seldes to Pauline Kael (two first-raters) may be charged thus with some slight justice. Van den Haag is a therapist, however, and his attacks against kitsch are not directed against their vulgarities or their qualities as art or debasement of art. He centers, instead, upon their psychological fallout, attacks that are more difficult to deny than those counter-weighing popular culture against élite culture, or that depend upon the slogan of "grass roots democracy", whereby it is legitimate to know nothing about art but to know precisely what one likes, no matter why.

In particular, van den Haag is lucid on the relationship of technology to mass culture and its methodical utilization as a persuasive power in Western society. Because he does not draw enormous morals from his insights, he is more realistic in his analysis than numerous other sociologically oriented critics who deal in cosmologies based upon severe moral value judgments. Step by step, we are introduced to the standardized, dehumanizing de-individuization inherent in industrial culture,[24] the homogenization of experience, the bleakness of our pre-fabricated hospitals, cafeterias, motels and housing developments, and our final personal humiliation, in the hypocritical idiocy of contemporary funerals with their efficient, slick, tape-recorded denial of flesh and blood reality. In van den Haag's words, "If one lives and dies discontinuously and promiscuously in anonymous surroundings, it becomes hard to identify with anything . . . The rhythm of individual life loses autonomy, spontaneity, and distinction when it is tied into a stream of traffic and carried along, according to the speed of the road, as we are in going to work or play, or in doing anything." [25]

[23] See G.N.G., *L C*, pp. 292–293. Van den Haag's general position is well stated in *Passion and Social Constraint* (New York: Stein and Day, 1963), a compendium of his most interesting analytic essays including those on mass culture.

[24] *Ibid.*, pp. 289–309.

[25] *Ibid.*, p. 303.

Mass culture is reflective therefore of *all* modern culture, in van den Haag's view. And it is obvious that he sees minor and temporary changes in mass culture itself as meaningless without broader metamorphoses first in society at large. He largely disregards the persuasive power of mass culture as an ally of technology, bureaucracy and capitalism, functions which are of secondary interest to a therapeutically oriented observer. What he sees, however, is significant: the *consumption* of culture as opposed to participation in it; the prefabrication of low common denominator experiences that cannot but please uncultivated tastes; the creation of external images and façades at the expense of the development of one's individual life-style; and other symptoms of contemporary *anomie*. He perceives a sense of pain behind the sleek façades of our entertainment heroes, fashion models and cultural pace-setters who, if they were a bit more intelligent, might well be considered among the saddest victims of our technological society. As it is, most of them—but not all—are insulated from their own superficiality by shortages of sensitivity and brain power.

At one point, van den Haag states, ". . . what art is presented (in contemporary society) is received as entertainment or propaganda." [26] His reasoning, as this chapter indicates, is valid, although his observation would be more incisive had he written "what art is presented is received as entertainment *and* propaganda." If the observations above are adequate, a propagenda *element* attends the *totality* of persuasion in mass culture, whether that culture serves man well by entertaining him, or poorly by corrupting him, or, in some miraculous manner, performs both functions at the same time.

Psychiatrists are fated, unfortunately, to observe *per diem* more cultural disaster areas than other types of modern social critics with the result that, frequently, their social psychology is unnecessarily dour. Sometimes, they overcompensate for the depressive tendencies of their profession in much the way physicians, nurses, morticians and others, forced into a daily round of gloom, attempt to preserve their own equilibria. Granting this proclivity, Ruesch, a medical psychotherapist, puts van den Haag's observations into a slightly different cognitive context but directed to the same end, emphasizing particularly how persuasive delusions of contemporary life are drawn to their logical conclusions:

> But when man gives up self-reliance . . . he has nothing but the system to turn to; and if the system has no solution, when it cannot provide further illusions, comfort or anesthetics, the individual feels lost. Self-esteem is bound to self-reliance, and self-reliance is based upon well-functioning personal relations. The insecurity experienced by many of our patients is an awareness of the realities which contrast with the picture painted by the propagandists of our day . . .

[26] *Ibid.*, p. 307.

> . . . Modern mass man is a creature without a past but with a boundless future. The future, however, is fantasy and fantasy vanishes at times of stress. Man's failure to be anchored in tradition and historical continuity creates a feeling of being adrift. Modern man . . . feels deeply insecure when nature and suprapersonal forces raise havoc with the order he has created. To cover this insecurity, modern man has acquired a public face; externally he presents the picture of a calm, smiling, relaxed individual who is always in control, even if he is ready to explode.[27]

Clinical experience, teaching and other social occupations that emphasize the qualitative considerations of personality in industrial societies (regardless of the orientation of their exponents) almost invariably teach that mass culture is essentially corruptive of individualism in contemporary life. A partial list of social critics who espouse this view indicates the catholicity of the range of viewpoints in which this concept flowers. Consider, for instance, the differences between Jean-Paul Sartre, J. K. Galbraith, Pierre Teilhard de Chardin, Aldous Huxley, Erich Fromm, Philip Wylie, David Riesman, José Ortega y Gasset, Hendrick M. Ruitenbeck and Paul Tillich in basic epistomological and ontological assumptions. Yet their view of mass culture (and the views of many others)—concerning its functional results in technological cultures—are similar, most noticeably in regard to the corruptive power mediated from its few owners and managers to the masses.

On the other side of the coin, individual thinkers and writers whose emphasis is upon objective social phenomena, and who are not basically concerned with subjective breakdown, neurosis or individuality, seem little impressed by the concept of corruption by mass culture. They are equally as mixed a grill, and are made up of such individuals as David M. White, Leo Rosten, Leo Bogart, Max Wylie, Solomon Simonson, Kurt Lang and Joseph Klapper. And, of course, add that impressive roster of individuals who, in one way or another, derive their livelihood from mass culture but, nevertheless, defend their own roles intelligently, like Frank Stanton, Yale Roe, and a few of the members of the Federal Communications Commission who have given thought to their responsible positions.

Judging from such a sample of authorities, the weight of dispassionate authority would seem to fall on the side of the believers in corruption. But the problem is not this easily settled. Whatever the effects of mass culture, the fact that they *may* be corruptive (depending upon one's definition of corruption) may be far less important that they are also—to some degree—the inevitable concomitants of capitalism, industrialism, representative government and mass education. If, on the other hand, they can be shown to cause no harm either to children or adults, to the weak or the strong, the normal or the deviant, the discovery may also be *irrelevant* to the *funda-*

---

[27] Jurgen Ruesch, *Therapeutic Communication*, pp. 111–112.

mental function of mass culture: energizing myths of our time by narcotizing a formidable segment of the public into accepting those inevitable disorientations in life produced by technical progress.

Two possibilities, therefore, exist concerning the corruptive power of mass culture:

1.) In general tone and flavor, mass culture may be corruptive of subjective life, causing, in the short or long run, individual aberrations and social breakdowns of a minor sort. Technological culture operating without such breakdowns is difficult, if not impossible, to imagine, unless one flirts with utopian totalitarian idealism.[28]

2.) Mass culture may be more or less harmless, from a sociological perspective, to our contemporary society. Its function may merely be to enhance and provide necessary sanctions for the many upheavals inevitable in the progression of technological culture. Mass culture may be defended (albeit far from convincingly, at present) by recourse to an ameliorative theory of some sort centering upon the primacy of human needs for "diversion," "play," or "entertainment."

Conclusion

Mass culture is no longer a new phenomenon. It is generations old and shows signs, despite its apparent vigor, of considerable stagnation and lack of the variety that once characterized its years of early growth and invention. One of the dreariest aspects of contemporary kitsch to the modern critic (who has little effect upon it) is its sameness, repetition and aura of *déjà vu*.

Many perspectives of mass culture are possible, but, from the orientation of this book, little doubt may be raised that mass culture serves a powerful purpose as a persuasive device in the service of contemporary technology and its handmaiden, commerce. Nor may the individual hide or insulate himself from this persuasion; it is redolent in all manner of life styles, fashions and intellectual currents, both inside and outside of the major acculturating agencies of school and family. The power of television on our lives is the best example, because it is derivative from old cultural forms and distributed in a new and near-ubiquitous manner. Nor does per-

[28] A prosperous, large, modern totalitarian state probably cannot at present ever come to pass. A close study of Hitler's Germany demonstrates how his supposedly "total" power had to be shared and counterbalanced between jealous rivals in the second echelon of Nazi command. What Hitler did cleverly was to keep his lieutenant's at each other's throats. Neither Castro's Cuba nor Communist China are today totalitarian in any specific sense; both are, in different degrees and different ways, bureaucracies where power is temporary, equivocal and shared. As the oligarchs of the USSR have discovered, a community dependent upon the technological geniuses of differently oriented people (in science, art, literature, industry, finance, etc.) wastes its own time and resources when it hankers after the romantic concept of totalitarian control—except in time of genuine, immediate national emergency. Stalin taught the Soviet Union a useful but bitter lesson in this regard.

sonal recourse to class culture exclude the rush of mass culture into modern life, regardless of social class, education, sex or financial status.

Mass culture has been defended as "mere entertainment" and irrelevant to genuinely serious social concerns. The notion of entertainment has been lionized and squeezed into a theoretical context which emphasizes *homo ludens* or "playing man," for whom diversion or relaxation is somehow at the spine of his systems of motivation. Both the nature and functions of entertainment are complex matters, partly prone to semantic misinterpretations, psychological enigmas and other obstacles. History appears to sever entertainment from the "narcotizing dysfunction" of cultural agencies like mass culture, but the issue has yet to be settled. Neither has the notion that mass culture is essentially corruptive or degrading, except insofar as its total relationship to contemporary culture is clear. The notion of eliminating (or improving) mass culture without simultaneous dramatic changes in the government, social life, economic structure, education and the value systems of the modern state is probably unrealistic, although arguments on this topic will doubtless continue for many years to come.

Chapter 7

THE MAKING OF A CONSUMER

American society, as popular advertisements portrayed it, was a nightmare of fear and jealousy, gossip and slander, envy and ambition, greed and lust . . . The typical American, as they pictured him lived in a torment of anxiety and cupidity and regulated his conduct entirely by ulterior considerations . . . To the advertisers nothing was sacred and nothing private; they levied impartially upon filial devotion, marriage, religion, health, and cleanliness . . . Love, as they portrayed it, was purely competitive . . . Friendship, too, was for sale . . . Advancement came not through industry, intelligence or integrity or any of the old fashinoned virtues, but was won by an astute combination of deception, bribery, and blackmail.

Henry Steele Commager

THE CONTEMPORARY art of salesmanship is an ever-acute and significant manifestation of American genius. Without its present development, it is doubtful, to this writer at least, that either technology, invention, contemporary education or popular democracy might have functioned as efficiently as they have during our short history, granting, of course, their many and serious imperfections. Most economists grudgingly agree that our peculiar (and sometimes apparently irrational) methods of marketing, sales and advertising are as important as any other factors in the function of the contemporary technological state. At least, few of them would be willing arbitrarily to recommend that these methods be severely modified without sounding dire warnings of possible devastating economic results. Their trepidations might be greatest in the matter of advertising where cause and effects and mechanistic relationships between output and public behavior are difficult to analyze and predict with precision.

The institution of advertising has had a curious social history and occupies a colorful corner of American cultural life. Words like "schizoid" and "ambivalent" may fairly be applied to general attitudes towards it in all of its manifestations. Commercial persuasion—the essence of most advertising—emerges so obviously and deterministically from the growth of competitive industry, the accumulation of personal wealth, mass production and modern materialism that one might expect it to be as broadly accepted—and acceptable—in a culture like ours, as sewers, traffic lights and roadways. Yet, advertising has been, and is, a topic of continual social controversy and literary exploitation about which feelings run high. Some years ago, at the end of a broadcast concerning advertising hosted by the writer, one of the then most respected consultants in the advertising industry noted aloud, "I have never been able to figure out why advertising, that devotes itself to selling other people's wares, has about the worst image of any industry in the country!"

Advertising and Morals

For all of his experience, he need not have wondered. The history of his own profession provides answers, not necessarily justified or rational, but answers nevertheless.[1]

First, advertising of some sort has almost always been intimately related to trade and commerce, neither of which, from the beginnings of mercantilism, ranked high in the strata of respectable occupations in the West, until the heroes of invention and production, like Thomas A. Edison and Henry Ford, began to capture the fancy of the public at the beginning of the twentieth century. Politics, education, warfare and medicine were socially acceptable. Business, unless it was carried on under the guise of statesmanship or philanthropy, was fit for Jews, the uneducated, the gross and uncultivated who had neither the time nor inclination to participate in better facets of Culture. Even such recent developments as the opening of the Harvard Graduate School of Business after World War I did little to improve a stereotype that had associated money-changing with usurers, factories with exploiters, and counting-houses with Scrooges.

Second, advertising could not claim even the status that business itself assumed (in the words of its own enthusiasts) because, apparently, it produced nothing: neither tangible goods nor significant consumer services. True, it did employ people, circulate currency, help to defray publishing costs, and provide the market with rough and capricious schedules of available items and reasonable prices, but its exact relationship to the market

---

[1] See E. S. Turner, *The Shocking History of Advertising* (New York: Ballantine Books, Inc., 1953). Starting with the first British periodicals in the early seventeenth century, Turner tells the story of this aspect of salesmanship with clarity and charm. But there is little *shocking* about the account, despite all of its color; nor does it deserve to be published (as my edition was) as one of a series of books on deceptions, frauds and confidence schemes. The excesses of advertisers it covers are little worse than the excesses of schoolmasters of the same periods, or of physicians, dentists, theatrical producers and politicians. The shocking history of *mankind* displays that some people are liar and others are apparently infinitely gullible, and that the two groups often pair off together neatly.

place was never clear—nor is it to this day. How many times has the statement been made (attributed to John Wanamaker, Lord Leverhulme and others) that "three-quarters of the money I spend on advertising is wasted, but I'll be damned if I know which three-quarters!"

Advertising's reputation for wind merchantry has been compounded in many ways. It is, for instance, axiomatic among most students of our current society that *all* consumer goods, if they are to be distributed to a national market and succeed in capturing the public's fancy, *must* advertise or fail in the market. Yet, the single exception to this rule is to some breathtaking. Aside from a short time during World War II (and for reasons having nothing to do with merchandizing), the Hershey choclate bar has never been advertised via any instrument of mass communication, in any manner, in the United States.[2] Brilliant advertising strategies, like the scientific analyses that preceded the birth of the Edsel, have failed in odd ways, and in the face of much generally accepted advertising mythology.[3]

Rules, laws and stratagems of advertising all admit of exceptions and provide an impression that caprice and charlatanry run rampant in the profession, and that, in the absence of hard-core production imperatives and irrefutable marketing tests (the best of which are presently equivocal), the advertising industry is corrupt—printed codes of ethics, industry protestations and published analyses notwithstanding.[4] And the impression, of course, is not entirely misconceived—nor is it generally true enough to derive from it dire moral consequences, or to sustain the weight of the fancies that have been spun upon it.

Third, advertising by its nature (including even such neutral announcements as those found in classified sections of newspapers), must always be selective, and often, to certain perceptions, distortive. Wherever

---

2 Readers may have seen announcements of the sales of Hershey products in local stores, paid for, I understand, by cooperating merchants and food distributors and circulated no further than local newspapers or throw-aways. A soap bearing the Hershey name, made in Hershey, Pennsylvania by a firm unrelated to the chocolate manufacturer, has also been advertised. Spokesmen for the Hershey chocolate organization have stressed that they have nothing against advertising; they simply feel that the company has little to profit from it, preferring to stimulate sales by other devices and attempting to attract as much attention as possible at the point of sales. Hershey bars, incidentally, have recently begun to be advertised in Canada. They are also, at last, to be advertised shortly in the United States, I am told at the present writing.

3 See John Brooks, *The Fate of the Edsel and Other Business Adventures* (New York: Harper and Row, Publishers, 1963), pp. 17–75.

4 Martin Mayer's *Madison Avenue, USA.* (New York: Harper and Brothers, 1958) is certainly *not* a blast at the advertising industry. If anything, Mayer twisted himself into benign attitudes when reporting some of the phenomena he observed in the big agencies, the overall attempt in his book being to correct common misconceptions about this aspect of marketing in America. His general thesis, that the sins of the advertiser are no greater (if no smaller) than those of the rest of our commercial community, is justified. His suggestions, positing a theory of the psychological utility of advertising (pp. 308–324), tip the scales of reason too far, I think, although the general tenor of his entire analysis—now unfortunately dated—is fair.

one finds advertising of any kind, in picture or narrative and regardless of the instrument by which it is purveyed, one also discovers drama or communication by re-enactment. When effective drama is employed, it utilizes showmanship, and the latter almost invariably requires a certain measure of hyperbole and deception, even when it may be regarded legitimately as dramatic license. All actors are, to the hard-nosed realist, liars, and so are novelists, painters, poets and advertisers.[5]

The result of this (perhaps) inevitable state of affairs, therefore, is that advertising must, at present, involve deception to some degree, no greater, in many instances, than those deceptions employed in other commercial affairs, in most education and in modern government. But deception it is, in fact, that encourages a vast number of otherwise sensible citizens to degrade both the nature and purpose of advertising and to maintain attitudes of aloof ethical superiority to it, even though they may personally be engaged in activities as shady as, or even more deceptive than, advertising. A physician who might not think twice about "covering" a colleague's ineptitude, or offering a precise but bogus physiological diagnosis and placebo for a condition he knows merely to be caused by nerves, may snoot at a mild omission (like rate of gas consumption) in an advertisement for an automobile. A college professor whose wife marks his term papers (unknown to his students) may criticize an actor who mouths a hair tonic testimonial for cold cash. A politician whose atheism does not prevent him from evoking God's blessing upon his party's platform may protest to his friends the irrelevancy of a windjammer in an advertisement for Scotch Whisky.

Hoist on their own petards of deception, advertising personnel usually resent this sort of hypocrisy with considerable justice, particularly in the light of their belief (never proven incorrect) that the capitalistic market owes much of its vigor and apparently unending potential for expansion to them. Their seeming ability to channel goods, create—within limits—demands for consumer goods and services and facilitating power for activating public faith in the economy are, to them, positive cultural contributions deserving of the same sort of laurels that are given to other captains of industry and public benefactors. Only their self-evident self-guilt keeps them from protesting more than occasionally in trade newspapers and letters to the editor. The advertising professional is rewarded financially a

[5] Here is a thorny problem of ethics and prompts consideration of how variable ethics confuse people, even when the ethical structures themselves are quite simple. Magicians believe it is ethical to misrepresent their behaviors and props in the interest of entertainment, but that it is unethical to share with a non-magician the truth—that is, how their tricks are done. To substitute shaving cream for whipped cream on a television commercial is considered by federal auditors unethical, even if the whipped cream melts under studio lights, and shaving cream makes a pudding dessert look real. Yet such a substitution is freely permissible in a television drama. Variations between backstage ethics and public ethics (not sheer greed) lay at the roots of the great television quiz scandals in the late 1950's, and still admit of numerous unsolved curiosities in mass communications.

good deal more benevolently, after all, than he might reasonably expect for services that, when boiled down to essence, are not (compared to other artistic and literary skills) either difficult or demanding creatively, industry protestations notwithstanding.

Packard has, in an over-stated polemic,[6] hit upon the major cultural problem of contemporary advertising persuasion. Simply stated, it is the peculiarity of responsible segments of this industry—or profession—that they have come somehow to believe their own myths, to credit with truth their own deceptions, and to swallow the rationalization of their own uses of sciences, particularly those derived from sociology and psychology, usually employing surveys, demographic studies and elaborate statistical computer print-outs. Add also the fact that some (but far from all) advertising practitioners have also accepted and postulated pseudo-Freudian techniques, unique selling propositions, bogus semantic notions, communications theories and human relations mystiques that belie the supposed ivy-league educations of the fish who swallow their consultants' and resident experts' bait.

A skilled magician usually does not believe in supernatural magic precisely *because he can* (apparently) perform supernatural feats, read minds, and, for that matter, make water flow upwards. He therefore knows how the tricks are done, and that they are tricks, not miracles of nature.[7] Commercial advertisers, for reasons irrelevant here, are not nearly as realistic. They feel constrained to pay obeisence to their success gods by defending the value of advertising for culture, not in sensible, justifiable, objective, economic and historic terms, but rather in dubious moral and spiritual ones. In short, they want not only to be important, well-remunerated people; they want also to be virtuous, beloved and cossetted, which is asking a lot in twentieth century America.

This situation appears to extract its greatest penalties in the psychological fallout from self-deception which sometimes renders skilled advertising professionals useless for any other human purposes. Certainly, the demeaning nature of their work does not cause this characterological erosion, because the labor is not all that demeaning. Many of us who suffer more menial labors than writing odes to laundry soap are able to surmount the tedium of our work. Advertising people (with notable exceptions) rarely

[6] See Vance Packard, *The Hidden Persuaders*. Recall that this volume was a run-away best seller in its day, but seemed to do no harm whatsoever to any aspect of the advertising industry in the United States. I imagine that it was probably read widely, and with masochistic glee, by advertising men and women, considering their usual proclivities for self-castigation.

[7] The most ardent opponent of astrology, witchcraft, ESP and other superstitious nonsense I have met was my friend, the late magician, John Mulholland, who would not countenance even the slim doubt in me that mind-reading *might* possibly occur or that any factual basis for the occult might exist. The reason, of course, was that Mulholland was perfectly competent at any moment to read my mind with astounding clarity and therefore knew that mind-reading is impossible, precisely *because* he could accomplish it so cleverly.

do, probably because the impetus of professional justification and rationalization requires an interiorized world-view which spills over from their working hours into the rest of their lives. And the individual obsessed with self-justification is not likely to relax long or well enough to employ his energies and talents wisely, especially if he carries also the burden of the guilt of unmerited affluence, a syndrome frequently displayed by the new rich.[8]

Advertising and the Marketplace

Criticism and denigration of the quality of American commercial persuasion, and advertising everywhere, for that matter, has long been a favorite international indoor sport. It is as old as the profession itself, but was given new currency in the United States after World War II with the publication of Frederic Wakeman's impressive novel *The Hucksters,* and by the development of the television commercial which managed, in its earliest days particularly, to carry quickly to absurdity everything jejune, insipid, and simple-minded that all other forms of advertising had painfully and slowly developed in a century and a half. These dispositions were deepened by the mythos of the advertising industry itself that its own exponents spread. It reflected as well an industry-wide guilt reaction and heightened sensitiveness among advertising personnel, amusing to behold, to criticism of any kind.

Other factors were also involved. With their almost limitless belief in the power of education and rational potential of the average man in the street, Americans have long cherished numerous colorful suspicions that a modern version of the classical Italian hand is everywhere at work in our culture. By and large, it is possible to sell much of the public almost *any* conspiracy notion, particularly if it is foreign, preferably Mediterranean. Despite our gullibility, the *idea* of mass persuasion for profit is repellent to most Americans on its face—theoretically a not unwelcome insurance policy against demagogery, except that the clever demagogue usually poses as an honest man exposing a conspiracy. Because ostensible competitive advertising is in fact so uniform in content, the possibility of a conspiracy of persuaders causes a cultural undertow that it is difficult *not* to feel when looking at our current marketplace with its imitative, repetitive numerous consumer brands, almost all identical except for packaging, and sold at similar prices and advertised in the same ways.

Numerous economists regard this problem in a different manner, but arrive at much the same conclusions using similar and more precise data.

---

[8] David Ogilvy, *Confessions of an Advertising Man* (New York: Dell Publishing Co., 1963) is an interesting and literate example of how a clever huckster explains his own success in respectable terms. To Ogilvy's credit, he has the common sense, as a displaced Briton to snoot a bit at the vulgarities of American life, but his "secrets of success" give away the clue that he probably believes his own persuasion in spite of his intelligence.

Large corporations, all with easy entry into the marketplace (the economists claim), utilize advertising merely to keep prices high and lure customers from one brand to another; in fact, to share their potential market (and wealth) between themselves. The consumer's choice is narrowed down to which product he buys. And his consumption is stimulated by minor model changes (as in automobiles, or proliferating, near-identical, lines of breakfast foods) that then become exploitable themes for advertisers who stimulate more—and unnecessary—consumption. Advertising is, on one hand, a system of corporate checkmate, and, on the other, a device for maintaining high prices and continually increasing consumption. It is, from this viewpoint, economic blubber, essentially wasteful, costly to consumers, and, if it were all eliminated in one instant, not essentially destructive to those large corporations that now spend millions (in costs passed on to the consumer) by simply maintaining an economic standoff with their competitors.

The construction of our marketplace above is obviously not a dynamic one, and does not take into account the interplay of many unseen variables that maintain our social and economic life. Galbraith's construction of the role of advertising in our present culture is far more sophisticated—and probably accurate—although it has appeared to have little effect upon contemporary attitudes and the thinking of most economic theorists.[9]

First, he says, demand is rarely static in a constantly evolving technological nation. In effect, both quantity and quality of consumption may be force-fed up to a point. A family that owns one car may be able to afford—and use—two. An individual used to hanging cheap, framed reproductions on his wall may be encouraged to purchase original charcoals—or to begin painting himself, for better or worse. A family may be encouraged to take a so-called "budget" vacation to Europe instead of a cheaper hegira to the local seaside. Advertising is probably the easiest and cheapest mechanism to affect consumer changes of these sorts.

Second, Galbraith notes that the homeostatic concept of brand loyalty obtains for a time, but gives away eventually to a form of operational "games theory" between competing advertisers with similar goods or services. Such strategy involves, of course, continual modifications of advertising that mean little. But it also may include changes in product design, services, value for price, voluntary price control, and even—at times—modifications in the fundamental nature of the product itself. These changes are far from meaningless; they are essential to the dynamism of the market, and, in many ways, also directive of cultural life.

A recent example (too grotesque and overt to serve as more than a caricature of the process) is the competition in both advertising and prod-

---

[9] See J. K. Galbraith, *The New Industrial State* (Boston: Houghton Mifflin Co., 1967), pp. 202–210.

uct between *Hertz* and *Avis* car rental services, although most similar "games" involve many more than two players and therefore have greater economic ramifications. Within its parameters, however, the *Hertz-Avis* gambit was both interesting and productive. Games like these also may rectify temporary slumps in business by producing new formulas for sales, with resultant stabilizations of industrial expenses, although the entire market still remains vulnerable to overall economic cycles.

Third, Galbraith regards this sort of management of demand as a subtle but effective social control, with the consequence that, "while goods become ever more abundant they do not seem to be any less important . . . Yet it might not have been. In the absence of massive and artful persuasion that accompanies the management of demand, increasing abundance might have reduced the interest of people in acquiring more goods. They would not have felt the need . . . ," [10] (a need induced, in part, by commercial persuasion) for the apparently unlimited profusion of goods which circulate in the market. This need is necessary for the maintenance and expansion of the industrial system, as well as the sustenance—in a highly competitive world—of the morale, prestige and health of the total culture itself.[11]

Galbraith concludes:

> For advertising men it has long been a sore point that economists dismissed them as so much social waste. They have not quite known how to answer. Some have doubtless sensed that, in a society where wants are psychologically grounded, the instruments of access to the mind cannot be unimportant. They were right. The functions here identified may well be less exalted than the more demanding philosophers of the advertising industry might wish. But none can doubt their importance for the industrial system, given always the standards by which that system measures achievement and success.[12]

Our next problem, from the point of view of the consumer and citizen, is the close consideration of these standards, the persuasion used to maintain them and their relevance to those facets of culture that reach beyond the marketplace.

---

[10] *Ibid.*, p. 209.

[11] Galbraith makes the excellent point that such prestige now depends upon the output and consumption of goods instead of yesterday's symbols of prosperity: the hyper-affluence of the capitalist class, and/or ownership and use of real estate or land. Even today, however, atavists like the Georgist economists continue the fiction that land is the focal commodity in our economic system. And various mythologists still concentrate upon the power of colorful, mysterious, manipulating capitalists like Howard Hughes. Japan's experience during the past generation provides an interesting microcosm in perspective, however, of how a nation has recently and quickly centered its economy both on the production and *ownership* of consumer goods after centuries of activities largely in other economic areas. Advertising, of course, has been intimately related to the recent Japanese experience.

[12] *Ibid.*, p. 210.

Consumer Culture

Before our cultural critics consign the contemporary marketplace to oblivion (as they often do), we had best ponder carefully the complexity of the contemporary technostructure. Since World War I, it has simply been too easy to fixate upon a few, certain aspects of culture in the West that show signs of inner rot, or worse, extended adolescence, and blame materialism and competitive capitalism for them. The later works of Freud combined with simplistic constructions of Marxist materialism have produced a strange and powerful fusion in modern thought.[13] Many of us who survived the ravages of the past generation salted our popularized Freud with fashionable socialistic discontents that were confirmed by paperback nay-sayers and the prophets of alienation discussed in Chapter 5.

The simplicity with which commercial culture and mass culture were equated one with the other as symptomatic of the failure of capitalism to provide for our people a humane psychological environment need neither be stressed nor repeated here. If we believed that popular culture was vulgar, the forces of commerce and the perversions of cash were the instruments vulgarizing it. The possibility that state-supported culture (Public Television, for instance) might one day be more vulgar than the commercial variety did not occur to us, mainly because we were not exactly sure of what vulgarity *was*. The theatre, arts, literature, films, social life, even education were apparently being destroyed by heathens of the marketplace. Avaricious movie producers, publishers and broadcasters were prototypical capitalists in high hats, smoking enormous imported cigars. They spit in the face of the masses and forced their peculiar commercial opiates down the public gullet, or so many believed.

The viewpoint had (has) the advantages of simplicity and naïveté. Like all such systemic discontents, it produced "good guys" and "bad guys," and its shallowness only becomes apparent after searching and careful study of the "good guys," and mature reflection on the "bad" ones. Whenever government and public spirited foundations did, in fact, begin to assume a tentative directive force in American cultural life, neither the quality of that culture nor the nature of life changed noticeably for the better. If anything, it became worse, in the opinion of many.

Eleemosynary high, low or middle-brow culture may lack the strident groping after popularity that marks much consumer-oriented culture, but it also lacks its verve, originality, daring and spirit. The American drama was not saved by public works; if any drama is being created today in the USA it is probably in the commercial crucible of off-Broadway free enterprise pro-

[13] See Paul A. Robinson, *The Freudian Left* (New York: Harper and Row, Publishers, 1969), for an excellent study of how psychological and economic theories from Hegel to Marx to Freud found their way into the radicalism of Wilhelm Reich, Geza Roheim and Herbert Marcuse, primarily, although other similar thinkers are also discussed.

ductions. Our proclivities for preserving the better things in life in public museums have stimulated the creation of far less significant pictorial art than the commercial galleries on New York's 57th Street. Municipal orchestras have commissioned countless symphonies, but important developments in American music are probably being made by the many commercial types who feed our burgeoning recording and hi-fi industry. And so it goes, in almost every corner of American life: the cultural output of the United States Government Printing Office, the Office of Education and similar arms of government—free from the pressures of the commercial market—are models of unimaginativeness. Foundation-supported culture analysts and political scientists pour out pedantic nonsense (neatly parodied in the spoof, *Report From Iron Mountain*), while the men who man the newsrooms of our networks and who slapdash together our many newspapers (in continual competition one with the other) limn for us, daily, a remarkably sensible appraisal of the world's newsfronts—better usually than we credit them, especially when we compare their output with their opposite numbers in nations with state controlled news services.

To many, however, advertising still epitomizes the vulgarization of art and culture in the service of commerce and is accepted this way with neither study nor qualification. Certainly, much truth lies in the conceptual fusion of commerce and mass culture as cheap, low culture, almost by definition of either or both. But much popular culture is highly satisfying, apparently harmless and technically excellent, even if it does not satisfy the need of refined sensibilities for special experiences. Advertising, on the other hand, appears (and has always seemed) to possess none of the spontaneity of the best of mass culture. It is usually damned on its face and withheld *a priori* from serious consideration as art or culture of any kind.[14]

The basic reason, of course, results from the assumption that commerce simply *could not and cannot* produce "Culture," at least Culture in the refined sense of the European leisure class and university world of the past century. It has been forgotten (or never known) that commerce has been involved in producing—quite directly—most of the fine Culture of the past: the Parthenon, the Mona Lisa, the Elizabethan theatre, Italian Grand Opera and the best of French Impressionism; that the greatest artists in our history (from Cellini to Shaw) have often been the greediest and sharpest commercially; and that many (or most) of man's most significant cultural advances have been motivated by private profit and the yearning

[14] Through the back door of highbrow culture, of course, advertising, over the years, crept into the galleries in such manifestations as "pop art," usually wearing the disguise of satire. University art galleries to this day exhibit pop art as "camp" or "spoof," unaware that considerable aesthetic and psychological gratification may be discovered in certain types of American package design, poster art and advertising layout work—particularly in the juxtaposition of shapes, forms and words. Nor is this gratification necessarily amusing, or any more or less amusing than other clear visual statements are.

for personal glory. But the secret could not be kept, because the artistic grandeur of contemporary technology was too enormous to contain and too obvious to hide. The Golden Gate and Verrazano-Narrows bridges were too impudently magnificent to ignore; a banking Boeing 747 was too dignified and thrilling to deny; and (most important) the Volkswagen magazine ad or the airline commercial on television was too clever, articulate and intelligent to bypass with condescension as nothing more than a sleazy by-product of commerce.

All of this is relatively recent history. And it is not the author's purpose to lionize advertising as the flower of a contemporary renaissance in design or high art. The problem is one of relative values, centering mostly upon the question of whether the truly public arts (highways, housing developments, stadiums, bridges, post offices, schools, etc.) bear a noticeable and distinctive superiority to the arts involved in commerce—particularly advertising—on view in contemporary life. The writer simply suggests that quite the reverse is frequently true: that the landscaped roadside, for instance, planted along a new highway is frequently inferior as design, art or culture (but obviously not as nature) to much of the old billboards and poster art that it presently replaces, and that it is undeniably far more tiresome for the driver to suffer and less diverting and/or amusing.[15]

To the eye of the contemporary Gnostic, however, postulating, as he does, that the market is corrupt, everything that emerges from it must also be tainted with corruption. His viewpoint is not unlike that fostered upon Soviet artists in the Stalinist era and upon Germany by Hitler—the latter, a man, by the way, who not only knew what he liked but also knew a good deal about art. To the determinist, particularly the Hegelian (be he Socialist, Fascist or voluntarist with naïve beliefs of human relations and brotherly love), one must first consider the source of an artifact before one evaluates it. To the social determinist, a play with a so-called "message" is superior to a play without one (or with the incorrect one), regardless of the skill manifest in conception or performance. To Stalin, expressionist art (at a certain period) was decadent, because it evolved in capitalist nations and expressed what he considered degenerate ideas. To Hitler, Jewish writing was corrupt, because it was Jewish. Intrinsic qualities, to the determinist, have nothing to do with quality. Life, for him, is literally lived on an extrinsic level.

Little wonder, therefore, that advertising's persuasion has been regarded as a ubiquitous evil in the West, likened by many to an epidemic, and symptomatic, supposedly, of a degraded culture and public obsession with materialism, especially, it must be added, by the guilt-ridden advertising industry itself. The culprits are, accordingly, forever trying to expiate

---

[15] Far be it from me to grow sentimental about old Burma Shave signs, but I do not think that it is an indication of my increasing antiquity to note here that I miss them.

their sins by attempting public service work that might often better be accomplished by public servants, and by giving each other awards. In this respect, they are not unlike educators, movie makers and architects. (The latter are probably the busiest award givers and receivers in the West.)

An *extrinsic* view of commerce, capitalism or technology necessitates an unrealistic, negative attitude towards, particularly, their (apparently) non-productive aspects, particularly in their most competitive, simplistic and standardized modes. While it appears not to be difficult to use and exploit the material benefits of capitalism and, at the same time, to deride the system that created them (like a Ford Foundation grantee expounding an elegant economic and social theory that mass production discourages the study of social theories), it is far more difficult to admire advertising and, at the same time, equate capitalist technology with sin.

What is even worse (from the extrinsic perspective) is the apparent truth that quite a number of intelligent people in contemporary Western society enjoy advertisements—or, at least, do not mind them. Fairfax M. Cone[16] reports a Roper study of the audiences of television commercials that indicates a number of things, among them the finding that about two-thirds of the viewing public seems not to mind commercials. One quarter finds them annoying, and ten per cent actually dislike them, presumably not enough to stop watching television because of them. Cone is an unusual advertising mogul, in that he occasionally punctures some of his industry's myths and treats his craft realistically. He notes that these same statistics indicate also that, while two out of three people show favorable attitudes towards television commercials, seven out of ten "find at least some commercials objectionable," which is exactly what the survey (made for the television broadcasters' persuasion front, the Television Information Office) does indeed indicate.

Granting even that three out of ten people *like* television commercials (the least inventive, amusing or interesting part of the advertising industry, in the opinion of many) one wonders what percentage of the public *likes* newspaper and magazine advertisements, billboards, car cards and radio spots (which are becoming increasingly interesting and clever). Certainly, a good portion do—or enough to justify the observation, made at many times and in many places that, were advertisements taken from the American scene, most of us would miss them sorely.[17] Popularity of this sort, in the

---

[16] Fairfax M. Cone, "What's Bad for TV is Worse for Advertising" in David M. White and Richard Averson, *Sight, Sound, and Society* (Boston: Beacon Press, 1968), p. 265.

[17] Of course, we would miss those ads which offer an orientation function, that is, tell us what movie is playing at the local popcorn palace, what is on sale at the supermarkets, etc. But, above and beyond this, I hope I am not hurting anyone's feelings by noting in passing that, these days, I enjoy the advertising matter in *The New York*

face of all of the cultural artifacts which social ameliorists *know* are far better for the health, education and welfare of our populace than advertisements, is, from an extrinsic view, inexcusable, and explains also the general cultural status of commercial persuasion today.

How defensible is this enormous cultural attention paid to advertising, and the possibility that it is, in some ways, the single most popular aspect of mass culture? Not defensible at all, if one thinks of it—as is often done—in terms of the displacement of other experiences. But does it really displace them, or does the general current of advertising serve merely as a vehicle of acculturation to a highly complex society where much special knowledge is demanded for basic survival? And who knows what role this orientation plays in the steps all of us must take in learning to sever the honest from the dishonest, persuasion from fact, and junk from gold.[18] As the movie critic, Pauline Kael has noted, "I don't trust any of the tastes of people who were born with such good taste that they didn't need to find their way through trash." [19] Many of us are open to the accusation that we have not progressed far in the cultivation of taste *beyond trash*, if we defend seriously commercial advertising's positive cultural functions. Perhaps. But, at least, we are progressing beyond patent satisfaction with sheer kitsch, and so may many millions of people, further and faster than even apologists for advertising's sins dare suggest.

Friendly Persuasion

Good or bad as culture, advertising is the merchant of consumerism, and our present consumer technology could probably not exist without it. When relevant arguments, therefore, are presented against advertising, they are not directed against persuasion itself, but instead, usually, against the need to consume as we do. Krutch, for instance, makes the simple and intelligent point[20] that man has not, in his long history, been primarily re-

---

Times Magazine, *The New Yorker*, and many similar upper-middle-brow fashionable publications more than the legitimate content. I may also be exceptional and the victim of foul taste, because I also prefer the kitschy copy and illustrations in mail order catalogs (especially the Haband Company, Spencer Gifts, Greenleaf Studios, Brecks of Boston, Walter Drake, etc.) to doctoral dissertations, commission reports, and educational research; but I imagine I am not alone.

[18] Advertising is frequently criticized because it is dishonest, which is naturally true of some of it. It is possible, however, that dishonest advertising, irrelevant sales claims, the bandwagon approach, testimonials, and the rest of the tricks of the trade help to sensitize many of us to the inevitable deception that I, personally, have seen in most marketplaces and bazaars around the world, not necessarily in technological-capitalistic countries. In my experience as a teacher, also, I have noticed that children at about junior high school age are often highly critical of the faulty logic in advertising, beginning, for themselves, an informal kind of consumer education or marketplace sophistication distinctive of modern Americans.

[19] Pauline Kael, *Going Steady* (Boston: Little Brown and Co., 1970), p. 115.

[20] See Joseph Wood Krutch, *Human Nature and the Human Condition* (New York: Random House, 1959), pp. 21–39. Advertising's relationship to education, a matter

garded as a consumer by humane arbiters of his social order. As the world became more materialistic, so the productive capacity of man and his talent for consumption increased in significance. Today, writes Krutch, " 'Scorn not the common man,' says the age of abundance. 'He may have no soul; his personality may not be exactly the same as his neighbor's; and he may not produce anything worth having. But, thank God, he consumes.' "[21]

Naturally, this view of advertising is extrinsic. And just as naturally it quarrels, not with what advertisers tell us, but with what they *mean* by the telling, although thinkers like Krutch do not center on the political or economic assumptions that advertising represents in its celebration of the success of technological capitalism. Like all humanists, the writer included, he is concerned about people. And it is hard to confront with much moral annoyance a statement like this: "One thing seems clear. When man's first duty comes to be consumption, he suffers a strange loss of dignity, and not only he but the coming generation comes to be valued chiefly in terms of its potentiality as a voracious consumer."[22]

A generation has one-half come of age since those words were written, and we have seen the youngsters who were ten at that time grow out of the children's market, into the 'teen age market, on to the young adult market and finally into one of the differentiated male and female adult markets, like "young swinger," "Playboy-type," "bachelor girl," "young married," "new parent," "black business man," "executive type" and others. Each has its appropriate mode of consumption, its appropriate costumes, make-up, home and work settings, its methods of transportation, food habits and sexual mores, all of which are closely geared to patterns of consumption. Do consumers demean themselves to play these roles?

One may search, as O'Hara has,[23] to note differential pressures from different corners of society, by different methods of communication to different people, and discuss in various ways the pressures that advertisers exert upon the people involved in the mass culture industries and contemporary schooling. True, the press is freer of advertisers' pressure than radio or television, and the movies are less dependent than any other arm of mass communications upon it, except that the cinema industry's progress depends, in some measure, upon the effectiveness of its own advertising.

O'Hara, Berelson, Steinberg, Siepmann, Emery, Skornia and others

---

no less serious than it was a dozen years ago, is Krutch's central and most poignant theme. If I fault Krutch's ongoing criticism of "modernism" (a term he has used in a book title), it is merely because he credits too little the frequent spontaneous antitheses that arise in American life and thought that modify the virulence of our fads in thinking and life styles. But he is a hard humanist to deny.

[21] *Ibid.*, p. 39.

[22] *Ibid.*, p. 38.

[23] See Robert C. O'Hara, *Media for the Millions* (New York: Random House, 1961), pp. 81–88.

who have attempted to characterize mass communications in our time (and whose works are too familiar to list here) all miss an essential logical point in their differing discussions of the variable pressures that mass communicators suffer—for better or worse—at the hands of commerce and the institution of advertising. This point centers on the fact that *all* mass communications in our culture are the *result* (not separate entities) *of the same commercial forces* that also created advertising. It was not a whim of history that joined the first newspaper with the first printed advertisement. They were both cut from the same historical clay, and both are inevitable, complementary components of the technostructure of our world.

The great persuasive force of advertising is not specific; it is general.[24] It is not locatable in individual conduits of communication; it *is* an uberconduit of communication. It uses, in various ways, and with various types of results, the press, films, radio, television, billboards, skywriting, supermarkets, electric signs and handbills to create a cultural climate whereby goods and services may be channeled in certain ways to certain markets to meet certain needs, some of them stimulated by these instruments of communication, not necessarily directly by advertisements.

One amusing but typical example of the process comes to mind. A contemporary sex novel on the best-seller list that the writer recently read (in response to a uxorial suggestion that he would abhor it; and he did) constituted a virtual lexicon of contemporary urban consumption. Set in New York City, telling the rather pathetic story of the sex lives of four young ladies under thirty, this weak imitation of Schnitzler's *La Ronde* contains more information about the various sex hygiene and contraceptive devices upon the market at present than even a gynecologist probably needs to know. In fact, attention to consumption potential of female genitalia—even to the extent of keeping it warm in winter—provides about the only originality discernible in the book. It is also a tout for expensive restaurants and stores in New York, something of a cookbook and menu guide, and it dabbles in interior decorating and available amusements in the big city. The volume might serve as a consumer's guide for almost any middle class, white, silly young female in town—and as something of a realistic rule-book for the sexually predatory male. It is, in short, a minor triumph of unpaid-for (one presumes) advertising.

On a more serious level, neither *Time* magazine, *The New York*

---

[24] Even the best specific stories about advertising, like the creation of *Lestoil* or the genius stroke that gave us *Alpha Bits,* are simply colorful examples of general cultural trends. The late, lamented *Lestoil* was the natural culmination, in its day, of the cleanliness cult that had been created for industry by advertising, among other forces. The whole breakfast cereal world, which *Alpha Bits* upset unmercifully (and curiously), is a facet of culture devoted originally to using surplus grains and by-products from other types of food production. It was created in its early days mostly by clever advertising and good marketing that developed a need for a product which I, personally, have never found much of a use for, except to feed to my gerbils.

Times, The Wall Street Journal or the *Chicago Tribune* may be evaluated as cultural artifacts without considering their overall roles in the friendly persuasion of consumerism. The short spots we see on television are, naturally, paid commercial persuasion; but the potent medicine is brewed in the longer video segments blandly called "programming" and are as likely, sometimes, to emerge from network news departments as entertainment factories. Hollywood movies help to create consumer culture, and films from all over the globe depict life styles for us to emulate, places for us to travel and objectives for us to imitate, if only in fantasy. American advertising is far bigger than Madison Avenue. It is also bigger than Wall Street, Hollywood Boulevard and Broadway. And let us not forget that our schools, from kindergarten to professional academy, adjust the young to our way of life and probably succeed better at making them consumers than at teaching reading and spelling.

Our purview, therefore, now transcends even Krutch's doubts concerning whether life as a consumer allows modern man the dignity he finds, or once found, in other cultures not devoted as avidly as ours is to fabricating consumers. Our vista is not only of society but of much history: not only of a few thousand men devoted to attracting the public to this or that product, but of millions of us in the contexts of our values, our recreation, our work, our style of living, mating and dying, as well as the continual noisy denial by many of everything these peculiar culture traits mean.[25]

Written, as these words are, at a moment of financial recession, inflation and (perhaps) impending profound disorientation of American industry (out of which the future of technological culture probably will be forged), one is impelled to refer discussions which derive *from* history back *to* history. Many of us have been, in the past, asked by our society to be far more than mere consumers. And many have fulfilled these requests, sometimes at the cost of their lives. We may yet be asked as citizens to become less *as* consumers, and much, much more *than* consumers in order to make peace with technology and modernity. This change, should it come, will require all the friendly persuasion the institution of advertising can muster. We may, some day, thank God for it.

Conclusion

Advertising has occupied a peculiar corner of American culture for a long time, because it is the subject of widely ambivalent emotional and cognitive dispositions. On the one hand, it is seen as a necessary lubricant of commerce. On the other, it is construed as annoying legerdemain, economic waste and cultural dross. Both points of view have meaning in contemporary life, and evidence exists that both are true—up to a point. The

[25] Hippies, teeny-boppers, SDS radicals and Black Panthers are as much by-products of technological culture as canned cat food and Elmer's Glue. They will be discussed in their proper context in Part Four of this book.

argument that centers upon them today is futile by virtue of the justifications to which both camps go to construe contemporary advertising (and salesmanship) as something which it is *not.* Justifications and techniques of the behavioral sciences, in one camp, are met by excess and irrelevant aesthetic and artistic rhetoric, in the other.

Advertising deserves a legitimate place in the technological capitalistic marketplace that can, in the construction offered in this chapter, satisfy champions of Keynsian economics and a planned economy (perhaps *especially* individuals so oriented) as well as those of more conservative economic dispositions. The question, mainly concerning the management of demand, of whether the marketplace *as we know it* will continue to function in its predicted ways is another matter with deep ramifications, not necessarily lethal, for the future of cultural persuasion by the advertising.

Most advertising is kitsch; some of it is amusing; some briefly brilliant; much is trash. But most criticism of the content of advertising stems from extrinsic dispositions towards the apparent useless success of advertising in contemporary industry, rather than intrinsic, thoughtful criticism of the output itself. Compared to much other American kitsch (and to public works and self-conscious attempts at American fine arts), a lot of advertising does not come off badly in respect to vitality, originality, spirit, technical excellence and—to the chagrin of many—popularity. The currently accepted American notion of class art, unfortunately, does not deal realistically with the way societies in the past have found to express their geniuses. And a good deal of resistance exists to the notion that a capitalist marketplace and materialistic incentives are *not* totally incompatible with art of any type, fine or popular.

The persuasion of advertising has been charged with having raised in the USA a nation of consumers. While this may have been true in some measure, most of us have managed to find objectives in life richer and more rewarding than consumption, although without question, it has been one of the main cultural imperatives of the past two generations. And the future may well see the decline of the present great age of American consumption. Whatever the fate of our society (unless it is extinction), advertising in its present ubiquitous forms, a facet of many parts of culture, will probably play a major role in it.

Chapter 8

POLITICAL PERSUASION

We do not have, as yet, a body of intellectual and moral habits, customs and attitudes to fit the realities of modern popular government.

Walter Lippmann (1930)

POLITICS is an invention born early in the age of simple mechanics and has united with technological developments of the West during the past century and one-half.[1]

Politics, dictionary definitions aside, concerns *power:* how it is conceived, how it is distributed, how it is used. It is, in many ways, representative of what appears to be a *middle* stage in personal and social development. Individually, we are neither competent nor permitted to act, in any frame of reference, in a political manner until we are mature enough to assume, at least, the physical and intellectual responsibilities and consequences of power. If we live long enough, nature and environmental erosion enervates our physical and psychic powers, and—if as our main bodily needs are met—we tend to retire gradually from political activity, conserving physical resources and maintaining our egos either by resort to memories of the past or fantasies.[2]

Societally, loose and primitive organizations tend to develop in man's first sort of crude political structures, highly stable in the long run (and in theory) but volatile from the short view. Political leaders expire or are murdered young; ruling families die out; warfare almost invariably involves personally, and vanquishes, the most powerful individuals; assassinations are not uncommon.[3] But societies mature, and, as people interact, sociopolitical habits—in many instances among the first techniques or technolo-

[1] I shall refer to "politics" in the singular in this chapter, although I affirm that, philologically speaking, politics are (sic) the result of many singular behaviors. In regard to politics and technology, their recent obvious proximity (neither startling nor

gies created—are institutionalized. The need for unity is the major requisite for government, and the latter is developed, usually, in the simplest way possible: along hereditary lines or in physical combat. Both methods characterize many of our contemporary political institutions, in vestigial form at least, having survived in an unexpectedly pristine state. Neither method long remains entirely stable. The politics of heredity requires biological exogamy (within limits) to prevent genetic dry rot,[4] and the politics of physical power demands immunity from the possibilities of destruction by technical invention, foul play, magic and collusion.

Intensive political sensitivity seems subsequently to characterize a culture in this particular period, after which it sheds the original main constructions of political forms, those that have been followed for a long and productive period of relative success and development of tradition. (In Rome, after the death of Julius Caesar; in Europe, from the founding of national states until the series of revolts that followed the American revolution; in the Near East and India, from pre-colonial times until the present; in China, for many centuries until the first years of the present one; and in Japan, for hundreds of years until General MacArthur.) At this period of rather sudden change, resulting usually from systemic breakdowns in the social order or military conquest by another state, much of the population becomes politically active. Among other things, binding consensus decisions are made as to who, in fact, *are* to be considered part of the political population. (In ancient Rome and the United States, for instance, slaves decidedly were *not*—constituting property similar, for instance, to horses.)

One way or another, political rights are usually first extended, in this period, only to those regarded as an enlightened minority, sometimes by

---

remarkable as they are touted) is a sub-topic of almost every extensive political essay written in the popular press today, and has been the subject of numerous fiction and non-fiction best-sellers, *The Selling of a President*, 1968, the most recent at this writing and, so far, the most popular.

[2] In this latter regard (the withdrawal from political action with age), I am reminded of the differential individual responses of some of the statesmen of our time: Lord Moran's account of Winston Churchill's final days staring into the fireplace, depressed and swallowing gall; President Eisenhower's self-assumed role as consultant to Presidents; Harry Truman's retreat to sentimental senility; Rudolph Hess' feigned (?) near-catatonic silence; Khrushchev's supposed bucolic isolation to pasture, and others. I think an intensive study of this phase of the individual political life of different notable people from the psychiatric perspective would be rewarding.

[3] The texture, brutality and inevitability of this primitivism (often found in cultures with sophisticated symbol systems, rites, relgions and totems) is clarified in Theodor Reik's *Myth and Guilt* (New York: George Braziller, 1957), pp. 117–155. While Reik is concerned most with those tribes whose stories are told in Genesis, his observations are drawn from, and relate to, many other primitive societies.

[4] Most of the hereditary political orders of modern Europe tried to circumvent this primitive requirement, thereby inducing feeble-mindedness, deformity, madness, hemophelia and other problems of inbreeding that were eventually instrumental in their downfall.

devices as sophisticated as those employed after the October Revolution in the USSR (to date), or as crude as those which enfranchised but a minute fraction of the population in the thirteen colonies of the American nation in the 1780's. But the people to whom the rights are extended *tend to use them.* Political activities also assume a significant and important role in culture. In fact, they give the appearance of being among the most vital and necessary aspects of collective life. The words of Jefferson may indicate some of the tonal idealism that invariably marks this period of political development: "We (the founders of the new American Democracy) believe that man was a rational animal, endowed by nature with rights, and with an innate sense of justice, and that he could be restrained from wrong, and protected in right, by moderate powers, confided to persons of his own choice and held to their duties by dependence on his own will." [5]

The next social and cultural step may indeed appear strange and difficult for many of us to observe, because of our own immediate engagement in the process. Historical models (Santayana's advice about reliving the history we do not understand not withstanding) are meaningless because of the fricative pressure of political games upon those immediately involved, particularly historians and political analysts.

Political activity, first, tends to spread and, if the state is a cultural economic and cultural success, the population also begins to increase, for many reasons. More people move into positions of power, politics becomes more complicated as a process, and more of the population (and more population) either is involved in political decisionmaking, or is led by various stratagems to *believe* that it is.

Society is not only a political entity. While this expansion occurs, so also do numerous other facets of culture develop: commerce, warfare, public and private arts, education, entertainment, sports and others. Although they influence, to a degree, political life, they also produce their own *apolitical* ends, and each constitutes, in some measure, diversions as well as occupations for many.

The societal result, therefore, parallels, in a general way, the terminal stage the individual's political engagement. In sum cultural total, political interest is widely spread; but its pith as a social institution declines. It merges with other activities like social climbing (in ancient Rome) or show business (in the USA). Ideals are blunted and obscured rhetorically, powers are divided and weakened, statutes and laws accumulate (many of them unused), and bureaucracy takes over as the operative arm of govern-

---

[5] Quoted in Aldous Huxley, *Brave New World Revisited* (New York: Harper and Brothers, 1958), p. 37. Huxley then follows this quotation with an excellent example of the kind of skepticism, cynicism and qualification that usually follows this peak period of cultural political ferment. Jefferson's idealism is salted by Huxley with strong doses of contemporary psychology, intellectual realism and uncomfortable information about the imperfection of modern man—all reliable factors in contemporary social analysis.

ment in order to "keep things going" while politicians argue and form committees and investigating commissions (ancient devices). Corruption is ubiquitous but rarely uncovered and more rarely halted; the population, therefore, believes either that corruption does not exist or that it is ubiquitous, with identical psychological results. Just as in the fate in the individual political animal, inertia results. Sentimentality, senility, madness and/or mere posture obtain. And death is near.

Politics and Technological Culture

Ferkiss, a sensitive observer of political aspects of modern life, puts the problem briefly and well. The growing political insenility of our own society is not too different from others in the past, except that technology and its retinue of societal handmaidens are engaged in the diversionary forces mentioned above. The common view of technology and technological culture held, two generations ago, that the newly harnessed forces of nature might agglomerate such enormous political power into so few hands that neither conventional political structures nor governments themselves might be competent to control them. "Existing political systems make such fears groundless," writes Ferkiss. "The political and governmental structures, even in the most technologically advanced nations, render man bewildered and impotent, a prisoner of his most primitive atavisms and a plaything of the fates." [6] What is evident is the process noted above: the slow decay of political life as it travels broadly through culture and loses its hold upon the consciousness of men.

One of the primary problems inherent in our modern political structures has been clearly identified by Cahn.[7] It is an old notion, that in all stages of political growth the state is subject to anthropomorphic interpretations, that is, it is almost always regarded as a human entity. Historically, such conceits as the statement "I am the state," the way sovereigns in Shakespeare's historical plays talk about themselves, cartoon representation of Uncle Sam (or Sap), John Bull, the U. S. Supreme Court and other such symbols illustrate this tendency, as applicable today, probably, as it ever was. In a complex technological nation like ours, the analogy of anthropomorphism still attracts the public. It simplifies things, and its appeal is similar to that of other symbols.

The contemporary state, however, is *not* a person and accordingly is not even vaguely similar to an anthropomorphological phenomenon, in most critical respects. It can, for instance as Machiavelli demonstrated, operate on a far broader set of moral standards than the individual may—or should. The state, for instance, runs a uniformed, economical (and not too

---

[6] Viktor Ferkiss, *Technological Man*, p. 196.

[7] Edmund Cahn, *The Predicament of Democratic Man* (New York: The Macmillan Co., 1961), pp. 18–23.

effective) protection racket with impunity. Local gangsters administer effective illegal protection rackets with no such happy sanctions. In some ways, the state is powerless to handle small options that are reserved for individual consciences. Legislators and law enforcers seem unable almost everywhere to enforce prohibitions against the consumption of liquor, drugs like cannabis, or gambling, prostitution, homosexuality and other unconventional behaviors of people in private. (Political force does not really influence these matters to any great degree, although the rash of such recent changes, for instance, the legalization of abortion in certain states—which will have little effect, probably upon the number of abortions performed annually in the USA—are brave attempts at denying this fact *post hoc.*) Yet, our favorite image of political instrumentation still remains the state as an individual (or corporate) fiction and construes the political process as subject to the same constraints as those that apply to individuals. At the height of popular political involvement, particularly when governments are new, such thinking is defensible.[8] As society matures, it grows less so, to ultimate absurdity.

Technology adds its mite to the problem in two ways.[9] First—and perhaps most important—an operant technological society is successful because it succeeds *at* technology, not because it has necessarily improved the quality of individual or collective life. Largely, the focus of this success is achieved outside the realm of political life, although politicians, representatives, legal agencies and all manner of irrelevant power groups do not hesitate to take some degree of credit for technology's accomplishments. And to a minor degree, they are correct, in that, by means of the passage of certain laws and the maintenance of ethical standards and fiscal regulations, the private sector of society (which constitutes, in capitalist nations, the core of technological culture) is provided with unobstructed fields in which to operate and expand.[10]

Because a technological society is a success *as* a technological society,

[8] The framers of the United States Constitution were not misguided in their anthropormorphic constructions of the thirteen colonies. Under such simple conditions, the representatives of the states *were* the states, or at least that part of their total constituency that they represented personally and politically, in much the manner that the citizens in the legendary New England village meeting each represent their own interests. This variety of hypothetical political body is truly anthropomorphic. (I have incidentally attended New England town meetings, and have yet to run into one that reflects, even remotely, the halcyon text-book ideal. The ones I have seen were almost as replete with wheeling, dealing, gamesmanship and intrigue as the 1960 Democratic Presidential Convention.)

[9] For a reasonable but differently oriented discussion of this matter, see Ferkiss, *op. cit.*, pp. 188–190.

[10] This "private" sector is merely a "separate" sector in such Communist states as the USSR, where this particular principle (but not necessarily the one that follows) applies in much the same manner to political life as in the USA, although some individual technologists in the USSR are given less independence to pursue their own destinies than in the USA, I assume.

however, does not mean that it is also a political or social success, and here is the essence of a prime curiosity. Because of political confusion—or naïveté—certain people may starve in the midst of technological affluence; outmoded, illegal and immoral inequalities (irrelevant to the GNP or unemployment) may exist in education, housing, mental institutions, hospitals, choice of career, or job availability according to absurd criteria of race, family background or sexual preference, as in the USA today. Citizens may live in slums and work in steel and glass palaces. Terror may prevail on the streets of modern megalopoli. And all politically oriented attempts to cure these social anomalies may be of little avail, resulting only in popular cynicism and publicly displayed contempt for politics. These have been the results, in many discouraging ways, of the United States' recent grasp after the Great Society and our misconceived War on Poverty, both of which were cast in the mold of the now irrelevant, obsolete and antiquated social theories of the New Deal of the 1930's. The latter was revolutionary in its time, but it is as relevant to the political amelioration of our present crises as a bag of camphor around the neck is to a cure for flu.

As a result, in a technological culture, politics is pursued on a personal basis, frequently for amusement, while important issues concerning technology itself are solved by industrialists and military experts, relatively immune from the publicity fallout from the political structure. For example, the American electorate has not been able to utilize its potential political power to determine whether or not their government should pursue its costly space exploration program, or whether they approve of research into the so-called "peaceful" uses of atomic energy.[11] Certainly, technology has kept few of its major advances secret, and they have been turned into a running science-fiction narrative with suitable heroes, tragedies and eleventh hour rescues, thereby producing the illusion (or reality) of public affirmation or what has been called the "bandwagon effect." In turning this trick (which is all it is), private industry has had the invaluable aid of the shrewdest enemies of conventional political processes in almost all cultures: the military establishment, the government's bureaucracies of privilege and judicial recipients of patronage. What serendipidity also brought the two main *non-political* forces of our technostate, the military and the technological businessman, into their present felicitous embrace![12]

---

[11] Of little consequence is the fact that space agency propaganda (and enthusiasts like our television network commentators) might easily have whipped up public enthusiasm for our moon flights to have them approved by referendum. The important point is that the whole matter of space exploration (as opposed, let us say, to the potentially *non-military* benefits of more intensive oceanographic studies) has never been open to genuine political debate, outside of *pro forma* flourishes in Congress and soap-box oratory from nay-sayers whose justifiable logic has been treated as satire or lunacy by the print and electronic press.

[12] See Chapter 18 for further consideration of these all-too-likely bedfellows. Industrial technology does, of course, respond to political processes in minor ways, as does

The long range results are typical of all societies where political action has been either stunted or attenuated, but demonstrate a particular important trend in technological states. Various issues and platforms that are highly relevant to the community are lost in the complexity of interacting government, industry, military power and news dissemination devices. They are too complex, too frequently and artificially oversimplified—and too important—to be placed before the electorate in any direct or meaningful manner. The result is apathy and indifference to the significant issues of the day on the part of much of the public, a phenomenon for which the public itself is frequently blamed by professors, authors and professional do-gooders. Those who are politically active may, in fact, just as well be apathetic for most practical purposes, because they are not consulted in the major thrusts of government and industry, but are instead kept busy with endless political games and entertainments, personality conflicts and little morality plays on "hot" issues (crime in the streets, the narcotics problem, *de facto* school integration, traffic problems and rent controls are examples), not unimportant matters, but largely beyond effective political control. In any case, they are much less significant than the directions taken by the industrial-military complex and the thrust of its exponents in state and national seats of power across the nation.

The second focus of interplay between technology and politics is a more discussed and popular issue, but, in the author's opinion, the less important of the two, although relevant enough to political persuasion for intelligent concern.

The one area where the McLuhanite mystique may relate cogently to life (long before the Canadian guru was born, and before the age of electric communication) is the mediating power of technology as used for the past

---

the Pentagon, but feebly and as infrequently as possible. Occasional government agencies and individual legislators, spurred on either by power blocs in their constituencies or dedicated private citizens like Ralph Nader, *do* also influence the nature and direction of some technological development. In this regard, an innocuous political manifestation concerning an inconsequential aspect of technology for the industrial-military duet is blown-up by their own propagandists into a major political imposition upon the Establishment. The best present example is the fuss being made today over the environment, its pollution, and the fad of ecology. With the consent (and encouragement) of producers of automobiles, gasoline, electricity, beer bottles and industrial haze, politically sensitive citizens (including the impressionable young and the usual menopausal sign-carriers and chronic protesters) are being manipulated to place political pressure in the interest of the "environment," upon legislators. The latter, in dramatic acts of pseudo-heroism, enjoin carefully selected culprits to stop practices which in most cases they had to (or had planned to) discontinue anyway. No fundamental changes in technology can result from this present, well controlled, ecological gambit. Where and when the military-industrial complex must continue to pollute the environment in what they call "the national interest," they will continue present practices. Few of us will be told much about it, because this complex controls, in a number of ways, most of the instruments for telling. What appears to be the genuine political and social issue of ecology is largely fake gamesmanship that also sells books and provides endless topics for television documentaries.

150 years in political processes. While the medium(s) is (are) not the message, the form of a communication may be a severe modifier of the message—as it has been for centuries. It may serve, in one degree or another, to distort the message in a number of crude ways, less because of the technology involved in transmission than because human interpretations intrude *into* images received by an audience, even those provided by the live theatre or lecture.

The early press in the United States, printed manually and employing hand-set type, was one of the first, and in some ways best, examples of this technological influence on political messages. These early newspapers were, for the most part, political broadsides, representing (like many European and Near Eastern newspapers today) an official line of various political interests.[13] The people of the new nation, most of whom were personally involved neither with the personalities nor the issues of the day, were, therefore, highly dependent upon these interpretive journals for political news. The newspapers spoke to this electorate (a literate minority) in a fairly erudite manner. They offered no claim to objectivity (the journalist's fatal conceit that was not born conceptually until well into the nineteenth century). And in order to receive a balanced view of political matters, the inquisitive, affluent reader usually read (and could afford) more than one newspaper.

In this context, did General George Washington move from Aristocrat to General to Statesman in the popular mind. The issues that stood between Jefferson and Hamilton were clarified and simplified (and, in this case, often distorted) by politically engaged editors. Only in the matter of the foreign menace of Britain (and aided by the Alien and Sedition Laws) was the American press unified.

Technology's influence grew as the press, harnessed eventually to the steam engine, reached a greater number of enfranchised citizens, dropped in price per issue and turned partly away from politics to other issues during the first half of the nineteenth century. The central political figure involved in this change, symbolically at least, was Andrew Jackson, America's first "image candidate," who was transmuted by the country's editors and reporters from the hero of the Battle of New Orleans (one of the few moments of American glory in the lost War of 1812) to the presidential champion of people's democracy. Jackson was the prototype for hundreds of champions of the common man in subsequent American history, individuals as different one from the other (but similar, in many ways, to Jackson) as Lincoln, Bryan, Franklin D. Roosevelt, Huey Long and, recently, George Wallace. Without the press and its power to purvey personality and subsume issues to it, neither the rhetorical skill of Jackson's closest adviser,

---

[13] See Edwin Emery and Henry Ladd Smith, *The Press and America* (New York: Prentice Hall Inc., 1954), pp. 107–190.

Amos Kendall (himself a journalist), nor the legal brilliance of Supreme Court Justice Roger B. Taney, nor the charismatic personality of Jackson himself might have wrought the bloodless revolution in democratic concepts that we understand today as the Age of Jackson.[14]

Little is proved by following the role of technology in politics from Jackson's time to our time, except to show that present—and far from new—interest in the way that television focuses upon people rather than issues and has encouraged advertising experts to merchandise political candidates are far from new issues. Nor is the fact that communications devices are devilish instruments for destroying personalities and political careers more than the continuation of an old trend. It is doubtful that network television cameras were any more cruel to the late Senator Joseph McCarthy than cartoonist Thomas Nast was to New York's Boss Tweed or to Horace Greeley. "Teddy" Roosevelt, rough rider, explorer and man of action was, in large measure, a merchandised, pre-packaged image that even the advertising personnel in Joe McGuiness' memoir, *The Selling of a President,* might wish to emulate. No President before or since was probably as free of the obligation to discuss issues and concentrate on the marketing of his personality as General Ulysses S. Grant—unless he was General Dwight D. Eisenhower. Certainly, as Hyman has pointed out,[15] the one chief executive who was elected to office almost entirely because of a slick image was Warren G. Harding, who owed much to the technology of print and photography.

At present, political candidates and legislators (among others in political life) are using the available talents and techniques involved in technology (and the technology itself) to win votes, provoke assent and enhance their reputations, just as they have been, *not* since the beginning of technology, but since the time that popular support and majority votes were introduced to government procedures. There is little unexpected, unusual or new in what we are observing today: political candidates on radio and television spot commercials, advertising types managing certain aspects of political campaigns and a President who, at this writing, appears to have more hair on his head today (1970) than he did ten years ago, when he was defeated by a candidate with a forelock.[16] There is nothing essentially

[14] *Ibid.*, pp. 192–245.

[15] Sidney Hyman, "What Trendex for Lincoln?" in Reo M. Christenson and Robert O. McWilliams (eds.), *Voices of the People* (New York: McGraw Hill Book Co., Inc., 1962), p. 365.

[16] Certain sensitive souls seem inordinately distressed when political figures worry about cosmetics or use show-business techniques to appear attractive. Most of our presidents have been old (and broken-down) enough to need false teeth. Some have worn hair pieces. And I have been told (and have observed) that male British monarchs have, for many years, worn make-up on ceremonial occasions. Rumors report that Lenin and Hitler frequently used cosmetics for various reasons. So careful was the press and newsreel coverage given Franklin D. Roosevelt during his presidency that it was possible for many Americans to live through almost his entire lengthy administration without knowing that he was a cripple, largely confined to a wheel chair.

alarming about a chief executive who takes elocution lessons from an actor (as Eisenhower did from Robert Montgomery) or an actor himself who uses his theatrical skills for political purposes like the late Senator Everett Dirksen or ex-Senator George Murphy. Neither does the salubrious utilization of flattering communications technology (or its opposite uses) portend either good or evil *per se*. A printed editorial panegyric in an influential news journal may gather more emotional steam and pander more to the public's visceral sensibilities than the best produced and slickest television campaign program. In fact, a candidate with enough rhetorical skill may be as effective live on a stump as on television—even granting difference in the size of the two audiences, but considering the possible influence (or wealth) of the smaller constituency. Old Huey Long might have failed on the television tube, but, considering the spheres of influence in which he traveled, he was a demon at a political picnic; and political picnics were the places where his fate was often sealed.

Harry S Truman probably won the 1948 presidential election (held well into the radio age) because of his personal man-to-man whistle-stop campaign across the United States. Without doubt, the present trend is for national candidates to stay close to the television studio rather than travel among the people while campaigning, so populous has this nation grown. But precisely *because* the public is rapidly becoming habituated to this kind of campaign publicity, the time may be ripe for an underdog candidate to repeat the Truman formula (by air rather than train, and extended, of course, to Hawaii and Alaska), making multiple, skillfully staged personal appearances in different places a number of times a day, holding forth to carefully selected drummed-up crowds of local politicos, especially if his opponent opts for the remote (and obviously lazier) device of campaigning by television.[17]

As to the charge that television technology has a peculiar effect on human personality that distorts the essential nature of a candidate and make it difficult to discover the real man underneath the exterior gloss, it is probably true, as far as it goes.[18] But a speaker's rostrum has a similar

---

[17] My services are available at a fantastically high price to demonstrate to any presidential aspirant how this objective may be accomplished at a fraction of the cost of the conventional television-era campaign. The only qualification the candidate must meet (aside from rough agreement with my own eccentric and inconsistent political biases) is that *he must be an underdog*.

[18] This issue is discussed well (if somewhat one-sidedly) via a number of case studies in Gene Wyckoff, *The Image Candidates* (New York: The Macmillan Co., 1968). Note also the opinions—or set of questions—posed in Kurt and Gladys Engel Lang's provocative volume *Politics and Television* (Chicago: Quadrangle Books, 1968): "Our studies pointedly suggest that television, like other forms of mass communication, presents a refracted image of the events it reports. There is, however, one major difference: television journalists regard their technology as an ally in the quest for actuality, so much so that they sometimes defer to the camera to report the 'facts' while denying responsibility if viewers misinterpret what is shown," (p. 295).

"peculiar" effect, and so does the translation of political personality to print, as in Kennedy's *Profiles in Courage*, or Nixon's *Six Crises*.

Has any electorate, in truth, penetrated to the real man underneath the gloss of political candidates in any period of our (or any other) democracy? If the television tube has a peculiar influence upon the projection of personality, so indeed does public life itself. The current myth about television is merely a recent manifestation of an old idea to the effect that once —somewhere, perhaps before anyone alive today was born—the democratic process of elections, winners and losers, and the will of the majority was a pure, pristine, absolutely fair and morally noncorrupt process. Here we find a Rousseauian strain in contemporary democratic idealism. When compared to actual political practices, such illusions invariably make the status quo appear depraved, unfair and possibly evil. What they signify is merely that faith in democratic processes still obtains, in spite of the fact that many of those most concerned about them know little of their history, assumptions, shortcomings, or the main requisite for their survival, the mythology of public opinion.

The Great Myth: Public Opinion

Nothing written about political processes in a democracy performs the delicate open-heart surgery found in Lippmann's *Public Opinion*, first published in 1922.[19] Lippmann penetrated so deeply into the vital organs of popular government that, in the time since *Public Opinion*'s publication (and despite thousands of his own qualifications), he, to this day, appears perplexed by the essential puzzles he discovered in the very notion of "the public" that he articulated so brilliantly shortly after the end of World War I.[20] In addition to identifying the limitations of stereotyped thinking which characterizes the greatest part of political speculation concerning the electoral ritual (thinking that was a decade or two later to provide the foundation for various theories in social psychology treated in Chapters 12 and 13), Lippmann subjected the entire electoral process to a hard-nosed sort of scrutiny that it had never before undergone, to the best of the author's knowledge.

What Lippmann noted—and what we still recognize with similar discomforts in our own knowledge—relates to a central assumption of democracy, derived in great part from Lockian and Jeffersonian thought, that the

---

[19] So many editions, in paperback and hard cover, of this volume are available that to list any one here is not prudent. The edition I am using is a Penguin paperback, dated 1946. A Macmillan paperback edition was also issued in 1960. The most useful general collection of Lippmann's enormous output is Clinton Rossiter and James Lare (eds.), *The Essential Lippmann* (New York: Random House, 1963).

[20] Lippmann's major books reflect his return to this theme through the years: *Public Opinion* (1922), *The Phantom Public* (1925) and *Essays in the Public Philosophy* (1955) are, in my opinion, his finest general analytic works, and are all basically concerning the enigmatic myth of public opinion.

will of the majority, in the selection of governors and the broad disposition of major issues, is a superior method of popular choice to any other yet devised. This assumption is probably true, but the numerous self-evident imperfections in the process bother men of ideals like Lippmann—process, that is, as it relates to the formation of issues, their distribution to publics, and methods for determining what manner of opinions those publics hold. As Lippmann puts it:

> The environment with which our public opinions deal is refracted in many ways, by censorship and privacy at its source, by physical and social barriers at the other end, by scanty attention, by the poverty of language, by distraction, by unconscious constellations of feeling, by wear and tear, violence, monotony. These limitations upon access to that environment combine with the obscurity and complexity of the facts themselves to thwart clearness and justice of perfection, to substitute misleading fictions for workable ideas, and to deprive us of adequate checks upon those who consciously strive to mislead.[21]

So much for the environment upon which the public acts.

What about the electorate itself? How does it handle the considerably "refracted" information it is given? Again, quoting Lippmann, "The notion that public opinion can and will decide all issues is in appearance very democratic. For when everyone is supposed to have a judgment about everything, nobody in fact is going to *know* much about anything." [22] Epigrammatic as it is, the statement offers a sobering thought, borne out in the experience of those of us who have traveled through and around the opinion-making process in our various social, economic and educational institutions. Nor may we cherish a belief that highly educated (or degreed) people are any more likely to base their political dispositions on reality than those who have not been lengthily schooled. Many people who have not suffered long at the hands of our educators are tougher auditors of facts than others who have been indoctrinated in the qualifications and suspended judgments that are fashionable in educational communities. Despite the bold concept that education somehow imbues democratic choices with integrity, contemporary schooling today is as (or more) likely to create gullibility and dependence upon Lippmann's "refracted" environment (and therefore greater deception) than the hard-nosed unsophisticated skepticism of many of our uneducated populace.

When one comes to the (eventually) terminal problem, the determination of *what* public opinion *is*, two main instruments of adjudication are today held sacred: the ballot box and the public opinion poll. The limitations of the former are obvious, but they are circumscribed in a nation like ours where the ignorant and apathethic are not likely to bother voting

---

[21] Walter Lippmann, *Public Opinion* (New York: Penguin Books, 1946), p. 56.

[22] Rossiter and Lare, *op. cit.*, p. 98.

either on issues or people. We are protected, in a way, by the sloth of the non-voter; compulsory participation in the electoral process might destroy the myth of the majority's wisdom.

The rising percentage of voters participating in national elections may one day provide blind enthusiasts for the democratic processes with cause for concern. May one qualify or rate the integrity or wisdom of a single vote and still abide by the mystique of a democracy? The "one man, one vote" principle appears to indicate that our best thinkers in Congress and on the benches of our courts believe we cannot, at least as far as geography and vested interest are concerned. But has anyone thought to measure the enlightenment content of *one* vote compared to *another* and *evaluate* them accordingly? The idea is not as ridiculous as it sounds, although it might start a nation like ours on the yellow brick road to fascism in short order. Voting in the USSR, incidentally, seems today to be conceptually reserved only for the "enlightened," as it was for a long time in the USA during the past century.

Concerning instruments for measuring public opinion by means of polls, mystiques and more mystiques are packed upon the dry bones of old myths.[23] Pollsters themselves have been vindicated in their activities in three ways, by Berelson,[24] who brings the social scientist's (as well as the politician's) interests to this aspect of democracy. In effect, first, theory and practice are hopefully tested, one against the other, by certain integral samples of quantitative measures of public opinion. Second, opinion polls also force us, says Berelson, to test our assumption about democratic processes in the matrix of reality. Third, they encourage us to reformulate many of our theoretical propositions concerning the role of governors and the governed in exact terms.

Perhaps. But let us center our attention on a typical instance, that occurred within a few days of the present writing. It concerns a *CBS News* poll, purporting to have sampled 1,136 people, representing the population of the United States. It presents the following information:

> The attitudes emerged in the answers to questions that posed key provisions of the Bill of Rights in terms of contemporary issues:
>
> "As long as there appears to be no clear danger of violence, do you think any group, no matter how extreme, should be allowed to organize protests against the government?" No, said 76%.
>
> "If a man is found innocent of a serious crime, but new evidence is

[23] See Lindsay Rogers, *The Pollsters* (New York: Alfred A. Knopf, 1949), which was written in the harsh light of the 1948 presidential election, in which the major pollsters had picked Thomas E. Dewey to overcome Harry S Truman by a landslide. Although it crows about this fiasco, Rogers' warnings concerning our trust in polls are, for the most part, still realistic and thoughtful.

[24] See Bernard Berelson, "Democratic Theory and Public Opinion" in, Bernard Berelson and Morris Janowitz (eds.), *Reader in Public Opinion and Communication*, Second Edition (New York: The Free Press, 1966), pp. 489–504.

uncovered later, do you think he should be tried again for the same crime?" Yes, said 58%.

"If a person is suspected of a serious crime, do you think the police should be allowed to hold him in jail until they get enough evidence to officially charge him?" Yes, said 58%.

"Except in time of war, do you think newspapers, radio, and television should have the right to report any story, even if the Government feels it's harmful to our national interest?" No, said 55%.

"Do you think everyone should have the right to criticize the government even if the criticism is damaging to our national interests?" No, said 54%.[25]

This particular poll was considered important (and shocking) by many of us interested in civil liberties, especially in the light of Berelson's now almost classical rationales for opinion inventories. On its surface, the poll shows what *Time* implies—that a majority of Americans reject five of the major notions included in the Bill of Rights. Closer scrutiny requires answers, however, to the following questions: How representative of all U.S. citizens (or any substantial part of them) may 1,136 people be in matters of opinion, no matter how carefully selected—or, for that matter, 10,136 people, 100,136 people or 1,000,136 people out of the total population? How well (or poorly) did the respondents understand the questions put to them? Did they assume a specific context for any of them, or did they treat them as general propositions? Did they know that these were rights, guaranteed by the Bill of Rights, or were they presented with no qualifications? With all but one of the reported percentages hovering around 50%, how significant (or reliable) is the implied assumption of majority choice? In terms of political life, what is the actual relevance of public opinion to these particular issues as they operate in society, even granting that the percentages may be roughly accurate? In other words, are they issues administratively and legally related to public opinion in our nation, or rather judicial and/or historical concerns? Last—from this same viewpoint—what does it profit CBS or *Time* (except to gain attention) by publishing such ambiguities and implying that they have profound significance? Will public opinion now be the same as it was before the news item was printed in millions of copies of magazines? That is, will these figures tend to distort the field and polarize other opinions, as already they have to this writer's, for instance? He, for one, is firmer now in his conviction that these civil rights must be maintained regardless of people, polls and the public. But might others, having read these statistics, possess rational (they think) reasons to conclude the opposite: that, because these liberties appear to be rejected by the magical majority, they should be eliminated from our Constitution? This conclusion is logical, as long as the myth of public opinion obtains in democratic thought. We have, if the poll is to be believed, simply clarified a

[25] *Time*, April 27, 1970, p. 19.

previously mistaken idea about the "will of the people"—thanks to CBS.

Germane to the set of problems above is this observation of Lippmann. "The Gallup polls are reports," writes he, "of what people are thinking. But that a plurality of people sampled in the poll think one way has no bearing upon whether it is sound public policy. For their opportunities of judging great issues are in the very nature of things limited, and the statistical sum of their opinions is not the final verdict on an issue. It is, rather, the beginning of an argument." [26] Possibly Lippmann's characterization of the accuracy of instruments like the Gallup polls (that, for many reasons, are not necessarily—as is commonly believed—validated or invalidated by subsequent official ballots) is correct. But the ramifications of his point lead to gentle—and obvious—testing points for democracy: namely, how well a nation may preserve necessary societal controls (or liberties) while they are subject both to argumentation *and* to appeals to the will of the majority *and* to the pressures of public opinion, or what the public imagines the latter to be? Lippmann (writing in 1955) may have been thinking of a far more stable republic than ours at the moment, a decade and a half later. Today, while arguments rage and are instrumented by the lockout, the sit-in, the protest, the homemade bomb, the police raid, the urban riot and the hysterical voices of fanatics, one ponders uncomfortably Lippmann's assumption that rational arguments about great issues may no longer be feasibly debated, on a large scale, in our society.

Yet the political game, it appears, cannot and will not take place without the myth of public opinion—or "general will," in another tradition. V.O. Key writes, "Fundamental (to our system) is a regard for public opinion, a belief that in some way or another it should prevail. Even those who cynically humbug the people make a great show of deference to the populace." [27] Key indicates that appeals to public (up until the time of his 1961 article) were circumscribed, in our nation, by decorum providing "certain restraints on political competition (which) help keep competition within tolerable limits," [28] usually observable beneath the surface nonsense and razzle-dazzle of political contests. Majority rule also serves similarly as an instrument of etiquette but as little more, considering, particularly, the close margins of recent victories in important elections and other factors (weather, fortuitous hard news, the stock market's behavior, rumor and the scandal mill) that appear to shift critical blocs of votes from one direction to another.

Is public opinion, therefore, a humbug? There is little question about its contemporary status as myth. But myths may constitute part of the sym-

---

[26] Rossiter and Lare (eds.), *op. cit.*, p. 88.

[27] V. O. Key, Jr., "Public Opinion and Democratic Politics" in Berelson and Janowitz, *op. cit.*, p. 127.

[28] *Ibid.*, p. 128.

bolic reality by which a society operates, as much a part of that reality as property, taxation, population, wealth and other quasi-symbolic artifacts. But humbug is another matter. It implies deception, manipulation and even control.

Conventional wisdom regards many elements of mass culture (narcotics, alcohol, sex obsession and the fun morality, for instance) as equivalent to Marx's opiate of the masses: religion. May conventional wisdom be wrong (as it often is)? May the symbol of public opinion, in fact, be a most potent social control, yielding large measures of political control to those who manipulate mass opinion blocs, by fair means or foul? They thus distill an elixer of apparent justice (the social narcotic) that the majority of our population accepts in order to maintain the status quo and ultimately to cede more power to the powerful—or to replace the presently powerful with a new, small number of manipulative and politically potent managers of public opinion.

Managing the Myth

There is, of course, no definitive answer to this question, merely faintly paranoid suspicions.[29] The picture is today, obscured by political bosses (a dying breed, but still operating backstage), political royal families new and old, (Roosevelts, Kennedys, Biddles, Cabot-Lodges, Stevensons, Tafts, Longs, etc.), pressure groups and lobbies (the China interests, the NAM, NAB, NRA, bird-watchers and cat lovers), legal, quasi-legal or illegal operators (the international currency gang, Cosa Nostra hoods, show business speculators, narcotics dealers, gamblers and others), power cliques and enclaves (Harvard brain trusters, CIA types, professional consultants, Rand Corporation geniuses, foundation pundits and the like) and other groups. Every power bloc maintains a politically oriented arm devoted to the management of public opinion, even supposedly secret government agencies. The possibility therefore, of any über-managers of the American public opinion myth—*à la* Huxley or Orwell—is unlikely. Diffusion of real power has apparently created also, in our society, a diffusion of influences on public opinion. More realistically, various interpretations of the issues dealt with by public opinion myths are manipulated by different sorts of communications, even in regard to how they are articulated and what personalities address various publics. This plurality of voices is probably a protection

[29] In a culture where sources of power remain as obscure as they are in ours, strains of paranoia run rampant. I have recently noticed that many of my students, some intelligent, some dull, are prone to believe that "everything" in our country (whatever that is) is controlled by the Mafia. Why shouldn't they? Half a dozen best sellers, fiction, and non-fiction, have recently developed this theme with conviction and clarity, as have an endless number of newspaper exposés and films. A paranoid delusion that someone is following you is not unjustified (or paranoid) if you are continually told by supposedly reliable sources that someone *is* following you. For a further discussion of this problem, see Chapter 18.

against the overaccumulation of power, although continual warnings of conspiracy (like Eisenhower's statement, upon retirement from the Presidency, concerning the coercive power of the military-industrial complex) somehow seem to fade quickly from memory.

Lippmann has long been aware of this situation. He has reminded us many times that "private interests seek to associate themselves with the mantle of the disinterested public,"[30] and therefore often masquerade as the public interest, especially at the hands of propagandists, press agents, public relations counselors or whatever it is fashionable to call professional political persuaders. In this respect, of course, the words "private interest" may be construed as political party interests, governmental agency interests, and, most elusive of all, the interests of social agencies, foundation interests and non-profit organizations devoted to the betterment of the human race—in addition to the peculiar interests of private capitalist industry, the usual whipping boy in popular conspiracy theories.

The overall situation is, of course, different in other modern states which may or may not be as open as ours is to the broad utilization of communications technology and to near universal education. Nor have they created similar myth structures concerning public opinion. The smaller the competing interests in a given society, the clearer the lines of persuasion are, and the more explicit are tests for its effectiveness and failure. Public opinion is important today as a myth in the USSR; and through that vast country, to the best of my knowledge, run many strands of it. Because its points of origin appear relatively clear (artists, students, intellectuals and the manager class, for instance), and because, by its nature, it must either run confluent with or against the Politburo's general line, its effects, even when whispered on our shores from clandestine sources, are relatively lucid. Those that are provided publicity within the Soviet Union are, obviously, considered controllable by the central government: the works of poets, playwrights, novelists, or artists approved by proper political arbiters of correct thinking.[31]

In the United States the picture is not as clear. Certainly not our federal government, nor even any of our power blocs, may realistically hope to challenge, as Terence Qualter puts it, "the total patriotic outpourings of the American parties, the cinema, newspapers and broadcasting industries . . . and the hundreds of self-styled patriotic groups." He adds that, while totalitarian nations may be able to create bodies competent to manipulate public opinion more extensively than the USA, "it cannot be greater than

[30] Rossiter and Lare (eds.), *op. cit.*, p. 91.

[31] The general picture of how diversity is permitted to some degree in the Soviet state and how it may coordinate with Communist propaganda policy may be found in John C. Clews, *Communist Propaganda Techniques* (New York: Frederick A. Prager, Publishers, 1964).

the total of public and private propaganda within the United States."[32]

Somehow and probably, the myth of public opinion itself is, in some manners, managed or manipulated—but to serve different interests at various times—except, perhaps, during the earliest days after a declaration of a war or in time of national emergency, when the voice of central government speaks loudly. In normal times, alliances of interest merge and separate. Just as similar social concerns tend to coagulate into congeries, so do persuasive political interests, and one special interest group will use another (or use each other reciprocally), creating and dissolving a multitude of long and short term alliances. When, for instance, it was in the interests of our broadcasters to support the tobacco industry (and their propaganda), they did. When legislation divorced their interests, broadcasters could then afford to join the persuasion campaigns of the public health, anti-smoking agencies. Public opinion alliances are no different from most others: conditional, temporary and constantly shifting.

We talk of strange bedfellows, and none are stranger, frequently, than such alliances. Gangsters and educators follow the same propaganda line, when taxes on legalized prostitution or gambling are used to build schools. Conservative foundations support revolutionaries, when the latter serve the former's short term goals and enthusiams for social reconstruction. Enormous oil interests cozy up to the wildlife societies, when they see opportunities for petroleum strikes at the cost of a little ecological beneficence. Antique dealers change their political orientations, when a First Lady decides to redecorate the White House. Such relationships often verge on the absurd, but so have the objectives of persuasion when viewed from the vantage point of public opinion throughout the history of democratic government. This is because public opinion, at any moment, displays only the political force that expediency and present policy permits it, and no more. Taken alone, public opinion means nothing. Taken as a variable cultural myth, it means a good deal, especially to the politician whose art essentially is the expedient management of social reality, an objective that he will only accomplish by creating the illusion of common popular assent, whether it exists or not.

Conclusion

Political activity is observable in the human behavior in two phases: personal and social. Both appear to mature in much the same manner, arrive at a zenith of activity at a certain point, and eventually decline and die out after having passed through a period of near total self-involvement and apathy. The process is remarkably similar from individual to individual, from society to society, and from individual to society.

---

[32] Terence H. Qualter, *Propaganda and Psychological Warfare* (New York: Random House, 1962), p. 140.

The state, the central focus of society's political interests, is generally regarded as an anthropomorphic entity, in spite of the fact that the rights and powers of nations transcend those of individuals. In addition, in technological societies, success at technology is frequently mistaken for political success. The result is political failure, political frivolity, political complexity, political apathy, and eventual preoccupation with the games involved in contests for office and clashes of personalities.

Technology has also—since the invention of the printing press—been the purveyor of political issues and personalities to the electorate and, in this capacity, has gone through numerous phases. At present, much attention is given to the supposed political power of television and its apparent tendency to emphasize personalities at the expense of issues. Close examination reveals that the new notion of the "image candidate" and prefabricated campaign practices antedates television back to the earliest days of representative government, and portends little of novelty for the future, except to encourage, in the short run perhaps, a return to old political styles. Present concerns merely perpetuate an historical illusion that a once pure democratic political process has somehow been fouled by modern technology.

The concept of public opinion is one of the main operative myths of democratic government. The entire notion is open to severe questions: what it is, how it is refracted in reporting, how it is formulated, what its relationships to majority and pluralities are, and what the relationships of these latter factors are to wise political choices and the function of government, and other enigmas. Neither public opinion polls nor the ballot box in a democracy answer these and other questions, vital to the rationales upon which most republics function. Nor do we understand entirely (granting we have defined and clearly articulated the quality of public opinion) what we most prudently should do with information concerning the general will, even were we competent to ascertain it with precision. Ironically, however, political life and political games cannot continue without a measure (or many measures) of faith in the ultimate correctness of public opinion. There remains, even, a possibility that much of the contemporary flux and flow of public opinion is the object of clever, covert manipulation, not of classic political tycoons, but of forces representing many types of public and private interests, acting with diffused powers, joining in numerous flexible minor conspiracies to create an illusion of unanimity, majority or plurality.

The process of political pressure acting upon and through public opinion varies from nation to nation where public opinion is a political force—but, in some degree, it probably is a factor in all, or most, cultures. The issue is particularly perplexing in our own plural state with its ubiquitous and protean arms of professional persuasion speaking for government, philanthropy, education, industry and other fragments of the commonwealth. New alliances are continually created and old ones dissolved. What this continual ferment adds up to is vital to the sustenance of our panoply of democratic mythology, the total of many necessary kinds of persuasion that insures continuous (and occasionally rational) maintenance of political controls upon a plurality of conflicting forces in society. Were these forces ungoverned, they would produce little besides chaos and a continuous chain of revolutions.

Chapter 9

EDUCATION, INDOCTRINATION, AND TRAINING

But are we not proceeding in a circle? Theoretical culture is supposed to induce the practical, and yet the latter is to be the condition of the former? All political improvements should result from education of character—but how can character ennoble itself under the influence of a barbarous civil policy?

Johann Schiller

THE MOST powerful *formal* system of persuasion in any society is probably its network of schools. The contemporary revolutionist knows that, even before he has subdued the militia, captured airfields and arms supplies, he had first better occupy the local radio and television stations to grasp *immediately* the attention of the populace—and perhaps to gain their temporary sympathy. But he is also aware that, *in the long pull*, the national system of education will be critical to the success or failure and stability of his conquest.

To capture a broadcasting station, an army or a city admits of problems, but not nearly as great as capturing the spirit of the educational institutions of a people. One of the most remarkable aspects of the Nazi period was the efficiency with which Hitlerism was introduced and accepted by all levels of German scholarship, from elementary grades to the university, by teachers and professors involved in one of the most sophisticated systems of education in Europe, at one time the model for our own schools in the United States. Some scholars and professors, of course, resisted Nazification, but (aside from Jews) their number was comparatively small. Most followed the philosopher Martin Heidegger and other academic luminaries who took well-published oaths in support of the Fuehrer and his wild constructions of European ethnic history and German national destiny.[1]

While most of us tend to maintain idealistic beliefs about education

[1] See William L. Shirer, *The Rise and Fall of the Third Reich* (New York: Simon and Schuster, 1960), pp. 248–258. Those who profess amazement at the lack of resistance today of our university solons to subversion might contemplate the relative ease with

and its potential powers for good, the fact remains that many or most educational institutions may rapidly be subverted to a wide range of special interests as efficiently as Hitler conquered the schools of Germany. They may also be harnessed as intimately to the service of the state, as the public schools of England once were to the class of administrators and governors required in the great days of the British Empire. They may follow the (much misunderstood) plural requirements of a multi-lingual and multiracial state like USSR, at the same time that they espouse one common political and social doctrine *and* may also meet the needs of vast agricultural, technological and managerial classes with considerable efficiency.[2] They may follow the apparent direction of contemporary Red Chinese schools where intensive vocational training is combined with Maoist doctrine and Marxist materialism.

In short, schools everywhere in the world are powerful conduits of persuasion. Even in countries like Afghanistan or Tibet, where only a fraction of the population ever see the inside of a schoolhouse, that fraction provides the political, economic and social leaders of the nation's communities; and what is taught them is crucial. In countries like India, where education is more widespread, but, in general, unbelievably ineffectual and confused, what little persuasion the schools exert upon the people is treated with exaggerated importance, and the formalities of education receive enormous respect.[3] Because, fundamentally, education is considered everywhere (even in fascist states) *the* prime device for uniting the material and intellectual progress of the past with the present (and therefore passing it on to the future), it is a symbol of the process of birth and reproduction of a culture's new generation. Like politics, its prototype is discovered in the life process of individual man, including man's ability to influence his natural world and modify his environment to meet his aspirations. As A. N. Whitehead and others have observed, education is fundamentally a spiritual process, and for this reason is of central significance in the current of persuasive practices that run through society.

Educational Ideals and Schooling

Next to the world of religion, education remains one of the last outposts in American life that discourages the satirist and the cynic with dead-

---

which the (probably) stiffer backbones of the German intellectuals were broken so quickly and easily by the Nazis' pseudo-philosophy and fanatic nationalism.

[2] The main directions of Soviet schooling are well explained in Division of International Education, Office of Education, *Education in the USSR* (Washington: U.S. Dept. of Health, Education, and Welfare, 1957), and/or George S. Counts, *The Challenge of Soviet Education* (New York: McGraw-Hill Book Co., Inc., 1957).

[3] An Indian student of mine returned to Senegal with calling cards so printed that his name was followed by that of an American university, followed by "B.S., M.A., Ph.D. (Failed)." Evidently, in India, evidence of having failed in achieving an American doctorate is a sign of greater erudition than never to have attempted the degree at all!

pan ostracism, invective or worse.[4] One can kid Wall Street brokers, ministers, soldiers, captains of industry, journalists, advertisers and even movie makers (most of whom take themselves unnecessarily seriously), but you will find little humor in the halls of ivy. True, you are allowed a few chuckles, if you clothe your barbs in nostalgia and sentiment and mend your ways by your exit line in the form of some sort of encomium to teachers or students or both. But, by and large, education (which employs the largest occupational force in the country) is a bleakly humorless institution. It is also a powerful one, more powerful in most circumstances than its own professionals know or appear to care.

The obvious reason for this humorlessness, of course, is that Americans *outside* of academia take education most seriously. Cremin has indicated this in a number of books and essays, but nowhere with the historical perspective shown in his quotation below from Jame De Bow, a contemporary of Horace Mann's:

> Let us diffuse knowledge throughout the length and breadth of this great country; multiply the means of information,—send the schoolmaster into every hovel,—dot every hill with schoolhouse and college,—let the Press, without intermission, night and day, pour forth its steady stream of light,—foster Science and the Arts,—let the civilizing and godlike influences of machinery uninterruptedly extend. Then will be the future of our country open boundless and great, beyond all example, beyond all compare, and countless ages bless its mission and acknowledge its glorious dominion.[5]

Written in 1854, in a nation expanding on many fronts, with an apparently limitless frontier and a growing industrial technology (seemingly infi-

---

[4] I am convinced this is largely an American trait. James Hilton's *Goodbye Mr. Chips* had its greatest successes (in book form and on film) in America. In Britain, it produced a good number of "replies," the best of which was the play and film *The Browning Version*. The British, in fact, have permitted, and encouraged, much satire of education at the hands of men like Wilde, Gilbert, Snow, Waugh and Shaw. The bitterest film I have seen about a school (but far from the sharpest) was the recent English import *If*. In America, we have brewed such weak tea as *The Blackboard Jungle* (where our faults lay in our streets, not in our schools) and *Up the Down Staircase*. Critics—even non-satirical critics like James B. Conant—are treated as pariahs in our university schools of education. I have personally been occasionally accused of anti-Americanism because of my published criticisms of present school practices. And I was once attacked as a "subversive" for failing, in a course, a Physical Education major at a distinguished university. ("Our nation *needs* dedicated girls like Deborah," her advisor told me. "Unless she passes your course, she won't be eligible to teach. Don't you know how badly our country *needs teachers*? What are you *accomplishing* by failing her?" shrieked this gym-teaching female to me over the telephone.) Deborah flunked, and the ship of state is, to the present anyway, still sailing.

[5] Quoted in Lawrence Cremin, *The Genius of American Education* (Pittsburgh: The University of Pittsburgh Press, 1965), pp. 5–6. See also Cremin *The Transformation of the School* (New York: Alfred A. Knopf, 1961), for a full-blown discussion of the extraordinary idealism that attended the development of the progressive movement in schooling, and how and why it eventually burned out.

nite in its capacity for creating wealth), this "high-flown rhetoric," as Cremin calls it, was the mere extension into a new mass society of the old Jeffersonian dream (a heritage of Lockean and Platonic wisdom) that the fundamental prerequisite for democracy was education. Government, unmuddled by the practicalities discussed in the previous chapter, was, to the enfranchised citizen, *the* most serious business in society—to the idealistic, even more serious than taming the frontier or developing commerce. And deified education was the prerequisite for wise government.

As the nineteenth century wore on, schooling remained important but more and more in a new way, overlooked today by many historians. On one hand, the education of an enlightened electorate became (apparently) less and less important, as it became obvious, due to some inherent quirk in the nature of representative government, that it was possible for ignorant fools to nominate and elect great statesmen (like many of our backwoods political heroes), at the same time that well educated sophisticates might cast the majority of their votes for fools and/or frauds. It seemed, in large measure, that the slogan "In God We Trust" was literally justified in the pragmatic arena of government. On the other hand, both the arts of finance and the skills demanded by growing technology also required education of a certain kind for certain people, depending upon fate and individual aspirations: reading and writing, certainly; mathematics, to some degree; basic technical know-how and/or science, also to some degree. And if a person was looking for upwards mobility in the class structure, it was also necessary to expose himself to a lot of "useless" subjects for character development and conversation with his superiors. Such studies included one or two foreign languages, basic music appreciation, classic painting and sculpture and literature and drama, involving the perusal of a few poets and the plays of Shakespeare, but rarely viewing the latter on a stage.

By the end of the nineteenth century, education was regarded as a vehicle for *success*, but not for financial success alone. Many of our immigrants from Europe had brought with them traditional respect for the teacher, rabbi, doctor or whatever they called their intellectuals, that was independent of their materialist considerations. Oddly, from the heterogonous grab bag of immigrants, only the Irish and the Negroes seemed in any way deficient in this tradition, although, in the case of the former, penurious Irish Jesuits rapidly established an intellectual beachhead in the New World that they have maintained to this day. Education was—and to some extent still is—variously denied the black man, but even the slaves and post-Civil War blacks evolved the symbols of the black preacher as a man of "the book," and that of the wise old Negro matriarch who possessed a mine of folk knowledge, more valuable than money.[6]

[6] For the blacks, this tradition continued almost until 1950, at which time the beginnings of a Negro intellectual élite, that had gathered about a handful of figures like Langston Hughes and Richard Wright, began an expansion into scholarship and the

The charge that Americans have, since the late nineteenth century, been given to construing schooling almost in exclusively materialistic terms is a common socio-historical error. In general, *public* education until recently, often served no more socially acceptable a purpose than training people for public service jobs, few of them comparatively well paying: teaching, public health, social work, and even journalism and government. Parochial education of all types could articulate no finer objective than to identify those young people who might be called to the seminary and monastery. Legends (and Leo Rosten) remind us that our urban night schools of two generations ago were filled with immigrants, suffering—with what effects we shall never know—through classes in Americanization, sometimes merely to be able to communicate with their own children or to avoid the onus of having to read a foreign language newspaper on a local streetcar. And some of these immigrants just wanted to be Americans, because they loved the ideals and promises for which the country stood.

Although they were not related to material matters, these motives were, in almost every case, extremely important to the people who read for the first time the words "Knowledge is Power" on the facades of our public schools. Not only did America offer the promises of wealth and freedom (so apparent in our mythology until World War I), it held forth to the politically, socially and intellectually impotent proletariat the gift of social and organizational power, often more magnetic in its way than either money or access to instruments of governmental choice.

The great educational reformers at the beginning of this century (whose influence was felt keenly in our schools during the 1930's) have been correctly called "pragmatists"; but the term "instrumentalist" most clearly dramatizes the coloration of their interests. Their philosophies and programs clearly coincided with the growing materialism of American life at large. Whether the common phrase, "To get anywhere you need a (grammar school, high school, college and graduate, as the century wore on) education," *resulted* directly from the instrumental force of this philosophy, as translated into curriculums and teaching methods, is an unanswerable question. But thought frequently follows action in culture, and ideals are tailored to realistic limits. In this writer's opinion, instrumental philosophy was more a *result* than the cause of those materialistic imperatives in American life which found their way via legend and popular literature (including radio, press and films) and popular thought into the writings and lectures of Dewey and to the subsequent behaviors of his educationalist followers.[7]

---

arts, culminating in the persons of such activist black intellectuals as the late, self-taught Malcolm X and Eldridge Cleaver and others. Persuasion by and upon the black communities will be discussed in detail in Chapter 24.

[7] Instrumentalism, its setting, and Dewey's somewhat ambiguous contribution to the progressive education movement, is discussed by Cremin in detail in *The Transforma-*

Many educators still wince at the equation of what actually became of progressivism in education with the thrust of materialistic motives in schooling. Dewey, in his enormous output, usually emphasized instrumentalism's role in facilitating individual development and the creation of an harmonious democratic state more often than the pragmatic uses of progressive education. Ideally, if education is an instrument, its role in culture is to free the young in democracy to pursue some more benign objective than the mere accumulation of wealth, the ultimate in materialism. In practice, progressive education displayed a strong and unmistakable pecuniary, materialistic bent, compatible with the classical cultural incentives of the nineteenth century. In fact, an instrumental, practical, pseudo-democratic, pupil-centered, vaguely non-authoritarian non-subject matter centered elementary and secondary school system that branched off into four directions—to blue collar labor; to liberal arts college, a gentleman's education or profession; to purely vocational education; or to child-bearing and home keeping—was probably the only kind of schooling that might, even imperfectly, satisfy the plural aspirations of our burgeoning, variegated technological culture. Despite the criticism leveled at them, if Dewey, Kilpatrick, Counts and the other apostles of progressive education had not been born, someone would have had to invent them to meet the materialistic expectations of the mass of Americans who, by now, viewed education, not only in idealistic terms but also—to put it crudely—as a device for making a heap of gold.

This motive, incidentally, has probably been heard more blatantly, more freely and honestly expressed by parents and students during the past ten years than at any time in our nation's history. High school valedictorians still hold forth in idealistic platitudes, and the young—particularly those who opt for rebellion for short periods against materialism, as they define it—are publicized in family magazines as dedicated, selfless socially-oriented angels. But college admissions officers and guidance personnel usually admit that the fundamental concern of our young people is how their education will serve best as a device for fulfilling their materialistic aspirations in life.[8]

---

tion of the School. A short but expert critique of this phase of educational life appears in the volume, Robert Ulich, *History of Educational Thought* (New York: American Book Co., 1950), pp. 315–336.

[8] Sometimes this occurs in bizarre ways. Some years ago I was involved in the production of a comic book (sic) designed to persuade young ladies to pursue the career of nursing. While the rewards of service were emphasized, the realists involved in the writing geared the main theme of their persuasion to the implication that a Registered Nurse had an excellent chance of capturing a physician for a husband. Another similar "public service" document I was involved in was a film designed to lure small-town talent to teach in big city ghettos. It employed (after experimenting unsuccessfully with the concept of the challenge of the work) an appeal, for men, of life as a playboy in a swinging metropolis and, for women, the number of available rich bachelors in urban (versus rural) areas. I have been informed that both persuasive devices worked well, but,

Dewey was probably as suspicious of the virtues of materialistically oriented schooling as any of his critics who subsequently opposed progressivism in the name of "liberal" or "basic" education. But Dewey had written enthusiastically, in his seminal essay on the "new" education, concerning "the educative forces of the domestic spinning and weaving, of the sawmill, the grist mill, the cooper shop, and the blacksmith forge . . . ,"[9] an idea which must have raised numerous eyebrows among the academic fraternity. Along with vaporous obeisance to the deities of intellect he also suggests:

> Though there should be organic connection between the school and business life, it is not suggested that the school is to prepare the child for any particular business, but that there should be a natural connection of the everyday life of the child with the business environment about him, and that it is the affair of the school to clarify and liberalize this connection, to bring it to consciousness . . . by keeping alive the ordinary bonds of relation . . . (T)here are plenty of real connections between the experience of children and business conditions which need to be utilized and illuminated. The child should study his commercial arithmetic and geography, not as isolated by themselves, but in reference to his social environment. The youth needs to become acquainted with the bank as a factor in modern life, with what it does, and how it does it . . .[10]

While these words do not seem unsettling today, in 1900 (the year they were first published), they might have constituted an agenda for the education of an Horatio Alger hero. They constitute but a fraction of the multitude of educational ideas Dewey was to propose in the two generations to come. Taken in sum total, they were to materialize schooling in America more effectively than any other power or force before or since. They were not, strictly speaking, examples of philosophical persuasion. Dewey as a formal philosopher and Dewey as an educational thinker are hard to reconcile. And suggestions like those above were often poorly implemented in classroom procedures by educationalists of less imagination and vision than Dewey.

It was not Dewey's objective, at any time, to undermine in any manner, the original democratic idealism of education as a liberalizing force, so central a theme to Jefferson and his contemporaries. What Dewey hoped to accomplish was to demonstrate that such idealism was relevant to the class-

---

like all propaganda, they were so closely articulated to circumstantial realities of time and place that they yield no general principles of persuasion, other than the apparent fact that the materialistic aspects of life and wedlock were attractive to many rural young people at the time of their composition. Both documents were, incidentally, stylistic horrors.

[9] John Dewey, *The School and Society* (Chicago: Phoenix Books, 1943), p. 11. The influence of this essay on education in the United States was enormous, an influence less the result of its ideals of spirit than of its practical suggestions, which Dewey did not offer his students and readers in such copious amounts again in his writings.

[10] *Ibid.*, pp. 76–78.

room—and American democracy and culture—if properly implemented, a century *after* Jefferson. What resulted from the attempt was, however, the partial de-idealization of education, seen less as an instrument than as a visa stamp that might destroy the border gates between the lower and middle classes. Enfranchised millions (or their children), raised in poverty, would now achieve new, high standards of living in a growing industrial society. For those millions, democratic idealism was a side issue. The American Way *worked*. This was what they were told in school, and this was what they found in the theatre of life. Should this happy eventuality square with idealism, so much the better. If not, what loss? To repeat, one needed (and still needs) an education to get somewhere, and getting somewhere was (and probably is) the major objective of the school population.

The Dual Paradox of Schooling

Among professional educators and certain portions of the lay public, a controversy has been percolating (slowly) for nearly a generation, broadly based on two apparently antithetical ideas of schooling, results of the historical factors described above. One has touted loudly and long the virtues, now in disrepair, they claim, of basic education, the three R's, liberal arts, and non-utilitarian, well-disciplined directed schooling. The other, more or less representing professional teachers, parents associations and educational organizations has endorsed education stressing adjustment to the social order, relaxation of discipline, the apparent diminishing need for what once were considered fundamental academic subjects, the elimination of competition and the encouragement of permissiveness. Clearly, the first is a relic of the élite school system of the past century. The second is a loose version of John Dewey's instrumental education.[11] Both polar versions (rarely found in their pure form) and all compromises between them (the education our children are currently receiving, regardless of where they go to school) are interesting and sometimes powerful persuasive instruments in contemporary culture. Let us examine them briefly to note their essential irony, not alone for the educational community but for society in the West.

First, the argument or antagonism between them is more apparent than real. Even in their extreme manifestations, ongoing tensions between "liberal" and "professional" (or "vocational") education, are largely a matter of terminology, not fact. Conant, for instance, indicates that *no* consen-

[11] The advocates of basic education are probably well known to most readers and include such writers and scholars as Arthur Bestor, John Keats, Mortimer Smith, Albert Lynd, and (sometimes) James B. Conant. Rather than discuss their various works, I recommend James D. Koerner, *The Case for Basic Education* (Boston: Little Brown and Co., 1959). The other side of the controversy is represented largely by that collection of educationalists teaching today in our Schools of Education, few of whom are competent enough at composition to speak eloquently for themselves. Their case is made fairly in Paul Woodring, *A Fourth of a Nation* (New York: McGraw-Hill Book Co., 1957), although Woodring is a "moderate" in the on-going argument.

sus exists today in the United States as to what a liberal education must (or should) consist of, how it should be taught or what its objectives are to be.[12] The same confusion faces one in delimiting and defining non-liberal or professional and/or vocational education,[13] even in those clear-cut instances, like law and medical and dental schools, where the exact nature of basic vocational objectives was at one time commonly understood. Today, however, law, medicine and dentistry as professions have proliferated into so many specialties and have crossed lines with so many other disciplines and professions that even the general corpus of knowledge and skill once understood as necessary for their pursuit has become increasingly (and in medicine, sometimes, unfortunately) difficult to pin down or define.[14] At lower levels of aspiration also, in the training of secretaries, machinists, butchers and hotel managers, much the same type of confusion may be discovered merely by examining the Bulletins of various vocational schools or talking to their inhabitants.

Second, in less clear examples, educators carry on unending waves of semantic warfare with startling innocence. Departments of art at our universities cleave into departments of art history (liberal) and painting and sculpture (professional); divisions of drama and speech offer historical and theoretical studies (liberal) and courses in theatre arts and broadcasting (professional), merrily tossing the subjects (and their professors) from one

---

[12] See James B. Conant, *The Education of American Teachers* (New York: McGraw-Hill Book Co., Inc., 1963), pp. 86–92.

[13] My dirty wash is little different from everyone else's. At this writing, I am employed by a university proud of its tradition of undergraduate liberal arts studies. But it runs a prosperous undergraduate School of Education and School of Business, both "with a strong liberal arts orientation," of course, according to the deans of each school. Within the university's liberal arts division, departments of Speech, Drama, Fine Arts, Communications, Engineering and others offer professional-vocational undergraduate courses of study as specialized as those found in trade schools and community colleges. The academic administrators of the school, of course, stress its "strong liberal arts orientation," meaning a handful of required courses (mostly electives) in one or another of the humanities that few professionally oriented students take seriously or concentrate on much. The Provost and President of the university, both wise and educated gentlemen, know exactly what is going on, but are forced to defend (except in private) the "strong liberal arts orientation" of a campus which has become, over ten years of rapid expansion, in fact, a collection of professional and vocational mini-schools, all with a "*strong professional-vocational orientation.*" This disclosure would be shocking, except for the sly fact that is well-known by everyone concerned with the university, including the cafeteria staff, with whom I have had the pleasure of discussing it. In general, they do not appear to approve of it.

[14] Medical schools, for instance, have remained more or less stagnant in concept and procedure since the Flexner report of 1910 which recommended the general format for medical education employed today. Over the years, of course, a multitude of new sciences and technologies (social, behavioral and chemical, among others) with direct bearing upon the education of the modern physician have found their way into the curriculum, affecting different medical schools in different ways, many of them presently overloaded with obsolete or irrelevant subject matter. See Martin L. Gross, *The Doctors* (New York: Dell Books, 1966), pp. 435–490.

university division or department to another. Inflated prose concerning educational objectives, the cultivation of the "whole man," ethics, ideals and creativity so pollute the air at curriculum committee meetings that any professor or teacher who wastes his time in such service is, to a sensitive observer, immediately suspect as a fraud. Such confusion is indicative of muddled heads that have never considered the actual objectives of schooling as a persuasive artifact, not an apparent on-going dialectic or amusing battle of wits between those who espouse hard or traditional education versus those who prefer soft or permissive schooling. In caricature, the conflict is polarized on every campus (and every schoolhouse) by the separation of most faculties into those who teach cultural subjects (English, History, Science and similar subjects) and those who teach practical subjects (Physical and Driver Education, Mechanical Drawing, Engineering, Physiotherapy and others), a caste schism so rigid that it even divides the staffs of single academic departments in high schools and colleges. Some hardy teachers are foolish enough, for a short time, to attempt to straddle the gap, a brave undertaking, so great is the semantic wedge between the two camps.

Third, not only is this dichotomy vaguely and arbitrarily limned in fact, but the polarity is bogus in theory as well. The idea that a liberal orientation excludes either specialism or practicality is an extremely modern misconception that has been articulated by schoolmen only since (approximately) World War I. The canard attended the development of practical sciences like biology and psychology, and was encouraged by the sudden emergence of multiple professional schools and departments in the world of secondary and higher education. The reaction of the academies—into a reconstruction of the liberal arts as somehow exclusive of specialism and technique—was purely defensive, illustrated today by the fact that on most campuses the liberal arts faculty constitutes a clique of old guard bureaucrats. They wield enormous power (mostly by forcing curriculum committees to list their courses as compulsory for non-Humanities students) and maintain a pose as guardians of so-called "high standards," their favorite but meaningless rallying cry.[15]

Fourth, professional education, as we know it today, is a comparatively *new* educational phenomenon; although most of the *first* colleges in the USA were, in some manner, professionally oriented, the orientation was

[15] The best discussion of the role of specialism and techniques in education on all levels remains A.N. Whitehead, *The Aims of Education* pp. 52–106. None of these essays, written in the 1020's and collected in 1929, reflect the liberal-professional education dispute. Whitehead takes it as natural that a professional education should be liberal, and that a liberal education is worthless unless it is professional. (His address to the students and faculty of the Harvard Business School is interesting in this respect.) Whitehead's ultimate aim, the promulgation of culture by "activity of thought, and receptiveness to beauty and humane feeling" naturally includes the necessity for the development (in school and out) of professional or vocational skills.

misty and poorly implemented. Purely vocational training (a replacement, largely, for the apprentice system of the past century) is even newer. On face, the apparent need of students entering trades and professions to pass through various quanta of non-utilitarian education is slight, contingent upon the particular profession or vocation and aptitudes of the individual student and the life-style for which he opts, or into which he will fall. It is a cultural luxury to spawn army officers who have read Ovid, physicians who can argue Hegel or dental technicians who have tried to make sense out of Talcott Parsons; arguments for the *necessity* of such training for the welfare of the state (or for the students' own welfares) are invariably weak. They fall back on lame generalities concerning the fabrication of cultivated citizens, not mere policemen, lawyers, housewives or actors, propositions difficult to defend by scrutiny and study of presently successful (and reasonably cultivated) policemen, lawyers, housewives and actors.

As Jencks and Riesman have shown,[16] no halcyon and highly productive period of effective liberal education (or vocational education) has ever existed in this country, at least on the college level. The two have always been in some degree mixed, and "purity of motive and single-mindedness of purpose have never been characteristic of American colleges, and . . . the question has always been *how* an institution mixed the academic with the vocational, not *whether* it did so." [17] Much the same observation also applies to our elementary and more recently invented secondary schools. The promise and availability of professional and vocational education have recently attracted large numbers of students to college, or induced them to stay in school, when, a century ago, they would have gone to work after learning reading, writing and arithmetic, perhaps, and studied their professions on the job. Now they attend (or stay in) school, and their rebellion against traditional non-utilitarian vestiges of the gentleman's education is understandable. Their grandfathers, schooled only slightly, would not have known (or cared) what the Humanities were. Now they are forced (under the sympathetic eyes of professional teachers) to take well-called "useless" courses in subjects unrelated to their interests, usually at the demand of a powerful liberal arts faculty that has taken directive control of administering the academic side of their high schools, colleges or universities. This near-total disregard, the writer believes, of the genuine needs and interests of college students, in the light of their professional objectives, by old guard, liberal arts professors (many of them young people, incidentally) is one of the main causes of the tendency of numerous semi-politically active students to side with campus radicals in such stormy college protests as those at Columbia, San Francisco State, Fordham, Kent

---

16 Christopher Jencks and David Riesman, *The Academic Revolution* (New York: Doubleday and Co., Inc., 1968), pp. 199–202.

17 *Ibid.*, p. 199.

State and elsewhere. The pity of this state of affairs is not that it might easily have been avoided, but that it was inevitable and therefore might have been foreseen, understood and contained by the faculties of these and other schools (including high schools), if they had been willing and competent to change their ways slightly and were equipped with a sense of paradox in regard to their own specialties.

The ideational properties of all schools are such that their persuasive influence upon the environment is dualistic, both conservative and liberal. And this tendency is visible at all levels in all kinds of instruction, even the kind given by barbers' colleges, driving academies and charm schools. Emphasis upon one or the other influence may, in fact, constitute the *only* qualitative difference in how two schools in a given community operate at a given time.[18] Viewing education as a whole, in the degree to which it serves a conservative function, it fails in liberality, and this is unfortunate and dangerous. In the degree to which it exercises its liberal thrust, it fails in conservatism, a situation which is also unfortunate and dangerous. The conclusion to this paradox is, therefore, that the results of the main forces of persuasion in *all* education invariably produce—along with occasionally reaching apparent objectives—social tendencies that are invariably unfortunate *and* dangerous. But they are also precisely the risks which attend all social institutions for innovation. Schooling is no exception.

In one mode, schools pass on the accumulated knowledge of the past to the future. Here, as Whitehead and others have noted, lies the great economy of education. Most individuals might have, for instance (had they the time, will and intelligence) worked out the principles of Greek geometry for themselves. Mercifully, most of them did not have to, because a teacher, steeped himself in a tradition of puzzle-solving, showed them ancient techniques of measuring angles, predicting distances and other Greek techniques. The elements of collective experience, cultural values, scientific knowledge, wise generalizations and (most significant in the entire process) techniques are the contents of schooling that were taken from yesterday's world and introduced to the present one, in the knowledge that, after a certain amount of change and pruning, they will be passed on into the future. To a degree, the fields of fine art, religion, law and government share also in this process of conservation, and the museum, church, courthouse and city hall are symbols of these aspects of society, along with the schoolhouse.

In another mode, schools, since Plato's academy, have also been instruments of social amelioration and cultural change. In addition, therefore, to

---

18 I am grateful here to my former colleague, Charles A. Siepmann, whose insight the following discussion reflects. It recalls vividly for me our weekly seminars when I first became his student in the early 1950's. Siepmann, like many other thinkers educated in Britain, spoke (and speaks) poorly of, but beautifully for, his school background, almost entirely devoted to the Humanities.

conserving tradition and keeping certain aspects of society as they were, education is a progressive, liberal and sometimes revolutionary force, wherein the speculations of philosophers, the findings of experimentalists and the experiences of empiricists are translated into practical programs of change. These programs may concentrate on modifying dispositions, techniques, life-styles or the production of new material artifacts. As they flow from the educational environment, in which they were born and taught, into society, it is difficult to predict their outcome. Our general orientation to, and concepts of, the welfare state were born in an academic environment. Their end products may be "creeping socialism," various urban problems (dramatized today by our burgeoning welfare rolls) and/or a heightened social consciousness of the majority of our population. Internationalist tendencies in the teaching of history after World War II somehow encouraged the violent pacifism (and the vague nonmaterialism) of the college generation of the late 1960's. The introduction of Freudianism and the study of sexual behavior as a facet of biological science have contributed to (or are producing) a sexual revolution, particularly in respect to behaviors once regarded as deviant or immoral.[19]

These changes did not emerge solely from the schools, of course, but most of the major cultural modifications of recent times have at least received assent (and nearly always cooperation) from the educational establishment. If it is today possible to purchase the works of an author whose words were yesterday considered unfit for us (or our children) to read, it is because various academic judgments have led to judicial moves that indicate a change of cultural disposition is brewing, in regard to literature—not all of them having to do with literature alone, incidentally, but calling into the forum the authority of psychologists, sociologists, theologians, criminologists and political scientists. In many ways, education is, in truth (as most revolutionists recognize and most idealists hope), the vanguard of reform in all cultures, particularly those that allow their teachers and professors fairly wide measures of individual freedom.

As education succeeds in its conservative function, it therefore fails as an innovative force. As it succeeds in leading to change, it therefore fails in its conservative context. The neat paradox results in the unhappy fact that schooling must always, accordingly, be a failure. But by the same standards of judgment, it must also always succeed. The central problem that teachers and administrators face is to facilitate this success on one hand, and to anticipate and channel the inevitable discontents of failure into benign cultural channels, on the other. This requires continual realistic appraisal both of the aims and ends of schooling as cultural persuasion.

---

[19] See Chapter 15 for the influence of the sexual revolution on contemporary persuasive tactics and modes of expression.

The Teacher as Propagandist

Thus far in this volume, we have found no need to distinguish, either in specific instances or generally, between *persuasion* and *propaganda*. The reader may find it odd (or amusing) that such a distinction is useful in discussing the role of *education* (of all topics) as an acculturating force, while it is more or less irrelevant to the discussion of politics, advertising and mass culture. The reason, of course, is that "propaganda" (as the term is most frequently used at present) is merely one class of persuasion, as noted in Chapter 4, and a relatively recent one, the nature and definition of which has changed considerably over the past three centuries. Most of the institutionalized and personal persuasion discussed so far in this part of the volume may or may not fit certain contemporary constructions of the word "propaganda." The matter is, in fact, irrelevant to its logical qualities as persuasion, because the term "propaganda" has not been used in any way *except* as a synonym for "persuasion" (like advertising).

For teachers in schools, there is realistic alternative between persuasion and propaganda. Teachers or institutions of education may persuade *or* educate, that is, they may influence dispositions *or* transmit (as far as can be ascertained) facts and skills. But few teachers are hired for, or function only, to disseminate facts and skills, even in technical institutes and professional schools. By precept at least, and exhortation at most, they are involved in orientation, even if to no more pressing matters than behavioral life styles and norms of conduct. In this sense, therefore, it is useful to distinguish between a teacher as an *educator* (mediator of facts and skills) and a teacher as a *propagandist* (agent of indoctrination). Let us bear in mind that every teacher in every school—no matter how objective he considers his work or detached he remains from the concerns of his students—is, in some degree, a propagandist by virtue of his very *being and doing*, from nursery schools to Army Officers' Candidate Academies, to bartending, music and driving schools, to courses taught in the early morning on television.

As a class of persuasion, propaganda, especially in schooling, is distinctive from other intentional communication, but the dictionary meaning of the word does not help us to clarify how. "Propaganda" has today a pejorative tone that it did not possess two generations ago, and advances in technology and methods of so-called "psychological" warfare have also lately given it new connotations.[20]

---

[20] The number of definitions for the word "propaganda" (aside from those in the dictionary) given by experts in the field over the past forty years is notable. The following are taken from Michael Choukas, *Propaganda Comes of Age*, pp. 13–18:

> *Propaganda Analysis Institute*: "Propaganda is the expression of opinions or actions by individuals or groups deliberately designed to inffluence opinions or actions of other individuals or groups with reference to predetermined ends."

For our purposes, we shall label that class of persuasion "propaganda" which 1.) sets itself to a clear institutional objective; 2.) reaches a formidable mass of people in the same general format (either by instruments of mass communication or large numbers of similarly trained person-to-person persuaders); or 3.) in one way or another, modifies or directs the cognitive, emotional and/or dispositional aspects of its subject matter so as to increase to the pragmatic maximum the likelihood of reaching its intentional objective.

Most teachers, as indicated above, naturally thus serve as propagandists, either by virtue of the similarity of roles they play in providing precepts for their students, or by the more or less identically oriented subject matter that each, on various levels of education in his discipline, imparts to the young. Most textbooks (excepting those concerned only with abstract skills) are, in different degrees, also instruments of propaganda. In theory, there is *less* necessity for a teacher to propagandize his students (in our terms) the higher one rises along the ladder of schooling, from kindergarten to graduate school. Young children require a good deal of direct, formalized persuasion merely to carry what social reciprocity is necessary to provide a decent environment for learning. The failure of many young (and some older) teachers to carry out this type of propaganda results in their simultaneous failure to create such a climate, frequently in many of our ghetto schools. Children, therefore, are not impressed by the precepts of their teachers and learn comparatively few of the facts or skills they are

---

H.L. Childs: "To propagandize is merely to propagate ideas and doctrines . . . to attempt deliberately to influence the minds of other people."

Leonard Doob: "Propaganda can be called the attempt to affect personalities and to control the behavior of individuals toward ends considered unscientific or of doubtful value in a society at a particular time."

Harold Laswell: "Propaganda is the control of opinion by significant symbols, or, so to speak, more concretely and less accurately, by stories, rumors, reports, pictures, and other forms of social communication." Also "There is a need for a word which means the making of deliberately one-sided statements to a mass audience. Let us choose 'propaganda' as such a word."

E. D. Martin: "Propaganda offers ready-made opinions for the unthinking herd."

Frederick Lumley: "Propaganda is promotion which is veiled in one way or another as to 1.) its origins or sources, 2.) the interests involved, 3.) the methods employed, 4.) the content spread, and 5.) the results accruing to the victims—any one, any two, any three, any four, or all five."

Maxwell Garrett: "We may define propaganda as any organized effort to make people think of something—whether concrete or abstract, simple or complex—otherwise than it would be thought of by a perfectly impartial person aware of all the relevant facts."

E.L. Bernays: "Propaganda is a consistent, enduring effort to create or shape events to influence the relations of the public to an enterprise, idea, or group."

Add also—

Charles A. Siepmann: "Propaganda is organized persuasion."

Of the definitions quoted above, I prefer the last for its clarity, sense and precision.

supposed to. Nor do they tend to develop attitudes that their middle-class elders (their instructors and administrators and frequently their parents) expect them to assimilate in school. Not only do they appear stupid, they are also rebellious, and frequently antisocial to the degree of delinquency. These results are seen as a failure of education, which they are not. They stem, rather, from a failure of persuasion and propaganda to provide the right kind of cultural indoctrination that makes learning possible. While many factors contribute to this problem, the main fault lies in the training of the teachers and administrators who deal with these youngsters. It may, therefore, be placed directly at the feet of our professors of education (many of them poorly or miseducated themselves) as well as our federal and state departments of education. It is also, ironically, a problem that is, possibly, quite simple to solve.

By the time students have advanced to high school or college, one expects, (in theory) that the need for propaganda in schooling will have decreased apace as they are competent to handle information in a mature manner and are able to draw relevant and logical conclusions from their inquiries. By the period of graduate or professional school (again in theory), one hopes that they will be free of most persuasion in their studies, except for that which derives directly from precepts provided by their instructors, and that, if propagandistic influences invade their classrooms, they will be able to recognize them and weigh them for what they are worth.

In most schools, this is far from present practice. How simple to find the propagandistic thread of the policies of the American Bar Association in our law school classes and the American Medical Association in medical schools. But covert persuasion is also hidden in many tangles of other types of advanced schooling, sometimes so obviously that it is difficult to pinpoint. A Keynsian, Marxist, Freudian or Piagetan who teaches a course in Keynes, Marx, Freud or Piaget is, of course, expected, in a graduate school, to show a good deal of enthusiasm for his subject and *amour propre*. But it also anticipated that he pay attention to the weaknesses and inconsistencies in the ideas of each and the arguments and positions of their detractors. Or is he justified in leaving this task of providing an antithesis to another teacher somewhere (to whom, he presumes, his students will some day be exposed) who is anti-Keynsian, anti-Marxist, anti-Freudian or anti-Piagetan? The question is so delicate that it is impossible to settle in generalities, depending, as it does, upon the school and students, with whom the teacher is working and other factors.

The inappropriate role of persuasion in much education—broadly speaking, too little in early schooling and too much in later phases of instruction—may strike close to the primary cause for the failure of free, universal education to live up to the idealism once held for it, and explain in some measure, also, the recent decline of the influence of all our schools as social controls in the orderly management of our culture. All of our schools, excluding perhaps the "Hollywood High" schools and some *avant-garde* academies, self-hypnotized by the excitement of experiment, seem chronically out of phase with the rest of society, just as they did two generations ago when they supposedly served as an ideal of middle class respectability to which the proletariat aspired and the middle class acquiesed. (The uppers took care of their own.) Today, urban minorities and other lower class citizens seem increasingly to reject the aspiration of entry into the middle class as important or educationally relevant to their long-range concerns. Middle class students and teachers have themselves failed in self-acceptance and nerve in maintaining the integrity of their own subject matter and life styles. And even the so-called upper classes (as represented in ivy-league institutions) seem presently dissatisfied with the main functions of their educational institutions in the web of modern culture.

In truth, one cannot help feeling that most of our schools and colleges exist in a dream world fundamentally unrelated to social reality. The word "irrelevant," used so frequently at present by revolting students, is not a bad one to describe what they are up to. Does one expect any other than a violent reaction when rich universities espouse classroom rationality in philosophy and sociology courses and spend millions on cyclotrons and libraries, all the while surrounded geographically by slums in which people starve, die of heroin overdoses and children are bitten in their cribs by rats; when timid biology teachers mince words about the birds and bees to groups of children that include 'teenage prostitutes, veterans of abortion and members of sex and "pot" clubs; when guidance counselors attempt to use human relations techniques to convince uncivilized, neglected ghetto children to assay a college education, while what they need is to learn simply how to make a living and achieve independence from a miserable environment?

Friedenberg has chronicled this failure (in our high schools) intelligently and sensitively.[21] His main points illuminate directly the present role, and present failure, of most of our schools—not only on the secondary level—to serve as instruments of acculturation and persuasion in the right ways for the right students. He writes:

> The public school is still the gateway to opportunity, but the opportunity is intrinsically less attractive to the young than it was, or appeared to be, fifty years ago. There is more of a squeeze on them, and the squeeze is more complicated than in the past.
>
> Not only is middle-class life too constricting to arouse much enthusiasm even among its own children, much less to win enthusiasm and ambitious converts from below; middle class roles are declining in scope and availability . . . (W)hat the school imposes is the pattern of

[21] See Edgar Z. Friedenberg, *Coming of Age in America* (New York: Random House, 1965), pp. 168–188.

> life and values accepted by its own staff who are mostly lower middle class, and which is generally in practice throughout the country.
>
> But this does not mean that the school imposes middle-class taste . . . (R)eal middle class taste . . . is as much a specialized minority taste as any other, and wholly out of place in a mass society. In their effort to serve uniformity, school personnel have been no more respectful of middle-class tradition than of any other.
>
> What they offer expresses the taste of no class, but a refusal to recognize that human experience varies according to the social and economic situation one lives in.[22]

Upon this failure rests the failure of educational persuasion today: propaganda for education itself, for civil liberties, for social welfare in its broadest sense, for humanism, for technology, for the responsibilities of the affluent society, for civic responsibility or any one of the hundreds of meaningful cultural objectives for contemporary education. Out of this failure has come a glut of wasted years and time-marking for millions of students, the symptoms of which have been falling standards of accomplishment and the decline in qualities of teaching and learning at all levels.[23] Today, some of the consumers of education who have been short-changed are fighting back—at this writing—on some college campuses and in some high schools. But shortly and inevitably others will join them in their own ways. And the rebellion of the young includes its own form of propaganda with a genuine potential to halt, change and reverse the direction of Western society as we know it today. The threat of this rebellion may be greater to the future of our state than either a polluted environment or nuclear destruction.[24]

Conclusion

Our institutions of education appear, in the long run, to operate as the most potent—or potentially influential—instruments of persuasion in modern society. In the USA, this persuasion is particularly important, because it is salted with traditions of serious idealism. Non-materialist (historically) in some of its major modes, schooling has become the talisman of political and social progress, as well as a practical device for the individual to achieve success, both materialistic and non-materialistic. Educational reform, how-

[22] *Ibid.*, edited from pp. 172–175.

[23] When one hears that a high school diploma is not worth what it was forty years ago, that a college degree means less than it did before World War II, and that professional and graduate schools are not producing the same calibre of MD's, Ph.D's, or Ed.D's that they once did, the observation is an indirect way of bemoaning objectively lower standards for completion of one or another curriculum. The true weight of the decline in standards often hides behind an enormous increase in school populations of the kind we have witnessed in recent years, and in an increase in the yearly number of diplomas and degrees handed out. This is educational inflation; diplomas and degrees are no more difficult to print than dollar bills, and are subject to the same sort of substantial devaluation.

[24] See Chapter 22 for further discussion of the problem of persuasion upon and from young people in contemporary life and its consequences.

ever, at the beginning of the present century brought the idealism of teachers and students closer to the pragmatics of social reality and, in many ways, polarized the objectives of schooling, leaving so-called "progressives" on one side and "basic education" exponents on the other.

Essential, however, to this and other controversies regarding educational persuasion is a clear perspective of the essentially ambivalent nature of the school as a cultural institution. While education must preserve tradition and act as a conservative force, it is also expected to stand at the vanguard of liberality and social change—or, at least, to provide the conceptual vision and instruments for that change in the person of graduates who have been, in some degree, radicalized.

At present, our schools seem to be more successful in the second function than in the first, but continual failure at both of these objectives must attend success at both, a paradox inherent in the educational process. Partly because he must somehow maintain a balance between these two, the teacher in our culture not only mediates persuasion but actually operates as a propagandist in most contemporary senses of the word. In addition to imparting knowledge and skills, teachers indoctrinate their pupils—from kindergarten to graduate school—with societal objectives, desiderata and values, either by precept or direct instruction.

Propaganda has an essential and useful role to play in effective modern education, greater for young students than older ones, and more fully in the dissemination of social controls than as instruments for rapid social change—as long as a consensus obtains concerning the maintenance of the basic structures of our current social and cultural institutions, particularly those which relate to technological life-styles in a free enterprise economy.

Educational propaganda is, unfortunately at present, out of phase with the rest of society in two ways. First, teachers and administrators usually show little awareness of their proper roles as instruments of cultural indoctrination and, accordingly, most of them, regardless of what they teach and to whom they teach it, are doomed to failure at this essential task. They are, in terms of understanding intention in communications, simply naïve. Second, teachers fail to apply realistic propaganda goals and persuasive techniques in their procedures, because they are also unaware of what places in the acculturative structures of contemporary education such persuasion is required, and in what directions it is supposed to lead their students. The result is an apparent communications gap between teachers and pupils on lower levels of schooling, and the inappropriate introduction of distortion and bias in much teaching on the college, graduate and professional levels. The total problem of misconceived and misdirected propaganda in our schools today is as serious a problem for the future of our state as any other in a mass society. It naturally relates intimately, also, to nearly all phases of life because of the tendency of schooling to influence the totality of culture in all its manifestations over long periods of time.

Chapter 10

NATIONS AND OTHER TERRITORIES

Man today is not safe in the presence of man. The old cannibalism has given way to anonymous action in which the killer and the killed do not know each other, and in which, indeed, the very fact of mass death has the effect of making the killing less reprehensible than the death of a single man.

Norman Cousins

WITHIN recent years, considerable speculation from various quarters has centered upon a phenomenon loosely called "territoriality," a word defined usually as, in one or another way, the attachment of organisms to particular territories.

Interest in the influence of territory, specifically, upon man's behavior (one major consideration of all environmental studies) goes back, of course, to antiquity. Man's fall from God's initial grace and original sin is associated with the removal of the first couple from the *territory* of paradise. Abraham shattered the idols in his father's house; but his discovery of God resulted in his defection from the *territory* of Ur. The fundamental quest of the ancient nomadic Hebrews was for a *territory* of their own—found once, then lost, seemingly irrevocably, and apparently regained in our own time. The wars of antiquity were usually, in part at least, territorial disputes. So were the schisms of the great religions from the abandonment of Mount Olympus by the Greek and Roman gods to the eventual sanctification of Rome, Mecca, Constantinople, Avignon, Palestine, and even London as holy places. Perhaps the greatest territorial series of events in Western history were the Crusades, adventures that destroyed much of the stability (including territorial stability) of the Middle Ages, and, in awakening the feeling of re-born classicism in the populace, set the stage for what, to date, has been the apotheosis of man's territorial inventions: the modern national state.

Territory, as understood in the West, is considered property, privately or publicly held. It, therefore, eons ago, became, for our ancestors, a personal, political, economic and spiritual object of utilization, depending upon the needs of their culture at the time. The ownership of land was (and is) often construed to be the prime unit of property to which the protective powers of government are enjoined in the interests of law and order. The territorial mystique was, for instance, one of the main binding elements that brought many of the seemingly incompatible interests of the original thirteen colonies together to form the United States, itself a territorial term. At the hands of later dynamic thinkers like Henry George, land would be viewed as *the* one ultimate, essential economic unit. And modern Georgists turn back to the Bible for justification of their unconventional view of history and commerce in maintaining, up to the present moment, that land is the fundamental unit of all economic activity.

It is within the wide ambit of the Georgist spirit, that modern men still frequently interpret the essence of ownership in terms of territory. Despite our general mobility, most of us feel a certain solidity about territory that we *own*, be it a cooperative apartment or a 50-by-100-foot city lot. Our place in the country may cost more, and be far less convenient and salubrious than, a yearly resort vacation, but that shack in the mountains is damn well *our* territory. Owners of large Texan ranches strut like caricature medieval barons on their sprawling territories—or burn up Lincoln Continentals or Cadillacs, exceeding speed limits, through *their* personal domains. Families in fiction and fact, in the plays of O'Neill, the novels of Edna Ferber or filmed sagas of depression era, anguish and argue over "the land," which they regard as extensions of their personal egos. When all else is gone, runs the cliché, the land remains.[1]

Published discussions of the influence on life of territory (some of which will be treated in the pages to come) have recently proliferated, most of them attempting to extenuate, usually by reference to the territorial habits of animals, many of our current social disturbances into the realm of theories of territory. The trend is justified by the observation that man's worst scourge, warfare, is similar to intra-specific aggressive behavior in animals that often appears to be related to their territorial instincts. Territorial ideas also seem to bear upon minority and urban ghetto problems, crime, delinquency and social anomie. In popular literature, particularly, analogies between animal behaviors and such human affairs, like those constructed by

[1] In the old American towns of New England and the South, old family names still mark the streets and avenues. But many of the families have departed. One will occasionally run into genuine descendants (usually grandchildren) of the original landowners, continuing to reside on old land in relative penury—partly because it is free, and partly because it is family land. They are not *Tobacco Road* peasantry; more likely, they are comfortably nestled in middle-class occupations that cannot support the old mansion, gardens, tennis courts, lakes and other opulent residue of the past. Occasionally, young offspring venture into the big cities, but the old homestead is waiting for them in case of failure or breakdown. Tennessee Williams has written knowingly about such people, implying strongly that such over-association with territory is a neurotic (and in some cases a psychotic) syndrome.

Robert Ardrey,[2] have called public attention to the issue, as has the publicity given the problems of population expansion and pollution, two of the safest social and political "do-good" causes on the market today. These latter, and similar social movements, are rooted in territorial matters and bespeak two *a priori* territorial values, generally beyond (and invulnerable to) consistent logical dispute: the sanctity of territory before it has been modified by man; and the need of every individual for a certain amount (rarely specified) of territory of his own. The resident devils here are ecological blight and crowding respectively, the virulence of which may be supported by selective historical and empirical evidence, and have thus become socially respectable evils.

Let us grant that all (or most) of man's territorial instincts or proclivities are psychological issues in the final summing up.[3] The Georgist myth of the sanctity of land is, however, sheer rot. Money, as much as soil, gives the modern individual room to swing his own peculiar cat. The laborers who build apartment buildings construct territory. And nature, as well as man, despoils territory. A square yard of a city with one working water spigot is worth a thousand square miles of desert without one—to most men. Nathan Leopold has discoursed beautifully upon the vistas of territory a fertile imagination may open for itself in the confines of a prison cell.[4] His experiences are provocative and revealing.

The *use* of territory is contingent upon many variables, and these constitute the critical elements of any territorial situation in which man is involved. Before and immediately after World War I, the motion picture moguls (having made, one presumes, a pact with Lucifer) bought for a song a lot of worthless real estate in southern California for the wrong reasons, in terms of their aims. Fifty years later, it had become some of the most valuable residential and industrial land in the world because of events that had nothing to do with movie making. When they drilled beneath its crust, they also frequently found oil and natural gas. The land changed, but the territory remained the same. And many of the descendents of the origi-

---

[2] Robert Ardrey, *The Territorial Imperative* (New York: Atheneum, 1967). Ardrey is a playwright with a flair for colorful prose who purports to have discovered all manner of social models in the animal behavior he has seen and/or read about. By carefully selecting observations and constructing fragile analogies about them, he has fabricated the kind of mystical non-fiction out of which best sellers are made. I personally prefer the more solid ghosts Ardrey once constructed in his thoughtful drama *Thunder Rock*, an excellent play, far ahead of its time.

[3] They will be discussed in this framework under the various psychological categories in which they belong in Part Three.

[4] See Nathan F. Leopold, *Life Plus 99 Years* (New York: Popular Library, 1958). Let me recommend this book to anyone interested in the psychological aspects of the deprived physical environments in prisons. Note especially pp. 102–115, and the continual battle by Leopold, a murderer condemned to prison for life (he thought), to utilize intelligence to extend the psychological dimensions of his incarceration, with almost unbelievable success.

nal investors have scattered to spend their fortunes elsewhere—some on the pseudo-territories of yachts or in the VIP lounges of the world's best airports. Consider also that the territory of a place like a "Hilton Hotel" exists apparently irrelevant to longitude or latitude. And young users of psychedelic drugs call their personal euphoria a "trip," presumably to a different territory bounded by the limits of the chemical reactions of their brain cells and individual talents for fantasy.

Territories, however, are also logical entities, land or water masses, bounded by genuine perimeters, rubbing usually against neighbors and subject to many delimitative expansions and contractions of human access.[5] No territory inhabited, even momentarily, by a human being lacks a potential psychological influence upon human dispositions. But logical elements of territory descriptively precede the psychological, and there is undoubtedly a wide spectrum of influence to which men are subject by the nature, size, and temporal constrictions of the territories in which they live—territories like countries, automobiles, airplanes, homes, offices, cities, highways, factories, rivers and oceans.

Nationalism: Inside Factors

In his study of the rise of contemporary repressive nations, Cassirer has shown clearly[6] how cultural pragmatics, human nature, primitive ritual and rite combine in numerous ways to transform shared territory into a political entity that eventually emerges as the corporate fiction of the state (or city or town or tribe), from and by means of which individuals achieve much of their sense of identity. The more clearly delimited the perimeters of personal behavior within such territories, and the more power used to exact conformity in them, the more stable any particular cultural unit appears, from an historical perspective. Stability is bought at the price of individual liberty in any culture, just as a sense of community is also purchased by limiting cultural differentiation and experimentation with it. Many of the chronic breakdowns we observe in contemporary society result, as Maurice

---

[5] The psychological extensions of territory do not apply only to humans, but to pets—like my various families of gerbils, for instance. My wife refuses to believe that the territory of an 8- by 14-inch cage may be increased enormously for its rodent occupants by, for instance, placing a treadmill in it. From our gerbils' point of view, access to yards of running space are thereby opened, and the animals' functional territory increases considerably. But my wife's concern for her pets is territorially limited by the macrocosm in which she lives. So she maintains that gerbils residing in such small spaces are crowded, true enough if they had no treadmill. The gerbils seem happy in the small space, as long as they have access to the treadmill. Deprived of it (and other toys which create new areas for them to poke about in), they become petulant, grumpy and bored, victims of territorial deprivation—nostalgia, I presume, for the wide Mongolian desert of their ancestors.

[6] See Ernst Cassirer, *The Myth of the State* (New York: Doubleday and Co., Inc., 1955), especially the anthropologically oriented summation and conclusions, pp. 348–375.

Stein has indicated, from the "fragmentation of social relations and the division of allegiances and affectations in our society," that produces in people a diminished sense of social responsibility, which may be the ultimate social cause of culturally deviant behavior. At two extremes, Stein notes, ". . . in primitive societies there are customary methods of dealing with . . . problems . . . of emotional adjustment by which they are externalized, publicly accepted and given treatment in terms of ritual beliefs. Society takes over the burden which, *with us*, falls entirely on the individual." [7]

The last sentence is critical. Primitive peoples, immigrants set apart by race, language or religion in physical or psychological ghettos, interdependent frontiersmen or conquering soldiers, among others, pool both their assets and liabilities and weaknesses and strengths for common welfare and protection. To this end, of course, individuality or eccentricity are forfeited for the common good. And impulses which press one toward nonconforming directions, as Stein indicates, are transmuted into certain common "rituals, symbols and rites" serving as crude social controls. As societies increase in complexity, and mutual interdependence seems (incorrectly) to be less critical for individual survival, these symbolic occurrences (most noticeably patriotism in its many manifestations) usually lose their ameliorative power. They diminish until an external event, usually in the form of warfare, natural disasters or epidemics, forces the citizenry to restimulate their dormant emotions of community.[8] Either this occurs or the state, whatever its political dispositions, disperses, decays or is consumed by another community and its cooperative nationalism.

Two *internal* viewpoints of the role of community in the life of the individual constitute viable dynamics for creating the climate for the sort of cultural persuasion we call, loosely, "nationalism." The first is anthropological (and anthropocentric) and explains, as Boaz, Benedict, Malinowski and numerous others have, how men act upon a specific environment to turn their own particular territory into a cooperative social unit, usually involving shared religion, laws, language, economy and other determinants

---

[7] Maurice R. Stein, *The Eclipse of Community* (Princeton, New Jersey, 1960), pp. 240–241. (Italics added.) Stein's review of sociological community studies, begins with those of Robert Park at the University of Chicago in the 1920's and continues to the present. His review of this labor clarifies many of the centrifugal and centripetal forces that are constantly at cross-purposes in binding people into communities and, at the same time, tearing them one from the one.

[8] When pressures to reformulate community occur in a territory that has been *permanently* and *artificially* torn asunder, the result is the intolerable kind of counterpoised love-hate relationships visible in the German nation (East and West) today, an apparently endless set of tensions that will be resolved only by the passage of generations, if ever. As a result, the two most horrible specters in Europe today are, in order probably, 1.) the possibility of a reunified East-West Germany, and, 2.) the continuation of the present schizoid Germany in the continental power struggle. See below for a re-affirmation of the persistence of German nationalism.

of life-styles. Because culture and society are, from this perspective, so obviously the *results* of collective human endeavor, it is assumed that even highly complex entities like the modern state, the city, the industrial complex or the cooperative farm, are, one and all, similar man-made devices and that the same general analytic principles apply to all of them.[9]

The tendency towards nationalism is therefore at root a sharing of common symbolism—usually spread within fixed geographical limits—manifest largely in personal *modi vivendorum,* irrelevant frequently to the forms of political or governmental control exercised upon a given society. Cubans were Cubans under Batista and Castro—and will be Cubans, should the present regime be overcome by a counter-revolution. Ukrainians were Ukrainians under the Czar, the Kerensky regime and Stalin. While nationalism appears frequently to be associated with various political factors, these are usually the last and least important persuasive impulses involving the love of territory in a citizen's life. Good examples of how similar roots of nationalism produce political flowers of different colors are Germany and Japan, our enemies in World War II. The political structures of both countries were all but destroyed after VE and VJ day, respectively, but neither German nor Japanese nationalism were eliminated, merely because two governmental structures tumbled. If anything, the common nationalistic symbols and bonds of each of these societies were *strengthened* by defeat and occupation, including the oppressive drain of Soviet hegemony in East Germany. Today, bifurcated German and unitary Japanese nationalism, including the force of patriotism in its numerous manifestations, is probably stronger than it has been at any time since the beginning of the present century.

Nationalism, however, is frequently confused with politics, the general belief being that patriotism is a political manifestation, an aspect of the common illusion that equates the values of the peoples of a culture with those demonstrated by their leaders, and with the political and governmental forms that they have approved by referendum or into which they have been coerced. Taking the Soviet Union today as an example,[10] one fre-

[9] Upon this assumption, sociologists and anthropologists have analyzed various facets of modern culture with differing degrees of success. Frederick Thrasher, Harvey Zorbough, Franklin Frazer, William Foote Whyte, Lloyd Warner and others approached, with pad and pencil, various corners of contemporary American society in precisely this spirit. Leo Rosten and Hortense Powdermaker assayed more-or-less anthropological studies of the natives of Hollywood, USA. Margaret Mead and Patricia Sexton currently buzz in and around ghettos and youth cultures in much the same manner. The results of such analyses, if they have accomplished little else, have provided copious reading matter (and filled the curricula) for university sociology and anthropology departments. These departments, in their turn, process graduates who generate more and similar studies. Some sort of higher purpose seems thereby to be served by all this activity. Its applications to social control have yet to be demonstrated.

[10] The observations below are based upon the slightly dated, but still relevant, study by Alex Inkeles, *Public Opinion In Soviet Russia* (Cambridge: Howard University Press, 1958), and numerous conversations I had with émigré Soviet scholars.

quently tends to equate nationalism in the USSR with Soviet governmental structure and political communism, although this is a largely unwarranted assumption. (It is, however, one central theme of much Soviet propaganda and international persuasion, based as it is upon a theme of ideological homogeniety among people of various national states, speaking different languages, living in different cultures and displaying different types of allegiances to their territories as remote as Lapland and as cosmopolitan as Greater Moscow.)

Only a minority of today's Soviet citizens are politically active, like most citizens of most nations. Of this minority, consistent political behavior (beyond voting) is rare—again, typically. Voting itself provides choices between different ideological stances, not only typical but invariable in most powerful modern nations including the USA. Many of the governmental choices made are beyond politics, that is, they are concerned whether bureaucrat A or bureaucrat B will administer present policy of a local or national agency, also typical. And failure to assent publicly, if necessary, to the general consensus of public opinion as defined by the ruling oligarchy constitutes a personal risk to one's livelihood and future, no matter what one's personal political feelings. In sum, the citizen of the Soviet Union may be a person of deep national commitment and feeling towards his territory. But he may also live continually and severely at odds with local and national governmental ideologies and practices.

Certainly, this state of affairs is common also in the United States. Some of our citizens with the deepest nationalistic feelings are also the most articulate critics of the President, Congress, the Supreme Court, state and local governments, military power and the influence of large corporations on American life. In fact, their criticisms of our institutions appears so extensive that they are frequently told to "go back where they came from." And slogans like "America, love it or leave it," may be hurled at them. The slogans miss the point that, in times of distress, such nay-sayers have often displayed (and some display today) most ardent forms of nationalistic behavior, signified by the significance with which they regard patriotic symbols. This is manifest, sometimes, by acts of defiling them, a most convincing form of symbol worship.[11]

The other (and second) major interior approach to nationalism views

---

[11] When a radical flies a flag upside down, or a personality like Abby Hoffman constructs an article of clothing out of the national banner, he is obviously affirming his belief in *that piece of cloth* as a symbol of a nation. If college students defile a statue of a long-dead general, they are affirming the symbolic relationship between that hero and the cause for which he fought. *The destruction of a symbol as a symbol (and not just a clearance project) demonstrates the acceptance of that symbol as a magical instrument, even if the ideology of the destroyer is entirely contrary to what the symbol stands for.* Symbols of all kinds will loose their power only when people are totally indifferent to them and treat them merely in terms of their intrinsic value. When a flag *becomes* just a piece of cloth, it, thereafter, *is* a piece of cloth, irrelevant to human feeling.

culture as *extrinsic* to individuals and operating as a determinative force *upon* them. This viewpoint is not so naïve as to construe culture as a spontaneous generation of nature—or even, necessarily, as a manifestation of some Jungian variety of collective unconscious—but it does not bear down heavily on the historical and environmental forces that have generated it. Rather than seek the roots of, and explanation for, the rituals, languages, symbols and rites that add up to a people's way of doing things, this *gestalt* is accepted *a priori*, and observational emphasis is directed instead upon how culture appears to influence the life styles of a given people in both subtle and dramatic ways.

One of the closest observers of this function of culture, fully deserving of the recent attention paid his work, is Edward T. Hall, an anthropologist with a wide range of interests in both those conventional aspects of culture studied by his fellow professionals and numerous other components of human interaction that they frequently ignore.[12] Perhaps the general direction of Hall's observations are best presented in his own words.

Basing his observations on the observation of linguistic cultural relativity described by Benjamin Lee Whorf and others, Hall first of all posits that "(e)xperience is something man projects upon the outside world as he gains it in its culturally determined form." [13] He continues:

> Until very recently, it was believed that the thing that every man shared with others regardless of culture was *experience*. Yet it now seems doubtful indeed that experience is shared or that there is a constant that one can call experience in terms of which everything can be judged or measured. All cultures, rather, can be said to be relative to each other on the pattern level. There is a growing accumulation of evidence to indicate that man has no direct contact with experience *per se* but that there is an intervening set of patterns which channel his senses and his thoughts, causing him to react one way when someone else with different underlying patterns will react as *his* experience dictates.[14]

---

[12] Hall's observations are well covered in his two major works, *The Silent Language* (Greenwich, Conn.: Fawcett Publications, Inc., 1959), a classic in its field, and a newer, less ambitious (but no less interesting) adumbration of his notions concerning the cross-cultural uses to which various people put space, *The Hidden Dimension* (New York: Doubleday and Co., Inc., 1969). Not only does Hall avoid the clichés and jargon of his colleagues, he displays an active and personal familiarity with the operative principles he discusses. The only weaknesses I have so far found in his conclusions are a few loose assumptions based on poor speculative leads from the Toronto Center for Culture and Technology, which specializes in loose assumptions. (See *ibid.*, pp. 80–81, concerning the supposedly primarily "visual" nature of art and the functions of man's "visual world." Any form of communication may be visual only insofar as, say, printing is visual, theatre is visual or radio drama is visual—which, of course, they all *may be* in a psychological sense, once one has eliminated the McLuhanesque cabal involving the word "visual.")

[13] Hall, *The Silent Language*, p. 111. (Italics in original removed.)

[14] *Ibid.*, p. 113.

In many ways, Hall's observations are not noticeably different from the now classical observations of Sapir in regard to the similarities and differences in the vocabularies of highly disparate cultures.[15] What Hall has accomplished, however, is to chart new vocabularies of communication in various societies, "cultural vocabularies," he calls them, of time usage, gesture, touch, dress, and, most convincingly, the vocabulary of space and its use in daily life, art and artifact.[16]

Perhaps wisely, and for all his astute observation, Hall comes to no earth-shattering, or particularly novel, conclusions about the force of culture upon the behavior of human beings, other than to observe that this impression is far more pervasive and subtle than commonly realized by conventional anthropologists. To Hall, the dimensions of cultural influences (and therefore cultural persuasion) are extremely broad and, it appears, function unconsciously in many covert aspects of human relationships. He uses the term "proxemics" to describe one critical aspect of this influence, the use of *space* as a "specialized elaboration of culture," [17] in Hall's words. To this end, he employs evidence from a variety of sources, the most convincing of which employ direct observation, literature and fine art. The least convincing are the arbitrary (and highly suspect) findings of experimental psychologists he cites, as well as analogies fabricated between human and animal behavior and habits—one pathway, frequently, to Hades in the behavioral sciences.

The web of communication that he exposes is an impressive one. It appears to offer its greatest challenge to the cultural lexicographer who, like Hall, is competent to utilize his specialized training and developed perceptions to determine *what* the proxemic differences in various societies are, what common institutions of culture they relate to and what regularities one can discern, to the end that this will provide for his method of inquiry a predictive value.

Hall's observations, which he obviously enjoys charting, illustrating, listing and diagramming, are not unlike the so-called "structural" cultural

---

[15] G.N.G., *L C*, pp. 43–44. Note also George Steiner's observation in *Language and Silence* (New York: Atheneum, 1967, p. 15), "Between verbal languages, however remote in setting and habits of syntax, there is always the possibility of equivalence, even if actual translation can only attain rough and approximate results." This is apparently quite the opposite of the conclusions of Whorf and Sapir that stimulated Hall to his studies of non-linguistic cultural interaction. Sapir, however, first observed this dual proclivity of verbal communication many years ago, but this particular insight has generally been overlooked.

[16] *The Hidden Dimension* is largely devoted to these latter concerns. The significance of the use of space as a method of communication is best indicated by Hall's observation that twenty per cent of the English words listed in the pocket Oxford dictionary (or more than 5,000 entries) "could be classified as referring to space." He writes, "Even deep familiarity with my own culture had not prepared me for this discovery." (P. 93.)

[17] *Ibid.*, p. 1.

methods of Claude Lévi-Strauss that have achieved considerable notice in recent years, and will influence cross-cultural exploration even more deeply in the decades to come. Steiner has written of Lévi-Strauss' approach in general (bypassing its most sophisticated subjective methodological novelties), "Lévi-Strauss has elaborated the view that all cultural phenomena are a language. Hence the structure of human thought and the complex totality of social relations can be studied best by adopting the methodologies and discoveries of modern linquistics . . ." [18] Lévi-Strauss regards all culture "as a code of significant communication and all social processes as a grammar . . ." [19] These observations might apply directly to Hall's investigations as well, with as much direct relevance as to their intended object, the work of Lévi-Strauss.[20]

By means of their clear exposition of the communication of various near invisible facets of cultural agreement (non-verbal languages of time, space and behavior), Hall, Lévi-Strauss and others have provided for the student of persuasion the skeleton of a mystery story by means of a closely woven fabric of clues (or, at least, specific instruction of where and how to look for the clues) that promises to reveal how bonds of behavior may unite organisms—animals as well as men—to specific territories and environments. The clues center also upon the adjustments in special relationships organisms agree upon, or are forced to accept, by some quasi-instinctual pattern, in order that their species and/or particular sub-cultural units survive. What exponents of cultural investigation, fashionably named "structural," offer us is a procedural scenario, less distinguished by present content or cleverness of insight than its promise for those trained to observe social interactions in new (and perhaps, as yet, undiscovered) ways, and from new vantage points. Whatever its outcome, this approach has already evolved a fascinating human puzzle that has not yet, to any major degree, been solved. Neither the victims, the detectives nor the culprits have even been clearly identified.

Proxemics and its allied studies cut close to the quick of nationalism. Local, regional or national feeling (and the behaviors that result from it,

---

[18] Steiner, *op. cit.*, p. 241.

[19] *Ibid.*, p. 242.

[20] Hall's methods are related to similar investigations by James J. Gibson on perception and optics, many of the speculation of ethnologist Konrad Lorenz and the work of John B. Calhoun, Gregory Bateson, Erving Goffman, Robert Sommer, R. Buckminster Fuller (naturally) and others, including numerous specialists on the social habits of muskrats, owls, canaries, deer, hares, fish, dogs, rats, gulls, hawks, walruses, crabs, monkeys, cockroaches and swans. For an amusing overview of current attempts to discover regularities in "body English," by means of the so-called science of "kinesics," and the work, mostly, of R. Birdwhistell, A. E. Sheflen and A. Kendon, see the article "The Way We Speak 'Body Language' " in *The New York Times Magazine*, May 31, 1970, pp. 8–9, 29, 31, 32, 34, 41–42, and Birdwhistel's *Kinesics and Context* (Philadelphia: University of Pennsylvania Press, 1970.)

including those that are institutionalized) are probably extrapolated from "silent languages" or "hidden dimensions" that bind together people with similar cultural experiences, or which set apart those born and raised with different experiential vocabularies. From this investigational stance, the assumption that personal and social adoptive patterns are generalized into institutional forms, both pragmatic and symbolic, appears valid, although the main emphasis of studies such as Hall's appears to center on the opposite relationship: the determinism of a culture upon the mind-lives and value systems of individuals born and raised in it.

In either case, nationalism is the objectification of the understandings between individuals that usually remain unspoken and are most frequently noticed when an individual travels from his territory (large or small) to another one. A city dweller in the north of the USA is, therefore, almost inevitably aware, not only of the cultural lexicon from which he is excluded when he visits, for instance, the rural south, but also his own social givens and values that are useless to him in a "foreign" environment. The greater the cultural distance in terms of language, mores, climate and general life style, the more acute, usually, will one's awareness be of the impress of his native culture upon himself, both overt and covert. Most travelers perceive this pressure as discomfort; some few enjoy, or even thrive on it. The majority adapt to the change by modification of their own behaviors with surprisingly little difficulty, if they are normal and the cultural change has been voluntary. Otherwise, one is forced to search out others who understand one's invisible vocabulary and, as in the instance of American military or corporate personnel abroad, form either official or spontaneous colonies of similarly acculturated individuals in which the many languages (including the verbal) of home are spoken, and in which the alienated stranger may feel at ease.[21]

---

[21] Americans who have shared my experience of relative isolation in parts of the globe where few—if any—fellow Americans reside or visit, know how hungrily one meets and shares the company of a passing countryman, even if the two of you have little in common and would certainly have remained strangers had you met on home ground. Some foreign nationals remain forever isolated and, literally, alienated from their new territory for many reasons. One carefully studied group of such aliens is the host of victims of Hitler's concentration camps who were admitted to the United States after World War II. The shock and disorientation of their prison experiences, their unusual personally felt guilts concerning their survival, and their hostility towards the Americans (particularly American Jews) who had been spared Nazi barbarism all tend to isolate these unfortunate individuals into withdrawn and sometimes near-psychotic states. They are prevented, psychologically, from submission to the life style and value vocabularies of an existence of freedom, much less permissive culture they discover in the United States. See Henry Krystal (ed.), *Massive Psychic Trauma* (New York: International Universities Press, Inc., 1968), for a symposium on these unfortunates, as well as the survivors of the atomic bombing of Hiroshima.

Nationalism: Outside Factors

In 1967 a document of considerable significance was published, written (probably) by Leonard C. Lewin.[22] It was intended as a joke, a spoof and a satire, apparently to serve a number of purposes, among them imitation of the deadly style of boondoggle studies and think-tank seminars of organizations such as the Rand Corporation. The *Report* is an immediate reminder that in the past years we have spent millions of dollars (most of them tax loot) on simulated fights, games and debates, and "systems approaches" to social, economic and cultural problems. In short, the book ribs, in deadpan style, the obvious ludicrous attempts through which we have been recently living to apply human intellect to subtle and enduring human problems by the positivistic arbiters of the "human" sciences—some sociologists, psychologists, economists and historians sitting high on the academic hog on various university campuses, investigatory commissions, and "task forces," the latter a new term from the vocabulary of high level trivia.

The other main purpose of the *Report* was to demonstrate how high level planning, devoid of moral or spiritual guidance or purpose, might be employed (by various scholars in the disciplines noted above) to defend not only the inevitability of warfare between states, but specific economic, political, social, cultural and scientific *benefits* that warfare produces for mankind. After a discussion of the inadequacy of any sort of contemporary substitutes for these beneficial functions, the document lapses off into the jargon of "suggestion for further programs of social adjustment" of our institutions (in maximum social benefits) by means of the continuation of controlled carnage, carefully directed by readouts from computer studies.

Meant as example of reduction to absurdity, Lewin's *Report* also serves other functions, some of them, perhaps, not intended by the author. While his humor is, in its quiet way, extremely wise, it does not seem to produce in the reader (or in reviewers) the intensity of shock of other far more modest proposals—Swift's suggestion that the Irish eat their babies, for instance. What it points to, on the contrary, is the affirmation of the entirely acceptable notion that territorial allegiances—nationalism, in the case of large-scale hostilities—is an inevitable precursor of abrasions between territories. That this friction, the collective extension of the very genre of cultural dissonances described by Hall, Mead, Whorf and numerous others, will *inevitably lead to* conflict of an extraordinary and eventually

[22] Anonymous, *Report from Iron Mountain on the Possibility and Desirability of Peace* (New York: Dial Press, Inc., 1967). This short book contains introductory material by Lewin, who, supposedly, was given the ensuing document by a professor involved in the preparation of the suppressed report, the security implications of which Lewin pretends to be more agitated about than the report itself. The entire document, however, evidently sprang from the mischievous cerebellum of Lewin, and—except for the occasional shocks of pain as it cuts close to reality—is delightful, poker-faced, contemporary satirical humor, in some ways, to quote Shaw, "Too true to be good!"

disasterous nature, appears justified, not only by history but the laws of logic and anthropological and sociological evidence of many kinds as well.[23]

This chilling concept may not only be underscored by the satirist's pen, rationalized or contained intellectually in myriad ways—Pangloss' advice to Candide to "cultivate your garden" is a common and effective one—it may also evoke the selective examination of the so-called "facts" of history that demonstrate that lethal combat between territories has been, in some ways, a progressive force and (at present) a deterrent from even greater evils for mankind in general than warfare.

Stanislov Andreski, an English sociologist, has compiled an impressive list[24] of the benefits that war has wrought for civilization. By combining some tribes into larger states, warfare may have had a good deal to do with the development of civilization itself. He notes that war has served as a spur to industrialization, collective government, democracy *de facto*, as well as a stimulus to technological inventions and innovations, too long, complex and irrefutably related to armed combat and peaceful use to repeat in detail. In some ways, arguments like Andreski's merely find rationales for phenomena that presently exist in culture, select the positive and excludes the negative. Famine, disease, crime, divorce, suicide, narcotics, alcohol addiction and every other form of human perfidy may be examined in terms of selected results, results which have led to *some* form (or forms) of benign social by-products or aspect of progress. The game is an ancient one. But the cogency of such observations provide, if merely because of their currency in the market of ideas today, some measure of the expectations that men believe their territorial habits will yield, in probable consequences, for the future. Few adults alive today are probably unaware of the risk of atomic slaughter and what the maintenance of nationalistic patterns of societal behavior entails. They seem willing, nevertheless, to accept counterbalances to this threat in arguments remarkably like those of Andreski. They also accept fictions concerning such obvious failures at keeping the peace as the United Nations, and take as reasonable bizarre reconstructions in present contexts of the games of war as played centuries ago by professional armies. These notions, repeated daily in newspapers and weekly in magazines, indicate the degree to which territorial determinisms are presently felt as *essential* to the maintenance of *all* other persuasive social forces

---

23 In man's history, he has been at peace only one year out of fifteen, on the average. Since World War II, I have been informed, more than thirty local wars have broken out on our planet. Over twenty million people are involved in military occupations at present. And the virulence of war is also increasing: During the nineteenth century nearly four million people were murdered in warfare. So far, in the seventy-first year of the twenty-first century, the total is already close to one hundred million.

24 *Time*, March 9, 1970, pp. 46–47. Other thinkers such as Herbert Spencer, Ludwig Gumplowicz, Jerome D. Frank, and Gaston Bouthoul have (and do) share a number of the ideas proposed by Andreski.

treated in the preceding chapters; namely, technology, mass culture, consumerism, politics and school, to say nothing of the focus of the next chapter: the will to religious conviction. Could we really imagine how any (or all) of these forces might operate today as they do (or as we imagine they should) unconstricted by nationalistic imperatives and controls?

One near insane example of the intensity of territorial obsession is contained in the paradigmatic nationalistic notion is demonstrated in the following report, printed verbatim from a national news magazine. While it might find its most interested readership among a group of psychiatrists, the territorial assumptions it bespeaks, and the extenuations of nationalistic impulses inherent in it, are, in some ways, more eerie than Lewin's deadpan assault on war psychology:

> Several hundred million peasants will rise like a mighty storm, a force so swift and violent that no power, however great, will be able to hold it back.
>
> —Mao Tse-tung, March, 1927
>
> Was the Chairman prescient? Could he have anticipated by more than four decades an ingenious scheme just conceived by University of Alaska Geophysicist David Stone? If Mao had carried his maxim a little farther, says Stone in a tongue-in-cheek letter to *Geotimes*, China could have threatened distant enemies with mass destruction years before the development of nuclear warheads and long-range missiles.
>
> If at a given moment, says Stone, all 750 million Chinese obeyed a command to jump from 6½ ft. platforms, they could constitute a "geophysical weapon." How? Assuming that the average Chinese weighs 110 lbs., he calculates, the energy released by this great leap downward would be equivalent to an earthquake of magnitude 4.5 on the Richter scale, causing extensive damage in China. But if the Chinese were organized to jump roughly every 54 minutes—just when the peak of a barely perceptible natural ripple that continually sweeps around the earth's surface passes through China—they might set up a world-girdling resonant ground wave that would cause even greater damage in distant lands. By properly aligning their millions and carefully timing the jump, for example, Peking could aim a ground wave along the Pacific-rim earthquake belt and possibly set off quakes in California far more devastating than the original shocks in China.
>
> Would there be any defense? Certainly, says Stone. By having its population jump between the peaks of the ground waves stirred up by China, a threatened nation could damp them out before they grew intense enough to cause damage. There is one catch: the target nation would, of course, be less populous than China. Thus, to effectively counteract the massive Chinese geophysical aggression, its people would have to jump from higher platforms.[25]

[25] *Time*, December 19, 1969.

A certain *über*-reasonableness attends the picture the item above conjures up, the thought, particularly, of every inhabitant on earth jumping periodically from a fixed height at various prescribed intervals in order to prevent the planet from eventually cracking into fragments. In his way, the Alaskan physicist responsible for this morsel of insight provides an excellent metaphor for the externally oriented picture of relationships between territorial units, particular nations that periodically display hostility one towards the other in the form of armed combat. By the date of the Great Jumping War, which should end the game forever, our earth's population will have resolved itself into the two focal components of national hostility: man and his own bit of territory—and, of course, a suitably adjustable platform.

The extrinsic versus the intrinsic view of territorial nationalism, however intense, and applied to whatever sized territory, highlights the *dual logical function* of nationalistic persuasion or patriotism or territorial loyalty (or any other name it is given). On one hand, the silent language of culture provides an educational vocabulary that unites men in common endeavors; provides defenses against natural and man-made disaster; produces many economies of effort by processes of sharing and specialization; prevents the need for each generation to derive anew the values, morals and techniques that make the environment livable; and—most important—in complex civilizations appear to provide a wide range for personal freedom, individuality, self-expression and creativity, consonant with the general welfare of society. In most of these manifestations, for most of the time, these are productive functions that offer reasonable chances for healthy, meaningful life to a majority of members of a given culture. If the latter do not grasp what is offered them, the responsibility is their own and not the system's, although it is the rare individual who is willing to admit that his personal discontents are of his own devising, preferring to extenuate his miseries into (or onto) existing socio-political structures.[26]

As we examine various territories around the world (past and present), the same dynamics perform numerous similar functions (from an extrinsic point of view), primarily in stabilizing the unique ways that people of apparently different pheno- and genotypes have adapted to different sorts of environments and managed to survive for considerable lengths of time in these locations. They have also permitted the development of extrinsic entities such as national states, that, by means of anthropomorphic personification, have evolved diplomatic channels and foreign policies to deal with one another, that, up to the present, have worked much of the time to

---

[26] This tendency, it seems to me, has reached an all-time high at the present writing, taking the form of ubiquitous student protests, so-called "peace" movements and the most interesting sight of all: the Women's Liberation Movement, a fascinating contemporary political projective device. See Chapter 21 for further details about the latter crusade.

avoid conflicts and maintain generally felicitous interterritorial relations.[27] Territorial imperatives yield various forms of nationalism that reason tells us are not incompatible with one another. Sometimes, reason has been correct.

We stumble at this point, however, upon the major deception that attends the persuasive powers of nationalism, and one that may rapidly be taking our planet to the brink of destruction. It is the myth—taught now as truth in schools and colleges around the world—that increased communication, better understanding and the ideal of a community of extrinsically different forms of nationalism (performing vastly different functions) will somehow achieve peace and prevent warfare in those specific cases in which *quite the reverse is likely, in fact, to occur.*

Because the writer has already discussed this canard in this volume (and elsewhere), the realistic intelligence of the late C. Wright Mills may, in the present reference, serve the argument better than his own words.

Writes Mills,[28] "(R)ecently, psychologists and anthropologists have ascribed war to 'misunderstandings between peoples' or, more sophisticatedly, to 'the tensions arising from differences in national character.' This is a very old view, although it now masquerades in the garb of social science."

Mills notes that the facile fiction has been widely espoused that wars are actually intercultural "misunderstandings," and "that peace is a matter of rationally convincing enough of the public that war is absurd." To hold such a view, he maintains, is to misread the role of public opinion and popular action in the destiny of nations. "It is," he notes "part of the nationalist trap"—as we have noted, an apparent extension of the findings of those who focus their thinking only upon internal cultural vocabularies that *bind* individuals *within* a culture together, far different from those forces that permit various cultures to survive side by side.

"Increased understanding," Mills notes, "may just as well lead to more intelligent hatred as to greater love. To have understood better the Nazi character and outlook would not necessarily have led to avoidance of war with the Nazis. Better understanding between peoples does not result in, much less determine, changes in the policies of their respective élites," that is, individual representatives of the anthropomorphic state.

Why then does extrinsic friction between cultures produce warfare? Mills' answer is uncomfortably familiar but, as yet, apparently unheeded by

---

[27] For two clear statements of the United States' successes and failures at this form of interchange discussed simply and directly, see the short volumes, Walter Lippmann, *U. S. Foreign Policy* (Boston: Little Brown and Co., 1943), and George F. Kennan, *Realities of American Foreign Policy* (New Jersey: Princeton University Press, 1954).

[28] C. Wright Mills, *The Causes of World War III* (New York: Simon and Schuster, 1958). The following quotes, direct and indirect, are taken from pp. 75–80 of Chapter 12, "On Psychological Causes," one of the genuinely provocative short essays, in my opinion, written in recent times on the nature and wellsprings of warfare.

the molders of opinion and persuasion in most places on our globe, neither more nor less in the USA than anywhere else:

> The issues of war and peace cannot be melted down into a naïve psychology of "peace through better understanding among peoples." It is not the aggression of people in general but their mass indifference that is the point of their true political and psychological relevance to the thrust of war. It is neither the "psychology of peoples" nor raw "human nature" that is relevant; it is the moral insensibility of people who are selected, molded, and honored in the mass society . . .
>
> As it concerns the thrust toward war, this indifference is best seen as moral insensibility: the mute acceptance—or even unawareness—of moral atrocity; the lack of indignation when confronted with moral horror; the turning of this atrocity and this horror into morally approved conventions of feeling. By moral insensibility, in short, I mean the incapacity for *moral* reaction to event and to character, to high decision and to the drift of human circumstances.[29]

Mills then lists such events as saturation bombing in World War II, Hiroshima, Nagasaki, Auschwitz and other symbols of contemporary dehumanization. But more recent atrocities may also be noted here: the Songmy massacre in Vietnam, virtual concentration camps for displaced Arabs, police harassment in the USA of Black Panthers, common conspiracy in high places to permit our syndicated traffic in heroin, the near paralysis of American education by well-duped students and teachers, border incidents in Manchuria, war crimes trials (in Germany and Israel, mainly) that pile vengeance upon atrocity, and a dreary list of contemporary cruelties with which we have learned to live, horrible less because they involve mass torture and murder than because they are so commonplace.

From the external perspective, the wages of territoriality and nationalism and its consuming persuasion are obvious. Mills says correctly, "In the expanded world of mechanically vivified communications the individual becomes the spectator of everything but the human witness of nothing . . . It is not the number of victims or the degree of cruelty that is distinctive (of our time); it is the fact that the acts committed and the acts that nobody protests are split from the consciousness of men in an uncanny, even schizophrenic manner."

Perhaps today (a dozen years after these sentences were written) the words "nobody protests" might be replaced by "nobody seems to have the remotest understanding of," because active and *mindless* protest is becoming the order of the day. It accomplishes little (if anything) and produces a new spectacle of meaninglessness and idiotic moral insensibility carried to vigorous extremes. The schizophrenia, however, remains; and atrocities multiply, populations expand and murder continues, including now increas-

---

[29] *Ibid.*, p. 77.

ingly generally legal license to abort fetuses who are not yet, after all, quite human creatures—rather like Jews to some, Negros to others.

If only out of fear, one suspects, our national territories may be safer at this instant than they have ever been in recent history, although we live in a time of constant personal cruelty and peril. Nor are sudden changes in this treacherous equilibrium to be anticipated. For, in the end, after we have gone, the territory will probably remain to tell its story, somehow, to our children's children's children.

Conclusion

In spite of recent popular interest in the territorial imperatives to which man appears subject (interest drawn largely from the study of animal behavior), the relationships of people to the portion of the earth they inhabit has interested students of collective behavior from many disciplines for countless generations. Economic theories like those of Henry George have today been replaced by psycholgically oriented efforts of naturalists and others to arrive at new perceptions into the behavior of contemporary national states, largely with in hopes of shedding some light upon aggression which interaction between these states appears inevitably to generate.

Studies of the internal dynamics of culture reveal many unsuspected results, in terms of a rich language of mediation of value and conduct by means of the manipulation of territory. The recent study of "proxemics," with its elaborate lexicon of sensual vocabularies, represents a beginning into the examination of the basic structure (by subtle cultural anthropological data) of a given society. The mediation of this structure may be viewed in one (or both) of two ways: either as the developmental vocabularies of men, interacting with their environments creating instruments for survival; or as the investigation of how given cultural determinants act upon a population to create their own national, cultural or sub-cultural identities. Both approaches are viable and rest upon the assumptions and conclusions of classical cross-cultural anthropology. But the amount and kinds of data available today for such speculation are increasing at a steady rate.

The external dynamics of territory are bound up with the concept of national states, and lead to consideration of the manner in which such entities, speaking by means of diplomatic channels and élite representatives, seem forever to hurl themselves into positions demanding the tragic solution of a war. This eventuality produces a victor and loser, and thereby, apparently, it eliminates the conflict. Warfare as a super-cultural institution has had its defenders whose arguments are carried to absurdity by the present potential of munitions competent to destroy the sovereignty of the very national state it has been employed to protect.

Common palliatives for ending warfare are, it appears, based upon shallow and demonstrably ineffective assumptions, particularly the notion that mutual understanding between nations or territories has anything to do with preventing hostility between them. The problem of warfare is, at heart, a moral one, in the sense that most cultures today seem to have abandoned moral idealism (if they ever maintained it) in favor of an insensibility that permits a population merely the selective political support of "right" platforms. One must therefore reject the "wrong" ones, no matter how unmoral or immoral the right, and humane the wrong. People who wear moral blinders are probably as, or more dangerous than, people who are morally blind, and therefore the inevitability of war in our time is not a likelihood. It is a present reality, a future inevitability and part of the history of the past twenty-five years.

It is deceptively simple to state that men should have learned better than this by virtue of their unfortunate past experiences. Nations and other territories, it is becoming increasingly clear, provide an overwhelmingly ubiquitous form of cultural persuasion (or determinism)—whether manifest in patriotism or rebellion matters little—varying from territory to territory, but potent far beyond utility or reason and, inevitably, far beyond hope or despair as well. But, to paraphrase a current slogan, this is our world. We must love it or leave it, a teleological choice that the fates have already made for each of us.

Chapter 11

MERCHANTS OF GOD

Perhaps the greatest solace in religion is the sense that one lives in the Presence of an Other.

R. D. Laing

How curious that one may, in today's scientific-technological culture, identify religion as an institution of such socio-cultural power as to merit, on its face, inclusion in the section of a volume concerning the main logical (and therefore institutional) forces at work in the contemporary world. Less important is the fact that the author has left it until last in this section for discussion—a reflection, perhaps, of an unconscious awe or desire for unity and balance in the concluding chapter of Part Two.

The history and drift of Western thought might lead an historian (from outer space) to predict that the power of religion (or at least the power of churches) over the minds of men should have diminished progressively from the invention of the scientific method to the present. It seems reasonable that, as occurrences once ascribed to the power of God were explained by natural laws, the influence of the idea of the will of God in nature—including the affairs of man—would diminish slowly, lessen and eventually disappear.

The pragmatist might answer that the main reason that this has not occurred, and that religion is still a potent force in the West, is that the scientific method has not explained yet the basic significant phenomena of nature with a high degree of precision: mainly the origins and purposes of life, the meaning of death and the nature of human consciousness.

The pragmatist would be partially right, partially wrong. The scientific method *has* brought us a long way in explaining *exactly these phenomena,* but not in the same terms of explanation employed in all religions that refer causes and purposes in man and nature to mystical forces. Mysticism cannot be explored profitably or explained by scientific methodologies. The positivists of the past have called it "irrelevant" to their concerns. But modern science is now demonstrating that it is *less* than entirely irrelevant, but not always or immediately relevant either. Much of what was once regarded as mysticism is now frequently viewed as actual components of non-deterministic macro and/or microscopic worlds that our new scientific sensors, methods and instruments of analysis have opened for us, nowhere more interestingly, for instance, than in the study of genetics (the "communication system" of life) and neurology (the "pulse" of life), but also in physics, chemistry and astronomy.[1] Much of the knowledge—and many of the insights—that science is now unfolding have neither been reduced to non-specialized parlance or communicated effectively to the public, but this is probably a temporary situation. Should the public discover what is indeed known about the essential nature of life and matter (beyond the feature story level of discourse that usually concerns technologies years behind the progress of science), it is doubtful that much impression would be made by this knowledge either on most people's belief in God or on the function of the church in our society.

A more germane, but less pragmatic, argument is the one advanced by Pierre Teilhard de Chardin, a Jesuit biologist whose ideas have never been popular either in the scientific community or in his own church. Wrote Father Teilhard:

> To outward appearance, the modern world was born of an anti-religious movement: man becoming self-sufficient and reason supplanting belief. Our generation and the two that preceded it have heard little but talk of the conflict between science and faith; indeed it seemed at one moment a foregone conclusion that the former was destined to take the place of the latter . . .
>
> But, inasmuch as the tension is prolonged, the conflict visibly seems to need to be resolved in terms of an entirely different form of equilibrium —not in elimination, nor duality, but in synthesis. After close to two centuries of passionate struggles, neither science nor faith has succeeded in discrediting its adversary. On the contrary, it becomes obvious that neither can develop normally without the other. And the reason is simple: the same life animated both. Neither in its impetus nor its achievements can

[1] Popular books on scientific subjects dealing with these matters tend to be dangerously misleading, and there are few that I recommend. Philip Wylie does creditably in *The Magic Animal*, but certain specialized volumes handle the problem of the outer limits of modern knowledge better, if less interestingly. See A. N. Whitehead, *Science and the Modern World* (New York: The New American Library, 1953), on the physical world; P. B. Medawar, *The Future of Man* (New York: The New American Library, 1957), on genetics; and José M. R. Delgado, *Physical Control of the Mind* (New York: Harper and Row, Publs., 1969), on neurology and consciousness.

science go to its limits without becoming tinged with mysticism and charged with faith.[2]

Teilhard's conjunction of "reason and mysticism" would seem to the positivist, of course, just mere mysticism, the latter engulfing the former with its amoeboid proclivity to swallow everything that comes near it, because the less structured a religion is, the more competent its disciples are to apply it to great congeries of motley phenomena.[3]

This is the central objection to the fusion of religion and science, voiced today by many working scientists and technologists who, from their work-a-day viewpoints, cannot see a relationship between their universe and the mystic's impetus. Nor, for that matter, can the followers of Ernst Mach, or the contemporary school of British linguistic philosophers who often seem peculiarly bitter and sensitive about what they regard as the anti-scientism of thinkers like Teilhard.

The Functions of Religious Belief

That religion survives today (begging the question, for now, of God's immediate health), despite what William James calls[4] the *je m'en fichisine* of analysts as witty and deft as Joseph Renan in the past century, and Sigmund Freud in this one, is little short of amazing, especially considering that profound directive role that the latter's other enthusiasms and anti-enthusiasms have played in the United States. The father of psychoanalysis' attack on what he called the "illusion" was quite specific and characteristically heavy handed. "I believe," he wrote, . . . "that when he personifies the forces of nature, man is once again following an infantile prototype. He has learnt from the persons of his earliest environment that the way to influence them is to establish a relationship with them, and so, later on, with the same end in view, he deals with everything that happens to him as he dealt with those persons." [5] Religion is thus neurosis, and, as Freud

[2] Pierre Teilhard de Chardin, *The Phenomenon of Man* (New York: Harper and Brothers, 1959), p. 283.

[3] If one compares the Eastern religions with the Western ones, the practical advantage of loose structure becomes apparent immediately, particularly in regard to Hinduism with its "many paths to the same summit." In this respect, the molders of the Judeo-Christion tradition were less realistic than the more protean Easterners, a difference in cultural perspective which may be more critical for the modern world in fifty-or-so years (after the Far Eastern religions have been more fully secularized, a process already begun to Mao Tse-Tung) than it is today. See Huston Smith, *The Religions of Man* (New York: The New American Library, 1958).

[4] William James, *Varieties of Religious Experience* (New York: The New American Library, 1958). p. 46–47. If one book on the universality of religion is essential to an understanding of most aspects of men's relationships to his deities, this is the one. It was originally published in 1902.

[5] Sigmund Freud, *The Future of An Illusion* (Garden City, N.Y.: Doubleday and Co., Inc., 1957), pp. 35–36. In all fairness to Freud's memory, it should be noted that this bitter and frequently bewildering book was written extremely late in his

states, "by accepting the universal neurosis, he (man) is spared the task of forming a personal neurosis." [6] The illusion of God is therefore not only a sickness, but, in large measure, also the palliative for the disease it causes, something, one supposes, like a homeopathic drug in a psychoanalytic context. Other mechanisms of the same sort exist in psychoanalytic theory; in fact, neurosis itself may be construed as a dual mechanism, both the sickness and cure of a psychologically intolerable state, and therefore difficult to dispel because of the equilibrium it frequently finds in the individual.

To Freud, the religious neurosis is, in this respect, no different from any other neurosis, merely more important because of its historical effect and immediate hold upon the minds of men. That Freud himself was ambivalent towards religion is evident in many of his essays, in many ways no more specifically than in the weary, guilty, almost apologetic tones in which he discusses the illusion of God in his last years, apparently in spite of his own better judgment at times. He notes carefully that men prefer illusion to reality, and that the destruction of illusions does not necessarily yield better *men* in the end.

This insight is a fine and important one concerning the role of religion as a persuasive force upon the dispositions of people. What Freud could not see in his final period of summing up, of course, was that psychoanalytic theory was to become shortly, in large measure, a deterministic philosophy itself, to be carried in implication far beyond the predictive and descriptive aspirations of its founder.[7] But here is the result of the extension of all determinisms into the social fabric of society, save, of course, deistic determinisms: *that a world view which excludes the function of a supernatural must therefore consign that supernatural to the function of diversion, illusion or hypnotic device, and assume unto itself some of the functions which religion classically served in society.* Certainly, this is true of psychoanalytic determinism, which now centers on the worship of Freud himself as the father of the cult and the roles of his priests, disciples and saints,

career and life, when he was in the throes of his terminal illness and after he had fled his beloved Vienna for the bleak aspects of London, British weather and English cooking. While it is popular with many contemporary Freudians and neo-Freudians, this essay is not characteristic of the master's usual sense of engagement, zest and consistent reasoning, although its intention as a final statement on the part of a devout atheist is unmistakable—and brave.

[6] *Ibid.*, p. 79.

[7] See Richard La Piere, *The Freudian Ethic* (New York: Dell, Sloan and Pearce, 1959), for a study of what becomes of a theory when it is transmuted first into a pseudo-law, second into a deterministic philosophy and finally into criteria for ethical behavior. I think La Piere carries his anti-Freudian case too far in this book, indicting Freudians for many contemporary problems for which they are blameless. But the volume is recommended as the rarely stated case against the general uncritical acceptance of Freudian theory in the United States, particularly, and the way in which the psychoanalytic vision of life has influenced many of our institutions in dubious ways with strange results.

various heretics, and the ceremonies (therapy itself) by which novices are indoctrinated in the priesthood.

To follow similar trends in Marxism is unnecessary; the fiction of the opiate of the masses has been told too many times. The story has not been told often enough, however, concerning the metapolitics of Houston Chamberlain and his best known follower, Adolph Hitler, but this is not the place to tell it, merely to note in passing the cultural similarities of *all* determinisms (particularly those derived from Hegel) as persuasion.[8]

As far as the author recalls, in fact, no political, social or psychological deterministic stance has yet been evolved which, in its application to groups of people, does not generate a metaphysic—or, to be more specific, does not deal eventually in spiritual and religious-ceremonial matters that usually become central to its own welfare, and, by extension, the welfare of the people at large. And this observation includes determinisms of a subcultural nature like those involved in General Semantics, Black Power, Alcoholics Anonymous, partisan politics, cults of youth, Progressive Education, Women's Liberation, and the Shriners, to mention a few.

From a cross-cultural orientation, James has given us[9] a summary of the characteristics of religious belief that ramify into any social order and that appear universal in application, not only for familiar religions but unfamiliar ones, and for the religious aspects, as well, of secular social movements. Modified slightly to fit the present context, they are:

1. The belief that the world of experience is part of a larger universe which gives the former its significance.

2. The belief that harmonious fusion with a higher power is man's true purpose.

3. The belief that communion (or communication) with the highest universal element is achieved in a process generally known as "prayer," and that the results of this union become perceptible parts of the world of experience.

4. The visible manifestation in the communicant of enthusiasm for life that manifests itself in breadth of character, through art, in contact with others and through selflessness.

5. The assumption of the bestowal of love, safety and eventual peace to the communicant and to those who share his belief.

In other words, what James has shown is that religion as a (possibly) instinctive or unconscious manifestation in man seems to arise in different sorts of cultures in much the same way. Nor are the values that religion centers upon either neutral nor random. Granting cross-cultual differences

---

[8] The best work on the religious and political aspects of Nazism is, in my opinion, Peter Viereck, *Metapolitics* (New York: Capricorn Books, 1961). The book was originally published in 1941 and therefore speaks with the insistence of contemporary alarm that still, unfortunately, applies to various cultures today.

[9] The following are taken from James, *op. cit.*, p. 367.

in the nature or meaning of abstraction like "law" and "peace," the natural processes of individual dependence upon our mothers (and, usually, fathers as well) is replicated in the rites of religious communion. Because these are mostly values of acceptance, love, peace and joy, religions center on these matters also.

A theologian might add that religious values, being so relatively clear, connote also their opposites: hate, war, pain and rejection, and therefore the outlines of hell are drawn in James' profile as well as those of heaven. In maturation, each of us discovers the anti-mother, the tribal enemy, the guilt and terror of the gift of life. But no religion has ever, on any great scale, offered or searched for its prime values in negative or destructive terms. The human condition has created more relevant problems about the meaning of consciousness and the purpose of life than have been yet, in any sense, solved. The individual, and subsequently his culture, is therefore impelled to the guesswork of establishing a rationale for life's enigmas. Because the very concept of "meaning" itself connotes value, the positive value structure observed by James necessarily follows. True enough, some profound thinkers, after having been tempered by life's most bitter and apparently meaningless experiences, have, and do, base a loose spiritual structure on the so-called "value" of meaninglessness. Nihilists and some contemporary existentialists and cultists are examples, and trends in modern art, the theatre of the absurd and a certain style in literature have been based upon these antivalues.[10] But they are invariably diversions from the mainstream of social and cultural progress, particularly the ever-evolving force of religion which grows as populations grow and is given apparent power as new stimuli, technology being the most important today, create in the consciousness of men the need for a sense of meaning in life.

Strictly in surmise, it was probably easier for an agrarian tribesman, whose life depended upon his crops and whose social contacts were limited to his family and a few neighbors, to induce reasons for his own being than it is for those of us who function in complex cultures where we are ever aware of the complexity of forces beyond our ken. Without those complexities, we could not live as we now do; but they also seem, at times and somehow, irrelevant to the pulse beat of our own consciousness as human beings. In other words, the search for meaning in life is probably more difficult in complicated social and economic structures than in simple ones. The former appear so deeply involved in matters of little relevance to individual purpose, and the latter deal directly with matters of vital personal importance. A metaphysic is therefore probably more difficult for modern

---

[10] Many pursuits of the meaningless are delightful, largely because they have meaning for their auditors, not their creators. The few nihilists and absurdists around at any given moment tend also to be talented, and, because they are apparently detached from their own creative output, attract attention to themselves. If they do not, they usually perish quickly.

man—particularly the so-called "average" man who believes the conventional myths of the technoculture—to accept than it was for his predecessor in societies where one had direct and daily contact with such patent miracles as birth and death, and one might observe directly and often either the "caprices of nature" or "the will of God." Faced frequently enough with the perils of caprice, God's will eventually becomes highly attractive.

Technology and science appear to diminish the random cruelties and favors of nature by introducing a high degree of predictability to life,[11] both intellectually, in comprehending how the world operates as it does, and operationally, in the construction of a culture that contains a multitude of controllable mechanisms from electric lights to lawn mowers to contraceptive devices to golf clubs to hydrogen bombs. But, despite earthquakes and power shortages that often appear to occur without visible cause (or appear to produce senseless results like the deaths of innocent people), belief in the will of God is often difficult to maintain in the face of an apparent iron control of man over so many aspects of life.

In matters of individual consciousness, in relationship to questions of being, sensing (particularly by autonomic sensors) and non-being (death most insistently), are technological men threatened by the chaos of the unknowable and therefore amenable to the comfort of mysticism. Today, however, technology is competent to quiet these fears by chemical[12] as well as surgical procedures, and even this area of spiritual motivation is probably losing its power over human dispositions. We have not found a way to encapsulate God in a pill (except in the momentary phantasies evoked by

[11] I think this is an *appearance*, not reality. A day in the life of an individual in a pre- or non-technological culture consists, of course, of many events, but a large proportion of them are unpredictable and therefore extremely important to him. The events, minor but frequent, that *are* predictable seem less important. In a technological culture, one is probably involved in a larger number of activities on a single day, and the percentage of them which are predictable are the *important* events, inordinate attention being called to them on the rare occasions when the predictions are *wrong*, for instance, when our automobiles do not start properly. In a technological world, many events remain unpredictable (providing scope for God's will), but they are either falsely considered predictable (like reports from the weather bureau and many medical prognoses), subsumed to vague systems which we will "understand in the near future" (like whether or not tumorous growth will grow to be normal or malignant or if a tornado will hit a certain city), expelled from consciousness (like the possibility of the reader-or-writer dying of a coronary incident after reading or writing this sentence), or recognized as truly unpredictable. With so many alternatives from the latter course, many of us accept the others much of the time.

[12] LSD, the rest of the family of halucinogenic drugs, and alcohol on a short-term, pay-as-you-go (in hangovers and depressions) basis naturally serve this purpose, in some measure. More subtle effects, however, are achieved by fairly new anti-depressant drugs, such as the Tricyclic derivatives (Imipramine, Amitriptyline, etc.) that, I have noticed, not only elevate the depressed but also seem to quiet deep existential fears (like that of death) and sustain these effects as long as the drug is used. The user of the drug is almost invariably unaware of this aspect of its power. See L. E. Hollister and J. J. Prusmack, "Psychotherapeutic Drugs in the Treatment of Depressions" in, *Clinical Medicine*, Volume 70, 1963, pp. 1805–1817.

some psychedelic chemicals in certain people under certain conditions), but we are becoming increasingly competent at keeping God at bay by eliminating the fear, or awe of life and death, in individual consciousness by chemical and surgical devices. This has become an important aspect of the technological control of society and will be of critical significance tomorrow, greater, perhaps, to the twenty-first century's ministers and theologists than to its psychotherapists. While education or indoctrination of a more or less rational nature, as attempted in the USSR, apparently fails frequently and noticeably in satisfying desires for mystical experiences, it is ironic that chemists and surgeons in the capitalist nations (that supposedly "trust in God") may have discovered the precise mechanisms to destroy Marx's "opiate" and Freud's great "illusion" entirely, with what ultimate results it is impossible to predict.

Religious Persuasion

Despite the obstacles with which they have had to contend in the past century (not only the general force of technology and science, but the potent specific theories of Marx, Darwin, Freud, Einstein and others), spiritual authorities of the various churches of the Western World are today able to look back comfortably upon nearly a thousand-year hegemony in the power plays of popular persuasion among the various social institutions in our Western tradition. The story of Thomas à Becket (brilliantly told both in Eliot's verse play and film of the drama *Becket* by Jean Anouilh) is, in many ways, paradigmatic of how, before the scientific age, church persuasion, in one form or another, would almost invariably manage to supercede secular power. As a friend of King Henry's, Becket was the king's natural ally in church and lay affairs. But as Archbishop of Canterbury, Becket was also a servant of God, and his conflict of interests (as we call his tragedy today) was resolved in favor of God, not the king.[13]

So did this problem re-occur, almost invariably, in our history when the forces of church and state met in conflict, until the period of the composition, of course, of the United States' Constitution. But by this time, Western society was already well along into the Age of Reason and into the era of science and technology.

As dissonant with this American doctrine of "separation of church and state"—a clever euphemism for "state supremacy" in a religiously pluralis-

---

[13] A later Henry also had his conflicts with the church and thought to subsume its power to himself by breaking with Rome and playing Pope's role as prince of God himself. Politically, Henry VIII's strategy worked in serving his short-term goals. *His* tragedy was the discovery, that servants of God remain servants of God, whether or not they report to Rome, as two other stage and screen dramas (*A Man For All Seasons* and *Anne of a Thousand Days*) have demonstrated for contemporary audiences. And history shows that, for all Henry's agonies over his resident clergy, the conflict between country and state religion in Britain has, over the years, been no less tortured than the conflicts between countries and *non-state* religions.

tic country like the USA—may seem, the United States, like most other Western nations, still invokes the blessing of God in its official slogans and seals, on its currency, and opens its legislative ceremonies with prayer to a specific deity. Presidents and perjurers still swear on Bibles, although a witness in court may (in New York State and others) merely affirm his veracity without mention of God. A President is also free to take his oath of office sans Bible and not to mention of God if he so desires, but none has yet had the nerve, or inclination, or both. More significant, perhaps, concerning the place of religious persuasion in the United States today, is the fact that few politicians, no matter how cynical or skeptical of religion they personally are, will end a major political address without a prayer or mention of a divinity, a higher power, a supernatural force or a direct plea to God. For all the fuss, also, that the American Civil Liberties Union has made over the matter, our public schools still officially recognize Christmas and Easter with pine trees and colored eggs and extended vacations from school. And the kiddies are still usually taught the words "under God" as part of their pledge to the flag.[14]

Who is America's God, and what manner of persuasion is consummated in His name?

He is, of course, a Judeo-Christian conception. The Roman Catholic trinity is as close as any major religion in our nation has ever come to theological plurality. And, although we are a Christian country, the God to whom our politicians pray is a unitary force, issues of church doctrine aside. Major determinants of the "secular" God (the "God" in "In God We Trust") have been, in rough order, the Puritan religion of the book; the high church biases of our founding fathers; deists, transcendentalists, and moderate religious reformers in the nineteenth century; Catholic and Jewish complications of ritual and rite from about 1880 to the present; and the liberal WASPish construction of the Godhead who speaks to Moses with an NBC baritone in the Cecil B. DeMille version of *The Ten Commandments* (second version).

This evolution baffles many foreigners and some Americans. When they hold our vague, permissive, Unitarian, Congregational, Reformed Jewish and Liberal Catholic versions of religion and ritual against their Old World equivalents, the United States does indeed look like a Godless nation.[15] Hence, the recent popularity of the "God is Dead" cult and the not-

---

[14] When I was taught this pledge nearly forty years ago at New York's Public School 6, I am *positive* that the words "under God" were not included. How, why and when they crept into it, and where they remain and where they have been dropped, would be an interesting research topic for someone with a lot of free time. By the time I had begun teaching in 1946, the pledge included the words. To this day, when I have occasion to pledge my allegiance to the flag, I invariably forget to say them, reflective not one iota of my religious beliefs but of the excellent (and permanent) conditioning I received at the hands of Miss Clark at P.S. 6 forty years ago!

[15] I remember my own cynicism, some years ago, after having given a lecture in which I

quite-incorrect notion of Aldous Huxley which anticipated, in *Brave New World*, that the word "Ford" would eventually replace "Lord."

The New World God has been fashioned of three parts: technological culture, a plural low common denominator of the Judeo-Christian religions and the spiritual needs of men in an affluent culture. He is acceptable to the great majority of Americans, no matter what faith they accept in the course of their daily lives. When in trouble or crisis, they may retreat to their Old World Gods for therapy. But more and more of them are seeking spiritual counsel elsewhere, frequently in the apparently godless world of psychiatry, which, in fact, is riddled deep at all levels with ritual and rites that are, in the author's opinion, closer to religion than to medicine.[16]

In strange ways, however, the churches themselves have maintained enough power to make their influences felt on society. The commitment—whether religious or resulting from guilt feelings of having been spared wide anti-Semitism in the USA, for instance—of American Jews to the State of Israel is one example, and an important one, of how effectively a minority church can influence even international policy. The Catholic Church and school complex has not been as effective as it might have been, for many reasons, in stemming the tide toward birth control and abortion, but Catholic influence upon laws in these regards, on the state level at least, is still noticeable.[17] (The election of a Catholic to the Presidency of the

---

severely criticized the materialist coloration of Christmas and the apparent loss in the confusion of the meaning in the holiday of Christ's birth. "What can we do about it?" asked a female student after my talk. My answer was glib. "Abolish Christianity!" said I. I do not think I would give that answer today, nor would I voice that particular lament about Christmas quite as emphatically.

[16] There is little need to repeat, or labor the point, that much psychotherapy has followed religious forms, particularly psychoanalysis. A minister friend of mine has commented upon the way that Alcoholics Anonymous and its imitators, although not formally religious organizations, resemble the meetings of the early Christians under the Romans. Newer therapeutic devices like existential therapy, Logotherapy, Encounter groups, nude therapy and mind-expanding cults are all mystical manifestations in many ways, sometimes quite self-consciously *not* Judeo-Christian but oriental or astrological in flavor. The main point here is that religious behavior in our culture is occurring more and more outside of our churches, not just in the Protestant sense, but in a way that makes church ceremonies of any and all kinds irrelevant to the spiritual experiences of millions (I suspect) of our people.

[17] The fact that lay Catholics and clergy have been, in the United States and elsewhere, divided themselves on matters of doctrine has done much to undermine this influence—to the delight, I notice, of many Catholics. Combined with the force of the ecumenical movement and the financial problems in which parochial education currently finds itself enmeshed, a devout American Catholic today is the victim of almost as many divisive forces within his Church as outside of it. The American Jew is in a different position, so complicated by ethnic, cultural and social factors that, unless the reader is Jewish, he will not begin to understand them without an introduction like the book by James M. Yaffe, *The American Jews* (New York: Paperback Library, 1969), or one equally as candid. Yaffe is a superb writer of Jewish-American fiction, incidentally, as well as an authoritative spokesman for today's Jewish cultural-religious *mish-mash*.

United States in 1960 was epochal in the light of the defeat of another Catholic popular candidate some thirty-two years before, probably on religious grounds.) The world of the Protestant churches is the great world of middle America, and so many are their fusions of interests with fundaments of the various power structures in the United States that the places where the church's authority ends and the world of finance, production, transportation, commerce or defense begins is blurred. The fit is nearly seamless.

Only certain significant side-diversions in culture are specifically non-Protestant: intellectuals are frequently Jewish or Jesuit in training, beyond the representation of either group in our population; show business is run mostly by Jews, although performers (particularly young ones) tend to look (Barbra Streisand excepted) like WASPs. The percentage of Catholics and Jews is also out of proportion to the total population in broadcasting, the newspaper and magazine world, and in the fine arts. But Jews and Catholics exert, mainly, cultural rather than religious influences on the institution they touch in work or social life. In New York City today, for instance, a gentile public relations man working with show business clients probably speaks a creditable Yiddish, and sometimes, when he thinks he is speaking English, he is, in fact, speaking Yiddish. A Jewish TV newscaster will wear a green tie on St. Patrick's Day "out of respect." Irish drinking habits have been emulated by Protestants and Jews, and the Jewish cuisine presently may be poisoning the entire nation, so widely has it been accepted, even in the South and Midwest.[18]

These cultural evidences of the American "melting pot" are sentimentally attractive, but they have little to do either with religion or the role of churches in American life. It is significant that in recent years, when young Negro Americans felt the need for a religion by which to set themselves apart from the white man's religious groups, they chose the Moslem faith, hardly represented in the white majority of the United States. That they did not understand Islam, and practised the faith incorrectly, was irrelevant to their refusal to join any of the white man's churches, as a sign of protest. They recognized clearly and well that Christian and Jewish churches in America are a close-knit complex, distinguished more by the cultural elements they share in common (as "whitey" practices his religion), than by their spiritual and doctrinal differences.

[18] Jewish cooking is not Jewish at all. It merely represents the dietary habits of the Jews of the diaspora who settled in the USA. Bagels and blintzes are Russian, brought to America by Russian Jews. Gefilte fish was made by all the people in East Europe who lived near fresh water supplies. What we call the Jewish "cuisine" was actually fabricated by immigrants on New York's lower East Side and in the Bronx. Its only unifying characteristics are its obesience to Jewish dietary laws and its difficulty to digest. But the same is true of other national cuisines. Pizza pie (now the American national dish, having replaced the frankfurter in popularity) was native to Naples (as a dessert) before it was Americanized, and lasagna was (and is) a local Italian specialty. Most Cantanese cooking originated in San Francisco, and some of the most noted French specialties extant were born at the old Waldorf Hotel in New York City.

Many other factors have caused this cultural-religious mix in addition to the three noted above, but continual inter-marriage and the ever-grinding influence of the Protestant majority will slowly but inexorably diminish the power of the extant churches in American life in the years to come, just as it has in the recent past. Catholics and Jews will see (and have been, and are seeing) the distinctive qualities of their faiths diluted in many ways. And they will also claim (as they are claiming) that many of the younger generation are returning to orthodoxy. Some young people, of course, are, and they become conspicuous by the eccentricity of, say, keeping a kosher household or taking vows and joining the priesthood. But the great mass of them are becoming, for practical purposes, functioning WASPs, while maintaining titular identities as Catholics, Reformed Jews and Ethical Culturists, or else they convert to the blandest of Protestant sects they can search out.[19]

The late Episcopal clergyman Bell saw the American church's contemporary function with clarity and breadth rare from inside the world of formal religion:

> Certainly no competent sociologist or political scientist, no scholarly observer of our country who is not himself a professionally ecclesiastical person, says or thinks that the Church has much to do with the contemporary American picture. Instead, their usual conclusion is that most Americans regard the church as promotor of a respectable minor art, charming if it happens to appeal to you, *its only moral function to bless whatever the multitude at the moment regards as the American way of life*. The Church may be relied on to advocate certain incidental improvements in the cultural pattern, though rarely does it initiate any of them. It cooperates, rather, with secular good works. The Church certainly is not generally expected critically to examine into what our way of life is like, much less to go about resisting it.
>
> . . . The world, hurtling on toward political, economic, psychic catastrophe, is not going to be saved, if it is saved at all, by the Church if the Church remains an uncommitted host of politely respectable people, willing to be led by professional ecclesiasts whose methods of promotion and administration are just about as worldly as those of the sick society they say they wish to reform but which, as a matter of fact, deforms them just as much as it deforms everybody else.[20]

These words were written eighteen years ago and explain much about the way religious persuasion has affected (or has failed to affect) life in the

---

[19] This does not, of course, apply to the Negroes, although the same sort of inter-marriage (inter-breeding is ancient history) will dull the distinctive traits of the American black man or woman. In time, they too will join the WASPs, as many Negro Americans have already. See Chapter 24.

[20] Bernard Iddings Bell, *Crowd Culture* (New York: Harper and Brothers, 1952), pp. 98–99 (italics added). Dr. Bell was not only addressing clergymen of his own faith but other Protestants, and Catholics and Jews in the United States in this polemic.

United States since then. Rumblings *within* our churches (including the "God is Dead" notion) were, and are, based upon similar discontents and were quite clearly predicted years ago by clear-sighted clergymen like Bell, often characterized by his critics as "gloomy." The public much prefers the upbeat optimism of the late Harry Emerson Fosdick and Norman Vincent Peale, both of whom often appear to view Christianity as an Adult Education Extension Course in Human Relations,[21] which is exactly the face and posture of most religious persuasion in the USA today.

The Men God Needs

Most noticeably in its approach to the young, the American Church (Protestant more than Jewish or Catholic) has compounded somehow the notion of middle-America, the YMCA and Four-H club movements into an old-fashioned evangelical matrix and emerged with the clean-living cults of such men as Billy Graham. A little showmanship and hocus-pocus (similar to the techniques by which magician Joseph Dunninger used to "read minds" on radio and television) are combined at mass religious services featuring apparent "decisions for Christ" on the part of repentent sinners.

The Graham Crusade has thrived, and has even proved attractive enough to lure away student sociologists sent out to study its dynamics,[22] an unusual outcome in the practice of the social sciences. It has also, at the present writing, spun close connections with the executive arm of the United States government, in what appears to be a personal relationship between the President and Dr. Graham, who resemble each other physically and in public style. Whatever the genuine and human points of contact between Nixon, the Republican lawyer, and the latter-day Billy Sunday may be, the mix is entirely commuensurate with a conservative executive branch of government (representing largely élite business and financial interests), allying itself with a predominately lower middle and upper-lower brow Americans who attend church regularly and admire men like Graham. And Graham's constituents, in large part, come from the hard-core middle Americans from whom Nixon, at this time of writing, seems to draw most of his popular support.[23]

---

[21] A friend of mine who is Communications Director (read Public Relations man) for one of the most influential Protestant churches in Washington, D.C. calls himself "God's flack." He is not, and he knows it. He is a "church flack," and a living display of Bell's characterization of the church's deference to the demands of contemporary culture.

[22] See Kurt and Gladys Engel Lang, "Decisions for Christ: Billy Graham in New York City" in M. R. Stein, J. Vidich, and D. M. White, *Identity and Anxiety* (Glencoe, Ill., The Free Press, 1960), pp. 415–427, in which a clear description of a Graham Crusade is reported by competent sociological observers. The student (or students) of the Langs who were apparently converted seemed later to have had second thoughts about their decisions.

[23] This paragraph is being written (in first draft) on a lovely June day of 1970, a period during which Nixon's domestic policies (to some degree) and foreign stance

According to most social investigations of religion in our culture, belief in God, church attendance and religious preferences have social, occupational, educational and other correlates that should be so familiar to anyone who has even flirted with sociology that they do not need reference here.[24] In short, church attendance, belief in God, "religiosity" and dependence upon religious values and spiritual directives in life are *least* likely to be found in people who are either psychologists or sociologists studying the correlates of religion in American life.

While this state of affairs may appear amusing, there is nothing improbable about it; and the apparent truth of it provides considerable insight into why and how religion appeals to certain kinds of individuals and not to others, and what values people believe spiritual beliefs display in a culture like ours.

First, religion is likely to be regarded by intellectuals as a culture trait, capable of discrete severance from other aspects of life and only tangentially related to belief in God. This belief is regarded as a class of experience different from the practice of religious symbolism, attendance at church or membership in a formal religious sect. This is a fairly recent construction (in any widespread form) of religion, the result probably of the influences of William James and Max Weber, in their respective fields of psychology and sociology, to the study of religion as conceived and so regarded, enhanced by the writings of the Freudians and others.

Second, religion so regarded, women seem more attracted to it than men; its appeal to old people is greater than the young; it is a middle class phenomenon; it is most likely to be an influence in the lives of people who have been indoctrinated least by our institutions of education. Churchgoers tend to be more stable in their marital relationships, less prone to deviant sex and less sexually active, than nonchurchgoers. Different sects reflect different class biases, the most noticeable being the preference of lower class church goers for salvationist religious activities. "Upper class denominations are more formal in their religious observance, lower class denominations more emotional," [25] and, broadly speaking, Episcopalians, Congrega-

---

in Southeast Asia seem to have gained the enthusiastic approval of those whom we now call "hard-hats"—day laborers, union members, blue collar workers, and lower middle class suburbanites, midwesterners and southerners. Many of the members of this constituency are new to the Republican fold (and temporarily visiting, I guess), having been maintained by the liberal thrust of the Democratic party since the Roosevelt years. The reason they find Nixon attractive at the moment, it appears, relates largely to their antagonism to the militant behavior of his intellectual elder and youthful critics. Political alliances are invariably tempory, and I anticipate that this alignment of interests will have altered considerably by the time this footnote is typed, corrected, re-typed, set in type and published. It will be interesting to observe if they change and how they change by then.

24 Anyway, consult at least the compiled finding on the role of religion in culture in Berelson and Steiner, *Human Behavior*, pp. 384–396, for a summary of these data.

25 *Ibid.*, p. 393.

tionalists and Presbyterians tend to be high working class sects; Methodists, Lutherans, Baptists and Jews, middle class; and the smaller groups (along with many Baptists and Catholics) are lower class in orientation. Catholics and Jews tend to favor liberal politicians. People generally assimilate to themselves their family's religious beliefs and tend (for many reasons) to marry people with church affiliations similar to their own. Once again, not only the assumptions of behavioral scientists but empirical evidence seems to indicate that it is possible to sever, for purposes of study, an individual or group's religious affiliations from his attendance at church and performance of religious rites, which in turn may be separated also from belief in God or the exercise of what may fairly be called "the spiritual dimension of personality." [26]

What the behavioral scientists' studies of religion reveal—both in their own attitudes towards religion and in the results of their various enquiries and studies—is quite clear and entirely consonant with observations concerning the role of religion as a persuasive force in contemporary life by other kinds of social critics, for instance, novelists like Sinclair Lewis, John O'Hara, Saul Bellow, James T. Farrell, John Steinbeck, Graham Greene, and many others,[27] as well as popular essayists.

In the first place, religion operates as a social control in the sense that it maintains the status quo of class and social structure. In this respect, it seems to justify the Marxian view as "the opiate of the masses," but only where and when artificial opiates are *required* to facilitate the adjustment of deprived individuals to their deprivations rather than encourage their revolt away from them. Religion is most definitely *not* an opiate (compared with sex and liquor, for instance) for the affluent, self-satisfied churchgoer who is contented with his life. Neither does it narcotize his rebellious offspring, simply because pot, motorcycles and other "kicks" work far better than church-going. In any case, most religion in society at present performs merely an adjustive function most of the time for most people, and serves as forms of "insight therapy" that teaches one how best to live in the social order by changing it *least*. Exceptions, of course, exist, but they are not to

[26] While little formal attention has been paid to this concept, both literature and history clearly indicate that a facet of human personality which (in the same sense as "sexuality" or "greediness") may be called "spirituality" appears to exist in certain people. It is not to be confused with other characteristics like "altruism" or "selflessness," although an altruistic or selfless individual may also (and is likely to be) spiritual in character.

[27] For the past decade, in the United States, a foreigner might believe that the only religion of literary interest to recent American writers has been Judaism. This is the result of the concordance of fates (or inherited talents and cultural aspirations) that introduced so many Jewish writers into the short story and novel writing fields, and also of the apparently large number of Jews who buy and read novels or who go to movies made about them. They therefore understand what Isaac Singer, J. D. Salinger, Philip Roth, Budd Shulberg, Irwin Shaw and the rest are talking about in the Yiddish-American fantasies and chronic ethnic guilts they project. What the non-Jewish reader makes of their in-group communication baffles me, as it must also baffle them.

be discovered in the passive oriental interpretations of the disaffected young from the now-extinct beatniks to the vanishing hippies, who are content to opt out of society rather than change it. Black Moslems, some Jesuits and others among minority communities, however, construe religion as a viable factor in social revolution, but they are few and rarely taken seriously by the rest of society.

In the second place, religion today is almost a natural enemy of non-conformity of many kinds. Because our churches have reached so far beyond the spiritual domains of life and into the social structure, there is little room in most of them for the genuine or pseudo non-conformist. The way of life of the former is immediately suspect in most religious circles, be it non-conformism in dress, sexual preference, intellectual style or political thought. Pseudo non-conformists tend largely to congregate in the intellectual centers of our medium to large communities, and the abregation of formal religion is usually one of the rights of passage into the rigid cultural and social cliques of "right" people inhabiting our universities, foundations and "think tanks," all of whom must affect just the prescribed amount of individuality and rebellion for their particular group, which rarely includes much church-going. If religion emerges in this environment, it manifests itself for a short time in the form of a passing interest in cultism.

Third, the relationship between religion in America today and its power as an institution shaping dispositions towards belief in God is a mystery at best, open to all sorts of speculation, most of it irresponsible. A good case has been made for the "death of God," or, at least, for His desertion from our churches. But a similar case might have been well made, on the basis of the visible corruption permitted or suffered by contemporary culture, at any period in history since Abraham left Ur. And it is no more urgent or impressive today than it has ever been. Noticeable appeals to God, mysticism and a wisp of spiritual orientation are manifest in numerous films,[28] on television, in literature, politics and even in philosophical essays. Occasional attention is given God in speeches and papers by both behavioral and natural scientists, but they rarely seem to be bothered by Godly beliefs in their actual research procedures and theory construction.[29] Belief

---

28 A recent film, based on the Depression novel, *They Shoot Horses, Don't They?*, was quite popular with the public. It is hard not to believe that the main reason was its direct allegorical relationship to the modern world, represented in the movie as a dance marathon during the 1930's. The most powerful (and artfully played) character in the film was obviously meant to be God—a mean, ironic, self-deluded, selfish, capricious, cynical and tired God, but God nevertheless. Gig Young's conception of the role was so brilliant, clear, and unmistakable that for once, Hollywood's Academy Award was given to a skilled artist for an inspired performance.

29 Even apparent non-believers like Albert Einstein and Robert Oppenheimer have had their moments of non-specific hortatary spiritual enthusiasm. Freud aside, I can think of few major scientists in relatively recent times who have not professed, at one time or another, a transcendental belief, if only faith in Man and Mankind, both words capitalized for obvious reasons.

in a higher power has been discovered to be almost essential in certain forms of psychotherapy, particularly by those self-help groups working to free from their compulsions that relatively small proportion of alcoholics and narcotics addicts who desire to control their diseases. These forms of therapy display a decidedly spiritual, although non-sectarian or omni-sectarian, bent. Much the same bias is evident in other forms of psychological treatment like logotherapy, existential psychiatry and the many mutations of group therapy that have emerged in recent years.

Fourth (as corollary to the observations above), little appearance of a belief in God, formal religion notwithstanding, colors institutional life in our culture. God's role at birth is confined to obeisance to ritual and hygiene by the rites of circumcision and baptism. The desertion of religious implications of death and burial by the undertaking industry has been the topic for both fictional and non-fictional exposés. In our schools, little of the "duty and reverence" which, according to A. N. Whitehead [30] marks a spiritual (to him "religious") education has been apparent in many of the institutions that the author has visited or resided in for many years, both as student and teacher. In government and law, the severance of church and state is discretely manifest in the blind eye that these essentially pragmatic institutions turn to spirituality of most kinds.[31] Divine intervention may be sought occasionally and informally in our stock exchanges, race tracks and gambling houses. And these citadels of chance are about the *most* likely places in our society where audible appeals to God are heard. The design, mood, style and function of our hospitals is purposely oriented toward efficiency and the pretense that the art of healing is an offshoot of the natural sciences. (Operating rooms and nurses' and physicians' lounges are less intentionally austere than the rest of most hospital buildings, because no public pretense is necessary in these quarters.) Occasional exceptions are the pitiful sights of otherwise idle priests, ministers or rabbis prowling the halls to find someone *in extremis* to practice their prayers upon. Doctors and nurses know that Morphine and Demerol have replaced God for most moribund patients and will do the same for them when their time comes.[32] At any rate, hospitals have been designed to be poor places to contemplate the wonders of birth, the force of life and the significance of death—one's own or anybody else's.

Fifth, we have built a lot of churches in the United States in a wide variety of styles and on some of the most valuable real estate in the country.

---

[30] A. N. Whitehead, *The Aims of Education*, p. 26.

[31] An exception is a recent decision of the Supreme Court of the United States that a conscientious objector to war does not need to belong to a formal church in order to verify his principles, and may be excused from the draft.

[32] Recent studies of dubious reliability indicate that physicians and nurses fear death more than the average man. But neither fear of death nor wonder at life seems essential for faith in God for most people. Medical personnel are probably about as religious and/or God-fearing as other members of their social, economic and educational strata.

We also have fabricated some amazing cemeteries, and the reader who has not toured Forest Lawn in Los Angeles (or its equivalent) is advised to do so at least once before the black angel overtakes him or her. Some of the most amazing architecture in the land has also been lavished upon places of worship—far more interesting, often, than upon residences, and infinitely superior to most other institutional buildings. Cemeteries in urban areas are eyesores. But they are pleasant places in small towns where space and affluence permit.

Neither churches nor cemeteries are essentially religious structures, regardless of their crosses, organs, eternal flames, books of religious instruction or hymnals. Nor do they or their props tell us much today (as they did in the Middle Ages) about man's concepts of a supreme being and his feelings about the human situation. If anything, they are surprisingly *inhuman* artifacts of culture, for the most part. Our churches, particularly, are rarely redolent with the glory of life or inspiring of awe, despite their architectual trickery, be it a contemporary novelty or imitation of the Gothic notion of majesty.[33] Men may bring their own beliefs in God to these buildings. To some, they may be transmuted by imagination into holy places by rituals and sanctification. To the cold observer it would be difficult, indeed, to determine precisely what role they play in the world, and what their influence upon it is likely to mean, say, a century from now.

Conclusion

That religion is still, in the technological age, a persuasive force is analogous to the wonder of the dancing bear: not how beautifully he dances, but that he dances at all. What the persistence of religion clearly indicates is that, while science and technology tend to obfuscate both personal religious beliefs and religious institutions, they accomplish little at the subjective level in providing either meaning and reason for life or insulation from the terrors of living and pain and apparent pointlessness of death. Scientific knowledge of the physical components of these processes neither intensifies nor decreases the pressure of the fears and doubts which persist, at least at present, in most perceptive men's individual consciousnesses, be they scientists, poets or day laborers. While the positivist speaks convincingly for the objective world, the mystic speaks for the subjective one, and neither, usually, speaks clearly or meaningfully to one another.

Many thoughtful and clever leaders have employed numerous strata-

---

33 Where the churches of Europe and the mosques of North Africa remain in something like their original settings, they convey some hint of what they *were*, but, like most American churches, little of what they *are*. I have been deeply moved by some churches, but never by a so-called "great" one. Some of the hovels of Latin America, one or two austere New England houses of worship (including a Roman Catholic whitewashed wooden structure), and some of the odd places in the urban ghettos where poor black people worship have touched me deeply. Perhaps they have even generated a mite of spirituality within me.

gems of reason against both belief in God and organized religion, undermining, apparently, neither, but creating a certain degree of confusion, thereby enhancing the pluralism of individual and institutional religious allegiances in the Western world. Marx, Freud and other quasi-determinists have had profound effects upon society by virtue of their atheism and anticlericalism. But the social functions of religion as described seventy years ago by James still apply in the modern world, even in the face of modern tendencies to advance nihilistic philosophies directly in the face of *both* scientific positivism and religious mysticism, putting the latter two in a peculiar tandem intellectual position.

In some ways, the need for religion is increased by the growth of uncertainties in a technological society, although technological means for control of the perception of these uncertainties are developing rapidly and may destroy entirely man's need for any notions of the supernatural. At present, however, religious persuasion, both from churches and secular forces, remains important in the conduct of our modern state. While we in America believe that we have legally separated church from state, it is doubtful that this schism has, to any functional degree, been accomplished except in statute. What we have done, apparently, is to secularize and pluralize religion, quite a different matter. Thus, to many we appear formally and informally godless, which is not accurate. Neither is God (in any sense) dead; He is alive and well and dressed in the latest fashion.

Culturally, America's melting pot has become more and more an accomplished fact, but the relationship of the pot to religion is questionable. In formal ceremonies and church attendances, orthodoxies and secret cabals are declining, and a meeting point of WASPish, middle class, Sunday, titular religion is, indeed, in the process of being evolved for Catholics and Jews who want to join—and will probably marry into—the great American middle-class world. To this end does the Catholic ecumenical movement, Reform Judaism and the Unitarian church (among other Catholic, Jewish, and Protestant arms, both religious and lay) seem to be moving. But culture is not religion, and religion is not belief in God or spirituality. And the melting pot tendency is viewed by perceptive churchmen and others as a diversion *into* culture *away from* humanistic Christianity or Judaism.

Sociologists and psychologists tend to regard religion—and its resultant effects on people's minds—as culture traits, amenable to their various precise methods of study. In this context, religious people today are made up largely of the older generation, non-intellectual members of the middle class, who display various conservative behavior patterns—with exceptions. A number of points are clear in this approach, namely, that religion serves today as an effective guardian of the status quo in many aspects of life, that it is an enemy of non-conformity in thought and action, and that we know little about how religious behavior (and the dispositions of churchgoers) relates to belief in a supernatural God. Evidence that such a belief is widespread may be discovered in both popular and class culture and in some accepted psychotherapeutic practices as well. But this belief does not appear to penetrate deeply into the functions of most of our institutions, neither into our schools, hospitals, nor, in vital ways, even into our churches and synagogues. The latter is a peculiar and contradictory manifestation, visible in our society for the first—and perhaps the last—time in human history.

Part Three

PSYCHOLOGICAL PERSPECTIVES

Why, I can smile, and murder while I smile,
And cry "Content" to that which grieves my heart,
And wet my cheek with artificial tears,
And frame my face to all occasions.
I'll drown more sailors than the mermaid shall;
I'll slay more gazers than the basilisk,
I'll play the orator as well as Nestor,
Deceive more slyly than Ulysses could,
And, like a Simon, take another Troy.
I can add colors to the chameleon,
Change shapes with Proteus for advantages,
And set the murderous Machiavel to school.
Can I do this, and cannot get a crown?
Tut, were it farther off, I'll pluck it down.

Gloucester (later Richard III) in
Shakespeare's Henry VI (Part Three.)

Chapter 12

MOTIVES, PERCEPTIONS AND MEN

The chief reason for our general hesitancy to undertake a serious study of psychological data themselves is that there seems to be no instrument to negotiate it; few people realize how excellent a presentation of such data is to be found in the arts. A few scholars have become aware of it . . . But no one, as yet, has pursued the revelation to the point of finding problematical facts never presented before, or recognizing vital patterns in pure art which may be keys to essential relations in the life of feeling.

Susanne K. Langer

In Part Two of this volume—and in much of Part One—our discussion centered on descriptions of how certain major institutions in culture, ours and others in the past, communicate certain of their persuasive aspects (or intentional qualities) in what we have termed "logical" modes to people individually and in groups in society. Our attempts have been to uncover, as simply as possible, the nature of the intentions of communications involving these institutions and, from a descriptive stance, to illustrate their powers, manifest and potential, as instruments of persuasion.

For these purposes, our discourse has taken generally structural, operational and historical paths for the most part, although psychological speculation (and subjective reports) have been entered in passing—whenever possible in first person footnotes to avoid excessive breaks in the narrative, a result of the author's intention to clarify for the reader his inevitable biases in the interpretation of history, social criticism and (sometimes) political matters.[1]

As demonstrated and explained (hopefully) in Chapter 1, the logical approach to the study of communication (or any aspect of communications in scientific or social history) tends to pass over in anecdotal fashion numerous manifestations of what we sometimes call "aspects of mind," concentrating best on what logic tells us most clearly: what people do and say, including what they *say* they are doing and thinking. Or *think* they are saying and thinking.

1 Some talented structural anthropologists, historians and social critics are far more competent than I am to accomplish this end without recourse to notes and side com-

The logical tendency has been evident in the past seven chapters: to exclude from serious consideration subtle and speculative manifestations of "mind" as it is understood by many (but not all) psychologists, centering instead upon the plot of long and short-term history and the *dispositions*—a word used whenever possible—that we may fairly induce people, alone or in groups, display towards culture, and how these dispositions appear to change as culture changes. We have also been concerned with apparent causes for these dispositional states and reasons for change. But searching questions concerning *how* and *why* these metamorphoses occur are fundamentally psychological matters. They have, therefore, not been so much avoided as treated in the descriptive manner of the social sciences rather than the implicit manner of speculative psychology.

As we shift epistemologies even slightly, so we must shift meanings, assumptions and concepts also. For the following chapters the notion of human "dispositions" as the outcome of persuasion, for instance, is too crude to be satisfactory for psychological analysis. What will be required is a more *exact* (but still inevitably imprecise) *anatomy* of dispositions, one that will center on notions of *belief structures, attitudes,* and *opinions,* the topic of Chapter 13. It has been necessary to speak loosely up to this point of all three types of dispositions. Definitions were understood to be those employed in common talk or implied in the text. Psychological notions of process, conscious and unconscious, were, for the most part, neither implied nor directly assumed in the discussion, because they were not needed. When the psychologics of beliefs, attitudes and opinions are, on the other hand, analyzed, process becomes all important, and concern centers on physical, mental, emotional and cognitive factors—at different times and under various circumstances. They are vital in the task of outlining psychological parameters of how and why persuasion works, fails to work, or produces unexpected results.

Psychological perspectives *in vacuo* are worse than useless, however. They are misleading—for instance, when one discovers personality theories intruding into otherwise admirable volumes of history, or when drugstore

ments. This is just *one* way in which their superiority is evident; they are also better writers than I am. In my opinion, though, a mere handful are adept enough at this personal-structural type of serious writing not to overbalance scholarship and research with their personal points of view. Many try; few succeed. They try because publishers and editors frequently favor serious books and articles (even for scholarly markets) that are not cluttered up with citations, references and footnotes, which they associate with academic dryness (and, probably, memories of their own distastes for their academic pasts). Their failure lies in misguided attempts to follow Socrates' admonition to "think like a wise man but to communicate in the language of the people," which even Socrates could not himself accomplish creditably. The worst work of this kind is done by successful popularizers of the arts and sciences who crack the best-seller lists; the best by less well known scholars whose structural method of analysis *includes* a recognition (and clear perception) of the instrument recording their data: themselves. In the latter group I include men of the stripe of Lévi-Strauss, Heilbronner, Eisley, Kahler and Edmund Wilson, among others.

notions of psychological motivation clutter up otherwise admirable community studies and sociological analyses. The few exceptions include reports of animal experiments and whatever evidence that laboratory "rat-running," for example, may yield for the study of human behavior. This sort of facile analogy fabrication, a great deal of it spurious in the author's opinion, requires merely self-sustaining, self-justifying psychologics to yield information, valid or invalid, that may be useful in the development of meaningful generalizations. Hence, this volume has, so far, kept a respectful distance from the psychologics of communication as described in the first chapter.

The only *caveat* entered here is that this future task is more difficult to accomplish rewardingly than the one through which we have just passed; and far more replete with competing doctrines, theories, assumptions and variations of method, all of which have legitimate title-claims to adequacy as instruments for the development of generalizations of psychological meaning. Such is the state of the psychological sciences and the arts of theory articulation in the major psychological schools of our time, including those of therapeutic psychiatry and neurology. Our objective, unfortunately, requires that we pay some respect to nearly all of them, less because of what they have demonstrated that is factual and reliable, but because so little that is apparently factual and reliable about what they have produced to date has satisfactorily withstood the contemporary examinations for proof. In the absence of such proof, it is unfair to play favorites in competing theories.

In sum, therefore, the *less* we know for certain about many matters, the more widely and deeply and longer we must investigate them, and the greater the risk is taken that the cash register of inquiry will register "No Sale."

Man and Motivation

In few fields of speculation must one start at so basal a point as the study of the psychodynamics of persuasion. Because of the reasons noted above, this is the result not from a shortage of available explanations concerning why people think, feel and behave as they do (and yield to influences changing thoughts, feelings and behaviors), but because of an excess of them, most of them making some intrinsic sense. They are almost all open, however, to numerous kinds of qualification, argument and responsible doubt.

In this period, when many of man's institutions are being subsumed by popular and powerful quasi-psychotic plans, benignly called "systems engineering" (to be treated later in a number of references), it is necessary to exercise extreme care in delineating a picture—or a number of pictures—of psychologically oriented epistemologies. The danger is that they may be misrepresented, or accepted or rejected, for the wrong reasons—that is, reasons which stem purely from their apparent utility in a society where tests of adequacy for use are constantly in flux. M. B. Smith has brilliantly (and bravely) posted a warning,[2] to the effect that anyone who pursues a psychological orientation that is not based upon the "mechanical determination of American psychology that still persists" [3] (particularly when the approach maintains more than a modicum of the voluntaristic affirmation of free will), proceeds at his own risk, and will probably be forced to end up anyway in some sort of compromise with one or another form of psychological determinism.

Determinism in American psychology has many faces, but the major aspect, as Smith indicates, follows roughly the path of William James—not the James of *Varieties of Religious Experience*, but a more intellectually constricted, less humble and extremely American James, courageously attempting to bring scientistic styles of thought to the grab bag of physiology and poetry that was known in his day as "psychology." [4] The type of analytic work he accomplished was characterized by James himself as "radical empiricism," although—to the author's surprise—many students of behavior, including psychologists and psychiatrists, do not appear to comprehend the nexus between psychological behavioral notions and Jamsian Pragmatism in philosophy, Instrumentalism in education, Conditioning in therapy and, most particularly, Behaviorism in psychological theory. (As A. A. Roback notes, the latter was not a direct product, as many believe of James' philosophical-pragmatic approach, but he certainly set the philosophical stage for its arrival.)[5] Nor are the motley crowd of American philosophers, educators and psychologists usually associated with the behavioristic coloration of psychology in our times—John Dewey, J. Rush, Irwin Edman, John B. Watson, F. H. Allport, Clark Hull, E. L. Thorndike, B. F. Skinner and others—easy to unscramble in regard to individual contributions to theory, experimental techniques and other matters. Most of these men simply lived so long, and their intellectual output was so enormous, that it is difficult to tell a clear story of the development of the behavioral idea either objectively[6] or perjoratively.[7] Add to this tangle the influence of Ivan Pavlov in

[2] See M. Brewster Smith, *Social Psychology and Human Values* (Chicago: Aldine Publishing Co., 1969), pp. 9–10. This is a thoughtful collection of essays on the current state of social psychology as seen from a number of viewpoints. Since World War II, Smith has been one of the quieter leaders in American social psychology, and he appears today, in retrospect, to be also one of the wisest, especially in his conservatism. His example and wisdom will hopefully be brought to bear upon many of the problems in the following pages.

[3] *Ibid.*, p. 9.

[4] See any one of the number of editions of William James, *Psychology*, originally published in the 1890's. It is available in a paperback Harper Torchbook edition, first published in 1961, and contains an Introduction by Gordon Allport who edited it.

[5] A. A. Roback, *A History of American Psychology* (New York: Collier Books, 1964), pp. 168–69, 270–71.

[6] See *Ibid.*, pp. 264–282 for a well written and fairly presented attempt.

Russia, whose experiments and theories of various types of conditioning[8] was, to many, neatly compatible with American behaviorist schools. And the end product, behavioral psychology, as understood today by American experimental, educational and clinical psychologists *and* American social psychologists, still displays today a certain unmistakable looseness in theory and practice.

Psychological history is fortunately not the subject of this chapter. The mighty and trenchant influence of behavioral theory upon American (and much European) thinking concerning motivation is considerable, as well as the fundamental ideas of human nature implicit therein. Even considering the effect of popularized Freudianism upon our culture, behaviorism has made what appears to be a near immutable impression on our culture.

Common experience and much of history records that men's motivations will, in a large measure, tend to be decided by what they believe their motivations *ought to be* as related to their behavior at a given time. In other words, the concept of motivational psychology they tend most easily to accept (and men accepted such concepts before the word "psychology" existed) provides, at least, a reasonable and simple *raison d'être* for the nature and direction of their obvious drives, impulses and incentives.[9] Thus, frequently, does psychology (and behaviorism particularly) truly create its own deductive proofs.

America, in this current period, is no exception, except that, at first glance, motivational aspects of the different sorts of people in our culture appear pluralistic and diverse, especially when one construes motives in a broad sense as the articulated causes or purposes in *life*. The author has previously discussed in detail some of the dynamics of such motives in another book,[10] where they appear as *Work, Progress* and *Happiness* symbols in a societal symbolic grab bag: retirement dreams, a good standard of material well being, productivity, respect, admiration of others, health,

---

[7] In his volume, *The Magic Animal,* Wylie spices the tale of behaviorism with considerable venom, but I can find little wrong in the spirit (if not the letter) of his attack on pp. 37–58. In fact, if more criticism of the behaviorists emulated Wylie's vigor, American psychology, psychiatry and social psychiatry might not display some of their present symptoms of identity confusion.

[8] Good books on Pavlov and his work in English are not difficult to find. One of the most comprehensive, presently in paperback edition, is the unfortunately poorly edited (or pruned), Michael Kaplan, *Essential Works of Pavlov* (New York: Bantam Books, 1966), which covers its subject with too many return trips to the same places. The editor does little to relieve the ponderous style of many Russians when they write about any subject of an essentially theoretical nature.

[9] The one area of success that psychoanalysis may justly claim, namely therapy for neurosis, derives in part from this phenomenon. The analyst, by means of many ruses and stratagems (some of which he is almost certainly not aware himself) may shift motivations—usually in the direction of permissiveness and loose criteria of judgment—so that a patient's neurosis, while untouched, may no longer conflict with his apparent motivations for behavior. In effect, a cure is the result.

[10] G.N.G., *L C,* p. 86.

sexual conquest, community involvement, diplomas, degrees, acknowledged philanthropy and other virtues.

What these assorted shared motivations have in common is that they involve perceptible *behaviors* of individuals, even when the behavior involves remote matters (like philanthropy) that only pay-off after death. (Here the justification of motivation behind the act often concerns the behavior by which the individual bequeaths to his estate the specific inclination for a memorial to himself.)[11] Lifetime motivations for some of us may, in fact, center upon covert, apparently non-behavioral factors like subjective self-fulfillment, peace of mind, a promise of something in an afterlife, communion with a transcendental life force or the joys of contemplation. Such lifetime motives are rare in our day, rarer perhaps than they have been in the past (considering population expansion), because, apparently, immediate gratifications in behavioral terms are more realistic objectives today than they once were—although this apparently satisfactory explanation may be too facile to be true. More important, motivations for continuing the struggle of life, or, when young, the impetus to make something of one's self, reflect a cultural implantation of goals, ideals, values and potentials to which all of us (psychologists, philosophers and teachers not excepted) are educated early in life. Cross-culture anthropologists have shown countless cultures in our own time where people appear *not* to be so motivated, in general. And we are able to observe with clarity how these alien values, so variant from our own, have also been inculcated by formal and informal systems of indoctrination and education.

Motivational factors in our culture are, therefore, in summation, usually behavioral factors, and amenable by a behaviorist orientation to psychological speculation, whether the speculation is undertaken by observers of an orthodox behavioral school or not, although the more developed one's sense of the adequacy of behavioral explanations of human peculiarities and irregularities, the more satisfactory (hence good or moral) these particular motivations seem. Their application has certainly been clarified in the novel *Walden II* by B. F. Skinner in a loose behavioral context.[12] But they are

---

11 A *George N. Gordon Memorial Armchair,* if so-dedicated at the social men's club to which I belong, might amuse or please me *now*. I am sure my ghost would treat it with indifference and not even bother haunting it.

12 As an admirer of fiction, I cannot in good conscience recommend *Walden II* to anyone who enjoys novels. Skinner's utopian effort is, at present, enjoying a successful revival, and young Skinnerian behaviorists, I hear, are setting up colonies along the lines suggested in the book. My personal preference would be for the now declining hippie communes, because of their sexual and pharmacological attractions that often appear anti- or non-behaviorial in orientation. (Since she is something of a primitive behaviorist, my wife does not look kindly upon my occasional suggestions that I examine these manifestations—congeries of hippie pads, not the mini-Walden IIs—at first hand for a few weeks or months. I have, accordingly, behaved myself.) Skinner's general orientation is expertly described in the kind of volume he writes best: B. F. Skinner, *Science and Human Behavior* (New York: The Macmillan Co., 1953), my suggestion for further inquiry.

even clearer in a daily newspaper and informal experiences, especially for those of us who work with young people at the stage of life at which they must face the problem of the behavioral consequences of their youthful ideals and ambiguously felt appetites.

One can hardly contest the validity of behaviorally based motivations as "good" or "bad," in fact, and participate profitably in contemporary culture in the West and in much of the East. Ethnocentric proclivities may neither be intellectualized nor willed into oblivion by even the wisest and most detached of us without severe consequences to one's perceptions of reality and an attendant threat of cognitive, emotional and behavioral derangement. In rough terms, madness looms on such a path. Overt behavioral motivations derived from cultural consensus are certainly adequate for the maintenance of our world today; whether or not they will be as adequate tomorrow is too conjectural for this discussion.[13]

Koestler comes as close as any modern thinker to this detachment,[14] noting that behaviorism in any form is a manifestation, in human terms, of the naïve positivism of mechanistic physics (long since subsumed to other systems) as articulated in the past century. Dealing (as does behavioral psychology) mainly with observed phenomena, it almost immediately runs into formidable obstacles when phenomena are uncovered which are not, in the accepted sense, observable. Behavioral psychology displays this difficulty when it encounters such notions as "consciousness," "mind" (or "mental events"), and handles them in much the same way that hard core positivists still treat any data they cannot fit into their systems. They ignore them or call them "irrelevant." Koestler describes the experimental aspects of behavioral psychology (apparently its most productive phase being the study of laboratory animal behavior) as consisting of "analysing bricks and mortar in the hope that by patient effort somehow one day . . . (your efforts) would tell you what a cathedral looked like." [15]

Behaviorism, or its methodologies, has, in recent years, led to complex experiments that deal with elaborate and elegant attempts to explain (and thereby control) how language develops, how it is used and how people learn, offering today's sophisticated experimental behaviorist almost uncontested leadership in sheer activity and assiduity of experiment concerning complexities of cognition.[16] Armed with relatively simple theories of various sorts of conditioning, he has developed complex mathematical, experimental devices not only to "prove" behaviorism (which, given its limits, is quite easy to do) but to apply conditioning techniques with circumscribed

---

[13] See Chapters 27 and 28 for some guesses, humbly (but possible also madly) submitted.

[14] Koestler, *The Ghost in the Machine*, pp. 5–18.

[15] *Ibid.*, p. 9.

[16] Piagetian theorists and interpreters are catching up, at the present writing, in these fields.

chances of success to certain aspects of human development. Behaviorists as clever as Arthur W. Staats[17] must not be—as Koestler and Wylie would have it—underestimated in their recent contributions to social psychology. Not only does Staats apply a brilliant critical scalpel to many accepted notions in linguistics, gestalt psychology, systems engineering and psychoanalysis.[18] But he is also always (and inadvertently) scrutinizing with intense honesty a critical facet of contemporary social life which accepts *concrete results* (i.e. behavior) as the *one main and relevant* manifestation of psychological value. The general viewpoint for which behaviorism speaks is, however, naïve, outdated and—in the light of the enormous variety of artistic, voluntaristic and spiritually oriented activities we experience in ourselves and see in others—apparently fundamentally incorrect.

In the academy, behaviorists are likely to make up the greatest single segment of the psychological faculty, thus giving college students the impression that behaviorist psychology is *the* psychology—except that their own personal therapists are likely to be psychoanalytically oriented. And professional psychiatrists and psychologists employed by universities to deal with students' problems are rarely, if ever, behaviorists.

The latter's position on a university faculty is easily explained, and a matter of importance. First, behaviorists provide the widest possibilities of all psychological schools for research and experiment and go to unbelievable pains to invent devices for torturing inbred laboratory animals, fish and, sometimes, children. The experiments and devices roughly follow Pavlov's doghouse gadgets. But Pavlov would not recognize them today. University administrators appreciate action, experiment, visible manifestations of research, publication of findings (if only by Xerox) and laboratory equipment to display to visitors. Behaviorists supply plenty of each.

Second, and far more important, universities are places where aspirations are catalyzed *into* behavioral manifestations, and motivations are given their first test before they are subsequently activated. Aspiring lawyers learn the behavior of lawyers (and some law); aspiring physicians learn the behavior of physicians (and some medicine). For most students, critical aspects of professional learning—or informal learning to grapple with the exigencies of life—will be gained slowly, and largely in non-behavioral ways,

---

[17] See A. W. Staats, *Learning, Language, and Cognition* (New York: Holt, Rinehart and Winston, Inc., 1968), for a complex but enviable adumbration of experimental behaviorism, carrying the various forms of conditioning into statistical experimentation of an extremely elaborate variety. Personally, I feel sorry for the author's daughter Jennifer who was the guinea pig (replacing, I suppose, Skinner's pigeons and rats) for many of his procedures.

[18] For excellent criticism of linguistics, see *ibid.*, pp. 154–158; of programmed instruction, see *ibid.*, pp. 200–202; pungent observations of gestalt psychology and psychoanalysis are found throughout the volume. Staats' consideration of motivation, *ibid.*, pp. 430–31, are consistent with the observations above. Motivational studies (and speculation) are one area, I think, where behaviorists are likely to maintain conceptual hegemony in the United States and the USSR for many years.

after graduation, over a period of years of trial and error. The university is one place where motivation is given concrete form in terms of today's social value structures, that is, as anticipated behaviors, and therefore the behavioral psychologists (and similar mechanists) thrive and gain status there.

Beyond the university, however, the impotence of their numerous sophistries becomes more obvious, particularly when behaviorists attempt therapy or modification of social processes—in fact, in any activity more testing than advertising, the profession in which the father figure for American behaviorists, J. B. Watson himself, ended his career. But a behaviorist may also prove useful in the mail-order world, correspondence school education, salesmanship, publicity, public relations and in talent agencies,[19] all occupations where motivations of human beings are of fundamental interest.

In no manner, is it implied here that behavioral notions, for all their shortcomings and potentially deadly misconceptions, are the only meaningful psychological devices available today to gain insights into the wellsprings of human motivation. On the contrary, numerous other instruments exist, from theories of raw instinct through the detective story analogies, symbols and clues in the Freudian system (as played frequently at social gatherings and dispensed by guidance counselors), as well as religious and/or spiritual concepts. The point is simply that the behavioral design, which regards motivation as learning and motives as pragmatic reflections *in action* of social values and aspirations, is the most *useful* one available today. It accurately describes, for the widest range of purposes (especially ours, associated with psychology in a social field), the reasons and results of the observable motivational aspects of human nature.

Possibly the concept of motivation as applied to collective phenomena *is* mainly a behavioral process in its psychological references. If so, we are dealing with a tautology, but one no more irrelevant to modern life than an ideal of "success" that is defined by "riches," and therefore elicits a subsequent analysis of how people succeed according to how they accumulate money, which is both relevant *and* meaningful in our culture, behaviorally, at least.

Perceptions of Perception

The study of perception—building blocks essential to our inquiry into the psychological aspects of persuasion—takes us to an area of discourse unfortunately beyond the productive application of behaviorism in psychology for a number of reasons. This is true simply because perception is simply not a behavior; it is a process, either defined physically, mentally or both. K. Koffka, the gestaltist, suggests that "things look (or smell,

---

19 One instance proves nothing, but an acquaintance of mine, a graduate behavioral psychologist from a midwestern university, is today one of the most successful and active talent agents in Hollywood. He rarely tells his clients about his background.

taste, sound etc.) as they do because of the field organization to which the proximate stimulus distribution gives rise," and because of the interrelationships of these stimuli.[20] As we move into the consideration of perception, our concern with fields, organizations and relationships (constantly in motion) shifts our framework of discourse inevitably to gestalt theory. This must occur, because behavior derived from individual perceptions, while interesting to us in the pages to come, tells us almost nothing about the *source* or *nature of the stimulus* of perceptions themselves, except in rigidly controlled situations unlike any involved in social persuasion, the exceptions, possibly, being so-called "hypnotism" and "brainwashing."[21]

To illustrate, let us imagine a man running up a flight of stairs. His behavior results, let us assume, from the perception of *something,* but we do not know what. It is unlikely that any examination, no matter how sophisticated, of his *running* will yield important evidence as to the nature of that perception. Neither will a verbal report to our question, "Why are you running?" if the perception involves a socially unacceptable factor, say, haste to get to a bathroom because of a sudden stomach cramp, flight from the sight of ghost, vampire or goblin, or a retreat from a sexual encounter with the wife of an armed psychotic who interrupted his dalliance. In each of these cases, a holistic explanation is required to make any sense of his behavior, much less understand it.

The physical aspects of perception center hueristically somewhere between the boundaries of neurology and psychology, and remain, at present, arcane subjects of conjecture and experiment, the data of which, even in their present crude state, require considerable special knowledge and skill, especially in the integration of the philosophical, anatomical, psychological and neurological factors involved.[22] The psychological aspects remain equally as inchoate in many respects, but the approach to them, at least, is more amenable to common discourse.

The psychological fundament of most (or all) persuasion is perception. Little argument denies that first, individuals perceive their environments by means of multiple mechanisms; second, these perceptions are somehow organized by sense organs and other segments of the nervous system; third, they are set against a framework of previous impressions of

---

[20] K. Koffka, *Principles of Gestalt Psychology* (New York: Harcourt Brace, 1935), p. 98.

[21] See Chapter 20 for further discussion of these phenomena.

[22] With trepidation, let me here suggest Warren S. McCulloch, *Embodiments of Mind* (Cambridge, Mass.: The M.I.T. Press, 1965), especially the introductory article and McCulloch's famous essay (written with others) "What the Frog's Eye Tells the Frog's Brain," pp. 230–255. This wide-ranging, fascinating, and (to me) sometimes unintelligible book brings the reader to the frontiers of psychoneurological speculation concerning human thought processes and perception, one of the late McCulloch's strongest interests.

many kinds and interpreted as meanings; and fourth, it is often surprisingly simple to distort this process at any point, most particularly in its initial and final stages. Perception, for instance, by touch is immediately befuddled when we finger a marble with crossed fingers and eyes closed, a novelty many of us learned in childhood. Perception is disoriented in its latter phases by a magician's apparatus that apparently displays a headless woman but, in fact, merely presents a woman with a set of mirrors covering her head. In any case, the words "initial" and "final" may be misleading here, because perception appears to constitute a holistic process, and the time sequences we use to explain is a result of the necessity, for descriptive and rhetorical purposes, of segmenting and mechanizing a totality.

What has interested social psychologists particularly since the early 1950's is an observation, hardly new to this century but stimulated by experiments performed on American soldiers during World War II. Despite apparent similarities among individuals and of their perceptual processes, for many reasons, perceptions tend to be variable, and subject to simple manipulation in different people under various circumstances, and even in the same people under similar circumstances. On the heels of this discovery followed an outburst of experimentation (mostly on university campuses) in order to study what seemed to be the variable distorting factors in the impressions individuals perceive: the arousal of fear, the prestige or credibility of the source of a stimulus, persistent or short-term prejudices, physical and temperamental and other factors. Citing these individual experiments and invariable theoretical by-products is unnecessary here;[23] they have become closely associated with the pioneers who conducted them, including Jerome Bruner, Solomon Asch, Marie Jahoda, Carl I. Hovland, Arthur A. Lumsdaine, Irving L. Janis, Leo J. Postman, Irving Sarnoff, Daniel Katz, Gordon Allport and H. A. Witkin, among others.

The evolution of the concept of "selective perception" emerged from this outburst of experiment, as did the concepts of "selective attention" and "selected retention." [24] Less important than the names or slogans involved, of course, was the observation, by now supported both by empirical and experimental studies, that the process perception is, in some measure, the function of an individual's own nature, which, in terms of perceptual possibilities, is a product of a distinctive background and a functioning immediate environment. Because one draws certain expectations from this environment, his perceptions are, in numerous ways, circumscribed by all

---

[23] Most social psychology text and books of readings, including the various editions of Guy Swanson *et al.*, *Readings in Social Psychology* (New York: Henry Holt and Co.), contain reports of these experiments. They are also expertly and briefly described and interpreted in the text of Tamotsu Shibutani, *Improvised News* (New York: The Bobbs-Merrill Co., 1966), which, in spite of its misleading title, is one of the richest compendia on the social psychology of communications lately to come my way.

[24] These notions were variously expressed by most of the writers above during the early 1950's.

these factors, occasionally in extreme and bizarre ways, but, usually, more or less predictably. The more charged the environment with emotional and cognitive factors, the greater the likelihood of distortion, it seems, even if that distortion requires that the individual erase certain perceptions entirely from the field, or at least from memory.

Nothing in the concepts evolved from these observations came as much of a shock to skilled playwrights, actors, magicians or politicians, because practical translations of these principles have been their stock in trade for years. But, under controlled situations and with rational (?) college students as their subjects, experiments, such as those performed by Asch,[25] seemed spectacular. In one of them, a poor victim solemnly swears that he perceives two unequal lines as being exactly the same size because of immediate collusive social pressures brought to bear on him. The principle behind the experiment (the coercion of "stooges" upon a "patsy") has been employed on circus midways and in medicine shows for many, many years.

Numerous theories, of course, appeared in order to explain these phenomena, each and all emphasizing the apparent perceptual tendency towards "consistency" or "balance." [26] Heider's entry centered on harmonies and disharmonies between individuals in relation to a specific object. Newcomb centered his hypothesis upon interpersonal relationships and the progress of subjective factors in perception to objective ones in social situations. Rosenberg and Abelson followed a somewhat different track, citing parsimony in the changes necessarily made to adjust one's perceptions to an imbalanced and/or inconsistent object. These constructs and others constitute interesting attempts to explain an ancient human quirk.

The bulk of this work, for all its passing interest, may be in its general thrust subsumed into Leon Festinger's familiar theory of "cognitive dissonance" [27] which, by the late 1950's was generally, if provisionally, accepted as the one most adequate explanation of the various perceptual curiosities demonstrated in the laboratory and as chewed upon in psychological literature. Frequently criticized for the difficulties it produces on its face in translating *verbal* notions into *human* processes and *events* (a ubiquitous problem of such theories), Festinger's concept, nevertheless, provides a clear background for the consideration of how persuasion and perception reciprocate with one another.

Briefly stated, the theory of cognitive dissonance assumes that an individual will not, perceptually at least, tolerate more than a minimal quan-

---

[25] The rationales and conceptual frameworks of these experiments may be found in Solomon E. Asch, *Social Psychology* (Englewood Cliffs, N.J.: Prentice-Hall Inc., 1952). See Chapter 16, especially.

[26] For a tense review of these theories briefly treated below, see Smith, *op. cit.*, pp. 89–92.

[27] See Leon Festinger, A *Theory of Cognitive Dissonance* (Evanston, Ill.: Row, Peterson and Co., 1957).

tum of psychological inconsistency in his perceived environment. When dissonance of certain magnitudes occur, and one is faced with inconsistent cognitive elements in the world around him, he appreciates the problem and resolves it by reducing whatever tension it creates as easily as possible. This may be accomplished by behavioral changes, minimizing the real nature of the inconsistency or by misinterpreting the data upon which he must act. What is being sought by the individual is psychological equilibrium, and this is purchased at the price of some kind of change, either in behavior towards, or perception of, the dissonant elements.

In common parlance, we might say that, faced with a situation that an individual perceives as inconsistent with his cognitive structures, he does everything he can, within the limits of the environment, to vindicate the rightness of that structure and the integrity of his own cognitions—up to a point. This difference between reality and his cognitive structures is understood to constitute the ratio of dissonant to consonant elements. And the degree in which cognitions agree with the new perceptions (and do not therefore cause dissonance) constitutes what is termed "cognitive overlap." In theory, at least, we are now able to explain and predict what will happen when cognitive dissonance occurs, and, if we are given enough data, when and where it will happen, to whom, and even how it is likely to happen.

In charting this course, it is necessary to specify the cognitive elements, obtain a clear picture of the environment, the magnitude of dissonance (which, if extreme enough, can, of course, force an individual to abandon entirely the integrity of his cognitive system), the impetus to resolve the conflict, and the methods used to decrease dissonance. The basic ways the individual usually accomplishes the latter are either by finding new consonant elements, modifying his behavior, or changing his internal and/or external environments.

While a theory like Festinger's will inevitably be modified and qualified in time and with application, it represents a functional approach to understanding many, if not most, of the formerly noted curiosities of perception, *including those of an organic nature* (whether as a result of illness or pharmacologically induced) that are relevant to the study of persuasion —or, more precisely, which permit certain individuals to *be* persuaded (or remain not persuaded), under certain conditions.

Personality and Persuasion

The psychology of personality is probably as old, if not older, than any other type of disciplined study. If the psychology of perception may be traced back to Socrates' allegory of the cave (". . . when such a prisoner came into the light, would not the brilliance fill his eyes so that he would not be able to do even one of the things now called 'real'?"), the psychology of personality was already clearly articulated by Greek dramatists and philosophers well before Socrates created the allegory. Although based on a crude system of human typologies, the ancient concept of humors has served as a basic handbook for storytellers and dramatists for thousands of years with remarkable relevance both to comedy and tragedy, and has been refined many times in the process, most frequently in recent years. Hooton, Sheldon, Kretschmer, Jung and Adler are probably among the best known modern psychological typologists.

Typological personality concepts (it is difficult to regard them as theories) are closed systems consisting of physical, behavioral or metaphorical variables which can, with various degrees of precision, be manipulated into a mix that will provide an immediate and provisional character description of a (usually) practical nature. These data are generally more useful for descriptive purposes than for either prediction or explanation. Two discrete stops on a scale are all that are required for a sophisticated typological system—if they are as rich in connotation as the ideas of *introversion* and *extroversion;* or *cerebrotonia* and *visceratonia.*

Students of personality theory today, however, tend to turn their backs upon typologies—in fact, ignore them entirely—in favor of more elegant constructions of personality as a relatively open system in interaction with internal and external forces. Character "type," if such a term is used, would therefore be related to the interaction of time, place and dynamic individual factors of acculturation, physical development, age, and more variables than it is probably possible to gather about any one person at any moment.

The psychology of persuasion today is better articulated in the loose universe of contemporary personality theory than in terms of typologies. One may, for instance, type an individual as gullible, a typical country gawk similar to Al Capp's Lil' Abner. And such bumpkins exist—but, in terms of persuasion, we are merely noting and generalizing *one* aspect of human personality at *one* moment of an individual's life. The same man who loses all his money at a three-shell game may be highly inflexible in his political orientation and impossible to seduce away from his wife and home. Although he is gullible today, it is also possible that he was not gullible twenty years ago, and will not be gullible in quite the same way next year. In more sophisticated terms, even the physical-typological balances of Sheldon's familiar morphologies seem to vary with time, diet, environmental stress and other factors, although they may be quite reliable at a given moment. But the psychology of persuasion cannot be primarily concerned with given individuals at given moments. They are not irrelevant to it, but its social psychology must operate in a broader temporal and characterological field of action.

One possible personality factor is, of course, immediately relevant to persuasion. It might be called the quality of "persuasability," which, according to Hovland and Janis,[28] does, indeed, appear to loom large in their

[28] Hovland's studies span many years of experimentation at Yale and considerable publication of results. The three main volumes that cover this work are Carl Hovland,

many years of experiments (on available student populations in New Haven, Connecticut, mostly). Hovland demonstrates variability between individuals, apparently as functions of personality, in the probability, or ability, of one to be persuaded. This personality factor is *unrelated to general intelligence* as measured at the time. Persuasability *is* involved with self-esteem, hostility and other psychological characteristics, as well as to sex differences. (That Hovland shows that females are more persuasable than males[29] is interesting, but may, in fact, constitute mere affirmation of what has been known for a long time about the role of women in American life.) Cross-media effects, such as print vs. face-to-face communications, were also studied.

Hovland and Janis' conclusions are summed up thus: "How important are personality factors in persuasability? If we attempt to answer this question from the correlational data already at hand, *it must be said that personality factors appear to play only a very minor role as determinants of persuasability*. Almost all the correlations obtained . . . are relatively low (statistically) . . ." [30] In general, many years of evidence seem to indicate that individuals of low self-esteem, the guilty (or guilt-ridden), the hostile, inadequate, isolated, lonely, dreamy, dependent individual is more likely to be generally persuasable than his opposite. But, with due respect to Hovland's efforts, are these factors elements of personality, or simply variable subjective behaviors? In more specific terms, were the numerous and questionable "personality inventories" employed by Hovland genuine and adequate tests of personality traits as the psychologist interprets them, a problem for which Hovland and his associates cannot be held responsible but which is of prime relevance to their modest conclusions.

Practical persuasion of many kinds has been carried on for generations with the assumptions of a "gullible-Gus" theory which echoes in the slogan, "Never give a sucker an even break." Given Barnum's estimate that one sucker is born per minute (a rate that must have accelerated since his day), it is odd that psychological science has not told us a good deal more about the behavior and personality of the sucker than it has to date, including Hovland's findings. One danger is that the orderly study of the quality of persuasability may lead to the methodical inquiry into a figure of speech, rather than to the investigation of a phenomenon of psychological interest.[31]

Irving L. Janis and Harold H. Kelly *Communications and Persuasion*; C. Hovland etc., *The Order of Presentation in Persuasion*; C. Hovland, etc. *Personality and Persuasability* (New Haven: Yale University Press, 1953, 1957, and 1959). Hovland and Janis' major conclusions—especially in regard to personality—appear in the final volume, pp. 225–279.

[29] See C. Hovland, etc., *Personality and Persuasability*, pp. 238–240.

[30] *Ibid.*, p. 248. (Italics added.)

[31] Still in the spirit of Barnum (and as a former pitchman myself), let me register my

Personality theory, however, offers us quite a range of theoretical formulations, many of which satisfy our demands for non-typological, non-specific delineations (or series of critieria and metaphors) of the origins and functions of personality. Mehrabian shows[32] that personality theories run a gamut today from modified versions of behavioral schema to a notion derived from computer simulations, the latter, "not a theory in itself," according to Mehrabian, "but . . . rather a method of using a computer as a tool . . ." [33]

(Because all tools are limited in application, it is clear from Mehrabian's discussion[34] that his modesty is likely to prove unnecessary in the long run. The computer approach will unquestionably modify theory by relegating the data that cannot properly be simulated to irrelevancy; if enough modifications occur, old theory will, in time, turn into new theory, a process already at work.)

What theory has to offer at present centers on concepts familiar to the student of contemporary psychology: Rogerian notions of congruence and incongruence (similar in many respects to Festinger's ideas of perception on pp. 224–5) between an organism and its environment ("phenomenal and organismic experiences," in Rogers' words), and concern with sources of the subjective experiences that affect this relationship.[35] Psychoanalysis, of course, also yields a theory of personality that may be formulated in many ways but invariably centers upon the maintenance of an ego structure continually dealing with conscious and non-conscious drives, resulting in such Freudian staples as reaction formations, anxiety, aggressions, regressions, and gratifications of various types.[36] Mechanistic theories of "instinct-need-

---

personal feeling that, if suckers exist, they are no less evident at a convention of behavioral scientists than on a carnival midway, and that university graduates are in no manner more difficult to "take" than the "gentle townspeople" to whom Barnum addressed his appeals. The present state of fractured "schools" of psychology and sociology, for instance, indicate that a formidable number of suckers must have been (and are being) fooled by one or another pseudo-scientific confidence schemes. It is unlikely that they are *all* correct, unless the various viewpoints of culture and behavior extant today can, like the theory of epicycles, be gathered into one, comparatively simple natural law. More likely, I think, suckers have swallowed moonshine. The question of determining exactly *who* the pyscho- and socio-suckers *are* must await, I fear, further investigation.

32 See Albert Mehrabian, *An Analysis of Personality Theories* (Englewood Cliffs, New Jersey: Prentice-Hall, Inc., 1968), for a well organized and clearly stated presentation of a number of personality theories, as well as a careful discussion of the problems that arise in their articulation and evaluation and criteria by which to judge them (pp. 1–30, 180–84).

33 *Ibid.*, p. 165.

34 See *ibid.*, pp. 174–178.

35 See Carl R. Rogers, "A Theory of Therapy, Personality and Interpersonal Relationships etc." in S. Koch (ed.), *Psychology: A Study of A Science*, Volume 3 (New York: McGraw Hill Book Co., 1959), or Mehrabian, *op. cit.*, pp. 33–51.

36 Note *ibid.*, pp. 53–84, but the psychoanalytic assumptions developed therein may

habit-trait-factors" in Mehrabian's words, from McDougall to Murray, also provide a selection of theoretical speculation[37] that appears moderately interesting to students of personality.

The adequacy or inadequacy of the theories briefly described above is, fortunately, not our concern. Their relevance to the psychologics of persuasion is. For our purposes, most of them fail to meet both descriptive and predictive requirements in comprehending more than superficial descriptions or vague analogies of personality. They tell little about the process of modifying human dispositions in various environments and under different circumstances, as related to human character. The fact remains, however, that a psychology of persuasion without an adequate foundation in a theory of personality may as well be entered simply as another chapter under the heading *Logical Perspectives*, and treated as either empirical knowledge or history.

How fortunate, then, that a more satisfactory approach than those above has been delineated recently,[38] employing (largely) concepts derived from the developmental psychology of Jean Piaget.[39] Based upon Piaget's familiar notions of *adaptation* (as commonly understood), *assimilation* (the

---

easily be modified to fit the demands of any neo-Freudian school. Curiously, Freud's own work, to the best of my knowledge and memory, does not move far beyond the study of personality characteristics limited by Freud's personal interests in his patients, his time and place, himself and his fellow European Jews. In naming the dynamics of these characteristics, Freud did, however, search out prototypes in drama and literature, but his speculation into the wellsprings of personality rarely traveled beyond the circumference of his own environment.

[37] *Ibid.*, pp. 86–118.

[38] See *ibid.*, pp. 121–162. As presented by Mehrabian, this theory draws heavily also upon H. Werner, *Comparative Psychology of Mental Development* (New York: International University Press, 1957), and Werner and B. Kaplan, *Symbol Formation* (New York: John Wiley and Sons, Inc., 1963).

[39] Three of the volumes presently available in English that adequately discuss Piaget's work in child psychology and its ramifications are, like many American books of Piagetian theory, not written by Piaget himself but by his students and disciples. (These creatures, incidentally, are increasing their numbers in the academies of the United States as rapidly as gerbils, at the present writing. I foresee, just around a corner, a burgeoning "Piaget industry" in the world of educational psychology, comparable, in terms of fame, glory and fortune, to the manifold "Freud industry," which, if I read the market correctly, is now declining.) The books listed below are all sensible and clearly written. How close they come to Piaget's psychology as Piaget understands it, I cannot judge. See John F. Flavell, *The Developmental Psychology of Jean Piaget* (Princeton, New Jersey: D. Van Nostrand Co., 1963); Herbert Ginsburg and Sylvia Opper, *Piaget's Theory of Intellectual Development* (Englewood Cliffs, New Jersey: Prentice-Hall, Inc., 1967); and John L. Phillips Jr., *The Origins of Intellect: Piaget's Theory* (San Francisco: W. H. Freeman and Co., 1969). The latter is written for teachers and reduces Piaget's notions to simple statements without (apparently) also reducing their value. For a fairly recently published book on Piaget *by Piaget*, see Jean Piaget and Barbel Inhelder, *The Psychology of the Child* (New York: Basic Books, 1969), which is, according to some of his students, inferior to the volumes of his interpreters. At the present writing, I have not had the opportunity to study the latter closely.

process of change an organism creates in its environment in order to incorporate what it needs into itself), and *accommodation* (the modification of the function of an organism necessarily to assimilate part of that environment), and finally translated into cognitive terms, the theory displays a Jonsonian bias, but it is both evocative and interesting.

Personality is understood to center, at any given moment in the life history of an individual, between what is *assimilated* from the environment and what is *accommodated.* When assimilation is dominant, the organization tends to automatize; when accommodation is dominant, it necessarily remains flexible. When a balance is struck between the two, the individual centers his pattern at a given point, and personality characteristics display irreversible tendencies.

As the individual matures, a certain pattern emerges in his development of concepts, percepts and other cognitive organizations, so that a *personal mode of differentiation and hierarchic organization* characterizes the way *he* adapts, assimilates and accommodates to the world. Naturally, training is involved and manifests itself in the similarities we find between people. But the Piagetian concept holds that intellect (in its broadest sense) is an autonomous development of the human animal that emerges only as the individual interacts in increasingly complex ways (due to the increasing complexities of his capacities) with the environment. This latter process is naturally individual and highly personal, but nevertheless dependent upon distinctive provisions in the environment to exercise *one's own* potential for development.[40]

---

[40] Mehrabian notes wisely that the environment, rather than individual, tends to dominate in the accumulation of what are usually regarded as "personality *crises.*" Thus, such crises display typical developmental stress episodes at specific periods in a given culture. In our own society, he suggests that they occur at about the age of six, in early puberty, in early adulthood and in the forties—when one reaches what is called on New York's Madison Avenue a "flame out." See Mehrabian, *op. cit.*, p. 147. But the environment is accommodated and assimilated differently for different people in a single culture. Having fortunately experienced my personal "flame out" in my thirties, I have (with the help of others) accepted (or accommodated and assimilated to) a mode of behavior which, in general accent, centers its focus on the present day rather than perceptions of past and future, both of which are germane to the etiology of all of these crises. Learning, quite literally, to live "a day at a time," produces in one personality changes of a startling nature, even when environments are changed only slightly, because one's process of accommodation and assimilation is, in large measure (but, naturally, not entirely) thereby centered on a small temporal environmental field: the present.

I have seen hundreds of people move comfortably from deep states of crisis to this degree to both flexibility and equilibrium at various adult ages, almost always as the result of a personal crisis, usually precipitated (*not* caused) by addiction to alcohol or to some other, but similar, drug that distorts or disorganizes conceptual functioning. In breaking their addiction (by accepting total abstinence), such individuals appear to regress sufficiently into reversible, labial relationships with their environments to effect for themselves reorganization of cognitive and affective processes that, one would imagine, had been automatized years before. The kind of therapy employed by Alcoholics Anonymous and similar organizations appears to operate along

The process is one which continues throughout life, involving a galaxy of contexts (as yet unspecified) and variable but interrelated degrees of disengagement, objectivity, centering and decentering and reversibility of orientations, all of which are positively correlated with the individual's richness of cognitive development and his skill at adaptation. Inadequacy of adaptation and cognitive regression are therefore also possible, marked by low cognitive development in various areas of personality. Development also tends to cease of its own accord when one has reached either a high level of cognitive growth or has maintained his individual personality structure for considerable time at a low cognitive level.

This perspective of personality growth displays a number of advantages over those discussed previously, because, first, unlike typologies, it is not fixed but highly maleable; second, it deals, broadly speaking, with intellect and conceptual development (including one's cognitive understanding of his emotions, needs and drives), all of which are matters critical and relevant to the concept of personality; third, notions of consciousness (and nonconscious influences) are easily subsumed into the pattern but are of little consequence to the existential explanation of personality; fourth, it centers on the individual's double-edged relationship with his environment—what he *takes* from it and incorporates into his self; the way in which he *manages* and *manipulates* his world for his own purposes—on a developmental scale as yet undeveloped (beyond Piaget's critical stages of conceptual development in childhood) to its analytic potential. It, therefore, and fifth, conceives of personality as highly variable throughout one's individual life-span and as circumstances change in the world around him. One maintains in the self ever present possibilities for personality modification at any time in

---

these lines, limited severely in application by the necessity for the individual in crisis to *want* to change his life style enough to give up his dependency upon the perception-distorting drug to which he has became addicted.

This kind of conceptual re-education of cognitions and emotions is not easily accomplished. Far from it. Its main difficulty, however, is often overcome by the simple recognition by the individual in crisis that his or her only alternative to such reorganization is the prolongation of the crisis, personal defeat, total personality disorientation, alienation (inability to adapt, accommodate or assimilate), and a degenerative death or institutionalization, all of the above usually occurring in rapid progression. This recognition is, nevertheless, a personally difficult step to achieve, calling into question one's ontological relationship to his own senses, his concepts of the environment, and, in Piagetian terms, the nature of his conceptual relationships that are direct functions of his personality. It is no wonder, therefore, that such a recognition is frequently described as a "miracle" or a "spiritual awakening." This is an almost universal phenomenon among such individuals, although it is frequently comprehended by them for what it is only in retrospect. They tend, therefore, frequently to associate it with their new world of spiritual cognitions and a newly found sense of growth associated with freedom from addiction. For this reason, movements such as AA are often incorrectly interpreted as religious in basic orientation. They are not, but most recovered alcoholics (the lion's share of whom are members of AA) and former drug addicts tend to accept, or find reasonable, personal cognitions of a power higher than themselves. This concept makes particular sense to them in the light of their former experiences with the tyrannical power of alcohol cr drugs.

life, a necessary criterion for a realistic theory of personality, useful in delineating the psychologics of persuasion.

Conclusion

In order to set the stage for the psychological perspectives of persuasion to follow, certain psychological considerations must be discussed. As discourse changes its emphasis, so do theories, assumptions, and frames of reference.

Contemporary psychology offers a wide range of speculation in many keys for the student of social behavior. Conventional social psychology tends to be eclectic. But, as taught in the university today, it concentrates on an unfortunately narrow area, most of it drawn from a small number of recent experiments that search for mechanisms applicable to the behavior of groups.

As satisfactory as this approach may be for the academy, the study of persuasion, unfortunately, does not fit neatly into the limits of contemporary experimental psychology or the traditional curriculum in social psychology. A more catholic approach is required, one that travels beyond matters of "attitude formation," "persuasability," and "propaganda techniques" into the many, variously articulated concepts of *what relationships human motivation, perception and personality have to modifications both of dispositions and behavior.*

Of the options open to the student of the subject today, a behavioral approach (for all of its conceptual and operational shortcomings) is probably the most revealing when applied to contemporary *motives* for most of the problems that involve mass communications and interpersonal persuasion in a technological society. On the other hand, experimental psychology has yielded a rich literature of *perception,* comprehensible to the general student of the subject (as neurological evidence, for instance, is not), particularly in the matter of cognitive dissonance. Theoretical speculation on this phenomenon appears to apply to perception of most kinds. The problem of personality, however, requires a somewhat more elegant structure. It is provided in the present chapter by the provisional acceptance of the developmental, conceptual-cognitive psychology associated with Piaget's work on the conceptual growth of children.

Chapter 13

ATTITUDES, OPINIONS, AND BELIEFS

After all, the only difference in life is your point of view, how you look at the world. The world does not change, you change. And how do you change? By your different attitude. Whether you see it from down here, like the frog, as Spengler said, or up above, like the eagle. Or still higher, like the gods.

Henry Miller

WE HAVE noted in the previous chapter that psychological inquiry into collective dispositions requires a precise (or well delimited) set of understandings as to what these dispositions are and how they may be used in forming assumptions, testing hypotheses (if this is our inclination) or theory formation and/or selection. Such understandings are particularly important in the field of social psychology, because much of it has, during the past two decades, concentrated less on the psychodynamics of human behavior—the preference of its pioneers from Gustave Le Bon to (roughly) George Herbert Mead—than upon dispositions or states of mind.

The shift in emphasis seems to have occurred for three reasons. The first is that collective behavior (even when observed in a context as dramatic and lacking in ambiguity as the social movement of the Nazis in Germany) is extremely difficult for inductive investigators to study with precision. Deduction had been the dominant method of most of the European social theorists, men like Oswald Spengler, Karl Mannheim, Ernst Cassirer, José Ortega y Gasset and others; and their psychological theorizing reads like historical analysis. Subsequent inductive investigators countered deductive theories of social behavior, political practice and national ideology (spun, as they were, into theories and sub-theories) with the question, "How do you *know?*" The European analysts (including Le Bon and Freud [1]) did not "know" in terms satisfactory to their (somewhat later)

[1] See Chapter 19 for a review, in modern terms, of these enormous, but almost entirely deductive, critical constructions of collective behavior.

American inductive counterparts. They had not *tested* and *measured;* they had merely *observed* and *speculated.*

In the second place, the inductive researcher found that it was more difficult than he had anticipated to test and measure the behaviors of groups of men without resorting to historical or journalistic techniques that he could not justify within the ground-rules of his science. One area which he *could* test and measure, however, was that of dispositions. He discovered that it was indeed possible to ask people what they thought and to receive in response relatively precise answers that made up "opinion" or "attitude inventories," neat inductive evidence from which measurable and testable evidence might be wrought. He developed this art to quite a high degree of precision in eliciting evidence by overt and covert methods. But it left him merely with personal reports of what people were thinking and feeling (or thought and/or said they were thinking and feeling) about various specified issues.

Third, the commercial and political communities, in the United States particularly, showed increasing interest in dispositions in the light of the magic that behavioral scientists seemed competent to perform with their inventories and questionnaires. Market research, radio program ratings and public opinion sampling all provided precise-looking data (frequently both invalid and unreliable) that might accomplish two ends: they offered a somewhat coherent conception of consensus to fill the vacuum caused by the common idea of "public opinion"; and, even in political life, they relieved tycoons and board chairmen of the burden of making critical decisions regarding such matters as public taste and therefore insulated their business decisions from much criticism. Commercial or political failures might now safely be blamed on the polls or research departments. Pollsters and researchers would then blame their instruments or methods and set vigorously to work on further refinement of them.[2]

The discipline of social psychology was naturally caught up in this tendency to the degree that most of its best exponents in the United States devoted their energies more to the study and analysis of dispositions than to social action. They assumed that dispositions (or attitudes or opinions)

---

[2] This juncture of interests is probably best celebrated by the historic moment in the 1930's when Dr. Frank Stanton, a psychologist knowledgeable in statistical techniques, convinced William Paley of the Columbia Broadcasting System that his procedures would provide for radio broadcasters a relatively clear picture of who was listening at a given time to what radio program. Since then, the number of sociologists and psychologists employed by communicators, advertising agencies (some offering personal services for politicians) has grown to mighty proportions. At least two-thirds of the (roughly) 1,000 members of the scholarly American Association for Public Opinion Research have, in recent years, been employed by commercial organizations whose main interests in collective dispositions have been neither academic nor political. Dr. Stanton, without leaving CBS, defected from the world of psychology to the pursuits of commerce and is reputed to have done quite well. He is *not* now a member of the AAPOR, according to its 1970 Directory.

presumably *precede* action and that they were devoting their attentions to what they believed were matters of primary significance.

The bulk of their studies, most of them conducted in the interests of commercial and political organizations, have never appeared in the scholarly marketplace. Mimeographed or Xeroxed from typescripts, they dealt with such esoteric subjects as whether men or women preferred pink or green soap, powdered or frozen fruit drinks, what images a trademark evoked and other trivia. Occasionally, one or two would fall into the hands of sensitive reporters like Vance Packard or Martin Mayer and provide grist for the mill of a polemic. The public—and academic community—also received considerable publicity from them about radio and television surveys (infamous devices for shifting the burden of programming from license holders to a mystical "will of the people") and political polls. The latter attracted public attention most widely at the times of their infrequent blatant errors, such as the 1948 Presidential election in the USA and the contest for Prime Minister in Britain in 1970.

Major studies relevant to social psychology were produced by a handful of psychologists and sociologists, some of whom worked part-time as consultants for what they call on campuses "industry." The inductive research efforts (and attempts at theory construction) of such first-rate scholars as Berelson, Lazarsfeld, Laswell, Cantril, Bruner, Newcomb, Jahoda and others cannot be underestimated. The main focus of their investigations, of course, centered on dispositions, called differently and arbitrarily "opinions" or "attitudes." They proved of immeasurable value in limning coherent pictures of what many Americans thought and felt about numerous issues during the past generation.[3]

A second strain of study concentrated on theory articulation, combined frequently with anthropological research, following Boaz, Benedict, Mead and Malinowski, that rarely stepped far beyond the range of inductive inquiry. Once more, its focus was upon dispositions and its theories were tentatively expressed. But it provided excellent material for academic speculation in university seminars and that might be tested somehow in doctoral dissertations by graduate students in psychology and sociology. It included Adorno's concept of the "authoritarian personality"; Kardiner's transmission model of basic cultural attitudes; Linton's notion of the survival values of primary institutions versus individuality. Powdermaker, Kluckhohn, Havighurst, Thrasher, Loeb, Vidich, Bensmen and others surveyed special populations and their institutions (primitive tribes, girls' col-

[3] For a detailed review of this research from a psychological point of view (which unfortunately tends to underestimate the contributions of numerous sociologists, particularly those involved in various "community studies"), see M. Brewster Smith, Jerome S. Bruner and Robert W. White, *Opinions and Personality* (New York: John Wiley and Sons, 1956), pp. 1–28. The general interest of attitude study and theory building is both clear and accurate in these pages, and is also indirectly reflective of minor influences from contemporary sociology and anthropology.

leges and one-horse towns) and brought together a mix of sociology, anthropology and psychology unique to this area of inquiry. The thrust of their interest was also towards human dispositions, most of it utilizing more or less precise questioning procedures, and some of it (wisely) informal and intuitive. Its attempt was to discover, in people of different backgrounds, regularities of general enough application to be labeled "attitude theories."

Measuring Dispositions

Historical theorists have always been interested in dispositions, particularly those that eventually catalyze into overt action: revolutions, revolts and *coups d'etats*. The methods they have classically employed, not unlike the general procedures followed in Part Two of this volume, have balanced empirical inductive speculations with deduction, depending on the data available. From these relationships, concepts concerning dispositions were induced. An example is the idea, repeated by many historians, that the American intelligentsia, until the Civil War, appeared to suffer greater and deeper pangs of guilt at our aggressive behavior towards Indians and Indian nations than at our brutality towards Negroes, because it was generally understood that the Indians' capacity for civilization (as Americans interpreted it) was greater than that of the Negroes. The results were manifest in the novels of James Fenimore Cooper and enormously popular dramas like *Metamora* of which the public never seemed to tire, despite their seemingly masochistic themes centering on the exploitation of the noble savage (Indians) by wily white men.

Are attitudes or dispositions so induced accurate? The question is apt but impossible to answer. Until the development of the random survey and psychological attitude inventories, this was, however, the only sort of data available to historians, resulting from rough indications of assent or negation, like the popular vote (which was rarely in fact popular), and those dispositions, like the Civil War Draft riots, that were precipitated into unmistakably directed action.

Despite the degree of subjectivism that was (and is) involved in such historical speculation—especially when it appears as part of a political column in a daily newspaper—its tenor is largely logical rather than psychological. True enough, *states of mind* are assumed from external evidence, including such obvious evidence as newspaper editorials and political speeches. But because of their lack of regularity and coherence as data they are usually regarded as bits of evidence to be utilized eventually for the gathering of a logical, coherent picture of the world "out there." When they disobey the assumptions of one or another constructions of history—or fly in the face of the logic of the accepted myths of the social, economic and cultural worlds in which they are found—they are usually discarded as spurious or irrelevant. In other words, their test for adequacy lies more in a frame of logical references than in a psychological one.

Not so, usually, with the inductive-empirical research of the behavioral scientist. His instruments do not (in fact, cannot) lie in giving him fit answers to the specific questions he has posed concerning human dispositions. It is possible that he was searching for the wrong kind of evidence for his purposes, or that his instruments were not, in fact, telling him what he wanted to know about his target dispositions but describing instead various other sorts of behavior. His instruments, especially when they apply to small populations or substitute statistical procedures for genuine investigation, may also be, in practical sense, faulty. Tautological though it appears, every device he employs (including statistical maneuvers) will, if used honestly, tell him exactly, and only, what it is competent to tell him about the attitudes of the population he is studying. His greatest challenge of intellect and wisdom comes about when he must interpret his data in order to determine what his results *include or miss*, and what his presumed attitude data *actually reveal* in terms of what he set out to discover in the first place.[4]

A number of methods are currently used in eliciting data which may or may not indicate what dispositions of individuals are. Social scientists usually employ them according to expediency or at the behest of individual biases in training (psychologists prefer one kind; sociologists another), rather than careful consideration of their applicability to the occasion. The first of them were obviously crude.[5]

The famous Thurstone scale depends upon the skill of supposedly impartial judges in evaluating various statements on certain issues which range (hopefully) from "favorable" to "unfavorable" positions. The statements are quantified by tabulating the consensus as to scale position by the judges and presented to a subject. He checks off his degree of agreement with the statement, which is then given a numerical value. The Lipert scale simplifies Thurstone's method considerably by requiring that respondents indicate their disposition towards a statement on a fixed point scale running from "Strongly Agree" to "Strongly Disagree." Guttman's Scalogram operates in a similar way, asking the respondent to arrange a series of attitude

---

[4] This is where, in my opinion, attitude measurement fails most gravely. So impressed are most social scientists with the print-outs of their data that they are loathe to infer (or hire people intelligent enough to interpret) what these data may or may not mean or may circumvent in various ways. Because they think of themselves as laboratory scientists, they also resist, frequently, the urge to speculate on their results, treating them as hard-core *facts* about human cognitions, which they are not. Opinion and attitude survey results (which look so neat when presented as percentages, medians, modes and standard deviations) are usually small *pieces* of a larger puzzle that requires considerable insight (and creative gall) to translate into material meaningful for social psychology.

[5] See Philip Zimbardo and Ebbe B. Ebbesen, *Influencing Attitudes and Changing Behavior* (Reading, Massachusetts: Addison-Wesley Publishing Co., 1969), pp. 123–128. This book, designed as a text for social psychology courses, is wisely and closely larded with well-chosen material on the psychology of attitudes despite its uninspiring textbook format.

statements on a given subject in order from "Least likely to accept" to "Most difficult to accept," after the statements have been refined (concerning discreteness and relevance) by pre-tests.

Most paper and pencil attitude scales depend upon these techniques devised and refined by Thurstone, Lipert and Guttman, but the number of possible ways in which they may be varied appears nearly unlimited. They may be offered as simple printed tests, on cards (to be arranged), and/or they may utilize any number of modifications in preparation and application. In fact, they may all be combined in one inventory. Their greatest virtue is that they yield statistical information that may be subjected to tests for reliability and validity, and be analyzed according to the variance in responses between individuals and groups with some precision.

Two other frequently employed devices for discovering dispositions do not rely on the direct assault of the individual with (in effect) demands for questions and answers on devices like the above scales. This quality is their strength and also their weakness, because the best explanations of exactly what these procedures show about attitudes is far from clear. But they do approach attitudinal matters in an indirect way that is likely to reduce the chances for dissembling or misunderstanding printed statements.

The first is the Semantic Differential instrument.[6] This is actually a two-dimensional model that places an individual's reactions to a word, idea or picture (or anything) in a grid which rates it on a (usually) seven-point scale according to evaluative factors (like "good" to "bad"; or "sharp" to "dull") that are relevant to the subject at hand and formulated frequently as adjectives. In its original form, the Semantic Differential was used to test reactions to adjectives placed in the three categories of Evaluation, Potency, and Activity, but any general concepts of human dispositions may be employed on the scale. The instrument is particularly useful in delineating how a single individual perceives words (and what the words stand for) and other stimuli, and may be given to relatively large groups. But it does not have the immediate salience to expressed attitudes of a simple opinion questionnaire. Its most useful application, it appears, is in the study of meaning rather than disposition.

The Q-sort (technique or methodology) is a similar instrument,[7] employing a set of cards which a subject arranges in order according to some evaluative criterion.[8] In practice, the factors involved may become quite

[6] For a detailed study of the application and use of this device, see Fred Kerlinger, *Foundations of Behavioral Research* (New York: Holt, Rinehart and Winston, 1966), pp. 564–580. Kerlinger, no fool, eschews the words "disposition" and "attitude" in his description of this procedure. "The semantic differential," he writes, "is a method of observing and measuring the psychological meaning of things, usually concepts"—which is a pretty safe and cozy sentence to my old eye.

[7] See *ibid.*, pp. 581–599.

[8] William Stephenson is the originator of the Q methodology which he has employed in the development of his colorful ludenic theory of mass communications. See pp. 105–6.

complicated, and a large number of cards may be sorted into piles signifying "For," "Against" and "Neutral," or any other attitudinal states. Propositions, concepts, names or other subjects may be written on the cards. The number of items usually runs from sixty to ninety, and the cards may be sorted into any number of piles, each signifying a slightly different value. Rated values are then assigned to the items in each pile, and the results are quantified. The test may be repeated in different references on the same person and/or given to different individuals. Statistical techniques permit judgments to be made concerning the various preferences of the individuals in terms of their characterological inclinations, and allow for factor analysis of the clusters of agreements that the technique produces.

While the Q methodology appears to be useful in many kinds of studies dealing with the preference of people or groups, its relevance to *specific* attitudes is limited by its tendency, apparently, to work best with concepts rather than issues. The instrument also accepts as given subjective interpretations that individuals give words. On the other hand, it is quite useful in checking (or noting) how attitudes or dispositions relate to different aspects of its respondents' verbal environment.

Do any of these instruments really provide the observer with a clear picture of how dispositions are held, their psychological functions, and their vulnerability to change? The answer depends, of course, on what instrument is chosen and how it is applied. And the selection of the proper subjects is also of critical importance. To find out that members of an old-folks bowling team have negative feelings towards permissive abortion laws is quite a different matter from discovering what Catholic teenagers or Orthodox Jewish rabbis feel about the same issue.

Let us not also overlook the journalistic method of eliciting dispositions that seems to satisfy many viewers of serious television: the interview or open-ended question and discussion, in which the investigator himself may or may not play a role. A questioner may be armed, like Kinsey's researchers, with a galaxy of cross-checking questions. Or he may merely carry on a loose discussion with his respondent and allow the latter to center upon his own interests once a frame of reference has been determined. The results may be extremely productive.[9] The data may be reported in the form of transcribed, edited taped conversations or as a summary on the part of the investigator or in any number of ways. As in the case of most anthropological research, it may be subsumed into a consideration of a larger issue of which the attitudes discussed are merely a part. Information elicited informally may also be quantified by a researcher, if he receives similar answers to the same enquiries from different people.

---

[9] This is a frequent method of sociological observation, although I believe that it has never again been employed as effectively as it was in Robert Merton's study of the appeals of Kate Smith to her radio audience in *Mass Persuasion* (New York: Harper and Brothers, 1946).

While some behavioral scientists do not approve of these latter methods of opinion investigation,[10] their main virtue lies in their potential for qualitative elaboration. If, for instance, one is unclear as to exactly what a respondent's notion of "civil rights" is, one may ask him directly to define the term or explain it further. On the other hand, quantifications of these sorts of data are quite difficult, and it is almost impossible to compare, with any accuracy, various dispositions of one group on a number of issues with another's. Nor may individual factors be analyzed or degrees of reliability be calculated with the same ease as when employing more precise measurements. What one may gain in potential precision and adaptability, one may lose in breadth and manipulability. A broadly spread, highly manipulable instrument given to 1,000 women chosen at random in one community, for instance, may provide a market researcher with significant information about the potentials of a new laundry soap. On the other hand, informal interviews with *five* housewives, all of them mothers in the same housing project, might elicit considerable attitudinal information on parental discipline which a larger group of parents and non-parents might overlook if they were confined to neatly formulated attitude scales.

The Anatomy of Dispositions

As indicated above, a critical and creative moment for an individual interested in dispositions arrives after his data have been collected and statistic legerdemain has been accomplished, and he is faced with determining what, if anything, his "research" (as he calls his findings) shows. They may—for various reasons—show very little, and this may be fit cause, as in the case of Klapper's study of the effects of television on people,[11] to publish

---

[10] See the essay concerning the meeting-points of sociology, psychology and anthropology in the discipline of social psychology, entitled "Anthropology and Psychology" in M. Brewster Smith, *Social Psychology and Human Values*, pp. 33–65.

[11] See G.N.G., *L C*, pp. 288–290. I have been respectfully and sagely criticized for my skepticism regarding Klapper's "null" findings concerning television's effects, but my fundamental objection to them remains. Klapper should have addressed himself to the problem of *explaining* something, at least, about those effects of TV on living styles, consumer behavior, language, disposition and celebrity worship, that are *visible to the naked eye*, not just deny their existence. The main problem today centers on what we *see* in attitudes towards violence on the part of young people, attitudes which are certainly effected somehow by television, among other factors. To conduct experiments on matched groups of "average" youngsters in this regard is absurd. Those who watch television will probably be no more or less violent than those who go to the movies instead. The children who need to be studied are those who live in environments where violence is a way of life day in and day out, for instance gang members in ghettos. *How* television influences *them* (and I'll bet it does) is what interest me, not the fact I already know, that television does *not* appear to influence my own youngsters, except in silly ways (the jokes they tell, the slogans they mouth and the games they play), because my over-protected offspring are interested in watching silly television programs. My discontent with studies like Klapper's, as both scientific research and social commentary, *is merely that the wrong people are asked the wrong questions about the wrong things, a guaranteed way to confirm the null*

a well reasoned volume showing that his cupboard is bare, coupled with an expressed hope that someone, someday may discover something.

On the other hand, such research may show smoke which may or may not indicate fire, as in Stauffer's well known study,[12] conducted in the middle 1950's. It indicated that a large percentage of Americans were extremely narrow-minded in their attitudes towards socialists, communists and atheists. Considering the period in which the questions were asked (known today as the "McCarthy era"), fair implication might be drawn from the results that the Senator from Wisconsin was helping to create a climate of suspicion and hostility towards political and religious nonconformists. This conclusion would in some measure be confirmed or denied by comparison with a similar enterprise conducted today. One may also use one's results as an ongoing record of changing disposition in changing environments, as Newcomb did with his classic study of a gaggle of Bennington girls over a period of years.[13]

Rarely does (or should) an attitude study produce results, or may implications be drawn from it, that are widely at variance with what common sense tells us about familiar populations. After all, one does, to a degree, wear one's dispositions on his sleeve, and one's life-style manifests them in speech, clothing, choice of possessions, relationships with others and small talk. People tend to discuss with each other matters of political and social importance to *them,* and an astute observer, even a sociologist or psychologist, should be able to find clues to dispositions in casual relationships.[14]

Many of us probably manufacture covert informal dispositional profiles of the people we know, highlighting their sensitive areas, the ways in which their notions seem to differ from ours, and on what matters we are likely to agree or disagree—and whether disagreement may injure our relationships with them. When dispositions are rigid, the common word we usually choose for someone who disagrees with our own biases is "opinionated." If we disagree, but the other party tends to a skeptical attitude and displays a readiness to consider arguments we reject, we call him "wishy-

---

hypothesis every turn at bat. This is a useful stratagem when and if you want to demonstrate statistically how harmless you are.

12 See Samuel A. Stauffer, *Communism, Conformity and Civil Liberties* (New York: Doubleday and Co., 1955).

13 See T. M. Newcomb, *Personality and Social Change* (New York: The Dryden Press, 1943).

14 The man who services my automobile, for instance, is largely a stranger to me, and yet, it occurs to me, I know quite a bit about his dispositions towards the critical matters that interest sociologists and psychologists: namely, matters of politics, attitudes towards racial minorities, students, intellectuals, local politicians, birth control, pollution and so forth. Neither, as I have discovered in my wandering, is he much different in his dispositions from the man who runs the next service station down the road. I doubt that an attitude study *on these topics,* therefore, of service station owners in Nassau County, New York (where I service my car) would contain many surprises for me.

washy." At times, we make assumptions about dispositions that we regard as true until disproved, for instance, the reasonable guess that a run-of-the-mill university professor will incline to a liberal political orientation and think more highly of Roosevelt, Truman and Kennedy than he does of Hoover, Eisenhower or Nixon.[15] In fact, the determination of dispositions according to sex, social class, education and economic status has been involved in most broad survey sociological research accomplished in the past generation[16] and has characterized the bulk (and best face) of that discipline's contribution to the study of collective behavior to date. For the reasons noted above, little of it contradicts generally accepted notions about the dispositions of the young, the rich, the farm or city dweller, Whites, Negroes, members of the middle class, and other segments of society.

In sum, people tend to show the kinds of disposition one expects them to have in our highly volatile society; they are mostly inheritances from one's background, parents, home and milieu, and they intrude into nearly every facet of life, where they are continually reenforced. Reaction formation as rebellion against, or modification of, environmentally enforced dispositions is rare, but it does occur—when, for instance, a middle-class youngster defects to the hippies, a wildcat oilman strikes it rich, one marries out of his faith or race or migrates to a new country, or when one undergoes a conversion experience as the result of a personal crisis of some kind.

Absolute dispositional determination is therefore a statistical fiction—or a statement of probability to which we can usually identify hundreds of exceptions, both in people found in the public arena and those we know personally. Such rebellion is rarely abstract and usually follows an overt action or behavioral change of some sort. The lower class youngster who finds his fortune as a television comedian learns to live (and think) like a rich man, deriving his values from the aristocracy (in his case, probably, a show business aristocracy) with which he associates. Change is slower and less certain on the trip down the socio-economic ladder, but usually visible.

---

[15] Of course, this tendency depends to a high degree upon where the university is located and the source from which it draws its faculty. I recall, however, certain college students trying in 1956 to arrange a debate, at a university at which I was then an instructor, between faculty members on the relative virtues of that year's presidential candidates. Plenty of professors were ready to speak for Adlai Stevenson, but they could not discover *one* teacher who would support (or argue for) Dwight D. Eisenhower. Finally the chairman of the Political Science department agreed to take Ike's side, *providing that it was clearly stated before and after the debate* (and in the university newspaper) *that he intended to vote for Stevenson.*

[16] Most of these determinants may be found neatly listed under their appropriate categories in Berelson and Steiner, *Human Behavior.* Time is almost certainly running out on some of the statements found therein (the notion, for instance, that "political attitudes are formed in rebellion against the parents is true for only a small proportion of the people," and, "There are two conditions of residence that affect the development of opinions, attitudes and beliefs: geographical region and urban-rural location"). But, for the present, most of them serve with reasonable accuracy.

Many a small-time captain of industry who was once convinced that his own financial welfare and that of his corporation were reciprocal with that of the entire nation has been reduced to bemoaning the mindless expansion of capitalism and the inflation through which we have lately been living. As he might put it, gazing wistfully at his Social Security check, "Old timers like me have to live on a fixed income. What is the government going to do about it?" The mighty do, at times, fall, and their attitudes frequently fall with them.

The main difficulty regarding the delineation of the nature of dispositions has, however, not been a lack of precision in constructing proper determinants, or even the problems (discussed in the previous chapter) of relating them to personality. Some believe that sociology has given us too much information about dispositional determinants over the past generation to make sound predictions or to stimulate useful analysis. Others note that the enormous amount of experimentation and theorizing by psychologists has left us with a few weak but reliable notions concerning dispositions and their relation to behavior and/or mind. These discontents may be merited, although it should be noted that neither definitive evidence nor theory accumulate in the behavioral sciences at the whim or direction of behavioral scientists. Extremely useful psychological concepts have emerged from experiments designed modestly for other purposes, and useful theory in both psychology and psychiatry is sometimes generated under unexpected circumstances.

One of the fundamental deterrents to both inductive and deductive speculation in social psychology arises from the fact that, as of the present moment, nobody has clearly indicated what a *disposition* is or how it operates as a process (or part of a process) of behavior or as a quality of thought. The word "disposition" reminds one of a recent Supreme Court justice who (like judges for 150 years before him) was completely puzzled by the nature of "pornography," because he could find no adequate criterion for judging it by comparing it to similar material that was held *not* to be "pornographic." His despair was expressed in his lament that, while neither he nor anyone else could define or describe pornography accurately, he would know it when he *saw* it. He was probably speaking the truth[17] and is similar to the behavioral scientist's use of the word "disposition."

---

[17] Thanks to the Supreme Court's decision in the Roth-Alberts case, jurists today have a working definition of "pornography," but its failure in precision is on view in a number of interesting movie houses, book stores and peep show parlors in the city in which I live—I have been told. Of course, definitions of pornography have been employed by judges since the Cockburn decision in the early nineteenth century in England, but their inadequacy stemmed from their rigidity and difficulty of application to matters of "social value" and "art." Today the problem is reversed; randy junk is peddled for its artistic and social values which it cannot be shown *not* to possess. Defining pornography precisely is as great a problem at the moment as it ever was—and will remain so. See Chapter 26 for further discussion of this problem.

In the same manner, most of us know what our *opinions* are and how they are differentiated from other cognitions and feelings. We may be less acutely aware of our *attitudes* but still conscious that we feel them in one way and may show them in another. Those of us inclined to introspections may also be able to put our fingers on our *beliefs* and the intellectual and emotional components of them. But, if the reader is anything like the writer, the nature of our dispositions—beliefs, attitudes, and/or opinions—seems peculiarly mercurial, subject to many factors associated with the roles we play in life, and they frequently change rapidly in critical situations and at the whim of subjective fancy. A poet has said, "The topical sin is doubt." But is there a churchman who has not, perhaps for extended periods, doubted his *belief* in God? Is there a reasonably intelligent atheist who has not doubted his *non-belief?* Do not our *attitudes* towards groups to which we do not belong shift according to our relationships with members of those groups? Are not most of our *opinions* provisional, changeable in the light of evidence, time, perspective and caprice?

Because they are made of such protean stuff, a generic term for or clear definition of our dispositions defies the lexicographer's scalpel. In practice, the terms "attitudes" and "opinions" have been used more or less interchangeably in the literature of the behavioral sciences to date. "Beliefs" have frequently been severed from the other two when referring to major abstract issues, particularly religious or highly emotionally-toned dispositions, like belief in God or freedom or the dignity of man. But even "beliefs" have been frequently thrown into the bin of "attitudes" by opinion samplers, less out of carelessness than confusion.

Smith *et. al.*, in their excellent work on the relationships of opinions to character, are disarmingly candid in speaking for the main currents of behavioral thinking about the matter. "Attitude, opinions, sentiment," they write, "all of these terms refer to the kind of predisposition we have in mind . . . In all honesty we must confess that we do not think the time is ripe to be theoretically solemn about the definition of an attitude . . ." [18] In the remainder of their book, they use the terms "attitude" and "opinion" *ad lib.*

The same problems arise elsewhere with less candor. Do "attitude inventories" test attitudes, opinions, beliefs, or some sub-numbered factor of each, contingent upon the time and circumstances under which the test was given, and modified by the fact that the test is merely an exercise in game playing, not a test in a social field of what one will *do* in a given situation? Do the same problems arise in laboratory settings where individuals express opinions and have them maneuvered by clever experimental designs, frequently involving students coached to dissemble certain reac-

---

[18] Smith, *et al. op. cit.*, pp. 33, 34.

tions in order to fool an unsuspecting subject? How adequate are attempts to quantify the tenacity or stability of all kinds of dispositions? Does one man believe in God *more* than another; and, if so, how? May one display a *variably* tolerant attitude towards racial minorities, especially in the light of the ambivalent attitudes one (presumably) notices among Jews (as treated by novelists) towards Negroes? What good is an opinion that X should be elected to the Senate if one intends to vote for Y, because he is convinced Y will win the election, and he "doesn't want to throw his vote away"?

The questions above, and many more like them, indicate a general confusion about the nature of dispositions, reflected, as most confusions are, in the very language in which they are couched. Nor is the issue any clearer when a particular writer states *his* definition of an attitude (and does indeed discuss attitudes, so defined, throughout an entire book) if his reader is likely to construe many of the sentiments he treats as opinions or beliefs, and therefore irrelevant to his discussion. The problem is *not* a semantic one, as most behavioral scientists maintain today, but germane to the productive discussion and analysis of dispositions.

Kretch and Crutchfield (and some others) have attempted salient definitions of "beliefs" and (or versus) "attitudes" but have been honored only by a flagrant misinterpretation of their attempts.[19] Their main distinction between the two is the implied notion that beliefs are more or less stable, while attitudes are processes which may or may not elicit action. They seem to regard opinions as certain, specific and special types of beliefs. But their distinctions, like those of most other behavioral scientists, are vague. The most amusing solution to the problem yet offered is the one concocted by Berelson and Steiner in *Human Behavior*. They call opinions, attitudes and/or beliefs "OAB's," an indication of the degree of desperation surrounding the matter.

The following constructions may therefore be helpful, if not to the field of attitude (or opinion or belief) study in general, at least to the discussion that follows in this volume:

Beliefs are relatively stable emotional and cognitive dispositions, usually directed at abstract ideas. They tend also towards homogeneity in pop-

---

[19] See David Krech and Richard S. Crutchfield, *Theory and Problems of Social Psychology* (New York: McGraw-Hill Book Co., 1948), pp. 149–174. The authors define a *belief* as "an enduring organization of perceptions and cognitions about some aspect of the individual world." An *attitude* is "an enduring organization of motivational, emotional, perceptual, and cognitive processes with respect to some aspect of the individual's world." Milton Rokeach in *Beliefs, Attitudes and Values* (San Francisco: Jossey-Bass Inc., 1969), also differentiates, both theoretically and experimentally, between beliefs and attitudes and characterizes values as components of beliefs in much the same way as in the discussion below. Note especially his discussion, pp. 124–132, his statement on the latter page, and his conclusions on p. 155 and p. 178. Rokeach is, correctly I think, skeptical of the usual thrust of most recent "attitude studies" in psychological literature.

ulations within primary institutions and also within sub-cultures. Occasionally they change—or may be modified—but rarely other than either a.) over a long period of time and considerable experience, or b.) as the result of a shock or experience of traumatic dimensions or both.

Attitudes are less stable dispositional relationships within certain aspects of the individual's experience, either mediated to him firsthand or by an instrument of communication. They may or may not be consistent with beliefs, and their relationship to behavior is entirely contingent upon the context in which an attitude is called into operation. While attitudes are determined by socio-cultural factors, they are also, to some degree, reflective of individual psycho-biology and are thus closely related to an individual's personality. They may shift with relative ease depending upon circumstance, but the main and usual factors that appear to influence them are a.) experiences, particularly those with high emotional content, b.) education (in-school and out) and indoctrination, and c.) novelties in the individual's perspectives of his relationship to society, caused in any manner.

Opinions, which may or may not be logically consistent with attitudes, are direct, usually malleable dispositions towards an object, institution, person or artifact in the individual's world of perception, mediated to him in any manner. They are capable of relatively precise articulation when compared with attitudes and beliefs, and are generally spun from, or involve further articulations of, negative or positive cognitions and feelings. Opinions relate, either in eventual outcome or fantasy, to probable actions an individual believes he will take when and if faced with a situation demanding choice between two or more alternatives, real or imagined.

Were human beings creatures who governed their thoughts and feelings in an entirely logical mode, the relationships between these three types of disposition would be linear, simple and consistent. Thus:

BELIEFS → ATTITUDES → OPINIONS → RELEVANT BEHAVIOR (OR ACTION)

Men and women who seem to operate psychologically in this consistent a manner do, in fact, inhabit this earth. Some are on view on university campuses and elsewhere. But such people tend towards dullness, lack of imagination, shallow perceptions and operate with little apparent emotionality. While their dispositions appear inherently characterological, they have probably accepted, over many years and bit by bit, a mechanistic credo of personal and social order in order to allay numerous fears that most other people face as conditions of the human situation and not demanding major alterations of psychic processes. Such rigid personalities may correctly be associated with persons displaying behavior usually called "psychopathic" and others who it is currently popular to call "paranoid." The behavior they show does not (apparently) warrant therapy, nor do their defense mechanisms differ greatly from other similar but transient neurotic manifestations commonly observed.

Such psychological consistency is fortunately rare—fortunately, that is, for those who enjoy diversity and inconsistency in human behavior and rebel against tendencies to mechanize the spontaneous proclivities of man. Most individuals appear to operate in continual fields of tension, each force pulling in an opposite direction, one from the other. One is the rational tendency (at whatever level of complexity the individual lives and however he construes rationality) to achieve a consistent flow of disposition from belief to attitude to opinion to behavior. In a manner similar to that which propels, in theory, Festinger's idea of the resolution of cognitive dissonance,[20] the individual (on behalf of what he regards as "sanity") seems constantly to be testing, in consciousness or fantasy, the rationality of his flow of dispositions. As we shall see, his tests often fail even his own standards of "sane" behavior. At this point, rationality turns to rationalization as understood in psychoanalysis. Should rationalization become impossible, either because of the apparent exciting drama of inconsistency or a permanent or temporary inability to resolve the dissonance, the result is withdrawal, either into apathy or bizarre behavior. The latter two attempt to reconcile what is psychologically irreconcilable, resulting in some sort of clinical display of a denial of reality.

The other vector of this tension is an equally rational systemic tendency which, it appears, recognizes the discrete notion of different types of dispositions, and demands that the individual structure each component—beliefs, attitudes and opinions—so that the system is self-consistent *per se, in spite of the fact that this internal consistency is purchased at the price of dissonance in the relationships of the categories to each other.* This tendency is also demanded by the requirements of so-called "sanity," and its disregard is also a form of dissonance. In other words, one's beliefs must be defensible regardless of one's attitudes and opinions, and the same requirement remains true for opinions, attitudes and, of course, actions. If they are inconsistent, the result is discomfort and psychological disharmony. But this discomfort must now be balanced against the satisfaction of harmonious belief, attitude, opinion and behavior processes on one hand, and self-consistent dispositions of different kinds on the other. The resolution of tension will depend, of course, upon the psychological characteristics of the individual and his social context. Recall also, that this process of balances occurs in countless references for most individuals most of the time, and that they are rearranged in momentary hierarchical orders of importance, depending on environmental demand and the flux of attention.

Again a diagram may illustrate the process:

---

[20] See pp. 224–225.

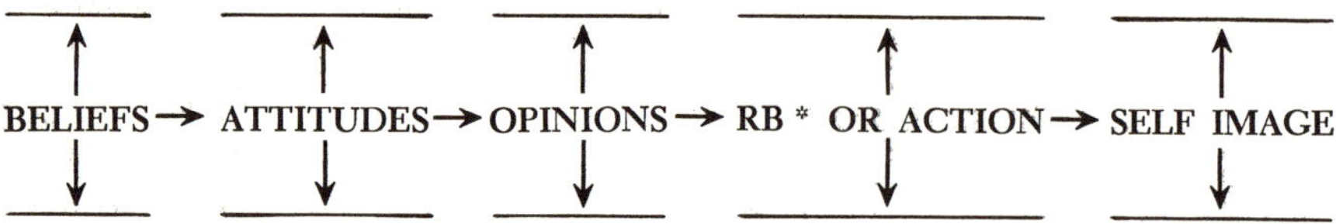

If we understand all arrows to be of about equal force, the directions in which the individual is pulled are clear. The horizontal stress is upon a consistent self-image, because one's beliefs, attitudes, opinions and behaviors are perceived as consistent. At the same time, other demands are being made upon the sense of those components which must be resolved. These resolutions affect the integrity of the horizontal flow, and forces and counter-forces now bring the entire system into a state of disequilibrium which may be resolved in any way imaginable (including dismissal of the entire process). But it is usually maintained by constant psychic adjustments, by learning, rationalization or exercise of the emotions. The process is, in effect, kept from disintegration, although it no longer manifests the neat closure of the diagram. (Such closure is the exclusive property of the mechanist-neurotic or psychotic described above.)[21]

For example, and in a simplified context, let us consider a Mr. A who *believes* in God. Following this belief is the *attitude* that the institutions (churches) man has created to signify this belief are generally healthy for society. His *opinion* of the Catholic Church is high. As a Catholic (let us assume) he therefore attends church. The horizontal component seems (deceptively) stable.

Mr. A also believes in God and so forth, but his *opinion* of the Moslem religion is low for various reasons. Because he has Jewish friends, he gives money to support the state of Israel against the Arab nations. Let us assume he recognizes an inconsistency now in his horizontal structure. But the tension is easily resolved! His *attitude* towards the Moslem religion may be modified, because Moslems do not go to churches as he knows them, and he does not credit that they *really* believe in God. His *opinion* in the matter of the Israeli problem is thus easily resolved by disregarding the religious issue and conceptualizing Israel as a socio-political entity with cer-

* Resulting Behavior.

[21] I think that this particular psychosis or neurosis here may be fragmented from the total life-style of certain individuals. In other words, I am familiar with apparently stable people living reasoning comfortable lives who display this neurosis only when they write articles for learned journals or lecture to students. The question of whether they are "really" being themselves when writing, teaching or living in their daily world is complex. But the inconsistencies in the displays of their various selves and their adeptness at role playing, makes me, personally, uneasy in their company under any circumstances. When I hear, as I frequently do, that they have in one or another manner cracked under the strain, I am sympathetic but rarely surprised, because the strain has been so apparent.

tain proprietary rights in the Near East. The system is stable again, and stressed. But the stress will not bother Mr. A until, somehow, the system is called to his attention anew; and its elements may be once again revised.

In a broader context, nothing is therefore fundamentally amiss in a society whose populace becomes fearfully excited when warfare kills a few of its number, but literally ignores the carnage that automobiles create on its highways. *Belief* in the holiness of human life is tempered by adjustments in attitudes, opinions and behaviors.[22] Individuals who display *attitudes* of kindness to animals and rebel against their use for scientific experimentation often demonstrate their *opinions* of a sirloin steak by their enjoyment of it. *Attitudes* towards the necessity of improving public health conditions will be expressed in *opinions* and *actions* centering on the horrors of cigarette smoking and narcotics addiction, while the highly visible problem of alcohol addiction (the nation's most severe health problem) is virtually ignored. The reason, of course, is that millions of Americans drink alcoholic beverages without toxic effects (which has nothing to do with the problem of alcoholism). Expressions of overt *opinions* in favor of aiding alcoholics and supporting programs to help them, accordingly, would require uncomfortable *attitude* adjustments (as well, perhaps, as *opinion* and *action* changes) that are not required in centering their attentions upon such comparatively minor (in public health terms) matters as cigarette smoking and drug addiction. The integrity of these *opinions* and *action* is enhanced cognitatively (vertically) by explanations centering on rationalizations—like the fact that drug addiction, although not very widespread, is a problem of young people, and cigarettes affect the unsuspecting and innocent.

These inconsistencies do not result from any psychological inadequacies. They are, in fact, evidences of the collective impetus towards adequacy on the part of individuals who participate in a complex society, each bringing his own dispositions into harmony with the "reality" that his environment presents to *him*. A local exponent of air-pollution control who chooses to drive his car, when alternate transportation is available, in his rounds to "do something" about foul air displays neither intellectual nor psychological ignorance nor disharmony. His *attitude* towards pollution is consistent. His *opinion* is that his own car does not make matters worse. And the end of his gas burning (lobbying for pollution control, let us assume) is more important than his means of accomplishment (polluting the air). His dispositions and actions yield highly consistent and self-justifying actions, from the psychological perspective. From a purely logical point of view, the man is a fool, a walking tautology and a hypocrite.

---

[22] The hot-rod that nearly forced my car off the Grand Central Parkway the other day (filled with setose, popular young adults of various sexes), and nearly forced me to take my chances driving up a tree, had a large so-called "Peace" sign painted on its rear. This is typical, psychologically defensible behavior—but damned annoying.

Before we consign him to the logical inferno, however, let us examine with care our own personal beliefs, attitudes and opinions, measure them against our relevant behaviors, and face squarely how we have resolved the tensions between the adequacy of the processes of our dispositions and the consistency of the characteristics and antecedents of these same dispositions. The true anatomy of the resolution is likely both to amuse and surprise us, if we possess the capacity for self-candor. The next step is to ask ourself what kind of persuasion will enhance this consistency, or will reduce the unresolved tensions we discover in our perilous explanations.

One possible solution is a *change* of disposition, a process given attention by such psychologists as Sherif, Hovland and Smith. The possibility of change, however, is a function of the ego involvement of the individual in the belief, attitude or opinion in question. The more ego involved, the less the likelihood that he will change; thus his *latitude of acceptance* will be smaller than his *latitude of rejection*. In order that persuasion, introspection, or the pressure of events change dispositions, therefore, one or all dispositions must come within his latitude of acceptance. In Smith's words, the individual is then "likely to minimize . . . (the new concept's) judged distance from his own position (*assimilation effect*) and be open to its influence." When the new stimulus falls into his latitude of rejection, "he is likely to exaggerate its judged distance from his own stand (*contrast effect*) and to resist influence." [23]

One assumes, also, that most people are more ego involved in beliefs than in attitudes, and in attitudes than in opinions; although one may possibly be more involved in behavioral manifestations of disposition than in expressed opinions. Under many circumstances, therefore, behavior (and the defensibility of it) becomes far more ego involved than more abstract matters or even one's deep beliefs. For this reason, people are sometimes forced to mediate or adjust their dispositions in order to face up to their actions, an observation discussed often in the psychological writings of William James and still directly applicable to the psychology of persuasion.

Conclusion

Social psychology, and therefore the study of dispositions, has shifted from the deductive mode of many of its earliest pioneers to an inductive mode of inquiry, at least in the USA. This tendency has occurred entirely in harmony with the development of the behavioral sciences in America and has been quite productive. The generality, or adequacy as theory, of much of this production is, however, questionable, particularly the articula-

[23] Smith, *Social Psychology and Human Values*, p. 88. Smith notes that the psychology of judgment, an ambiguous matter at present, is involved here, and that explanations of how individuals adapt to dispositional changes has, as yet, not been thoroughly explored by psychologists. While this is true, we shall, unfortunately, have to make some broad assumptions in this regard in the remaining chapters of Part Three on an operational common-sense basis.

tion of principles applicable to the understanding of how dispositions are held and what forces influence them—including both mass and person-to-person persuasion.

Our thinkers have evolved some interesting and clever devices for measuring dispositions in various ways, but they are qualified by basic confusions in exactly what they measure and what their implications, both clinically and culturally, are. Sociologists have correlated dispositions with cultural factors and noted clearly some of the societal forces which they think change dispositions. Psychologists have tended to associate dispositions with manners of perception first, and personality configurations second, and have discovered certain regularities of process in certain kinds of people. A general theory of "persuasability" has even been, on the basis of experiments with relatively homogeneous populations, tentatively articulated, but, as in all theoretical work in this field, the theory leaves enormous gaps to be filled before it becomes either adequate enough for predictive purposes or sophisticated enough to provide groundwork for further theory development. Theory, as a matter of fact in the study of dispositions, is frequently best referred on the perceptual level to the notion of cognitive dissonance, and on the operational level to the sociologists' near-endless anthology of respondents' replies to questions relating social variables like class, education and sex, to beliefs, attitudes and opinions.

One problem facing this type of inquiry is the simple differentiation of various *kinds* of dispositions, a problem frequently dismissed as mere semanticism and apparently solved by loading all kinds of disposition into one category such as "opinions." Some psychologists (and others) have made progress in defining various parts of the dispositional universe, but usually to their own satisfaction and nobody else's.

Our analysis brought us first to a definitional separation of *beliefs, attitudes* and *opinions*, following loosely those already accepted. A tentative theory of function was then presented, more in an attempt to clarify the natures of the categories than to explain psychological phenomena. Briefly, beliefs, attitudes, opinions and behavior were presented in two contexts, one continually in a state of tension with the other. In the first, they make up a cognitive-emotional process that interacts with the individual's coherent view of his environment. In the second, they are seen as discrete categories which continually demand discrete psychological orientation for self-consistency. Individual and collective behavior, regarded in this context, is therefore by implication amenable to persuasion that reduces the tensions induced in the enormous range of personal disposition, whether supplied by mass communications or live interaction. In addition, one's latitude of acceptance of such persuasion will be an inverse function of his personal ego involvement with his beliefs, attitudes, opinions or ongoing behavior.

Chapter 14

THE POWER OF FEAR

Not the acknowledged fears, the fears that are advertised. More dreadful than those: the private fears of childhood. Fear of the height of the high-dive, fear of the farmer's dog or the vicar's pony, fear of cupboards, fear of the dark passage, fear of splitting your fingernail with a chisel. And behind them, most unspeakably terrible of all, the arch-fear: the fear of being afraid.

Christopher Isherwood

THE conventional—and often useless—explanation of fear centers on certain easily detectable neurological and behavioral data. It is (possibly incorrectly) mechanistically oriented. Fear is understood, in fact, as a "protective mechanism."

In the *Psychiatric Dictionary*, at least 214 specific types of fear,[1] each with its proper name, is listed, from fear of air (aerophobia) to fear of sitting down (kathisophobia) to the fear of writing (graphophobia). They are not of equal value, either psychologically or semantically, but merely, one supposes, a list of the main things that enough people are afraid of (burglars, feathers, large objects, northern lights (sic), stairs, rectums, time etc.) to call themselves to the attention of psychiatrists who coin and/or list terms. To regard them all as operational protective mechanisms for the individuals who are cursed with them requires imagination; but the idea is psychologically defensible.

The general tendency that one faces when discussing emotions and other complex psychological phenomena is to prefer simple and overt descriptions of a *result* to speculation concerning *processes* or *causes*. Fear is particularly prone to this proclivity, because its behavioral manifestations are dramatic, both as felt and observed, a trait it shares with few other aspects of human feeling. Plutchik sketches[2] the usual and accepted dimensions of fear in his study of emotions by reaching into a grab-bag of

[1] See Leland E. Himsie and Robert Jean Campbell, *Psychiatric Dictionary*, Fourth Edition (New York: Oxford University Press, 1970), pp. 296–298.

[2] Robert Plutchik, *The Emotions* (New York: Random House, 1962), pp. 72–78.

scientists and poets who serve as well as any other sources to limn a relatively clear picture of what fear *looks* like, what fear *feels* like, and, in some measure, what happens to the human organism when it is afraid of something or somebody.[3] His picture is drawn from such various sources as Freud, Kempf, Shakespeare, Darwin, William James, McDougall, Homer, Aeschylus, Dickens, Virgil, Chaucer, Mower and Harry Stack Sullivan, among others.

The mechanistic model postulates fear as a function of the "fight or flight" response of those animals (the human being among them) that are competent either to fight, flee or both. To this end, moderate quanta of fear increase adrenalin secretions in slight amounts, and the organism is raised in the direction of its highest muscular and cerebral potential, either to flee or fight as effectively as possible—as well as to decide as cogently as it can which choice to take. Where this model leaves a puzzle (if we must construe fear merely to be a protective mechanism) is in the curiosity that more than moderate doses of fear *interfere* with activities of mind and body and induce panic characterized by trembling, fainting, and the inhibition of both realistic thought and relevant action.[4]

While fear may indeed offer one more moderate degrees of protection in the course of his normal activities, it is an extremely *ineffective* mechanism on those precise occasions when man needs it most—in extremely fearful situations. Also, the notion of protection—even when construed as a non-cortical, intensive atavistic activity that impedes goal-seeking behavior by throwing man into physiological conflict with his objective—[5] is of little psychological value when discussing fear in the social settings of most hu-

---

[3] We notice in most animals certain types of behaviors which we understand to be fear, at least by analogy to similar manifestations in human beings. Perhaps a philosopher may explain whether the analogies hold true enough of the time to be valuable for psychological research. The psycho-biology of animal fear is, of course, an apparently significant matter when the analogous animal (an ape, for instance) shares overt behavioral characteristics with humans. A tranquilizing agent that apparently subdues fears in a gorilla will probably perform a similar function for a frightened human. I have noted, however, that meprobramate, which seems to dispel fear in humans, often increases its apparent symptoms in animals as similar, in some ways, to people as cats.

[4] These observations are qualified by further complications. With intense fear, blood vessels close to the skin surface tend to contract, therefore protecting one (presumably) against excessive bleeding in case of injury. A rapid pulse and low blood pressure may accomplish the same ends, but this speculation appears that the protection offered by extreme fear is, at best, defensive and at worst potentially destructive. See *ibid.*, pp. 74–75.

[5] This construction is well discussed in Desmond Morris, *The Naked Ape* (New York: McGraw-Hill Book Company, 1967), pp. 149–153, particulary because of Morris' delightful (but usually misleading) ability to describe the behavior of monkeys while apparently convinced that he is discussing human beings. The aggressive-fear reactions Morris has treated on the pages cited above is therefore a particularly clear and well ordered construction of them as socio-biological processes, written with a bent for animal-human analogies that will hopefully dismay thoughtful psychologists.

man affairs. While the roots of human fear may one day in the future be traced accurately to protective emotions or biological processes in organisms *other* than man, human fear cannot be dismissed (or regarded mainly) as an inept attempt of our endocrine systems to cope with environmental or psychogenic threats. In its journey up the steep incline of physical and cerebral sophistication, the feral roots of fear are as irrelevant to most of man's present social functions as Mark Twain's moustache was to the dermatological welfare of his lip or the color of the reader's eyes to his capacity to read. Unfortunately, it is precisely this construction of fear which has interested most of the classical, and highly regarded, psychologists of emotion like Bull, Freud, Cannon, Dunbar, Hebb, Tolman and Young, among other writers (including those noted by Plutchik above), whose contributions to the general understanding of feelings in the psychic life of the individual has—in other respects and taken together—been formidable.[6]

The Nature of Fear

What we may reasonably accept from mechanistic theory and psychobiological descriptions are certain simple hard-core facts concerning manifestations of human fear, many of which were, in numerous ways, as obvious to the ancients as they are to us today, although the former could not record or measure them as expertly as we can.

First, fear is an *emotion* or *feeling,* related to—but not identical with —two corollary emotions: namely, anxiety (a generalized form of mild fear, in psychiatric terms) and aggression (a behavioral result of specified fears, in biological terms).

Second, fear is a frequently visible function of *behavior* on one hand, and physiology on another, in many complex ways, depending upon how, when and in whom it is aroused.

Third, fear is often a *learned reaction* (conditioned, if you wish) to factors in the individual's environment.

Fourth, because fear is aroused differentially in various people, it is necessary to conclude that the nature and degree of fear-arousal that people manifest is also a *function of* their unique psycho-biological *personalities,* similar insofar as personalities in a given culture or sub-culture tend to be like one another, but different in many of the ways personalities appear to vary.

Fifth, fear is experienced by most people as *unpleasant,* producing a unique kind of pain, whether or not it intrudes into consciousness. Nonconscious fears, according to rough psychoanalytic analogies, are felt as discomforts which manifest themselves in congeries of related emotions: anxiety (mentioned above), guilt and depression, all of which are perceived as operational impedimenta by most people. Certain neurotics and psychotics

---

[6] See G.N.G., *L.C.*, pp. 176–77.

aside, most individuals try to reduce the unpleasantness of fear as effectively as they are able by the most convenient circumstantial and psychological means available.

Sixth, fear is *not necessarily* related to any sort of *physical modifications* of the human environment, either internal or external. In other words, it may be created, sustained or terminated by *purely psychological* means. While this is sometimes true of other emotions also, its significance in comprehending the function of fear in persuasion is central. The recognition of this curiosity concerning fear is quite clear in the short quotation from Isherwood's novel, *Prater Violet*, at the beginning of this chapter. It is also evident in the success of such catch-phrases, essentially meaningless in psychological (and, to some, circumstantial) terms, as Roosevelt's emotionally charged phrase, "The only thing we have to fear is fear itself," or the battle-cry during World War II, "Freedom from Fear."

As in the analysis of all human emotions, one is naturally required to consider how feeling relates to circumstantial reality and under what circumstances covert impressions of that reality (or deceptions derived from it) arouses feelings, pleasant and unpleasant. From a psychological view, fear is one of the few emotions that is more interesting most of the time (to the student of persuasion) when it is aroused by language than when it is aroused by physical means. The fear experienced by a neophyte sky-diver before he jumps for the first time from an airplane 2,500 feet above the earth is genuine—and dramatic enough,[7] but it is the almost inarticulate, seemingly unreasonable fears—like those of witch hunters of devils—that are of primary interest to the social psychologist.

In a functional way, also, the nature of fear is fundamentally ironic, explaining, perhaps, why dramatic communications of classical stature have yet to produce a hero who does not specifically manifest fear within the plot structure of the story in which he appears. "Fearless" heroes are reserved for fairy tales and children's stories, and, even in melodrama, the prototypically "brave" protagonist is usually vulnerable to fear—of an immediate and visible environmental threat, in his case, rather than an internally aroused fear. The absence of the latter sort of fears in melodramatic heroes is one of the non-realistic elements in the thriller on stage, film or printed page.[8]

---

[7] I have tried this sport—once. Because, for me, the fear of jumping was greater than the subsequent elation of surviving the fall (and because it is an expensive recreation), I have no desire whatsoever to repeat the experience, unless necessary.

[8] See G.N.G., *L.C.*, pp. 150–152. Prototypes are not difficult to find for these fictional creatures, immune to inner fears but apparently vulnerable to those in their contrived environments. The stage, films, comic strips and television are replete with such creatures from Gillette's *Secret Service* to Chandler's Philip Marlowe stories to my old favorite *Tarzan of the Apes* (old and new style). Most of these heroes display a single inner "weak spot" that may arouse in them covert psychological fears—like tender feelings towards a sex object, loyalty to a cause, or love of animals or children—but these excep-

The clearest manifestation of fear human beings experience, and the most simply perceptible, is the fear of physical disorientation, either in the form of pain or death. Pain is a subjective experience; future or impending pain is an extrapolation (often reflexive) of past experience, conditioned or learned. Death is objective, except insofar as one guesses that dying is likely to entail pain, an idea derived from observation. Because death does not articulate with one's own sense of consciousness and desire for immortality, it apparently represents for most people an ever-coiled instrument for the production of deep feelings of fear. Pain and death are essentially physical matters relating also to profound *beliefs* concerning the relationships of consciousness to body functions, rendered *attitudinally* variable by means of certain controls, the most frequently used of which are presently chemicals that apparently block a spectrum of sensations of pain and different types of perceptions of impending death.

Even in such elemental manifestations of fear, the emotion remains an enigma. It is puzzling first, because various people perceive *both* pain and death differently and therefore manifest their fears, even in biological-organic terms, differently. For some, pain is part of past experience and therefore less fearful than death which is unknowable and unknown. For others, pain is part of past experience—*horrible* experience—and therefore far *more* frightening than the existential notion of dying, a process through which one goes but once and, apparently, often in peace. And for many of us, fear of pain is also apparently a far more dreadful experience than the actual pain itself. In some, fear of death appears negligible at certain times in their lives. Reasons naturally relate to the deeps of beliefs, functions of nature, nurture, accident and age.

Discussing the relationship of pain to fear, London's insights are helpful. "Fear," he writes, "is a more effective control method than punishment, because there are fewer practical or moral restrictions on the extreme use of fear than on the use of pain." Resistance to pain, he notes, is often possible, and therefore a measure of choice is left to the person in agony; he may bring inner resources (or external devices, if available) to bear upon his state. A degree of choice remains to him. But, London continues:

> (F)ear does not offer the same options for resistance that pain does, because it is invoked before anything painful has happened. Fear is aroused by threat, which works wholly upon the imagination, so the object of resistance is often more varied, diffuse, and harder to control than is the case of pain . . . Fear works on expectations of the future, and people's judgments of their prospects, for better and for worse, are cloudier and more intense than are their memories for what has passed.[9]

---

tions are undimensional and allow the author to plot occasional gratuitous thrills in his thriller.

[9] Perry London, *Behavior Control* (New York: Harper and Row, 1969), pp. 108–9.

London has articulated clearly the ironic miracle of fear: that the human being is often more deeply touched by apparently unreal factors in his environment than real ones, no matter how terrible the genuine threats may be. Most emotional states are associated directly either with goal seeking or avoidance reactions. *Fear apparently need not be primarily associated with either or*—just as strangely—*with both.* This is because fear is accepted as an alternative to a realistic construction of the environment (the one choice open to the individual) and, at the same time produces negative reactions towards the environment *and* its potential dangers. The individual who fears anything cannot, therefore, in a loose sense "win," except by eliminating somehow his fears. But even in this case, he takes the horrible chance that his fears are justified by reality (and they may be) and may deal with him even more harshly than he anticipates. The common notion, introduced into consciousness at this point, that fears are protective will probably only increase them. When one grants a need for protection, one accepts the notion of impending danger. When one accepts the notion of impending danger, one also, perforce, realizes that the danger *may be greater* than anticipated. Fear is therefore not allayed but frequently increased.

Psychoanalytic attempts at reconciling the individual with his fears attempts to reduce the generalized states of anxiety in which some people appear to live much of the time by achieving a relatively adequate appraisal of the patient's world, in which appropriate and inappropriate fears are severed one from the other, relevant to the patient's potential for productive operation. The analyst in these instances is rarely dealing with fears of intense or psychotic proportions. Nor may he, should he be treating a patient who lives in an environment which indeed *does* threaten his physical or psychological welfare,[10] often accomplish more than (hopefully) lead his patient to voluntarily attempt to change his environment and thereby eliminate the threat. At its most effective, this fundamentally rational approach —for all its usual methodological symbolic rituals—to the generalized disorder of anxiety is an uncertain form of therapy, time-consuming, expensive and sometimes more destructive than ameliorative; that is, more fear-producing than fear-allaying.

One can easily see, therefore, how impermeable and rigid fears, especially those even faintly redolent of paranoia, are—and how difficult they are to dispel. In normal individuals, specific fears may be held as deeply and

[10] Not all anxieties, of course, are fundamentally psychological problems. The most obviously and apparently anxious man I have ever met was, at the time, a stilt-walker in a circus who had grown, over the years, extremely frightened of falling. He was supporting various ex-wives and children and therefore needful of his profession's lucrative stipend. Fate changed his environment. He fell one night from his stilts, and, after a painful recovery, presently works as a mediocre clown. He is no longer anxious and frightened of falling. He is anxious and frightened, now, about paying his debts and supporting his dependents.

closely as those of the psychotic, if they are in some ways justified by the person's environment or past experiences. They simply cannot be diminished by facing up to "reality" and weighing the logic of circumstances against the reactions of one's own emotions, either at one's own initiative or at the counsel of another—except perhaps momentarily. Little wonder, therefore, is the fact that many psychiatrists, faced with a patient apparently consumed by fear, still turn to such archaic methods as electroconvulsive therapy (or one of its variants) rather than start a trial-and-error course of tranquillizing drugs which, in some instances, take a number of days or weeks to produce noticeable and uncertain results.[11] And the sight and presence of fear has a frightening effect even, the author has seen, upon the hardened physicians and nurses who work daily with deranged people in institutions. Fear in another person, it appears, almost invariably stirs latent possibilities of fear in one's self.

Again, what *else* might we expect? "None of us stands outside humanity's black collective shadow," writes Jung as he indicts us all for the crime of human vanity of the "*fear* which we involuntarily and secretly feel for our own evil . . ."[12] Poets and dramatists may seem less frightened of reaching into the wellsprings of human fear than most other people, but occasionally a philosopher or social analyst will muster sufficient courage to look deeply into the chaos and problematic nature of all human life and particularly in his own self.

Fear, it seems, is more comfortable a companion to man in the role of poet or artist than man as a psycho-biologist. But it walks inevitably beside both poets and scientists, cowards and heroes, young and old—close at some times, distant at others. Neither self-hypnosis (if it exists), surgery, chemistry or any manner of diversion appears able to keep it at bay for long, simply because it *is* indeed a fearful experience to live *at all*. And, like eventual death, fear appears for most people to constitute one of the elemental conditions of life. To hear it denied in polemical or therapeutic terms is to be exposed to one of the ultimate human follies and absurd vanities. The wise man might study such a speaker well: he is either narcotized, intoxicated, stupid beyond salvation, deeply injured or so afraid of the shadow behind himself that he dare not glance up, down or even to his own side, lest he notice it. He—like many others for many reasons—has been, in truth, broken by fear.

What Are We Afraid Of?

A direct answer to so difficult a question is the best one.

First, people may be afraid of *things* or *processes*. Hence, the taxon-

---

[11] *Ibid.*, pp. 115–117.

[12] C. G. Jung, *The Undiscovered Self* (Boston: Little, Brown and Co., 1958), pp. 96–97.

omy of "phobias" by which psychiatrists label the symptoms of fear displayed by their patients.

Second, we may be afraid of *being*, or the consequences of being, hardly a phobia but a simple consequence of life.

It is fashionable to believe that all of us display certain relatively benign phobias and constant ongoing fears related to being. But we attempt not to let them interfere with the "serious business of living," by which is meant the pursuit of a living, raising families, sustaining social relationships, trying to figure out ways to participate in cultural affairs and having "fun" of various kinds. The same fashion also dictates the credo that such fears are "normal and healthy" except when they cause individual dysfunction, an arbitrary matter, because normal function varies so from individual to individual. Dysfunction is frequently open to various opinions, sometimes irrelevant to the problems of the individual involved. In other words, a man or woman regarded as pathologically fearful in one setting may appear normal in another, a problem that extenuates into legal and psychiatric practice in numerous ways.[13]

This simple knowledge has provided a useful, common sense tool in any and all types of persuasive situations yet created by man. Roughly, people will tend to move away from confrontations with fearful situations, no matter how trivial the fear appears, in favor of those which offer an illusion of security. When fears are aroused, advertising copywriters tell us (and experiments confirm),[14] we had better allay these fears with safe "solutions" if we wish to accomplish the persuasion for which our objectives are set. This is elementary rule-of-thumb psychology, as evident in Shakespeare's *Julius Caesar* as in the latest speech by the Secretary of State on the international crisis.

Fear, as we have noted, is, at the same time, a more ephemeral irony which resists objectification, at least in our society. When it lacks specificity, it is called "anxiety," understood by therapists usually to appear in two manifestations, as either "*anxiety neurosis*, a general inner tension manifest . . . as a constant freely floating anxiety (that) is specifically connected with a special situation, which represents the neurotic conflict." [15] In

[13] Thomas S. Szaz has written thoughtfully and as well as—or better than—any other writer on this controversial problem. See, for instance, his *The Myth of Mental Illness* (New York: Harper and Row, 1961), and *Law, Liberty and Psychiatry* (New York: Macmillan Co., 1963).

[14] See, but please do not accept entirely at face value (because of the special nature of the topic involved and subjects used), the classic experiment of Irving L. Janis and Seymour Fesbach, "Effects of Fear-Arousing Communications" in Daniel Katz *et al.*, (eds.), *Public Opinion and Propaganda*, *op. cit.*, pp. 320–336. There exist, naturally, numerous special situations where fear arousal does *not* need to be resolved within a given persuasive context for a message to accomplish its objective.

[15] Otto Fenichel, *The Psychoanalytic Theory of Neurosis*, p. 194. In my opinion, Fenichel's discussion of the specific etiology and symptomology of anxiety neuroses

this framework, and considering the attention given it by psycho-social analysts of the stature of Fromm, Riesman, Kahler, May, Erikson and others, the fear we call "anxiety" may be the most common and virulent disease of contemporary Western society, well ahead in its destructive capacity (but not unrelated to) warfare, highway deaths, cancer, circulatory disease and alcoholism.[16] It may be our "number-one public health problem," if indeed one equates anxiety with abnormality and illness. This construction is apparently a semantic problem, but, even so, it constitutes a significant one for students of culture.[17]

The status of anxiety specifically as a neurosis (or any other kind of sickness) has only indirect relevance to its psychological influence on beliefs, attitudes and opinions, except insofar as it may be reflective of social pathology of the moment or of the collective curiosities of society, matters we shall explore in Parts Four and Five of this volume. The etiology of fear, including anxiety, implies, however, numerous critical relationships to human dispositions, particularly when considering chances of modifying them.

We have seen that neither psychological nor biological constructions bring us close to the sources of fear except in poorly adumbrated operational terms. To this sort of etiological explanation, the question, "Why?" is devastating. It is answerable only if couched in assumptions concerning mankind's (sometime dubious) need to survive or inevitable, mysterious conditions of fate.

Our choice, therefore, in answering the question "What are we afraid of?" with any incisiveness is either to turn to those poets and artists who have already answered this question with brilliant acumen countless times, or to another unorthodox source of investigation. Our answer is visibly triangulated at the meeting points of psychology, philosophy and theology. Specifically, the writings of P. Tillich and R. D. Laing constitute the frame-

---

deserves close study by all students of persuasion. It is, unfortunately, too elaborate to discuss fully here, although I have drawn upon it in my discussions in this chapter. See especially Fenichel's analysis on pp. 193–215, for material that I have personally found most useful.

[16] The wide range of opinion that equates anxiety with psychopathology is clearly covered in Hendrik M. Ruitenbeck, *The Individual and the Crowd* (New York: The New American Library: 1964), pp. 53–110, particularly. Ruitenbeck expertly skims the discontents from most of our contemporary philosophers of *angst*.

[17] The problem is serious because the definition of "illness" and "health" remains so nebulous. James once noted that once a condition is described as an "illness," the chances for ameliorating it increase considerably. This has been the experience of many working with mentally "ill" individuals, especially alcoholics, narcotics addicts and functioning neurotics. Whether this experience is analogous to so enormous and widespread a condition as anxiety is moot. Anxiety, even in moderate manifestations, is frequently treated by physicians as a sickness, in that they prescribe medication for its relief. Millions of people also medicate themselves freely with aspirin, alcohol or other drugs for this condition, which they probably regard as an "illness."

work upon which the suggestions and discussion that follow are hung.[18]

In the first place, we must differentiate anxiety from fear, more fully than in the statement above: that the former is a generalized condition of the latter. Generality is but *one* attribute of anxiety, either when observed (or felt) in its neurotic or hysteric forms, the latter apparently centering more upon *degree* than *kind* of anxiety. At first glance, much anxiety does not seem highly generalized at all. We are anxious over the outcome of *specific* issues, it seems, most of the time. But it is also clear that such specific states partake of, and are fashioned after, psychological models and experiences intimately involved in anxiety "about the human situation as such," as Tillich notes. This is perceived as a threat that signifies, at first, an absence of control over some aspect of the environment which, because of its concern to us, connotes also in extenuation a loss of control over ourselves—that is to say over our own human direction and destiny. Specific anxiety is therefore invariably a recognition of the slim thread of control (or imaginary thread) that one possesses over the course of external events. One's simple (and, in the following case, oddly pleasurable) anxiety over the outcome of a horserace is an excellent example. The fact that one cannot control the outcome of the race—unless he knows it is "fixed," in which case he would not be anxious—offers also a simple, covert reminder that one's being, destiny and fate are beyond one's control in *all* matters, including life itself. The horserace is a specific, contrived reminder of this fact.

Under more spontaneous and typical circumstances, the generality of anxiety induces, usually, some of its most uncomfortable aspects. Most of us will simply not allow ourselves to suffer generalized anxieties for long; the discomfort is too great and the resulting dysfunction too noticeable. One way of solving the problem is then to dismiss the anxiety, if that is possible, frequently either by a shift in behavior or by intervention of drugs. Another way is by self-analysis: that is, to specify the components of the anxiety—asking one's *self* exactly what it is one is afraid of. In the words of Tillich, "Anxiety strives to become fear, because fear can be met by courage. It is impossible for a finite being to stand naked anxiety for more than a flash of time." [19] Fear is therefore a possible *outcome* of anxiety as well as a specified and directed form of anxiety—when and if we attempt to face generalized anxiety squarely.

---

[18] Tillich is the main source here, particularly, *The Courage To Be* (New Haven, Conn.: Yale University Press, 1952), pp. 32–63. Some of the discussion is influenced by observations on ontological insecurity in R. D. Laing, *The Divided Self* (New York: Pantheon Books, 1960), but it concerns more directly Laing's clearer restatement of this problem in *Self and Others* (New York: Pantheon Books, 1969), pp. 35–38. Influences notwithstanding, I must take full responsibility for errors of interpretation in the ensuing discussion.

[19] Tillich, *op. cit.*, p. 39.

Achieving this outcome, however, is a shallow victory for most of us most of the time. True enough, with or without guidance, if an individual can conjure up his dragon, screw up his courage and slay it, he is temporarily relieved of his anxiety. But, more frequently, he fails in this heroism, at least in part, and cannot resolve anxiety into sufficiently specific fears, thereby heightening the residue of anxiety because of his impotence. Or, facing his true fears, he finds them so insultingly negligible that he can muster no courage to face them, nor the will to eliminate them. He is therefore hurled back into his generalized anxiety state. Or, facing his true fears, he finds them *truly* fearful and unconquerable, irrelevant to his courage, and chooses to rush back into the relatively comfortable generality of anxiety.[20]

The latter road is the one we seem to choose most often in our culture. "The Age of Anxiety" is not an overstate shibboleth; it is barely adequate to describe the societal and spiritual tone of the West today and the generalized social anxiety (most of it neurotic) peculiar to our time and place—a longer time and a wider place than "The Age" slogan connotes. Neither statistics nor authority need verify the phenomenon, because it is not raised here in comparison to any halcyon vision of a "non-anxious" past or contemporary happy primitives gamboling on tropical islands. Our world speaks eloquently for itself through a single copy of almost any daily newspaper.

Tillich centers his analysis of anxiety upon the notion of "non-being," a prototypical fear, held by most of us at the depth of a belief (although "belief in extinction" is a strange-sounding phrase) that manifests itself in three clusters of attitudes. Laing adds a fourth. They are all existential in orientation; that is, they bespeak psychological pressures of *now* into which we subsume (as opinions perhaps) the petty and specific fleeting fears and undulating anxieties that accompany our waking hours and play their practical jokes in our dreams.

First, fear of death itself cannot but be re-emphasized here as the prime anxiety-producing element in most people's lives. Even in the heightened consciousness of living and the achievement of what Maslow calls "peak experiences" of happiness and joyful emotion, fear and anxiety may diminish almost entirely, but consciousness of death and non-being

[20] If my experiences with dying people (all too frequent for a man in a peaceful profession) and my own subjective reactions mean anything, this is precisely, I think, the way we must face the specific fear of our own personal deaths. In consonance with psychoanalytic theory, we expose ourselves in fancy to the fear. The result is so devastating to our egos that we *reculer pour mieux sauter* (a Freudian "retreat in favor of the ego") into a generalized, but rarely debilitating, anxiety state. Our best recourse is therefore not to dwell consciously too long or hard or often upon notions of death. Should one not *reculer*, for one or another reason, he is condemned to an on-going panic state which may result in derangement, "psychogenic" death (far more common than many of us—including physicians—realize) or suicide.

remain part of one's awareness.[21] "Certainly the anxiety of death overshadows all concrete anxieties and gives them their ultimate seriousness," says Tillich.[22] Coupled with this anxiety is the accepted concept of fate, in the form of our knowledge that the ultimate disposition of each of us is preordained and that it is both a function and consequence of each particular moment in which we are engaged. "Fate would not produce inescapable anxiety without death behind it," writes Tillich. "And death stands behind fate and its contingencies not only in the last moment when one is thrown out of existence but in every moment within existence." [23]

Second, anxiety is produced by attitudes involving feelings of emptiness and fears of meaninglessness in life. Our struggles to "create" something (in their various manifestations) are efforts to overcome these essential attitudes apparently felt by nearly everyone.[24] Accordingly, we make money, raise families, indulge in hobbies, take adult extension courses, write poems, paint pictures and meddle in the lives of others to give meaning to existence. If we cannot love enough to *be* lovable, we, at least, desire to be liked or accepted, or indulge in a thousand postures and conceits, ending, at their most ludicrous, in attempts to become immortal.[25] Unless we achieve the trick of total self-absorption, our efforts always fail to a degree. And if the spectre of emptiness is glimpsed even for a moment, we often realize the shallowness of our travail. Logan Clendening, the physi-

---

[21] See Abraham H. Maslow, *Toward a Psychology of Being* (Princeton, New Jersey: D. Van Nostrand Company, Inc., 1962, pp. 97–108.

[22] Tillich, *op. cit.*, p. 43.

[23] *Ibid.*, p. 45.

[24] There are exceptions. An intelligent, charming and pleasantly endowed boyhood friend of mine (born to some wealth, fortunately) has spent his life in therapy because, after a drastic early marriage, he simply and apparently gave up attempting to "create" anything. When asked what he is "up to," he replies accurately, "Nothing," and means it. A mutual acquaintance, a psychiatrist, claims that this individual is, due to some obscure cause, simply not anxious or fearful of meaninglessness and emptiness, concepts that have been accepted by him as an inevitable condition of living. Early suicide attempts (when such anxiety was present) have been replaced by a placid acceptance of existential nothingness. Psychotherapy of many types was (and is) useless in the face of so devastating a withdrawal from what most of us consider reality. Yet my one-time friend does not require institutionalization. He is simply vapid, equally unconcerned about all aspects of his existence. Even when he must function, he appears to go through the motions of whatever activity it is he is engaged in (buying clothes or reading a newspaper) merely to kill time. Neither do the numerous diagnoses of his condition that have been entered into his casebook by psychologists and psychiatrists over many, many years appear to have done him much good, as I perceive his welfare.

[25] Arthur Miller mentions in a poem the elaborate statue the late Al Jolson had ordered for himself in California's Forest Lawn Cemetery, a good place for this sort of idiocy. Someone pays also to keep fresh roses on Marilyn Monroe's grave at all times. Many people spend good portions of their lives erecting memorials to themselves that will bloom after death, for some, an effective but amusing way of keeping the demons of meaninglessness at bay.

cian-author of the classical volume on physiology, *The Human Body,* ends his narrative in the following way:

> No, there is nothing so horrible as old age. When wrinkles begin to come, and vision blurs, and the breath comes short on attempting an incline! . . . So far as I am aware, medical science has no wisdom on these matters. You may be perfectly sure that if you live long enough, you will grow old, you will be unbeautiful and unattractive, and that surely death will come. When it comes, you may be certain you will disappear like all the rest and you will not be missed nearly as much as even in your least sanguine moments you have been inclined to suppose.[26]

It is the last sentence that chills, particularly because Clendening died as a victim of his own hand.

When opinions, attitudes, ideas and values lose their stability because of changing times, the virulence of anxiety caused by emptiness and meaningless increase apace in intensity. One's sense of creativity requires stability, usually with its roots running into the past and to prospects for the future, the reason, probably that raising children (or "brain-children") is regarded as one of mankind's most meaningful creative activities. But, in periods of unrest and rapid social change, even values such as these are called into serious question. Threats of nuclear warfare are psychological threats to our very creative capacities via our children (or "brain-children").

In stable times, the axiom that art is immortal may ring true. But in volatile periods, books are burned, museums bombed and "art" itself is redefined. One's life's work, even if it had centered on the labors of ideation, may be wiped out in an instant before one's eyes, leaving emptiness and nothingness. And no exception is made for those values which people label "spiritual." The best evidence we have is that our spirit (if we have one) dies with our body. The result is nothingness. Neither nuclear explosions nor dynamite make special cases for sacred objects or saints, as far as we have been competent to ascertain to date.

Third, man is threatened by anxieties derived from a sense of universal guilt, previously discussed. The question of *why* man feels guilty and exactly what his crime is (or was) is best left to poets and dramatists, although the efforts of Theodor Reik and others (mostly Freudians) have constructed a colorful mosaic of rite, ritual and religion that explores the configurations of myths of the past and their residues in consciousness today.[27] The reader may prefer Kafka's less elaborate symbol of *The Trial.*

In any case, the artist (and sometimes the psychologist) often succeeds

---

[26] Logan Clendening, *The Human Body* (New York: Pocket Books, 1943), p. 479.

[27] Freud started this exploration, and Reik followed. But the latter has been most productive in following the lead into primitive religion. Reik's enormous output—little of it uninfluenced by the current of his concerns—is too enormous to list here. So are the many other Freudians who have walked similar paths.

at illustrating the ways in which we dispose of this fear. We treat it either, on one hand, by a defiance of the "rules" (or morals) we must follow in order to exist and therefore alienate ourselves, like Camus' *Stranger*, not only from society, but also from all other human beings. On the other hand, we may accept this guilt and attempt to allay anxiety by adhering so closely to "right" thinking and "correct" doing that we sacrifice our humanity to the rulebook of a "proper" life. In either case, we free ourselves from anxiety of guilt at the cost of the virtual destruction of our personalities: our *selves* as individual, viable significant components of a meaningful world.

Clear psychological precedence exists for the etiological idea of universal guilt, incidentally more obvious and elemental than the psychoanalytic unearthings that are spoken in arbitrary symbolic languages. Most of us perceive death and its accompaniments (old age, pain, infirmity and unattractiveness) as inappropriate final rewards for a life from which we have attempted to grasp some decent measure of meaning and substance.[28] The inevitable may therefore be construed as punishment. If it is man's fate to be thus punished, a crime must lie behind his final disposition, a crime of which he is guilty. And, in fact, one does; and he is! The crime is the *hubris* or impudence to live at all; and the guilt is intrinsic to the painful process of surviving the "stages of man" in order to live long enough to be ironically punished by death and its handmaidens. Guilt is thus a condition of existence.

Tillich tells us that our guilt derives from an existential skepticism of the moral principles by which men must live. This doubt, says he, is perceived as guilt. To this observation let us add the qualification that living itself is cause enough, in this construction, to punish one, like Kafka's K— even if the bill of particulars against him does *not* include the specific sin of doubt.

Fourth, Laing points to the possibility of what he calls "ontological insecurity," a form of anxiety wherein "a person encounters non-being in a preliminary form, as a partial loss of the synthetic unity of self, concurrently with partial loss of relatedness with the other (another), and, in the ultimate form, in the hypothetical end-state of *chaotic nonentity*, total loss of relatedness with self and other." [29] We are driven by this anxiety to the

[28] A geriatric community is, to my eyes, the saddest sight our culture offers, and, thanks to the miracles of modern medicine, more of them exist today than ever before. The more vigorously social workers and psychologists try giving them (necessarily bogus) meaning, the sadder they look. And what other perception can one's aged, dying, feeble friend or relative cosset except the bitter realization that *this* abomination is the fruit of a lifetime—*this* being Fort Lauderdale, a nursing home, a hideous "elder citizen's" housing project, a wheelchair or a bed with guard rails on either side. If God is good—and if He reads footnotes—He will spare me the wheelchair, the cane, the bedpan and their attendant indignities by taking me before the masters of medicine turn to extending my life into the humiliation of senility by means of their surgery and pills.

[29] Laing, *op. cit.*, p. 36. (Italics are Laing's.)

obvious outcome, notes Laing. Within ourselves we cultivate the subjective impression of sincerity. What we search for in others is security. The result in the long run, once again, is inevitable failure. Because we are motivated to sincerity by anxiety (called "hysteria" by Laing), the more sincere we *try* to appear, the more false our behavior rings; the more like acting or pretense (or worse) becomes the "frantic desire to make pretenses real." Security desired from others is doomed, because our faulty grasps after sincerity cool all honest attempts of others to make us feel secure, or in our self-conscious, involuted state we think they do.

We are, therefore, alone and afraid on two fronts: within ourselves and in company with others. Anxiety is produced, and our fear now generates a new cycle of inept searching for relatedness. The round-dance continues in a fugue of anxiety, self-detachment, seeking, failure and anxiety, all the while tempered by fate, which changes the setting and cast of characters (but not the leading actor) in our little game every so often, until the major role, our own, is eliminated from the drama by death.

Fearful Persuasion

Little discussion, fortunately, is required at this point concerning the role of fear in the psychodynamics of persuasion. For some people, at certain times in history and under certain orientations towards consent, fear may be understood as the *only* psychologically viable force by which to change behavior, qualify opinions, moderate attitudes or tamper with (or touch) beliefs. And, in part at least, this view may be correct, particularly in matters relating to beliefs. Our own time may also be one such period where fear plays a critical role in much apparently moderate and rational persuasion. So-called logical assent or dissent may be the *rationalization* of specific fears or anxieties, rational merely *post hoc* and in the light of impending terror.

Tillich has remarked that "all human life can be interpreted as a continuous attempt to avoid despair." [30] *We* do not require existential philosophers of *désespoir* to remind us that such a construction of living is not only possible, it is the only one conceivable to millions for whom existential anxiety has become their single relevant, given datum of the moment. Such an orientation was, of course, the philosophical stance of many Europeans a generation ago, detached as they were from the past and future by Hitler's storm troopers and concentration camps and the fire of military chaos that raged across their continent. Existential philosophy is less interesting construed as the brain-child of Kierkegaard in a burst of nineteenth century genius than as a sympathetic reaction to a twentieth century liberal-humanist tradition that had been brutally assaulted and dehumanized by

---

[30] Tillich *op. cit.*, p. 56.

World War II. The physical realities of Europe of the 1930's and 1940's left little recourse for the intellectual but to fear and despair.

We have seen that warfare is not the only cause of fear, however, and that modern man's rapidly changing environment is prone to peculiarly disguised and socially sanctioned forces that tend to exacerbate and extenuate what might be considered the "normal" fears attendant his human condition. Non-being is not so terrible if one can conceive—as poets often do—of never having been born. Neither is it more than personally and moderately threatening in a stable world managed by benign and equitable gods, a world which has "always been" the way it is and will "always be" that way—*the* world, incidentally, in which most of the world's population, most of the time, have believed they have lived. The threat of non-being *is* formidable, however, to the concentration camp inmate who is robbed not only of his name but his title (Doctor, Professor, Mister), his family, his home and all the things, tangible and intangible, that he and his family have treasured for generations. Perhaps the threat is even more frightening to the middle class American WASP (who cannot accuse fate of congenital anti-Semitism and thereby achieve a sense of martyrdom) for whom non-being entails relinquishing to nothingness his 3.5 children, credit cards and brilliant technology, along with the trappings of a culture that he views as the epitome of all historical progress.

The only genuine escape from fear and anxiety—and fearful persuasion—lies, of course, in suicide. The decision for suicide modifies all personally felt social issues for the simple reason that one dies alone. It may quiet one's fear of death, because one has conquered it. But, as Tillich notes (and Christianity teaches), suicide does not release one psychologically from guilt, because, paradoxically, guilt seems to continue after death: The example of history shows the living that the wages of guilt produce more telling monuments than all other memorials we may erect to ourselves. That suicide is chosen by thousands as a way out of fear—and fear is probably what the successful suicide is most frequently escaping from—is therefore remarkable.[31]

The rest of us, neither brave nor stupid enough to kill ourselves (despite the hours of thought most of us have given the prospect), opt for life, and with it, the acceptance of fear. We range typologically on a psychological continuum that spans the distance from psychosis to normality, but one

---

[31] For a terse analysis of suicide as a social problem see Jack P. Gibbs, "Suicide" in Robert K. Merton and Robert A. Nisbet (eds.), *Contemporary Social Problems*, Second Edition (New York: Harcourt, Brace and World Inc., 1966), pp. 281–321. Considering the discussion above, it may interest the reader that Gibbs points out that "Catholics and Jews are much less prone to take their lives than Protestants are," (p. 302). See also Emile Durkheim, *Suicide: A Study in Sociology* (New York: The Free Press, 1951), for what is considered a classic study of suicide proposing an interesting but questionable hypothesis relating suicide rates to social integration.

that the parameters for which have not yet been clearly drawn. Our vulnerability to persuasion which affects these accepted fears will result from the unique concatenation of two factors: relevance of specific persuasion to them, first, and the place on the continuum at which we find ourselves, second. And vulnerability does not mean that fearful persuasion must pull our dispositions in its intended direction. Such persuasion may—and often does—frighten us into retreat and/or call forth previously discussed selective and distortive devices of perception, attention and memory that modify the activation of fear in a manner impossible to predict.

Of one point we are certain: men are motivated by fear and activated by anxiety. A construction of history based upon concepts of fear as a motivating force is not only possible, it is as convincing as an interpretation from any other starting-place. Fear—cold naked fear—is probably at the core of most of our dearest beliefs. Our attitudes are tempered by the ever-glowing heat of anxiety. Our opinions probably reflect peaks of specific anxieties, refined and rationalized for argument and self-affirmation. And our behaviors frequently betray rabbit-like sensitivities to unexpected "things that go bump in the night" and to a million possibilities for instants of personal terror that we create in fantasy while we juggle the potential threats of our most mundane activities. We bolt our doors, or keep a gun in a secret place, and prattle about "security" and—for brief moments—may even evoke a transient feeling that we have indeed found it. When the feeling subsides, however (as it must), we are alone again, not only with the possible, but also the inevitable—and we are, quite sensibly, afraid.

Conclusion

Time has run out, at least in this investigation, for the conventional description of human fear as a "protective mechanism" on the psychobiological levels of human operation. While this explanation makes apparent sense, it is contradictory in practice, largely because fear is not a mechanical practice or analogy of one, nor is it neessarily protective, even when considered as a vestigial trait of an autonomic nervous system left over, somehow, like a vermiform appendix, in the human organism from an earlier evolutionary stage.

Fear may, in fact, be described with some precision regarding its nature and function. Its main curiosity in human beings is that it need not be reflective of any apparent environmental situation, and it often produces effects of considerable irony. It is closely associated with psychological perceptions of pain but, in effect, is frequently more painful or frightening than pain itself. Thus, fear may be both a cause and effect, a cause of more fear and the effect of imaginary possible dreadful events or circumstances. In this respect, people are often moved more forcefully by unreal aspects of their environments than real ones, and therefore much fear is extremely difficult to dispel except by means of chemicals or surgical procedures.

Causes of specific fears are often easily determined, but causes of anxiety (both "neurotic" and "hysterical") tend to be more general and relate to the ambient consequences of living in a given culture at a certain time. The genesis of such anxieties, as discussed by Tillich and Laing, are found in fears of non-being, expressed in anxieties concerning 1.) death, 2.) meaninglessness, 3) guilt and 4.) chaotic nonentity in relations with others. They present elaborate problems for the social psychologist that ramify beyond the objects of his discipline into his own intellectual and personal orientation to existence.

Persuasive appeals directed to human fears, while manifesting curiosities like "boomerang effects" and retreats from fields of conflict, are often highly effective. They probably occur differentially as they act upon clusters of human beliefs, attitudes, opinions and behaviors. They are particularly important, the author believes, in the warp and woof of modern technological societies, where the objects of fear (or anxiety) are perceived less as specific threats to the individual from his environment than as a generalized feeling that a complex, sophisticated and powerful culture is in an unseen manner robbing the individual of his identity—that is, reducing his being to non-being, despite his personal best efforts to prevent it. Suicide is one logically and psychologically satisfactory solution to the problem. But an attempt to maintain certain fixed ideas and values in a rapidly changing social order is the feeble but viable alternative (from a pragmatic viewpoint) that most of us accept, along with its inevitable concomitant of living with our fears.

Chapter 15

THE POWER OF SEX

Throughout the Western World, we have all got sex on the brain, which apart from any other considerations, is a most unseemly place to have it.

Malcolm Muggeridge

A CONTEMPORARY CYNIC might be justified in observing that it has taken precisely one hundred years for sex to make the journey from sin to instinct to culture trait to scientific object to recreation to joke.

The statement is too facile, not because it is untrue, but because, at least from pre-Aristophonic comedy to the present, sex has *always* been a joke. Various types of sexual behavior have also, everywhere, and for as much history as we have recorded it, been sinful, although the aspects of sex conceived as funny and/or sinful have been and continue to be widely different throughout time and over distances.[1]

While their exactitude may be questioned, various studies published over the years indicate roughly that sex is the topic that most people, over pubic and under late-middle age, think about more of the time than anything else—in excess of fifty per cent among college students. Certainly, awareness of individual sexual attraction is the dominant image that one receives on the streets of our cities and towns, on our instruments of mass communication and in the world of commerce. To affirm, as some do, that our culture is "sex mad" is neither more nor less correct than saying we are "money mad," "automobile mad" or "education mad." Wherever one travels, he sees human transactions involving money, automobiles and education—and other cultural institutions, of course. He or she, if at all perceptive, also observes the ubiquity of consumed, proposed or fantasied

[1] This observation has been made by Margaret Mead a number of times, most particularly and clearly in her article, "Sex and Censorship in Contemporary Society," in Kingsley and Eleanor Widmer (eds.), *Literary Censorship* (San Francisco: Wads-

sexual transactions, or, because they are frequently homosexually as well as heterosexually oriented, what may better be termed "human communications with erotic content."

The tendency to compare this phenomenon with other cultures and former times—usually for self-excoriating reasons—serves no purpose. Unconvincing arguments like those of the late Sorokin of Harvard,[2] that our preoccupation with sex is destroying us, based upon comparisons between sex-obsessed cultures and eras of social decay, may serve social functions by framing in differential contexts various life-styles and reminding us of the Puritan heritage of the New World. In a more popular (in every sense of the word) vein, and from another perspective, the therapeutic realism of men like Albert Ellis is equally as removed as Sorokin from the true dynamics of the culture complex they purport to treat. Following and exploiting our sexual permissiveness of the moment, they appear highly liberal and emancipated from prudery, their stance sustaining the myth that we are today throwing off shackles of outworn moral and ethical codes and moving into a new, liberal world of sensual realism, wherein sexual behavior will, or should be, regarded as little different in moral connotations from other forms of interpersonal transactions.[3]

Both arguments (and their possible ramifications) contain portions of

---

worth Publishing Co., 1961), pp. 140–151, and is a sub-theme of Bronislaw Malinowski, *Sex, Culture, and Myth* (New York: Harcourt, Brace and World, Inc., 1962), one of the richest cross-cultural analyses of various moral interpretations of sexual behaviors available.

[2] See Pitirim A. Sorokin, *The American Sex Revolution* (Boston: Porter Sargent Publisher, 1956), for a sociological polemic that will warm the heart of the contemporary puritan. Sorokin's idealism bespeaks strong cultural ties with a kind of old world intellectual style that had gone out of style long before he died. Vance Packard, however, stepped into Sorokin's shoes with *The Sexual Wilderness* (New York: David McKay, Inc., 1968). Packard's arguments lack Sorokin's authority, the former being a journalist who has devoted his recent years to professional "viewing with alarm" various American institutions. Inevitably, he finally centered on the problem of sexual license in a readable but unconvincing volume, overloaded with trivia and lacking in conviction that the "new morality" he attacks is, in fact, leading us to perdition, or anywhere else, for that matter. Packard, an extremely astute student of culture behind his repertorial masquerade, knows better, I think.

[3] Ellis' works are numerous and freely available. As complete a statement as he has made of his position may be found in Albert Ellis, *American Sexual Tragedy* (New York: Twayne Publishers, 1954). Ellis' skill as a psychotherapist appears, at first glance, formidable, but one must remember when evaluating such healers that they, for all their protestations to the contrary, are fundamentally helping people to adjust to values that society itself has been attempting to force upon them since adolescence. A therapist's admonition to follow one's nature in the release of sexual tension is precisely the same message that the "fun morality" of today implies, in a less apparently reasonable fashion. What a therapist *may* accomplish is to provide sanctions and bolster nerve to conform to accepted socio-sexual values alien (for various reasons) to his patient. The patient perceives this process as a liberation, when, in fact, it constitutes little more than the acceptance of, and conformance to, the specific ground rules of an old and familiar game.

relevant truths, and both may sometimes prove curiously therapeutic to individuals who are needful of sanctions for their personal dispositions and behaviors. Because the attitudes and opinions of men like Ellis more closely accord with today's apparent public consensus, they appear more therapeutically satisfactory than those of men and women like Sorokin, an illusion resulting from relevance rather than cultural logic or psycho-social wisdom.

Various psychological orientations naturally construe problems of human mind and function in different ways. But the variance in psychological approaches to the sexual part of man's life probably admits of more fundamental and furious controversies than any other single topic. The main reason, as even high school students know today, is that Freud chose the concept of "libido" as the propelling force for life in his theoretical formulations: an instinct, appetancy or what have you, opposed by a thanatotic power, to provide (quite late in Freud's career) the Hegelian thesis and antithesis that yielded in synthesis the operant, individual, ongoing ego. At the other pole of psychological investigation stands Pavlov and the American behaviorists who accept an instinctual component to the sex drive, comparable in many ways to other raw drives, that is conditioned through life in various ways to respond to certain stimuli. But, for them, the entire process results from environmental happenstance in the form of learning, and constitutes part of the individual's socialization process.

In one way or another, and with the possible exceptions of those espousing holistic views of psychology, the two viewpoints have divided the behavioral sciences into what, at times, appears to be totally irreconcilable factions. When attempts to fuse them are made, they appear as ineffectual compromises, such as the claim that Freud did not truly construe the term "libido" as the sex urge but as a generalized "life-force" (which is patently and obviously untrue); or that behaviorists generally regard sex as important, but not as important as Freud did (equally untrue).

The resolution of this problem has taken the following form in the United States: Psychoanalysts, whether physicians or laymen, tend to follow original Freudian interpretations. Psychiatrists tend to accept the Freudian notion in theory, but prefer, in practice, to follow a biological-neurological course that has unearthed little or no evidence of the invariable primacy of the sex drive in the etiology of neurosis or psychosis. Experimental, educational and clinical psychologists were, two decades ago, largely committed to Freudian sexual theory and resultant methodologies. They have lately been breaking away from the notion of libido and have instead shown a preference for the ideas of various neo-Freudians, particularly Piaget, Bruner and others whose positions in this critical regard are difficult to determine. In other words, they have deferred the matter for future consideration and as largely irrelevant to their present concerns. Others have been influenced by non-Freudian, generally behavioristic, sociological evidence concerning sexual behavior as it is practiced and accepted in society today. Sociologists, who usually prefer inductive surveys, polls and statistics to deductive techniques, lean decidedly towards the behaviorists, following the example of the former entomologist, Alfred Kinsey. Those who deal in theory (small or grand) in the manner of the European sociologists often share the Freudian view of the primacy of the sex drive in apparently unrelated human behaviors, particularly those involving important individual or social dysfunctions. There are, of course, few but significant exceptions.

Sex and Society

Sexual beliefs, attitudes, opinions and probably behavior have changed considerably in the past century, as our imaginary cynic has observed. Much has been made of the apparent reasons for these changes, particularly those Victorian morals and attitudes from which our present sexual notions are supposed to have been liberated.

The history of the Victorian period in the West contains many contradictions, little of it providing evidence that its code of sexual morality, double standards, and its world of elegant gentlemen and ladies functioned more than superficially in a dress-up world of manners (apparent opinions, shared attitudes and slyly inconsistent beliefs) by means of which the apparently secure members of the upper classes presented an image of solidarity to the rest of society and to each other. It seemed covertly understood that almost everyone knew what was going on beneath the surface. The theme that one does not discover, as he reads through stacks of dreary real and make-believe Victorian pornography, is that of social or cultural self-recrimination stemming from the apparent hypocrisy of a culture that dressed one way, spoke another way, and fornicated in yet another.[4] This incongruous behavior, of course, was only standardized among the gentry. The lower classes evidently pursued their sexual objectives in quite an abandoned manner and, if we are to believe D. H. Lawrence and others, with considerable permissiveness and joy. Brothels abounded at the time in nearly every civilized (or semi-civilized) community in Europe and Amer-

[4] See Steven Marcus, *The Other Victorians* (New York: Basic Books, 1966), for a contemporary evaluation of the sexual habits and reading preferences of the Victorian gentlemen (and ladies) who visited the licentious underworld of the period. This demi-monde was given notoriety in its own day, incidentally, by such philosopher-writers as Oscar Wilde, W. S. Gilbert, Robert Louis Stevenson, Bernard Shaw and many others in England and America. As for Victorian pornography, it is difficult to separate fact from fancy, but *My Secret Life* (in any one of its editions) and the collected editions of the pornographic periodical, *The Pearl*, give one a clear picture of what preoccupied the consciousness of some Victorian roués. Other samples, like *A Man and A Maid* abound today in paper editions on drugstore bookstalls, and are worth scholarly investigation if you have time to waste. The clearest orientation to the psychology of pornography, including the Victorian variety, remains Eberhard and Phyllis Kronhausen, *Pornography and the Law* (New York: Ballantine Books, 1959), written before the Drs. Kronhausen embarked on the present, more public sexual adventures in print and on film.

ica, only a small fraction of them operating as pleasure palaces for the rich. Most of them were common, inexpensive and extremely active cat houses, from which, of course, any but "fallen women" were barred almost entirely, at least as working girls.

Our much discussed liberation from Victorianism merely amplified new soundings from Dr. Freud's clinic in Vienna: information, for instance, that erotic feelings might be aroused in unlikely people in unusual ways. The unlikely people were women and children, illustrating the fact that, from the author's reading of Victorian, pre-Freudian pornography, the Victorians understood clearly that women (even whores) and many children appear to enjoy sex with remarkable avidity, an observation entirely at variance with most common psychological and historical opinion. The unusual ways were those *not* associated with standard heterosexual intercourse, but with homosexuality, neurotic behaviors, symbolic activities and a galaxy of startling insights into relationships between parents and children, brothers and sisters, and infants in cribs with themselves.

Only the uninformed will underestimate the impact on Western culture of Freudian *morality*, a popular novelty induced from his theoretical writings and case studies. For psychologists to date the start of the present period of sexual emancipation from Freud's series of lectures in 1909 in Worcester, Massachusetts (upon the occasion of the twentieth anniversary of Clark University) is not to overstate the significance of an historic occasion. Freud and his work were well known among the psychological fraternity in the United States before his journey to Worcester. The Clark lectures, and their subsequent publication, however, introduced Freudian notions to the rest of the academic world. With remarkable rapidity, they were popularized for the masses in literature, in the theatre and by the new art of the motion picture.

The moment also collided with other events in America that made Freudian pan-sexualism an ideal battle-call for the generation born at the time of the Clark lectures. World War I, while of short duration and involving limited participation by the United States, spawned the myth best encapsulated in the song title, "How Ya' Gonna' Keep 'Em Down on the Farm After They've Seen Paree." True, few American soldiers *saw* "Paree," but writers and artists had, and they were to visit it again and again during the "lost generation" period to follow. What they saw, of course, was not "Paree" at all, but a European sucker-trap *seulement pour les Americains* that they mistook for the genuine item.

At home, Babbitry of various sorts became a national joke, and Prohibition turned Americans of all classes into lawbreakers. Corruption of one kind tends to breed corruptions of other types, and, if constitutional law, on one hand, could openly and easily be contravened, might not private morality, or at least the open discussion of it, be violated to the same degree? In a nation in search of sexual and ethical guidelines, Hemingway's suggestion that that which was moral was what "felt good" held particular appeal for people who broke the law daily in their battle with the noble experiment, Prohibition.

The aftermath was a period of depression, confusion and disorientation. The 1930's became the great period of Freudianism in American popular culture, theatre and the films, but it took shape as anti-intellectual Freudianism, most prurient and frequently silliest when it took itself most seriously. The films of Mae West, exalting libidinous female pleasure by her literal *use* of such sex objects as the young Cary Grant or Randolph Scott, such seriously intended melodramas as *The Children's Hour* by Lillian Hellman that treated a lesbian relationship (or the possibility of one) on the stage, and the adulation of quasi-nymphomaniac heroines like Scarlett O'Hara were all fundamentally non-intellectual translations of psychoanalysis into American argot.

The generation since World War II (a sexual interregnum that has received too little analysis by our arbiters of erotica) has also witnessed an assault upon former sexual conventions from a number of quarters. Automobiles, the motel industry and novel contraceptive devices have produced the impression of an increase in pre- and extra-marital sexual behavior, although the latter techniques have not affected either our birth rates or rates of illegitimate births.[5] The impression of increased sexual activity may have little basis in fact. The automobile and motel have merely helped to fill the need for trysting places created by close living in urban centers and by the diminution of privacy in suburbs and exurbs. For reasons the author cannot fathom, except for the possible truth of an ancient adage he learned as a youth that "an aroused male penis does not respond to restraints of conscience" (or words to that effect), there exists little evidence that contraceptive devices, including chemicals, effect frequency of intercourse, and/or choice of partner, or influence severely the psychological consequences of most sexual activity.

Second, a scientific vanguard of quasi-medical investigators, like Kinsey and his associates, Masters and Johnson and many others, invaded domains of private behavior with cold, boldly stated, statistical and observational reports about the social and psycho-physical aspects of human sexual behavior. Their naïveté concerning the generality of their investigations merits

[5] Whether or not new liberal abortion legislation, like that currently adopted by New York State, will effect either is a moot point. My guess is that both birth rates will probably remain stable. Procuring an extra-legal abortion for those who wanted it (and could pay for it) has not been a problem for any but the dim-witted since the invention of anti-biotic drugs that reduced nearly to zero the chances that even an amateur abortionist would be apprehended by a botched curettage. Many thousands of once illegal abortions will now be performed lawfully, more competently and (hopefully) more cheaply. There is also a current of opinion that holds that illegitimate children are usually covertly desired offspring, and the question of legitimacy is of no consequence in the sub-cultures into which most such babies are born, especially in ghetto communities.

qualification and criticism. Smith,[6] among others, has pointed out the ethnocentric frailties of much of the tunnel vision displayed in their research. He notes correctly that the title of Kinsey's *magnum opus, Sexual Behavior in the Human Male,* exposes the project's basic fault on its title page. The study does not concern the *human* male at all, or even the American male and his behavior, but a segmented and selected sample of verbal replies by white Americans of the sort who would willingly and honestly expose themselves to the questions of Kinsey's researchers—and nothing more, except by implication. Exactly the same problem, in sharper form, attends the pseudo-generality of Masters and Johnson's volume, *The Human Sexual Response.*[7] For the authors of this latter tome to comprehend that their subjects are by no means representative, even in physiological matters, of all (or most) "humans" under all conditions is asking for a degree of detachment unlikely to be discovered in the community of sexologists, particularly in the light of the troubles to which they went to gather their data and the instrumental ingenuity employed in studying it. By no means, does this criticism imply that Kinsey's or Masters and Johnson's data may not be useful to many students of human behavior. It merely means that the impression readers receive that their conclusions relate either to normal or average (the two are different) behaviors of human beings—or American men and women—is erroneous. *And it is precisely this impression that has characterized the greatest social and intellectual influence of their work, and of others who have followed their leads, especially in academia.*

Third, the present period has seen a frontal assault upon censorship of materials once held to be obscene that have lately received protection of the First Amendment of the Constitution of the United States, and are today protected by judicial interpretations of the nature of free speech.[8] The application, in practice, of this freedom varies in different parts of the country, but it is sufficient in this chapter merely to indicate the limits to which this new protection seems to have extended, as of the present mo-

---

[6] See M. Brewster Smith, *op. cit.*, pp. 46–47, for his wise discussion of the values of the cross-cultural anthropological approach to all research purporting to possess psychological generality.

[7] At this writing, two of the Kinsey volumes (on human males and females) have appeared. Reasons for abandoning or postponing Kinsey's original research design for comprehensive studies of various races and national groups, pornography and other phenomena are unclear, and I do not wish to give credence to rumors. The Kinsey Institute at the University of Indiana today flourishes under the guidance of the late Dr. Kinsey's associates. It is shortly, I have been informed, to be the subject of a book by my friend John Tebbel who somehow and invariably manages to find lively subjects for his scholarly scrutiny. The original Masters and Johnson volume published in 1966 by Little Brown and Co. was followed in 1970 by a self-help, do-it-yourself book of what I imagine I should call "sexual therapy." Because I am uncertain either of its value or accuracy (pending further investigation), it will not be cited here.

[8] See Chapter 26 for further discussion of this phenomenon.

ment—in New York City, for example—without apparent overt legal interference:

1.) Any type of pornographic printed material *in words* may be purchased freely and openly in the city, including graphic descriptions of such sexual novelties as homosexual coprophagy and similar diversions.
2.) Films showing nude males and females performing the sex act, including scenes of male orgasm and ejaculation, female and male fellatio, cunnilingus, and, if the author's eyes served him properly, analingus are displayed in peep-shows and motion picture theatres. A number of the latter specialize in male homosexual films. Three films at present show these acts explicitly but set them in a documentary format as serious studies of sexual behavior and pornography in Denmark. Others are less pretentious.
3.) Picture magazines and books openly for sale are only slightly less explicit than pornographic novels, but they cover a wide range of interests, both homo- and heterosexual. "Underground" newspapers advertise the promised consumation of commercial and amateur sexual relationships in a somewhat obscure but unmistakable language of euphemisms. The author has no idea of whether they are genuine or bogus.
4.) In addition to a number of "adult," well-publicized legitimate plays featuring nude performers, an intimate burlesque follies (performed in a former dance hall on an improvised stage) operates openly (and apparently without judicial interference), presenting nude female performers who masturbate in full view of the all-male audience. Live simulations of nude men and women producing a "stag film," and other such novelties, come and go. Most of these performances continue for about twenty minutes, and admission is usually five dollars.
5.) While there has never been a shortage of prostitutes in New York City, most of them have, for the past generation, usually operated from "inside," that is, as call girls or in bars and cafés and by means of pimps acting as steerers. Within the past year or so, it has been literally impossible for a reasonably well dressed lone male over thirty to walk through certain segments of the city at any time of day or night (except perhaps in the early A.M.) and not be solicited directly by at least one attractive, and usually youthful, streetwalker.

The observations above represent the confluence, of course, of many social factors. But the role of the courts (particularly the Supreme Court) in implying, and sometimes directly stating, new criteria for freedom of speech and attendant behavior has provided immediately effective legal sanctions for the phenomena noted above, and probably many others that have escaped the writer's notice, because he has not gone out of his way to search them out. They are listed without opprobrium, neither in outrage nor with shock. Nor does the writer feel that restraints upon them necessarily either bode well or ill for the future of our culture.[9] They merely represent departures from *legally sanctioned* sexual communications of, say, a decade ago in *one* city. New York has for years been the scene of the *illegal* exchange of pornographic pictures, books and films in massive supply. *Illegal* sex shows, quasi-public or private, have never been difficult to locate, nor have prostitutes, sex circuses and similar diversions. Whether the apparent legalization of these items has increased patronage for them, it is impossible to determine. Possibly not. Their prices now appear somewhat lower, at any rate.

Legalization, however, is also currently producing changes, partially in attitudes, certainly in opinions and possible in behavior, in all communities where similar degrees of license obtains. It is too soon to draw any conclusions about them, even of the supposed effects of such exposure upon the young and impressionable. Changes in common vocabulary and the use of once taboo words are noticeable, as is a new pseudo-frankness in discussion, even between students and professors, about sexual matters. But similar changes have occurred in the past without the confluence of social, scientific and legal forces that give them the authority they have today, nor have they been spread by sophisticated instruments of communication that give them wide currency. They unquestionably provide a colorful background against which to hold the contemporary psychodynamics of sexual behavior and feeling as they influence our capacities and proclivities for persuasion.

[9] I would not be fair to the reader if I did not record some of my personal value judgments of these overt changes in my native city. My experiences as a teacher lead me to doubt that the widespread distribution of pornographic texts or pictures hurts (or helps) anyone much; too many millions of people have been exposed to too much of it and survived to live normal (or non-destructive) sex lives to justify its evil reputation. I myself enjoy printed pornography, in moderate doses if it is cleverly written. Most pornographic films tend to be abominations from every criterion of judgment *except* as pornography, including the so-called "documentary" and "art" films openly shown today. I do not think they are corruptive for adults, but they certainly do not help to develop tastes for superior cinema experiences. Again, moderate doses are all I am able, personally, to take. The legitimate plays sold as art which exploit nudity also exploit *my* gullibility, and, therefore, having been burned once by an enormous ticket price (and having seen enough nude people in various places to last for *this* lifetime), I tend to stay away from them. The sight of living girls or men indulging in sex play (masturbatory or otherwise), on the other hand, usually makes no pretenses to be anything more than amusement for *voyeurs*. As long as it does not hanker to be art or theatre (and if the performers are attractive), I have indeed the capacity, at times, to enjoy it. I am in hesitant agreement with those who claim that prostitution serves a legitimate social purpose for certain people (a matter discussed in Chapter 26), but I *most decidedly* do *not* believe that the general tone of any city—not London, Paris or Calcutta—is enhanced by strolling and talking prostitutes. If they *must* stroll, let them at least not verbalize.

Sex and the Individual

Despite the wealth of our phenomenological, empirical and theoretical speculation on the topic, the nature of human sexual feeling mostly remains unexplored, as do other basic human functions like the healing process, cerebral cognition and other common physiological and psychological processes. But sexual emotion is regarded as more dramatic than most of them. The drama derives from two human conditions attendant our sexuality: First, one is usually not clearly aware of the emotional power and force of the sexual drive over one's cognitive processes until after the point in life at which these latter have been developed to a high degree of sophistication and apparent autonomy. Second, cultural impetus, as well as (probably) biological appetites, lead one's first *individual* perceptions of sexual feeling (in the form of tensions and masturbatory experiences) eventually, and usually, into *social* experiences whereby emotions are somehow stimulated and shared between individuals in a manner that remains, to date, a matter of chance and mystery. (A popular romantic love song states the puzzle in terms of, "How little we understand what touches off that tingle;/That sudden explosion when two tingles intermingle," and expresses the mystery as clearly as it is found anywhere.)

Human curiosity has, throughout history, been stimulated by the inherent mystery of the sexual process in its two major phases,[10] both of which share psycho-physiological elements, but are nevertheless discrete in experience. The first phase centers on germination as its end, but impels immediate attention to erotic gratification as an illusory or pseudo-end in itself—symbolized by male ejaculation and female orgasm, the latter a less specifically understood dynamic than the former. The second phase is dominated by the female and entails fertilization of the ovum, uterine development of a foetus and the birth of a new individual, the second "sub-end-product" of the sexual process.

The two phases, however, are differentiated sharply most of the time in most cultures that have been studied by anthropologists and historians.

---

[10] See G. Rattray Taylor, *Sex in History* (New York: The Vanguard Press, 1954), for an excellent history of sexual behaviors in the West. Also note the mistitled (for purposes of exploitation, apparently) work, James Bellah, *Anal and Oral Love* (Los Angeles: Ultima Books, 1970), a less scholarly volume than Taylor's, but more candid and replete with cuts (mostly drawings) of erotic practices from antiquity to the present in both the East and West. The latter volume is currently sold as mail order pornography, but (except for some arbitrary diversion into morality and half-baked, impromptu psychoanalysis) is both interesting and accurate, and recommended to readers over twenty-one, as the advertisements say. It is about as pornographic as *David Copperfield.* See also Fernando Henriques, *Love in Action* (New York: E. P. Dutton and Co., 1960), for a sociologically oriented study of the history of sexual attitudes and behaviors; and Richard Lewensohn, *A History of Sexual Customs* (New York: Harper and Bros., 1958), for another historical journey through the same territory. The final two chapters of the latter, on contemporary sexual problems (pp. 369–409), make a number of interesting points about sex problems in our own culture.

In fact, in some societies, the connection between sexual congress and subsequent birth is dimly understood, if at all. One might expect that the relationship between the two would be experienced mostly in biological contexts. On the contrary, the hinge between any single act of male-female intercourse and the subsequent birth of a baby is almost invariably psychological, and enforced, legalized, symbolized or romanticized entirely by one or another cultural institutions for creating and maintaining families, and, especially, caring for children until they are competent to care for themselves.[11]

The first phase is the one we identify in common parlance as "sexual," and, because its ends are separated by time and bio-mechanics from the second, has accumulated by custom certain orders and clusters of sterotypical feelings and behaviors that are similar in different cultures—but, at the same time, distinctive differentially in legal, moral and sensual tone in each. Their main manifestations, however, are understood best in behavioral rather than psychological terms, and admit therefore of considerable cross-cultural distinction. They are 1.) masturbatory sex; 2.) passive and active homosexuality; 3.) procreative or heterosexuality; 4.) non-procreative passive or active heterosexual sex; 5.) passive bizarre sexual variations; and 6.) active bizarre sexual variations. The latter may be homo- or heterosexual, scatological, verbal, sado-masochistic or bestial, and may include any of the former six behavioral categories in their performance. "Bizarre," is, of course, a culture-bound term, but in most societies it may be applied to behaviors not generally performed, or essential to, commonly practiced masturbatory, homo- and heterosexual patterns of erotic behavior, and therefore are usually considered unnatural or perverse to a greater degree than behaviors in the first four categories are.

The little evidence we possess on the topic indicates that most people —in our society at least—usually select certain types of sexual behavior patterns and, at different ages, and for numerous and different motives (with occasional excursions) tend to regard them as proper and satisfactory for themselves for life. A smaller number shift behaviors from one to another category with considerable latitude, depending upon the flux of endogenic and exogenic factors upon them. Fewer still (and including male and female prostitutes whose interest in sex is primarily financial) are psychologically equipped at all times to play—within their physical capacities—any role demanded of them with equal vigor and enjoyment, or detachment and disdain. Social opprobrium, moral disapproval and legal restraints naturally qualify the picture by construing certain of these behaviors either as

---

[11] Even in a culture like ours, most of us would probably find it difficult to identify *the* single act of coitus which produced any or all of our children, except in instances when special circumstances created the parameters for a clear cause-and-effect situation. Neither —and oddly—do we generally appear curious about the matter, except when questions of paternity are in doubt. Maternity is never, of course, in doubt.

offensive and/or unavailable for practice on one hand, or as attractive forbidden fruit on the other, again depending upon individual inclinations and circumstances.

The time span of sexual behavior, also, covers a much greater period of life's activities than had been, until recently, generally believed. In the first place, cross-cultural studies indicate that Western males apparently do not often live up to anything like their individual potential for sexual activity. In terms of number of orgasms per week or span of sexual activity, males in other cultures are often far more busily immersed in sexual activities, including masturbation and homeroticism, than Westerns, for a variety of reasons left for the reader to induce. Second, potentials for sexual activity in both males and females continue unabated well into old age with considerably more effective force than conventional wisdom (and off-color jokes) would have it. Third, sexual malfunctions are usually (but not always) psychological, not physically determined manifestations. In this connection, evidence also indicates that sexual neurosis (in the form of inability to achieve one's own ideal of sexual satisfaction, regardless of the form or category into which the attempt falls) may be one of the most widespread neuroses in our culture, affecting, at one time or another, the majority of people who live a normal life span.

Quasi-scientific research is, at present, arriving at the above conclusions, none of which were unfamilar to poets and playwrights for many, many years, but which had been lost in the multitude of confused folklore and oddly oriented beliefs, attitudes and opinions concerning sex.[12] One viewpoint, popular today among the psychological community (and bespeaking the orientation of Ellis and others), attributes these neuroses to the apparent misunderstanding and confusions that individuals display concerning the biological and psychological "realities" of sexual behavior. Correcting these impressions by teaching the physiological and empirical "facts" in schools and encouraging the elimination of laws and morals that are incompatible with the apparent behavior of millions, will free one, according to this orientation, from the guilt and fear that (it is assumed) generally causes psychological sexual malfunction. An opposing viewpoint (not necessarily compatible with the outrages of Sorokin and Packard) does not wish to equate either legal restraints on certain types of sexual behavior or sexual morality with empirical evidence of behavior or with physiology. It con-

[12] How strange that the world had to wait for a Masters and Johnson to confirm the simple relationship between vaginal secretion and female sexual arousal, and to slay the dragon (still popular with contemporary pornographers) of the copious fluid female orgasm, another other of their observations. I imagine that most laymen—like me—who read *The Human Sexual Response* found absolutely nothing in it at variance with their experiences. What, then, is the matter with gynecologists and physiologists? The only explanation for their backwardness that I can offer is the hypothesis that, for some esoteric reason, members of these professions make love exclusively in the dark with gloves on.

strues laws (partly) and morals (almost entirely) as guidelines which most people do *not* (and cannot) forever live by, but that at least serve as ongoing references by which to judge the qualitity of their present behavior and dispositions. This view equates present sexual neurosis with a breakdown in morality rather than ignorance, and sees the rise of directionless permissiveness as encouragement towards confusing, and therefore frustrating, sexual freedom and experimentation of many sorts. This occurs in the absence of external guidelines (in the form of moral ideals rather than statistical averages) to tell one, in effect, whether he is likely to be following a pathway to reasonable happiness or to sure despair in the exercise of his sexual feelings.

Regardless of which of these viewpoints is most suited to our society—and it is possible that each contains a portion of a larger, satisfactory vision, or that both are inadequate—one factor qualifying their influence is the inordinate degree of gratificatory expectation that our culture affirms *must* attend the erotic or sexual behavior. It is possible (and the consideration should influence those who advocate nearly total sexual permissiveness) that elements of social rebellion and personal individualistic affirmation are often necessary if personal sexual pleasure is to live up to the expectations that myth and song have created for it in our tradition. In addition, divested of what might be called the "sin" or "mischief" factor, sexual activities frequently tend to serve psychologically as mere surcease from tension, therapy and mild pleasure—sometimes not even the latter as people mated with one another for long periods can testify in discouraging hoards. At this point, each partner frequently begins a search for novelty, classically solved by deceptions involving mistresses and lovers, and recently displaying what is apparently a revolt at such boredom in the form of sex cults made up of married people, replete with wife-swapping, exhibitionism and sexual party games. These outlets are cheaper for men than maintaining mistresses and less risky for women than taking lovers. They are construed by their participants as mischief. Their rationale is that such organized sexual variety frequently stimulates the sexual aspects of married life thereby consolidating dissolving marriages, a claim which is probably often justified. Should infidelity be the recourse both partners in a marriage take from their ennui, frank, open and mutual infidelity is likely to be more morally acceptable to our valve system than hidden infidelity should it be uncovered, as it often is.

Whether or not the quasi-scientific approach to sex combined with sexual oversell in our culture at large leads many people to sexual weariness is difficult to guess. The latter, the equation of sex with "fun morality" and the myth that it is ultimate experience in life, undoubtedly raises expectations higher than human experience can possibly meet. Under these circumstances, adolescent masturbatory fantasies are often more satisfying than one's first sexual encounters, and progressive sexual sophistication (sometimes marked by a temporary or permanent satyriasis or nymphomania) continually fails to make good the promise of transcendent pleasure sustained by cultural attitudes and expectations. The main problem here is *not* the much inflated physiological problem of the inability to achieve orgasm (especially for women). It *is* the progressively haunting discovery that grinds into attitudinal states as one wakes up to the fact that, for some reason, individual sexual behaviors and gratifications are simply *not*, for most of us, the extraordinary, meaningful, overwhelming experiences that social myth has implied they should be for the normal person. When the individual is faced, under such circumstances, with the question of whether something is the matter with *him* or with his *culture*, he is likely, often, to place the blame upon himself. Rarely will he have the competence of cultural observers like Malcolm Muggeridge, Edmund Wilson, Louis Kronenberger, Dwight McDonald, and Pauline Kael to indict the environment rather than himself for his disenchantment.[13]

The result of this disillusionment is cynicism, boredom, guilt and self-hate—torment born of the vain hope that the solution to one's quest may be within grasp, coupled with the near certain knowledge that it is not. In a sense, the individual has short-circuited the possible development of his own sexual fulfillment—and the difficulty applies equally, the author believes, to heterosexual and homosexual relationships—that is his biological and cultural heritage by accepting a generalized notion that sex and salvation are one and the same.

Reik notes,[14] however, that contemporary sexual attitudes in the West have been slowly built, first upon a premise of gratification and relief from tension. Secondly, and "slowly," Reik notes, "the qualities of the object, especially the physical endowments, were acknowledged and appreciated." The idea of "sin" (in the sense noted above) resulted from Christian belief and subsequently offered a "new obstacle . . . to be conquered. A resistance had to be overcome and with that new enticement the sexual desire became intensified. The forbidden object enhanced the attraction . . ." Finally, romantic love as we know it evolved in the Renaissance,[15] empha-

---

13 Reading civilized commentary about sex in our culture is a therapeutic venture. The Muggeridge quotation at the beginning of this chapter is from his article "Down With Sex" in *The Most of Malcolm Muggeridge* (New York: Simon and Schuster, 1966), pp. 32–45, a fine article. The other writers mentioned extend their civilized attitudes towards sex as it is used and abused today by instruments of mass communications into much of their critical writing.

14 See Theodore Reik, *Myth and Guilt*, pp. 238–39.

15 The beginnings, for instance, of romantic love in our modern tradition are clear in, of all plays, *Romeo and Juliet*, when one considers the dire warnings of the Chorus who offers the drama as a case study of the folly of romantic love at the behest of sexual attraction. Shakespeare's prescience is not shown in the wisdom of elders in his play (including the Chorus) who are suspicious of the power of romance (and sex) to overcome social proscriptions. It is rather the romantic and poetic nature of the scenes between the two children in love—some of the dialogue of which also

sizing the virtues of chastity and chivalry, giving sexuality "a new stimulus, and the object seemed to have an augmented lure." [16]

Contemporary "fun morality" now supervenes this tradition with scientistic liberation, existential hedonism and the insidious cult of popularity, a phenomenon discussed elsewhere in this volume. True, immediate liberation from old traditions serves some individuals well. For a greater number, it merely produces disorientation, alienation and confusion. Sex has, of course, always been possible without a recognition of "the other" in Reik's (and Laing's) terms, and without love; just as love of various kinds was, and is, known in many cultures in contexts unrelated to overt sexual experience. But the individual today calls into personal service his or her sexual capacities for many purposes: enjoyment, proof of attractiveness, confirmation of love, release of tension, proof of virility or masculinity, indications of youthfulness, release from worry, affirmations of selfhood, competition with others, relief from boredom and a host of other motives, including the cold-blooded manipulation of other people for money, position or career advancement. Perhaps we are asking too much of a relatively simple organic process, the primary function of which, human reproduction, seems to be beside the point for most of us during the major portion of our active sexual lives.

As far as sexual morality is concerned, Crane Brinton notes[17] that our culture still has far to go to rival the moral permissiveness of Rome and numerous other cultures, past and present. Brinton, like the author, is doubtful of inevitability of dire consequences from allowing considerable margin for sexual experiment and error (or "sowing of wild oats") among young people—and sometimes older ones, too—in our secular moral structures. The "deadly sin" of *lechery*, in the history of our race, apparently is far less destructive than myth would have it—or than the other six. But it is far less spectacular (and sinful) also, and this disenchanting truth is of greater moral importance today than the oversold wickedness of most of the pathetic lechers in our contemporary cultural zoo.

Sexual Persuasion

In light of the fact that the American advertising industry has practically been built upon appeals to sexual charm,[18] (a self-evident discovery

---

appears in Marlowe's *Tamburlaine* written ten years before *Romeo and Juliet*—that are indicative of the wave of romanticism that was to engulf the West in the ensuing centuries.

[16] *Ibid.*, p. 239.

[17] Crane Brinton, A *History of Western Morals* (New York: Harcourt, Brace and Co., 1959), pp. 384–386.

[18] I am constantly amused at the ubiquity of irrelevant sexual appeals in advertising, sometimes in unlikely places. A friend of mine, a college professor, tells me that he cannot look through the advertisements in *The New York Times Magazine* without experiencing an erection, and I tend to believe him. I do not, fortunately, have any such

that outraged Packard in his first and angriest exposé, *The Hidden Persuaders*, one might think that the dynamics of persuasion by sex had been accurately charted by the professionals who manipulate them. This is not the case. Covert and overt sex appeals are apparently employed *ad lib* by advertisers, except in instances where motivational researchers sell what they claim to be non-conscious sexual symbols to advertising agencies that have been evolved from supposed depth studies of a psychoanalytic nature from panels of "average" consumers.

The main paradigm for sexual persuasion is, of course, quite simple, and one example of a behavioristic model of a stimulus-response situation is adequate to explain it. An individual is stimulated sexually, and a promise is given or implied that, should he modify his disposition or indulge in a specific behavior, tension will be released in the form of provisional sexual satisfaction. The modification or behavior is accomplished, and the satisfaction is given.

Like most paradigms, this one is rarely seen in pure form—except in specific transactions as unsubtle as those employed by fictionalized Mata Haris in spy stories. In daily speech, we often say that an individual is "seduced" into a modification of a disposition or behavior rather than "persuaded," and the word, under the circumstances, quite satisfactorily explains the transaction. The only unusual aspect of such seductions is the willingness of certain individuals to be seduced sometimes into extravagant and self-destructive behaviors, particularly when the tension created is not only sexual tension but also involves ancillary factors discussed above, like guilt, doubts of attractiveness and chagrin at aging. In sum, more than one old goat has made a fool of himself over a pretty young girl (and old women with young men), and will continue to despite all the strictures of logic. In such instances, the issue at hand is rarely, if ever, purely sexual. Many other psychological factors are involved, and, if the young man or girl is looking for a substitute father or mother, such liaisons may turn out to be discouragingly satisfactory to those who predicted their logically horrid consequences.

In other, more subtle types of persuasion, the paradigm is less apparent; in fact, questions arise, frequently, as to whether it is present at all. Most important, human attention is quickly diverted from almost any other focus of interest *to* a sexual attraction. Vision plays an important part in sexual stimulation, but sexual calls to attention are not limited to visible objects. They may include sounds, textures and caresses. Sexual attraction may be brought into the individual's perceptual fields in one of three ways: either by direct attraction or by a dramatic simulation or both simultaneously. In other words, the sex *object* may be exposed *directly* to the individual in one case. Other individuals *involved* in sexual activities may be

---

trouble with the *Times*, but occasionally my wife brings home copies of *Harper's Bazaar*.

exposed to him in another. In either case, attention will probably be attracted. In the third instance, a slightly more ambiguous situation involving sex objects and sexual behavior may be created, but, because the appeal is ambiguous, it lacks a psychological certainty of gaining attention, and it does not necessarily combine the strengths of the former two devices. It may also fuse its weaknesses, depending upon the context in which it occurs and the vulnerabilities of the auditor.

Sexual attraction also enhances persuasion by *precept*, as in instances where film and television sex idols endorse consumer products, or an attractive political candidate defeats a homely one for no other ascertainable reason than his good looks. Under these circumstances, the element of sexual attraction is more complex than it at first appears. A heterosexual male may indeed be attracted by a female sex object attempting to persuade him of this or that. But he may prefer (and also respond to) an appeal by an attractive male with whom he can identify. (The homosexual variants of this principle tend to become complicated, but they seem to have equal substance.) The popularity of Hollywood's sex gods, particularly men, appears often to be greater among members of their own sex than either latent homosexuality or admiration of histrionic ability explains. The reason, of course, is that individuals are not only attracted by sex objects. They may also empathize with them, one of the explanations why these stars of yesterday (and some today) influenced the styles of dress, make-up, and behavior of members of their own sex so noticeably.[19]

Another perspective of this phenomenon follows thus: societal pressures (noted in this chapter) have enhanced the sexual roles that people play to such cultural significance that, for certain periods of their lives, their identities relate critically to these roles.[20] Most of these roles are fairly com-

---

[19] Clark Gable's influence on the undershirt industry in *It Happened One Night* (he was not wearing an undershirt in a disrobing scene) is, by now, a legend. The undergraduates I teach, members of my generation will be glad to hear, are similarly indoctrinated. My lecture sections contain various Beatles (I can identify which is which), Donovans, Sean Connerys, Steve McQueens, Joni Mitchells and enough variegated youth idols for a spontaneous rock festival. *Plus ca change, plus c'est la même chose.*

[20] Freud's familiar description of oral, anal, phallic and genital traits of characterological development served as models for the equally well known orientations of Erich Fromm as described in *Man for Himself* (New York: Rinehart and Co., 1947), especially pp. 54–82. Fromm's concepts of "hoarding" and "marketing" typologies are not unlike Riesman's familiar "inner" and "other" characterological orientations. Granting the validity of much on-going criticism of Freud's developmental theories and Fromm's interpretations of them, the hoarding (masturbatory) and marketing (predatory) typologies display counterparts in terms of the erotic images we have of ourselves and others in today's society. Returning to Freud's original developmental stages, notice how profanity in speech follows his original orientations: the phallic character is perjoratively (and neatly) characterized as a "prick" or "cunt." The more generalized genital (or marketing) individual is referred to, in terms of process, as "a good lay" (female) or "a hot stud" (male). Much other profanity follows this crude wisdom with considerable aptness and relevance. The point is that both Freud's and Fromm's typologies have *socio*-sexual equivalents in our culture that undoubtedly relate both to

mon, drawn from conventions of culture including family life, peer influence, mass communications and other relatively homogenous influences in society. (Even the patterns for certain kinds of overt homosexuality, male and female, demand conformity of a characterological nature to learned behaviors that, in the West, are quite homogenous.) Communications which *challenge* the integrity of these roles or self-images will create hostility at worst, tensions at best, both of which may, under some circumstances, be exploited for persuasive purposes. Communications which affirm them will be acceptable and perhaps coveted, if they are appropriate.

Image building of this sort is most obviously seen in magazines like *Playboy* and *Vogue*, neither of which fixate upon one proffered self-image, but leave a certain amount of freedom within a broad type of sexual image that their writers and editors intuit will be receptive to their readers. In a more serious context, Adolph Hitler adumbrated both masculine and feminine sexual prototypes of Nordic perfection with which a population, most of whom were as characterologically unlike the Nazi ideal as the consumer of *Playboy* is from Heffner's image, might associate. Feminist organizations, including those at present promising women the dubious joys of "liberation," also deal in these sexual images, calling attention to the female's specific sexual attractions in our society by denying them, in much the way that a "swish" male homosexual centers his on-going satire on certain culturally accepted male sexual traits by making fun of them.

The psychological dynamics of these types of persuasion are too ambiguous, too mingled with the languages of symbols, and, most important, too personally threatening even in the hands of objective investigators to provide a general scheme for the formal analysis of them. We must, instead, impute sexual implications to certain prototypical individuals or culture complexes within the framework of selected analytic assumptions, as Leites and Wolfenstein did in their now classic study of the American and British (mainly) cinema.[21] What they accomplished, and what similar analysts, including the present writer, have done since constitutes essentially the *critical* study of some aspect of general sexually oriented behavior, with an accent upon what particular sexual images seem to predominate in the selected output.

In much the same manner, the advertiser or politician who wishes to use sexual persuasion operates by rule of thumb, often effectively. The more closely he watches the manifestations of sexual vulnerabilities in his constituency, the more likely he is to be able to exploit them. But sexual caprice is frequent. Blonde women (even unattractive women) may turn southern Italian and Sicilian men into simpering adolescents, just as dark

---

the sexual images that one has of others and also his or her own sexual self-image, as gutter argot indicates.

[21] See Martha Wolfenstein and Nathan Leites, *Movies; A Psychological Study* (Glencoe, Illinois: The Free Press, 1950).

hairy males seem inordinately attractive to Scandinavian women. But preference formulas like these rarely work in the USA and, for all the author knows, may have little value any longer in southern Italy or Scandinavia. The constituents of the sexual appeal of the late Marilyn Monroe, Brigitte Bardot and Racquel Welch may seem as obvious as those of the late Clark Gable, Yves Montand and Clint Eastwood. But when one is faced with sexual cynosures of as wide a range of types as Twiggy, "Ringo" Starr, Arlo Guthrie, the late Humphrey Bogart and Judy Garland, among many others (from Senator Eugene McCarthy to Charles Manson), it is obvious that formulas or pat methodologies for the public exploitation of beliefs, attitudes, opinions and behavior utilizing sex appeal alone are few, if they exist at all. Sexual persuasion is made up of part art, part sensitivity and part chance. How much easier it is to explain critically the factors involved in the sex appeal of the late President Kennedy in retrospect than to have predicted what they would be before he entered public life!

Most of us project our own sexual preferences into those we impute to others. Were the truth told, we probably, each and all, have constructed for ourselves a sexual profile as distinctively our own as our fingerprints, variable over the years and continually conditioned by many unforeseeable factors. One great mystery of existence is, of course, thereby enhanced, but so also are its perils, incongruities and ironies. Bernard Shaw once estimated that it takes at least seventy-five years to arrive at a stage of rational maturity in which one has outgrown the compulsive and basically adolescent tyrannies of the human endocrine system. His estimate may be, in the light of recent evidence, conservative. Shaw, the old fox, tricked fate into giving him time to grow up. But most of the rest of us will die as we have lived, bemused victims of that "tingle" and the complications of its results.

Conclusion

Sexual transactions are among the most vital and ubiquitous that people experience. In our culture, they are exploited by and for the technology in which we live, a phenomenon that certain observers see as an obsession with sex to the exclusion of more significant matters in life. Others blame residues of Puritanism, Victorianism and outworn moral codes for a socio-sexual neurosis which most of us display when we strive to obtain even greater scope and freedom for permissive sexual behavior of all kinds in our culture. The latter view is generally an extension of, or variant upon, the Freudian viewpoint of the libido as the driving force in life and of neurosis as the arbitrary constriction of this force by social restraints. Other psychological perspectives view sexual desire as less central to basic human concerns, while still others attempt a compromise with what they regard as Freudian extremism. Their viewpoints have ramified into many aspects of the behavioral sciences.

In culture at large, the Freudian notion (on the heels of Darwin's introduction of the human race to the animal kingdom) has, combined with other historical factors like World War I, prohibition and the great depression of the 1930's, left a definite impression upon sexual behavior and morals in America. At present, we are living in a period in which curiosity about sex is taking a quasi-scientific, supposedly objective turn, and we tend to judge sexual matters by evidences of extant behavior and practice rather than the authority of morality which is considered irrelevant to actual practice. New methods of contraception and new legal freedoms, including the restraints of censorship of books and entertainments, have created a climate in which (at the verbal level, at least) permissiveness concerning individual sexual satisfaction, whether within or outside marriage or in one or another unconventional manifestation, receives tacit social sanctions nearly everywhere in the United States.

Sexual satisfaction may be achieved in many ways, and individuals tend to cluster their behaviors through life into certain patterns which are direct functions of their beliefs, attitudes and opinions as well as other aspects of their personalities. The range, intensity and span of human sex life appears, at present, to be broader and longer than had been previously believed. Whether the new apparent permissiveness will have an effect on behavior, and exactly what its effect will be upon sexual attitudes and opinions in the future, it is difficult to predict. Problems arise from the loss of the sense of "sin" or "forbidden fruit" once associated with sexual behavior, as well as the equation of sexual feeling with the "fun morality" of our culture that insists that sexual activity be a source of play, even for those who are not inclined to be playful, as opposed to older notions of romance and love as *sine qua non* for a satisfactory sex life.

Sexual persuasion, viewed in this light, seems a relatively simple matter of arousing and then satisfying certain appetites, but the issue is not this clear or elementary. Sexual tastes vary; individuals are not only aroused by, but also identify with, a sex object under certain circumstances. Individual sex roles also change in many ways as life continues, depending upon internal and external experiences, the most important of which are frequently unexpected and which often happen by pure chance. While the potential of employing sexual motives for all manner of changes in beliefs, attitudes, opinions and behaviors is great, such changes are probably restricted only to diverse aspects of these dispositions, and frequently occur by lucky accident or inspiration. Criticism *post hoc* of the influences of attempts at sexual persuasion are therefore far easier to accomplish than to predict a stimulus-response relationship in the future.

Chapter 16

THE POWER OF LOVE

Some—perhaps most—human beings never know deep love until they experience, at someone's death, the preciousness of friendship, devotion, loyalty.

Rollo May

THE PSYCHOLOGY of love is often kept by behavioral scientists at arm's length. They refer to it frequently, but with little decisiveness. The idea of love connotes the love *of something,* and it is that *something*—erotic fulfillment, mothers, friends, pet animals, hobbies, self and ideals—upon which they justifiably center their attentions. Hence, they rarely speak explicitly of love itself.

Until quite recently, in fact, most non-psychological reflections on love—except for those sometimes provided by poets and musicians—have centered on beloved objects or individuals, at least in the Western world. In the East, however, the concept of love as a transcendental experience is compatible with any of the known Oriental philosophies, or from our perspective, religions and mysticisms. We are also familiar with the cultural wisdom of the Greeks that differentiated, by means of vocabulary, erotic love, brotherly love and love of society. From antiquity we have also received the convenient expression "platonic love," defined more clearly by what its object is *not* (sexual) than what it is (companionable). We are also aware, in both popular and scholarly literature, of the origins of what we call today "romantic love," a corollary to sexual attraction salted with elements of sentiment and predestination and a handy social control, now operating mainly in the service of the institution of marriage.[1] This eventuality is curious from an historical point of view, because romance, as far as

[1] See any of the volumes cited in Chapter 15 on the history of man's sexual behavior for their inevitable digressions into the history of human love. I have yet to discover

we know, seems to have had its origins in the dalliance of the troubadours and minstrels with married women, their poetry and songs serving as façades for a direct assault on marital chastity.

The spirit of these adventures was continued by many devices well into the Renaissance. In this highly productive setting, romantic adoration blossomed, yielding the modern notion of "falling in love" with its folklore, myths and mystiques and literary concept of Romance, with a capital "R," epitomized by men like Cellini and Villon and fiction's Quixote, the swashbuckling tradition of which did not necessarily call much attention to sexual activity. In the persons (and traditions) of Don Juan Manuel and (later) Casanova de Seingalt, sexual conquest and literary romance were combined, usually and oddly underscoring, in the world of literary adventure, the antagonism between romantic love and genital pleasure,[2] a difference that to this day is still unclear enough to confuse most of us at least once in our lifetimes; and once is more than enough.

Max Lerner, something of a romantic himself, notes,[3] that this romantic-sexual idealism is regarded as part of "America's life cycle as the harbinger of life's fulfillment with a violence of expectation of a culture built on promise." Lerner cites as evidence such indicative songs as "Love is Sweeping the Country," the phenomenon of the famous Hollywood happy ending, and the "boy meets girl" myth in the Great American Dream. Socio-political liberals like Lerner are frequently ambivalent about love, because of their tendency to generalize romantic illusions into social and political life. A vision of romantic love is integral to their convictions that social evil can be turned, by their platforms and stratagems, to social good, and love (in a broad sense) will ameliorate group schisms and indeed "sweep the country" clean. Typically, the liberal scoffs at love when it is held as a personal ideal *à deux*, but he manages to love the cultural underdog for his "top-cat" potentials and the romantic ideals of freedom and the brotherhood of oppressed minorities. Like Herrimann's Krazy Kat, he loves, in effect, the caricature of social evil incarnate, Ignatz Mouse, a grimy little schemer who rewards Krazy's undying affection with a brick to the cerebellum. Love, in the liberal's world of social change and idealistic reform, is usually rewarded in the spirit of Ignatz.[4]

---

a sexual history that does not extend freely its interests into the role of love in culture, almost always including non-sexual types.

[2] These themes, in reference to these figures, have been beautifully handled in the relatively contemporary theatre by Shaw in the *Don Juan in Hell* scene of *Man and Superman* and Tennessee Williams in his most misunderstood (and best, in my opinion) play *Camino Real*. Their treatment in both instances reflects centuries of skeptical analysis of important romantic symbols.

[3] Max Lerner, *America as a Civilization*, p. 582.

[4] Liberally oriented love is also the theme, in an educational setting, of Robert Marasco's superb melodrama, *Child's Play*. Without giving away the point of the play or the plot elements that create its almost painful suspense, the playwright comments incisively upon

Lerner's illustrations (of 1957) might be replaced today with the *schmaltzy,*[5] waltz-time observation, "What the world needs now is love, sweet love" and the hippies' admonition to "make love not war." Any member, or pseudo-member, of the "Woodstock nation" will tell you that what the young want most is love: "beautiful" love, if possible. While there is a free-flowing, more or less non-discriminating sexual content to this version of love, it *is* mainly a romantic conception, highly self-absorbing (and therefore socially meaningless), often accompanying subtle progression from sex and beer to marihuana, to psychedelic mushrooms and LSD, to hard drugs like heroin. But it is an exaltation of love nevertheless, practiced, at the start, at least, *en masse* by packs of young people, and here is its novelty for those of us who are not part of its manifestation. When it dies, it leaves a pitiful collective hangover, intimations of which contributed to making the film, *Easy Rider,* realistically attractive not only to young people but observers of youth,[6] while the somewhat similar movie, *Alice's Restaurant,* came across as a patent older-generation fraud, or in today's terminology, a "put on" by the old moralizing to the young.

The credo of the two Hollywood writers in Sam and Bella Spewack's *Boy Meets Girl* to "put your money on love" still applies in America. Sexual elements aside, "love" is the miracle catch-word in the American vocabulary and a panacea for all ills. If children misbehave at home or school, they do not require "avoidance therapy" (a fancy name for spanking) but love. Parents must bestow unconditional love on their young, lest they go astray; and when they eventually *do* go astray, it is because they did not receive *enough* love or the *wrong kind* of love. A young person who has not fallen in love with someone of the opposite sex by the age of twenty-one is generally regarded as abnormal, a dictate driving the Lord knows how many confused children to search for love among members of their own sex where it is often most easily found. Success at loving or being loved is as

---

the latent evil in the romantic conception of love when it is only ego-enhancing, sentimental and alienated from realistic humanitarian or (in this case) educational objectives. The play is, of course, a parable of great power, surprisingly popular at the moment with the audience of New York's professional theatre, considering the usually liberal social orientations of that group of theatregoers. It is a frontal attack upon much of the "best thinking" of the liberal educational community and bespeaks a complete turn-about from the political liberal theatre of recent history. Because it also attacks (mildly) the Catholic Church and organized religion, it probably contains enough fashionable liberal comment to blur its main point for those who are disposed to misunderstand it and concentrate instead upon its dramatic values as melodrama.

[5] I am using Leo Rosten's spelling of this gorgeous Yiddish word.

[6] The progress and destinies of the hippie communes in San Francisco and New York's East Village were clear examples of love gone astray. From "flower children" to "acid heads" to, finally, "freaked-out," hard core main liners, the community "trip" was rapid and downhill from the start, leaving its sick, dead and maimed—children who were victims of overdoses, jaundice and rampant venereal disease, exploited by hardened professional pimps and pushers for whom the idea of love was (and is) unknowable. Most urban hippie communities are now loveless slums and dangerous jungles.

highly regarded, and not independent from, success at making money or achieving celebrity status. As Lerner states, "It is as if the two circuits had become crossed, and the way Americans feel about money and success had got tangled up with the way they feel about love." [7] Regardless of the imprecision of the phrase "tangled up," Lerner is on the right track, and it is a different path from the one that conventionally deals with contemporary attitudes towards sex, although they both frequently lead to the same place and leave, in their wakes, indistinguishable manifestations of disillusionment, despair and feelings of self-loathing.[8]

What one might add to Lerner's observations, and the Hollywood formula, is that love in the 1970's is rapidly splitting into a dichotomous illusion. Whatever psychologics apply to it, therefore, follow two channels, one of which does not preclude the other but which simply makes it difficult to contain both in the same frame of reference.

On one side, love is still "hip" and likely to remain in the forefront of the near illiterate sloganizing and pseudo-philosophy of the underground press, avant-garde film makers, pacifists, country-style rock singers and action therapists. On the other, it is a quixotic idealization of the romantic ideal that is today (and always has been) a parody of the emotion that is required for close and honest human relationships.

The two approaches demonstrate the ease with which we can resolve many contradictory points of view concerning love when they are dramatically portrayed for us. The hero of many current "hip" films or plays from Britain is often totally alienated from both types of love. (In the prototypical movie *Morgan*, he was plain crazy.) After failing at making "hip" love meaningful, he or she encounters the quixotic kind. The resolution of the prototypical drama portrays either the hero's failure to succeed at or find romantic love, in which case he is shown alone and alienated at the end of the drama, or, in Hollywood fashion, the implication is given that quixotic love, somehow, will eventually conquer all. Because this latter ending has become more and more psychologically unsatisfactory for our time, we shall probably see many alienated, disoriented heroes and heroines at the fade-outs and final curtains of our movies and dramas in the years to come.[9]

---

[7] *Ibid.*, p. 585.

[8] Much has been made of the fact that the word "love" does not appear in the index to Masters and Johnson's *Human Sexual Response*, and that it apparently is not found in the text. (Having no time to waste looking for it, I have not verified this observation.) The fact is highly indicative, not that sex has been severed from love in our culture, but that we regard the love component of many (or most) sexual relationships as an occurrence of a *different quality and genre* from the sexual part. Forty years ago it was possible for the first person vocalist of the lovely Cole Porter melody to advertise "Love For Sale." Today her market would just be for sex, and she would have to seek out a different way to elicit love. This may be progress.

[9] Other notable recent films and plays come to mind, including *Inadmissible Evidence, The Homecoming, The Sterile Cuckoo, Georgie Girl, The Prime of Miss Jean Brodie, They Shoot Horses, Don't They?, Midnight Cowboy*, and others. While a good many

The Non-Psychology of Love

As de Rougement notes[10] modern love finds its strongest precedent in Christianity, particularly in various interpretations of the New Testament. (While sexual love has often been subsumed to other ideas of love, one does not find in the Western tradition the kind of holy, sanctified eroticism —or religious sex education—exemplified in the literary tradition of the *Kama Sutra*, the *Anganga Ranga* or *Koka Shastra*, or in graphic art and statuary that to the Oriental is holy but to the Westerner is merely obscene.) Building upon evolutionary models from Old to New Testament, Jesus Christ became, to his disciples, the ultimate symbol of non-romantic love in their time.

The religion that followed Him, in ideals at least, personified and worshipped that love, most obvious the affirmation of the reality of divine love in *people:* specifically Christ of course, but also the Virgin Mary and the apostles. The Judaic God of vengeance, righteousness and submission had been replaced by *human* symbols whose apotheosis, Jesus Himself, epitomized love towards other men, even His executioners for whom He asked forgiveness. *What* Christ loved—and what Christian idealism professes—is a relatively simple vision of man and his society. It is manifest best in simple relationships, such as those of monks, priests and nuns to God, or Christian to Christian, or in the sexual communion of marriage and within individual families or stable socio-cultural units.

Contradictions are immediately apparent in even so simple construction of the Christian ideal, and have been for centuries, explaining, perhaps, the failure of a satisfactory psychology of love to evolve in any Western speculative school, either in the teachings of the great Christian thinkers (and doers), or from secular observers for that matter. The Crusaders hardly loved the infidel Moslems they slaughtered in the name of Christ, just as we kill and are killed in God's name today. Apparently Gnostic notions, from medieval philosophy to the modern psychotherapeutic clinics of Vienna, have fouled the perfection of the ideal "love of man" with no end of contradictions born of lust, harlotry, shamefulness, sin and other ceaseless works of the Devil.

These particular corruptions have for centuries been overcome by the Christian view of love of one's *self* as the highest form of human good, demonstrated, not in self-absorption or detachment, but by means of per-

---

dramas of this kind come from England, Hollywood and Broadway both seem to be catching the dominant mood of their audiences. The American theatre, both on and off-Broadway, is, as usual, a generation behind the times, which is exactly where it has been for the past thirty years.

10 Denis de Rougement, *Love Declared* (New York: Pantheon Books, 1963), pp. 4–11, 206–208.

sonal sacrifice to achieve God's grace. As de Rougement states, "To sacrifice one*self* to one's *true self* . . . is to sacrifice *as one is to become* by the action of spirit. It is to rejoin the unmortal form of one's being through a transfiguring 'death to oneself'." [11] As mystical and clouded as such a statement appears at first, it so beneficently constricts the Christian ideal of love to one's *own* personality that it effectively does away with the subversions of lust, the irrelevances of holy warfare, and other such inconsistencies, and construes Christian love as a purely personal *act*, achieved by the sacrifice of one's own self for the other. Psychiatric and psychological taxonomists might simply call this "masochism" and be done with it. But the demonstrable power of this ideal in the affairs of men (to say nothing of its history) does not allow such facile disposition of it.

Metaphysics, mysticisms and songs to the praise of love are not difficult to compose.[12] Definitions are. The concept of love has probably been more fully generalized in France than anywhere in the West—confirming, probably, folklore that the French are the greatest (read "most non-discriminating") lovers in the world—but even the Gallic de Rougement offers us the concept of "reciprocal relation," evolving first *within* one individual, thence moving out to encompass two individuals, and finally between the loving couple and their culture. In other words, one moves, from self-love to shared love to generalized love. "Such is the fulfillment of love," writes he, "and its marvelous rarity! But our arts have always retreated before it. And our literatures . . . have lived on its diseases."

While others claim, as we shall see, that most artists anticipate love rather than retreat from it, injured love has unquestionably been the stuff of literature, and most (if not best) inquiry into it has been left to poets and novelists, not behavioral scientists, except for a handful who, like Reik,[13] have the souls of poets and the brains of therapists. Reik's words are, accordingly, clinically startling, set as they are against the present milieu of so many psycho-physical investigations of sexual relationships. "Sex and love are so different," says Reik, "that they belong to distinct realms of research fields; sex to the domain of biochemistry and physiology;

---

[11] *Ibid.*, p. 207. (Italics de Rougement's.)

[12] Ninety-nine out of one hundred popular songs are love songs. Unless films and plays are written solely for children, they contain themes of love; drama without a "love dimension" is considered, usually, not worth producing. I have not counted the love poems in *The Stevenson Home Book of Verse*, but over 800 pages of the volume are devoted to them, excluding those involving love of country, love of nature and various other non-erotic types of love. In sum, certain communication instruments seem employed almost entirely in the service of messages of love, an interesting curiosity that I refer to Dr. McLuhan and his followers.

[13] See Theodore Reik, *Of Love and Lust* (New York: Farrar, Strauss and Cudahy, 1949), for a full-blown Freudian overview of sex and love—more sex than love. The volume is less a critical analysis of libido than a fascinating venture into Reik's value system and the value system of psychoanalysis itself.

love to the domain of the psychology of emotions. Sex is urge, love is desire." [14] Love, Reik concludes, "is an illusion like every search for human perfection, but it is a necessary illusion. It comes nearest to the ego gratification we all need in pushing the ego aside . . . to make life worth living. Wise men warn us again and again not to expect permanent and serene happiness from love . . . It is not love's fault that we demand too much of it . . . We should know that on earth. It is even doubtful if there is heaven in heaven." [15]

Other therapists approach the subject differently. Rollo May[16] derives his concepts of love from the late thinking of Freud, noted in the previous chapter, by which time the concept of libido had been modified to play its role in the dialectic between the life force and the will to death, Eros and Thanatos. May thus juxtaposes, as given fact, sexual love versus erotic love, eroticism understood to cover a range of non-sexual pleasures accompanying numerous types of experiences. Carried further, his concept encourages the familiar analytic idea that it is possible to *eroticize* many non-sexual human activities. According to this tenet, the present writer has eroticized writing and teaching; thus he finds sensual joy in them beyond their expected, normal psychological limits. Americans appear to eroticize clothes, hair and gadgets. Germans apparently often fall in love (in an erotic sense) with their automobiles. For May, therefore, love has four faces: erotic love (not, in May's terms, sexual love), brotherly love, and love of others—culture or society—as well as love expressed in specific, episodic sexual feelings, as opposed to the three selected for consideration in this chapter.[17]

Erich Fromm, whose short book on love is as close as he has come in his writing to a popular self-help volume, construes the emotion of love, or love's feelings, in a still broader manner.[18] Love is not merely the symbiotic relationship between organisms. It centers on a broader non-sexual, quasi-mystical, individualistic and integral concept that includes brotherly love,

---

[14] *Ibid.*, p. 22.

[15] *Ibid.*, p. 194.

[16] Rollo May, *Love and Death* (New York: W. W. Norton and Co., 1969), pp. 37–38, 81–88.

[17] May might call my act of severing sex from love, and preceding this chapter with the previous one (calling the former *The Power of Love* and the latter *The Power of Sex*), "sexual puritanism" on my part. This may be true. See *ibid.*, pp. 45–52, for Dr. May's amusing analysis of some modern attitudes with which I cannot quarrel too hard or long. In May's construction, most modern sexologists are puritans. So I am in lively company.

[18] Erich Fromm, *The Art of Loving* (New York: Bantam Books, 1967), pp. 38–68. This small volume was originally printed in October, 1956, and has gone through nineteen editions in hard cover, at least. The paperback which I am using is dated September, 1967 and is in its twentieth printing. On the cover, I see that the publishers claim that it has been translated into seventeen languages, and over 1,500,000 copies in the English language have been sold. Benson and Law, those writers in *Boy Meets Girl*, are still correct: "Put your money on love!"

motherly love, erotic love (by which is meant sexual desire specifically), self-love (not to be confused with selfishness) and love of God, which unmistakably displays many of the characteristics of the preceding four categories. This attitude towards God is odd, because, despite Fromm's mature refutation of Freud's rejection of religion as dealing only with that part of spirituality based on love of God as a father ("a childish illusion" in Fromm's words) and his sophisticated argument that all of love is reflected in mature and unselfish God beliefs, Fromm affirms himself an atheist or agnostic. In his words, "I want to make it clear that I myself do not think in terms of a theistic concept, and that to me the concept of God is only a historically conditioned one . . ." [19] The ironies of love are infinite!

At this point, it should be clear that the main preoccupation (and cause for hostility) manifested by modern schools of psychology centers invariably upon the single migrant element (or court jester) in nearly any broad psychological description of love. The culprit is sex, whether generalized into the ideal of elegant and elaborate erotic relationships or a pure, greedy, self-fulfilling hunger. A "roll in the hay" or the paid ministrations of a prostitute may seem far removed from love in any sense, but, psychologically, they are but a step away from the most sophisticated spiritual and beautiful formulations of self-love or love of God in its most ecstatic form. The wedding ring on the nun's finger is one of the most obvious and clearest symbols of this nexus and/or juxtaposition.

Yet the psychology of our own senses—internal psychologics, if you wish—affirms that there is more to love than masquerading erotic pleasure, for all the cleverness of Freud with his surrogate father and mother figures and the pseudo-scientific rationales of his imitators. Unless we are ill or poor observers, most of us have either seen or experienced love of a transcendental sort that will not permit reduction to the kinds of psychological formulations that work so well for other emotions.

Love Is Something Else Again

A brilliant, well-known scholar and writer of the author's acquaintance (who will remain anonymous) was, for a time, thrown into an incredibly bleak depression at the death of his closest companion (next to his wife) of twelve years: his dog. His stratagems for covering the hurts of his lost love were painful for those around him to watch, and the proffered suggestion that another dog might take the place of the dead one, as any animal lover (note the term) knows, was treated by him as absurd.[20] Some people appear

[19] *Ibid.*, pp. 60–61.

[20] I am certain that this personal observation would sound ridiculous to most of the thousand students and friends who are acquainted with this man. Yet it is true. Love of animals is indeed a strange manifestation, sometimes considered merely projective anthropomorphism, but somehow also much more than that. I own five cats that I suppose I love, and who I fancy love me, primarily because I pet and feed them. (I pet them; my wife feeds them.) I also own numerous gerbils who reproduce so prolif-

to love institutions, houses or even ships.[21] Some of us may also have experienced the type of love that anonymous, selfless giving generates—not in ego-building terms, but simply in the affirmation of shared living. We may also have seen to what inspired heights the love of God has raised artists, sometimes beyond the love of truth, the love of science or even the love of money. Many of us have experienced and survived the death of love, or someone or something we loved, finding only meaningless dregs of consolation in near identical substitutes for that which passed or died, much to our own bewilderment.

Lerner suggests[22] that such loves as these require but two external characteristics, and that they are unique to the West, a facet, in fact, of romanticism—a questionable assumption. That, as he claims, each love combines *uniqueness* with *fatality* is less debatable. In its most trivial aspect, uniqueness manifests itself in acquisitive "love at first sight" with a "one and only" anything, sexual or otherwise. In its more profound setting, it is the recognition of Heraclitus' self-evident proposition that you cannot put your foot twice into the same river, or Wolfe's sage homily that "you can't go home again." It is, in short, the tragedy of existential love, as sere and unrelieved in its particular aspect as existential doom.

Fatality has a spectacular side as well: the destiny that brought together Bonnie and Clyde, Leopold and Loeb, or Rhett Butler and Scarlett. A Hollywood image of love, Lerner claims, but part of contemporary human experience, nevertheless. All love occurs at the behest of "the infernal machine" as Cocteau calls fate. Oedipus is brought into his mother's bed by the machine's workings. And the familiar tale that brings Death and the frightened man together in Samara underscores the timeless power of fatality. The most absurd characteristic of the fatality of love is the very tautology of its absurdity—that it adheres to few regularities, although some tunnel-visioned sociologists claim otherwise and then are frequently hurled themselves into one of its absurdities. And, even in societies where a person's earthly destiny, including his marriage, is supposedly arranged at birth, the free play of fate and love destroying the arrangement is a frequent and popular topic of mythology, song and story.

---

erately that their number is never constant: they come and go so fast that they are difficult to love. They are entirely a source of wonder and amusement to me. But the closest I have come to a deep feeling of love for an animal, I feel towards my California desert tortoise who, housebroken as she (an arbitrary sexual determination) is, roams my apartment for eight months each year and hibernates for the other four. In this tortoise, my family and I somehow find the encapsulation of life's unbelievable tenacity and talent for adaptation and—but how can one explain love?

[21] One of the most memorable scenes in Wouk's novel *The Caine Mutiny* occurs when the first-person narrator leaves the destroyer-minesweeper *Caine* for the last time and recognized that love grows in strange places.

[22] Lerner, *op. cit.*, pp. 583–584.

For Russell,[23] love is simply the companion of the good life: a fusion of delight and well-wishing, so simple a combination as to contain considerable psychological value for our inquiry. In terms of emotional altruism, the opposite of the feeling of love is the feeling of benevolence (or sympathy, perhaps): well-wishing *without* delight. On another metaphorical axis, rape may exemplify delight without well-wishing, almost invariably a cruel manifestation.

The "good life," says Russell, requires love, a proposition with which all modern schools of psychology would agree on its face. But they would be startled by his qualification: that *knowledge* is necessary to temper love. Says Russell:

> Neither love without knowledge, nor knowledge without love can produce a good life. In the Middle Ages, when pestilence appeared in a country, holy men advised the population to assemble in churches and pray for deliverance; the result was that the infection spread with extraordinary rapidity among the crowded masses of supplicants. The late war afforded an example of knowledge without love. In each case, the result was death on a large scale.[24]

In short, love's greatest challenge is directed to the intellect, as Plato observed centuries ago. And the fusion of love and knowledge is not only necessary for the individual's good life but for the continuance of culture. Well-wishing, caring and intelligence, on face, may be all that men require to create civilization and pass it on. True or not, either of the two without the third gives man the moral self-justification—or allows him unknowingly or by crass accident—to *destroy* his culture, his home and himself, either intentionally or because he lacks knowledge to recognize his real enemies.

Love in a Cold Culture

Love is much abused in our culture, despite sentimental pap in best selling novels, movies and on television. Most of this vapor is romantic diversion and has as much to do with real life as the comic strips. If we have managed to dehumanize sex in modern culture, we have fantasized love. And once what is actually possible is condemned to fantasy, it is unlikely that this possibility will ever regard it as real again.

In none of its constructions may the roots of love freely and spontaneously grow in a mechanized technology. Both giving and receiving become difficult. Interchangeable parts, modules and standardization reside at the heart of our industrial machine; so also are human beings implicitly and frequently regarded as interchangeable and standardized. Without individ-

---

23 Robert E. Egner and Lester E. Denonn, *The Basic Writings of Bertrand Russell* (New York: Simon and Schuster, 1961), pp. 372.

24 *Ibid.*, p. 372.

ualization, love is hardly possible. It is, many believe, becoming increasingly difficult for us to think of ourselves as individuals or find individuality in others as technology's hold over our destiny increases. Of course, human beings still serve as sex objects; but seen as components of a lonely crowd, any single sex object manifests all the uniqueness of an individual automobile or jet airplane.

Our defense against mechanization has become withdrawal, either into the perpetual motion of a schizoid state or into apathy—not the apathy of political and social non-engagement but the apathy of an inability (or fear) to give ourselves to others with love and to accept it in return. Apathy in a cold society is, as May notes,[25] a sort of insurance policy against defeat, depersonalization and relegation to a number in a computer. Few of us are competent to survive the anonymity of the mass state without making some assertions of our individual being. When the assertion includes giving or receiving love to or from anyone or anything, we take a fearful risk, however. The alternatives are apathy among the experienced (who have known the pain of futile love) and protest among the young. Protest requires commitment and lashes out in spurts against cold culture, but it requires only temporary commitment, not love. In fact, as young protesters discover, what began as an act of love often ends shortly in premature disillusionment.

One fashionable enigma of our moment in history is the question of why so many of our people, young and old, appear to be rushing headlong into a drug culture and choose to spend much of their lives literally narcotized. This phenomenon is not reserved for the young with their ubiquitous marihuana, LSD and (despite rising figures), the relatively rare use of heroin and other opiates. Millions of older people live much of the time in an alcoholic haze and show neither the desire nor impetus to emerge from it. Anti-anxiety drugs, anti-depressant drugs, anti-psychotic drugs, as well as sedatives and stimulants, are prescribed and marketed so freely that *not* to find a pill box containing one or another of them in an adult's medicine cabinet, pocket or purse is today an exception rather than rule. Call them what you will and defend them (in part justifiably) by whatever clinical rationales are available, these agents are distorters of, and insulators from, cold reality and the individuality—for better or worse—of the person who uses them. If love is not possible, then one may choose a mild or strong dose of chemical euphoria. Even if one is wise enough to know that total euphoria is sometimes addictive and often physiologically dangerous, he can—quite safely it seems—pharmacologically soften periodically the hard pangs of love's denial and the worse consequences of modernity's conquest of the individual.

True enough, some chemical agents serve mainly to diminish the cultural boredom of impersonal sex but have little to do with the absence or

[25] May, *op. cit.*, p. 31. May follows Harry Stack Sullivan's construction of apathy here.

evocation of love, except superficially. Alcohol usually increases sexual appetite while diminishing capacity for performance, an ideal copout. "Hard" drugs simply destroy the sex urge; tranquillizing agents permit one to relegate sexuality to irrelevance in life's major concerns. But the implied and stated relationships in the popular press between sex and drugs has been exaggerated.[26] The inability to love, however, remains a significant etiological factor in our drug culture and will remain so, the author suspects, for many years.

Curiously, there exists a phase in the manifestation of love that opens one also to the vulnerable reality of death. May observes that our culture has erected few psychological barriers to the fear of death (discussed previously) similar to those in other societies where beliefs in reincarnation or immortality dull one's perceptions of the grim reaper. Love in *any* context is a wide-open affirmation of life (far more so than the momentary sexual spasm): a statement of being of the self, a statement of significance of individuality, and a statement of the presence of others as symbolized by society. All of these deep commitments, for commitments they are, are demanded by one's acceptance or giving of love and recognizing its attendant perils that are always at the mercy of death's unpredictabilities.[27] Risk to the ego, even in instances where, as parents for instance, we are hurled into love-evoking situations, is so enormous that our retreat is, in substance, a flight from the consciousness of impending death. Once again, emotional coldness, apathy, self-absorption, sex or drugs are called into the service of the psyche. *Any* emotion, it seems, is frequently preferable to love, even sentimentality over other lovers on soap operas, in films and in books by female novelists whose busy prose is just gossip about love. Anything *but* love!

The other great cultural obstacle to love is puritanism. Heaven knows that the argument that we are a nation of old-style Puritans in regard to sex has run down its natural course. Quite the reverse obtains today; and if traditional sexual Puritans live among us, they are sequestered in nursing homes and/or rock gently on front porches somewhere. A few of them

---

[26] See *ibid.*, p. 60, for instance. Huxley in *Brave New World* came closer to describing the problem *now* than most so-called "experts" on alcoholism and narcotics addiction. The error of their conclusions is the ancient one that imputes causes and effects to adjacent phenomena. A male chronic alcoholic is likely to make sexual advances to every sex object he encounters when drunk *because* he knows he cannot perform. Female drunks who solicit men for "kicks" have a way of passing out during coitus, or at least relegating their sex acts to blackouts. Women narcotic addicts, who are practically sexually anesthetised while using hard drugs, frequently become prostitutes or indulge in sex games because of their need (and the need of their pimps) for the quick and copious cash required to support their habits. Male prostitution—within limits—also frequently accompanies addiction to expensive drugs in the same way. In the cases of active addicts to hard drugs, sex, like love, becomes meaningless, neither enjoyable nor disgusting nor, in fact, relegated to anything except earning capacity as a source for obtaining drugs.

[27] *Ibid.*, p. 106.

appear somehow to get into the Congress of the United States. But outrage at permissive sex, pornography or sex talk is as passé today as the whalebone corset and Lydia Pinkham.

The new puritanism is spelled with a small "p", and is discussed by May.[28] But it is by no means a phenomenon that he alone has identified. It appears in the guise of a scientistic attitude toward sex as discussed in the previous chapter, but now applied to love. Love is alienated from the spontaneous activities of body and emotions and is utilized, employed or administered, machine-like, as a form of therapy, an index of mental health (a most disturbing term[29]) and a conduit for something called "creative expression." We are referring here to a cultural attitude not unrelated to sex, but, just as it is, to a degree, alienated from every other human function, it is alienated from sex as well. May describes the problem well. "The Victorian person sought to have love without falling into sex; the modern person seeks to have sex without falling into love." [30] Substitute the word "life" for "sex," and you have the broader manifestation of the problem and a more serious one, equally as common.

Symptoms of this version of puritanism center on the individual's self-consciousness of his own emotions, smugness of moral stance (usually described as "new," "realistic" or "modern"), an awkward worship of freedom, and the utilization of sex and other pleasures in the spirit of exercises or games like golf and tennis, not for enjoyment but because they are good for one. Better than any other word, "enlightened" describes the new puritan as he sees himself because, in human matters, he is entirely in the dark. He is also identified by his depersonalized vocabulary and pseudo-rational frame of discourse. Self-abnegation or sublimation are only considered acceptable in living if they produce something creative; art in any form that is not therapeutic is, to him, merely a benign form of neurosis, never a symbolic expression of love. Thus the puritan *cultivates* art as a hobby, attends museums and concerts to be *broadened* and because he is convinced that exposure to truth and beauty is *healthy.*

The new puritan is incapable of love until and unless he discards his puritanism. He is the unknowing victim of subtle cultural influences drawn mostly from the worlds of contemporary psychology and sociology. The influence is unintentional, because the behavioral sciences have been bent over backwards in their efforts to avoid any implied or stated obligation to articulate values when they described individual and social processes. As

---

28 *Ibid.*, pp. 45–52.

29 If the terms "mental hygiene" and "mental health" are as offensive to you as they are to me, see Theodore R. Sarbin, "The Scientific Status of the Mental Illness Metaphor" in Stanley C. Plog and Robert B. Edgerton (eds.), *Changing Perspectives in Mental Illness* (New York: Holt, Rinehart and Winston, Inc., 1969). pp. 9–13, as well as the two following articles in this anthology by Perry London and editor Edgerton.

30 May, *op. cit.*, p. 46. (May's italics removed.)

troublesome as the problem has become, physicists, biologists and natural scientists who are playing dangerous games are demonstrating an awareness that the search for scientific truth may often have much to do with the search for human values. Thoughtful members of the scientific community are therefore frequently called to act in two distinct capacities: first, to use their intelligences to achieve the scientific end of truth about natural processes and, second, to use that same intelligence, in quite a different manner, to articulate values so that men can survive along with the truths they bring into society.

Behavioral scientists have, until the present, faced no such critical schism, because values (like mental health programs) were implied by their activities even before they had even erected the procedural safeguards necessary for the conduct of their scientific investigations. Biochemists were at least restrained for reasonable periods—sometimes too short—before their serums were hurled into human blood streams, working their way up from mice to apes to convicts to small experimental populations. Behavioral scientists, on the other hand, found their notions leaping directly from journal articles to the therapeutic couch, usually through no fault of their own. Because they were dealing with matters of mind and behavior, along the way every tenet produced or accumulated a stratum of values due to their peculiar position. Most therapists, for instance, have gone in the past, and go today, out of their way to *avoid* value judgments or moral attitudes towards their patients. Yet what they do and say—and, more important, what they *do not* do and say in their non-directive techniques—are often perceived unwittingly by their patients as value construction and moralizing. That their patients then carry the banner of what they interpret as moral and ethical wisdom is not the fault of the therapist, although he is often blamed.

Behavioral sciences which, therefore, have attempted to achieve neutrality, in matters of sex and love especially, have violently affected the moral temper of our society, and the role of love in culture, by generalizing (via their popularizers) subtle insights, complex theories, and therapeutic gambits satisfactory for disturbed people but unsatisfactory for the normal. At first glance, the result has been a liberation from outworn moral codes and the sticky illusions of romanticism. Closer study (and time) has revealed instead that no new values have taken the place of outworn, so-called "prescientific" codes, and what has been left is a vacuum filled avidly with, first, mechanized sex, sad in itself, but coupled with, second, puritanized (or purified) love as a therapeutic tool.

Love is, unfortunately, simply *not* therapy, any more than art is therapy or music is therapy. Indeed, love may *produce* behavioral and dispositional changes in people, just as painting or exposure to art or music may also. But, as even psychotherapists are finally gleaning, play therapy is not real play, merely an analogy for play, often of passing (and questionable) value. Art and music therapy, passive or active, are not genuine encounters with art and music as they epitomize human "receptiveness to beauty and humane feeling," in Whitehead's phrase. They are tricks of diagnosis or devices that employ paints, modeling clay and recording and/or musical instruments. As creative experiences they are pathetic, with few exceptions.

Therapeutic love—and this is perhaps the only universally acceptable kind of love available any longer[31]—is to genuine love as art therapy is to art; or, as the title of a recent book notes, military music is to music. In the first place, therapeutic love connotes that one requires a *reason* for falling in love, in the face of the fact that the power of love lies precisely in its *unreasonableness.* Second, it is not spontaneous, self-generating and free of self-consciousness, but answerable to a "correct" interpretation of psychic hygiene, even when that interpretation is broad enough to include eccentric and unconventional love. Society's values, in the last analysis, dictate the appropriateness of one's feelings of love, and it is to society we are forced to look for the benign nod which will allow us to love our sex partner(s), families, societies, selves and even our country.

Most manifestations of love in our culture, therefore, seem hardly worth the effort; and those that are worth it, we are all too aware, are at the mercy of the two great arbitrary factors of disasterous change: time and death. To love is therefore to become vulnerable, engaged in life and to play the patsy, either for extinction (the best of two choices) or heartbreak, for lack of a better word. How much more satisfactory to play it cool—and safely.

Love's Labors Exploited

If the contemporary Westerner is to be persuaded *to* love or *by* love, he must be convinced that the love he gives or receives is, accordingly, safe. Most forms of safety (except a few elemental physical ones) are, at bedrock, illusions. Our contemporary mythology has, however, institutionalized safety in various contexts, the most significant one, in the author's opinion, the illusion of safety that society itself offers the individual by means of what we call "social welfare." Associating socialistic statist protection and safety with the words "womb to tomb" is psychologically revealing. The modern mother-like progressive nation not only protects us from womb to tomb (supposedly) but supplies for us as well the psychological equivalents of both. Both physical and psychological safety is therefore apparently as-

[31] Romantic love is today usually equated with idiocy. Self-love must usually be purchased at the price of non-conformity or ostracism. Platonic love is usually treated as a cover for closet homosexuality or some other deviant behavior. Patriotism is old hat and unrealistic in the light of the present crisis, whatever it is. Loving one's children, we are told, produces Portnoy's complaint. Loving animals is self-indulgent. And loving nature ritualizes obeisance to the great outdoors leading to such corruptions as lobbying for anti-vivisection and camping in mosquito bogs, nose-to-nose with other nature lovers.

sured by the strongest instrument of culture available: the modern technological nation.

Our attitudes towards private property, investment, insurance, medicine, psychiatry, marriage, the names our children bear, our hobbies, photographs and newspapers are all, in part, manifestations of this need for safety. Perhaps if we can convince ourselves—or if others are able to convince us—that we are indeed safe *now*, we may be able to give or accept love. Thus is the actual fact of death itself euphemized—beyond phrases and manners of speech—by the art of the mortician and funeral director, who make corpses as life-like and their disposal as lively as possible.[32]

Persuasion directly addressed to the need of man for love is therefore ambivalent, and just as likely to exacerbate tensions as to resolve them. From one side, love threatens, because it increases human vulnerability, as we have seen. On the other, it promises freedom: freedom of emotional play, freedom of self-discovery, joy of life and what Whitehead calls the "zest for living." In intimacy with a loved one, it offers either the freedom of sexual-erotic play and mutual pleasure, or, in a non-sexual context, affirmation of one's own being by the recognition of one's human worth in the mind's eye of another. Love may also offer transcendental freedom. The concept of love of country has widened a thousand multiples since the Greeks applied it to the *demos*; today it encompasses amplitudes of distance and time that the ancients could not even conceive of. Love, in other words, may be a *condition of social awareness* and therefore a perceptual freedom—for many, in a religious context, sometimes in a spiritual one, and sometimes in a purely secular one. This freedom has been captured expertly in the prayer of St. Francis. Note that nothing prevents the accomplishment of what is asked except dispositions of the individual praying: "Lord, grant that I may seek rather to comfort than to be comforted—to understand than to be understood—to love, than to be loved."

The risk remains, however. Other surrogates—sex, for instance—are safer and, to the puritan mind, healthier than love. The abnegation of freedom, as Sartre explains, is escape from the intolerable for those incapable of exercising free choice. Most modern persuasion therefore announces that we may see love, smell love, taste love—but not *feel* it, because the persuader knows only too well that were he to love us (or were he to seek our love for him), we would cringe and shrink away from him. And there are other risks.

The Kennedy family, for instance, is justifiably loved by much of the American public. But when, as recently occurred, a Kennedy is caught in a scandal involving the possibilities of criminal negligence and/or intent of

[32] See Jessica Mitford, *The American Way of Death* (New York: Simon and Schuster, 1963), a generally accurate account of the theatrics of the funeral industry, suitably provocative, stimulating and frightening.

adultery, that love can backfire. New York State Governor Rockefeller's divorce and the unfortunate circumstances surrounding it, on the other hand, did little damage to the feelings of the Governor's constituency; but "Rocky" was, and is, little loved, although generally admired. Hitler elicited and knew how to attract the love of his people with an intensity and on a scale seldom seen in the modern world—not comparable with feelings evident in other nations during the period towards Mussolini, Churchill, Roosevelt or even DeGaulle. Hitler, however, was an unusual master at managing mass emotions and did not hesitate to take many kinds of psychological risks. And the extraordinary love that he elicited was accompanied by his total personal (as well as public) devotion to his status as *Führer,* clearly demonstrated in his disciplined life-style. Hitler's suicide represented to Hitler (if we may believe accounts by Trevor-Roper and others) more a failure of the power of his own love for Germany (warped as it was), and the failure of the love of the German people for him, than a military defeat. Like all intense lovers, when Hitler's love failed, his actual identity was challenged, and suicide remained his only course.

A form of benign love does tend to agglomerate about public figures over a period of time, but it too has its risks. Jimmy Durante, deservedly I feel, is one of the best loved (and most lovable) American theatrical figures today. When Durante's agents, some time ago, encouraged him to perform in a number of breakfast food commercials, they were criticized for exploiting the aged Durante in what looked like a mercenary context. One does not enjoy seeing one's love object used by others for their own ends, although in this instance the Schnozola was ostensibly trying to assure financial security for his extremely young child who will probably pass through the formative years without a father's love.

Vicarious love—not vicarious sex—is probably, however, one of the most widely exploited forms of public persuasion employed presently in the United States and much of the rest of the Western world. To dwell too long on it is absurd, because there is so much of it. One finds the image of love somehow dredged from the lives of almost all public figures, in fiction and fantasy, in newspapers and novels and almost everywhere one turns. What is described is invariably manipulated love, as inherently vulgar as the wedding of singer Tiny Tim on a network television show. Public love invariably shows all the earmarks of a plot, which is exactly what it is—a plot to limit the exercise of freedom in love in order to use its power to manipulate opinions and behavior, more often and successfully in trivial contents than important ones.

The young naturally recognize immediately when love is manipulated. They follow the natural inclination to feel and give love with emotional freedom. They are unquestionably romantic (the films and TV shows they favor, from *Rosemary's Baby* to *The Mod Squad,* fairly drip with romance), and they seek spontaneity, uniqueness, fatality *and* risk in their love, because, in their inexperience, the young have not yet learned to fear spontaneous behavior. They feel that every surge of emotion within them is happening for the first time in the history of the world. Neither are they much afraid of fate; death is an apparently unreal construction of the old to the eyes of an individual whose endocrine system has just begun to blast off. Nor do they fear risks—either in "hot-rods" or in investments of psychic energy. Everything they want from love is natural and affirmative, and, from a middle-aged perspective, enviable.

The young are thus satisfied by the *appearances* of love that meet these conditions. Drugs, particularly marihuana, efficiently and quickly stimulate the illusion of spontaneity. Nudity, long hair, bizarre costumes, even voluntary retreat to a ghetto world of poverty and filth, may affirm, for some young people, their own uniqueness and grit in the face of fate, as well as provide a sense of risk. Certainly, their philosophers and folk heroes know how to exemplify these qualities, as do their protests and strident denunciations of the fearful and insecure conservative establishment of the aging.

What the young—particularly those who echo the hippie psychology—miss, as May points out,[33] is the overly generalized nature of such love, well-meant and emotionally pure as it seems to be.[34] It is directed to the incomprehensible notion of "mankind" and culminates erotically in more or less casual (but intense) sexual (and sometimes non-sexual) communion with other youngsters on a fleeting, promiscuous and chance basis. This is love that attempts to consume all of humanity and settles for intensive interaction with a minute fraction of it. Love so experienced precludes the enduring quality that allows relationships, no matter how immediately intense, to deepen and individualize, both for the lover and loved one. Individuality, in fact, is sacrificed to the loving commune; and the hippie way of life reduces the choice of to whom love is given and how. To choose means to discriminate, and, as May says, "to choose someone (also) means *not* to choose someone else. This is overlooked among the hippies; the *immediacy* of love in the hippie development seems to end in a love that is fugitive and ephemeral."

[33] May, *op. cit.*, p. 279.

[34] My seventeen-year-old daughter, like most children her age, has been affected by the youth cult and hippie mentality. In her room hangs an enormous photographic poster displaying a number of unattractive, aged derelicts and unidentified males in a setting suggesting urban blight. The ironic caption reads, "We have all come from lovers." In its way, this poster signifies all that is both good and bad about the love cultists. On one hand, it speaks for the universality of love and the possibility of its generalization. On the other, it relegates to a slogan and a simplistic psychological formula the complex problem of the unloved and unwanted in our cities, a social problem that young people, for the most part, are *incapable of understanding* will not be solved simply by loving or wanting to help someone or something. In their naïveté, they evade confrontation with the technical complexities of the society in which they live, and upon which they depend. Urban blight may indeed be removed from our land, not by force of youthful emotion but by force of mature intellect in the service of enlightened self-interest. This, the children will not, and cannot, comprehend.

Fugitive and ephemeral by all means, but understandable and attractive as well, because such love is the one kind that may often be given without vulnerability, the potential of pain and heartbreak or fear. Love, in other words, remains a pervasive and momentary reality for the young in our culture. For the rest of us, it is rapidly becoming a spectator sport.

Conclusion

Faced as we are, in the midst of much psychologically oriented talk about love but possessing merely an inchoate psychology of love, we have literally to clear out our own path through a forest of myths and verbiage in order to consider the nature and power of persuasion by appeals to love in our culture.

Love has been, and is, an American myth-dream of importance, equally attractive, at first glance, to the revolutionary and the arch-conservative in socio-cultural matters, although little agreement seems to exist on the relationship of love to sex, or whether eroticism is essentially a manifestation of the former or the latter. Christianity and medieval culture provide the major precedents for modern ideas of love that still center—as they did for the ancient Greeks—upon love partners, friends and the totality of society.

Love, however, connotes ironies that enhance its dangers as well as its attractions. It is allied with individuality and the inexorable fate that separates every man eventually from what he loves. For cultural viability, love must be tempered by adequate knowledge, lest it destroy not only the lovers but the world in which they love.

In our culture today, mechanization and depersonalization make the act of loving difficult, especially when fear of love takes on the face of apathy. This is a protective device, because the acceptance of love in a mechanized world reminds us forcibly of the failure of our techniques to deal with the basic data of existence, the facts of birth and death. Scientism of a sort has also developed for us the new puritan, for whom love, like uninhibited sex, is therapy, or a form of psychic hygiene, an interesting value he picked up during his destruction of older value systems that once governed human relationships in a less enlightened era than ours. Therapeutic love remains acceptable for many of us, however, less because of its intrinsic attraction than because it does not involve the degree of personal vulnerability or risk that other, softer, warmer forms of love do.

Love may, at times, be personalized by a politician or performer who, in a general sense, renders himself by one or another ruse extremely loveable. This also entails risks, because a lost love is rarely regained. Vicarious love is the main avenue to persuasion by love, except for the young who still cherish illusions of personal romance and openly resent the manipulation of love's image that they see around them in the adult world. In their search for love, they accept the worst, frequently, in rejection of the bad, understanding little of the enduringness of love by accepting a fleeting, casual love affair with the human race that ends in the promiscuous devaluation of the attributes of choice and discrimination. As they grow older, therefore, love's labors yield disillusionment, and, like their elders, they usually join the great hoard of adult *voyeurs* who watch love manufactured and manipulated from a comfortable distance.

Chapter 17

THE POWER OF LAUGHTER

Cats talk to each other by mewing, frum whence we get the word "Commewnicat."

Arthur H. Euwer

LIKE LOVE, laughter is a form of behavior often avoided by the serious analyst of human behavior. There is little that he may quantify in laughter and even less to qualify, although broadcasters, not scientists, have attempted to measure the intensity of collective laughter by the use of "laugh meters." A search of the records of contemporary American and European sociology indicates that neither humor nor laughter are topics of much interest to scholars in this field. Anthropologists, of course, encounter laughter in their casebooks and give it passing attention. Psychologists, on the other hand, seem more willing to discuss humor, following, probably, the interests of Freud in what we call today "black humor," and the continuation of his work into the psychodynamics of Jewish humor by Reik.[1] The former appeared to lack much of what we crudely call "a sense of humor"; the latter, at times, appears more interested in amusement than psychology—by no means an unwelcome surprise in a field in which sombre, humorless drones often achieve status as auditors of the human condition.

This author has previously attempted a superficial analysis of how humor is communicated,[2] following conventional literary and psychological precedents, with a degree of success, except that this kind of analysis tends to become tedious. Meredith, Bergson and Freud,[3] each representing a different phase of Western culture, produced three literary landmarks in

[1] Freud's main essay on wit and humor is, of course, a classic and central to the understanding of psychoanalysis. See *The Basic Writings of Sigmund Freud,* (New York: The Modern Library, 1838), pp. 633–803. Theodor Reik, *Jewish Wit* (New York:

the analysis of humor, each bespeaking the values of a different era and social orientation.

In brief, Meredith looked back at the theatre of the Restoration, French court comedies, and particularly the satire of Molière. He concluded that laughter served, in general, as a social corrective. Bergson concentrated on humor of a less elegant sort, apparently tempered by the psychological pressures of the industrial revolution he saw around him. The humor he describes grew out of the attempt to mechanize qualities that are basically not mechanical but human. (The author considers Charles Chaplin as the clearest Bergsonian comic of the twentieth century. But he will cross swords with anyone who claims for Chaplin, an essentially serious performer, more than honorable mention in the roster of great non-Bergsonian comics of the recent stage and screen.) Freud looked ahead to the twentieth century in which social strictures and widespread anxiety neuroses permitted the psychoanalytic view of laughter as a release from the tension of repressed emotion, particularly laughter that takes the form of off-color or bizarre jokes. For Freud, laughter, like symbols in dreams and preconsciousness, was a clue to the workings in the non-conscious of repressed feelings translated into consciousness in disguise.

Recently, ethologists have also shown interest in human laughter, based upon their observations of analogous behaviors of animals. In *Languages of Communication*, discussion in some detail centered upon the ideas of Konrad Lorenz[4] in this regard, particularly his suggestion that laughter may be an obverse form of human aggression, basing his arguments on the physical appearance of human laughter and the ways it is communicated in large and small groups—as well as some of the startling similarities of laughter to thwarted aggressive behavior in certain animals. The author's enthusiasm for this construction in his former volume may have been precipitous. But its freshness of approach, relevance to contemporary mass communications (where, on television, for instance, violence and laughter are today the two dominant moods), and adequacy in comparison to previous constructions, made Lorenz's idea seem attractive, in theory at least. The concept also, in some ways, specifies the Freudian notion of repression as the source of laughter, and stands at variance neither with Bergson's socio-psychological theories nor Meredith's cultural orientation.

Gamut Press, 1962), is a diversion from this prolific psychoanalyst's most significant work—although he discourses sagely on guilt and masochism in ethnic humor. The latter book is interesting, well argued and occasionally (and intentionally) quite funny.

[2] See G.N.G., *LC*, pp. 219–233.

[3] The volumes recommended for these and other familiar studies of humor are: Willis Sypher (ed.), *Comedy* (Garden City, N.Y.: Doubleday Anchor Books, 1956) and Robert W. Corrigan, *Comedy: Meaning and Form* (San Francisco: Chandler Publishing Co., 1965). These essays are also printed in numerous other collections.

[4] See Konrad Lorenz, *On Aggression* (New York: Harcourt, Brace and World Inc., 1963), pp. 177–178, 292–297.

As warmly and convincingly as he presents them, however, Lorenz's concepts will require considerable qualification and refining before they become generally acceptable. It is unfortunate that today too many theories and explanations for animal violence (particularly man's) have figuratively clogged serious socio-psycological consideration of aggressive behavior.[5] Psychoanalytic theories, reflexive theories, territorial theories and cultural theories compete and complicate the issues involved, throwing neither heat nor light upon them. The author has, accordingly, become increasingly suspicious of ethological analogies (some of them tentatively presented in the pages to come), including and especially those of theorists like Lorenz who depend upon selective evidence of animal behavior interpreted through the distortive lens of a human value system. They are, in the long run, self-consistent, self-generated, closed to experiment, and therefore sophistic. They are witty and, in a literary sense, wise. But they are really parables, not evidence in either a legal or scientific construction.

The Need for Laughter

As for the psychological function of laughter, Niels Bohr has been quoted as replying to a student, annoyed by his professor's general disposition of levity in the light of the lethal aspects of his work, "But there are some things so important that one can only joke about them." The cultural case for laughter (as if one is needed) in almost any society within our historical experience is, on its face, exactly Bohr's point. The ancient emblem of the Mimes of Thalia demonstrates the wisdom of the ancients in recognizing an obvious datum that we, their descendants genetically and culturally, frequently contrive to forget. Their point referred to the drama, but drama as a re-creation of life. The essential human condition admits of two possible ultimate emotions: either we laugh at it or cry at it. Any and all other emotional alternatives are actually evasions, and, if we live long enough to perceive the full course of any social or personal situation, we shall indeed end up either laughing or crying, depending, one supposes, upon the nature of the situation and our orientation to it.

A crude polar psychology like this (if psychology it is) has certain philosophical advantages over the complexities of explanation that are given by various theorists—including Hobbes, Nietzche, McDougal, and Max Eastmen, as well as those noted above and others—concerning the origins and functions of laughter. Those of us trained in the behavioral and social disciplines expect complexity, and sometimes we equate beneficent simplicity with naïveté and/or untruth. A man like Bohr cannot be accused of being naïve. He also knows the face of truth when he sees it, and the alternative he presents is both apt and realistic. The nagging question behind it, of course, is "Why?"

---

[5] See Chapter 23. See also the discussion of Ardrey's notions on pp. 172–173.

Let us, for the time being at least, beg the question of the origins of laughter by means of the observation that it seems to have feral beginnings and is discovered in relationships between mothers and small children, as Morris suggests,[6] and that laughter has been maintained in adult culture, and sustained in social evolution because of certain preferred abilities it provided laughers over non-laughers in the development of our species. Montagu notes that "(t)hose who possessed the ability to express their pleasurable states in . . . laughter would tend to be socially preferred over those who were not so capable." [7] Certain advantages, including in many instances even survival, were, therefore, accorded to them. In addition, and corollary to these causes, laughter, Weston Le Barre claims, is transmuted into an individualistic device that serves as a "tension-release of now 'innocently permitted' expression of otherwise forbidden aggressive erotic . . . fearful and embarrassed . . . states of mind." [8] Thus, he bows formally in the direction of both Freud and Lorenz and their colorful etiological theories.

So much, then, for causal factors—at least here. Human beings begin laughing, on the average, at about the age of three months and keep laughing at varying intervals, usually, until death. To the best of the writer's knowledge (and for reasons he cannot fathom), few inquiries have as yet been made of this pattern of behavior, even in its obviously normal or average aspects: whether, for instance, college students appear to laugh more under certain circumstances than high school students under similar circumstances; how laughter varies in quantity and quality with age, education and sex; whether it is possible to distinguish by psychodynamic evidence laughing *at* someone or something from laughing *with* him or it. Neither has anyone yet satisfactorily defined a "sense of humor," if such a sense (in any sense) exists, beyond the self-evident proposition that it seems to include the ability to detect what is funny in numerous aspects of life and to communicate easily these insights to others in a mirthful way.[9] How then does this so-called "sense" develop, and how does it change through life, if indeed it does change? These questions cannot be answered at present, except by conjecture, and one man's conjecture on laughter seems about as good as another's, including those of comedians whose profession it is to

[6] See Desmond Morris, *The Naked Ape*, pp. 117–118.

[7] Ashley Montagu, *Man in Process* (New York: New American Library, 1961), p. 196.

[8] Weston Le Barre, "Paralinguistics, Kinesics, and Cultural Anthropology" in Matson and Montagu, *The Human Dialogue*, p. 462.

[9] This definition presents problems, because identical abilities are detected in numerous people diagnosed as schizophrenic and are therefore confined to institutions and dehumorized chemically or by shock therapy. See A.F.C. Wallace's terse description of the semantic derangement of schizophrenia in "Culture Change and Mental Illness" in S. C. Plog and R. B. Edgerton (eds.), *Changing Perspectives in Mental Illness*, pp. 76–77, which includes, of course, a discussion of the *wrong kind* of sense of humor. But, "Wrong for what?" is the vexing and unanswered question.

make others laugh,[10] as well as the writers and other artists who create and mount their performances.

What the author has attempted below, however, in the absence of reliable etiological evidence that might clear up a number of unanswered questions, is a list of the specific functions that laughter seems to perform for most people most of the time. From them one may derive implications concerning the needs which laughter appears to meet—needs, incidentally, that may also be met in other ways quite satisfactorily. Excluded from this inventory, however, are the problems of what we might call "bizarre laughter" or "deviant laughter," most especially laughter which precludes humor, such as the laughter portrayed in fiction—and sometimes seen in life—of a sadist who enjoys watching people or animals suffer, or victims of manic hebephrenia who giggle, gush and laugh at almost any stimulus, as long as it is *not* funny.[11]

First, laughter is a form of shorthand communication.[12] A logical and functional evaluation of what laughter *does* centers on its main accomplishment, transaction of cognitions between people. Laughter is, in fact, apparently a facet of speech, although it is generally understood to be more an emotional reaction than a cognitive statement. But as a statement it signifies, both by sound and gesture, a good deal. Laughter indicates, first, understanding of a certain event, story or sight; second, the ironical or unexpected element of its object; third, approval of some aspect of this meaning (even of the proverbial man slipping on a banana peel); and fourth, joy in that approval. In the words of Montagu, laughter is quasi-verbalized speech, used on "occasions producing the sudden experiences of pleasure" of certain kinds. It is also frequently employed as a qualifier of speech, although laughter may occur without other verbal speech and still serve its function as communication.[13]

---

[10] An interesting book has been brought to my attention: Larry Wilde, *The Great Comedians Talk About Comedy* (New York: The Citadel Press, 1968). It contains well structured transcripts of tape-recorded interviews between the author and such outstanding comedians as Jack Benny, George Burns, Maurice Chevalier, Jimmy Durante, Bob Hope, Dick Gregory, Jerry Lewis and the late Ed Wynn, among others. What they have to say is sometimes fascinating, warm and revealing about themselves. (George Burns' tribute to his late wife's talent as a comedienne is particularly perceptive and moving.) But none of these humorists has anything more at his command than familiar folklore to explain why people laugh at the things they do and say—or why they do *not* laugh at certain times. Not that these comedians are either reticent or unintelligent about their skills. They simply—and quite correctly—accept laughter as a given human quality they stimulate by doing and saying odd things that members of their audience would not normally think of doing or saying.

[11] In hebephrenic schizophrenia, semantic derangement is as clear and notable as in any phase of the disease because of the presence of laughter at the meanings of words and situations that are obviously perceived or received distortively.

[12] See Montagu, *op. cit.*, pp. 195–196.

[13] It was with this facet of laughter—its nature as a modifier or quality of communications—that I was mainly concerned in G.N.G., *L C.*

Second, one aspect of laughter upon which almost all authorities agree is that it has power to release tensions. Physiological evidence exists for this observation as well as empirical data. But, mainly, we know that laughter will relax individuals in a relative undifferentiated manner and, under almost any circumstances, make them feel better. Hence, the fact that gallows humor exists and serves its purpose of tension reduction, as those who have served in warfare can attest. The prototypical black joke about the mutilated soldier on the brink of death who, when asked if his wound hurt, replied, "Only when I laugh!" *is* funny, not only because it is ridiculous but because it contains a measure of truth. Laughter's therapeutic element does not show much sticking power, but it is an impressive and effective characteristic of the phenomenon,[14] and supplies the main supporting datum, incidentally, for both ethological and psychoanalytic theories of the etiology of laughter.

Third, laughter communicates a stance or disposition of non-aggression and tends to diminish whatever degree of threat a situation poses for oneself or for another. A minor manifestation of this function is the smile that is normally exchanged between strangers upon being introduced. A major manifestation (aside from tension reduction) might be the miserable joke that a professor cracks at an oral examination for the doctorate, or in the face of a frightened class of college freshmen. In both cases, the teacher is euphemizing the idea that he is (or will be) less of a threat than expected. A laughing policeman approaching your automobile does not portend his giving you a ticket—although he may. A laughing obstetrician approaching an expectant new father says, in effect, "Mother and baby are doing well." When General Patton, in the excellent film biography of his World War II career, stands in front of his troops to apologize for his misconduct in slapping a shell-shocked soldier, he says, "I thought I'd let you see just how big a son-of-a-bitch I really am!" He thereby eliminates with laughter the possibility of vengeance upon his subordinates. There exists also little threat of aggression from an individual who has learned sincerely to laugh at himself.

Fourth, laughter is a signal that, commensurate with reduced tension and diminished threat, *playing behavior* is now a permissible form of communication. Cognitively, it is a sign not to take what is said or done too seriously. The President of the United States is likely to joke and laugh

---

[14] Some comedians say that the easiest audience to start laughing is a group of convicts, continual tension being one of the most unattractive aspects of prison life. Laughter is usually a significant aspect of effective self-help therapy like that of Alcoholics and Gamblers Anonymous, weight watchers, etc. Attending their meetings, one frequently wonders how individuals can laugh at the gruesome misadventures of fellow human beings, until one comprehends the significance of laughter as part of therapy, not only for momentary relaxation but in the development of a humorous attitude towards one's affliction (alcoholism, gambler's neurosis and obesity) in order to appraise and manage it objectively.

when personal questions are asked him at a press conference. When discussing national policy, he is likely to be stern. Many an elementary school teacher learns, to his or her regret, that any laughter is interpreted by small children as instruction to play. What he or she must teach them is to control the cue that laughter brings and to "turn it off" in the interest of discipline. A group of laughing people, regardless of their age, are usually considered at play; it is unlikely that they are discussing serious business, although they may all be bankers, educators, diplomats or counterfeiters. Lear's fool, of course, disguised much wisdom and serious psychology in play. And play, as the late Dr. Eric Berne taught us in *The Games People Play*, may have serious secondary psychological functions. Thus may tragedy unfold behind a curtain of laughter, but the function of the laughter remains, nevertheless, playful.

Fifth, and without drinking too deeply of the psychoanalytical cup, laughter is an immediate device for handling repressed and potentially dangerous threats—mostly felt as uncertainties within the individual.[15] When the function is apparent, we call the result "nervous laughter." When it is indistinguishable from other laughter, we do not call it anything but "laughter." Yet, its function may be identical in both cases. In this sense, laughter is a signal to one's self, not unlike whistling while crossing a graveyard, that whatever discomfort one feels is unfitting, and funny rather than serious. Such laughter may seem inappropriate when witnessed by others, but it makes psychological sense and is never the neurotic or psychotic symptom some observers may take it to be, unless it occurs in excess.

Sixth (and perhaps this observation is merely a sub-category of the manifestation above), laughter is a device that can mask oversensitivity, overt and covert, both to one's self and to one's perceptions of others. Should we be injured by a remark or direct attack, one immediate diversion, although there are a multitude of ways one may protect himself from such hurts, is laughter. Cripples, deviants of various sorts, people with speech defects and other infirmities like blindness, have mastered the laugh that signals to another the information that the other is not to worry too severely about hurting the individual in matters referring to his stigma. Laughter, in this instance, indicates that the stigmatized individual is willing to indulge in the pretense (it is almost always a pretense) that, regardless of his infirmity, he will be treated as a normal member of the other person's world. This laughter operates in reverse as well, signaling the

---

[15] When, many years ago, I presented myself to a highly perceptive psychoanalyst for fixing (a task beyond his art and science—but no fault of his), I recounted many of my grimy problems at our first meeting with what I thought was enormous candor. His reply was simply, "Why do you laugh so much?" He was perfectly correct and most insightful, of course. My monologue had been a transparent, sarcastic, laugh-loaded, defensive operation and a futile attempt to neutralize that miniscule portion of self-threatening material (or information) that I had chosen to offer him. My response anticipated Niels Bohr's by some years and was identical to his.

pseudo-acceptance of a normal person into a deviant or stigmatized society.[16]

In short, those who (following Meredith) emphasize the cognitive, cortical, civilizing, and distinctly humanoid thrust of laughter (and might hold a play by Oscar Wilde or Bernard Shaw as its apotheosis) are, from their point of view, correct. On the other hand, those for whom laughter seems mainly a bond between in-groups (like traveling salesmen at a bar exchanging dirty jokes) emphasize (following Freud) the tendency of instinct (or the id) to assert itself in a civilized context and to demonstrate the foolishness of man pretending to be less of an animal than he really is.

Neither viewpoint, in terms of the functions noted above, is entirely correct—nor is either wrong. Laughter, it appears, is the synthetic result of an ongoing tension between emotion and reason, instinct and thought, repression and cognition, or feeling and cortical activity, whichever one chooses. A basic incongruity remains regardless, and it remains funny. Apparently cerebral drawing-room comedy is funny because a group of "naked apes" (in Morris' term) are discussing and handling their fundamentally ape appetites as if they were playing a game of chess or bridge. The incongruity is funny. In his many humorous roles, the farce comedian regresses to childhood and exposes a facet of his existential animality; provoked by fate, the clown is invariably caught in a literally "reasonable" situation. The incongruity is funny.[17] In fact, identical incongruities displaying different emphases are, as one would predict, equally funny.

A dual process obtains. When reason shackles instinct, the result may be funny. When instinct shackles reason, the result may also be funny. In both cases, if the dominant mood is not that of frivolity, laughter will not result. Every function we have seen that may be performed by laughter may also be achieved by other psychological stratagems or devices. In this respect, therefore, laughter is indeed a cognitive, cortical process, because it serves in lieu of one or another form of speech or complex communication, all highly sophisticated activities. Laughter is also a form of expression that man must have learned in a social context, perhaps between mother and

---

[16] See Erving Goffman, *Stigma* (Englewood Cliffs, N.J.: Prentice Hall, Inc., 1963), for a remarkable study of the ways in which disabled and/or otherwise injured individuals manage their problems of identity in groups of other stigmatized people and in the company of "normals." Goffman's concept of stigma includes people who are psychologically as well as physically abnormal, and his book provides deeply human and sharply observant analyses of their problems in living and maintaining their identities.

[17] This juxtaposition of basic appetites with the amenities of civilization is epitomized in an ancient burlesque skit which, I have been told by a burlesque comic, goes back in plot to Ancient Rome. I have seen it in the United States, Italy, France, Canada and England, in various versions. It centers upon a low comic who is under the impression that he is visiting a house of prostitution, but has in fact wandered into a fancy girls' school, a nurse's residence, convent or what have you. The audience is privy to the "reality" of the situation, but the comic is not. Humor derives from the enormous and visible misunderstandings that result.

child, perhaps in forms of sex play, perhaps in adult imitation of infantile responses that reach back, the ethologists claim, into feral experiences. Laughter has become also one of the factors that, for many, makes life worth living; it is also one of the factors that has come, in the evolution of human experience, to make life bearable.

Social Aspects of Laughter

We have seen that laughter depends upon a social dynamic for its psychological effect. How trite to observe, then, that man is the only animal in whom antagonisms between emotion and reason (or any analogies for these terms) are likely to be generated. But also, how true! And how devastating to ethological theories of laughter, although, accidentally perhaps, one of the outcomes of these antagonisms may well be the diminution of aggression in man.

In addition to requiring an organism in which the proper tensions are contrived, laughter also asks one more factor in which to operate, namely a social field. Here it is *directly* analogous to speech. Neither speech nor laughter appear to have much value or meet, to any reasonable degree, man's social needs unless they are regarded as communications. True enough, they both contain what might be termed a "masturbatory value," but this value, like that of masturbation itself, introduces a fantasy social field into a solitary act. It is difficult, for instance, to perceive of a clever ventriloquist as a monologist, because, in a psychological sense, he is not one person but two: himself and his dummy. The latter creates an "other" in surrogate; all ventriloquists (except in fiction) are more like themselves in their personal lives than they are like their dummys.

In the progression of culture, therefore, laughter has probably been evolved in much the same way that other communications have. Because of its essentially autonomic nature, it has, wherever we see it, come to signify *truth* in reaction. It is difficult—but not impossible—to feign laughter. It is more difficult to persuade others that one is really amused by means of artificial laughter. The specific truths that laughter tends to illustrate, as we have seen, have two sides, both of considerable social relevance. On one side, we see how tyrannical are the cultural complexities that man has created to sustain society and culture. On the other, we observe how indestructible is the essential nature of man, even in the light of his complicated social inventions. The comedies of W. S. Gilbert reflect the former phase. The genius of W. C. Fields reflects the latter. Both humorists provided situations that are, however, socially intolerable, because they either penetrated the false front of society (Gilbert) or diminished man to a mere creature of appetites (Fields).

The result is tension, social tension, because social harmony is endangered by the meeting of these forces. The tension may, as the ethologists suggest, be associated with aggression, but whether it is or not is irrelevant from society's viewpoint, if laughter results. The HAHA reaction, as Arthur Koestler calls it,[18] transmutes what is essentially a *felt* tension into laughter. In Koestler's words, "To put it differently, laughter disposes of emotional tension which has become pointless, is denied by reason, and has somehow to be worked off along psychological channels of least resistance." [19]

Feeling is therefore neutralized, and the result is a new *insight* into either man's condition, his social controls, or both. The insight is intellectual, thereby justifying the observation that receptivity to laughter *is* a form of intelligence. The laughter is also likely (but not necessarily) to provide an insight into a culturally significant matter, thereby confirming the view of those who regard social satire as the highest form of humor and subsequently view humor as a societal palliative. One more step is, however, necessary (but not inevitable) to see clearly the function of laughter in group dynamics. Insight must be followed by something else that may vary as to time and place and depend upon circumstance. The "something else" is what most fully justifies laughter in both literature and life. Koestler calls it the AH reaction, but the syllable does not capture its essence. Freud wrote about "oceanic feeling: that expansion of awareness which one experiences on occasion in an empty cathedral . . . ," [20] but such metaphors gild a lily and turn what is a common experience into something of transcendental significance, which is exaggeration. The AH reaction is assertive, creative, integrative and, most important, educative. What occurs is a spontaneous discovery, usually quite minor, which allows one a *new* perception of the relationship of society to man. As far as the writer can determine, this is *always* the result of satisfying laughter, and the result is remarkably specific almost every time: One *learns* something new about how people relate to the culture in which they live in one or another context.

The explanation of the joy of laughter is therefore quite simple. We enjoy laughter—and jokes, funny stories, comedians, farces and clowns (sacred or profane), because we *learn* from them, and the instant of discovery, combined with an investiture of knowledge about man's social state, *must be pleasing.* "Tell me another," we plead, not entirely because we enjoy the sensual pleasure of tickling. Were this true, we would hire people to tickle us when we wanted to laugh. No, tickle laughter is strangely unsatisfying, because it lacks the pay-off of real laughter. We plead for another, because we want to discover and learn *again,* and discover and learn *more,* about one of the most important aspects of life: our reciprocal relationship with culture.

This is also the reason that society values (almost everywhere) comedians and funny people so highly. They are the teachers we *like.* The

---

[18] Koestler, *The Ghost in the Machine,* pp. 184–189.

[19] *Ibid.,* p. 187.

[20] *Ibid.,* p. 189.

schoolmarms and professors we encountered in our formal education are, for the most part, the teachers we *dislike* or are forced to like. As opposed to formal learning and other types of education, the entire experience of laughter is voluntary. In other words, we do not have to laugh (or learn) unless we want to. The HAHA insight makes us want to, combining spontaneous insight and the freedom to discover with the pleasure of self-justifying learning. In this respect, also, laughter gives us a sense of freedom on *two* counts: freedom to enter into the new discovery (that is, a learning process); and freedom to gain a little more control over society in a usually unexpected or novel way. This is the reason that so much laughter is understood as irrelevant, and why laughter is least appropriate at those times when individuals give up their psychological freedom in favor of some essentially serious cultural occasion, like a funeral or income tax audit. Under these circumstances, culture is dictating decorum to the individual, and he is not allowed the freedom of discovery that laughter brings, except (sometimes) covertly. He had best keep his insights into societal processes to himself. He must guard against a spontaneous accident or a slip of the tongue, because such insights sometimes demand expression. That is, the tension they create in generating spontaneous AH reactions (and laughter) is so great that the emotion perceived is transmuted into a sense of empathetic embarrassment most of us have, at times, felt at a squelched laugh, but which it is difficult to describe.[21]

One point is certain: comedians, comic writers, cartoonists and individuals fabricating comedy will generally deny that they are, in fact, educators, teaching their audience to share their clear perception of certain aspects of man's battle with society. This stance is critical to their effectiveness, because to admit as much would implicitly rob them of their freedom to explore matters that to others are sacred. Most educators, teachers, and professors will deny, with the same vehemence, that their own teaching arts are in any way like those of the comedian if their purpose is to teach students of any age almost anything of significance concerning man's "social problems," a term *sui generis* that often puts one in a bad humor. But the record demonstrates that the great humanistic teachers (and some in the sciences) have almost *always* possessed sharp comic senses that they were not afraid to exploit in the interest of their subject.[22]

21 The inauguration of President Kennedy in 1960 comes to mind, when, in front of the dignified assembly of politicos and statesmen, the heater under the Presidential podium started burning and began to exude smoke. A little laughter was elicited from the party on the dais and probably from most television viewers. When, subsequently, the late Robert Frost found it impossible (because of the wind and light) to read the script of his own poem written for the occasion, no laughter was heard, although the situation (under other circumstances) contained the seeds of comedy. The embarrassment of the spectators was obvious, and was set to rest, to the relief of all concerned, when the aged Frost ended with the inspired recitation of an older poem he remembered well, thus saving the occasion from chaos.

22 I cannot think of one of the really talented professors under whom I studied (or to

The idea that a laughing student is a learning student is repellent only to a pedant. But American educational institutions are fortresses of pedantry and foul humor, where professors frequently cultivate a relatively frightening kind of didactic style, characterized by humorless specialization on one hand and deadpan stupidity on the other. They are easily recognized by their inability to give or take laughter seriously. They have unfortunately raised generations of students (many of the present generation, most noticeably) in their own images.

Rather than belabor these points in many contexts and extropolate from them conclusions concerning laughter and society, it is fitting to give a first-rate humorist his say in the matter. Writes Malcolm Muggeridge:

> In a healthy, civilized society, it seems to me, everyone and everything should be open to ridicule. Indeed, I would further contend that the degree of health and civilization in any given society bears a direct relation to the degree in which this principle operates. Taboos, where humor is concerned, are an admission of doubt, and derive from a sense of weakness and insecurity. The truly religious take no offense when attention is drawn to the absurdity necessarily inherent in the dogmas to which they subscribe and the ceremonies in which they participate. Protests invariably come from the conventionally religious, from the formalists for whom dogma and ceremonies constitute the whole content of faith. It is the same with politicians. Those who most object to being ridiculed have least confidence in the policies they advocate. It is the same with moralists. If they complain that some cherished principle is blasphemed by the humorous treatment of its application, then it is certain that in their hearts they doubt the principle's ultimate validity.[23]

Muggeridge's principle applies to every aspect of social life. He is as amused by the starchy, hard-headed rigidity of the conservative as by frivolous infatuations and faiths of the liberal. The Queen of England, to his eye, cuts as absurd a figure as a growling, discontented, petulant "teen-aged anarchist." True humor, if it is to live up to its own civilizing potential, must be, in the broadest sense, non-partisan and anti-didactic, and the same requirements must be held for true laughter. For this reason (and others), laughter often manifests the psychological potential of a highly effective, occasionally also fundamentally unmoral, device for influencing, in a highly specialized manner, human dispositions.

---

whose lectures I exposed myself) who did not have a first-rate sense of humor and did not exploit it in his teaching. This includes one or two chemistry and physics teachers at Stuyvesant High School in New York and at Princeton (where I studied engineering under Army auspices). Professors Gilbert Highet, Walter Prichard Eaton, Charles A. Siepmann and others knew how to be extremely funny about the right things at the right times. And, of course, the transcripts of the lectures of great teachers, from Socrates to Conant, are almost invariably spiced with a comic sense.

[23] *The Most of Malcolm Muggeridge* (New York: Simon and Schuster, 1966), pp. 320–321.

Persuasive Aspects of Laughter

If the psychology of laughter has been neglected in our annals, then the serious consideration of humorous persuasion has somehow been more than neglected. The field is a wasteland. What information we have on how humor persuades, and why, is fragmentary, cursory and suppositional. This is strange, because humor has been employed for cultural persuasion since the satires of Aristophanes, and some of it constitutes the bitterest (or bitter-sweetest) political, social and cultural statements in mankind's ledger.

After Aristophanes, one probably discovers the first self-conscious use of humor, in its quasi-didactic form, in Roman literature and drama: writings like those of Petronius and dramas like those of Plautus, particularly his *Amphitryon*, labeled the first "tragi-comedy"—an ironic story that has haunted the Western theatre to the present day. In our tradition, we are familiar with the socio-religious thrusts of Chaucer and the numerous European comic exposés of corruption in church and government in the late Middle Ages and early Renaissance. Shakespeare's comedies—once one puts aside the banalities of *A Midsummer Night's Dream* and *As You Like It*—follow Roman, not Greek or English, models in their satirical thrusts. A *Comedy of Errors* is pure Plautus—plus Shakespeare's remarkable satiric eye. His best comedy (not funniest, but sharpest) is *Measure for Measure*, in some ways a humorous version of *Hamlet*, exploring with both seriousness and frivolity life from the palaces to the bawdy houses of the wide-open city of Vienna. It is, from the moralist's viewpoint, a brilliant tragi-comedy in the Roman tradition.

The funniest Elizabethan, though, was Jonson. And *The Alchemist* and *Volpone* still rank among the wittiest jests of money, rank, caste, class and professional vanity in our tradition. They compare favorably with the best of the amazing Molière, except that the latter composed his quack doctors, misanthropes and bumbling aristocrats for the self-flagellations of nobles of the court, an audience of specialized and acutely refined risibilities, while Jonson apparently wrote for the groundlings.

British literature is, of course, filled to the brim with the persuasion of "satire," an unbecoming term[24] but aptly descriptive of Dean Swift's modest proposals, the best of the comedies of the Restoration, and a few of the literary events of the past century, most notably *Alice In Wonderland*. In America, the burden of humor has been borne by playwrights of present

[24] I believe it was George S. Kaufman who said, "Satire is what closes on Friday night." And if he meant by "satire" persuasive humor in which the persuasion was too obvious and heavy-handed (as I suspect he did), he was placing his finger neatly upon cause for the decline of satire in our time. Much unfunny searching for humor, displaying inept writing or dull development, is accepted because it is supposedly satirical. *Macbird, Red White and Maddox* on stage, *Portnoy's Complaint* among best-sellers, and *Putney Swope* among many other movies, fall, as far as I am concerned, into Kaufman's "Friday night" category.

obscurity (Royall Tyler and Anna Cora Mowott Ritchie, for instance) and better known prose artists like Washington Irving and Mark Twain, to say nothing of Thomas Nast, America's first (and, in some ways, still best) graphic comic artist.[25]

No purpose is served, however, by continuing beyond this thumbnail sketch into the history of persuasive comedy. It is still ubiquitous, sometimes more comic than persuasive, or vice-versa, but a list of persuasive comedians in our present culture is impressive and worth a moment's consideration: The *Laugh-In* people on TV; Al Capp, the recently deceased Rube Goldberg and Herblock in the press; monologists like Bill Cosby, Flip Wilson, Pat Paulsen, Godfrey Cambridge, Dick Gregory, Buddy Hackett, Myron Cohen, Alan King, *et al.*; the young political types like the various former *Second City* theatre companies; female comics like Phyllis Diller and Carol Burnett; young film makers like Larry Tucker and Paul Mazurski; old timers like Red Skelton, Jackie Gleason and others who seem to deal in subtle persuasion by introducing social, cultural or sexual points of view to humorous contexts mercifully clear of didacticism.

As Muggeridge has indicated, laughter is also a function of freedom, confirming to a degree the psychological hypothesis of this chapter. The dominant mood in totalitarian countries is somber, and, when freedom of any kind is constricted, laughter is suspect. Comedy and the comic spirit are difficult to control. Even when it is controlled and directed against certain objects, therefore, laughter is likely sometimes to get out of hand and turn subversive—or it fails to amuse. Comedies today, for instance, are written and played on stage and screen in the Soviet Union and Communist China. But, from all accounts, they are usually either shallow and harmless or heavy-handed, not-too-funny attempts at satire.[26] Laughter in Nazi Germany was eventually and frequently construed as a symptom of psychosis. Some of Streicher's anti-Semitic pornography was supposed to be funny, but its appeal was directed, it appears, to the deranged. In our own culture, laughter does not fare well where and when liberties are constricted or individuals are bound by dogmas and determinisms. People who devote their energies to doing good to other people (including many educators) culti-

---

[25] Nast is best known for his comic newspaper drawings. But his fine oil painting of theatrical comic William Burton is his masterpiece, and, in my opinion, ranks as comic portraiture (or art) with the best of Daumier, Lautrec and Hogarth. The picture hangs in The Players' quarters on Gramercy Square in New York City.

[26] Gogol excepted, most pre-revolutionary Russian comedy was not very funny either, but neither was Tsarist Russia a particularly free society. We often forget the generally dark nature of the Russian and Ukranian character. Chekhov was, fundamentally, a comic writer, and his one-act plays are still delightful to read or see performed. His dramas, some claim, are also Russian comedies because "at least, everyone dies happily." Evaluating what pre-Maoist Chinese comic theatre and cinema I have seen is impossible, filtered as it was by time and cultural and language difficulties. I have been told, however, that laughter is frequently interpreted in the value system of the Red Guards as a sign of incipient deviation.

vate a superficial lexicon of dinnertime jokes and sometimes play with invective and sarcasm, but the seriousness of their mission in life blunts their satirical experiments. Teachers, frequently both dull and frustrated, raise our young in those humorless fortresses previously described as schools. In most bureaucracies, laughter is a sign that someone is cracking under the strain. Freedom *to* laugh, it seems, is also freedom *for* laughter, and when the dominant mood of a people is free the atmosphere is uninhibited, and laughter is heard, as in a children's playground, for instance. When the reverse obtains, the symptoms of oppression are difficult to detect, because one is rarely conscious of the laughter he does not hear.

The element of freedom is therefore necessary before persuasive laughter reaches attitudes, opinions or actions. (It is doubtful that beliefs are much affected by laughter.) And, because a free climate is necessary, the unpredictable outcomes of laughter must not constitute a threat to the status quo, or, at least, they must not be regarded as an uncontainable threat. Certain humorous communications have been distributed underground or by "the grapevine" in the most tyrannical of states, usually in the form of jokes. They are treasured precisely because they *are* a breadth of freedom in an otherwise constricted environment, for instance, the rash of anti-Hitler jokes that began to surface in Germany after (approximately) 1943, and the occasional satires that are reported circulating in today's communist nations.

American ethnic humor—Jewish, Italian, Negro, Swedish etc.—once symbolized this kind of climate, but, for reasons treated subsequently, the atmosphere for telling them in the United States has lately changed. It is less free in this respect than it once was. Negro humor is acceptable, if Negroes tell or perform it. Homosexual humor, jokes at the expense of the unwashed young and the square establishment are generally permitted. Also acceptable are political and military humor and twice-told moron jokes. The latter are sometimes pinned vaguely onto ethnic groups like Italians or Poles, or given a sadistic context and called "black" humor. ("Momma, what's a vampire?" "Shut up, and drink your blood before it clots.") Even in so-called free countries, freedom shifts its locus with remarkable speed. Contexts for sexual or scatological humor have widened rapidly in recent years, both in professional entertainments and general discourse.

When humor's edge slices into consciousness, it is often remarkably effective. The Canadian broadcast, *The Investigator,* saturated the recording market in the United States in the 1950's, and its serio-comic barbs were unquestionably related to Senator Joseph McCarthy's downfall as an anti-communist witch-hunter. Vice President Spiro Agnew has had greater political trouble to date with the opposition of laughter than the opposition of serious criticism, although he himself uses laughter effectively in his speeches. An historical case may be made for the concept that once a people have laughed at an institution or individual, it is extremely difficult ever again to take them seriously. Charles Chaplin's futile attempt at serious political statements on film (and in other ways) some years ago was an example, and, to some degree, so was the general satirical thrust directed against Lyndon Johnson during the last two years of his administration. Noel Coward's frivolities have kept the public from due consideration of the formidable serious side of his creative gifts, just as they insulated him from a British peerage until he was seventy years old.[27]

Wielding the rapier of humor is a difficult art, chancy even in trivial contexts like advertising, and more dangerous the greater the stakes of the game. William Joyce, Germany's Lord "Haw Haw" during World War II, was, most authorities agree, a poor propagandist. But, in his broadcasts to England during the "phony war" period in 1939 and 1940, he *was* funny. In a rush to post-war vengeance, and in the face of uncertainties concerning his nationality (he may have been an American), Joyce was executed by the English as a traitor. He was punished, not because of what he had accomplished for the Nazis (which was probably little), but because he had made people want to laugh at what they regarded as serious. His case is a good lesson in the vagaries of comedy and the seriousness of laughter.[28] While contemporary theories emphasize its benign and therapeutic qualities, laughter, like the freedom to which it is so intimately related, portends at times both power and danger in the hands of a fool. A fool may be pitiable, but there is also a chance that he will be laughed at, loved and even worshipped for his gift of evoking humor.

Joyce and others like him were fools. The laughter such people stimulate usually and eventually destroys them. Psychotic laughter has been mentioned above, and a poet has written, "Madness, we fancy, gave an ill timed birth/To grinning laughter and to frantic mirth." Lacking sufficient data, we cannot discuss such laughter in detail. It is sufficient to note here that laughter not only requires freedom—and gives one a sense of freedom—but it may also be used to fabricate an *illusion* of freedom. This is a psychological danger that is characterized best, perhaps, by the stylized laughter of the Devil (personified in drama by mad doctors from Faust and Frankenstein to Strangelove), that wily spiritual psychopath whose anti-morality personifies evil. Clinical laughter and Gothic laughter, both versions of the Devil's mirth, are widely understood in our cultural tradition. They symptomize a grasp after a transcendental, monumental freedom that liberates the possessor (or possessed) from all obligations of every sort, be they social,

---

27 That Coward had produced, written, directed and performed in one of the finest serious films ever made in England, *In Which We Serve* (about the British navy in World War II), did not forgive his heresy in composing the song *Mad Dogs and Englishmen* years before. A generation of colonials had to die off before he was finally knighted. He deserved a peerage, incidentally, in 1943 for his finest satirical song "Don't Let's Be Beastly to the Germans" on *its* merits alone, a masterpiece that is today too sadly prophetic to be funny.

28 See Gordon, Falk and Hodapp, *The Idea Invaders*, pp. 43–46.

moral or spiritual. Such freedom, we know, is impossible for rational men living together to achieve. But this does not prevent the irrational from attempting to reach for it, laughing all the while they try.

Conclusion

The orderly study of laughter in human affairs follows the interests of a few essayists and investigators, all of whom appear to offer equally satisfactory (and unsatisfactory) theories concerning why men laugh. That laughter is related both to aggression and repression seems clear, as do the feral antecedents of laughter in the socializing process of man, on the journey along the recent part of his biological evolutionary trail.

Functionally, laughter displays a number of traits. 1.) It is a form of communication. 2.) It releases individual tensions. 3.) It usually diminishes aggression and impulses to violence. 4.) It is often a signal that "play behavior" is about to begin. 5.) It may release repressed feelings. 6.) It may cover up sensitivities and social gaucheries. Laughter, seen thus, permits two general viewpoints: One emphasizes the cerebral, intellectual quality of laughter; the other its emotive content. In any case, laughter represents an ongoing tension between feeling (or emotion) and reason, or their symbolic equivalents.

In a social field as well, laughter releases tension in much the same manner, yielding insight; and, it is hypothesized, a form of *learning* is the result. This educative factor is essentially pleasant and creative—and provides a perception of freedom from the strictures of some aspect of culture, also felt to be pleasurable. Scope for such activity relates intimately to the tonus and mood of a culture in its social and political aspects, not only in regard to the static cultural climate of a society but its capacity for change as well.

Laughter is a persuasive device but difficult to employ in a regular manner. Cultural history books highlight the way satire has served as an institutional corrective. Social restraints have been applied to humorists in countries where fears of change in the established order have dominated. Areas of permissible and non-permissible laughter must exist either in a free environment, a free segment of a restricted environment, or within the borders of an illusory field of freedom in an individual's own consciousness. Laughter free of all social and moral strictures, however, is probably psychotic and dangerous, although few developed insights into sadistic and schizophrenic amusement are generally available to date.

Chapter 18

THE POWER OF POWER

Essentially all depends on me, on my existence, because of my political talents. Furthermore, there is the fact that probably no one will ever again have the confidence of the whole German people as I have. There will probably never again in the future be a man with more authority than I have. My existence is therefore a factor of great value.

Adolph Hitler

THE MAIN REASON that power holds such fascination for men is simply because its uses and abuses ramify into every facet of social life, involving the roles people play in their common work-a-day and domestic settings. Power shifts, undulates, gathers and dissipates almost everywhere, in an endless game, inducing in the spectator a fascination not unlike that of staring into a fire and watching the shifting configurations of flames.

The family (or orphan asylum) in which each of us was raised responded to configurations of power. As we matured, we personally gained power, physical, psychological and intellectual. Exercises of our power are related to the way we earn our livings and our relationships with each other in all phases of life. In each context, power has its place, its significance determined by situational and psychological factors. Knowledge, as the old saying goes, *is* power. But talent is also power. Money is power. Sexual attractiveness is power. Momentary control of a motor car is power. Motherhood and fatherhood are both power, and so forth, in an endless list of factors by which we exercise measures of control over our environment and/or other people.

Most theorists of power, from Aristotle to the present—with the exception of a psychoanalytical deviationist or two—have construed power primarily in the partially mythological and partially realistic context of political exchange.[1] The philosopher's tendency has been to depersonalize power

[1] The study of power theory is not for the casual reader. The *Politic* of Aristotle, however, represents the best starting point, followed by Plato's *Republic*. Some of the

and relate it to social affairs in a more or less abstract manner. When Hitler, later in the speech quoted above, indicated that he *was* Germany, his intent, most probably, was not to advocate the apparently foolish notion that any man may *be in fact* a state. He probably meant quite the reverse: that the political entity of Germany, as he saw it, was encapsulated in his own person in exactly the manner that hereditary monarchs have been holding power (and judges, addressed as "the court," hold theirs) for thousands of years. The Bishop signifies the power of the church; just as the principal signifies the power of the school and father (sometimes) signifies the power of the home.

The major construction of the term "power," and the one employed by theorists, is therefore political. This is the result partly of the historical heritage of the Greeks who developed a highly sophisticated political system and were intensely and sagely curious about it. For them, in both drama and philosophy, strictly *personal* problems were of too little consequence, and ultimate *ontological* problems were of too great a consequence, for extensive direct personal consideration. A compromise was effected in the evolution of the *political* problem.[2]

Antigone, for instance (in the tragic drama of Sophocles) has involved herself in an enormously difficult personal problem with her uncle Creon by virtue of her insistence she bury the dead body of her brother, Polynices, who was killed in warfare. The complications are unimportant here. She is also engaged in an enormous philosophical-ontological (and theological) problem concerning the action which she *knows* is "right." Sophocles has neither the ability or inclination to arbitrate the situation on a personal or philosophical-religious level. Instead, like most Greek thinkers, his approach is political: He sees Antigone's problem as a conflict of essentially ritualistic interests between a King of Thebes (Creon) and his niece, each of whom is acting in what they understand to be, broadly speaking, "the public interest." Although the conflict eventually kills Antigone and crushes Creon, the political problem is solved in a dramatically arresting

---

modern theories will be discussed below, but among the great philosophers of power were Rousseau, Nietzsche, Marx, Weber, Veblen and Mannheim, bringing us almost up to the present moment. See C. Wright Mills (ed.), *Images of Man* (New York: George Braziller Inc., 1960), for excellent selections from the writing of some of the latter thinkers. Note also such studies as William Withers, *Freedom Through Power* (New York: John Day Publ., 1965); Robert M. MacIver, *The Modern State* (London: Oxford University Press, 1964): Carl J. Friedrich, *Man and His Government* (New York: McGraw-Hill Book Co., 1963); Robert A. Nisbet, *The Quest for Community* (New York: Galaxy Books, 1962); and Ronald V. Samson, *The Psychology of Power* (New York: Random House, 1968). Other volumes on power theory will be cited in the chapter when references are made to them.

2 The rise of the concepts of the "public" and "private" domains of behavior through Machiavelli (see below) is expertly summarized in Hannah Arendt, *The Human Condition*, pp. 23–69.

personal manner and a resolution satisfactory to the requirements of the gods, in other words in a *philosophically* valid way.

The heritage of the Greek philosophers and dramatists is still with us. When Machiavelli picked up the classic threads of power theory in the Renaissance, he entered into an enormous revival of ancient modes of thought, social and cultural as well as artistic. *The Prince,* as we noted in Chapter 4, was a corporeal being. But he also stood for the abstract despotic political power of the state. In a sense, Machiavelli was in his text designating limits of personal conduct for a man. But in a larger context he was, also like his classical mentors, holding the Prince's soul up to God, seeking divine sanction for the ruler's conduct. The clash between these two forces, the personality of the Prince and his immortal soul, resolved by abstracting and detaching power from the man, disregarding theological problems, and construing power as a political matter—again, for the good of the people—is probably the most ancient, honorable, and frequently perverted idea in the history of Western thought.

Hegel, hundreds of years later, de-personified whatever vestiges of personification remained in the notion of political processes, and nearly all theorists of power to the present day have followed his main constructions. Marx was his most noted disciple, but political power, as we conceive of it today even in non-Marxist nations, is fundamentally Hegelian. Academic political science and sociology, no matter how they color their constructions with the flavor of human personality, generally evaluate political life as the confluence and conflicts of *forces,* not *men.* Vectors of force may be drawn along class or caste lines, act as functions of economic or religious interest, race, occupation, age and status. But their most significant aspect is that they are basically depersonalized forces: the aged, the young, the urbanites, Republicans, Democrats, anti-vivisectionists and on and on, from one impersonal category to another. And, in the modern lexicon, one group will only achieve power (if it is to be recognized by others as power) if and when its force is translated into political terms—that is, when that force is objectified in such a way as to influence phenomena of social significance.[3]

---

[3] The mythic Howard Hughes is a good example here. Because he shuns publicity, the personal Hughes hardly exists from a political perspective. Like other men, I am sure he acts personally in ways commensurate with his mortal state. The fact that he, personally, is very rich has no political significance, however. He may wear custom-made suits and live on a diet of lobsters; or he may, as rumor has had it, dress like a slob, eat in diners and drive a broken-down, second-hand car. On the other hand, when he becomes an economic vector, and buys and sells airlines, motion picture studios and a good portion of the city of Las Vegas, he suddenly achieves enormous political power, and grown men quake in their boots at the mention of his name. Howard Hughes is, however, little different from the average man in a modern state from the Hegelian viewpoint, except that he wields more power in a specific context than does the average man. Politically speaking, he is "somebody." Personally speaking, he is "nobody," which is apparently just the way he wants it.

Deep in our consciousness, however, we evidently are not put off (or fooled) by the old illusions of political power. We tend too generously to personify the Hegelian forces of thesis, antithesis and synthesis into "good guys," "bad guys" and "compromisers," and are too copiously prone to accept the dream of political power as it acts upon the persons of the men and women in public life. Nor would we find as much satisfaction in terms like "power structure," "power politics" and "black power" as we do unless we believed that they were anthropomorphic or embued with the spirit of life. For we continue to believe, in Arendt's words, that in the public (or political) world an alchemy occurs that "gathers us together and yet prevents our falling over each other, so to speak," [4] and thereby achieve a resultant force that we call "power." And, for most of us, although (like Browning's dragon) we cannot see, touch, hear or smell power, we can observe what it *does,* and therefore we intuit strongly that it exists and that we live in the wake of its handiwork.

Conspiracies of Power

For political power to become psychologically viable it must first, be concretized and second, personified. The consequences of ths processes are many, one of which is the illusion that the miracle works the other way around: that men holding power for various reasons, acting in concert, become political forces. This is our conventional wisdom, at one with certain (or most) historical viewpoints. It is entirely consonant with commonsense. It happens, however, also to be almost entirely false and creates strange consequences when people believe it.

Its temporal error may be demonstrated in many ways, but a study of the history of any major institution of power reveals that its political power is a scenario at the mercy of the socio-cultural winds of its time, and that the men who personify that history are distinctively cast actors, called from the infinite varieties of a human intellectual and physical power pool available at any moment. For example, the history of Catholic power in Europe is *not* the history of the power of Popes (although some were colorful and variously powerful) but a political history. Changes in the ruling oligarchy in the Soviet Union, too well known to retell here, indicate how leaders serve political causes by playing inevitably determined roles, and, like Stalin, Trotsky, Beria and others, occasionally die or vanish from the scene at propitious moments.

From the perspective of those of us who lived through Hitler's hegemony in Europe, we may find it difficult to lower our adrenalin level long enough to see him *both* as a deranged pawn *and* an innocent dupe of political history, but this is precisely what he was. *Der Führer* was the creation of the Versailles Treaty, the Weimar Republic, Prussian militarists, Rhur

---

[4] *Ibid.*, p. 48.

industrialists and a Teutonic proclivity towards scapegoating, among other factors. Any number of alternate "Hitlers" might have played the role, some perhaps *more* effectively than Hitler, as horrible as this idea is to contemplate.

The consequences of this particular viewpoint are many, and they have recently been clearly expressed by such politically antagonistic individuals as the late President Eisenhower, on one hand, the late sociologist C. Wright Mills, on the other. Ike, in his farewell address (or speech writer Malcolm Moos) cautioned us to beware of the aggregation of power by the military-industrial complex lest it upset the balance of political powers at the time (1960) in the USA. Certainly, President Eisenhower had had wide experience with both parties, and excoriated the very military establishment to which he belonged and from which he had gained his fame—and power.

The American public subsequently elected one of the most powerful politicians in the nation to its presidency, a Catholic liberal who belonged neither to the industrial nor military establishment and is reputed to have called our captains of industry "sons of bitches" (or words to that effect) more or less in public. Implication of cause and effect are left to the reader.

Eisenhower merely voiced a view that had first gained respectability in Europe in the past century and has been generally associated with the philosopher Proudhon, that power, class conflict and conspiracy are to be expected as natural outcomes of representative government. Proudhon excoriated property holders as thieves. But modern conspiratorial theories lump together various people representing different interests into congeries of compound and complex conspiracies. These are either lateral combinations, like Eisenhower's military-industrial complex, or vertical combinations. The former are usually overtly identifiable. The latter impute powers *behind* other powers, operating covertly. (Thus we hear that student revolts are not spontaneous; Communist agitators, we are told in whispers, *must be behind* them. The Black Power movement is a cover, supposedly, for this or that subversive agency—and similar rumors.) In other words, conspiracies are either open or closed: *lateral conspiracies are generally open; vertical conspiracies are usually closed.*

Mills chooses, however, to warn us of an open conspiracy that he believes is closed to the common man, because he cannot or will not observe it.[5] The conspiratorial constituents encompass slightly more broad territory than Eisenhower's: the military, the industrialists *and the politicians*. Mills charges that they each are made up of the same people. In a sentence, albeit a long one, the conspiracy he has found centers on an "inner core of the power élite (consisting), first, of those who interchange commanding roles at the top of one dominant institutional order with those in another; the admiral who is now a banker and a lawyer and who heads up an impor-

---

[5] C. Wright Mills, *The Power Elite* (New York: Oxford University Press, 1956).

tant federal commission; the corporation executive whose company was one of the two or three leading war materiel producers who is now Secretary of Defense; the general who dons civilian clothes to sit on the political directorate and then becomes a member of the board of directors of a leading economic corporation." [6]

Somewhere vertically behind this élite (on far broader terrain than the core indicated above) perform a batch of court-jesters and hangers-on, the power blocs of entertainers, educators, prominent citizens, newsmen and celebrities who live off fallout from the activities of the élite and provide the impression, mostly via mass communications, of wide popular support for a conspiracy which is never treated like one. In effect, these satellites interpret for the masses the doings of the power élite—meaning that they lie about its conspiratorial nature for public consumption.

The people, it is understood, cannot either appreciate or understand the complexity of this conspiracy. A sentient public might. But Mills would have us believe that we, the common citizens, conceive of ourselves as "public" in the somewhat sentimental nineteenth century tradition of idealists like Jefferson and Comte. In truth, however, we are not a "public" but a "mass," quite a different matter. We are fundamentally impotent politically, duped by our mass communications industries (branches, in many cases, of the industrial complex) and unable to translate any counterforce we may individually generate into action, because the channels of activation are controlled by the élite.[7]

Mills' version of power conspiratory sounds familiar on two counts. First, it is obviously drawn from the prescribed pre-revolutionary stance of the garden-variety Marxist. Economic determinism, control of the proletariat and a duped bourgeoisie are all entries in the agitator's handbook—familiar, trite and probably irrelevant to contemporary politics, even for graying liberals. Second, Mills' élite echoes suspiciously the present campus rebel's vile "Establishment," except that today's hirsute college protestors are unable to employ Mills' almost talmudic ratiocinations of dialectic argument in their catch-all rebellion against everyone—including old Socialists—who looks to the past to understand the future.

More important, it is the common-sense logic inherent in such a conspiracy concept, not only the conspiratorial nature of agglomerations of power, but *the way that the rascals are supposed to get away with it* that seems quite reasonable. It is the *psychological* validity of the simple model,

---

[6] *Ibid.*, p. 288. The general outlines of the power élite, while described in detail in Mills' entire volume, are summarized on pp. 269–297.

[7] Mills discussed the "public" and the "mass" in great (and interesting) detail on pp. 298–324, in his usual trenchant and apparently reasonable manner. So much of Mills' genius was, however, dissipated into Marxist clichés that they frequently befog his erudition, keen feeling for history, sociological idealism and sense of humor. What a pity he did not live to outgrow his deterministic fervor, the direction in which he seemed to be moving at the time of his death.

however, that is suspect, first, on the grounds that may contradict what we have already observed about the psychology of political power: that power is a projection and personification of forces, not a result of the combination of personal powers turned political. Second, the concept is suspect—merely suspect--because it is clearly redolent of paranoia.

One of the most bewildering aspects of the classical paranoid—contrary to general impressions—is the extraordinary reasonableness of the patient's explanations for his delusions; they are part of a system which is invariably sophistic and self-consistent. The result is one of the major difficulties in diagnosing paranoia, frequently, and it ends occasionally in gross errors: what is taken to be a paranoid fancy turns out to be true.[8] The difference between the two is a thin, light line that makes psychiatrists uncomfortable, and the same risk occurs in the diagnosis of *any* construction of political life as faintly paranoid. Conspiracies *have existed* in politics, but one is hard pressed to find historical precedence for Mills' particular mischief-makers, except in the works of obviously paranoid historians.

A. A. Berle, in his recent and, in some respects, definitive study of power[9] is correctly skeptical of conspiracy theories of power, in contemporary Western society at least. His view is based on an initial rejection of the social myth of "class power," in his words.[10] He repeats clearly the usual non-Hegelian principle that classes, as the social theorist understands them in the power games he plays, are each invariably abstractions of but partial social and psychological allegiances for most people. Strict divisions into class interests may have been a viable undertaking in simple societies where each human being understood his social role unilaterally as a Jew, a craftsman, a farmer, a worker or a teacher, to the necessary exclusion of other interests.

Today, for many reasons, most of them obvious, the matter is more complicated. And, as Berle notes, "Almost any class line that can be drawn intersects and overlaps some other class line" [11]—one, at least, and often a number of them. Because our culture is now so pluralized, and because the effects of that pluralization have been so completely integrated in the psychologies of our peoples (and here the effects of the mass instruments of

---

[8] One main peculiarity of paranoia is that, to the objective observer, a person's report that conspiracies are being incubated against him in dark places, that FBI agents are tapping his telephone and the Mafia is trying to chloroform him is a paranoid delusion *only when* these facts are untrue. If, on the other hand they are true—as they may be —the poor patient is not paranoid. When they are *partly* true—or true enough to be extenuated neurotically into a more elaborate scheme than reality provides—we are still faced with a difficult clinical problem, sometimes impossible to solve. The latter manifestation, the extenuation of reality into paranoid-like delusions while under stress, is commonly seen both inside and outside of the clinic.

[9] Adolf A. Berle, *Power* (New York: Harcourt, Brace and World, Inc., 1969).

[10] See *ibid.*, pp. 67–73, 159–161, for a discussion of "class power" as Berle sees it.

[11] *Ibid.*, p. 70.

communication have had a crucial effect), class interest is, at the outset and at the least, a concept requiring many qualifications that its exponents, like Mills and others, rarely give it.

What Berle would have us consider is that class theories—based on economic, hereditary or geographical deterministic forces—may aptly have described feudal societies to the present day, nations moving into simple technologies; and they may apply directly at the moment to certain Latin American dictatorships and a number of Asian countries. They also manifest relevance for our culture; we do, naturally or unnaturally, produce communities of interest and welfare that may be categorized in such elemental terms as "labor," "industrialists," "merchants" and similar terms. But their application is rarely either unilateral or clear cut, with the exception of a relative handful of individuals living voluntarily in their atavistic illusions of societies that have long passed. Most especially, Berle notes that the once all-pervading power of economic determinism seems rapidly to be losing force—both as a revolutionary slogan and a social vector—the result of Keynesian economics, welfare programs, unbelievable material prosperity and a historical climate of economic uncertainties that seem often to tumble established empires and hurl the most unlikely people into positions of affluence, apparently more at the will of God than the ghost of Marx.

As Berle indicates, if the conspiracy of class power in a number of ways smells strongly of fiction, it is not for a dearth of impulses by the rich and the powerful to conspire for their common welfare. What the rich and powerful discover, however, is that, in a society marked by plural psychological class loyalties—and, to a degree as well, by apathy and confusion that such cross-interests generate—conspiracy is more difficult to accomplish than activists of the left have led them to believe. When we talk of "communities of economic interests," we are usually indulging in wishful thinking. Other cohesive factors like race, religion, profession, taste, place of residence and age, all shift so rapidly and infringe upon human consciousness in so many ways (with variable strength from numerous directions) that the preconditions for conspiratorial power manipulation are simply *not met*. Some communities of interest, of course, form provisionally unified blocs—like conservationists, associations of entrepreneurs, high-tariff people and similar groups. But they are limited in power, first, by counter-groups, and second, by mixed loyalties within their own ranks. Even the military establishment is held together more sturdily by the bureaucracy of the Pentagon than a communality of mutual interests between Army, Navy and Air Force and high (within or between their own branches of service) echelon officers who span differences in socio-political orientations from Admiral Rickover to General Le May.[12]

[12] As far as "captains of industry" and "capitalist, imperialist war lords of Wall Street are concerned, their collusion with political bigwigs is so egregious that they

If power, then, does not rest ultimately upon a community of class interests, and, as we have seen, if all power is essentially political (regardless of how we create analogies for it or personify it) what are the sources of power in man's culture? Berle argues that all power eventually ends up as a personal quality of the men who hold it.[13] He does not underestimate the force of politics—and plural class interests expressed in various ways—but for Berle, men and women are the instruments who finally exercise power. Once gained and once affirmed, and as it accumulates, it is therefore the distinctive personalities of individuals that determines how power is used—with a reservation that, if it is not apparently so used to satisfy the political wants of his constituency, the individual who holds power will lose it, either by default (as other individuals crowd him out), by the ballot or by revolution.

Power and Personality

The will to power is not exclusively a human characteristic. Its analogies appear in the animal kingdom. But power-drives in antelopes, walruses or prairie dogs are of no more than passing interest in the study of how the urge for power influences human personality. Despite speculation by ethologists, observed power in other species speaks to human beings in a language of metaphors. If the will to power rests in our chromosomes, we possess no device yet (short of fancy) to describe through what process it emerges. If the behavior of animals has influenced man's power structures, as far as we know, it is because, consciously or unconsciously, men have been influenced—as ethologists decidedly have—by looking at animals and imputing humanoid motives to their behaviors.

The possibility of a human power instinct is another matter, as reasonable a concept as the construction of libido or any other particularly noticeable appetency that seems to be widespread. Certainly, an infant's education in the control and management of the environment is also an introduction to the delights of power. The expression "born leader" makes common sense; individuals seem to control their environment differentially—or allow it to control them differently. Such variations appear at ex-

appear to prosper only when their liberal enemies have power; and they suffer their defeats, recessions and depressions exclusively at the hands of their friends. A Republican fiscal policy, directed essentially by Nixon, the capitalist lawyer, caused the present (at the moment of writing) collapse of the stock market and current recession. Policy, that is, combined with the chief executive's genuinely heroic (but misunderstood) efforts to get our troops out of the Far East and move the nation out of what has been, in effect for years, a wartime economy. At present, the political "big business conspiracy" in Washington seems to be dealing nothing but blows to the jugular at those captains of industry who have been living by government contracts for military materiel, off and on, since 1940. If this sort of behavior indicates a political-military-industrial conspiracy, it is the most unusual conspiracy since the Tsarina and Rasputin.

[13] See *ibid.*, pp. 59–67.

tremely early ages and, as those of us who have taught very young children are aware, frequently seem quite stable factors of character.

In the mature adult, the drive to power may be, under certain circumstances, associated with neurosis. Examples abound where petty bureaucrats are allowed free run: in government, industry and particularly in the administrative ranks of schools and colleges.[14] The fictional Captain Queeg in *The Caine Mutiny* is one of the most familiar power neurotics in contemporary letters.

Power psychotics are better known and more obvious—either when they succeed, or fail, or both. Megalomania makes headlines, mostly because it is nearly always accompanied by that ultimate gesture of power: the murder of other human beings. Frequently, this destruction is hurled back at the megalomaniac, and he becomes the victim of murder. Psychotics tend to surround themselves with other psychotics or pre-psychotics, and the impulse to kill is peculiarly contagious among paranoid and psychopathic personalities. The power psychotic (and sometimes, inadvertently, the power neurotic) is invariably playing a dangerous game, but danger is precisely its appeal for him. As copulation is required by the satyriasist, so manipulation is needed by the power psychotic. Apparently, he only feels he is living at times when he is exercising power.

Some men seek power, others have it thrust upon them. Berle, from his position for many years next to men of great power, observes that the experience of power is one that seems to display a primarily emotional thrust. A person in great power must place power's obligations above those personal concerns about which most of our lives center. This, in itself, may be extremely disorienting. "Some men go to pieces under the experience," writes Berle. "One of the first impacts is realization that the obligation of power takes precedence over other obligations formerly held nearest and dearest. A man in power can have no friends in the sense that he must refuse to the friend consideration that, power aside, he would once have accorded." [15] Some men find the pressure intolerable and simply break. Others grow in wisdom and effectiveness. Some gain insight, expressed by Tolstoy, that no amount of power can control entirely immediate events or the whims of fate and destiny. Yet this is always a surprise to those who discover it, in power or out.[16] And the inability to recognize it often forces

[14] My favorite fictional treatment of the academic power neurosis is C. P. Snow's *The Masters* (New York: Doubleday and Co., Inc., 1951), a novel with a British setting that describes what I am afraid is a universal neurotic disorder.

[15] *Ibid.*, p. 65.

[16] One of the most graphic recent illustrations of this principle was the transmutation of President John F. Kennedy from one of the most powerful leaders of state to a mere corpse practically in public view in a matter of seconds. Why was *his* death so much greater a stunning blow than thousands of others before and since which may have been fundamentally more tragic? The spectacular loss of power involved may be one explanation.

the power holder to construct a world of illusion that he *can* control, at least to his psychological satisfaction of the moment.[17]

Power is lost in one of four ways: by death, by abdication, by replacement or expiration of office, or as the result of a revolt or revolution. Again, replaced power holders' behavior may vary, even under similar circumstances. After being succeeded as President, Harry and Mrs. Truman drove alone back to Independence, Missouri where they have lived to this day. Truman's retirement from power neither embittered him nor apparently left him with an unusually inflated ego. He went about the business of being an ex-President (writing memoirs, doing party chores and erecting memorials) with dignity and grace. If we are to believe Lord Moran, Winston Churchill reacted quite differently, suffering deep depressions and melancholy states, venting considerable spleen upon the public for its ingratitudes to him. Khrushchev, unlike the exiled or murdered Soviet leaders before him, appears content (presumably aware of the alternatives) to take up a bucolic life with equanimity and display what appears to outsiders as happy senility. Rudolph Hess, his life spared at the Nuremberg trials, has survived his prison sentence into what is by now probably genuine senility and sustained his pretense of madness—begun shortly after his flight to England in 1941, supposedly to negotiate peace with the British.

The exercise of power invariably leaves its mark on people, and few men of power are the same after they have experienced it as they were before. For this reason (among others), some people resist the temptation to assume power because of what they fear it may do to them personally. Others strive for it avidly. Failure to achieve it yields bitterness. Success yields uncertainty.

Still others are apparently propelled into power by forces greater than themselves. This is usually an illusion. If men like Lyndon Johnson (or Andrew Johnson) appear to have been sucked into a power vacuum by fate, it is because they carefully manipulated themselves into a strategic position and then took their chances on being called to serve. General MacArthur was playing such a role—and biding his time—on Pearl Harbor day. Fate dictated, with peculiar irony, that the Japanese bombs which fell on an American naval base on December 7, 1941 would be the prime causal agents for bestowing upon MacArthur, eventually, the power of a totalitarian ruler of Japan. Such strokes of ironic fate, carefully foreseen and planned for, are common matters in day-to-day affairs where petty powers continually exchange hands.

What are the personality characteristics of the man of power? We do not, unfortunately, know with certainty. But speculation would be irre-

---

[17] According to H. R. Trevor-Roper, this was the state to which Hitler was finally reduced in his Berlin bunker in 1945, fighting battles with armies that existed only as flags on a map and planning illusory victories that were never to be. See *The Last Days of Hitler* (New York: Berkley Publishing Corp., 1947).

sponsible without some discussion of what we *do* know (or think we know) about the rigidities of attitude and incisiveness of opinion—to say nothing of sureness of action—that characterize most successful men of power. These personality characteristics (and others) surfaced in the famous "California studies" of Adorno and others, published two decades ago.[18] Adorno had set out to rank on a scale attitudes and opinions (the two were not well differentiated at that time) of a rigid and supposedly prejudiced nature, representing what was then called "authoritarianism."

Looking back upon the entire venture, one notes in the study's assumptions an unquestionable persuasive (even propagandistic) bias. The scale was known as the F (for "Fascist") scale and the immediate *raison d'être* of the enterprise was to track down, if possible, the specific roots of anti-Semitism. This was apparently accomplished for different types of populations, as confirmed by subsequent reports of the study's applications.[19] But somewhere along the way, the initial anti-Semitic rationale was misplaced, the word "authoritarian" became dominant, and the foolhardiness of attempting to measure what are really political *opinions* on a scale designed to investigate ethnic *attitudes* became clear.

As Smith indicates,[20] the F scale did not measure much—or enough. Those who rated as "high" authoritarians turned out to be rather cocksure, super-patriotic, moralistic and rigid types of people—individuals prone to black-and-white thinking and therefore vulnerable to simplistic irrationalities *like* anti-Semitism and similar pat notions. The California scale, however, implied strongly that these irrationalities appeared in a context of political *rightist* orientations, hence the "Fascist" implications. But they were also discovered to apply equally and as neatly to irrationalities of the *left* among those we call "Radical," "Red" or some other pejorative name. The authoritarian "lows" were (presumably) rather fair-minded, permissive sorts of folk, best characterized by the political rubric "liberal." The "middles" remain something of a mystery—presumably sheep-like individuals who would follow clear directions from either the "highs" or "lows," depending on circumstances.

Whether or not the F scale is, in fact, a "psychological formula for irrationality," [21] as Smith claims, has not yet been determined. But if his main point is correct, the following is suggested: Despite (or because of) its apparent instinctual flavor, the will to power is fundamentally a manifes-

---

[18] T. W. Adorno, Else Frenkel-Brunswik, D. V. Levenson, R. N. Sanford, *The Authoritarian Personality* (New York: Harper and Bros., 1950).

[19] See R. Christie and Marie Jahoda (eds.), *Studies in the Scope and Method of "The Authoritarian Personality"* (New York: The Free Press, 1954), and H. E. Titus and E. P. Hollander, "The California F Scale in Psychological Research, 1950–55" in *Psychological Bulletin*, Vol. 54, 1957, pp. 47–64.

[20] Smith, *op. cit.*, pp. 72–73.

[21] *Ibid.*, p. 73.

tation of political irrationality in a public psychological context. In other words, the man who achieves power and holds it must, first, have accepted and interiorized a certain ideology and/or specific platform without equivocation. He must appear to believe[22] what he says he stands for. Second, he must view his constituents as "we" and his opponents as "they," leaving opportunities for "they's" to become "we's," and vice-versa. He must clearly see his side as the psychological in-group, the opposition as the out-group. Third, his own ego defenses must be developed sufficiently to externalize (in psychoanalytic terms) his unresolved inner problems into fully resolved external platforms, programs and politics that are clearly expressed as "correct," "right," or "true" by him. He is permitted, in private of course, a certain amount of ego deflation and doubt, but this harmless option is one that few men of great power seem to take if we are to believe their biographers.

In sum, the man of power is, therefore, likely to be the kind of personality described by the California inventory and its interpreters as a "high" authoritarian. This does not mean that his political beliefs or ideologies or platforms *must be* irrational. Not at all. But the man of power, in order to serve as a convincing leader, must be ready to hold and maintain the integrity of his professed attitudes, opinions and actions *as if they were irrational and/or in the face of almost inevitable opposition and evidence that they are by means of some irrational rationale.*[23] Note that we are not referring to beliefs here, nor are we imputing the necessity that the man of power must be *covertly* convinced that what he is doing or saying is right, although such a conviction may be personally helpful to him in maintaining psychological equilibrium. What we are concerned with is the public, political display of his attitudes and opinions, and the actions taken in support of them.

Political Persuasion

The dynamics of political argumentation and contests for power by means of modern instruments of communications technology are probably the single aspect of persuasion that interests the general public most. Best

---

[22] This interiorization in our culture does not require the long term commitment that it does in more politically sensitive societies. Our leaders and potential leaders switch sides and allegiances with remarkable rapidity, particularly in the short periods before party conventions. A most interesting example of such a change was that of Wendell Willkie, who, a few months before he was nominated for the Republican presidential candidacy in 1940, was (and had been all of his adult life) a registered Democrat. So great was the desire of many Republicans to find a candidate who had even a chance to defeat Roosevelt (running for his third term), that a little matter like party loyalty meant nothing to them. Willkie played the game until his death, but never having gained much political power, he was never put to the ultimate test of maintaining his public stance in the heat of office. Many other examples exist today.

[23] In our current age of sophism, this is not nearly as difficult or infrequently done as it first may seem to the reader.

selling books, academic analysis, experiments, magazine articles and numerous studies have centered on them, some achieving popular success, others more limited recognition among scholars and politicians. The nature of this literature, reasons for high public interest in it, and its effect upon the American life-style will be discussed in various contexts in the ensuing part of this volume.

In treating such matters as fear, sex, love and laughter, a dearth of both insight and evidence prevented us from expressing fully articulated theories concerning their psychological roles in human persuasion. A glut of speculation, however, in regard to power impedes our progress in this respect, along with the many constructions of the human power-drive which different methods of analysis yield in psychologically viable frameworks.

Of primary importance is the fact, though, that the concept of power (and the very word) is of greater specifically cultural importance than any of the psychological factors discussed in the preceding six chapters. The importance derives from our modern social and political constructions of power, into which all the tiny rivulets of most other sorts of power flow. Political and social power are felt violently and dramatically. Its impression is made not only on individuals but enormous segments of society, and, since the invention of modern "total warfare" and "unconditional surrender" in this century, these effects may occur rapidly and totally, excluding no one from their consequences, neither women nor children nor the feeble nor the deranged. We all probably intuit this factor about power drives in people (including ourselves) and recognize its critical significance in our time and place.

By no means are congeries of power in the political arena (that today knows no boundaries) in any sense new in our time. Berle comments upon the antiquity of time-worn models for today's apparently novel concepts of black power, student power, the liberated powers of art, philosophy, liberal theology and other ancient novelties. "Their history," he notes, "too often has been written in bloody chronicles of revolt and repression. The late twentieth century offers the United States no immunity from problems that have beset Europe through the centuries, rising to revolutionary intensity in recent generations." [24] A feeling of intensity surrounds these problems precisely because *they*—not the powers of fear, sex, love and laughter—for many of us, portend upheavals of societal dimensions in the form of revolt and repressions or both.

First, therefore, one must understand the power of the *concept* of power. Semanticists describe it in a number of ways, referring to intentional and extension meanings, and so forth. "Power" is better described simply as a "loaded term" in a "trigger happy" society, not loaded like the words "sex" or "guilt" (because most of us are all too self-consciously aware of

---

[24] Berle, *op. cit.*, p. 268.

their semantic power), but loaded because most of us are ready to believe any superficial evidence that this or that group or individual has power, *real* power, political or otherwise, and that they will not hesitate to use it.[25] The ubiquity of semi-serious terms like "flower power," "gay power," "love-power" and others is symptomatic of more than infatuation with figures of speech.

Second, in our culture we are ready to relate a display of power to almost any culture trait. But the major socially sensitive areas of personified power are (in no particular order) political (in fact, governmental) power, economic power, technological power (including the power of firearms), police power, legal power (or influence), the power of celebrity ("big shot" and "inside" power) and the power of fabricated publicity. This power is personified, and therefore the people who speak for it hold considerable persuasive potential.

Third, any one theory of power agglomeration is about as useful as any other, as long as a belief of *significant publics* is maintained in and by it—from the pragmatic, persuasive perspective. We have seen some of the particular problems involved in the class theory of power. Many believe that theories of this sort are today both naïve and irrelevant to Western life. Yet, many people still believe in one or another class theory, or at least hold more-or-less positive attitudes towards them—particularly academics of middle-age or older—and therefore their power—as a power play in power games—is considerable.[26] The theory of personal power, ideas of power vacuums, conspiracy theories, or deterministic theories of power distribution and control are indistinguishable one from the other *as long as people believe in them.*

Fourth, because the flow of power is so nebulous, one usually has to *disprove,* somehow, a person's previously held beliefs or attitudes about power before he can suggest new ones to him. The former, upsetting previous beliefs, is usually harder than the latter, leading an individual to accept new ones. Our personal concepts of power were developed very early in life along with our cognitions of fear, love and laughter, but long before

---

[25] Reactions to "bomb scares" telephoned to police and other similar wild grasps after power are good examples of our sensitivity to imputations of its irresponsible or destructive exercise. We cringe at any hint of power run wild, whether the reaction fits the stimulus or not. But we seem to have no choice. How significant that those of us who live in the Northeast pass our summers cringing in the face of portending power failures by electric companies. At the writing, the day-by-day operation of Con Edison in New York is a running front-page newspaper story.

[26] Elder liberals appear to believe, at this writing, for instance, that the laboring class in the country speaks for Nixon's so-called "silent majority" vis-à-vis the "student class." They base their concept on a handful of skirmishes in New York City and the fact that the President invited some union officials to the White House. Class conflicts have never in history been built on evidence of this kind, but the lion's share of liberal class theorists believe that a genuine class conflict may be building now on the basis of these slight confrontations. The issue will, I think, be dead by the time this paragraph appears in print.

our knowledge of genital sexuality. When discussing or appealing to a person's ideas of power, therefore, one is usually touching rigid and well implanted attitudes or beliefs. They are far easier to *exploit* than to *change*.

Fifth, the promise of power in any of its manifestations is, for some people, the most persuasive instrument in the psychological arsenal of a manipulator of human affairs. People seem particularly (and variably) sensitive to the promise of power under certain conditions: When they perceive that individuals around them of equal status are moving upwards socially, economically or educationally. When certain factors in their own lifestyles have changed dramatically while others have not, for instance, economic expansion without concomitant new educational or social opportunities, or increased social viability without economic progress. When individuals are given certain powers under law but are denied them in fact by social custom or gentlemen's agreements. When people feel the threat of a once impotent sub-group rising socially or interfering economically with their welfare. When people, proud of a tradition or life-style, have suffered a circumstantial or psychological defeat *because of* that tradition, or lifestyle and yearn for exculpation in their own eyes for their own downfall. In these instances, history demonstrates that assurances of future power take precedence often over promises of economic security, material welfare, self-esteem or any of the old propaganda appeals once accepted as basic persuasive tools.

Power, of course, may open prospects by which a single individual may project for himself new prosperity, security and status. But the raw love of power, of and by itself, may sufficiently motivate certain people, under certain circumstances, to follow unlikely courses of action, or to modify their attitudes and opinions in direct contradiction to the guesses of even the most clever social or political analysts.

Conclusion

Power of one sort or another is a human developmental factor active from birth on through life. Most human transactions and communications involve power shifts of some kind. In social matters, power is depersonalized, institutionalized, and then personalized once again in those individuals who represent men's institutions. Power is therefore most noticeable when it is political and refers primarily to public aspects of life, as it has been since antiquity.

Historically, Hegelian concepts de-personalized and abstracted power into "forces" that interact, via individuals as pawns, in certain predetermined and predictable ways. Class power (particularly economic class) was understood by nineteenth century Hegelians to be the single most significant natural expression of these forces and therefore to hold the great power over the lives of men. A human tendency, however, has continued—even in the face of wide acceptance of economic determinism—to identify power instead with the people who wield it, rather than abstract forces.

In the West, the notion of class power has been particularly attractive for many reasons to politicians and sociologists, as well as others as apparently disinterested in political theory as the late President Eisenhower. True enough, class theories of power provide copious data troves (like money) for scholars to enumerate and count. But the appeal transcends convenience in the articulations of power class conspiracies that snatch power and run social organization from behind the scenes. Such conspiracies have existed (and exist today), but they tend to become less and less significant in the industrialized West because of a plurality of classes and the tendency of individuals of personal power to belong to a number of interest groups, often at cross-purposes one with the other. At times, these conspiracy theories reach paranoid dimensions, but little evidence supports these views today, particularly as they relate to the economic aspects of culture.

Although power is objectified into public or political power, it falls eventually back into the hands of *men* who give its exercise coloration by virtue of their own psychological orientations and personalities. Power makes a lasting impression on almost everyone it touches, frequently breeding neuroses and even psychoses, and the risk that it will destroy the holder is always present. For this reason, some people shrink from power, although others rush towards it. Power is rarely given and accepted by accident. The use of power (as a personality trait) seems also related to the notion of "authoritarianism," or willingness to the conceptualization of one's programs, policies and rights of leadership as absolute. Power helps one build ego defenses against doubt, at least as expressed in public.

In matters relating to persuasion, appeals to, and on behalf of, power are potent, largely because of the extraordinary sensitivity of certain individuals in this regard who feel that they have not gained (or cannot use) the power to which they are entitled. Appealing to them is apparently simple by re-enforcing those beliefs and attitudes about power that they already have, whether or not these dispositions are logical or true or even relevant to the situation at hand. It is far easier to exploit notions of power than to change them, in almost every instance. But people are variably vulnerable to power appeals on a circumstantial basis as well as by virtue of their individual natures. Under certain circumstances, the desire for power is far greater than the desire for material comfort, prestige, wealth or even self-esteem *per se*, although power may promise any or all of these ends to those who seek it.

Part Four

CONTEMPORARY DYNAMICS

(S)laves, when inquired of as to their condition and the character of their masters, almost universally say they are contented, and that their masters are kind . . . I have been frequently asked, when a slave, if I had a kind master, and do not remember ever to have given a negative answer; nor did I, in pursuing this course, consider myself as uttering what was absolutely false; for I always measured the kindness of my master by the standards of kindness set up among slaveholders around us. Moreover, slaves are like other people, and imbibe prejudices quite common to others. They think their own better than that of others. Many, under the influence of this prejudice, think their own masters are better than the masters of other slaves; and this, too, in some cases, when the very reverse is true. Indeed, it is not uncommon for slaves even to fall out and quarrel among themselves about the relative goodness of their masters, each contending for the superior goodness of his own over that of the others.

Narrative of the Life of Frederick Douglass, an American Slave, Written by himself.

Chapter 19

"THE CROWD" REVISITED

The destinies of people are determined by their character and not by their government.

Gustave Le Bon

THE PURPOSE of this chapter is to define and delimit the subjects of Part Four of this volume to come: group phenomena in society today and the ways in which members of groups are influenced by persuasive communications, both as individuals and in their roles as members of groups.

Since Herodotus nearly all philosophers and historians have been concerned with people in their collective roles. Because we tend to think in sociologically subtle categories of nationality, race, profession and economic class today, we tend also to think that people have always been grouped or regarded similarly. A moment's reflection indicates, of course, the error of this notion. Until a comparatively few years ago, for instance, concepts of nationality and race were hopelessly blurred, even by the wisest philosophers—and still are, as a matter of fact, when terms like "Jew," "Arab" and "Russian" are used supposedly by sophisticated political writers. Nationality has, from pre-history, been a discrete device for indicating group membership. So, in the past centuries in the West, have terms like "gentleman," "freeman," "worker," "craftsman" and "slave." Distinctive groups of people have received distinctive titles when historians, politicians and sociologists (most lately) have required concepts of operative collectives for their particular purposes.

Modern Western sociological thinking about group phenomena follows the numerous visions of numerous theoretical pioneers: Marx, the class theorist; Spencer, the first genuine sociologist in today's classic tradition; Weber, the Cassandra of capitalism; Durkheim, the father of *anomie;* Veblen, the eccentric anti-economist—and others who followed. They created, in a period of less than 100 years, a group of concepts by which Western man might be examined culturally, in a relatively orderly and consistent manner, a way that was formerly and almost solely within the grasp of the playwright for centuries and the novelist for 200 years.[1] While the visions of the classical social thinkers varied according to individual *Weltanschauung*, they all displayed certain common elements.

First, their viewpoints were all scientifically oriented, that is, detached from *a priori* value assumptions about the role of man on earth. Second, they were concerned with collective existential human functions rather than titles, figure-heads, myths or mysticisms. Third, they were investigations of causes for collective behaviors that might not be explained by conventional and extant theories of history or philosophy.

Each of these giants, and his disciples, was incorrect in some part of his sociological vision. And yet, in some measure, each was also correct. The one greatest sociological error they made was their tendency to believe that any *one* single manifestation relevant to a given culture is likely also to be true of all cultures. On the other hand, their great sociological contribution was the identification of certain dynamics which *were*, in some measure, relevant enough to *most* similar cultures to justify the articulation of reasonable theory. The story of contemporary sociology is told in greatest part in terms of the efforts of inductive and deductive verification and modification of the theories from this heritage that have survived to the present. In the process, it has become the sociologist's dream to exert a measure of humane control over that which he has at last begun to understand. To his credit, he is apparently not easily dismayed by the distance that remains between him and that goal in nearly all of his main concerns.[2]

Group theory, in the sociological tradition, however, ran beside another strong current of behavioral study during the late nineteenth and early twentieth centuries, a particular point of view which would today be considered social psychology rather than sociology. The Langs have called this latter approach to collective behavior that of "pathological regressions." [3] The term is not unduly pejorative and, from their perspective, quite justified, having divided, as they do, the main sociological purviews of

---

[1] A good introduction to the major threads of the classic tradition in sociology is the anthology, C. Wright Mills, *Images of Man*, previously cited.

[2] I was confirmed in this opinion the other day after completing study of an excellent 1151 page anthology of the latest and best thinking by American sociologists on juvenile delinquency, crime and its attendant evils in our society. Benumbed as I was with fatigue, and with all respect to the criminologists represented in the volume, I could only conclude (in a note to myself on the fly-leaf that I do not remember writing), "As criminal behavior increases in the United States, we certainly seem to understand more and more about it—at roughly the same rate of increase." My proposition will stand up statistically, I think, based on the numerical data and criminological history cited in the volume itself. The book, which I recommend to the hearty and brave, is Donald R. Cressy and David A. Ward (eds.), *Delinquency, Crime and Social Process* (New York: Harper and Row, 1969).

[3] See Kurt and Gladys Lang, *Collective Behavior*, pp. 31–36.

group behavior into categories emphasizing either *social progress* (following Bagehot, Wallas, Cooley and Dewey), *natural history* (following Park, Blumer and Von Wiese) or *pathological regressions.*

The first category construes social history in essentially affirmative, evolutionary terms. The second assays objective descriptions of social process. The third, and the subject of this Chapter, centers on one basic question not easily trivialized by putting it bluntly; namely, "Why do people, who behave rationally when they act as individuals, turn into such damn fools when they function in groups?" Or, looking at the problem in a more serious context, the late psychologist Lindner wrote in 1956:

> For at least thirty years, and perhaps more, our civilization has been demonstrating behavior that, were the same to be discovered in the solitary human being, would cause the forces concerned with public order to remove him to an asylum for the mentally deranged. The world, in short, has run amuck. As a species, we are exhibiting exactly what the most profoundly disturbed psychopathic personality shows . . . The whole tale is contained in a few geographical place names—Madrid, Munich, Buchenwald, Warsaw, Hiroshima, Kargopol, Los Alamos, Seoul, Hanoi . . .[4]

(Would Lindner's ghost be surprised if we add to the list Poznan, Budapest, Prague, Havana, My Lai, Berkeley, Chicago, Detroit, Washington, and on, and on and on?)

This issue, one of the gloomiest facing contemporary social analysis, runs as counterpoint to all other (and perfectly legitimate) analyses of group behavior, including those in the classical mainstream of modern sociology. But no other one is as directly relevant to our culture now. Neither is any other as sensitive, responsive and directly related to the nature and quality of the conduits of persuasion functioning in this culture: mass communications, education, and the jungle telegraph of rumors, symbols, legends, jokes and bits of conventional wisdom that political analysts call "climates of opinion"—which are not "climates" and deal in far more significant items than "opinions." Collective or pathological regression is easily visible in the real world, apparently, in some ways, a condition of modernity. That we are able even to discuss it in precise terms is one of the cheerful manifestations of the progress of the behavioral sciences.

The Nature of the Crowd

A more subtle and sensitive mind than the writer's might explain convincingly why *so many* of major social and psychological currents of thought in the West emerged from that dramatic series of power struggles we call the French Revolution. Other upheavals, seemingly as significant, might have been just as heuristically germinal during the early nineteenth

---

[4] Robert Lindner, *Must You Conform?* (New York: Rinehart and Co., 1956), pp. 19–20.

century. But the record of the French Revolution is impressive. From its chaos emerged the modern ideas of totalitarianism, collectivism, communism and the psychology of the unconscious. It also spawned the concept that groups of people were not just herds of human protoplasm but organic gatherings, first conceived of as mobs, then as crowds, and finally (in our day) as masses, subject to scrutiny similar to that applied to individuals.

Where and how did the concept of the organic crowd start? Marx and Engels had euphemised and sentimentalized their class notions into "mass movements," and had identified the proletariat specifically with the masses. But the mass they described displayed little distinctive psychological coloration. It was mainly a vector of a class war or power struggle. Keener organic observations were made towards the end of the nineteenth century by Gabriel Tarde in France and Scipio Sighele in Italy. Tarde conceived of the entity of "crowd opinion," or collective dispositions of specific mobs of people under certain circumstances, dispositions which might change somewhat as individual opinions do when subjected to various stimuli. Sighele moved one step further into the articulation of an actual psychology of the crowd. His work provided the stimulus (or text) for Gustave Le Bon's remarkable book, *The Crowd*.[5]

Le Bon, a French physician and sociologist, may have been as avid a plagiarist as Sighele claimed; or the Italian may have been following Le Bon's leads in his own supposedly original delineations of crowd psychology. Or the two may have both been stimulated by Tarde to the same conclusions. The matter is academic today, because it was Le Bon in *The Crowd*, published in 1895, who influenced directly and indirectly a whole school of subsequent social theorists, most notably José Ortega y Gasset, Erich Fromm and David Rieseman, among many others, with his powerful concept of collective recidivism. Le Bon also stimulated Freud to design a crude outline for the psychoanalytic theory of social attitudes as a direct answer to his book a quarter of a century after its publication. In short, Le Bon identified and attempted to describe *crowd behavior*. Freud apparently accepted Le Bon's descriptions, and set himself to explaining *why* the curiosities Le Bon observed were true.

The chronology of Le Bon's influence is significant. At about the same time that Freud was theorizing about the psychodynamics of crowd behavior in Vienna, Ortega, in Madrid, was predicting (with unhappy accuracy, it turned out) what European crowds then gathering in Rome and Berlin would be up to in the next generation, both the former and the latter basing their views, apparently in some measure, upon the observations of Le Bon.

In the United States, however, it was possible, twenty years later—in 1941—for one of the then most highly regarded social theorists to write

[5] Gustave Le Bon, *The Crowd* (New York: The Viking Press, 1960).

from his insularity at exurban Princeton, New Jersey, in his book on social movements, " 'The fact that men who are put into a crowd puts them in possession of a sort of collective mind,' wrote Le Bon in 1895. Such a notion is no longer tenable." [6] This distinguished scholar, of course, had not had the opportunity to study the waves and surges of collective insanity and violence that were to straddle the globe in the three decades to come and were to revise the bases of his rational, empirical and paternalistic visions of social behavior. By 1961, the Langs were seriously weighing (tentatively) the relevance of *The Crowd* to the collective behavior they were then currently scrutinizing.[7] Now, in 1971, the present author suggests a re-visit to the world of Le Bon and his ingenious constructions.

With grudging admiration, Merton, in his Introduction to a fairly recent American edition of *The Crowd*, compares the volume in prescience to *The Prince*, and writes, "This end-of-the-century portrait of man pictures him as readily susceptible to manipulative control, as a strangely willing victim of deception by others." [8] He calls Le Bon's work an "unfinished portrait," indicating that, on one hand, Freud may have completed the picture by solving the problems posed by Le Bon and, on the other, displaying faith that nineteenth century man's capacity for self-deception has been today counter-balanced by new social devices and counter-forces of an essentially rational and humane nature. In short, Merton's contention is that Le Bon took his concepts of the crowd far for his time, but not far enough to deal with the generally sanguine new evidence in the field of sociology during the past three generations.

Le Bon's discussion may be reprised quite easily, shorn of its contemporary illustrations, particularly the travails of the French Third Republic and the study of the career of the prototype dictatorial personality, General Georges Boulanger, who, for a time, was an enormously popular hero in France (on a par with Napoleon) with little to explain his rise except his superb facility at mass persuasion.

First, Le Bon identifies the crowd as a *significant* mass of people, that is a group of individuals capable of exerting power *and who know their own potentialities*. In his words, "The destinies of nations are elaborated at

---

[6] Hadley Cantril, *The Psychology of Social Movements* (New York: John Wiley and Sons, Inc., 1941), p. 118. In this volume, Cantril articulates on quasi-Freudian crowd dynamics, and then reports considerable empirical data in the usual sociological key (questionnaires, percentages of this and that, interviews and speculation) concerning lynching mobs, the followers of Father Divine, the Oxford Groups, the Townsend Plan and the Nazi Party.

[7] See Kurt and Gladys Lang, *op. cit.*, pp. 111-150. The Langs appear to resist the notion of crowd consciousness or a mass mind, and hence, ten years ago at any rate, remained somewhat skeptical of those thinkers who followed Le Bon to that date. How they feel today, I am uncertain, and everybody is entitled to change his or her mind.

[8] Le Bon, *op. cit.*, p. XV.

present in the heart of the masses, and no longer in the council of princes." [9] This change in the direction of social power (protestations of democratic idealists to the contrary) contains inherently, in his view, the threat of a return to barbarism.[10]

Second, a crowd appears to generate an organic personality different in sentiment and nature from the individual personalities of those who compose it. For purposes of analogy, this personality may be regarded as a "collective mind." The actions of people in a crowd, also, differ markedly from these same people when observed acting individually.

Third, this change is part of an unconscious dynamic whereby intellectual and/or cognitive processes appear to lose primacy to emotions, most particularly a sense of invincibility, a loss of individual responsibility, the contagion of emotion and heightened suggestibility to messages of an emotionally toned nature.

Fourth, critical facilities are diminished, and members of crowds turn credulous, their main mode of cognition being successions of images. Differences in intelligence between crowd members are minimized in this process as their perception of cognitive matter is dulled, so that, in a crowd, people are more easily deceived than as individuals.[11]

Fifth, crowds are most impressed and most easily moved by leaders who contrive to present themselves as individuals of extra-humanity and legendary dimensions. This ruse requires showmanship rather than statesmanship, and may be accomplished by such diverse figures as military heroes, politicians, secular saints, magicians, actors and other charismatic figures. Great intelligence is not a required attribute of such a leader. Conviction is. In fact, education and intellect may militate *against* both his effectiveness and power.

Sixth, as a consequence of the diminution of their sense of responsibilities, crowds are easily maneuvered to violence; less easily restrained from it. Their moral codes are simple: black and white; good and bad. Accordingly, crowds respect displays of strength and force, decisive leaders and clear-cut paths of action.

---

[9] *Ibid.*, p. 15. This notion, and the twelve to follow, have all been derived from points made by Le Bon in *The Crowd* in more discursive fashion.

[10] This theme is developed in great detail by Ortega y Gasset in *The Revolt of the Masses*, where its intrinsic logic is discussed and affirmed in a number of ways socially, politically and culturally. See also Robert McClintock "Ortega y Gasset Rediscovered" in *Columbia Forum*, Summer, 1970, pp. 33–36 for a more recent evaluation of the kind of regression Ortega and his followers bespoke—a regression far ahead of its time.

[11] Professional magicians are aware that spectacular deceptions work best before large audiences. Simple card and parlor tricks, while often ingenious, rarely employ obvious ruses. On stage, or with a large audience, it is possible to get away with almost any deceit. The late magician, John Mulholland, often told me (to his constant pleasure) that the hardest audience to fool is a small group of little children, and the easiest, a large one of college professors.

Seventh, crowds think primitively and accept new ideas slowly. They are manipulable by means of spurious reasoning of causes to effects. They tend to believe unrealities, lies and untruths—if they fit in with patterns of previous ideas. The promise of miracles, impossible victories and dreams of glory are more easily accepted than modest, qualified and realistic suggestions.

Eighth, much crowd reaction seems similar to individual manifestations of religious belief and spiritually motivated behavior. Programs presented to the crowd should therefore be framed in a mystical aura of illusion of some sort.

Ninth, crowds tend to cling to traditional ideas, and therefore new programs had best be cloaked in traditional trappings. Traditional beliefs, however, do not stand much scrutiny from a crowd, and when they are questioned they may easily be discarded in favor of new and "better" programs.

Tenth, education is no defense against the intellectual regression of individuals in a crowd. A mob or mass that has been educated unwisely, that is, to no realistic purpose or end, is likely to be even more emotionally voluble than a merely uneducated crowd.[12]

Eleventh, the new crowd that rises in each new generation experiences each of these phenomena *de novo*. One generation, *en masse*, does not learn from the experience of the preceding one.

Twelfth, crowds are usually moved by three emotional-rhetorical stratagems: affirmation, repetition and contagion. The latter is a manifestation of the influence upon the masses of an urge to imitate, either each other or their leaders. The leaders, on the other hand, imitate nobody, but cover themselves with as much external, acquired or personal prestige as possible.

Thirteenth, these general principles of crowd analysis apply variantly to homogeneous and heterogeneous crowds, juries, the electorate (either in physically proximate groups or as recipients of mass communications), parliaments, congresses, committees and variants of spontaneous crowds.

Le Bon was a canny realist, and, as Merton notes, he was to score best as a prophet, almost as astute, as a matter of fact, at anticipating history as reading it. Ahead of him were to be born a new breed (or new versions of ancient types) of charismatic leaders who fit his conditions precisely: Lenin, Stalin, Hitler, Mussolini, Franco, deGaulle [13] and others each play-

[12] Le Bon is most specific on this point and his words might well be hung on the administration buildings of our universities. He writes, "The acquisition of knowledge for which no use can be found is a sure method of driving a man to revolt." (*Ibid.*, pp. 93–94.)

[13] I have heard that Lenin, Hitler, Stalin and deGaulle were, at one time or another, all close students of Le Bon's work. *The Crowd* has probably had as much practical influence on modern political behavior as any single document, including *The Prince*.

ing the role of "man on horseback." And the crowds of Europe behaved much as he had anticipated, unfortunately for the many millions of people who perished as a result of their atavism.

Crowd Dynamics and The Mass

In the light of our brief survey, it should be clear why careful sociologists, political scientists and psychologists have been inclined to reject the ideas of Le Bon. His intellectual crimes were numerous: He tended not to bother differentiating crowds, one from another, by means of the usual socio-psychological categories of class, education, sex and similar criteria. He did not credit individual members with much influence on the crowd *gestalt*. He made few provisions for the observation (or effect) of interactions within crowds, of cross influences, of the developments of sub-groups and their components. Most notably, he attempted few guesses as to *why* crowds act in accordance with his descriptive analyses. In general orientation, he observed both past history and future prospects with a skeptical and pessimistic detachment.

Le Bon stands guilty of all of the above counts—and more. In some ways he displayed extreme naïveté when compared to the average sociological drone presently gathering statistics for an advertising agency on laundry soap preferences in a medium-sized community. In the end, the agency will possess reams of data concerning its "crowd" but will probably trust to chance, luck and creative vision in its actual persuasive assault on the housewives it has so closely studied. Le Bon would have scoffed at sociological jot gathering and the elegant quasi-science it bespeaks. In his naïveté, he might also commit the further crime of predicting, more or less correctly, the course of history for the next three generations, much less anticipate preferences of housewives for various laundry soaps.

A generation after the publication of *The Crowd*, however, Freud, searching for a skeleton on which to hang his new interest in social psychology, came upon *The Crowd* which he regarded as "brilliant" and "deservedly famous."[14] He was undoubtedly attracted strongly by Le Bon's implied and stated applications of the concept of the unconscious, the keystone of psychoanalysis, that had come to Le Bon via the same route it came to Freud: experiments with hypnosis of the medical psychologists of France during the late nineteenth century. Copiously quoting Le Bon and the British-American psychologist McDougall,[15] Freud qualifies Le Bon's propositions in a number of significant ways.

---

[14] See Sigmund Freud, *Group Psychology and the Analysis of the Ego* (New York: Bantam Books, 1965).

[15] See William McDougall, *The Group Mind* (London: Cambridge Press, 1920). While McDougall pays respects to Le Bon, he denies entirely the manifestations which the latter associated with mass hypnosis, a doubtful concept at best. Hypnosis itself is discussed in Chapter 20.

Le Bon's notion of the unconscious does not deal, as psychoanalysis does, with repression, says Freud. To the Frenchman, the crowd's unconscious signified a mere mass of primitive traits. For Freud, it represented repressed feeling, unacceptable to consciousness because of their conflict with the super-ego or conscience. With conscience *hors de combat,* therefore, the crowd is free to violate its own standards of behavior. The charismatic leader becomes the ego ideal in surrogate, and the crowd member thus falls more or less under his hypnotic spell. The tie that binds is, of course, libidinal energy that flows from the members of the crowd to the leader who is himself the ultimate narcissist, loving no one but himself. Thus he is the perfect ego ideal.

Group behavior, says Freud, appears regressive because it *is* regressive and shared, an analogy to, or re-experience of, the childhood influences that members of the crowd have undergone with their parents. They renounce their parental image (the original source of the superego) and transfer it to the group leader. So great becomes this dependence that, in time of danger when and if the leader fails, the result is panic. Precedence for this process is found early in the history of the human race, notes Freud, in the tribal family that has been extenuated in modern culture into the crowd, mob, mass or what have you.

Granting that Freud's analysis takes us deeper than Le Bon into the wellsprings of crowd psychology, it does not cover as wide a territory or even contrive to underscore significant features of the terrain. Freud's monograph succeeded in opening the field of social psychology to psychoanalysis, to the reward of all who found in his analysis a refreshing view of culture. Freud's essay was the antecedent to the work of such familiar social analysts as Fromm, Erikson, Kahler, Reik and, in some measure, other thinkers who wandered as far away from the master as Koestler, Jung and Frankl, among many others.

In sum, the Freud-Le Bon concept of the crowd emphasized, by 1920 (the date is significant), a repressive-regressive concept of the mass, in which, by means of various psychological mechanisms, individuals lose their power of conscience, identify with a leader and are moved by appeals directed to feeling (id) rather than reason (super-ego). A crowd is thus bound together by common empathy with a leader or cause, and is both highly manipulable (in the manner of a subject in a so-called "hypnotic trance") and potentially dangerous on two fronts: first, when the crowd is agitated by the leader to violent action, and, second, when its leadership fails and fear and panic are produced.

Crowd behavior is analogous to family behavior, and the differences in crowds in different cultures (noted crudely by Le Bon) is therefore essentially reflective of family patterns by which the crowd constituents were raised. A German crowd is different from a Japanese crowd; just as a rural white crowd is different, in the USA, from an urban Negro one, but mainly on the basis of family history, sociology and psychology, not upon the basis of intelligence or rational similarities and/or differences of interest, except in superficial ways or exceptional instances.

In the fifty years since 1920, little has occurred to qualify or change the Le Bon-Freud construction.[16] What *has* changed is the nature of the crowd. In the time of Le Bon and Freud, and for well into the next decade, prototypical crowds were street corner mobs, ardent political enthusiasts in a stadium or meeting hall, crowds in village squares or piazzas,[17] or the gatherings rounded up by local politicos to honor a visiting dignitary.

Le Bon also mentions the tendency of the press to influence crowd behavior, most specifically "the recent development of the newspaper press, by whose agency the most contrary opinions are being continually brought before the attention of crowds." With eerie prophecy, Le Bon assays the results of this innovation. "The suggestions that might result from each individual opinion are soon destroyed by suggestions of an opposite character. The consequence is that no opinion succeeds in becoming widespread, and that the existence of them all is ephemeral." [18] As prescient as this statement seems in the light of recent developments in electronic communications, Le Bon could not anticipate the development of the radio, film, television, mass distribution methods of newspapers and the technology of communications that were to follow him. Freud might have in 1920, but did not. The latter's interests, even where group psychology was concerned, centered on internal psychic processes, not the environmental novelties he observed around him.

What has occurred in the past seventy-five years is the extenuation of

---

16 The recent spontaneous crowd groupings that have coagulated on our college campuses have provided excellent study models for this projection, especially when numbers of speakers in succession address youngsters employing variant cognitive and emotional appeals. These informal, usually out-of-doors, gatherings are, in some ways, as close as we come these days to duplicating the kinds of crowds Le Bon and Freud apparently described. See the discussion of the spellbinding hypnotic aspects of crowd behavior in the analysis of Le Bon in A. Koestler, *The Ghost in The Machine*, pp. 250–251.

17 Mussolini was something of a genius at handling and manipulating the piazza crowd, taking advantage, of course, of an Italian tradition going back to the *Forum Romanis*. The Duce's stage managing usually involved building up suspense by means of delaying his talks well past their announced starting time, supplying symbols of Roman history and strength and military bands and squads of aircraft flying over the waiting mob. He created a suitable Caesarian background for his histrionics that were unfortunately distorted (and therefore not taken seriously) by newsreel editors in the USA. In some ways, Mussolini was a more astute master of crowd psychology than Hitler, Lenin, Churchill or Roosevelt. His downfall, as Shirer makes clear in his history of Nazi Germany, lay mainly in poor judgment in personal alliances and ineffective diplomacy. Mussolini's larger vision of the fate of Europe turned out to be devastatingly accurate, but he was not able to convince Hitler to share it. As a public hero, however, he cut a figure in the tradition of the Borgias, Medicis and Caesars, even on that fatal day his corpse was found hanging upside-down at a gas station in Milan. But leadership in the environs of Rome has always involved risks.

18 Le Bon, *op. cit.*, p. 149.

the crowd out of the village square and auditorium into the fabric of society at large. The devices which have accomplished this have been technological, but not confined solely to instruments of mass communications. When Hitler, in 1932, campaigned across Germany by aircraft, delivering countless speeches to crowds brought together by local party lieutenants, or when Harry Truman accomplished substantially the same end in his railroad "whistle stop" campaign of 1948, technology was at work changing crowd dynamics. There is little doubt, as Le Bon recognized, that the printing press became, by virtue of its prestige and durability, one of the main agencies for creating new kinds of crowds, components of which were separated by time and distance. But Roosevelt's invention of the informal political narrative on radio (used by every president since and modified in the 1950's to accommodate the instrument of television), Hitler's innovation of the symbolic political cinema, Eisenstein's political films in the USSR, debates between candidates on radio, press and television, and press conferences involving radio and television journalists, all unquestionably have changed the substantive nature of crowds.

What exactly changed? At present, answers to this question are speculative. One difference is semantic. "Crowds" became "masses." The former had been a precise term indicating physical, and usually psychological, contiguity. The latter is imprecise, a variation of the concept of a "public" or "community of interest." Upon close examination, it also reveals a metaphysical rather than physical object of interest or discussion. Le Bon might have defined a "mass" as a "crowd extended to its limits by instruments of technology," and defended his construction with the claim that masses seem to behave much as crowds do. The sociologist Shils has taken the giant conceptual leap of delineating a "mass society" by carefully describing our contemporary culture and subsequently suggesting that whatever a mass society is, this is *it*.[19] Other distinguished sociologists, philosophers and social critics have had their fling at defining a "mass" and have done little better than Shils. The term remains basically ephemeral, imprecise and slightly mystical.

Semantics aside, the "new crowd," "mass," or whatever-it-was-called, differed not only physically and, presumably, psychologically from the crowd of Le Bon, but also strategically. By virtue of the special nature of a physical crowd gathering, it might be addressed on one or two topics, but the range of dispositions with which it was competent to deal was limited. This was true of all physical crowds—on street corners, in opera houses or in classrooms. The context of the setting prescribed the limits of discourse. Sometimes, of course, they may be stretched a bit. When a specific crowd, in the days of the author's youth, gathered to see a burlesque show, they would almost invariably find themselves victimized by a "candy butcher"

---

[19] See Edward Shils, "The Theory of a Mass Society" in Philip Olson (ed.), in *America As A Mass Society* (The Free Press of Glencoe; 1963), pp. 30–47.

during intermission. Few patrons of the burlesque palace objected to this imposition; it was understood to constitute a harmless addition to the artistic-cultural enterprise for which the crowd had gathered—and paid its forty cents. But a single bout per show with the candy butcher was all the audience would countenance. So it occurs with other live crowds that contexts of discourse are invariably limited.

Newspapers to a great degree, radio and television to a lesser extent and films least, modified severely the contextual nature of the meetings of their peculiar, ephemeral crowds. Large minorities of interests may be brought together by a feature story in a newspaper or a radio talk on a relatively esoteric subject. Opinions on political matters may range in a spectrum from left to right on one television program, but they are all exposed to the same mass audience, give or take a few who tune in or out. Exposure was naturally broadened by print and electronic technology, and, as Le Bon notes, the involvement of the new crowds with individual issues, to some degree, decreased—due to the neutralizing counter-forces of antithetical ideas spread by mass communications. Like so many of the present college generation raised in the wide-wide world of television culture, it is now possible for an individual to belong to a number of different "new crowds" and display a great but superficial knowledge concerning a lot of topics, but to ingest little important information about any *particular* subject. Whereas formerly, members of crowds had carefully selected the particular group they joined and given it full attention, "new crowd" members are literally served their gatherings on a platter, attend them only casually, and then slide on to liaison with new publics in, perhaps, entirely different contexts.

Certain occasions remain today similar to the crowd gatherings studied by Le Bon, but they are rare. In recent years, such enormous groups have gathered as mass television crowds giving intensive concentration to such specific occasions of national interest as presidential inaugurations, space voyages, state funerals and interviews with inebriated actors and athletes. When they gather (albeit singly or in family groups) in such concentrations, both Le Bon's and Freud's observations still seem applicable. When they fragment, these principles still apply, but, rather than require further qualification, they are simply less meaningful. As one would expect, fragmentation of attention combined with increased exposure yields merely decreased personal involvement.

It is important, therefore, to remember that, on one hand, the ideas in *The Crowd* are *more* trenchantly relevant to masses today than they were in 1895, because large crowds concentrate on specific events by means of technological instruments of communication. On the other hand, they are *less* relevant to societal processes because the mass is fragmented into smaller crowds by means of these same instruments, and they appeal to a plurality of interests. In this manner, they often reach smaller crowds (many of formidable size), the members of which are less interested (or involved) in the topic of discourse than large mass audiences exposed to what they believe is important, or smaller live groups similarly motivated. Both the unrealized potentials of this paradox and its sly, subtle influence upon our culture in the last two generations is one of the most significant—and often missed—cultural manifestations of contemporary society. Other matters concerning mass communication and group behavior *appear* more important (the amount of violence shown on television, for instance, or the accuracy of political reporting), but in far-reaching consequences, these are but matters of momentary interest. The nature and disposition of the new crowds or masses create a general and over-arching problem of which these issues, and others discussed in the chapters to come, are merely immediate, specific constituents.

Crowd Persuasion

Neither crowds nor masses, naturally and usually, gather for the purpose of being persuaded of anything. The interest of social scientists has been, however, directed largely in attempts to study influences on the beliefs, attitudes, opinions and actions of crowds and masses, regardless of the reasons they have formed—or think they have formed. Artists, like painters, scene designers, actors and writers have been more concerned with crowds in a relatively non-persuasive context, unless one is inclined to consider the evocation of suspense or laughter a form of persuasion. The broad field that we might call "audience psychology" (which includes audiences for mass newspapers, magazines, movies and television shows) is therefore bifurcated into two fields or foci of interest, related but quite discrete.

One is concerned with dispositions and—broadly speaking—a political context: how an individual will react as a crowd member in exercising whatever power he has, including the power of his vote, his power to spend money and his power to influence his children. The other is concerned with dispositions—just as broadly—in an internal, emotional and artistic context, whether or not an individual crowd member perceives an event as exciting, funny or stimulating.

The two interests of course merge in many (or perhaps most) instances.[20] In benign form, the star-studded yearly rally held in New York

[20] See G.N.G., *L C*, pp. 205–210 for a discussion of persuasive motives, particularly in the drama. The main difficulty that I have encountered with the analysis of persuasion by sociologists and psychologists is that they cannot understand collective behavior in its artistic, internal emotional contexts; to their perceptions, every crowd is basically a political crowd. By the same yardstick, artists often refuse frequently to recognize their audiences as socio-political bodies who may construe tears or laughter as politically oriented persuasion, although the objectives that the artist pursues are, he claims, politically neutral. This defense, by the way, was recently and insistently mouthed in the New York press by the producers of a documentary stage drama purporting to dramatize the innocence of convicted spies Julius and Ethel Rosenberg. Their repeated affirmation of motives merely to provide the public with an exciting

City to sell bonds for the State of Israel is as persuasive a gathering as may be found anywhere in the world. It is also an impressive emotional experience. In malignant form, the famous Nazi propaganda film, *Triumph of the Will*, is an excellent example of superb film making and editing, combined with explosively convincing emotional evidence of the virtues of Adolph Hitler and his followers in the days immediately following the blood purge of 1934. A purview of either of these two highly similar spectacles solely from a political or from purely internal, emotional and artistic orientations, would be as misleading as any other sort of examination of their logical characteristics without considering their psychologics, or vice-versa.

Such naïve analyses of crowd stimuli and reactions, it must be added, are presently the *rule* rather than the *exception* in the scholarly world. They are not inaccurate or untrue. In fact, psychologists and sociologists take great pains in preparing and testing the validity of their methods of content analysis and other devices for judging audience reactions like questionnaires and opinion inventories in order to elicit information they think is significant.[21] On the other hand, contemporary artistic criticism may not today be dispensed by Bernard Shaws or Stark Youngs, but much of it is interesting and relevant—but almost entirely *to art alone*, particularly motion picture criticism which seems frequently held captive by an art mystique privy only to the initiated. Social scientists (and what are called "propaganda analysts") call this kind of analysis naïve, and, from their perspective, they are correct, sensitized as they are to the persuasive aspects of communications.

Should a crowd or mass be exposed, then, to persuasion, either because it wants it (as in the case of the individual who attends a political rally) or in spite of the fact that it does *not* want it (as in the case of the captive television audience's exposure to a commercial message), what are the possible outcomes of such experiences?

In the second instance, if the persuasion interferes with the initial objective of the crowd (let us assume enjoyment of a television program), the result will be obvious and inevitable. The crowd will object, either by turn-

---

drama (regardless of its moral or political stance) was indicative either of extraordinary innocence of the dynamics of crowd behavior, sheer stupidity or duplicity in peddling persuasion as art. This trend, incidentally, is now increasingly evident on the American stage, where so-called "documentary" dramas have re-written the history of the Vatican, the Atomic Energy Commission and other politically sensitive institutions. Were they more satisfying artistically, these dramas might justify the aesthetic rationales given for their showing. Social plays of the depression and the various "epic" dramas of Brecht (and his immediate imitators) fared better. One did not need to agree with them politically to enjoy them as art or theatre, the true test of the success or failure of social drama. Neither did one need to enjoy them as drama to accept and be moved by their political persuasion, a test of a different kind.

[21] For as good an overview of the nature and spirit of this kind of investigation, centering mostly upon persuasion in the 1940's, see Chapter XVI, written in collaboration with Paul Lazarsfeld, in Robert Merton, *Social Theory and Social Structure*, pp. 563–582.

ing off the persuasion, or by turning its attention to something else, if it is available. Should it not interfere, the second crowd is much like the first, except for the critical difference that it is subjecting itself to a persuasive communication for a different reason.

Persuasion is usually directed to crowds or masses with the intention merely of *stimulating* their attitudes, beliefs, opinions or actions in some way. Contrary to common wisdom, the intention of much persuasion is not to *change* dispositions but to *activate* them *in a specific context for a specific objective*. The only result that persuasion is almost never designed to produce is probably the one most frequently encountered: that is, failure. It is almost axiomatic that, considering our two kinds of masses (assenting and the accidental), most persuasion is directed at people who did not request it; and most messages of a persuasive nature, falling into the perceptive field of most people most of the time, do not stimulate their dispositions in any manner.[22] It might not exist, for all the effect it has. This is a most difficult principle for behavioral scientists, writers, advertising personnel, and social critics to comprehend.

Should dispositions be touched, the manner of their stimulation varies between two poles: that of stasis and that of change. The former is more frequent than the latter.[23]

First, persuasion may leave dispositions as they were. It may have been designed to accomplish just this, as in the instance of a political party with a plurality of potential voters on its side which campaigns vigorously merely to insure that people will *not* change their anticipated votes. This outcome may also result from the tendency of individuals to enjoy having their beliefs and attitudes stroked and their opinions confirmed.[24] Should they not receive such affirmation, the possibility of drift away from their present stance emerges. Confirmatory persuasion is therefore usually as necessary as it is frequent.

Second, persuasion may move agreement from one category of disposition to another. A belief may be extended to an attitude. An attitude may be crystalized into an opinion. An opinion may be turned into action. Under these circumstances, it is inaccurate to claim that a change in disposition has occurred. It has not. What has occurred, for example, when one

---

22 Estimates as to how many appeals of a commercial nature fall into the average person's field of vision or hearing in the course of a single day run from 500 to 1000. In my case, it is an unusual day if I remember one of them, and I think I am as gullible a sucker as the next man—perhaps moreso.

23 I am grateful to Charles A. Siepmann for, as a small favor in company with many large ones, suggesting most of these outcomes of persuasion to me in various versions during our decade working together at New York University.

24 A joyous childhood memory of my late father centers on his proclivity to listen only to radio broadcasts of political candidates with whom he agreed. Whenever I asked him if he was going to listen to the opposing viewpoints, his response invariably was, "Why should I bother with those liars?" He was a man of extremely rigid dispositions.

donates money to a charity that he had intended to support anyway under the stress of immediate solicitation, is that a new and relatively specific disposition has been precipitated out of a former, more general disposition. The example above is of an opinion turning into an action. In an instance where concern about water pollution is focused by a newspaper article upon a particular industrial plant in one's own neighborhood, one discovers an attitude moving to an opinion. Should a motion picture like "Z" direct one's beliefs about democratic governments to suspicions concerning the role of police departments of countries in turmoil, an attitude has been formulated.

Third, beliefs, attitudes, opinions and actions may be modified—"changed" is too harsh a word. Anyone who has attended a Billy Graham meeting, or spent any time on carnival midways, knows how easy it appears, under certain circumstances, to influence actions. The urge to agree, to conform, to do the right thing is strong. Opinions are more difficult to reach, at least with an influence that may be sustained over any reasonable period of time. Great pressure is usually required to modify attitudes, combined with time and experience, but sometimes attitudes do indeed change, some slowly, others relatively quickly in extreme and dramatic situations. Beliefs also change, but the consideration of how, when and why hurls us into the next chapter. Suffice it to note here that when beliefs are modified, we are discussing such ill-comprehended phenomena as conversion experiences, the influence of so-called "brainwashing," psychological traumae and similar manifestations.

Fourth, persuasion may enter a wedge of doubt into one's actions, opinions, attitudes or beliefs. The wedge is usually the smaller as one moves from actions to beliefs, but the object of any discrete attempt at persuasion may be quite modest. When the individual holds his dispositions in the manner of what we (incorrectly) call a "prejudice"—that is, when a person inclines to thinking in all-inclusive categories or blacks and whites—a wedge of doubt may be all the structure of his fantasy requires to tumble it at some future time. In matters of persuasion, individuals who are absolutely convinced that their dispositions are correct constitute a peculiarly vulnerable class of individuals. Call them "true believers" like Eric Hoffer, or "authoritarian personalities" like Adorno, or "inner-oriented" men like Riesman. They are, collectively or individually, prize targets for persuasion because, in their carefully maintained fantasy, they confuse the shadow of a doubt with a high explosive. And if that doubt can be assimilated into their dispositions (as experiments have shown it may)[25] the explosive may someday be activated.

---

[25] See Eunice Cooper and Marie Jahoda, "The Evasion of Propaganda" in Daniel Katz (ed.), *Public Opinion and Propaganda*, pp. 313–319.

Conclusion

In the seventy-five years since Gustave Le Bon wrote *The Crowd,* the integrity of his principles have stood the abuses of time and doubt remarkably well. Le Bon, of course, spoke merely for only one viewpoint of collective behavior: that of pathological regression which assumes, on the basis of historical study, empirical investigation and experiment (where and when possible) that the behavior of groups is more primitive, emotional and less civilized than the behavior of individuals. In this context, group behavior is implicitly regarded as a variant of individual behavior and responsive to the same sorts of analysis as individual behavior.

A quarter of a century after the publication of *The Crowd,* Freud personally confirmed Le Bon's principles by explaining them in psychoanalytical terms. The total impetus of his analysis—and that of others like Ortega y Gasset, who, from different starting points, attempted similar investigations—was to explain *why* crowds display an organic nature of reciprocal relationships with their leaders, why they seem suggestible, and why civilized restraints of conscience are often diminished in their behavior. Within the limitations of psychoanalytic theory, explanations for these phenomena were provided by Freud.

Le Bon's theory of the crowd was generally rejected by American sociology in favor of analytic constructions that associated crowd behavior with group alliances of the members of the mass and their social roles. Ideas of crowd or audience psychology appeared superfluous at best, erroneous at worst. What Americans (and others) accepted, however, was the mystique of "the mass" or "new crowds," anticipated by Le Bon. The members of this mass drew their communality from shared experience by means of instruments of communication of enormous output and breadth of distribution. Mass man was understood to be a sociological unit (a group member) in whatever social role he played, as influenced by ubiquitous instruments of mass communication.

Persuasion was inherent to the function of the technology of communications in numerous contexts, both important and trivial. Le Bon's insights appear, upon re-examination, to apply with fair relevance to mass as well as old crowd psychology, and they applied easily to patterns of persuasion that had evolved in societies using mass instruments of communication.

The dynamics of persuasion themselves center upon possible outcomes of suggestions made to masses of people in various contexts. And the degree and nature of the stimulation of their dispositions will occur, in all probability, according to the limitations prescribed in the principles of crowd psychology delineated by Le Bon and Freud.

The persuasive aspect of crowd persuasion is often distorted in discussion and study because of a tendency to regard crowd reaction as *either* socio-political *or* artistic-emotional in bias, whereas the two are actually combined in various ways when persuasion works. The process may, however, be analyzed either by means of political or artistic criteria—or both, if possible. Outcomes of persuasion center on the stimulation of beliefs, attitudes, opinions and actions that run on a scale from "no response" to "conversion," passing through points of limited modification and shifts in dispositions, as well as the introduction of the wedge of doubt, a critically important result of crowd persuasion in certain instances.

Chapter 20

ILLUSIONS

Since men are so slightly amenable to reasonable arguments, so completely are they ruled by instinctual wishes, why should one want to take away from them a means of satisfying their instincts and replace it by reasonable arguments?

Sigmund Freud

No purpose is served by asserting—or proving—that man is a credulous creature. Or, more specifically, that modern men, despite their education, access to science and mass communications are as gullible as (or more gullible than) peasants of the Dark Ages, the ancients, or the superstition-ridden, non-compulsorily-educated souls who still live in remote places on the globe in small pockets, relatively untouched by time or progress.

All persuasion presupposes some degree of natural receptivity and possibilities of accomplishing objectives in terms of behavior, opinions, attitudes or beliefs. A superficial look at contemporary persuasion in any form indicates that credulity is, in some degree, a pre-condition of much of this receptivity. As children, our individual credulity was near limitless. Curiosity was assuaged by answers to questions that our parents and other adults and "authorities" provided. The answers were acceptable, *because* they came from elders, no matter how incredible they might have seemed to our childish, but often keen, minds. Teachers and authorities were later substituted for parents,[1] but the patterns of reference had been, by then, in many ways fixed. As various as our curiosities were, we learned by adulthood those particular methods by which we might limn for ourselves a reasonably satisfactory way of comprehending our individual environments.

Obviously, any coherent description of persuasive dynamics requires a theory, model or at least hypothetical evaluation of the degree and nature

[1] For a whimsical but accurate discussion of all kinds of authorities, see John Mulholland and George N. Gordon, *The Magical Mind* (New York: Hastings House, 1967), pp. 35–39. Many years ago I taught a class of junior high school boys, including the

of the credulity of various publics to which persuasion is addressed. No such description, theory, model or hypothesis exists today in more concrete form than the various tenuous conceptual frameworks discussed in Part Three of this volume. At best, they are (like the theory of cognitive dissonance and the concept of "persuasibility") tentative grasps at segments of principles that may some day be organized into coherent and systematic theories—or may not be. In the meantime, we are left with such folk wisdom as that of the mighty Barnum, aphorisms such as, "Nobody ever went broke underestimating the intelligence of the American people," and similar home truths.

Lacking a coherent set of paradigmatic principles, serious discussion tends to center not so much on *whether* we are credulous or *how* we are credulous but the appropriateness of our illusions and obvious persuasibility to political, social, economic and personal aspects of modern life. Bernard Shaw arrived, again and again in his criticism-as-drama, at the fact (as he saw it) that modern culture was almost entirely built upon a substratum of illusion, and that civilized man was simply incapable, in the important matters of life, of facing up either to social or personal reality. With equal integrity and intellectual candor, Eugene O'Neill seemed to have left us the message, in *The Iceman Cometh* (after years of searching for truth and reality in many corners of contemporary thought), that illusions were, and are, all that man really possesses to propel him from this day to the next. If the only way that man may survive, O'Neill seems to be saying, is by virtue of his pipe-dreams, he had better keep dreaming.

Shakespeare knew we were fools (and knew why), but the thinkers of the Enlightenment, the Age of Reason, and the nineteenth century apostles of science, empiricism and positivism had great hopes for our intellectual potentialities. Technology itself, because of its disinterest in emotional or moral matters, also held out considerable promise that men might be guided in earthly affairs by rational criteria, not dreams. The ultimate symbol of this latter faith is, to date, found in the concepts of cybernetics, games theories, systems' engineering and in the utilization of computers to handle swiftly great amounts of data in a rapid and (perhaps more important) an impersonal way in order to utilize our intelligences in all relevant contexts and possibilities. Far from liberating us from illusion, computers themselves have given birth to a new genre of illusions and myths that

---

son of a Japanese-American Buddhist priest. As I understood his tradition, a Japanese youngster does not challenge the authority of his father, especially if he is a Buddhist priest. The latter gentleman explained to me that I was upsetting his household by my teaching methods. After the father had settled some controversial matter for his wife and children, indicating that it was not closed by parental authority, oriental wisdom and Buddha himself, the 'teen-aged son (my student) would cheerily pipe up, "But Dad, *you're wrong!* Mr. Gordon says it didn't happen that way!" The son, now adult, has since learned that Mr. Gordon was *at least* as likely to be as wrong as the Buddha, if not his father's oriental wisdom.

simple-minded programmers, technicians and touts now employ to bilk the gullible for fun and profit, or both.[2]

Education and communications were understood, and continue to be advertised, as civilizing instruments in the service of reason that reduce credulity by teaching methods for obtaining (as far as possible) truth and accurate descriptions of the world around us. Their apparent failures at these tasks are due to many factors, some of them related to human negligence. But the basic assumption that increased available knowledge is somehow the key to reason, let alone wisdom, is sheer fallacy. Quoting W. R. Ashby, neuro-physiologist J. M. R. Delgado states clearly:

> (W)e must "dispose once and for all of the idea . . . that the more communication there is within the brain the better." As we know by personal experience, one of the problems of modern civilization is the confusion produced by a barrage of sensory inputs. We are optically and acoustically assaulted by scientific literature, news media, propaganda and advertisements. The defense is to inhibit the processing of sensory stimuli. Conscious and unconscious behavioral inhibitions should not be considered passive processes but active restraints, like holding the reins of a powerful horse, which prevent the disorderly display of existing potentialities.[3]

If Dr. Delgado is correct, one curiosity is, at least, explained: how it comes to pass that the best informed, most intensively educated generation of youngsters in the history of the world, exposed since childhood to such sophisticated communications as trans-continental color television, seem to display, *en masse*, many more active, visible symptoms of stupidity than their less-blessed predecessors. Delgado's observations, based largely upon studies of brain function and capacity, also lend credence to the arguments of many over the years who suggest that educators follow Whitehead's advice to teach fewer (far fewer) subjects to the young, but to teach what they teach *more thoroughly*. Lastly, these surmises are a direct blow to those who still maintain, despite evidence and over a century's experience, that the solution to most of society's problems will inevitably be achieved by educating (somehow and one day) a full generation of civil human beings, and it is even *reasonable* to maintain that new technology, particularly modern instruments of communication, will somehow facilitate this process.[4] Our experience in the United States has in no manner (with the

---

[2] A sophisticated computer installed in New York's Grand Central Station plots individual horoscopes according to variables like moment of birth, sex and other esoteric information. As far as I know, it does as well—or better than—other computers I have met that perform similar tasks.

[3] José M. R. Delgado, *Physical Control of the Mind*, p. 156.

[4] This viewpoint has a remarkable number of exponents, even excluding those realistic educators who espouse this line because their livelihood depends upon it. They are best spoken for by idealists in books like William Clark Trow, *Teacher and Technology* (New York: Appleton-Century Crofts, 1963), and by other humane proponents of audiovisual education. The best book containing civilized, but far from

exception of our development of a few arts of leisure and the use of gadgets) vindicated these assumptions, although they are still treated as facts, and sacred facts, by politicians, educators and social service leaders. Nor have similar experiences in any other nation in the world, including the USSR, other than replicated our experience and Delgado's observation.

This disheartening problem will be subsequently agonized over further.[5] For the present, let us draw perimeters for a (more-or-less) organized analysis of specific illusions as they bear directly upon persuasion. For persuasion itself is frequently the child, or step-child, of illusion, fashion and fad. Except possibly for religion and education, no cultural phenomenon displays quite the history of illusory biases as the arts of persuasion as we have examined them. Today's space myths and technological ritualism run no closer to our collective cultural nerve than the illusions pertaining to the practice of persuasion in the days of Barnum. There is also a special perfection about them, a wicked closure that produces a snowball syndrome.

Illusions about persuasion have, since pre-historic times, by themselves increased human credulity in much the manner that illusions about primitive magic enhanced the power of the sorcerer. Here we meet the familiar story of the emperor's new clothes: If people are made to believe that this or that individual, process or symbol has the power to render them persuasible, then this or that individual process or symbol *will*, in most instances, *render them persuasible*. Call this tendency by a recent cognomen like "the self-fulfilling prophecy" (to be discussed in Part Five), prattle about hypnosis and suggestibility (and we shall), or relegate it to any one of countless psychodynamics, it remains an ancient and well-exploited curiosity of behavior and mind. Credulity, therefore, is most easily enhanced in the credulous, a tautological but extremely practical observation. Upon it is built the structure of most modern political and social propaganda as well as some important (but not essential) aspects of commercial advertising.

This function of myths about persuasion (or credulity) would present to us nothing more than an amusing aside concerning quirks of human nature were the most persuasible and credulous among us somehow obviously set apart from the rest of the population by costume, skin color or tattoos. But this is not the case. In fact, the reverse obtains. We have noted that orderly experimentation does not convincingly set apart individuals defined by psychologists as "persuasible." Neither does common sense, simply because persuasibility (if it exists) appears not to be a function of the indices by which we ordinarily tend to categorize people. Like wisdom (in many ways its opposite), it seems to occur anywhere and everywhere and to

---

encouraging, analysis of implications of this faith is Charles A. Siepmann, *Radio Television and Society* (New York: Oxford University Press, 1950). Although dated, it bespeaks a deep, humanistic belief in man's ability to use technology for the pursuit of reason, a stance which I envy Siepmann.

[5] See Chapters 22, 26, and also refer back to Chapter 9.

have nothing to do with conventional signposts like education and/or intelligence. Also like wisdom, it appears to be most active in individuals who do not believe they display it.

Roughly speaking, the most persuasible and credulous people are therefore those who fancy they have mastered reason and hold their dispositions as naturally correct—that is, as cognitive and emotional extensions of perceived reality. The man of doubt will not only doubt his own conclusions, but he will also doubt persuasion designed to manipulate those conclusions, as well as affirmations that he is, in fact, persuasible. He is therefore difficult to persuade of anything. The savant, the oracle, the politician, the specialist, the professor, the activist, the pillar of society and the "true believer" will look at others and wonder how and why certain fools manage to sustain their silly notions in the light of the reality to which *he* is privy. The answer he gives himself *must* be that some people (not himself, of course) are persuasible and highly credulous. Ergo: Persuasion is powerful medicine; credulity is a harsh vice. Having thus been set up for an assault upon the bases of his opinions, attitudes and beliefs, he may be activated in many ways by persuasion, *providing always that such a person is assured of the intelligence and correctness of his dispositions and their relevance to the cultural realities to which he is committed.*

Persuasive Illusions

Freud claimed that the main and major neurosis of culture was religion. His argument is closely reasoned and persuasive in its bitter way, and according to one's personal spiritual beliefs, differentially convincing. If God exists, the futility of arguing him away is obvious, because the arguer is a mortal man. Freud, however, accomplished two things in his essay: he identified from a psychoanalytical perspective the source of man's need for God (which can easily be subsumed into either theological or anti-theological value systems), and he identified, by implication, a general human disposition towards mysticism in which God-beliefs are but a subcomponent. At the risk of oversimplifying a heroic intellectual feat, the critical insight in Freud's work is the proposition that "(B)y accepting the universal neurosis he (man) is spared the task of forming a personal neurosis." [6]

One matter is therefore clarified: the problem of how ideas, as removed from most human experience as those in full-blown mysticisms, have, for as long as we have had a record, been widely accepted, although they center on apparently irrational and uncritical notions concerning the most important elements of man's environment. The psychoanalytic view holds that these ideas have been crude grasps after what we today call "mental health." And, if one has ever experienced the subjective consola-

[6] Sigmund Freud, *The Future of An Illusion*, p. 79, previously cited and discussed in this volume on pp. 192–194 in reference to religious persuasion.

tion of religion, one is aware of the ways in which mysticism, at times of personal disorientation, helps the individual to deal with reality instead of deserting it in favor of derangement or suicide.[7] If they illustrate nothing else, both theory and experience indicate that man has a deep capacity for belief in extremely unlikely things when such beliefs serve a valid individual, subjective function.

Our task is not to evaluate the worthiness of any of these beliefs. Clearly, all mysticism is not of one piece. Even in its most bizarre manifestations, it may turn out to be merely a symptom of an organic derangement, the result of introducing a foreign chemical into the body, a consequence of a nervous system under stress or an apparently unmotivated spontaneous occurrence. There is also a great difference, for most people, between believing in the miracle of lucky charm, a belief in astrology, belief in God as a concept, and belief in the immediate grace supposedly achieved by an act of religious obeisance, although some would hold (crudely, in the author's opinion) that they are all essentially the same, on the grounds that they deal with non-perceptible, largely non-measurable psychological phenomena. As *acts* of belief, certainly, they *are* similar. But, as these beliefs crystallize into attitudes, opinions and actions, their differences become increasingly apparent, due to their relationships with cultural consensus regarding the adequacy of available knowledge and the weight of relevant authority.

Proceeding one step further, it is possible, using temporal-cultural criteria, to qualify such illusions on many dimensions, but our discussion here does not concern the quality of mysticism or human spirituality, merely persuasive illusions.[8] In short, there are two main kinds: first, those illusions that individuals think are illusions but in which they believe regardless; and, second, those illusions that are not comprehended as illusions but as genuine sense data.

In the first group, we might place the God beliefs of many of us who maintain our spiritual feelings (in spite of our doubts) on the basis that the cosmos may indeed contain the unknowable about which men may achieve strong feelings but glean little substantive information. Certainly, the personal realm of fantasy, from childhood onwards, usually belongs in the first category. And so do those transcendental experiences through which we live from time to time that may be explained *post hoc* by adequate sense data, right or wrong.

---

[7] This issue has been previously treated, but it is worth restating the fact here that there is no shortage of evidence that people with firm and well-interiorized spiritual beliefs weather crisis situations better than those without them. See Bruno Bettelheim, *The Informed Heart* (The Free Press of Glencoe, Illinois, 1960), for an excellent discussion of this phenomenon in the Nazi concentration camps, one among numerous other studies of this truism.

[8] See Chapter 11 for a discussion that takes the role of spiritual persuasion (in our tradition) as far as it reasonably extends without moving into the realm of metaphysics.

In the second group, we have already discussed the fundamental persuasive illusion in our culture: the belief that man is a highly persuasible creature. Like all essentially mystical notions, little if any sense data supports this proposition except rough empirical evidence, manifestly tautological: Man is persuasible, because he is easily persuaded; to be persuaded we must believe he is persuasible, etc. (Similar arguments have been made for centuries concerning the existence of God, based on empirical evidence that illustrates the apparent operation of a divine intelligence; and off one runs into another tautology.) In the end, the concept of man's persuasibility remains a common-sense proposition that, quite justifiably, psychologists are, at the present writing, trying to prove, disprove or qualify, just as, at the present writing, equally keen minds are still exploring the viability of God.

History is replete with flamboyant examples of the second types of illusions, fortunately no longer involved, in their journey through time, with syllogistic or tautological traps. Illusions of the most outrageous sort have been and are accepted by masses of people, including, frequently, intelligent individuals who possess both enough information and ability to judge them adequately. Sometimes they result from hoaxes, either sheer mischief or con-schemes, and find their way, like Piltdown Man, into the annals of science. Sometimes, like flying saucer illusions, they appear spontaneously generated by many different types of people, usually responding to similar stimuli at the same time. Sometimes, it is difficult to tell whether they are hoaxes or not; more than one illusion has been metamorphosed into fact by history.

The record, however, of the lengths to which man's fancy may lead him is one of the most interesting aspects of that history, increasingly incredible as one moves into the age of science and universal education, because of the previously noted and generally accepted illusion that science and education are safeguards against gullibility. If anything, both the methods of science and the spread of learning seem to *expand* the individual's potential *for* accepting illusion as fact: Science indicates, even to the scientist, that things (particularly cause-and-effect relationships) are rarely what they seem. If invisible microbes cause diseases, may not then invisible monsters inhabit the moon? Science and technology merely open new imaginative possibilities for deception and illusion.

Education therefore often widens one's *potential* breadth of credulity. If one studies the weird physiology of the duck-billed platypus, then may he not also accept as reasonable the notion that a race of reptile-men once ruled the continent of Atlantis? Both science and education, therefore and by their nature, increase the general ability to *be* hoaxed. More than this, in our culture, it is specifically *highly educated, scientifically oriented* individuals who are frequently among the first and most ardent dupes of illusion masquerading as fact. The casebook is replete with the story of the tendency, seemingly incredible, because it is often educators and scientists who lend their prestige to fantastic conclusions that their "open minds" have accepted, and they are then responsible for the spread and maintenance of illusions that the so-called "average man" has no way of evaluating fairly.[9]

At this point, the reader may be nodding his head in agreement, but perhaps he will stop when the writer lists a few of what *he* regards are important current illusions, generally regarded as truth that will, he believes, before the year 2,000 A.D. be identified generally as deliberate or misguided hoaxes: the writings of Alfred Korzybski and the study of general semantics;[10] the theories of Wilhelm Reich;[11] the concepts (or whatever they are) of Marshall McLuhan;[12] all records of children raised by wild animals;[13] extra-sensory perception;[14] brainwashing;[15] (hold your breath) hypnotism;[16] and many, many more equally as sacrosanct modern truths. The latter three are particularly relevant to the climate in which persuasion operates. Let us examine them briefly.

Concerning extra-sensory perception or ESP, the facts speak for themselves,[17] and center mostly on the futile efforts of Dr. J. B. Rhine of Duke University to demonstrate scientifically that mind-reading is possible. Rhine failed, but mind-readers still do remarkably well as entertainers, and occasionally their miracles are still taken seriously by scientists. That men *appear* to read other people's thoughts is not curious; the art is not simple, but it is not too difficult to accomplish either. It requires some study,

---

[9] Keeping track of this folly is a minor hobby of mine. I recommend the following books to those who, like me, find gullibility not only amusing but humbling. An excellent work on the psychology of illusion is J. P. Chaplin, *Rumor, Fear and the Madness of Crowds* (New York: Ballantine Books, 1959). Bergan Evans, *The Natural History of Nonsense* (New York: Vintage Books, 1958), is, by now, a classic in the study of common illusions, many of which are still generally believed. Concerning deliberate, unintentional hoaxes, the most complete, easily available volume is Curtis D. MacDougall, *Hoaxes* (New York: Ace Books, 1958). Martin Gardner, *Fads and Fallacies* (New York, Dover Publs. Inc., 1957), covers far fewer illusions but treats them in greater detail. If your interests lead you into the study of imposters, chiselers, swindlers and confidence men, see any of the anthologies by Alexander Klein (ed.), such as, *Grand Deception, The Fabulous Rogues, The Magnificent Scoundrels* (New York: Ballantine Books, 1955, 1958, 1960), and also the classic on con-schemes, David W. Maurer, *The Big Con* (New York: Pocket Books, 1949).

[10] See Gardner, pp. 281–291, and read Korzybski.

[11] See *op. cit.*, pp. 250–262, and read Reich.

[12] So many articles have treated this foolery that I hesitate to pick one. The best, I think, is Roy Huggins, "It's Time to Turn Off McLuhan," *Television Magazine*, March 6, 1968, pp. 30–43, and read McLuhan.

[13] See Evans, *op. cit.*, pp. 85–97.

[14] See below.

[15] See below.

[16] See below.

[17] See Gardner, *op. cit.*, pp. 299–314. Also note Milbourne Christopher, *ESP, Seers and Psychics*, (New York: Thos. Y. Crowell Co., 1970).

dexterity, a sense of showmanship and nerve.[18] What is of concern is why ESP is accepted by many intelligent people, and why the issue of the possibility of mind-reading remains today an all too open one. In other words, how is such an illusion sustained?

The answer is deceptively simple should we place the blame (if blame it is) upon those working performers who give us convincing demonstrations of thought transference. After all, they advertise that they are performers, and even Dunninger never really *said* that he was able to read minds; he simply *did not say* he could *not.*

But the reasons this illusion is acceptable are more subtle than charlatanry and concern evidence we experience in our relationships with others that frequently tells us more than we think we should know about them. What occurs results in part from ongoing sensitivities to the kinds of perceptive cues covered by Hall in his work,[19] and other types of non-verbal communication already discussed. They center, first, upon the use of spaces between people, so-called "proxemic" cues; second, upon apprehensions of temperature change in others by means of detectors in the skin, acuity of smell that increases with heat and closeness, and other visual manifestations of bodily temperature change like blushing; third, by overt physical contacts, extremely revealing mediators of sensual cues; fourth, by kinesthesia, kinetics or "body language," as well as directly active visual cues such as moustache stroking or ring twirling; and fifth, by the interplay of all these cues in a given situation within conventional social intercourse that reveal more about individuals than might be expected.[20] The total effect yields a more or less justified assumption, that, considering these overt "extra-

[18] In my youth, I worked odd hours and part-time as a professional magician and mind-reader. I was a better mind-reader than magician, and like may of them, I passed off my skill as a "gift." (Dunninger the magician was employing the same euphemism on radio in those days and had achieved enormous popularity.) I shall not expose any magicians' secrets here; they are all in the proper books for those who want to search them out. But I shall affirm that apparently reading a stranger's mind (telling him his 'phone number, what letters he has in his pocket, the serial numbers on his cash and similar tricks) is no more difficult (or incredible) than forcing a card or multiplying billiard balls or sawing a woman in half. The end product of them all is illusion. In the case of the latter, we reject the evidence of our eyes, because we know that bisecting a living woman and putting her back together again is impossible. In the case of mind-reading, we often do not reject what we see, because we have accepted the illusion that extra-sensory perception is, perhaps, possible. Let me assure the reader that neither I, nor any of my magician friends over the years, have ever seen one human being truly *read* another's mind. On the other hand, I have met a number of psychologists and psychiatrists who *have!* Let the reader judge why.

[19] See Edward T. Hall, *The Silent Language* and *The Hidden Dimension,* previously cited.

[20] Professional mind-readers employ these devices, either knowingly or unknowingly, but they are almost entirely auxiliary to the specific *modus operandi* of any particular demonstration of mind-reading. A professional mind-reader *cannot* take the chance of not being able to perform his miracles, so cues of these sorts are extra bonuses for him that, handled properly, may prove both amusing and bewildering in performance. But every mind-reading illusion has its own specific method of legerdemain.

sensory" perceptions that are visible to normal individuals, a *super-normal* person should therefore be able to obtain, in the same manner, even more explicit information. In effect, we hoax ourselves by an apparently reasonable, but quite impossible, extenuation of a valid proposition.

"Brainwashing" is one of the few phenomena known to have found its way into the Psychiatric Dictionary almost exclusively because it is an intriguing and colorful word, loaded incidentally with political connotations.[21] It achieved currency in our language due to treatment given American prisoners of war during the Korean conflict by the North Koreans, treatment brutally designed to convince them to cooperate with their captors. While such practices have long been common in warfare, the type of pressure used by the North Koreans was a comparatively new experience for the United States' military forces. Intensive solicitation of feigned and real ideological cooperation with the enemy on the part of prisoners of war had never before been publicized as it was during the Korean conflict.

In truth, most of our captured soldiers were treated poorly by the North Koreans, and they received extra privileges if they went through the motions of a Marxist-Maoist conversion. Quite a number pretended to. A mere handful, in fact, "converted" sufficiently to request to remain in Communist territory after the truce. But the word "brainwashing" emerged from the episode.[22]

The soldiers had actually behaved much as American prisoners captured by the Japanese in World War II had, but the word "brainwashed" was not at that time applied to defectors, because it had not yet been invented. Two books with provocative titles, one treating the new mystique of "brainwashing" from a Pavlovian point of view[23] and the other from the Freudian perspective,[24] gave the term psychological currency. The result is that, to this day, the technique of "brainwashing" is believed by many—in-

---

[21] Political experts agree that Governor George Romney inadvertently rendered himself ineligible for the Republican presidential nomination in 1968 bcause he admitted having been "brainwashed" by U.S. military personnel during a trip to Vietnam. Presumably, any man whose "brain" could be "washed" by public relations flacks is unfit to run for the office of President of the United States. Had Romney known a little about the psychologics of communications, he might have picked a happier term.

[22] See Edward Hunter, *Brainwashing* (New York: Pyramid Books, 1958). The subtitle of Hunter's well researched volume is "The Story of the Men Who Defied It." His report of the treatment of American P.O.W.'s in North Korea is grim. But, except for the implication in the title of his book, he reports nothing unusual in the treatment by their captors given these men. Most who survived kept their brains, and loyalties, intact, although, like most people under stress, some had been driven to bizarre extremes of behavior.

[23] See William Sargant, *Battle for the Mind* (New York: Doubleday and Co., Inc., 1957).

[24] See Joost A. Meerloo, *The Rape of the Mind* (New York: World Publishing Co., 1956). Richard Condon's science-fiction novel *The Manchurian Candidate* (and the film made of it) also contributed to the currency of the magical power of the term "brainwashing."

cluding psychologists—to entail a foolproof method of manipulating beliefs and attitudes.[25]

As these reasonably legitimate books above (and others) make perfectly clear, "brainwashing" is simply a new term for a collection of ancient techniques. (The publishers, dust jacket designers and promoters of these volumes, however, kept this a secret. They stressed the mystique of the new term rather than the contents of the books.) Many of the artists of interrogation during the holy Inquisition from the twelfth to seventeenth centuries developed numerous highly effective methods for modifying, changing or annihilating beliefs and attitudes in colorful ways.[26] Methods included racks, application of molten lead and fire, starvation, use of whips, thumbscrews, spikes, branding irons, water treatments, and various other techniques that produced some of the most remarkable confessions of odd behavior from the unlikeliest people that have ever been recorded. (The North Koreans were somewhat more subtle; but not much more.) Regardless of the elegance of the technique used, the combination of torture and fear reach a climax at a psychological saturation point for most people. They are, thereafter, extremely "persuasible." In Europe, Communist inquisitors of the past generation have also apparently employed new drugs and theatrical hokum as well as physical coercion to extract confessions and modify dispositions, but essentially the same suggestive methods have been used since antiquity.

As long as it was known as the "third degree" or "the treatment," coercive modification of dispositions was generally understandable. When it became "brainwashing" two results followed: first, it was now a mystical phenomenon (and many types of conversion experiences throughout history have apparently been stimulated by mysticism *alone*); second, the task of coercion became easier by mere recourse to the word "brainwashing." In the latter instance, the Communists thereby won a round in the cold war. Convinced, as many in the West were, that the Communists possessed sophisticated methods based on esoteric psychological principles to perform black magic called "brainwashing," their own vulnerabilities were accord-

---

[25] A well performed British film called *The Prisoner* is based on the arrest and subsequent confession of Cardinal Mindszenty in Hungary to apparently false charges of treason and espionage. In the film, the Cardinal's confession to crimes he did not commit is shown as the end product of stresses created in a complex relationship with his Inquisitor. The term "brainwashing" is not used, but a mystical process is implicitly involved. The reasons the real Cardinal Mindszenty confessed to similar charges remain obscure, but his confession merely demonstrates that Cardinals are human. Any small-town police chief with a rubber hose knows well that he can probably extract a confession of anything from anyone if he really wants to and has enough nerve, guts and time. Nor does he need to use the rubber hose as long as he can display it to his victim.

[26] See the description of these devices and the reasons they were employed in Homer W. Smith, *Man and His Gods* (New York: Grosset and Dunlap, 1952), pp. 230–296, especially the graphic descriptions of brainwashing techniques recommended in the fifteenth century *Malleus Maleficarum* of Pope Innocent VIII, pp. 281–292.

ingly expanded. If one believes he is going to be "brainwashed," and that there is no defense against this mystical process, one had just as well begin convincing himself of the integrity of a bogus confession and new dispositional state and thus save his inquisitors time and trouble, and himself acute discomfort. Much psychological double-talk accordingly surrounds "brainwashing": "equivalent," "paradoxical" and "ultraparadoxical phases of cortical activity and similar terms provide for it a peculiarly modern and sinister flavor. The word and the concept unfortunately remain with us to this day, along with the mystique.

Concerning hypnotism, the author treads a more dangerous path. If hypnotism does not exist—or is in some manner a sham—what was Mesmer up to in France? What was Freud studying in the Paris that led him to his concepts of neurosis? What about the present enormous medical literature on the use of hypnosis in psychiatry and for anesthesis in dental surgery and childbirth? What about the films that have *actually demonstrated* vaginal anesthesia of the labia, pins pushed painlessly into human cheeks, spikes run through flesh and other miracles? What about dramatic exhibitions of hypnotic control of autonomic nervous and muscular processes and control of blood flow and cessation of human heartbeat in self-hypnosis?[27] What about post-hypnotic suggestion?

The answers to these questions are similar to those which explain ESP. First, most of us have witnessed various physical miracles that we accepted as illusions, because they were performed by a magician. Lesser miracles, performed by men or women called "hypnotists" appear even more amazing, because we believe they are genuine. Frequently, also, honest psychologists and medical people are drawn into accepting hypnotism on its face by over-cooperative subjects who enjoy (or perhaps need) the attention that is usually given a supposedly good hypnotic subject. And simple suggestion—minus the hypnotic trance—was certainly inducement enough to persuade the poor mental patients in Charcot's Paris clinic (and others in thousands of clinics since) to placate an authoritative, if somewhat deluded, doctor for whatever privileges and approval are received from such cooperation. As a matter of fact, Freud subsequently discovered that he could accomplish what the French mesmerizers accomplished in neurosis-transference *with-*

---

[27] In all modesty, I can easily demonstrate any of the above, providing that *I* set the conditions for the demonstrations. Professional hypnotists ask the same concession, on the basis that, first, an individual cannot be hypnotized against his will (therefore excluding me, for instance, as a potential subject), and second, that a proper environment for hypnosis must be obtained. I am also (under certain conditions) prepared to give demonstrations of self-hypnosis, like stopping my heartbeat, as anyone competent to take my pulse may discover. I am also a whiz at self-anesthesia. Let me aver, however, that, precisely because I *am* competent to demonstrate that hypnosis *does* exist, I am extremely skeptical that it is possible. What I *can* arrange are conditions for exercises of showmanship and theatrical, magical illusions—to my thinking, far more miraculous phenomena than hypnosis.

out so-called "hypnosis," and thus was born the present couch-bound technique of psychoanalytic free association.

Time magazine sums up the present status of hypnosis with pith in a report of the work of Dr. Theodore X. Barber of the Medfield State Hospital in Massachusetts who is, at present, demonstrating the obvious: that no valid tests have ever existed for the presence of the hypnotic state or trance, and that anything accomplished by a subject supposedly under hypnosis may also be achieved with one who has not been hypnotized and is wide awake, often by the simple expedient of direct, overt, verbal, non-mystical suggestions. Notes *Time:*

> In one experiment, he subjected two groups of student nurses to identical degrees of pain: excruciating but not injurious pressure on a finger. The first group was "hypnotized" and instructed to listen to a tape recording of a story as a way to ignore the pain. The second group was simply told "that if they kept thinking about the story during the pain stimulation, they would not experience pain." Both reported equivalent pain reduction . . .
>
> Hypnosis allegedly cures warts. So does suggestion. Barber reports that the wart count among some New York school children fell dramatically after their warts were painted with chemically inert dyes identified as effective medication. Barber also discounts feats of strength under hypnosis, such as the ability of a man to make his body so rigid that he can be stretched like a plank between two chairs. "Practically all normally awake persons can remain suspended between two chairs while supported only by the head and ankles," Barber says.
>
> Barber notes that hypnotists have claimed the ability to produce and inhibit labor contractions and allergic reactions, to improve vision and to change heartbeat rates, blood-glucose levels and stomach-acid secretions. But, he says, "in each case there is evidence that the same things can also be obtained by suggestion alone." . . .
>
> The ultimate power of suggestion is reflected in the subject's own conception of hypnosis, he believes. People "know" that hypnotized subjects are supposed to act like glassy-eyed zombies. Thus, when it is suggested that they are hypnotized, they obediently act as expected. To demonstrate the point, Barber cites an experiment by Philadelphia psychiatrist Martin Orne. Orne told a class of introductory-psychology students that, under hypnosis, a subject's dominant hand automatically becomes cataleptic—that is, it cannot be moved. That is simply not true. Nevertheless, when he put the class under "hypnosis," 55% of his students were unable to move their dominant hand.
>
> Barber's arguments lead to the conclusion that hypnosis may be no more than a fancy name for human suggestibility. The same preconditions are required in both cases: a willingness to do what the suggester asks, the belief in one's ability to do it—*plus* the ability to do it. The importance of the latter is often overlooked.[28]

[28] *Time* Magazine, July 13, 1970, pp. 54–55.

Stage and nightclub hypnotists use methods more dramatic and subtle (and certain of outcome) than those employed by Barber, but these are neither more nor less clever than the feats of any other magicians. In fact, a hypnotist's audience is generally easier to deceive than one a conventional conjurer usually faces. The latter deals with a group of highly skeptical individuals who dare him, in effect, to fool them. The stage hypnotist generally performs before an audience that *knows* that hypnotism is possible and *expects* to see it occur before their eyes. They are, therefore, often unusually cooperative, accounting for some of the stage hypnotist's effects, but not all of them. The lion's share of hypnosis, in and out of the scientific laboratory (intentionally and unintentionally) is performed by ancient devices of theatrical legerdemain, well known to most professional (and some amateur) magicians.[29]

Once again, as *Time* indicates, the myth of persuasion itself creates the conditions for that persuasion. And the conditions also increase the power of persuasion. Credulity and suggestibility seem to know few limits, and a profound truth resides in Freud's concept of illusion: that men require illusions by which to live; discussion of whether they are good or bad, moral or immoral or ethical or unethical is frequently beside the point. As one illusion is shattered, another takes its place, and no amount of education or persuasion will change the matter. In fact, both or either may simply increase the ubiquity of the illusion and the capacity of people to accept it, no matter how unreasonable it seems. Most of the illusions we laugh at today are those our grandparents took seriously. And many of *us* have, or will have, grandchildren.

The Manufacture of Illusions

One issue must be clear, and Freud himself is the object lesson for it. Excluding the pragmatic view of life, scientific ontology or the logical positivist's epistemology, there is no historical or propositional statute that states that the worship, acceptance or promulgation of illusion is bad, immoral, unethical, lazy or fattening. As we have noticed, certain thinkers have counseled us to cosset our illusions, the only things some of us own exclusively. To respect reality (as defined by self-determined realists) as the most adequate form of provisional truth we know, and to respect sense data is reasonable. To *worship* sense data and/or reality to the exclusion of every other type of human experience is, in the opinion of the author, naïve, foolish and sometimes psychopathic—just as unwise as to worship illusion. *The Future of a Reality,* if the "Reality" is construed as strictly scientific proof, would make as provocative and danger-laden a title for a monograph as *The Future of an Illusion,* in a manner Freud might not have under-

---

[29] Ask any stage or nightclub hypnotist how his "horses" are, and be prepared for a quick get-away.

stood, but which has been made brutually clear to us by a number of his followers.

If, for instance, an illusion may be sustained in people who are (for reasons we do not understand) apparently addicted to alcohol, that they suffer from a disease called "alcoholism" (displaying few of the characteristics of any other familiar disease),[30] and if this illusion helps such people to stop drinking (as it frequently does), well and good. It is, for such people, a *valuable* illusion, and it constitutes, along with other equally viable and salubrious illusions, the *only* form of psychotherapy (not employing shock treatment or drugs) that may be shown with statistical regularity to *work:* specifically the techniques of the Alcoholics Anonymous fellowship. AA is simply *one* example out of thousands in which facing up to reality, under certain circumstances, is self-destructive—and where accepting illusion constitutes a rational, sane alternative, given the social matrix in which the reality and the illusion are judged.

On the other hand, and unfortunately in more dramatic contexts, when ideas (similar to those employed by AA) exploit mere suggestions from the embryo sciences of proxemics and kinesics into faddist illusions such as the cult of so-called "sensitivity training," the results are usually not healthy. As London notes,[31] sensitivity trainers are usually "expositors of moral doctrines, bearers of ideologies and secular priests" for mystical hedonism rather than therapy. And the technique of adults feeling and groping at each other in the hope of reducing neuroses constitutes an absurd, hair-raising fraud in the eyes of Edward T. Hall, the father of proxemics himself.[32] Illusion here becomes a confidence trick, in the opinion of many, albeit one with few prospects for long-term profit.

To encourage—even exploit—man's illusions is therefore neither immoral nor unethical *per se.* Questions center on *what* illusions, the *motives* for their exploitation and the probable end-product of the process. For all we know, the most unrealistic illusion which man has ever contrived is the concept of a peaceful order between societies and nations; a fine historical case (bolstered by ethological, anthropological and other evidence) may be made that constant warfare is a universal reality, given by nature to the human condition. Should this insight stay the hand of *one* man who might contribute towards the achievement of peace where war exists, the price of reality would be too high. By all means, let us encourage his illusions and our own illusion, perhaps, that we *are able* to encourage them.

An endless principle of closure, however, attends the acceptance of

---

30 See Craig MacAndrew, "On the Notion that Certain Persons Who are Given To Frequent Drunkenness Suffer from a Disease Called Alcoholism" in Plog and Edgerton, (ed.), *op. cit.*, pp. 485–501.

31 London, *Behavior Control,* p. 162.

32 See the interview with Hall on this subject in William Braden, *The Age of Aquarius* (Chicago: Quadrangle Books, 1970), pp. 246–247.

illusion in civilization. The luxury of accepting benign illusions frequently includes the acceptance of malignant ones as well. Although psychology has not yet confirmed the point, it is doubtful that people tend to be selectively credulous and choose only to believe those fancies that are good for them. Nor are our priests of science, religion, scholarship or government presently wise enough to distinguish one from the other. Many contend that the price of the God illusion includes, inevitably, the illusion of organized religion: saints, priests, churches and the chronicle of evils (as well as benevolences) performed in God's name. Right or wrong, the example applies also in many other instances. The price of the illusion of free will is a panoply of superstitions, from astrology to voodoo. The price of the illusion of human equality is the illusion of representative government and all its impediments. The rest of the pages of this book might be filled with further examples.

The worship of illusion, being the apparent "natural" (and the word is used cautiously) state of all cultures we have known, its exploitation into manifold cultural fancies is therefore inevitable. Cynics claim that nine-tenths of the beliefs that are held by most people today may be shown, by more or less scientific methods, to be bunkum. The observation is gratuitous, because at any point in human history, and in any culture one chooses, nine-tenths of the beliefs of most people may, using that society's method of reality-testing, be shown also to be bunkum. The issue is never contestable. What is critical is *how* the bunkum is employed. And the criteria for judging its value do not differ markedly from those used by the historian or sensitive observer in judging the values of any other culture trait.

Our society is no exception. We have learned that the triad of contemporary lodestones—science, technology and education—do not appear to diminish proclivities for cherishing illusions one jot or tittle. In fact, they seem to encourage them. In a more optimistic period, it was considered "a mark of an educated man" that he did not believe the egregious illusions of his time.[33] Today, the more educated a person, the more likely he seems prone to extend his illusions with foolhardy gall into areas beyond his competence. No more liberally educated segment of our society exists than the members of the advertising and public relations community and other similar merchants of feathers and eyewash. That they have—almost to a man and woman—swallowed their own mystiques and illusions is apparent in their memoirs, which frequently climb to the best seller lists, simply because they so effectively re-enforce the same illusions which advertisers spin.[34]

---

[33] See Albert Edward Wiggam, *The Marks of an Educated Man* (Indianapolis: Bobbs-Merrill Company, 1930) for an interesting study of common superstitions and misbeliefs forty years ago.

[34] I mean here the supposedly reliable writing of such artists as David Ogilvy, Fairfax

The temptation to end this chapter with a case study not yet in the literature of fads and fancies is too great to resist:

Americans have, during the past two generations at least, been extremely sensitive about normal body odors.[35] To the best of my knowledge, it was the hucksters of Lifebuoy Soap who coined the term "B.O." for body odor in the interest of their product: a blood-red bar of soap smelling of carbolic acid that was supposed to replace "B.O." with its own foul odor. "B.O." being an illusion, the illusory power of Lifebuoy soap was obvious. It succeeded naturally, in eliminating odors that did not exist (or were not unpleasant), and everyone concerned was made happy. Consumers loved the soap. Soapmakers thrived. Advertisers grew rich.

During the years before World War II, it was discovered that the application of an aluminum salt to the armpit areas of both men and women (a portion of the body uncomfortably close to certain sensitive and important lymph nodes) would decrease slightly the smell of perspiration from said armpits. The deodorant industry followed in the wake of this scientific breakthrough with a wide range of armpit lotions.

In developing both of these markets, illusions of guilt were aroused by advertisement: guilt concerning body odors of one type or another. Palliatives of questionable effectiveness (compared to a good scrub in a tub of water) were eventually widely accepted by the public as necessary to diminish this guilt. Illusion neutralized illusion. Demands were created where once they did not exist. Wheels of commerce turned. People continued smelling more or less like people, but they were convinced they did not. Stockholders thrived, employment boomed and children and their aged parents were supported by the profits. What was basically an illusion was now an integral part of our economy.

In 1969, absurdity had reached a new dimension.

In our environment, women have always been sensitive concerning vaginal odors, a problem, I am assured, easily solved in most cases by salt water douches and, during menstruation, frequent changes of sanitary napkins or tampons. So much for the gynecology of the issue. At the end of the second decade of our century, Town Unlimited, a subsidiary of McKesson Laboratories, employed the services of a well known advertising agency, to tout their new product *Cupid's Quiver*. *Cupid's Quiver* represents the ultimate illusion in smell prevention: it is a sachet of vaginal douche which

---

Cone, Jerry Della Femina and company. Eventually, nearly every advertising genius writes a book about how he turned the trick that brought him riches and fame. But nothing is clearly explained. Still living under the mystiques of his profession, his insights are useless illusions, generally accepted by his peers and naturally childish.

[35] For an authoritative study of the taboos and habits in regard to cleanliness and pollution since antiquity, see the volume by Mary Douglas, *Purity and Danger* (Baltimore: Penguin Books, 1966), which explains most of the historical background of the American pseudo-cleanliness fetishes that provide impetus for many of the goods and services presently on the consumer market.

comes in two flower odors, orange blossom and jasmine, and two flavors, raspberry and champagne. Sold at cosmetic counters, *Cupid's Quiver* has, to date, been quite successful.

You read it here first: the smell prevention industry has not yet hoisted its weirdest fancy and most grandiose illusion. There is more to come, gentlemen, and *we* shall be the victims next time! The women have *Cupid's Quiver*, but what about masculine illusions? Wait and see, ladies and gentlemen, just wait and see. The new show starts in about three years!

Conclusion

Man's credulity seems to be something of a constant factor historically and cross-culturally. While one type of credulity appears to attend ignorance and ethnocentricism, another is developed by institutions of education and communications, both supposedly indicative of intellectual and social progress. Inevitable as this state of affairs seems, its morality—or desirability—remains a moot point, argued more by poets than scientists and educators, although science has shown us some of the reasons for the sources of this problem without offering much information about how to change it if we wanted to.

The art of persuasion itself has been, and is, the focus of many illusions that increase credulity and enforce the likelihood that persuasion will work. The result is that some quite knowledgeable people with rigid dispositions are likely to be, also, among the most credulous. Illusions, however, are not cut-and-dried moral matters; they function frequently, as Freud has shown, as psychological safeguards against near-inevitable developments of certain personal neuroses. They require, in effect, the acceptance of one specific cultural neurosis in favor of an individual one. Illusions, especially illusions about persuasions, may be qualified on other value dimensions as well.

The major *persuasive* myth (or illusion) is the proposition that man is a highly persuasible creature by nature; to the degree that this proposition is held, he is. Ancillary illusions may easily be demonstrated to be frauds, and yet they are maintained by some of the so-called "best thinking" of our time. Among them, one discovers such "facts" of nature and "proven" phenomena as Extra Sensory Perception, the concept of "brainwashing" and the practice of hypnotism, all of them in varying degrees and in different ways illusions accepted by knowledgeable (but usually highly specialized) people.

Illusions are manufactured and transmitted concerning nearly every aspect of culture, including institutions regarded as bastions against them: the press and its electronic extensions and the world of education, in and out of school. Some of these illusions are cohesive social instruments; some of them are culturally and morally ameliorative; some are foolish; some are heinous by any man's criteria. The differences between them are not clearly drawn in terms of value. It is doubtful, however, that men have ever had for themselves clear choices of accepting good illusions and rejecting the bad. The price of maintaining a salutory illusion usually demands that the door be opened for an unhealthy illusion. This state of affairs is apparent all around us, but nowhere is it more noticeable than in the art of modern advertising, where illusory needs are met by consumer products that produce a counter-illusion and therefore actually *work*. Accordingly, they make good, in a general way, the promises that their servants, the advertising professionals, have made for them.

Chapter 21

WOMEN

It is women who set the stage and largely control the players in important sections of American life. America is a woman's world, a world in which, as a Chinese woman, Helena Kuo, remarked, women have succeeded in everything except the art of being truly feminine.

Eric John Dingwall

A DISCUSSION of contemporary persuasive dynamics must consider, at some point, the role of women *as* women in Western culture.

"Role" is the right word. The grand myths of femininity in our culture center upon two equally powerful, but equally irrelevant—and in degree absurd—propositions. The first, reflected by Dingwall above, and discussed in his book on women in American society,[1] centers on the common folk wisdom that "the hand that rocks the cradle rules the world." Women—as caricatured in the comic strips and as reviled by mysogynists—are construed as managers of the nation's economy, the power behind apparent male hegemony in commerce and culture. They are, in effect, innocent-looking witches who somehow oil the wheels of society while keeping their maleable males oblivious to their occult powers. Mrs. Macbeth is their prototype.

The second myth, newer and more respectable today, construes women as second-class citizens in a male dominated culture. It centers not upon what they do, or have accomplished, but what they have *not* done and *not* accomplished. Broadly, the myth understands the word "men" in the Declaration of Independence to include females (a dubious contemporary reading of the eighteenth century mind) and emphasizes largely the arbitrary exclusion of women from their societal rights. These rights have been understood variantly over the past century and a half, but have concerned mostly political matters, social position, occupational opportunities,

[1] Eric John Dingwall, *The American Woman* (New York: New American Library, 1958).

and, presently, roles in sexual behavior, home care and child bearing and raising.

The latter orientation heavily, and the prior slightly, both rest their cases upon a mighty body of physiological and psychological evidence, salted well with cross-cultural anthropology, which indicates that, except for a few physiological factors, similarities between males and females are far more impressive than whatever differences may exist between them, and, at any rate, they are not basically relevant to the human female's protean potentials. Historical cultural differences between men and women are, therefore, largely ascribed to societal influences.[2] For instance, there has never existed a great woman musical composer, because society has always discouraged women from writing music; female fine artists are few, because they are kept out of the atelier; there has never risen a great woman chef, because women have been discouraged from cooking, and so forth.[3]

Both myths accept the concept that women are substantially different from men, although the differences vary between and within the two orientations.

---

[2] There is little point in reviewing in detail the supportive literature for this point of view. Margaret Mead in *Sex and Temperament* (New York: New American Library, 1950), and her *Male and Female* (New York: Morrow Publishers, 1949), covers the issue about as well as any other authority. Ashley Montagu, *The Natural Superiority of Women* (New York: Macmillan Company, 1954), would probably today be accused by many women of male chauvinism (or unnecessary largesse) for his hyperbole, but Montagu's physiological and anthropological arguments are still worth considering.

[3] I am sorry. Let me enter here my own views, right or wrong, in regard to this sensitive issue, so the reader knows where I stand. First, I admit prejudices; but I have yet to meet an individual characterized as "male" or "female" who did not display biases concerning masculinity or femininity. Second, I accept both myths as selective, operative societal truths. I have known many women many ways, a tiny fraction of them in the biblical manner. They cover a wide range of sociological, psychological and biological typologies. (For example, they include a former lady acrobat who was competent to pin me to a wrestling mat in less than seven seconds, if she wished.) Their characterological range seems about as wide as for the men I have known. Third, I am the victim—somewhat defensively at this particular moment in history—of a certain emotional partisanship towards the male of our species on the arbitrary grounds that men have, like it or not, had the dubious privilege of exercising their talents in doing most of the sweaty and dirty work that Western culture has demanded to date, except bearing children. Fourth, I believe it is unwise to proceed into the future without according proper credits and debits to the past. Fifth, I see no reasons why former patterns of culture need shackle us to future social conventions concerning so-called "proper roles in society" of the sexes. But, in this matter, I am conservative, because we are traveling into the unknown and should, I think, move with caution. In a lighter vein, the reason that women have not become great professional chefs (there exist many magnificent amateurs) is largely because of the brute strength necessary to serve an apprenticeship in a first-rate commercial kitchen. Women are generally too frail for this labor, or so a superb chef I knew once told me. While they usually cook at home, women in the West have been discouraged from entering the world of *professional* cooking as a result of the same sorts of cultural restrictions that kept them for so long out of medicine and dentistry. A professional, *haute cuisine* chef is regarded, almost by definition, as a man.

The *first* emphasizes mystical differences rather than physical or psychological ones. Women are reputed to have keener insight than men, to be brighter in a practical way, to be more intuitive, instinctively alert and pragmatic. Like Cassandra, they are also mystically prescient, and like Pandora they are supernaturally capricious. Good or evil may emerge from either of these qualities. In the film version of *Wizard of Oz*, the two witches played by the late Billie Burke and Margaret Hamilton, respectively, exemplified the schizoid qualities of this single female mythic mysticism as well as the complementary aspects of its wholeness.[4] Witches, good and bad, are today usually abstracted from myth for literary purposes. But in real life as well, the notion remains that somehow contrary aspects of personality are manifest in the "whole woman" (whatever the term means), regarded usually as a sexual object for men and as a potential mother of males and other females. This whole woman is different from man in both essence and existential self, and, in a transcendental way, superior to him on every count. As a witch, she conspires with angels and devils who men cannot know. As an earth-mother, she is the vessel that replenishes the race. Men are expendable: Let them fight their foolish wars and kill themselves in pursuit of progress. Both are illusions. Women manipulate men anyway, and have since Adam's fall. Women bear men, raise them and educate them into culture. The role of men in the important business of living is therefore both ancillary and mundane. The female is critical to the more important spiritual and biological life of the race.

The *second* myth accepts differences between the sexes too, but they are far more concrete and specific, and are not seen as particularly relevant to female roles in culture. Some of them are implicit in the myth itself; some are so obvious that they may be accepted explicitly. As far as we know (at our present state of ignorance), they are all open to qualification but admit of little responsible debate:

1. Women and men are differentiated by primary and secondary sexual characteristics, although genital differences are variants of the same embryological prototype, and secondary sexual characteristics vary widely as manifest within each sex.
2. Women are able to bear children and breast feed them (although this latter function is today optional). Men cannot, although they are competent to raise children as well as women in every other respect.
3. Men and women differ also, on average, in skeletal and muscular endowment. While these differences are frequently slight, women's physical structure is essentially oriented to child bearing and endur-

[4] The Bergman film *Personna* also employed the same sexual dichotomy in a more obtuse but dramatically rewarding thematic context. Examples abound in literature and drama.

ance. The male structure appears better suited for predatory activities, flight and tasks involving the immediate application of muscular strength.

4. In almost every society known, past or present, male and female social roles differ. True, the female role varies as vastly from culture to culture as does the male role, and what is female behavior at one time or place may be male behavior at another. But within each culture, the roles are clearly differentiated; and, where clothes are worn, so, usually, is costume.

The second myth centers also on the irrelevance of all of these differences, except perhaps the child bearing function, to contemporary Western life. Genital and secondary sexual characteristics provide greater aesthetic than functional significances. Modern technology has eliminated effectively differences between men and women as fighters or flighters or pushers, except in presentational events like athletic contests. Cultural models of sex roles in other societies today (and in the past) are too arbitrary and variant for the clear definition of them. Women may play *many* roles; and so may men.[5] Whatever differences exist, therefore, in sex roles in our society —including vocabulary in the use of the words "man" or "mankind" to symbolize the human race—are arbitrary culture traits for which no reason exists other than custom, and, were enough people willing, might be modified. In this sense are women, in the words of Simone de Beauvoir, "the second sex," treated generally as inferior to men in most matters, consigned to mundane tasks of family raising and housemaking, and kept effectively from the active, exciting, productive aspects of civilized life.

The first myth is ancient, and may be traced back to the Greeks but is also found in the traditions of many cultures, particularly those of Japan and other oriental people. The origins of its roots is a matter of lively conjecture, of interest in our time to mythically oriented psychoanalysts like Jung and Reik and writers like Brigid Brophy. Perhaps this orientation belongs among our list of illusions in Chapter 20, but, if it does, it is an illusion as old as religion itself—possibly older than religion, for man's first gods may well have been female.[6]

---

[5] Our American culture and the USSR are two societies apparently rapidly blending these two roles in matters of dress, behavior and employment. As to whether or not either nation will eventually establish "Unisex" in clothes and social behavior is anybody's guess. I predict not, and see the present trend, at least in clothing, as another oscillation of a faddist pendulum. Marshall McLuhan thinks otherwise, or so he wrote in an article for *Look* magazine in 1967. See George B. Leonard, "Why We Need A New Sexuality" in *Look*, January 13, 1970.

[6] Female cave drawings and prehistoric statues of women have set off no end of speculation on the part of anthropologists, psychologists and historians concerning the role of women in pre-history. Perhaps these assorted, strange representations of the human female have survived only by chance; what they mean remains a mystery. See the fascinating story of the discovery of the "Venus of Willendorf" and her friends in Herbert Wendt, *In Search of Adam* (Boston: Houghton Mifflin Co., 1956), pp. 358–

The second myth has a shorter history. It is political in origin and a direct extension of the three notions energized by Jacksonian democracy in the USA and Jacobin and Marxist ideologies of Europe, among other sources. It is a direct consequence of theories of popular participation in government, universal education and statutory equal rights to pursue, at least, the materialistic aspects of happiness. Although women constitute a majority of the population of the USA (and the world), and probably spend the greatest part of private incomes in the West, they are often described as a minority—or marginal—group attempting to achieve status in a man's world. The myth has its full retinue of dead martyrs like Lucy Stone, Lucretia Mott, Susan B. Anthony and other masculinized heroines, as well as live agitators, old and young, like Betty Friedan and Kate Millett, both of whom will be discussed below.[7]

Why regard these two orientations as *myths?* They are mythic primarily, because *neither* describes, either generally and accurately, the true social roles of a large enough segment of the female populations in the West to be, in any construction, accurate assessments of life-styles of a dozen women drawn at random from our population. Like most myths, however, each contains a measure of truth, even the first and mystical one, in terms of what is generally believed by most of the population, including women. And attitudes and opinions that accept the first notion of the supernatural female gift of mystical superiority may be quite consonant with the second political orientation that accepts women as slaves of men, household drones and second class citizens. On the other hand, while each myth may have countless adherents, the second does not run deeply enough in the current of contemporary social life to account for more than passing enthusiasms, transient opinions, loosely held attitudes and counterpoint to other, more insistent beliefs, including the ancient one of supernatural female superiority.

In other words, the issue of feminism has in recent history generated more heat than light, although, as long as it remains active in the current forum, it will manifest considerable motivation for many types of persuasion.

The Female Rebel

Female rebels may be drawn from either the mythic or feminist traditions. Few factors may bind together such figures as Mae West, Dorothy Parker, Marian Anderson, Edna Ferber, Althea Gibson, Barbara Ward,

---

379, which adheres to the facts and does not attempt either speculative artistic or psychological interpretations of these odd relics.

[7] A well written history of this political manifestation is Eleanor Flexner, *Century of Struggle* (Cambridge, Mass.: Belknap Press, 1966). Flexner is a competent historian of liberal politics in history and art, and this book reflects a careful and unbiased scholarship rare in the literature of feminism.

Sophie Tucker, Lillian Hellman, Zsa Zsa Gabor, and Claire Booth Luce *except* femininity, but as recent female public figures, living and dead, they are all lineal descendents of the mystical earth-mother myth for different reasons. Obviously, they are all superwomen of some kind; for our considerations, the nature of their superiority is irrelevant. They also, in one way or another, have competed—directly or indirectly—with men, and won. They have all also *used* men inferior to them to achieve their successes. The maintenance of their positions of stature has depended, as well, upon contemporary acceptance of the myth of female excellence.

Their manner of rebellion has been more by precept rather than action. Many effective rebels operate in this manner, be they male or female. Simply by *being* or *doing* rebellion occurs, not necessarily the result of assuming either a masculine role or pursuing manly work as our culture defines it, but by locating a distinctive variant of any social role (even a feminine one) and subsequently imbuing it with a personal, feminized quality and unique style. Nor does such rebellion need to be set in a serious context. It is often most effective and lasting in a satirical vein, as illustrated by West, Parker, Tucker, Gabor and Luce (as a playwright). They were and are rebels, because they would not accept the female mystical myth as merely implicit or understood in society. Instead, they had to *show it* (meaning themselves) to the world: personifications of feminine witchery in one or another context. And this display—antagonistic unquestionably to real *male* chauvinists (who the other type of rebels, discussed below, are incapable of recognizing)—was and is convincing enough to reward them with prizes for excellence.

In no manner does the writer construe women of such qualities (and rebels of such victories) as *masculinized*. Whatever they create is truly feminine in the most benign meaning of the term—not in a political sense alone but in the mythic sense of our Western tradition, a mythos that includes historical, theological, social and political factors. In fact, a mystical-religious figure, Joan of Arc, is probably one of the clearest paradigms of the mythic female rebel, at least as her story is told today: Joan was chosen by God to achieve the impossible, and she achieved it; she led a male army into battle and victory without compromising the masculinity of her soldiers; she put a weakling on the throne of France and stiffened his backbone; deserted and friendless, she endured inquisition and torture designed to force a confession that she was both a fraud and a witch (an unlikely combination); after confessing, she recanted, choosing martyrdom, the affirmation of her femininity, the integrity of her mission, her own mystical power and the perfection of God to imprisonment. In spite of all the things that poets, playwrights[8] and bishops have done to her memory

[8] I must except Bernard Shaw here. He is, unfortunately, the only recent male writer who seems to possess a genuine understanding of the mystical female rebel, not only in *Saint Joan* but in *Mrs. Warren's Profession, The Millionairess, The Doctor's*

for nearly half a millennium (including canonizing her in 1922), there remains little doubt that she was a magnificent female rebel in the mystical mode.

The other female rebel, the politically oriented one, is a somewhat grimier proposition, but no grimier than the male chauvinist against whom she is usually found railing. In the author's opinion, these particular antagonists deserve each other and cannot succeed in battling beyond a stalemate. Friedan, in her book,[9] articulates some socio-psychological sources of the rebellion, depending, unfortunately, to such measure upon Freudian and anti-Freudian propositions as to weaken what constitute, in fact, a trenchant set of keen arguments.[10]

Friedan is at her best when she is not battling with psychological theory, sociology or what have become, in fact, trite gripes about the state of women in American culture, as familiar (and as essentially irrelevant to the rebel's best arguments) as housemaid's knee.[11] When, however, she writes

---

Dilemma, Man and Superman, Heartbreak House and other plays, major and minor. If more women had *listened* to Shaw instead of writing love letters to him, their sex might be faring better than it is today!

[9] Betty Friedan, *The Feminine Mystique* (New York: W. W. Norton and Co., 1963). Like many university administrators, I still teach classes and lecture. When, recently, I raised my eyebrows at a paperbound copy of this book a pretty co-ed student was reading, she misinterpreted my *moue* as a snicker of disapproval and asked (rather nastily) why I was sneering at a "classic." Her construction of the word "classic" amused me, because I had assigned Mrs. Friedan's volume as a textbook (one of many) for a course I taught at New York University from 1963 to 1965. Eventually, however, this particular co-ed got around to calling me a "male chauvinist" anyway, an epithet for which I had already braced myself.

[10] Freud and psychoanalysis cause female rebels nothing but trouble. Mrs. Friedan's tilts against Freud's "scientific religion" of male supremacy in a superficial manner, and displays both a deep (and probably incurable) misunderstanding of Freud's concepts of penis envy, castration fixations and similar ideas, as well as a severe neglect of the cultural milieu that necessarily distorted (but illustrated functions and processes) in all of Freud's notions. See *ibid.*, pp. 103–125. Kate Millett bravely faces the same problems but handles them even more ineptly than Freidan. See below.

[11] I should like to dispense with the present Women's Liberation movement as rapidly as possible by affirming its basic thrust, approving of it, giving it my blessing and the promise of a right arm if it is ever needed. The offer is made in the same spirit that has placed my name on the list of available blood donors in my neighborhood—not that a pint or two of my blood will accomplish much, but so that a neighbor of mine who may one day need live blood will damn well get it. As I understand the Women's Liberation program at present, the girls want to be paid the same money as men for the same work. If it *is* the same work, and if the man is not being *overpaid* because he is supporting a couple of families, why not? (If a female is supporting a couple of families, *she* should certainly receive the *same* consideration that a man does.) The girls also want copious abortions. How much better, I think, that they employ contraceptive pills, diaphrams, foams, suppositories, buttons, wires and other esoteric items, but let them be aborted, *ad lib* if they wish, by all means! (Legal and inexpensive abortions, incidentally, seem to me more specifically related to *male* liberation than *female* liberation! Having lived my fecund years in the era of expensive, illegal abortions, I am qualified to speak on the matter with some considerable authority—and shall, in my memoirs.) The "Libs" also want day care centers for their children so that they can trot off to work. If they need to work, or are foolish enough to prefer work to the

about the blocking of a women's basic human needs for "self-respect, self-esteem, and for the esteem of others," and the need for a sense of achievement and self-realization trapped on the dead-end street of the occupation of housewife, she has put her finger upon a genuine, familiar and meaningful problem.[12] Nor does she need to quote Maslow's ideals of a "self-actualizing" life, because one does not require psychological theory to work up righteous indignation against social forces which condemn sensitive people to lives of drab repetition, dull, mundane tasks and frustrations, be such individuals men or women.

Friedan's argument, however, raises many questions, also applying both to men and women. The first is whether the implicit assumption that such productive ways of life are possible for the majority of *men* in our culture is justified. In fact, they are not. They are merely *more* accessible, at present, to men than women; how much more, we are not sure. Second, there rises the problem of individual competence, and the risk of dooming countless women to the same frustrating experiences that presently affect millions of men, turning them old before their time, so amusingly described as *The Peter Principle*, but far from a joke. Opportunities for women to *succeed* in the professions offer equal or greater opportunities for them to *fail* also. Should women prefer to live their "self-actuating" lives at their "level of optimum incompetence," in Peter's words, to domesticity, they will be making a poor choice—or giving up a precious one. There are many reasons to admire profoundly those women who *have* achieved significant proficiency at a most exacting profession: housekeeping and child rearing in an industrial society. Third, and most disillusioning of all, is the unconvincing assumption that, because one can achieve so-called "success" as a writer, jurist, physician, politician or in any other male dominated field, the world of self-respect, self-esteem and self-actualization will suddenly open to one. Statistics concerning mental illness, physical and nervous breakdowns and suicides demonstrate that this romantic notion is not even a dream; it is simply another illusion. Even Maslow (whose study population was atypical) indicates clearly[13] that these rewards are frequently achieved under quite modest and unlikely circumstances. The writer wishes that he might share Friedan's faith that the death of the feminine mystique would provide for women what *neither* men nor women in the West seem even to comprehend as a meaningful *modus vivendi* at present.

At the present writing, considerable attention is being paid to a far less

---

joy of the company of small children, such centers, I think, are mandatory and should be built and run at state expense, as in the USSR. In many instances, the children, I am sure, will inevitably receive better care at the centers than they would have at home.

[12] *Ibid.*, pp. 314–326.

[13] See A. H. Maslow, *Motivation and Personality* (New York: Harper and Bros., 1954), and *Toward a Psychology of Being* (Princeton, N.J.: D. Van Nostrand Co., 1962), for the experimental evidence and theory concerning the concept of "self-actualization."

interesting polemic centered on myth number two by Millett,[14] which purports to be a literary, critical and historical study of the role of women in patriarchal societies. This it indeed is, in a pedantic shotgun fashion: a little second-hand history along with some criticism (from the sexual angle) of carefully selected nineteenth and twentieth century British and American essayists, poets and novelists. Millett's nineteenth century representatives are John Stuart Mill (one of her "goods"), John Ruskin (a "bad"), Tennyson ("bad"), Engels ("good"–"bad"), and others who, one way or another, treat in their work the notion of male dominance and female repression. After dismissing D. H. Lawrence (a "bad") and other recent supposed apostles of sexual equality, she dives (with fascinating fixity) at Henry Miller ("bad"), Norman Mailer ("bad") and Jean Genet ("good"), quoting copiously from their lusty prose, somehow indicting their books and plays as archetypes of common male attitudes towards female sex objects. Considering her stance as an exploited female egghead (a metaphor to ponder), it is not surprising that Millett finds the homosexual illusionist Genet the most realistic of the male authors she skins alive. Millett's literary preference in men is clear; her vision of life for the political, involved female is less lucidly delineated, and much less interestingly illuminated, than Friedan's.[15]

The sticking-power of Millett's disorganized diatribe is, in the author's opinion, slight. At the present moment, *Sexual Politics* has become a maypole (or priapus) about which some misled sisters of female liberation are, unfortunately, dancing. From a pragmatic viewpoint, the task of organizing the diverse types of women who accept the second myth seem dim. Even the notion that Millett might unite them somehow politically is unrealistic. It is difficult, in fact, to determine whether or not Millett comprehends much about contemporary politics, or exactly where her political orientation differs from other leftists, except for her substitution of the adjective "female" for the words "black," "poor," "oppressed" or "neglected." Mil-

---

[14] Kate Millett, *Sexual Politics* (New York: Doubleday and Co., 1970).

[15] While *Sexual Politics* is a respectable polemic (as polemics go these days), I am puzzled by the information that this document originally constituted a doctoral dissertation at a notable university. Now, I realize that standards for doctoral research have changed in the sixteen years since I wrote my own document (no masterpiece, God knows), but for the life of me I have been trying to figure out what part—or how—any of *Sexual Politics* might satisfy the rigors of critical-historical research, granting wide latitude to the word "critical." In no manner does Millett cover a universe of discourse, but simply selects various axe-grinders and pretzel-benders for approval or disapproval in a somewhat literate manner. While this sort of meandering may serve an informal purpose as criticism, it is far removed from my understanding of the type of generalizable scholarship necessary for a contribution to knowledge at the doctoral level. I have not been able to find out whether Millett actually *received* her degree, but were I on her sponsoring committee, I fear that my head might be bloody and bowed, although my signature of approval would not appear on her document. Also, because *she* brings the matter up so consistently, Millett's repeated complaints about other people's bad writing in no way improves her own tiresome prose.

lett's strongest argument in support of the myth is the oldest: the appeal to what she calls "functionalism," which constitutes a well reasoned and accurate essay concerning the way men have mistreated women in the recent past. But even this creditable position is presented without the sense of humane urgency displayed by most other feminist writers. Despite her *Postscript,* attempting to ally the Women's Liberation Movement with other agitation for cultural change, Millett's persuasion is unfortunately both pedantic, and, the writer believes, potentially unattractive to most women too. Throughout recent history, they seem themselves to prefer, unhappily, the mystical vision of femininity to the anti-exploitative, political one of masculined polemists like Millett. Millett is doubtless a heavyweight agitator, less as a writer or social psychologist[16] than as a gutsy and contemporary symbol whose arguments during the next decade or so, may cause considerable misunderstandings both of women in our culture and of the Women's Liberation Movement.

Considering its probable future as a persuasive manifestation, discussion of the Women's Liberation Movement has extenuated too far into the discussion. As noted above, far more women in our culture are rebels in the tradition of the first myth than the second, although the latter type direct more public attention to themselves playing roles of revolutionaries.[17]

Female rebellion in the West also transcends the American experience and is spreading, at the moment, to South America, Europe and Africa. This is a result of technology and economics for the most part. It is technological by virtue of the increasing control women are assuming over machines (the female driver is a puzzling example) and in their use of techniques of chemical contraception today—and instant abortion by suction tomorrow. It is economic in the sense that, increasingly, consumer goods and services (not large industry or the money market—yet) are falling under the effective control of women as consumers. Put another way, the instruments of manipulation and persuasion involved in these technological and economic activities are presently directed at women *in their roles as women.*

In fact, it is the author's contention that we *are* indeed living through a "female rebellion" (if these are the words that satisfy the activist), but modeled more on the image of James Thurber's war between the sexes than that of the militant suffragette. Susan B. Anthony's rebellious granddaughter is just a comical figure by virtue of her humorless mien and floppy mam-

---

16 See *ibid.,* pp. 220–233. Like Friedan, Millett also takes the knife to Freud's gonads. (I usually laugh at the concept of the castrating female, but recent research is causing me to reconsider.) Freud's penis-envy theory is attacked this time with new, hyper-thyroid vigor, as well as his concepts of female masochism, passivity and narcissism. Read and enjoy pp. 176–203. Millett sometimes shows she knows how to swing a scalpel.

17 It was, after all, a woman who served as spearhead for the Communist revolutionaries of the Russian revolution. Neither Rosa Luxemburg's sex nor religious origins militated against her revolutionary fervor. She was a political animal in every sense of the term.

maries, hardly a political figure to be dealt with seriously—especially when she humorlessly intrudes into such masculine domains as men's bars and/or Turkish baths in the name of civil equality.

The Nature of Femininity

That proper norms in our culture for the female role should still be matters for serious debate—to say nothing of intensive argument—is less the result of the masculine vanity that perceives women as somehow inferior than the insistent competition between the two contemporary myths of womanhood. Note that neither myth relates fundamentally to the biological role of women in the function of maintaining the race, too obvious a process to permit much discussion. They center instead on philosophical matters in two keys: The first is metaphysical; the second concerns ontology, destiny and self-realization. Both take pains (and in so doing add zest to the discussion) in order to avoid answering precisely, in socio-cultural terms, the basic question of what femininity in the West actually involves.

One might, of course, make the same point about the concept of masculinity, and bump into just as many myths—or more—and end up with other delicious arguments. The discussion, however, would not relate as closely to the issue of cultural persuasion. In truth, much of the present volume—particularly discussion of politics and economics—*has* centered on male roles, in that males almost entirely dominate these and other aspects of contemporary life. Nor do males in general usually display the same types of sensitivities about their maleness that females do about femininity, an important factor in vulnerability to persuasion. It is true that a small percentage of male homosexuals seem to possess—and publicize—prescient insights into the hypocrisy of masculinity cults. Plays like Anderson's *Tea and Sympathy* have explored some facets of the essential nature of the cultural notion of maleness with insight, and books like *Men in Groups*[18] occasionally evoke interest in intra-societal variations of male role manifestations. But males generally accept their implicit societal dominance in the West. And its responsibilities, lethal proclivities, boredoms, frustrations and idiocies are usually integrated into their personalities with mute stoicism—perhaps, also, *unwarranted* stoicism—but maleness *does* frequently include such unattractive aspects as comparatively early death, alimony payments, family support, work and its discontents and similar millstones, as well as access to men's saloons and social clubs, on the brighter side.

To note that femininity in the West seems often to involve symptoms of neurosis, frustration, unhappiness, exploitation and similar dysfunctions proves or implies little, because these conditions are not only universal among Western women, and they are suffered also by many men. Certain other straws in the wind may signify deeper meanings: Alcoholics, or at

---

[18] See Lionel Tiger, *Men in Groups* (New York: Random House, 1969). We shall return to this interesting but questionable document subsequently.

least individuals seeking treatments for alcoholism, today include greater proportions of women than heretofore. Discussions with numerous internists have indicated to the writer that the lion's share of prescriptions written for anti-anxiety tranquillizing drugs are handed to women; these particular chemical agents are presently almost universal specifics for such female complaints as post-partum depressions and menopausal blues.

Although Erikson's concept of differences in spacial perceptions of men and women are open to doubt (and are attacked vehemently by the feminine liberators),[19] the following paragraph provides, the writer believes, a realistic statement of the prototypical female role, for better or worse, in many Western sub-cultures:

> Women, through the ages (at any rate, the patriarchal ones), has lent herself to a variety of roles conducive to an exploitation of masochistic potentials: she has let herself be confined and immobilized, enslaved and infantilized, prostituted and exploited, deriving from it at best what in psychopathology we call "secondary gains" of devious dominance. This fact, however, could be satisfactorily explained only within a new kind of biocultural history which . . . would first have to overcome the prejudiced opinion that women must be, or will be, what she is or has been under particular historical conditions.[20]

This "devious dominance" is, of course, also mythic, although it evidences pragmatic aspects. As Tiger notes,[21] for instance, despite the small percentage of women around the world involved actively in political life, many of those who *do* opt for grand scale politics follow in the footsteps of dead male relatives, a devious but effective gambit. Mrs. Roosevelt, Mrs. Neuberger, Madame Sun Yat-sen, Lady Astor, Mrs. Indria Ghandi and others are examples.

To some, the issue of patriarchy in societies of the West is the single major psychological, and significant situational, determinant of female functions that our culture takes for granted. It is impossible to argue that ours is *not* a patriarchal society,[22] but so are most of the world's cultures

---

19 See Millett, *op. cit.*, pp. 210–220.

20 Erik H. Erikson, *Identity, Youth, and Crisis* (New York: W. W. Norton and Co., 1968), p. 284.

21 Tiger, *op. cit.*, p. 73.

22 Portions of American culture, however, tend to operate in loose matriarchal ways. Many northern female Negroes have moved into the American middle class more rapidly than Negro men with both psychological and economic results. One of them is the existence of numerous more-or-less matriarchal middle-class black families, presided over, usually, by a strong-willed grandmother or great-grandmother whose daughters, daughter-in-law and small children reside in her household in comparative stability, considering the resources the ghetto has to provide its black residents. The males involved (sons, sons-in-law, legal husbands, common law husbands and relatives) remain transients in the household; their financial contributions are meagre, and their moral and ethical influences are usually far less uncompromising and dominant than those of the women, particularly "grandma." See Chapter 24 for a discussion of this sub-matriarchy.

today, and it is difficult to imagine the outcome were the scale to overbalance and some large and powerful nation somehow suddenly converted to matriarchy. The results would probably be more interesting to observe than to experience, both for men and women.

Much is often made in sexual terms, also, of the national image of various countries: John Bull for England; Mother Russia and Mother India; Germany, the Fatherland, and similar metaphors. To the social analyst, rubrics like these are more than rhetoric, but how much more is difficult to judge, except in extreme instances at certain times, such as the period of Nazi Germany. At any rate, patriarchal influences upon our image in the USA reflect ambiguous attitudes: Uncle Sam, the Revolutionary trio, and the flag raisers at Iwo Jima are, of course, men. But so is the cartoonists' taxpaying citizen and "boobus Americanus." Columbia, the Gem of the Ocean and the Statue of Liberty are both women (not very sexy ones), and the America of apple pie and milk (for which our soldiers supposedly fight) smacks more of Wylie's "momism" than true patriarchal imagery.

The major offshoots of cultural patriarchy are symbolic. And it is mainly symbols that cause either the passive, masochistic, or exploitative phenomena mentioned by Erikson, on one hand, and activate angry female revolutionaries, on the other. All participants are aware that patriarchy is involved, but like Friedan, Millett and other even more militant anti-patriarchists, they remain at a loss to know what to do about it, except to attack—more or less willy-nilly—arbitrarily selected symbols of patriarchy in speech, advertising, literature and the mass arts. They utilize the one genuinely futile revolutionary cry, "Down with what's up!", because patriarchy versus matriarchy is not a political platform or social cause. It *is* a manner of perception that, fairly or unfairly, begins its cultural influence on page one of Genesis, follows our history from sword to cross to factory megapolis. To attempt to expunge patriarchy is as futile an endeavor as attempts by the General Semanticists to antisepticize the way we talk and, according to them, therefore think. And fools usually follow fools' missions. So the future of patriarchy remains well assured, if we are able to project into tomorrow on the basis of the past. Profound cultural movements in the West towards the direction of matriarchy are not only unlikely at present, they are pragmatically impossible.

Women in Western Culture therefore remain in a far from satisfactory position, seen as individuals and from the perspective of both concerned males and society in general, in the author's opinion. The most significant *social* event in a Western female's life remains today the precise moment she gives up her name (and part of her identity) in favor of a male. Her most critical *personal* moment—and perhaps the only "self-actualization" experience that most women achieve—is when, narcotized and draped in toweling, a new life is expelled from her distended reproductive canal. Everything else, including the raising of her own children, is often, for her, a battle or fight against cultural givens and against the odds, the latter called by males, usually with many losses and only occasional gains.

Unmarried women find themselves in a slightly different situation, but not so great as their own legends lead them to believe.[23] Single women may be categorized either as male dependent or male-independent. (The type who take seriously books like *Sex and the Single Girl* are usually male dependent; women who do not necessarily require such sorts of counsel are male independent.) Male dependent singles usually marry eventually, or else manipulate themselves in successive, tentative pseudo-marriages.

Male independent women usually fear most the stereotypical images of lonely old age, a childless life, and other horrors that marriage may or may not, in any manner, protect them from. But, all in all, their lives are not as bad as fiction portrays them. Among reasonably stable and satisfied single women (including some prostitutes, who neither invariably live miserably degraded lives or possess hearts of gold), a state of existential acceptance of life's caprices seems often the rule rather than the exception. But such women are few, so great is the impetus to marriage. Of all the female typologies in our patriarchal culture, however, such women frequently come close, in the author's opinion, to achieving self-actualization without undue reliance upon their culture-determined femininity.

Many (if not most) married women fare next best to their unmarried sisters, because marriage, in a patriarchal society, is always to some degree a compromise between self-fulfillment and a subservient social role. Married women take their compensations where and when they can find them, and these grasps are not fit for male merriment; they are too pathetic. They search in reading, adult education courses, great book lectures, television, the movies, coffee-klatch sessions of current events and pseudo-Freud, and in attempting to establish (sometimes vainly) a few points of human contact with their children after infancy. Their grasp includes, quite frequently, an occasional extra-marital affair (usually rushed, delusive and sleazy, but an experience as near to the illusion of romance as they will ever again come) and travel with their husbands in attempts to gain a sense of self-fulfillment above and beyond just "being a housewife" as they perceive the role. That they succeed in part (never, or rarely, as fully as they desire) in their quest is astonishing, but succeed they sometimes do.

Unmarried male-dependent females fare worst of all, because, in most instances, they are continually exploited by men in numerous ways to their

---

23 Personal impressions are deceptive, but among the women I know, the unmarried ones seem less chronically troubled and are apparently less disturbed by the rigors of living than the married ones. It is possible, of course, to hypothesize that they live in a regressive fantasy world. But this sort of response reminds me of the story of the man who was not *really* happy; he just *thought* he was.

own psychological extinction. And when they are gone, no one cares, an eventuality of which they are usually depressingly aware during their lives.

Female Persuasion and Persuaders

We have seen that Hovland's studies of persuasiveness (as defined for his experiments) indicate that young female Americans seem slightly more disposed than males to change dispositions in expected directions in coercive situations.[24] This, Hovland and others have assumed, occurs because the American middle-class girl (from which most of his female experimental population was chosen) has interiorized a life-style that emphasizes the need to please others, particularly men, by agreeing with them in opinions and behaviors at least, and generally conforming to their dispositions. Little hard evidence supports this concept beyond Hovland's (slight) statistical differences. But the concept of young females as more "other oriented" than males (in David Riesman's terms)[25] is part of our cultural folklore, along with the notion that, in sexual matters, every girl has her price, and that the right man can somehow effectively exploit any girl, no matter who she is, if he possesses certain bio-chemical gifts.[26]

Middle-class young girls are, of course, not all Western women. And it is also reasonable to suppose that men are often exploited in our culture as frequently and easily as women, but in different ways and contexts. Folklore, in its contradictory way, supports the stereotype of the strong-headed, intransigent female as well as the malleable sex kitten. And folklore, in its way, is probably correct. As for beliefs and attitudes, it is doubtful that women are unreasonably vulnerable to persuasion relating directly or indirectly to their sexuality, a matter that historical evidence seems to indicate is of deeper concern to them than to men in the kind of culture Hovland studied.

Female preoccupation with personal sexuality is simply the result of the deterministic proposition that, in a culture like ours, there are less alternatives for a woman to *be* anything significant, besides being a woman, than there are for a man (besides being a man). Femininity is, in a way, an occupation. There exist no equivalents for women's experience of patri-

---

[24] See Chapter 12 for a discussion of Hovland's findings.

[25] Evidence is not only found in Riesman's famous work, *The Lonely Crowd*, but is more apparent, I think, in the interviews upon which the volume was based, published as *Faces In The Crowd* (New Haven: Yale University Press, 1952), which, being less open to Riesman's interpretative sociology, allows his respondents to speak for themselves about their roles as females. They are—mostly—"other oriented."

[26] The late Alexander King used to talk about men he called "fluegels" (I think) who were sloppy, idle, indifferent, broken-down, broke, dirty and unshaven males who were able, somehow, to look at your wife, mistress, girl friend (or just friend), and seduce her away from you with a nod of the head. And there was absolutely nothing you could do about it. The most famous "fluegel" in fiction, I suppose, is Charles Strickland in Maugham's *The Moon and Sixpence*. But I have run into such real-life natural female exploiters over the years a number of times, invariably to my loss.

archal marriage and childbirth in the male experience. Male identity, in terms of name (the symbol of self) remains intact at marriage, and childbirth—while psychologically shattering to male smokers and nail biters—is an experience that even hardened male obstetricians will swear remains for them an absolute experiental mystery.

Critical moments in personal life for a male, as a male, are less auspicious: his first orgasm and/or homo- or heterosexual experience, his first paycheck perhaps, the burning of his mortgage, his first extra-marital fling, his daughter's marriage (maybe) and his funeral—all more or less trivia. Male identity is achieved by adventures (from the feminine viewpoint) in the so-called "outside world," to repeat Erikson's notion. They include belonging to service organizations, achieving status at work, spending money on automobiles and boats and coaching Little League teams, among countless options. Few of these activities are *intrinsically* male, and therefore maleness for men need be less a matter of attitudinal concern than for women. Belief structures, however, of men in patriarchies are firmly rooted in the acceptance of masculinity as a biological reality, even among homosexuals—excluding that small percentage who cherish a psychotic belief that, somehow, they are biological women masquerading as men.

Because of this determinism, the attitudinal stance of much persuasion of a relatively insignificant nature—most of it advertising—*is* currently directed to female attitudes and, therefore, on its face, is of little interest to men. While many women, for instance, appear to enjoy the commercial promotion in *Playboy* and *Esquire* (directed to the wide-ranging male, not merely the predatory one), it is the rare man who can stomach a large dose of the advertising in *Woman's Day*, *Vogue* or *Cosmopolitan*, even excluding ads for clothing and feminine hygiene materials. The reason is clear from an attitudinal perspective. The male magazines are full of ads for cars, high-fi equipment, liquor, novelties for bachelor "pads" and assorted technological gadgetry that spans a wide range of interests in the world "out there." The women's ads center on specialized items for the home like linens, furnishings, prepared food mixes, jewelry, articles for children and other items for the "world inside," meaning the world of the home and family. On the attitudinal level, we therefore find some degree of empirical confirmation of Erikson's notions of female "inner space" versus male interests in "outer space," less the condition of psycho-biology, as implied by Erikson, than a situational response to differing cultural roles.[27]

Sex relationships to opinions and behavior are less clear, although political analysts try to extrapolate broad theories from the popularity of at-

---

[27] This theory—a tentative one at best—is the topic in Erikson, *op. cit.*, pp. 261–294. It is based upon observation of children at play (pp. 268–271) and extrapolated into adult sex roles (pp. 271–279). Even while judging the behaviors of small children, I think that Erikson observes the *results* of the male-female socializing process (already interiorized at an early age) and confuses them with the *causes* for them.

tractive male politicians like the Kennedys and ex-movie actor Ronald Reagan. They are hard pressed to explain the appeal of the not-so-sexy ones, particularly among the young, like the late Adlai Stevenson and Eugene McCarthy, the best recent examples. Diehard political analysts keep insisting that there exists a women's vote; merchandisers prize the concept of a women's market. The difference between the two, however, is obvious. The women's market is an extension of the female life-role in culture. No such life-role exists for women in the political realm.

In all probability, female opinion—and much female behavior—is a psychological extension of male opinion and male behavior, either following or leading influences on the dispositions of a single dominant male in the individual household in the West. In regard to counter-influence, in the words of editor Webb in Wilder's *Our Town* (referring to the era before women's suffrage), "All males vote at the age of 21. Women vote indirect . . ." Women no longer "vote indirect," but unquestionably influence male opinions upon many matters, particularly if we believe the persuasion that professional persuaders print about the power of women as consumers.[28]

An enormous share of cultural persuasion is certainly directed to, at, or around women, but its exact influence on the precipitation of opinion and direction of behaviors is usually questionable. A reasonable sociological assumption, in fact the concatenation of many factors, leads one to posit that women have greater influences on opinions and behavior in middle-class than in lower or upper class homes. Middle-class women are more active in their communities, have more time, and are free to live less structured lives than upper- or lower-class women. But exceptions may occur in urban ghettos where the force of female opinion is frequently as much in evidence as that of males. Philip Wylie's famous "mom" (if, when and where she exists) is, of course, a middle-class animal, and mom—in her role as mother or mother-in-law—is probably an opinion influencer wherever she holds court, frequently in the family constellation of her married children if they cannot ship her off to Miami or Europe.

The most important factors in the analysis of female dispositions, however (in whatever images one prefers to evoke of the Western woman) center upon three incontrovertible aspects of her cultural condition, hopefully clarified by the discussion in this chapter.

The first is that most women are conscious of their second-class state in a patriarchy and therefore must necessarily opt for one or another (or

---

[28] A relevant old joke bears condensation and repetition: A couple remained happily married, the husband told an inquirer, because he made all the important decisions, and his wife made all the unimportant ones. When asked what kind of decisions his wife made, he answered, "Oh—when we buy a new car, where we go on vacation, what colleges the kids go to—trivia like that." When asked what important decisions *he* made, the husband replied expansively, "*I* decide whether or not we are going to invade mainland China!"

both) of the myths of female rebellion and/or female supremacy. To call this option a "belief" decision may dramatize it unnecessarily. But it certainly hovers near, or over, attitude structures—particularly attitudes towards men and male dominant endeavors that are rationalized into opinions and behavior—sometimes as futile (but interesting) as a Mother's March for Peace, or into as formidable and concrete an institution as the League of Women Voters.

Second, women tend to be ambivalent about their own sexuality: immensely and mystically possessive concerning its psycho-biological aspects, and indignant and/or repulsed by its situational impositions that stand in the way of their ideal of self-actualization. This is true not only of married women with children but of married childless women and single women as well, and, in the author's experience at least, most lesbians also—once again, excepting psychotics who believe that they are biologically incomplete males.

Third, to deny women the psycho-biology of femininity is to deny them identity; *but to deny women the role of martyr to the man's world is to deny one of women's most dearly held illusions in Western Culture.*[29] (Were the situation reversed, if we lived in a matriarchy, there is no doubt that men would demonstrate a similar ambivalence for exactly the same reasons.)

Persuasion directed at women is, therefore, usually effective if and when, sometimes in contradiction to logic, it travels a somewhat schizoid path. It must affirm, first, female superiority on the grounds of one of the two myths (the mystical one is most generally preferred and employed), at the same time that it infers that females are, in effect, operationally treated as inferiors by society-at-large, meaning men. Second, it must affirm the psycho-biological excellence and joy of womanhood, as it also affirms both a measure of guilt and repulsion against those cultural impositions that society has erected against the full expression of these human assets—meaning the self-image of Western women as whole, independent and spiritually self-sufficient human beings, competent to share male love rather than merely receive it and incubate its germ plasm. It must, in cold truth, tell her that she is a martyr to the progress of the human race.

Conclusion

The mythology of womanhood in contemporary Western culture was, in two phases, both old and new, fabricated first in ancient times (in all

[29] The Women's Liberation girls are great at dramatizing this ambivalence, shedding their dainties, storming men's clubs, whistling at day laborers, and, in the wild logic of feminism, acting like women *ad absurdum* by the natural (to them) display of the psycho-biology of the female. In fact, they are acting like rather infantile men who are light-years away from the promise of self-actualization and are closer, psychologically, to fraternity-row twerps or Shriners-on-the-loose than political rebels.

probability) by male story-tellers, and, in the recent past, mostly by women themselves. The old myths relate primarily to the legends centering on Cassandra and Pandora and the mystical excellence of females at occult arts, intuition, animal magnetism, manipulation and extra-sensory perception, as well as their involvement with unearthly spirits. The modern myth centers on the irrelevance of femininity to life in contemporary technological society and the supposed equality of women, intellectually and characterologically, to men (that generally, in the telling, becomes superiority) and minimizes the obvious physiological differences between the sexes, confining psychological variations to the realm of cultural influence.

Both mythological traditions produce female rebel roles, antagonistic one to the other. The former rebels implicitly by precept. The latter rebels explicitly by direct action, demonstration and, in today's parlance, "confrontation." The latter attracts, at present, a good deal of attention by stridently disguising a century and one-half old cultural trend as a modern liberation from the male dominance that she discovers (correctly) in all of culture, including literature and political life, the two main foci of her current interest. The transient intensity of her present call to attention, however, probably portends less for the long-term future of feminism than the first and older form of female rebellion.

Women (like most men) have much to rebel against in our culture, if the issues concern the matter of rights guaranteed by statute and tradition. Modern Western culture is unquestionably patriarchal and male dominant, and will continue this way into the foreseeable future. (Were it matriarchal, the shoe would simply be on the male foot, and the present inequities would then center on the role of men in our culture.) Rarely do women today achieve status comparable with men, and when they do, they are not always judged by male standards. The role of wife and mother is, to many women, highly unsatisfactory as a means of self-actualization, but so, unfortunately, are most of the options open to unmarried females, except that of professional rebel. When a woman makes observations such as these, she is a realist. When a man makes them, he is a male chauvinist.

Because of the ambiguity of their status, the intensity of the desire for self-fulfillment, confusion of roles and frequent dissatisfactions with their own femininity, women are peculiarly receptive to certain kinds of persuasion, as advertisers, particularly, have long known. Women consumers are highly manipulable as long as they are addressed in the contexts of one of the two myths by which they manage to achieve some sense of social worth. Female persuasion is generally based upon affirmations of the excellence of female social roles, including those that are traditionally feminine, ancient and mystical, as well as those that affirm the equality or superiority of females to males in both psychological and biological matters. Because ideas of feminine martyrdom are cherished by most women, and feelings of female equality, excellence and dominance are so avidly needed by them, communications that affirm variations of both themes at the same time usually offer considerable potential for effective persuasion in terms of the goals discussed in Chapter 19.

Chapter 22

YOUTH

Youth is imaginative, and if the imagination be strengthened by discipline, this energy of imagination can in great measure be preserved through life. The tragedy of the world is that those who are imaginative have but slight experience, and those who are experienced have feeble imaginations.

A. N. Whitehead

SENTIMENTALITY is an unlikely psychological by-product of power and technology. But the two nations that today, with any degree of justification, may be called mawkishly or sentimentally "youth oriented" are the USA and the USSR. Next to patriotism, the most sacred national cause in both nations is education and the welfare of the young. Spokesmen for the official destinies of both highly materialistic cultures pour out unlimited clichés about the critical importance of the young in determining the quality of the future.[1] In both countries, the concept of youth has spawned near tyrannical myths of the young as *classes* of citizens in contradistinction to their elders. Ortega y Gasset, in the 1920's, saw the developing power of the young in Europe as a burgeoning *chantage*.[2] And in no other countries do the young possess the supposedly "natural rights" that indeed approach cultural blackmail that they exert today in the United States, the Soviet Union and a few other highly industrialized states.

The analyst of persuasion, of course, is not surprised if and when the price of sentimentality includes blackmail or some sort of extortion. A lady novelist friend of the writer's maintains that the weak of the world appeal to the sentiments of the strong, and cling so tenaciously to the latter that eventually the strong are destroyed. Thus do the weak assimilate their strength. The notion is itself slightly sentimental, and, although this particular authoress has produced numerous successful stories centering on this

[1] See the study of Soviet family life and education in Alex Inkeles and Raymond A. Bauer, *The Soviet Citizen* (Cambridge, Mass.: Harvard University Press, 1959).

[2] José Ortega y Gasset, *The Revolt of the Masses*, p. 189.

theme, weak and strong people in life are not so easily identified or differentiated.

The young and the old are. And in a youth-oriented culture, a crude parallel to weak and strong makes sense. Nations in the West—and other large industrial states—have become lands of young turks, young jackals, bright young men and women, and myths of the neo-Rousseauian perfection of childish innocence. The graying executive, businessman, professor or functionary eventually peeps bitterly over his bifocals at a fresh and vigorous crop of recent graduates from somewhere who will inevitably unseat him from his desk and subsequently tender him his gold watch and retirement scroll. One viable alternative to bitterness is sentimentality, and in a technological society, the concrete symbol of youth may, if viewed sentimentally, stand for abstract symbols of progress and assurances that all the ailments of culture will improve when the visionary young invade the bastions of the cautionary old.[3]

In truth, in these countries today, many of the old seem afraid of the young—apparently, in fact, terrified by them. No other explanation accounts for the behavior of college professors, administrators, policemen, politicians and journalists in the face of recent and continuing student disruptions, youthful riots, saturnalias disguised as rock festivals, narcotics orgies and other outbreaks of disruptive mass juvenile behavior that receive implicit social sanction, if not approval. The precipitating occasions themselves are not at issue; their causes and functions vary. What *is* notable is the reaction of the old to the young when the latter behave contrary either to the law or to other cultural standards and norms. The response takes one of two forms: apparent paralysis and abject terror; or uncontrolled rage—leaving little middle-ground between the two.

Reactions of this variety by the mature population are generally *not* observed at times of international crisis, in the face of adult urban riots, prison revolts, or most other disturbances of the peace, and there have been many of these by which to judge them in the past decade. True, such grown-

---

[3] Films and television are the cultural indices of this trend, highlighted clearly and recently in *Wild in the Streets, Privilege* and such TV dramas as the *Mod Squad.* But this morning's newspaper lists, in the New York area, the following films that treat, in theme, plot or subplot, the supposed revolution of the young against the old: *Performance, The Wild Child, Suppose They Gave a War and Nobody Came?, M*A*S*H, The Grasshopper, Zabriskie Point, Five Easy Pieces, Joe, Catch-22, Goodbye Columbus, The People Next Door, Woodstock, Loving, A Walk In the Spring Rain, The Sterile Cuckoo, Easy Rider,* and probably two or three more with which I am not familiar. The same theme is equally ubiquitous on television. Note that this is the basic premise of the above mentioned, brilliant British film *Privilege,* a movie that attracted too little critical or sociological attention in its initial showings in the United States. Its fictional extrapolation of youthful "privilege" is based upon such documentary cinematic records as Riefenstahl's *Triumph of the Will,* the Canadian film *Lonely Boy,* and other movies, developing the premise (also evident in the American *Wild in the Streets*) that a popular youth idol is catapulted into national political and social prominence and power.

up occurrences are often marked by confusion and disorientation. Riot situations are particularly prone to capricious and thoughtless reactions, but stands are usually quickly taken and clear limits of behavior are drawn in reaction to the subversion of authority. Eventually quiet—if not peace—is restored. When the young are involved in such occasions, however, no such standards seem to obtain. Inflammatory situations either progress inevitably towards mismanaged tragedy (as at Kent State University in 1969), prolonged confusions of ploys and counter-ploys (as at San Francisco State College, Berkeley and Columbia University in New York), or sheer chaos (as in Chicago in 1968 or the sentimentalized Woodstock Festival at Bethel, New York shortly after).

To place the blame for these affairs entirely upon the educational establishment, the police or any single institution of society is to simplify their dynamics into meaninglessness. That these phenomena are genuine social problems today is, in fact, but a symptom of attitudes and beliefs prevailing in our culture in regard, literally, to the sacrosanct, exquisite and holy status of the young. The corpses of four typical post-adolescents killed by stupid accident on a midwest campus are more likely to get (and *have* elicited) strong public sympathy than dozens of adult Negroes killed and injured in ghetto uprisings, despite the fact that the blacks in general are not shy in exploiting their general image as cultural underdogs.

In short, attitudes and opinions of adults towards youth are myth and guilt ridden. As William Braden notes,[4] "Every period has had its privileged age," a period of growth in which the individual, for a certain time, is placed on a pedestal and given cultural obeisance beyond his or her worth. In our culture, it is the late-adolescent who has been (and is) so treated. At the instigation of the clothing industry at first (in search of new markets for bizarre styles), a specific term was created for these children shortly after World War II. It grew into one of the most devious concepts in our vocabulary—and value system. The word is "teenager," a locution new to the past generation. It connotes a period of privilege that neither starts nor stops now in the " 'teen" years, but sometimes continues as a psychological phenomenon (in the eyes both of adults and youth) well into middle age if circumstances demand.

Some authorities maintain that the causes of this phenomenon may be discovered in the permissive upbringing given today's children by their parents. The psychiatrist Bettelhein claims,[5] among other points, that the recent over-protective upbringing of middle-class youngsters has rendered them peculiarly vulnerable to appeals of pseudo-élitism, and has caused

---

[4] See William Braden, *The Age of Aquarius*, pp. 46–47.

[5] See the article by David Dempsey "Bruno Bettelheim is Dr. NO" in *The New York Times Magazine*, January 11, 1970, pp. 22–23, 107–111, for a succinct reprise of Bettelheim's positions concerning accepted modern methods of child rearing.

their resentment towards a technological culture that has provided them with no clear moral or ethical guidelines by which to live. Others blame our educational systems, current quasi-scientific moral relativism, the influence of mass communications, the legacy of the brutality of World War II and similar pat causes. In almost every case, it is the older generation *that blames itself*—or members in its age group—for supposedly corrupting the young. "Where did *we* go wrong?" is the typical lament of middle-class parents when they confront what they are convinced is their valueless, amoral, rebellious, frequently drugged and invariably confused offspring.

Once again, we discover a social illusion resting upon two premises, neither justified by recent history. The first is that the problems we observe today emerging from enclaves of young people are the direct fault of their elders. Few of us think to blame the young themselves for what they are (and what we fear they are becoming), because youth in our world *is* both privileged and sacrosanct. The idea obtains that the young cannot be evil *per se* but must have been taught their misconduct. The second is that the problems in living of today's young are, in substance and symptom, different from the problems of yesterday's young—in fact, unique in moral, ethical or value colorations when compared to the existential crises that formerly faced the present older generation.

J. P. Miller's television play and film, *The People Next Door*, implies these premises—without stating them with much dramatic vigor. (So does the popular movie, *The Graduate*.) When frightened, bewildered, unhappy, alienated, hedonistic, sex obsessed semi-alcoholic fathers or mothers, whose own lives are imbued with no spiritual values, no moral or ethical structures and no zest for life look upon replicas of themselves in crude miniature (displaying in bizarre dress and behavior their own internal confusion) in the person of their own "teenage" children, the confrontation is neither tragic nor pathetic, as our social dramatists would have us believe. It is comical, because the confrontation is not symptomatic of a severe social disorder or the decline of culture, but merely irony in the face of human ignorance and self-delusion.

The Generation Gap

Most discussion of conflicts between young and old begin with the pseudo-truism that many societies display conflicts apparently based upon age differences. This is a half-truth, not applicable, anthropologists tell us, to many highly stable social orders where there is little flexibility in the social roles among members, at least concerning matters of age. Since the beginning of the present century, options for variable and novel behaviors of youth have, in the middle-class world, been wide. One cannot say they have increased. The stereotyped, immigrant father of fifty years ago was extremely anxious—in fact, in certain Jewish, Irish and Italian circles it was *demanded*—that the young cultivate a life-style different from their parents almost from birth.[6] Parents and children discovered eventually that they were living according to different standards. And confrontations between the old and the new (symbolized by the old and new worlds) became not only literary, but psychotherapeutic clichés.

These older conflicts are *not* what we refer to when we speak of the "generation gap" today.[7] The present conflict between old and young is supposed to center upon the inability of the older generation to communicate viable interiorized values to the young. Neither are elders supposedly competent to comprehend the idealism of youth, its revulsion at the strictures of a conformist society, warfare, bureaucracy and the usual roster of other contemporary evils, all of which are placed on the doorstep of anyone of middle age or older.

For all the talk one hears about the New Left, contemporary youth does not seem to be a generation of ideologists to a greater degree than the American young have ever been. A small percentage (smaller than those similarly involved in the depression years) *are* the intellectual step-children of the multi-faceted Marxist movements during the 1930's. In many instances, they are the blood children of depression era and post-war radicals. Another small group follows the eccentric liberalism of such middle-aged gurus as Norman Mailer, Noam Chomsky and Paul Goodman, although it is doubtful that they are generally appreciative of the quixotic vigor of the first, the idealism of the second or the civil intellectualism of the third.

Another segment defers obliquely to the writings of Herbert Marcuse, a turgid, almost Talmudic Marxist loyalist whose published applications of dialectical materialism to capitalist technology are exquisitely obtuse. Marcuse, one imagines, would be the *last* ideological hero in the American political stable attractive to the excitable and volatile types involved in today's student revolts. And the actual potency of the revolutionary impetus of his writings is best demonstrated by the fact that Marcuse is, at this writing,

---

[6] A whole school of literature has developed from this generation gap of yesterday, its main exponents Jewish novelists like Saul Bellow, Lillian Ross, J. D. Salinger, Philip Roth and others, who are all (and invariably) concerned with a passing type of domestic conflict that is decreasing in social importance with the years as the immigrant older generation dies off. Among Jewish circles, it might be called the "My son, the doctor" syndrome, but it is by no means typically Jewish. Other ethnic groups that have experienced it have not spawned as many novelists as have the Jews, but Mario Puzo has done, I think, a creditable job in his best-selling novel *The Godfather*, where the theme of contemporary crime is less interesting than the conflict between first and second generation American Italians.

[7] I have no way of knowing whether the book by Richard Lorber and Ernest Fladell, *The Gap* (New York: McGraw-Hill Book Co., 1968), is a fraud or not. It rings hollow as an honest confrontation between a middle-aged man and his "hip" nephew and deals mostly in soap opera trivia. But it does, by cliché, indicate what the generation gap is *supposed* to be: the casual, amoral acting out and acceptance by the young of the etiology of what are life's frustrations for their elders. Like the gap itself, these symptoms of the gap are also nonsense.

alive and well and teaching (and on the public payroll) in the state of California.[8] His main attraction undoubtedly is the deft manner in which he interstices a Freudian vocabulary with Marxist outrage and fabricates an implicit revolutionary social psychology. Both his thought and persuasion are insistently political, however, redolent of an upbringing in the traditions of German political scholarship in both its most intellectually incisive and humanistically lethal manifestations.

Genuine ideologists in the rank and file of the New Left are rare, and their numbers will decrease as they grow older, disenchanted and/or run afoul of authority. A revolutionary stance, if it is genuinely ideological, requires a high degree of sophistication—whether on the left or right. This is a hard fact that each generation of revolutionaries everywhere seems forced to discover anew. Only the likes of Lenins, Castros, Francos, Maos and genuine intellectuals survive as leaders; the rest are conveniently lost or disposed of in the rise to power, as the Weathermen, Panthers and militant Birchites are discovering today, as if for the first time. The true Western ideologist of the left today finds himself in a peculiar position, far too testing for its present few quasi-charismatic leaders, whose names will probably have changed by the time this paragraph is printed. They must be, in truth, as sophisticated as a Marcuse. And few, if any, are.

It is not enough, for instance, for them to favor peace and oppose capitalist imperialism in the Far East—notably in Indochina at the moment. Leftist ideologists must also apply the same deterministic principles to Israel's conquests in the Near East and to political alignments of Near Eastern powers with Western imperialists, both capitalist and communist. (Some New Leftists—particularly Negroes who profess an affinity for the Moslem faith and dislike Jews on not entirely irrelevant grounds—have managed this particular problem consistently.) They must also deal justly with Soviet and Red Chinese economic and military imperialism. And other difficult ideological problems still await to snare them, because they are not both political realists and mature ideologists. They suffer, in fact, from the same sorts of confusions of ends and means that have plagued revolutionaries in the West for more than three generations, and have eventually deactivated most of them. They are, in many ways, more like their grandfathers ideologically than they are like themselves.[9]

---

[8] One's best and clearest introduction to Herbert Marcuse's writings is *One Dimensional Man* (Boston: Beacon Press, 1964), which brings together most thoughtfully Marxist and Freudian currents that pervade his earlier works such as *Eros and Civilization* (Boston: Beacon Press, 1955; new edition 1966). See also the generally fair evaluation of Marcuse's role in the New Left in Paul A. Robinson, *The Freudian Left*, pp. 147–244, which emphasizes Marcuse's clever transmorphologies of Freudian constructs into Marxist socio-political terms, distinctive from similar attempts by more familiar neo-Freudians like Fromm and others.

[9] See the anthology, Mitchell Cohn and Dennis Hale (eds.), *The New Student Left* (Boston: Beacon Press, 1967), for a somewhat dated, but still typical, potpouri or the variegated aims, means and variously interpreted ideological themes as interpreted by

The cornerstone of any generation gap is usually political, and, in ideological constructions, no such gap exists in any wide measure today. The Militant Left (including the New Left) exists, but it is a movement dominated by middle-aged intellectuals and tired radicals left over from the depression period. On the right, what militancy one discovers is a relic of the America Firsters of the late 1930's. As in the days of the author's youth, commitment to political revolution engenders a certain romantic appeal for the young, about as great (in the USA) as their built-in distaste for the genuine, blood and guts ideological commitment. European revolutionaries overcame this distaste and, like Hitler or Lenin, accepted prison as the price of commitment or, like Trotsky, fled into exile. If New Left revolutionaries go into exile today, it is likely to involve a short trip to Canada to avoid the draft, not to organize a revolution.[10]

Most other indices of the value gap between generations follows the same pattern as the supposed political gap. Multiple studies of our youth (biased fiercely in sampling techniques towards college students, supposedly the most radical segment of the young) indicate that the majority of them reflect almost exactly parental values in political, social, economic and other matters.[11] The greatest divergence between young people and their parents appears to center on opinions in regard to sex and drugs. Exploring further, however, one discovers that this divergence is almost entirely in the realm of *opinion*, and not concentrated either on beliefs, attitudes or actions.

In regard to sex, there is little evidence that either attitudes or behaviors, by and large, of the present generation are much at variance from the one that preceded it. As Adelson states, "Most close students of the sexual scene seem to agree that the trend toward greater permissiveness in the United States probably began in the 1920's . . ." [12] The one big difference today is that the young (and the old) apparently *talk* much more about sex than they ever did. And the spread of soft- and hard-core pornography is far greater, although this trend does not seem to influence actual behavior or attitudes much. For all the publicity concerning The Pill, it accomplishes nothing more remarkable than the condom did for the previous generation, and, for today's young, is often more tactically difficult to procure and use properly than a package of "safes" was when the author was a blade. Ob-

stable (mostly) spokesmen for the New Left, and interpret therefrom the integrity of their revolutionary zeal in terms of social and political theory as well as potential for activism.

10 Among the Negroes, Eldridge Cleaver is an exception. See Chapter 23.

11 The following estimates are taken from Joseph Adelson, "What Generation Gap?" *The New York Times Magazine*, January 18, 1970, pp. 10–11, 34–36, 45, which is a review of interviews with and studies of young people and their parents made by the author, a University of Michigan psychologist, psychiatrist David Offer, Vern Bengston, Samuel Lubell, *Fortune* magazine and other keepers of the national pulse-beat.

12 *Ibid.*, p. 34.

taining an abortion is quite simple (and legal) in many states at present, but so it was (but not legal) ten, twenty, thirty or forty years ago—although these ubiquitous illegal operations were not a that time covered by medical insurance. In short, today's youth seems, sexually, to be performing about as their parents did, displaying the same attitudes they had (and have), but expressing them more freely and in blunter language.

The drug problem is another area of apparent schism between the generations that does not indicate a genuine difference either in attitudes or behavior. The only assumption required to comprehend this consonance is to accept what is self-evident: that an enormous number of youths are today using marijuana (and probably amphetamines) for ends that previous generations achieved by alcohol in various concentrations, probably—and here the matter is moot—with less physiological damage and/or risk of subsequent addiction. This assumption is challenged, usually, by those who minimize the present role of alcohol in American adult life and are not acquainted with its potential for physical destruction. They do not realize that alcohol is one of the most insidiously addictive drugs known, both physiobiologically and psychologically. Because marijuana is illegal, and because amphetamines and tranquilizers are supposedly obtainable only by physician's prescription, they are immediately classed with hard, dangerous drugs like the opiates or psychedelic agents such as LSD. Little is known about the long term effects of the latter, but it has gathered about it a rich folklore (much of it nonsense) based upon isolated reactions and brewed in a climate of adult fear of, and for, the young.

In general terms, therefore, the use of drugs (including alcohol) is sanctioned attitudinally by the majority of our adults and by their young. Eighty million adults do not hesitate to dose themselves, in varying degrees at different intervals, with alcohol. Their children share their attitudes, but in opinion (and sometimes in action) extend their affirming disposition to cover cannabis and allied chemicals. Sons and daughters, of teetotalers tend not to use drugs of any kind, including alcohol.

The "hard drug" problem is another matter, practically epidemic in our Negro ghettos and presently moving into certain domains of the middle class, where isolated instances of heroin use invariably attract considerable attention. For all the publicity hard drug addiction receives, the number of addicts in the United States, including the young, remains low: about 160,000 persons are arrested as drug addicts per year—including marijuana users. On the other hand, about a million and one-half are arrested for drunkenness. The number of hard drug addicts in the USA is difficult to calculate, but it probably cannot, at present, exceed 200,000. The number of chronic alcoholics is somewhere between five and ten million. And most of *both* types of addicts will eventually die or be institutionalized as a direct or indirect result of their addictions.

In short, most of today's youth tend to reflect parental attitudes in the areas of life about which the legend of the generation gap has developed—areas related to basic values and life-styles. The figure of convergence, or statistical similarity, is remarkably similar in most extant studies: about three-quarters of the young are, in most respects, dispositional carbon copies of their parents. They may dress differently (as the young often do), may use a different vocabulary (again, a common stratagem of youth), and they may find profound verbal communication with oldsters difficult. But they probably find communication with one another difficult also. And typical (literary) American families from Sinclair Lewis to the radio soap opera to *Portnoy* have classically displayed severe problems in clarifying their feelings, aspirations and values between their members.

The other one-quarter are rebels in one or another sense, sometimes, as in the instance of a daughter who marries outside of her parents' religious faith, of such stylistic quietude as hardly to be noticeable, even to next-door neighbors. In a society as volatile and mobile as ours, the fact that so *small* a percentage of acorns are blown away from their parental trees is, to the author, more surprising than the phenomenon of a generation gap and its attendant mythology. Within that one-quarter, however, one discovers individuals of considerable *panache* and talent for attracting attention to themselves. Many are obviously quite gifted and do not hesitate to speak for their generation on occasions when they are merely speaking for themselves. Others attempt, metaphorically and realistically, to play with explosives and, one way or another, manage to blow themselves up, along with a few innocent bystanders. Others become severely disaffected and disoriented psychologically, join cults whose diversions range from venereal matters to selective murder, and in effect, replicate in group patterns the same behaviors usually pursued by older psychological washouts on our nation's skid rows. These youngsters make excellent subjects for Sunday newspaper feature stories and exposés in paperback.

For the rest, and in a larger perspective, psychologist Adelson writes:

> The young have always haunted the American imagination, and never more so than in the past two decades. The young have emerged as the dominant projective figures of our culture. Holden Caulfield, Franny Glass, the delinquents of the Blackboard Jungle, the beats and now the hippies and the young radicals—these are figures, essentially, of our interior landscape. They reflect and stand for some otherwise silent currents in American fantasy. They are the passive and gentle—Holden, Franny, and now the flower children—who react to the hard circumstances of modern life by withdrawal and quiescence; or else they are the active and angry—the delinquents and now the radicals—who respond by an assault upon the system.
>
> In these images, and in our tendency to identify ourselves with them, we can discover the alienation within all of us, old and young. We *use the young to represent our despair, our violence, our often forlorn hopes for a better world.* Thus, these images of adolescence tell us something,

something true and something false, about the young; they may tell us even more about ourselves.[13]

Perhaps the generation gap is simply an alienation we, as parents, teachers and, supposedly, ego-ideals for the young, feel in ourselves, the results of our own compromised ideals and the unrealized dreams of our childhoods that haunt the rest of our lives. Most assuredly, the gap is *not* a syndrome of modern youth or contemporary culture. If it exists at all—and if we *think* it does, it *does* to some degree—it is but one facet of a more general condition of cultural confusion and disorientation.

Children in School

Another perspective of the so-called "gap" opens a different area of conjecture. As Walter Lippmann said in a recent interview:

> The technological gap and the generation gap are the same thing. And the young people today are coming into a world for which there was no preparation in custom. There never was a world like this. Not that any revolutionist made it. It was created by technology and science. They don't know what to do about it, and the older people don't know what to do about it, either. They don't understand it themselves. That is absolutely the core of our problems. How will we be able to create a capacity to govern this enormously new and enormously complicated and very rapidly changing social environment? That is the problem. And there's no answer. We may not solve it in a generation. That's the problem today. The revolutionary—all that business—is of no importance except as a byproduct of that . . . *We might as well be honest about it with ourselves: we are not in a position yet to re-educate the masses, because we don't know what to teach them. And that is one of the critical conditions of our time.*[14]

The candor for which Lippmann asks is perhaps a richer self-honesty than we can presently afford (and at the same time sustain our illusions), because it may open alternate wellsprings of the guilt and panic that the older generation so often displays when called to confront the younger, reactions more dramatically displayed by educators and so-called "leaders" of the young than rank-and-file citizens. Individual elders, of course, are individually often responsible, not only for the irresponsibility of their children, but also for their own self-destructiveness. But guilt and panic are unnecessary and destructive.

Children may be raised in many ways. And, if, for instance, the permissiveness advocated in Benjamin Spock's handbook justifies for some the neglect and indifference of some parents towards their children, the blame falls neither upon Dr. Spock nor his book. Too many productive and

[13] *Ibid.*, p. 45. (Italics added.)

[14] Walter Lippmann, "On Understanding Society" in *Columbia Journalism Review*, Fall, 1969, p. 9. (Italics added.)

healthy youngsters have been raised "according to Spock" to blame a book or its moderate guidelines for domestic social problems. The parents who have failed their children are also failing themselves, and the end products, in terms of disoriented lives, would have been the same had they substituted, for their copy of Spock, manuals of child care written fifty years ago. Unquestionably, many adults have earned well the guilt they now attempt to exculpate by attacking Spock's handbook. But the fault lies in forces more insidious than a mere book on child care, forces that originate in the total drift of the social order, as Lippmann notes.

Occasionally, the essential absurdity—and seriousness—of our older generation's proclivities for self-castigation (the psychological source of the generation gap myth) offer a spark of justified indignation and thoughtful insight. One such example (and there are others) is the widely reprinted letter to his brother by the politically liberal History Professor K. Ross Toole, in which he expresses in blunt terms his feeling of being "fed up" with the arrogance of the young in the face of their elders and betters.[15] What Toole presents is the picture of a rational man and father, himself a social idealist, who has simply grown weary of feeling guilty about the highly publicized revolutionary behavior of our young radicals and their followers, a disposition probably shared by many of Toole's generation—and many young people as well.

Toole's tirade is an assault upon symptoms, not causes. And his alarm centers upon the general tendency of many politically uncommitted young people first, to believe the generation gap myth and the fiction that youth constitutes a socio-political class. Second, a large number of the young, influenced by mass media promulgation of this myth,[16] seem passively to support the rhetoric of overt rebellion mouthed by no more than one-fifth of our young people *and also*, in all probability, *one fifth (or so) of the population who are well over thirty and have been for many years (and continue to be) radicalized*, who form the apparent, well publicized (but bogus), coalition of the young.[17] Toole also points to the irresponsibility of the mass

[15] The letter has been published in paperback with other observations by Toole. See K. Ross Toole, *An Angry Man Talks Up To Youth* (New York: Award Books, 1970). Parts of this document have been reprinted in *U.S. News and World Report* and the *Reader's Digest*. The reference below is to the book.

[16] Numerous articles in magazines on the youth problem and gap feed this fire. (The teen age market is being presently exploited far beyond the clothing industry to other commercial fields, almost entirely by older people.) Television seminars that polarize young against old also feed these flames. I listened recently (in private consultation) to a menopausal female editor of a national magazine explain how she planned to pitch her highly influential publication to the young—in other words, to exploit this myth in the interest of circulation and, hopefully, also to interest adults in "now" things. All myths are self-generating to some degree, but, stimulated by fast earning potential and mass distribution, myths in a technological society are easily exploited for circulation and cash.

[17] A bit of personal history: I spent a recent so-called "student revolt" with a group of college students operating a university radio station during the fracas. I could not

communications' industries in interpreting the behavior of the young, the idealistic poverty of the young militant's idealism, and the tendency of the immature to demand instant gratification (under the guise of a search for relevance) combined with their scorn for the considerations of history.[18]

Toole is correct in his diagnosis as it applies to a fraction (again, about one-fifth) *of our total population, not necessarily the young.* And this social psychopathy, like all psychopathy, is contagious *especially* among the young—and especially, also, among those whose education has not included the study of persuasion and myth in history, or have not been provided with a properly disciplined curriculum to allow them to muster sufficient intelligence, moral fibre, operative internalized values and critical intelligence to stand aside for a moment from Le Bon's crowd and think for themselves.

But why should they? Are we not asking the impossible from the masses, no matter how reflective they are of civilized backgrounds, when we expect them not to behave like members of a crowd? Upon the answer to this question probably depends the destiny of all technological societies. And, unfortunately, it is at present unanswerable.

The etiology of honest but well-meant failure, however, on the part of the older generation towards the younger one remains, however, quite clear. It is not an issue to hide behind verbal smokescreens like "generation gaps" or the "now generation," or to consume in polemics like Toole's or in paroxysms of guilt, simply because our children dress like clowns and smoke different kinds of cigarettes from adults.[19] Ortega y Gasset noted long ago

---

have asked for more civil company and companionship. I report this without condecension, because those youngsters taught *me* a lesson in perils of easy generalization on the basis of Sunday supplement half-truths. Of course, they were inexperienced (and knew it) in socio-political matters, but remarkably open-minded, including those of their number who had legitimate complaints against both the social order and their own university. Had they not been occupied with broadcasting, they would have been among the student protesters, but as seekers, not as radicals. Also, I suppose, one or two of them might have been manipulated in this or that political direction by the activist twenty-percent. What occurred to me during that incident, among other things, was that, on the average, neither the young nor their elders need assume in any measure that they have raised a generation of malcontents. They have raised *average* youngsters who may or may not be competent to handle new challenges culture presents to them. Our main fault as parents and educators (mostly the latter) is clear in Lippmann's observation above: we did not foresee that we *should* have provided better and more explicit education in value formation in order to raise our *normal* youngsters above the *average* to discover in each his own potentials for uniqueness. Instead, we let our youngsters "be themselves," to the degree that they emerged at puberty as highly manipulable protoplasm, many of them, therefore, sitting ducks for simple-minded activist persuasion.

[18] Toole, *op. cit.*, 40–43.

[19] Once again, why the guilt? In my travels around the nation, the adult dress I see generally is no less clownish than children's dress; in fact, middle-class female and (now) male devotees of beauty-shop culture seem to me far more ludicrously garbed than flower children. Nor are adults any more or less generally drugged than youngsters. I have not been able to prevail upon my local druggist to disclose how many prescriptions for tranquilizing agents he fills per week, but he tells me that "everybody

that the two major indices of youthful rebellion were "caricature and violence," [20] and we should not be disturbed when we discover that the wise speak prophetically. Prophets, however, rarely deal in causes. Nor does the discovery of the cause of a symptom necessarily imply its cure.

Let us, however, examine some probable causes:

First, obscured by rhetoric about youth is the hard fact that, especially as they are now schooled in our society, young people, for the most part, do not *know* very much. Suggestions, therefore, from politicians and educators who should know better, that we begin to *listen* to youth (as if we have been doing anything besides listening for decades) are sheer nonsense, unless we are foolish enough to believe that we are able to utilize what they say for psychoanalytic purposes of some sort. Social ameliorists spend much time, energy and money at present listening, as do so-called "public service" mass communicators who accomplish little more than broadcasting widely ignorance, vacuous opinion and the charm of youthful drama. Associated with the major causes of the youth problem is the problem that we elders (educators and parents especially) *have,* in recent years, *listened too much and too long and actually done too little* for youth on our own initiatives.

Much has also been made of the period of identity crisis of the young, but on a superficial basis and rarely with sensitive attention to its implications. Fashions in child raising aside, our youth—like most young in all mobile societies where multiple options for careers, life-styles, values, morals and other existential anchors exist—face the same sort of options that most of us over forty once faced. But they are now multiplied in intensity at least one thousand per cent: They offer a plurality of possible future *selves* demanding choices of a critical nature at relatively early ages. This demand, enhanced by symbolic cultural pressures of many kinds, is insistent and unbelievably confusing to children. What is more, it is frightening—most frightening in the face of the knowledge that one's choice will probably destroy whatever cultural security one has previously found in childhood. The problem is thus greatest for upward ascending, lower and lower middle-class youths. It reaches near-hysterical proportions where the challenge of choice is greatest: among minority groups (including and especially Negroes and females of all races) and among those whose present family life-style, for any reason, is perceived as reasonably secure, on one hand, but ultimately unsatisfactory, on another.

With little or no preparation and on the basis of little experience, therefore, our young are required to make deep and usually misperceived

---

around here is 'on' the damn things, including me." And the busiest automobile in by suburban neighborhood is the truck (sic) that makes instant booze deliveries. I am often too free with advice to parents, but if one wants his or her youngsters to develop aesthetic, moral and/or behavioral values he admires, he can do it, but only *one* way: *by example.* A frequently overlooked educational truism is that most effective instruction *of all kinds* is accomplished by precept.

[20] Ortega y Gasset, *op. cit.*, p. 188–189.

personal ideological commitments in order to resolve the confusion and crisis of deriving for themselves a personal identity. The process is clearly summed up by Erikson:

> (W)e can ascribe to ideology the function of offering youth 1.) a simplified perspective of the future which encompasses all foreseeable time and thus counteracts individual "time confusion"; 2.) some strongly felt correspondence between the inner world of ideals and evils and the social world with its goals and dangers; 3.) an opportunity for exhibiting some uniformity of appearance and behavior . . . 4.) inducement to a collective experimentation with roles and techniques which help to overcome a sense of inhibition and personal guilt; 5.) introduction into the ethos of prevailing technology and thus into sanctioned and regulated competition; 6.) a geographical-historical world image as a framework for the young individual's budding identity; 7.) a rationale for a sexual way of life compatible with a convincing system of principles; and 8.) submission to leaders who as superhuman figures or "big brothers" are above the ambivalence of the parent-child relation.

Details aside, Erikson states, "Without some such *ideological commitment*, however, implicit in a 'way of life,' youth suffers a *confusion of values* which can be specifically dangerous to some but which on a large scale is surely dangerous to the fabric of society." [21]

This latter need is not met by our systems of education, most conspicuously not by our colleges and universities, and specifically in the precepts of the men and women who teach our students. The worst offenders are youngish, local celebrity professors who have mastered the art of spellbinding at the price of substance, and theatrics at the price of thought. Their open-mindedness and eclecticism (usually a cover for a lack of knowledge of their subjects) breed in their young student a pleasant confusion. Pleasant, because, as a student slides from past to present, over centuries, in and around schools of literature, drama and into and about psychological and sociological fashions, he receives a bogus sense of command over the miserable fantasy we call "human knowledge." Confusion, because the disciplined, insightful requirements for the acceptance, rejection or construction of ideology (except in simplistic radicalized social melodramas of "good guys" versus "bad guys") are absent almost entirely from this type of flashy schooling.

Our schools perform certain functions quite well, particularly the teaching of technology—or that part of it which involves techniques. Engineering, legal and medical training are good examples. But techniques are the *last things*, educationally, that the masses of freshmen presently invading the campuses of our nations need or *want*. First, these youngsters must discover who they themselves *are*. Second, they must learn what, realistically and sometimes unfortunately, they may (or may not) *become*. Third,

---

[21] Erik H. Erikson, *Identity, Youth and Crisis*, pp. 187–188.

they require a wide range of testing situations in which they may experiment with options. And fourth, they need guidance in choosing from among multiple options the components of experience that will yield, eventually, a perception of reasonable objectives in life. Fifth, they must, indeed, master techniques.

When this sort of sequence is not followed, or followed in letter but not in spirit, pleasant confusion yields eventually an unpleasant confusion that in turn yields hostility. In the light of this progression, one broad social question arises and should be referred immediately to suitable social psychologists: Why did American university students *not* begin tearing down their schools and colleges until the 1960's?

The answer probably centers on the fact that, until then, a mere handful of the total population entered college at all, and that handful was too stupid—or frightened—to speak up and/or be counted. The situation is different today.

Youth and Persuasion

The social revolutions of the past century have forced us, for numerous reasons, to extend for years the period of time that youngsters stay in school. To expect that a social change of such potential psychological dimensions would *not* create numerous kinds of social upheaval is but one symptom of the blindness of our educators, busy as they were in the belief that they were pursuing the laudable objective of opening wider the doors of our colleges and universities, in effect, to our total young population. The impulse to create the first college educated population in the history of the world is an altruistic ideal,[22] but the conviction that it may somehow be accomplished without changing both the nature and meaning of a college education—and without subjecting various segments of our educational institutions to severe, and in some cases mortal, stresses—is ludicrous. All young people possess neither the potentials—nor the desire—to become civilized *in the way that school teachers would civilize them;* and much valuable and contributive work in the modern world may be, and is, done, by people who have exercised their option to drop out of formal schooling

---

[22] The most civilized argument I have read in favor of this trend is found in a volume by Milton Schwebel, *Who Can Be Educated?* (New York: Grove Press, 1968). Schwebel thinks, in effect, that everybody can (be educated), and along specific lines that are generally approved by today's educational establishment. Lack of intelligence, non-conformism, dearth of initiative and other factors that once eliminated young people from our schools are seen by Schwebel as induced almost entirely by cultural determinants that may today be controlled and corrected. His argument is strongest in breaking down notions of the specific limitations that society does indeed place upon talented youngsters in deprived environments and who may well profit themselves and others by the further schooling that they do not, at present, receive. The consequences of Schwebel's general impulse to share what he—as a professor and educated gentleman—regards as the "good life" with everybody else are not, however, given complete or realistic consideration in his arguments.

at an early age. The virtual elimination today of such dropouts—or the social opprobrium heaped upon them—is one tragedy of our time resulting from the idealism that permits no graceful exit from the institution of education for those *too dull or too smart* (in their special ways) for overlong confinement in school.

One result of what, in substance, is turning into an open admissions policy running the gamut of colleges and universities across the nation is that we are extending the period of youthful moratorium, or era of youthful privilege, for longer periods than ever before and permitting it to continue, in many cases, well into adult years. Young people these days (motivated by many factors including a desire to evade military service) may attenuate their lives as students for years, even making something of a career of college, taken at a leisurely pace. Graduate studies may be delayed by one or another ruse until they are well into their thirties, and they may become, in effect, "professional students" in their adult years.[23] (In former times, this was a privilege of a mere handful of rich youngsters, many of whom demonstrated the efficiency of their training by later pursuing careers as playboys.)

The consequences of this cultural innovation are numerous, but the most dramatic stem from the fact that our schools themselves have, by and large, taken little cognizance of this change and continue in their time-honored ways. They simply multiply sections of *Freshman Sociology* and *American Literature I*, call into the fray ever larger echelons of green, young teachers—many of them ignorant of the fundamentals of their own fields—to meet larger and larger sections of new undergraduates. The syndrome of identity confusion is thereby attenuated, exacerbated and collectivized among these masses of students. Although physical adults, many of them are psychological children in their present cultural roles, an old American problem but carried now to absurd lengths.

Some of them, including the more intelligent, impatient and generally hot-headed, have terminated their own moratoriums and privileges by accepting jejune radical ideologies and joining revolutionary movements. But the greater number are still thumb-sucking and—naturally—playing sexual

[23] I have seen this process at work in the East, but it is apparently accomplished most easily in the State of California. A former elementary school student of mine is, at present, an aging professional student who started his college career in New York State and New England. Eventually, he moved to California where, a mature man now, he continues to study for various degrees in assorted subjects, teaching classes when forced to, and living on his wife's earnings and various scholarships and stipends that he manipulates from what I gather are state funds. He has also written a book which provides him modest royalties. He has, it appears, contrived for himself an extremely stress-free manner of living. When in California a few years ago, I stayed with him at his "pad" and enjoyed his hospitality. He explained that a good number of professional students live as he does, well into middle age and beyond. He personally had, at that time, no plans for the immediate future, except to try to find a university with more comfortable beach facilities and better ocean swimming than the one at which he was presently operating—in California, of course.

and pharmacological games with their own and each others' mature physical and psychic organisms. They seem forever to be getting dressed to go out to accomplish something, but are forced, in the straw-man world of the classroom, to play games at a time when they might be living. At least, they should be, by their late adolescent years, well on their way to carving out relevant identities and ideologies by which to live. But most of them are not given the opportunity, and are prevented from doing just this by an educational system and cultural imperatives designed to serve a society that no longer exists.

All of this may be a long-winded way of stating what the business world and entertainment industry has long known: that, in a raw sense, persuading teenagers of nearly anything is discouragingly simple; and that the teenage period of life, of itself, has little to do with chronological age. It defines merely an attitude or, in most cases, the absence or tenuousness of mature attitudes. This is because among youth, as among no other segment of the population, we are faced at present with a population of human beings who have learned to *disbelieve* more than they *believe*. Their basic attitudes, as we have noted, reflect their home environments, and, if they are in school, these feeble precepts are continually being tested by the confused and variegated attitudinal flack they receive from their peers and teachers.

Young people have been taught in school that to have opinions is a good thing, a sign of adulthood, and the external indication of one who has achieved identity as a thinking man. They therefore generate easily seething masses of opinions on every conceivable subject, including matters that do not lend themselves intrinsically to opinion formation. These opinions, of course, are not held deeply and are quite malleable. But the young are persuaded best and most by the opinionated or opinion-giving manipulator, even if the opinions he offers are apparently antithetical to supposedly youthful values.[24] The young are also intensely biologically active and therefore appear to be continually busy. Their actions are frequently irrelevant to, or inconsistent with, their opinions, although they may follow the direction and impetus of those opinions for relatively short periods of time.

Appeals to the young that promise them popularity, sexual activity, respect and the desiderata of adults are potent in minor contexts. But the major unmet area of need in the life of today's children is the need for ideology, which is essential to them in their search for identity. Because of their general scorn for history, young people are likely to accept ideologies that have been discarded by former generations, especially those that provide simple solutions to existential problems gleaned from textbooks or lec-

---

[24] The highly opinionated cartoonist Al Capp is a favorite campus lecturer, his act consisting largely of insulting his youthful audiences by means of direct and occasionally vulgar assaults at their behavior, dress and values. For obvious reasons, young people love such treatment.

tures at school or college. Their recent choices have been near inevitable: simplified Eastern cultism, astrology, witchcraft, psychological quackery, Scientism, Orgone therapy, Encounter groups, drug mysticism, musical orgiasticism and similar foolery, as well as a neo-Rousseauism that has (more out of desperation than ignorance), in recent years, been on display in new forms of Bohemianism—like the now defunct "beat" scene, hippie culture, post-hippies and flower children. This Bohemian culture bespeaks laudable aims in almost every instance, but its exponents lack both the raw knowledge of human affairs and the socio-political ideology that might raise their sub-cultures to the level of genuine social movements, not merely infantile responses to obvious evils.[25]

In these matters, the pragmatic wisdom of the post-World War II clothing manufacturers still applies with annoyingly direct relevance. There exists today an enormous market for *ideology substitutes*, and the wilder and more ridden with charletanry the better. These pseudo-ideologies must, however, serve as functional, simple and acceptable substitutes for genuine ideology, and provide near instant identity—or the illusion of it—to unknowing, naïve and confused minds. Hence the appeal of Dr. McLuhan and his "media" mysticism, the psychedelic cults, double-talking film-making gurus, disaffected clergymen and other representatives of the fundamentally alienated section of today's culture: that segment (and it remains a segment) of the young who have chosen for themselves the pitiful epithet, "the *now* generation." What a pathetic rubric to look back upon when "now" becomes "yesterday"! Not "shook up," "beat," "lost"—or "anxious"—but "now."

Conclusion

Because it is difficult to be young, and because all members of the older generation have survived such difficulties and tend to romanticize them, youth, in our culture, is less a period of growth than a source of myth and legend, believed mostly by the old, but frequently by the young themselves as well. Like other technological cultures, Americans idealize the young and are therefore apparently also afraid of their potential collective charismatic power.

---

[25] Bohemianism serves a societal and artistic function related to youthful grasps after ideology. See L. Douglas Smith, "The Beats and Bohemia: Positive Social Deviance or a Problem in Collective Disturbance?" in S. C. Plog and R. B. Edgerton, *Changing Perspectives in Mental Illness*, pp. 578–593. Bohemia is frequently an unhappy recourse for the disassociated young who join forces, in effect, with older, disturbed societal washouts, genuine but jaded *avant gardists* and dissenters from the social order who are motivated by rigid ideologies. In such company, the freaked-out flower child, regardless of age, is usually mercilessly exploited by sophisticated, older exploiters. This latter factor is one main cause of the dissolution of the various early hippie communities, publicized as they were by the mass press, television, resident sociologists and fast-dollar film makers. They also fell victim to the gangsters who gather around most urban Bohemias, greedy for the fast dollar from tourist trade, prostitution of various types, of course, a lucrative narcotics traffic.

We believe that they are given to radical activism; we therefore fear their revolutionary power. We believe that youth and natural perfection are closely related; we therefore fear the mysticism of inate youthful superiority. We are continually and vaguely dissatisfied with (and afraid of) our own offspring; therefore our fear is set against a background of guilt, when we discover that our children have not become the sort of people we hoped they would. We will not believe that our young may be essentially imperfect, or that they may be led astray by forces beyond their, and our, control. In the end, we conclude that we must have "spoiled" (a fortuitous word) them. We are willing also to believe that, somehow, we also spoiled the world into which we brought them and encourage them to remind us of our crime at every conveniently cruel instance.

The period of youth in the West is a time of moratorium and privilege, extended lately by the prolongation of the years we keep youngsters in schools. It is also a period during which people search for identity in accepting ideologies, out of which they may carve adult identities. Most youngsters solve this challenge by eventually accepting the ideological stance of their families. But a small, although highly visible, proportion do not. The latter either act out their confusion in apparently senseless rebellion, or join those whose commitment lies in some form of political or social radicalism.

In fact, phenomena like the generation gap are social fantasies. Differences in life-style and difficulties in meaningful discourse are probably far greater between young people themselves than between the young and their elders. The myth of the gap also results from the distorted illusion older people receive when viewing the almost invariably highly visible behavior of the approximately one-fifth of our young people, who are, in one degree or another, authentic rebels from their own pasts.

In short, the young and the old in America are today remarkably similar, except that the young are currently forced to face deeper problems than their parents encountered, in accepting and interiorizing values by which to find identity as adults. Our schools on all levels might help to resolve this problem, but they have not to date. And there exists no reason to believe that educators will be competent to solve it tomorrow, should they decide to do so by some miracle. They will continue to pursue traditional but unclear objectives in their old, odd ways, because neither most teachers nor most administrators possess either the training, intelligence or inclination to do otherwise. Thus, they will probably continue first, to prolong youth's period of moratorium, and second, teach merely various academic and vocational techniques with some efficiency, as they have done for more than two generations.

The young, on the other hand, will listen to those voices beyond the school and campus which give form and structure to those dispositions that are most in need of directive influences: beliefs and attitudes. In their special way, the young are highly persuasible, both in regard to the important matters of life and in the trivial ones. While fortunes have been spent to create minor appetites in youth and subsequently to satisfy them (for a price), far greater rewards await those who meet more fundamental youthful needs and provide for the disaffected segment of them a sense of purpose in life and significant keys to their own identity. In recent history, Hitler, Mao, Castro and others have differentially succeeded at this task. So, of course, and in different contexts, have the late Robert Kennedy, Eugene McCarthy and a host of mass communications celebrities who, by means of entertainment, have established crude identity models for emulation. Examples are The Rolling Stones, Joan Baez, The Beatles, Bob Dylan, Leonard Cohen, Phil Ochs and others in various fields.

From the perspective of the persuader who is competent to reach the young, one's deadliest errors are either to sentimentalize their social role and/or to believe the myths (especially those concerning sex and drugs) by which they are supposed to live. If one pays due regard to youthful confusion, fright, disorientation and panic at life's multitudinous options, he is on his way to striking a vital, communal responsive chord in them.

Chapter 23

VIOLENCE

Unfortunately, the concern with violence is directed at a myth. It demands an ocean where there are islands; it constructs a monolith in place of diversity; it calls for formulas to cover complexity; and it presumes cure-alls where we have no diagnosis.

Hans Toch

NEARLY EVERYBODY with anything to say on the subject of violence seems already to have said it, not once but many times. The constituent aspects of violence *per se* have been blown dry by the plenitude of investigations it has recently undergone.

The library of violence is enormous. Instead of dispatching the best thinkers to tackle our worst problems, Americans tend to think we will solve them by employing teams of second- and third-rate minds (and echelons of ghost writers) as "Commissions" which produce multitudinous reports in thick volumes that, by virtue of density alone, mean little to anyone.[1] Such compulsive documentarianism produces mere talismans, icons of sacrifice of labor to the gods of social justice. In cliché, they indicate that "somebody cared," and the initial problem is therefore "under control" in an entirely magical sense.

In this chapter, we shall not center concern on theories or methods of preventing or inciting violence. The former demands too extensive a study of alternatives; and the latter is apparently too easy. We shall, however, examine some responsible conjecture as to the cause of violent behavior among men and women, including socially sanctioned violence like that involved in sports and play, violence in warfare and law enforcement, as well as illegal, disruptive violence, which is usually what is understood by the term in common parlance. As we have in the previous dynamic contexts, we shall attempt, then, to relate violent behavior to the manipulation of dispositions by means of persuasion.

[1] In front of me I count three formidable documents that represent but a fraction of the spin-off from the work of the recent President's National Commission on the Causes and Prevention of Violence, headed by Dr. Milton S. Eisenhower who, I

Despite the literary proclivities of the Eisenhower experts, there exists (and can be) no discrete historical study of man's violence toward his fellow men, because violence is but one essential component of the full scope of conventional history. The story of British civilization, for instance, is meaningless if the violence is removed—as meaningless as Shakespeare's history plays would be without it. Conversely, the study of the violence alone would also signify little—as little as the hodge-podge of all the British battles fought upon the stage of the Globe. The first case would produce sound without fury, meaning nothing; the second, fury without sound, just as issueless.

The psychoanalyst, Storr, conjectures,[2] as do most students of the subject, about the feral roots of violence. Because violence and aggression are so dramatically demonstrated in the behaviors—particularly herd behaviors —of various animals, the empirical viewpoint leans to the association of violent behavior in humans with animalistic tendencies. Conversely, cooperation and non-violence are accordingly likened to so-called "higher" or distinctly human proclivities. What is forgotten or overlooked in this metaphor, is that cooperation and non-violence are also on display in most corners of the non-human animal world. But they are not dramatic and pass usually unnoticed by observers *except* when they are somehow humanoid, as in the case of a tribe of beavers building a dam or bees doing whatever bees do.

Digging into the fanciful and metaphorical literature of ethology, Storr suggests (among other alternatives) that higher animals—including man— have substituted forms of what he calls "conventional competition" for what were originally struggles over limited food supplies. He observes that Wynne-Edwards "goes so far as defining society as 'an organization capable of providing conventional competition.'" Culture, therefore, rather than reflecting a need for brotherly love, is seen as a "defense against aggression;

---

wager, has not himself, to date, studied the entire output of his own Commission, because nobody can read that fast. The books are *To Establish Justice and Insure Domestic Tranquility*, A Final Report, etc. (New York: Bantam Books, 1970); Hugh Davis Graham and Ted Robert Gurr (eds.), *Violence In America, The Complete Official Report*, etc. (New York: The New American Library, 1969); and David K. Lange, Robert K. Baker, Sandra J. Ball, *Mass Media and Violence*, Vol. XI, A Report to the National Commission, etc. (Washington, D.C.: U.S. Government Printing Office, 1969). I have attempted to scan these monsters and can assure the reader that they constitute an enormous garbage bin of so-called data (charts, statistics, lists, snatches of history, theories, laws, studies and statutes) both relevant and irrelevant to the recent history of violence at home and abroad, real and fancied. They provide *not one reasonable inkling* as to the substantive causes of the problem (specifically: violence) based on any firmer evidence than romantic conjecture. And they avoid scrupulously discussion of reasonable and practical ways to solve it, other than the plea that the problem be understood as a component of other problems. See below.

[2] See Anthony Storr, *Human Aggression* (New York: Atheneum, New York, 1968), especially pp. 31–37.

and . . . animals and men learn to cooperate and communicate, because they would destroy each other if they did not."[3] In the long run, Storr notes, most human groups have until the present day depended upon adult males for food gathering, fighting with animal or human enemies, and keeping the necessary harmony of the tribe by the use of violence against the disharmonious. In this manner, of course, is our culture nearly identical with most other cultures. If one social trait rarely appears among symptoms of ethnocentricity, it is the ritual application of violence to preserve cultural order, behavior which probably requires less cross-cultural translation than man's mating and eating habits.[4]

Violence is therefore intertwined with almost every human institution and tradition. As one of the National Commission's volumes indicates,[5] its ebb and flow, and direction and intensity, remain something of a mystery. But a topical review of the same study reveals where, with profit, delimitations for an historical study of violence must be drawn: anywhere. The subjects treated in the volume include European Violence, American Violence, Political Violence, Frontier Violence, Vigilante Violence, Literary and Folklore Violence, Working Class Violence, Labor Violence, Black Violence, White Violence, Southern Violence, Urban Violence, Domestic Violence, War, and other variations on the same theme set in contemporary historical and operational contexts. The great area of controversy in regard to violence seems to relate not to its ubiquity, necessity, desirability or control—but simply to its semantic relationship to various adjectives. In other words, profitable questions (in that they may be answered) may be posed concerning the application of terms like "legitimate," "legal," "justified," "necessary," "harmless" and others to the word "violence." Quite a stew may also be brewed from the process of categorizing violence into its euphemisms and synonyms like "protest," "force," "defense," "retaliation," "conflict," "aggression" and so forth.[6]

While such issues are debated hotly, people continue in their violent ways to imbue the full range of their cultures with beatings, shootings, stabbings, explosions and torture, the propositional synonyms for violence. As one lives in and/or through violence, however, it is not perceived in textbook terms. One feels first its impact upon the emotions in terms of fright that yields, first, the intoxication of activated glandular and muscular re-

---

[3] *Ibid.*, p. 31.

[4] The extreme violence (of a conventionalized nature) in Japanese films since World War II comes to mind. Most of these films are set in special periods of Japanese history, and yet Americans understand their ubiquitous violence easily, more easily than they comprehend their love themes, concepts of honor and family patterns. I am thinking particularly of such movies of *Rashoman*, *The Seven Samurai*, *Throne of Blood* (*Macbeth*, Japanese style), *Yojimbo* and others.

[5] Graham and Davis, *op. cit.*, pp. 792–795.

[6] *Ibid.*, xvii–xix.

sponses, and eventually a defensive, drugged stupor, not unlike the cozy warmth that overcomes those who freeze to death. In the interim, violence may activate in one many things, pleasant and unpleasant: perceptions of danger, exercise of caution, pain, and exhilaration, wild, near-orgasmic spasms of energy, feelings of potency, command and vigor, depression and derangement and many more bizarre subjective experiences.

Whatever functions these reactions serve, they appear to occur in men and women everywhere when they are involved in violent activity. Toch has observed,[7] and various other studies bear him out, that certain sorts of people seem to find greater rewards from violent behavior than others, at least when we examine that portion of criminal behavior in our culture associated with violence. In fact, such "(v)iolence takes place predominantly in certain circles, in certain settings, and on certain occasions, and usually involves at least two people who manifest their overt hostility in relatively formal patterns similar to those employed in games." [8] Or the situation may occur the other way around: game rules and regulations may constitute formalized versions of overt, informal violence.[9] Warfare, particularly as practiced until the invention of aviation, is largely a spectacular application at a highly theatrical level of the interplay of spontaneous violence, usually carried on throughout history over the same sort of issues: proprietary rights to commerce, territory, insults to sacred objects and similar causes.

On the personal level, Toch also states, "We have suggested that two types of orientation are especially likely to produce violence: one of these is that of the person who sees other people as tools designed to serve his

---

[7] See the major general argument in Hans Toch, *Violent Men* (Chicago: Aldine Publishing Co., 1969), pp. 183–248.

[8] *Ibid.*, pp. 4–7. Naturally, when a man throws a bomb into the cellar of a building —occupied or unoccupied—the "game" aspect of violence is immediately minimized. The bomber is, however, usually involved in a larger game: a conspiracy of some kind, real or imagined, in which his act is a ploy that will inevitably create a counterploy.

[9] A memory from the past may throw light on this point. I seem to remember, while an enlisted man in the army, playing an odd game that I have not seen described anywhere. Two sides were chosen; it did not matter how many were involved in either, although both were supposed to contain roughly the same number. Team A removed their undershirts; team B kept them on for identification. Two indefinite goals were decided upon at either end of a given area—not necessarily a field. An object of any kind was used as the "ball": a beer can, a towel, a helmet or some improvised flotsam. The game then began. The interesting element of the competition was simply that *there were no rules.* No innings, downs, fouls, methods of play or any other restrictions. One ill (or frightened) neutral observer usually kept score of the number of times that the "ball" found its way into the A or B goal area. The rest was violence, continued until enough players on one or another team had dropped out to necessitate terminating the action and declaring a winner; or until we were caught (and often disciplined) by an officer. I still carry a scar from one of these games that I oddly and dimly remember as *fun.*

needs; the second is that of the individual who feels vulnerable to manipulation." [10] One immediately senses symptomologies of the psychopathic personality, the paranoid and the paranoid-masochist. But conclusions of aberration must not be drawn too quickly. Similar symptoms are seen in fully rational, benign social types and perhaps in the reader himself. Some of Toch's respondents were undoubtedly pre-psychotic. Others were full-blown, classical, paranoid-masochist personalities. But, on the average and for all their quirks, they did not appear to be very different from the normal range of the prison populations from which they were drawn, or, for that matter, from the non-prison population at large. Thus, while they fell into personal typologies as "violent men," the sources of their violence were as likely to centralize upon exogenic environmental factors as upon endogenic personality traits. The process, therefore, of identifying and isolating the violent men in a community will not necessarily reduce violence there. In fact, our present penal system, in its crude way, *does* isolate violent men, but it does not appear to discourage much violence in those areas of sub-culture where it breeds best.

The will to violence is neither a sickness nor necessarily a symptom of a personality disorder. Nor, as Jung and others have suggested, is it other than as a latent predisposition of all men, although, for most of us, it remains subjected to social constraints for the greater part of our lives. Considered in this way, society is made up of pacified aggressors, a concept that cannot cheer exponents of theories of men as brothers under the skin. But if proneness to violence is not a sickness in the psychiatric sense (a moot point among psychiatrists), and if it is not definitively and invariably related to environmental circumstance (another not-quite-so-moot point), what is it?

Violence and Ecstasy

One answer centers upon those environmental phenomena which *cause* violence among men.

The first and most obvious one is tradition, the source, from an operational viewpoint, of most socially sanctioned violence. Games, competitions and dances containing violence and ritual combat are found in many primitive cultures; and they are also obvious in ours. The pseudo-violence of theatre and cinema shows a counterpart in every theatrical tradition of both West and East. Warfare, regardless of its psychological, social, political, religious and economic precipitants, is traditionally sanctioned universally, despite the existence of treaties, alliances, international laws and the United

---

[10] *Ibid.*, p. 183. These self-inflicted roles have parallels in the games that nations play by means of warfare. In any given instance, the identification of personal style with a given nation will depend upon from which perspective you judge its wars. History offers some objectivity here as does the passage of time, but so does the judgment of a court when two or more individuals are involved in less spectacular acts of violence.

Nations. In one degree or another, society smiles upon and approves of this sort of violence and has done so into the deeps of pre-history.

One may hope, with the authors of the Charter of institutions like the UN, that some of these sanctions, particularly in regard to international combat, will at some future date be eliminated or modified. But a hard look at the past does not augur well for the future. In respect to warfare, one may perhaps most realistically foresee the day that the world returns to the kind of regulated professional combat it knew before the inventions of total war, unconditional surrender and non-negotiable demands. Should wars, by the year 2,000, be conducted as they were in Europe from the twelfth to nineteenth century—that is, as regulated contests between more-or-less professional combatants observing certain rules of fair play—we shall be spared the inevitable end of total war: total destruction. Particularly do the potential violence of atomic weapons, rockets and lethal chemicals require strict control, as well as the involvement in warfare of masses of civil populations remote from battlefields, supply lines and production facilities. If we can achieve these modest ends during the next generation, the violence of war will not destroy modern civilization. Sad to state, if we opt for unrealizable, idealistic dreams of "total peace," history's pronouncement upon us, the author believes, will be inevitable doom and the extenuation of war without rules to its absurd and final conclusion.[11]

Non-sanctioned violence is another matter in which tradition plays a smaller part. The National Commission has identified certain cultural phenomena that seem to encourage violence.[12] Right or wrong, their conclusion is that the control of these social behaviors will in some manner reflect upon the incidence of violence in our culture, hopefully reducing it. They are that we: 1.) reduce military spending, 2.) increase crime prevention and control facilities programs, 3.) solve the problem of narcotics addiction, 4.) isolate and treat violence prone citizens, 5.) solve the problem of unemployment, 6.) provide decent homes for everybody, 7.) extend government welfare, 8.) save our cities from urban blight in its protean manifestations, 9.) strengthen local governments, 10.) stop the migration of the poor from rural to urban areas, 11.) provide better medical, legal and educational services for the poor, 12.) organize decent, peace-loving citizens for mutual self-protection, 13.) diversify the control of news dissemination outlets and improve their services, 14.) encourage schools to teach history bet-

---

[11] I write these words in cold blood and beneath a "peace" symbol on my wall, but I fear their point has been written too infrequently in the past two decades. In grasping for total peace we may, I fear, end with the worst that destiny has to provide us. Should we settle merely for war, we will end up badly, but possibly be spared the worst. This is hardly a poetic or idealistic vision of the future, but I personally would trade all my illusions for a guarantee that man's future will include the presence of men in societies as we now know them, fighting, if they must, according to rules.

[12] The following are taken from *To Establish Justice, To Insure Domestic Tranquility,* especially as reviewed on pp. 229–236.

ter, 15.) strengthen our judicial system, 16.) encourage research into the cause of violence, 17.) enforce civil rights legislation, 18.) purge television cartoons and dramas of violent representations, 19.) study the film rating system to insure that minors are protected from exposure to violence, 20.) solve the problem of campus violence, 21.) lower the voting age to eighteen, 22.) reform the military draft, 23.) institute more federal youth programs, and 24.) try to communicate and understand each other better.

The reader may ponder the pith of the *eighty-one* conclusions of the Commission, boiled down above to save space. (We shall return shortly to some of the specific assumptions they accept.) The Commission focuses most intensively upon problems of controlling the sale and possession of firearms, federal and state programs for urban ghettos, and the control of violent scenes in television and movies, in about that order of significance. The inference here is clearly that violence is a social problem arising out of environmental stresses which may be solved by the conventional anodynes for all ills: legislation, education and better human relations—although the need for police control of violence *is* occasionally noted in passing.

The following observations are not directed at the Commission's recommendations *per se*, which, with minor changes, are perfectly safe remedial steps for *any* social problems the world has ever known, and patently beyond the capacities of present knowledge and probable means of implementation. They concern, rather, the Commission's assumptions of *cause*, the same trite causes of every other social dysfunction we suffer: the lack of proper education, poverty, bad housing, narcotics, easy access to lethal weapons, lack of medical, dental and psychiatric care, poor law enforcement methods, legal inequities, penal shortcomings, racial discrimination and the irresponsibility of mass communicators. In sum, the seeds of violence are construed *as pressure of manifold external deprivations that corrupt vulnerable populations*. The process may be halted, therefore, in two ways: first, eliminate or decrease the deprivation, and, second, reduce the potential vulnerability of the people affected.

Others would search elsewhere for causes and around different corners. Fromm notes[13] that most societies provide outlets, via artistic creation, wherein the individual may, in his words, be "brought in touch with himself as a human being, with the roots of his existence." What he means is that, employing the dramatic medium of communication, men may conduct rituals of excitement, competition and pseudo-violence. The closest that we come to this particular use of the dramatic medium in our society is in lodge and fraternity initiations and in competitive sports, *not necessarily spectator sports*. Deprived, as we are, of many more meaningful secular rituals in the dramatic vein, we then search for *substitutes* elsewhere: in spectator sports, comic strips, novels, animated cartoons, films, television

---

[13] Erich Fromm, *The Sane Society* (New York: Rinehart and Co., 1955), pp. 144–146.

drama and similar experiences. But they are weak tea, and subsequently our impulses bring us back to reality—not immediately perceived reality, but reality as mediated to us by such devices as magazines, newspapers and news broadcasts. Here our obsession is with drama also: the drama of human interest stories, the lives of celebrities, airplane crashes, rapes, murders, suicides, robberies, natural disasters, and, as an advertisement for a bygone film most correctly put it, "all the things that make life worth living." But, unfortunately, they do *not* make life worth living, at least not when communicated to the individual in a passive environment and context by a technological instrument. Says Fromm, "All this interest and fascination is not simply an expression of bad taste and sensationalism, but of a deep longing a dramatization of ultimate phenomena of human existence, life and death, crime and punishment, the battle between man and nature."

For many of us, particularly the most naïve, poorly educated and those incapable of deriving deep dramatistic satisfaction from such experiences as theatregoing, poetry, narrative literature, hobbies, music and (especially) spiritual exercise, this "deep longing" is simply not satisfied by the insipid world of kitsch, a world in which, incidentally, our ghetto dwellers and poorly educated citizens are immersed more deeply than others in our nation, as the result of their lack of alternatives, both for economic and cultural reasons.

Many observers have examined the roles of dramatic communications in performing a defining, ritual function in life. Goffman contrasts "backstage" and "on-stage" roles in significant informal social performances with skill and insight.[14] Burke,[15] Bronowski[16] and others[17] have also identified the dramatistic thrust of life that may, one way or another, be ritualized into extremities of action, including violence. These approaches, in fact, reverse generally accepted notions, reflected by the Commission, that associate extreme and dramatic manifestations of a human assault with atavistic, malignant, social and psychological states. This view associates them instead with attempts to create a personal social field around the individual and his group of excitement, significance and of dramatic value.

Arthur Koestler, for instance, denies explicitly that violence is a manifestation of social pathology,[18] suggesting that it is futile to try to ameliorate violence either by providing in his words "harmless outlets" (games, sports and sex) or "appeals to man's better nature." His reason is that this "better

---

[14] See Erving Goffman, *The Presentation of Self in Everyday Life* (New York: Doubleday and Co., Inc., 1959), especially pp. 106–140.

[15] See Kenneth Burke, *Language as Symbolic Action*, pp. 44–45, 54–55.

[16] See J. Bronowski, *The Face of Violence* (New York: George Braziller, 1955), pp. 9–62.

[17] See my discussion of the nature and function of dramatic communications in G.N.G. *L C*, pp. 143–158.

[18] Arthur Koestler, *The Ghost in the Machine*, pp. 233–235.

nature," as it is generally understood, includes "self-sacrificing devotion to a flag, a leader, a religious faith, or a political conviction. Man has been prepared not only to kill but also to die for good, bad or completely futile causes." On the other hand, Koestler denies that—in either the long or short run—the vices of selfishness, greed or self-assertive tendencies are not at root cause of much minor and inconsequential violence. But, in regard to major displays of violence, he quotes Pope's epigram, "The worst of all madmen is a saint run wild."

A moment's consideration of the nature of the violence that we observe around us these days—*excluding* the almost entirely preventable carnage on our highways, the results of what are supposed to be motor "accidents"—permits confirmation of this perspective and makes difficult the association of violence in man with animalistic regression. This violence is caused by man's utilization of his higher, cortical and strictly human thought processes. First, much of this violence is intentionally dramatic, occurring in highly visible places, constituent of spectacular acts, and obviously stimulated (and sometimes intended) for photographic or television cameras and/or repertorial coverage which it is sure to receive if it is theatrical enough.[19] Campus riots and political fracases are noticeably (and usually) staged occasions, in which rioters, by extending the nature of the threats they portend, eventually stimulate over-reactions of equally dramatic intensity from guardians of law and order, be they police or soldiers. Even the willful destruction of property has an intrinsic dramatic quality. Less drama attends apparently spontaneous street riots, but, when described after the fact, they display a more or less novelistic plot, usually starting with a small confrontation and ending with the total engagement of an entire neighborhood.

Second, these violent episodes (not violence associated with rape or robbery) are the result of the instrumentation of almost invariably simplistic ideals rather than thrusts after personal gain or selfish motives, except in the instance of street looters who are frequently non-participants in violence itself but seek its spoils. If one draws up lists of the kind of individuals involved in the early stages of recent riots, one sees immediately that the motives for their actions are determined by a *cause* of some kind, not material or personal gain. Such lists include policemen, black militants, student activists, national guardsmen, campus police, liberal intellectuals, student conservatives and others. Whatever else one may say about them, they cannot be accused of operating from what are generally considered base or selfish motives.

Third, the violence we see around us propels the participant into a special kind of ecstasy. His life, his cause and his actions take on meaning that may, perhaps, find their way into one of the countless books written on

[19] This point is well but ironically made in a number of contexts relating to the Chicago riots of 1968 in the superb film *Medium Cool.*

contemporary violence (or he may write a book or article himself). His glory may be preserved on film or television tape. At the least, his participation will be discussed and reviewed by and with others. Words like "Chicago," "Newark," "Detroit" and "Watts" have a magical, near mythic significance at present in contemporary folklore among many people. To have lived through violence of any kind is analogous to the mystique of having survived combat in war, and this mystique has, through the ages, displayed greater sticking power than the enormous revulsion many people feel at the actual moment of engagement.[20]

Corruption to Violence

The claim that the roots of violence are planted entirely in its raw enjoyment oversimplifies the subtleties of cultural history. Most superficial students of violence are content to evaluate it as a manifestation of man-as-beast and society reflecting its worst and most highly degenerate side. To them, outbreaks of violence are indications that the social bonds between men are coming loose and that civilization is falling apart. Violence, accordingly, may therefore be prevented (as noted above) by strengthening these bonds and applying the usual cultural panaceas for social problems: better communications between groups, higher standards of living, the stimulation of joy, better education more widely spread and purposeful, creative activity for the idle.

Others, less given to the admiration of conventional social uplift, are not so sure. In the broad historical theatre, violence has apparently been responsible more frequently for the strengthening of social bonds than the weakening of them. Careful study of such recent history as the behavior of the belligerent nations in World War II appears to confirm this, especially in respect to the response of the citizens of the USSR to the German invasion. (In many ways, the defense of Stalingrad was one of the most remarkable social occurrences of recent history.) True, happy, phlegmatic, belly-filled and opulent people are rarely collectively violent; but happiness, phlegmatism, full bellies and opulence have been socio-historical exceptions rather than rules. And even this truism admits of exceptions in the small but visible segment of college rebels today who come from affluent environments. They may frequently be seen driving to and from protest meetings in new sports cars! Disaffected intellectuals of a revolutionary bent (including Marx, Lenin and Trotsky and most others) tend to be distressingly bourgeois in their personal lives.[21] These observers are less certain, therefore,

---

[20] An interesting first person experience of this revulsion, as expressed by a sensitive Negro broadcaster during the Newark riots, may be found in George N. Gordon and Irving A. Falk, *TV Covers the Action* (New York: Julian Messner, 1968), pp. 101–110. This chapter, originally written for young people, has been reprinted in *Something Else* (Glenview, Ill., Scott Foresman and Company, 1970), pp. 76–80.

[21] The Fidel Castro who came from the hills with his rebels was, of course, a carefully constructed image of a man who had been, before the revolution, a middle class

that ameliorative steps based upon garden-variety social idealism may accomplish little more than exacerbate the problem of violence wherever it appears.

Neither are they as certain as conventional empirical students of the subject that it is so-called "corruption" which causes violence—in other words, that people are led to violence by anti-social influences and persuasion. As a significant example, the Commission's experts were generally explicit about the role of violence in newspapers, films and television as a contributive cause to recent displays of violence in our society. They state (factually) that "(t)here is sufficient evidence that mass media presentations, especially portrayals of violence, have negative effects upon audiences . . . ," and that "the majority of the American public believes that there is too much violence of which they disapprove, and believe that television portrayals have undesirable effects." [22] (The balance of the Task Force's recommendations relate mostly to establishing a research Center to apply brakes to free enterprise in the communications industries and encourage them to respectable conduct. Such a Center would, ironically, also devote itself to conducting research into the validity and reliability of the data that the Task Force offers as valid and reliable.)[23] These conclusions are accepted by the Commission, which recommends, as we have seen, purging televised animated cartoons, crime shows and westerns of their violent content.[24]

Certainly, television and other mass communications have effects on people, although some researchers claim that they do not and that they merely enforce the *status quo*.[25] Regarding violence, the matter is in dispute, and by no means a matter of *fact*, as a discussion held in 1966 between sociologist Klapper, psychologist Berkowitz and the psychiatrist Wertham indicate.[26] Their enlightened opinions run the gamut from Klap-

intellectual and lawyer. Cigar and beard were (and are) props for an intellectual who wants to look like an anti-intellectual, in the manner of many other revolutionists, including Lenin. On the other hand, Che Guevera—no intellectual—was closer to being an authentic anti-bourgeois revolutionary. But at the time of his visit to New York some half-dozen years ago, I was delighted to observe that his guerilla uniform was obviously tailor-made of high quality broadcloth.

[22] D. Lange, R. Baker and S. Ball, *op. cit.*, p. 381.

[23] *Ibid.*, pp. 384–393.

[24] *To Establish Justice etc.*, *op. cit.*, p. 235.

[25] See G.N.G., *L C*, pp. 287–290 and Joseph T. Klapper, *The Effects of Mass Communications* (Glencoe, Ill.: The Free Press, 1960), which, as discussed in Chapter 13, indicates that presently we do not apparently have enough evidence to say that mass communications influence anybody to do anything. Basing my observations upon the obvious and immediate effects of commercial announcements and advertising in our culture alone, I obviously (and increasingly) disagree strongly with the generality of Klapper's non-conclusions. See the discussion that follows.

[26] Otto N. Larsen (ed.), *Violence and the Mass Media* (New York: Harper and Row, Publ., 1968), pp. 273–293. A wide range of arguments and differential data concerning the effects of vicarious violence upon children and adults are presented in this anthology.

per's bland views to Wertham's contemporary diabolism. In other words, even the so-called "experts" are at odds about the influence of televised and filmed violence upon people, from the impressionable and young to the rigid and old, and they are frequently able to muster enough convincing arguments to propel one either to the middle ground or utter confusion. (The latter is the strategy of the-sadly-numerous social scientists "purchased" by the television and film makers to exculpate their industries.) Like exposure to pornography, dramatized violence is understood, therefore, to do something to somebody, somehow, sometimes, but little concrete evidence indicates at present what, who, how or when.

That mass communications influence people is today beyond reasonable dispute. Too much money is spent upon advertising, too many direct results are visible of the outcome of exposure of new personalities, catch-phrases, styles and fashions in films, the press, and television to quibble about the issue. And far too many surveys—albeit many of questionable value when examined singly—indicate that a major proportion of the news and other information—or what the broadcasters, journalists and the public consider news—comes to the public specifically from television. It is also reasonably certain that the totality of these impressions influence behavior, including political behavior, in decisive ways. If this were *not* the case, if the instruments of mass communications merely enhance values in the status quo, then fierce amounts of money are being wasted every second by commercial advertisers and politicians, among others, to say nothing of time and talent running down the drain of futility. (Such a sacrifice of national manpower might itself demand full investigation by Congress.)

Crude truisms of this sort, however, do not answer directly fundamental questions of public concern about violence. First, one encounters the entire matter of the nature and direction of mass communication's influences upon beliefs, attitudes, opinions and actions. Second, differential instruments of communication operate differently at different times. The contrasts are wide. For instance, reason tells one that a staged fight in a television western *means* something different from a photographed genuine fracas on a video news broadcast, even if the specific nature of the violence shown is similar. Violence involving a deceased movie actor on late night television is different from that indulged in by a popular star in a contemporary dramatic video-taped play. Newspapers report violence (and everything else) differently, one from the other; and news magazines, literary journals, and books also cover the same events in different ways. Third, audiences differ according to time, place and age. It is difficult for the author to comprehend precisely how *Bugs Bunny* or *George of the Jungle* engender impulses towards violence in normal children. And the question of

---

At the present state of the art of determining cause and effect in these matters, you "pays your money for the book and takes your choice" from numerous different conclusions.

whether standards for children's fare should be set by possible harm to the severely abnormal is another vexing problem. The author's children seem to have survived years of televised cartoon violence admirably, and so do most other youngsters.

The unilateral and unsophisticated charge that television and filmed violence, as well as violence in print, is sometimes, and in slight ways, *involved* in the cause of social violence is probably true. But the significance or utility of this truth is clear only to the fanciful or gullible. The study of American History in schools—including concern with assassinations—probably was *involved* in the psychological motivations of Lee Harvey Oswald, Sirhan Sirhan and James Earle Ray. But even a simplistic do-gooder would not suggest, therefore, that we eliminate coverage of the Lincoln, McKinley and Kennedy assassinations from our history textbooks in order to save the life of some future public official. One does not require a federal committee hearing, involving a barrage of sociologists and psychologists, to hypothesize that violence is somehow related to environmental factors that influence people, and that the devices of communication are among these environmental factors—*as well as* schools, universities, pool halls, football fields, bowling alleys, libraries, families and, for those who still read, books.

What is really at issue here is the question of whether people, generally, may indeed be *corrupted* to violence, and if so, how, a question that has not yet been faced in more than cursory fashion. If the word "persuaded" is substituted for "corrupted," we have returned to the specific concern in this book, and the reader is therefore cognizant of the hazards of facile answers to such a problem.

Most normal human beings may be provoked to violent actions by exogenic, and sometimes endogenic, causes, and the differential boiling points of each of us is a function of individual psychological factors as influenced by the setting of the provocations. In the heat of summer, in our urban slums, that boiling point is lowered for many, and this affects individual psychological states in noticeable ways. That our mass communications lower this boiling point as well, particularly in the young, is possible. But evidence that it does would only achieve significance considered in comparison with the many ways other cultural factors like boredom at school, involvement in sports, the exercise of parental authority, membership in youth groups (including street gangs and those run by social workers) and other experiences that may affect it. In all probability, the evils of mass communications, in this respect, are merely duplicated or exceeded by other cultural factors, particularly schools, youth centers, corrective programs and other experiences that tend to institutionalize people, a frequently noted possible etiological factor in the brewing of violence.

That *groups* also have boiling points is a valid empirical observation in social psychology. But, because they are moderated or stimulated by interactions within the group, they are more complex than those of the individual members taken alone. When the question arises as to the effect of, say, televised violence upon a group's sensitivity to the provocation to violence, the problem is more vexing than when posed for an individual. The Commission's Task Force claims it knows that a generalized climate created by the modern instruments of mass communications increases the likelihood of group violence. Others are not so sure, but granting the Commission's assumption, would the enforced replacement of that violent climate by a non-violent climate on television and in other mass communications change matters?

Let us assume that henceforth our televised western gun slingers play chess instead of shooting each other; that spy stories substitute panel discussions for their inevitable chases; that animated cartoons dwell mainly upon love stories between cats and mice; and that every melodramatic villain on film and television expresses his evil nature by mouthing nasty words instead of employing guns, knives and brass knuckles. Let us further assume that radio and television newscasts are purged of displays of physical hostility and warfare. Were this metamorphosis decreed by fiat, what then?

The author, personally, would be impelled to near homicidal rage by such changes, but his reaction is perhaps atypical. In general, such a move would certainly eliminate the function of the arts, as described by Fromm, as vicarious violence, but to what end? Would it produce a rush to spectator sports, perhaps, or to the underground cinema (unless it were similarly purged), to tabloid newspapers, and to the commercial theatre (where entrepreneurs might profitably revive the *Grand Guignol* and productions of the seamiest Elizabethans)? Would such a climate of non-violence modify violence in society?

Let the reader who is certain that the change would be a healthy one consider his reasons. To the best of the author's knowledge, even Dr. Wertham, arch foe of televised and comic strip violence, has not even cogently as yet attacked the basic question of *what the elimination of violence from the dramatic and narrative mediums of mass communications might actually accomplish, if anything.*[27]

---

[27] See Frederic Wertham, "School for Violence," in Larsen, *op. cit.*, pp. 36–39, as well as his two books, *Seduction of the Innocent* (New York: Holt, Rinehart and Winston, 1954), and *A Sign for Cain* (New York: The Macmillan Co., 1966). The first centers on the corruption my generation received from what we believed were innocent pleasures of reading about super-heroes. The second is a more general analysis of how people are led to violence in literature and life. The Task Force that prepared *Violence and the Media* kept Dr. Wertham and his ideas at bay, largely by concentrating upon content studies and other globs of loose empirical data concerning violence in television, films and print rather than allow a forum for deductive analysts like Wertham. When a professor of sociology discusses the role of violent action in the drama, however (see *op. cit.*, pp. 444–446), in naïve, mechanistic and jejune terms, sensitive readers who have either studied, written or acted in plays or films are justified in entertaining temporary, murderous impulses. Just as dramatists, for their own good, are well advised to moderate in their on-stage constructions of the social sciences, so it behooves sociologists and psychologists, unschooled children in

Despite the urging of pacific behavioral experts like the vitriolic Dr. Wertham and others, the author tends to agree generally with the opinions of Storr, who states that "there is a wide gap between the actual experience of violence and aggression in childhood and its acting out in fantasy," [28] in the first place. If small children feel reasonably secure in their environment, and if older ones live in a milieu that is not overly abusive, the distinction between reality and fantasy appears to be simple for them to comprehend even when they are quite young and particularly when fantasy is part of a theatrical event. They learn to recognize, in other words, that *re-enactment*, as a means of communication, is not equivalent to the enactment of an event, just as they understand that a narrative account of behavior is not that behavior, and that a picture of an object is not the object. A certain amount of confusion is evident in their first attempts at these distinctions. But, by the time they are as old as Dr. Wertham, most people (barring perceptual or integrative breakdowns) comprehend, both emotionally and cognitively, the difference between dramatic fantasy in any form and reality with considerable acumen.[29]

According to Storr:

> There is little convincing evidence that reading of heroes slaying dragons, or even of gangsters shooting cops has a disturbing effect upon, or provokes displays of violence in, those children who are not already predisposed; and, whilst we may deplore the vulgarity of "horror comics," we are not justified in supposing that such reading matter has accounted for murder or other aggressive actions in later life. This is not to deny that an exclusive diet of violent literature and television programmes may give a distorted picture of reality, or have a harmful effect upon those children whose actual experience of the world has been one in which physical violence plays a notable part.[30]

---

theatrical matters, to shut their mouths rather than attempt dramatic criticism. In this respect—and in the tendency of its researchers to extend their moderate competencies too broadly—the Task Force acted poorly. Had they been as chary of the art of the deceased Stark Young as they were of the opinions of the living Wertham, their documents might have been, in these matters at least, more impressive.

[28] Storr, *op. cit.*, p. 46.

[29] The degree of this acuity in untrained people (especially children) is sometimes remarkable in determining whether a televised episode or film clip is "real" or "fake." The professional actor's eternal problem involves repeating conventionalized constructions of reality at will, an art that changes style over the years as the constructs change. In our relationships with others, those of us who are *not* actors often discover that it is difficult for us to dissemble actions that are not genuinely felt, and that our efforts to do so are frequently transparent. Professional actors also usually have this problem in their personal lives, their talents for on-stage dissembling notwithstanding.

[30] Storr, *op. cit.*, p. 45. My experience as a teacher of many types of children for 25 years, and as a father, give me little reason to challenge Storr's viewpoint. Perhaps more important is my own deep interest (going back to childhood) in murder mysteries, horror tales and films, witchcraft and man's concern with the occult that has taken me both into the popular and specialized study of these phenomena. A psychiatrist would not have a moment's difficulty in determining *why* my interests have followed this

The problem of Storr's *caveat* in his last sentence is large and of wide social dimensions that transcend the issues of corruption and persuasion. The main danger, Storr and many others (including the author) believe, presented by the *possible* corruptive potentials in the vulgarity of horror comics, television, films, books and magazines centers on their innate vulgarity rather than their incidence of violence.

While many film enthusiasts disagree, it is possible that an essentially (to the author) vulgar, exploitative, shallow and silly film like *Bonnie and Clyde* is *redeemed* in some measure from tiresome mediocrity by technically well-contrived time-stop violence and gore. The same observation applies to other poorly characterized and dramatically dishonest films like *The Wild Bunch* and *The Dirty Dozen*. The combination of virtuoso dramatized violence and shoddy theatre is, possibly, much less corruptive of sense and sensibility than weak characterization, childish plotting, and dime-novel moralizing when offered *without* artful violence. To many, dramatized violence for its own sake is, at least, honest soap-opera nonsense, unfortunately disrespectful of the intelligence of its audience, but little more heinous.

On the other hand, when expert art and violence combine fortuitously, their fusion may be bewilderingly civilized. And the names Goya, Poe, Dickens, Grimm, Griffith and Eisenstein head a lengthy roster that includes many of the finest dramatic artists from antiquity to the present. But presidential commissions rarely examine closely the obvious.

Violent Persuasion

Beyond the specific problem of corruption, the relationship between violence and persuasion occurs at other facets of contact. Violence itself may be, or be involved in, many types of persuasion. Threats of violence, as previously noted,[31] are frequently as, or more effective than violence itself. By the same token, a threat of violence may neutralize persuasion, or produce what appears to be a boomerang effect that may, in time, resolve merely into a tactical and temporary evasion or delay in persuasion. Sustained violence may well alter belief structures, especially for individuals who are not used to it, either in reality or fantasy. Single displays of violence may also, as few other stimuli, modify or change attitudes easily. At

---

direction (among others), although the record shows that (recently, at least) I have been quite a peaceful citizen, far less violently inclined, I think, than some individuals I know who collect sea shells, read little scholarly magazines and attend more symphony concerts, museums and ballets than I do. Let us also remember that the most flamboyantly violent Nazis (Julius Streicher excepted) possessed developed, refined and non-violent tastes in reading and drama, although Hitler's personal love of children and animals (one of his final serious concerns in 1945 was for the welfare of his constant companion, the Alsatian dog, Blondi) was more than counterbalanced by his crude taste for Wagnerian opera.

[31] See Chaper 14.

the sight of violence, pacifists may turn into warmongers, and vice-versa. Opinions are extremely sensitive both to the threat and presence of violence; and behavior responds to violence in so immediate and intensive a manner that the lack of subtlety involved should gratify even behavioral psychologists.

The call to violence has naturally under-ridden every revolutionary attempt that history has known. Today's common wisdom—repeated by social scientists of many types—insists that violent persuasion as an impetus to revolution is most effective when directed towards groups that are moving upward in social, economic, educational and other aspects of life but who are not improving their lot fast enough to suit their aspirations. Some evidence supports this claim. Obviously, segments of a population drained by starvation, constricted by tradition and/or embrued with apathy, are unlikely to respond to the revolutionists' call to arms. On the other hand, scholars of revolution have also demonstrated that it is not always potentially mobile segments of populations that have responded to revolutionary persuasion, but rather those psychologically and culturally browbeaten individuals who can muster faith that their revolutionary violence will not have been expended in vain. In few words, most revolutions are fought by individuals *who believe that they have a chance of winning their battle*[32] regardless of their mobility, and sometimes regardless of their theoretically all-important socio-economic statuses.

The persuasive force of violence, however, is invariably translated into psychological factors that exert pressures upon dispositions and behavior. The *threat* of violence, we know, engenders fear. The *promise* of violence may, in certain people, turn into hope, excitement and a generalized stimulation of the *elan vital.* The *sight* of violence—or participation in it—may create *anomie,* despair or withdrawal from society.

Like the so-called "media" of communications, the "medium" of violence says nothing of and by itself. Its quality and nature will depend, in large measure, upon whether it is real or fantastic, whether it is threatened or actuated, and will eventually be determined by the mind-sets and circumstances of the populations against whom it is directed.

Much discussion has concerned the question of why the violence of the Nazis precipitated such seemingly different results when directed against Jews, Gypsies, Jehovah's Witnesses, Danes, Norwegians, the

---

[32] The notion of the revolutionist's involvement in slow upwards socio-economic mobility is apparently derived from the study of recent revolutionary groups in Europe, South America and the United States and has been given recent publicity in the writings of Eric Hoffer. The dynamics of revolution are far more complicated than these theories indicate, however. For two thorough historical surveys of some of the unlikely apparent causes of revolutions and their conduct, see Hannah Arendt, *On Revolution* (New York: The Viking Press, 1965), and Crane Brinton, *The Anatomy of Revolution* (New York: Random House, 1965). The latter was first published in 1938 but revised and expanded to cover revolutionary activity and recent violence in Latin America.

Dutch, Poles and other national, ethnic and religious groups. Most of the argument is fatuous. For each group, Nazi violence occurred in different ways, was perceived differently, and encountered different situational and psychological circumstances. Little about the inherent nature of each group *per se* (the resignation of the Jews, the tight-lipped courage of the Norwegians or the saintliness of the Jehovah's Witness, for instance) is revealed in its behavior, except as they enhance the auditor's prejudices. The main—or, in some cases, only—common factor to which the groups were exposed was violence, or the threat of it. Other complex variables were primarily responsible for their reactions.

In our time and place (at the writing), violence, real and implied, is gathering impetus as a major integument of persuasion and as a myth of growing power. We have, of course, in recent years, been exposed to a good deal of bizarre violence, originating from apparently unlikely sources, occurring unexpectedly, and manifest in unorthodox ways.[33] But, as the Commission scholars on the government payroll delight in repeating *ad nauseam*, America is no stranger to violence. The cinematic version of the adventures of General Patton reminded us that ours is a violent nation, having survived long periods of extraordinary militancy. The counter-illusion that we somehow maintain, however, pictures us as peace-loving, violent only when necessary as a means of achieving peace. The price we pay for this conceit is the constant state of cultural shock at the discovery that *now*—at this instant—we are either recoiling from violence immediately past, immersed in violence or facing the fearful threat of it in the near future.

The result is an attitudinal condition, expertly described by Knopf,[34] rarely noticed, and deserving of attention here. It centers upon the persuasive influence, not of violence, but of those disturbances that our invariably astonished reaction to our own violence engenders. Knopf refers specifically to black violence. But her observations have implications beyond the ghettos and the specific evidence upon which they are based, especially considering that the reporters and editors she attacks are, in addition to being professional journalists, citizens, whose beliefs, attitudes, opinions and actions replicate on a large canvas those of the publics they serve.

Common (and uncommon) sense notwithstanding, we perceive, in Knopf's words, violence (or the report of it) as invariably "meaningless, purposeless, senseless, irrational," while in certain instances, the assassination of Martin Luther King, Jr. being a case in point, *any* reaction *less than* a

33 Bizarre, unlikely, unexpected, unorthodox—maybe! Psychopathic assassins are not novelties. Black violence has been visibly brewing for nearly a century. Did we think that our urban slums were—or might ever be—oases of peace? How long did our college and university administrators believe that they might sustain outworn educational systems and disciplinary assumptions before they would begin violently to fall apart? And so on.

34 Terry Ann Knopf, "Media Myths on Violence" in *Columbia Journalism Review*, Spring, 1970, 17–23.

stimulus to overt violent rage might cast severe doubts upon the sensitivities and sanity of the black (in this case) community to the symbols, hopes and opportunity that were apparently stilled by an assassin's bullets. The collective standards by which manifestations of violence are perceived are invariable and stereotyped by most of us: violence is shocking and wrong, at least so says our myth of the moment. The standards, however, from which the single peaceful citizen measures his own *personal* need for recourse to violence are *not* invariable, nor are they stereotyped. They stem from ideals, ideologies and other factors described above, reflected in every disturbance American society has undergone from colonial times to the present.

The facts behind the myth of our cultural repulsion against violence indicate that *certain* manifestations of violence are (commensurate with American traditions as bespoken by patriots from Jefferson to Lincoln to Kennedy and Nixon) meaningful, purposeful, sensible and, by present standards, rational. As Knopf writes, "Both the general public and the (mass) media share the same dislike of protestors; both are unable to understand violence as an expression of protest . . . both prefer the myth of orderly, peaceful change, extolling the virtues of private property and personal decorum."[35] They detach themselves from the realistic roles of violence in our past, and extol mechanically the cozy virtues of passivity and order—especially when the violence to which they are reacting is undertaken by people they fear for reasons they do not understand or with whom they disagree. They are also usually and conveniently able to justify violence when it accords with their biases or upholds what they believe right.

In point of fact, as Knopf notes, much of the recent violence through which we have lived that has occurred in the ghettos—and which we often assume is senseless—has resulted from the accumulation of long-term, deep grievances. It is expressed, in large measure, by fairly well-educated people involved in political movements striving (all elements considered) for relatively moderate and necessary social changes. Contrary to popular beliefs (and the differently oriented behaviors of most university protestors), instigators of urban riots know exactly what they are doing, are not activated by outside agitators, and construe violence as a *last resort* in achieving changes long overdue. They are also aware that in accomplishing the end of social amelioration they are likely to destroy themselves and others, to say nothing of their own property. The prospect does not cheer them, but they see no alternative action to violence—and they are probably correct.

Senseless violence, of course, also occurs. So does the activistic political nihilism which construes *any* form of destruction as good, as long as it disturbs some corner of the status quo. Yesterday's anarchist with beard

---

35 *Ibid.*, p. 22.

and bomb is the prototype of this psychotic typology, although today such an orientation often appears to be associated more closely with immaturity, identity confusion, drugs and alcohol than simple mental disarrangement.

What is important, however, is that our current dispositions towards violence do not admit of exceptions or evaluate the many stops on the scale of violence in reality. As a result, the mythic concept of violence *per se* as a social evil obscures what is relevant about it: its causes, its relationship to ideology, its social functions and its psychological dynamics. Instead of turning our attention to such matters, we attempt stratagems that enhance the integrity of our myths. The appointment of investigating committees, arguments concerning gun control legislation, and campaign promises of law and order are all defenses of myth, not realistic adjustments of circumstances that will eliminate the sort of violence that neither the times nor circumstances can afford. To do the latter, we would have to accept certain forms of violence and reject others, both by force and in disposition. Far worse, we would have to admit that we cannot always be peace-loving, that we cannot eternally abhor violence and mayhem, when, in fact, it is a powerful and dominant heritage of both our society and our species.

Will our schools, churches, social agencies, legislatures and universities muster courage to face such realities? Of course not. We shall remain, therefore, peculiarly vulnerable to the persuasion of peace and anti-violence —campaign themes and promises of ubiquity, ease of delivery and guaranteed success. The tragedy of such persuasion is that it is managed best by men with bloody hands, because the *real* peace makers, although they may be blessed, invariably must speak softly and are usually ignored.

Conclusion

Reasons for man's violence are many, and, if they admit of controversy, it centers on the question of whether centrifugal or centripetal forces hold society together: that is, whether culture keeps man, the violent animal, at bay; or whether violent man is an eternal deviant who continually disrupts his peaceful culture. The proposition is not likely to be resolved soon, and, in the meantime, attention is better paid to the way in which violence has played a vital role in the cumulative experiences of almost all of our institutions.

Non-sanctioned violence in our culture has been the cause for concern by many who are convinced that its recent increase (a debatable issue) results from corruptive influences. In fact, conjectured causes of violence span such a range of social etiologies that one might believe, if he studies the recommendations of a recent government Commission, that persuasion to violence occurs as the direct result of every currently fashionable social malaise in the case-worker's handbook from indolence to education to naughty movies and more.

Others believe that violence and pseudo-violence are inherent to certain kinds of common psychological gratifications, and that the needs for these gratifications are usually met, either by resort to sanctioned violence (as in street fights) or vicarious violence (as in spectator sports and drama). The latter, especially, seems to be the way that these impulses are handled by the majority of our population, and an over-chewed dialogue continues between those who view re-enacted violence either as a social palliative or as a corruption. Some of the discussion centers upon newspapers, books, and magazines, but most of it is reserved for incitement to violence by television and films, particularly as they effect children. Cases put on all sides—and sides of sides—tend to run to extremes.

The role of dramatized violence in the arts and in society is a complex matter. The corruptive possibilities of art were first discussed by Plato (who accepted them) and answered by Aristotle (who rejected them). The argument has matured since antiquity, and the specific issue of the creation of an environment of violence for the young by mass communications strikes responsive chords among many today. Resort to purgation of mass distributed dramas of their violent content appears to be a non-viable solution to the problem, if problem it is. Further investigation into the psychology of fantasy and its differentiation from perceptions of reality, however, might lead to profitable avenues of inquiry.

Persuasion employing the direct use of violence, or the threat of it, is also ancient and effective. In our society, however, myths concerning violence and non-violence have assumed such ubiquity and force that a realistic appraisal of appeals, on one side to peace and on the other to salutary violence, runs up against a strong cultural consensus, oblivious both to history and the tide of current events that construes social violence entirely in polar terms.

Chapter 24

BLACKS

On the other hand . . . minorities can try to solve the(ir) dilemma(s) by admitting being different. Those who are choosing this . . . way feel that, even if this choice should lead to being rejected as a kind of a stranger, it is still more honorable to be rejected for what one really is than to be accepted for what one really is not. They prefer to preserve the integrity of their personalities and are willing to pay the price of not being accepted.

Gustav Ichheiser

Among the variegated, cross-hatch of American minority groups, the one that best symbolizes the outsiders' problem in the modern Western world is the American black community. Blacks, at present, are probably both the source of and recipients of more intense persuasive thrusts than any other large group with common interests in our culture. Like most of these publics, the persuasion travels two ways and rides on the wings of myths not unlike those attending other similar cultural phenomena of current significance.

That America contains a *black community* is, on many counts, the first myth the analyst of persuasion encounters. The semantics of the word "black" are in themselves two-edged and persuasive, the term being the newest incarnation of equally unsatisfactory rubrics like "Negro," "colored," "darky," "spade," "dinge" and/or "nigger," all of which are still used freely in different places by blacks and non-blacks. To note that blacks are not black is as self-evident as to observe that whites are not white. To maintain, however, that the terms "black" and "white" permit freely a kind of linguistic-psychological polarity that terms like "Negro" and "Caucasian" do not, or is impossible by the entirely pejorative "nigger" (except as occasionally used by blacks between themselves), brings us immediately to the subject of influencing dispositions.

Nor is the black community a "community"—or even a group of "communities"—in any stable sense of the term. Americans of various non-Caucasian and non-Oriental backgrounds have, after all, descended from families with New World origins of greater longevity than those of many who make up the "white establishment" (a less ambiguous term than "black community"). Between blacks, there is but one frail, cohesive biological factor: bundle of genes of (probably) African origin (exceptions admitted) that found their way to the USA by way of slave ships, Caribbean Islands and desultory migrations from other temporary stopping points. The cohesive function of the unprovable genetic heritage has been unusually strong, considering the way other, more dramatic inheritances have been thrown in the metaphorical American melting pot.

The number of genetic blacks who have flipped their individual psychological coin to white and passed into the larger culture cannot be counted; nor should it be underestimated. So also has the notion of "Negroness" been subject, over the past fifty years especially, to so much stress that the objective plethora of sub-cultures that make up our rhetorical "black community" are not difficult to observe in almost any part of the nation. The recent consolidation of many blacks in support of, and against, various political figures has, among other things, called attention to the plurality of Negro culture, a large part of it barely distinguishable from non-black culture of the same relative social, economic and educational strata. This is not to minimize the differences that exist between, say, the black and white middle classes—particularly the fact that the whites have greater potentials for upwards mobility than the blacks—but the life-styles of both are similar. And among these similar groups, disturbances concerning race rarely occur except when questions like *Guess Who's Coming to Dinner?* are asked. And, even then, while inter-marriage may create problems for those who attempt it (if they wish to retain former life-styles) sub-cultural allegiances are frequently maintained primarily by all parties involved.

To speak of "the blacks," then, is to some degree inaccurate, and to another impudent, whether the speaker is himself black or white. Nor is he helped by recourse to euphemism. The many eloquent voices today discussing Black History, Black Power or Black This-or-That are speaking for themselves and the constituents of their particular sub-groups. And the generalities that they articulate are, in their way, as stereotypical as (and not too different from) Amos n' Andy, Abie the Agent or Charlie Chan.[1] Fortunately, many American non-whites today are aware of their own plural characteristics and more frequently remind the public of the fact than whites do.

[1] To write a chapter on the dynamics of black persuasion is equally as impudent—and inaccurate. I call the reader's attention therefore to the *caveats* below. I also suppose that such an analysis may even be considered worse than impudent by some, because the writer is white (or gray-pink in my bathroom mirror) and has perforce lived more or less remote from the so-called "black experience." But if the black experience is, as will hopefully be shown, in good part myth, my own psychological trepidations alone motivate this aside. The application of an individual's experience and background, be he black or white, to black persuasion needs no more qualification than my similar latitude in speaking, in this part of this book, both for and about women and/or young people.

The majority of the nation's twenty-three million Negroes, of course, constitute the so-called "black community," and also constitute about eleven per cent of the total American population. What segments, in truth, are represented by their most publicized spokesmen is a matter of conjecture. On the whole, the main myths of Black America have been directed to and generated by young people, urban dwellers (almost invariably raised in slums), more usually men than women, individuals of better-than-average education and/or intellectual potential, and people who reject two long-term, culturally sanctioned *desiderata* of American Negroes: entrance into the American socio-economic middle class in tacit agreement that they will quietly remain there; and the broadly articulated ideal of civil rights, itself a culture myth whereby legal stratagems are accepted as indices of symbolic social, political, educational and other equalities with Caucasians.

More than rhetoric and persuasion has naturally emerged (or re-emerged) from the construct of blackness. In somewhat cold-blooded terms, the problem of a high visibility minority of (mostly) former agrarians and cheap labor finding its place in an increasingly technological culture run by a majority of a different skin color was clearly limned by many as our most severe domestic challenge as long as a generation ago in both its circumstantial and psychological contexts. The argument has almost always been presented from the perspective of the white establishment.[2] As Braden explains,[3] and as the well-known Kerner Commission officialized (not entirely to satisfaction of black and white Marxists), that racial antagonism, or hostility on the basis of those non-Caucasian genes whatever their ancestry, lies at the root cause, not only of black unrest, black poverty, black violence and black persuasion, but of every apparently unrelated social conflict that springs from them.

A social upheaval—which is what the contemporary black is living through—based upon race is a peculiarly unsatisfactory state of affairs in a democracy, because it exposes weaknesses in equalitarian idealism (as expressed in the American Constitution), our judicial system (and its impotence to affect change by constitutional construction), our enforcement agencies (in their inability to augment civil rights legislation) and many

---

[2] Gunnar Myrdal, *An American Dilemma* (New York: Harper and Bros., 1944), has been required reading in sociology courses for a generation and clearly anticipated the social and moral problems to come. The black psychiatrist from Martinique, Frantz Fanon, also heard (in an emotional context) more specific rumblings in *Black Skin, White Masks* (New York: Grove Press, 1967), some years ago, as did other prescient writers from the political far left like W. E. B. du Bois, and white historian Herbert Apthekar in *A Documentary History of the Negro People in the United States* (New York: Citadel Press, 1951). The latter has written voluminously on the American Negro from a Marxist perspective and, within his ideological limits, comes to the issue ably, armed with a lifetime's experience and perspective.

[3] William Braden, *The Age of Aquarius*, pp. 198–222.

other difficulties involved in squaring practice with profession. In common parlance, American racism boils down to the unhappy truism that "You can't legislate people's attitudes towards each other," and this bit of cracker barrel social psychology applies equally to blacks and whites.

Set, therefore, in the context of considerable ignorance concerning what race is, what its genetic and physiological sources are and what genuine differences, if any, it signifies between people, recourse to the scientific evidence is futile. And few people, even those of some intelligence, listen closely to scientists who claim that race is irrelevant to most human activities. Nor is it likely that public opinion would readily accept concrete findings that demonstrated that it is *not*.[4]

Racial persuasion, in other words, intended either to disdain racial differences or identify and heighten their significance is yesterday's social propaganda. In the absence of much new to say about cross-racial difference (by-passing occasional spurts of opinion on one or another side), and in the light of a host of tensions and conflicts apparently sustained mostly by skin pigmentation as well as other cosmetic factors, the issue of the ways that blacks and whites may be racially different from one another is no longer relevant to what the law, long-held dispositions and political action are *doing* and *not doing* about an ongoing societal upheaval affecting millions of American citizens.

Many blacks, therefore, are ready to by-pass the anthropological issue of race, and, to the consternation of numerous white liberals whose attitudes were based on integrationist notions of racial brotherhood, turn the problem of the Negro in the non-Negro's world into a *political class* problem. This trend is first reflected, as we have seen, in the actual semantics of the words "black" and "white." Second, it found for the blacks, numerous

---

[4] For reasons that they may have (and have had) cause to rue, the Anti-Defamation League of the B'nai Brith has gone to great lengths to employ numerous sociologists (and others) who take exquisite pains in devising statistical and other intellectual acrobatics to demonstrate that the evidence that exists that demonstrates so-called racial differences between people does not exist. See Melvin M. Tumin (ed.), *Race and Intelligence* (New York: Anti-Defamation League), Mary Ellen Goodman, *Race Awareness in Young Children* (Cambridge, Mass.: Addison-Wesley Press, 1952), Peter I. Rose, *The Subject is Race* (New York: Oxford University Press, 1968), and such pamphlets as Ashley Montagu, *What We Know About Race*, Thomas F. Pettigrew, *Negro American Intelligence*, as well as Martin Deutsch's reply to Arthur Jensen's controversial thesis that race and intelligence are related entitled *Happenings on the Way Back To The Forum*. When an occasional dissenter like Dr. Jensen unearths a bit of evidence that racial influences *may* have something to do with the capacities of men and women for various endeavors, such data appear in a scholarly journal or two and find their way into the Sunday supplements and some magazines. And then the boom of silence is lowered on source and data, while other experts find ways to show that they are incorrect, or that the wrong conclusions were drawn from them. *It is impossible that, for the next generation at least, any findings demonstrating that racial differences in type or nature of intelligence, aptitude, or personality will be taken seriously by American scholars, regardless of what race is shown superior, or how the data and conclusions are derived.* Perhaps after 2000 A.D., scientific investigation into these possibilities, and the objective analysis into their findings, may become culturally viable.

allies among Caucasians (including North African and other Muslims) who, by virtue of their opposition to the American white establishment, may reasonably be included in the cause of black rebellion: Cubans, Maoists, North Vietnamese and others. Third, if the black issue is a class issue, it is now amenable to class-oriented revolutionary politics, largely Leninist, and dialectical historical solutions.[5]

As victims of a race problem, Negroes found themselves in a *cul de sac*. They were promised equality but knew, just as the whites knew, that if it was to come at all, it would come painfully slowly, perhaps educationally first, then financially and last socio-sexually. Granting the full weight of liberal civil rights persuasion, two generations, at least, might pass before racial intermarriage was sanctioned by the major institutions of the country. The liberals could, perhaps, make good the promise of the Supreme Court that separate education must not be considered equal, but they required time, and the result would have to be accomplished in the traditional white, liberal manner—and in peace. Under these circumstances, black children today might grow old to die in a *de facto* world of gradualism and tokenism.

With an impatience that is remarkable only because it took one hundred years to collectivize and become active, the new Negro, the black, rejected an integration he might never know, civil rights he might merely hear about but not experience, social ameliorists who might benevolently lead him to their peculiar concepts of social progress, and opted for the creation of a new class based on the historical fact of race but moving into the future as a black political (or power) class, *all the more potent for being highly visible.*

---

[5] As individuals, most of the black leaders have experienced personally the same transitions as the Negro population itself has, with the notable exception of diehards like Elijah Muhammad and intellectuals like James Baldwin. Elijah cannot give up the essential racist thrust of the legends of the Black Muslims that cast the white man as a devil and the black as God's chosen race. Baldwin, and other highly educated and talented Negroes, desire largely to compete with white intellectuals, artists and highbrows on fair terms. (Like black athletes and musicians, they know their strengths.) Class war will not help them. Eldridge Cleaver, the most articulate of the living black class advocates, began life in the old Negro world playing by its rules. Later, he became a fierce Black Muslim racist and anti-white, but eventually recognized that a class position was the most profitable one to encourage social change. Cleaver replicated the experience of Malcolm X, who lived for a greater period of time as a ghetto stereotype than Cleaver, and eventually dipped deeper and more publicly into unabashed racism. Malcolm's recognition of the necessity of class conflict rather than paranoid racism was clarified during his trip to Mecca, and, because of it, he was killed. Details of these personal changes may be found in Eldridge Cleaver, *Soul On Ice* (New York: Dell Publishing Co., 1970), and *Post Prison Writings and Speeches* (New York: Random House, 1969), as well as Alex Haley (ed.), *The Autobiography of Malcolm X* (New York: Grove Press, Inc., 1965).

New Negroes

Part of the change among groups of today's young ghetto blacks is apparent in the images that many have chosen to signify their class status. The revision of appearance, even granting that black life-styles have remained fairly stagnant, is a wise choice. It dramatizes their class awareness, solidarity and uniqueness in much the way that a uniform does. One important factor is the discontinuation of the practice of "conking" hair by both black men and women and allowing it to grow in Afro-styles, as well as rejection of skin lighteners and other cosmetics in imitation of the white aesthetic ideal. Another is the association of black sartorial garb with African clothing and jewelry instead of bizarre caricature extremes of white middle- and upper-class fashions, a trend that reached its epitome in the "zoot suit" of the pre-World War II era.

While the change of imagery, along with suitable symbols, is confined largely to the new blacks, and especially those who have chosen the Muslim faith or African traditions, the entire profile of the urban black, particularly, appears to have changed as well. In point of fact, however, numerous Negroes continue to imitate white styles. Although many of them feel sympathy for the black ideal, circumstances force them into an unwillingness to detach themselves entirely from the stylistic ideals of the whites with whom they frequently work and sometimes live.

This bastion of reaction is found in the black middle class and so-called black "society," actually the upper segment of what whites would regard as upper-middles. But the Negro middle-class was and is directly oriented to the culture at large, from both black and white perspectives."[6] Negro women have had less difficulty than men in rising, psychologically at any rate, to middle-class status via the professions of nursing and teaching. Also, in their roles as domestics for whites, they have achieved status in their homes and communities according to the status of their employers, as well as opportunity for more, more frequent and better paying employment, frequently, than black men. That these women, as well as male Negro professionals in white collar jobs, resist the move away from white styles of cosmetics and dress is not surprising. Plenty of black hair is still de-kinked, and skin lighteners still enjoy a brisk sale.

Nor does the old Negro matriarchy join lustily in with the present thrust of the new blacks. Old ladies who have raised generations of families, seen their daughters become professional and "make good," are not inclined to give up their own authority, and the measure of it they have

---

[6] See E. Franklin Frazier, *Black Bourgeoisie* (Glencoe, Ill.: Free Press, 1957), a somewhat dated but still interesting analysis of black middle-class life including a skeptical look at the potential economic power of black communities. See also the same author's *The Negro In The United States* (New York: The Macmillan Co., 1957).

passed on to their daughters, simply for a racial class cause and a promise of identity. Millions of Negro women over thirty *have* clear identities, families and jobs, and can compare their lot in life quite favorably, if selfishly, with white counterparts who do *not* work as professionals, do *not* have status as matriarchs, and do *not* perceive their middle-class status as *personal* accomplishment the way the Negro women do.

For these reasons, largely, few mature Negro women have found the Women's Liberation Movement interesting or show much enthusiasm for the likes of Millett and Friedan. Their cultural experience has not included patriarchal hegemony, even, frequently in the matter of last names. By the same token, neither does the political activism of their own sons seem particularly attractive. Should one of these matriarchs admire a black leader, he will not be a Panther or ideologist but, most probably, a minister of the Christian faith like the late Martin Luther King, Jr.; certainly not Huey Newton. Chances are that she will read both *Ebony* and *Life* and straddle both American middle-class worlds, black and white, content that she has, in many ways, achieved the better elements (professional status, family control, and respect, a decent income security and paid vacations) of both. And she is, by common standards, not deluding herself.[7]

In short, every black community in the USA contains its bastion of conservatives whose force must not be undervalued, particularly the influence of Negro women of middle age or older. Middle-class or "white" blacks are less apparently influential than the new blacks, involved as they are in the rat-race of white commerce, but their money talks. When and if these middle-class citizens move to managerial positions, the significance of the move is frequently exaggerated, because, even granting some remarkable successes, there appears to exist at present natural ceilings upon the potential power of black capitalism, personal or institutional, in relation to the enormous totality of American commerce upon which its fate depends. Much the same observation concerns the formidable number of resident or show-window blacks hired by white firms, not on the basis of competency but simply because they are black. In high visibility positions, they indicate the liberality of the organization—supposedly. The broadcasting and advertising industries, for instance, put their blacks where they can be seen—in front of cameras. In backstage work, technical jobs, executive echelons, management and creative jobs, one notices few blacks, except those used as

[7] In New York City, for instance, were the black population (largely female) suddenly removed from the professional sections of our hospitals and nursing homes, the functioning structures of both would collapse in an hour. Let me add that those of us who have suffered the inefficiency and indolence of run-of-the-mill white nurses and technicians have thanked the gods that so many Negro women, raised and trained in matriarchal family units, sprinkle so much of the sympathy, compassion and gentleness (learned at home, not at nursing school) into the application of their professional skills to the infirm of all races. If such words are construed as patronizing, so be it. But I personally see nothing demeaning about the recognition of general professional excellence, even if it is based on race.

resource personnel to tell white management what the Negro community's reaction to some project is likely to be.

Old style Negroes are considered by the blacks, in one degree or another, "Uncle Toms," a male epithet and usually a fitting one. With what degree of subjective, self-conscious simulation one never knows, the Toms continue their servile roles as bartenders, waiters, porters, bell boys, and other conventionally black occupations in white establishments, much to the chagrin, usually, of the new blacks. While their roles may be subservient, the edge of bitterness has been removed from the circumstances of many Toms. They often earn respectable wages, and, if the author's perceptions are correct, derive a measure of ironical psychological satisfaction and humor from their ante-bellum acts of extravagant obeisance to the white man's largesse. Written largest, the most successful show business and professional athelete blacks have always played the Uncle Tom game (and have appeared to win at it), especially those affluent national idols like the late Bill Robinson, Louis Armstrong, Cab Calloway, and (during his heyday) Joe Louis. (Muhammad Ali is one of few exceptions.) Even the younger black commedians play Uncle Tom to a degree, selling themselves as colorful ethnic prototypes with at least as much, or more, dignity than white show business sex symbols (male and female) market the accoutrements of their sexual potentials. From the new black's point of view, the Uncle Toms represent a peculiarly difficult constituency to activate politically, because being a Tom and working for "the man" is frequently and simply too psychologically and economically profitable to permit stimulation of class discontents.

The new black is himself part of a fractured community in which the Muslim movement, Afro-Americanism, political revolution and the dynamism of certain personalities have been periodically jumbled together and re-aligned in uncertain ways. Certain stable elements emerge, the most visible being the cosmetic one that takes on an honest and organically pure form in visible matters. But it presents innumerable problems on the conceptual level as signified by the words "Black is Beautiful." As a slogan of persuasive potential, this one demonstrates a cohesive tendency until it is examined, as it inevitably must be, by blacks and whites alike. It contains the same old buckshot backfire that has harassed Negro communities for generations. Are less-black Negroes less beautiful than blacker ones, thus reversing the antique hierarchy of the skin-lightened values of yesterday? Are black Toms, black "pigs," black FBI men and black capitalists beautiful? And what is the relationship of beauty to the black heritage, black history, black literature and black art? The slogan obviously replaces the center of interest of new Negro movements from class back upon race, an eventuality obviously at cross purposes with the present class need of the new blacks.

From a social-psychological perspective, the new blacks recognize that they have, at last, an opportunity to clarify and create a constructive role for Negroes in the West, but at present face two major questions, the second stemming from the first. Is that role compatible with white capitalism? And, second, what precisely is that role to be? Spokesmen for the best organized segment of the new blacks, the Panthers, answer a modified "no" to the first question, but point to the decadence and imminent decline of capitalism regardless of the black's role in its future. To the second question, they respond that promises of equality mean nothing in a game where equal opportunity is an illusion, given the American Negro's history as a second-class citizen and the not-so-silent racism that still pervades the national air.

What the black today wants is not meaningless equality but to be treated as a human being, which is quite a different matter. And, as a human being, the black American also wants, of course, his due share of the materialistic jackpot of functioning capitalism. The promise of equality, in the latter regard, has formerly been interpreted by blacks and whites alike as an equal right to *try* to get the gold. But simple statistics and a look at the standards of living in the black ghettoes demonstrate the multitude of obstacles that a white dominant society has placed in the black man's path to material success. When one treats a person as a human being, on the other hand, one does not safeguard his statutary rights of competition for prizes in commerce, and, at the same time, fix the game so that he cannot possibly win or play to a stalemate.

This subtle point bewilders many white liberals who would treat blacks as equals and expect them to be grateful for receiving a part of what they should have received nearly a century ago *and have already learned to survive quite admirably without*. In essence, one admits one's equality to his *guest*. But one shares one's humanity with another human being with whom he *lives*, and the raw issue of "equality" is irrelevant. The American liberal, especially behavioral scientists and similar intellectuals, find it difficult, if not impossible, to understand this. Nor do they seem to comprehend how neatly they themselves have already fixed the materialistic game.

Grier and Cobbs describe[8] the psychological roots of the situation in startling and clear terms, granting that their patients (upon whom much of their evidence is based) are as selectively drawn from the black community as similar individuals would be from any other one. What these two black psychiatrists demonstrate is *not* fundamentally a race problem, thereby drawing a picture that coordinates and runs parallel with class antagonisms presently expressed by black political polemicists. Black Americans, say Grier and Cobbs, in effect, suffer from a special *class* neurosis, the result not of any inherent racial factors, but relevant to their self-perceptions as a class construed as both different from and inferior to the white man. The

---

[8] William H. Grier and Price M. Cobbs, *Black Rage* (New York: Basic Books, 1968).

neurosis they describe is not new, although its distinctive manifestations in blacks are unique. In one degree or another, the neurosis has touched all minority groups in their contacts and conflicts with others in their cultures, most reently the American Jews who have generously spilled the imagery of their galloping identity disorders so freely into American literature.

But the critical difference between the Jewish neurosis, the Irish neurosis and the Italian neurosis, on one hand, and the Black neurosis on the other, is simply that the Negro has had a longer, more static, and self-reinforcing history than any of the former, and is, accordingly, far more difficult to place in perspective and treat. When Theodor Reik (or Freud himself) analyzes dispassionately symptoms of Jewish neurosis—or when Roth, Bellow or Salinger write their stories—they have already successfully moved away from the storm center of their problem—in fact, surmounted it. And, in the process, they help to manage it for their patients and/or readers. In some measure, this also is what Grier and Cobbs have done. But their accomplishment is far more heroic; and the problem, because it is basically an issue of black perceptions of white attitudes, opinions and behaviors of long standing, cannot be solved merely by recourse to insight or stepping aside. Grier and Cobbs take clinical advantage of the calm in the eye of a still active hurricane.

The black neurosis is dominantly a class neurosis, true only in transitory manifestations for most other groups. For many reasons, Jews, Irish and Spanish-speaking Americans display class mobilities that Negroes do not, and have not, since emancipation. One major avenue of therapy is therefore at present largely closed to them,[9] except in the rare examples of black capitalists and mass culture heroes and heroines. But their similarity, in many ways, to other classes of people who perceive their environments as functionally hostile is striking.[10] For such individuals, their own class and/or

---

[9] Even in such antiques as the plays of Clifford Odets or the books of James T. Farrell, the hint of a *class* solution was invariably given for the situational ills and manifest neuroses of the characters involved. In both writer's works, it is stated or implied that solutions to the social problems of their concern lie in class mobility. In Odet's best plays, some of the keenest characterization is given to Jews who have "made it," that is, found their way to economic salvation in the upper middle class and an apartment "downtown," while their relatives still chew their fingernails in poverty in the Bronx. (I am thinking of *Awake and Sing* particularly.) Rich relatives appear in Farrell's novels too. In no way, are these upwardly mobile characters necessarily admirable from the author's perspectives, but these characters have clearly surmounted the worst self-conflicts and minor desperations of their minority status as Jews and Irish Catholics.

[10] See Henry Krystal (ed.), *Massive Psychic Trauma*, previously cited. This volume is devoted mostly to articles and symposia on survivors of German concentration camps and the atomic bomb at Hiroshima. Most interesting are the psychological and psychiatric problems displayed by ex-concentration camp inmates living presently in the United States who feel alienated from the culture around them in attitudes and manifest behaviors not unlike those identified in blacks by Grier and Cobbs.

racial status (in truth, their senses of self) as they believe it is perceived by the dominant majority is the major, and in some instances only, reality of life. For Negroes, therefore, nearly the full range of existence is modified by blackness, not always (hopefully) as negatively as Grier and Cobbs indicate (with their more than the usual psychiatric interest in dysfunction), but enough to generate, in a social realm, involuntary defensiveness of a pre-psychotic nature and of near-epidemic proportions among the young particularly. Write Grier and Cobbs:

> Black men have stood so long in such peculiar jeopardy in America that a *black norm* has developed—a suspiciousness of one's environment which is necessary for survival. Black people, to a degree that approached paranoia, must be ever alert to danger from their white fellow citizens. It is a cultural phenomenon peculiar to black Americans. And it is a posture so close to paranoid thinking that the mental disorder into which black people most frequently fall is paranoid psychosis.
>
> Can we say that white men have driven black men mad? [11]

We can, of course, say just this—with some justice. But the statement is just rhetorically true (like the Kerner Commission's easy resort to white reactionary racism as the fundamental cause of today's black unrest), in that it implies an unrealistic solution that is as fanciful as the Negro's image of white culture frequently and unfortunately is. Of this difficulty, Grier and Cobbs seem distinctly aware.

Black Power and Politics

"Black power" is a fine slogan and, unlike "black is beautiful," provides a reasonable foundation for merging the sorry truth of black history in white America with a viable popular eschatology. Contrary to the beliefs of some, the major force of black power is, and will be, neither economic nor military, at least for the foreseeable future. Frazier,[12] among others, has shown clearly the limits of black economic force. Even the power of blacks as consumers is relatively small; countervailences to boycotts and other similar economic stratagems are too easily applied by white antagonists.

The Panthers are the main militaristic arm of the new blacks, and, at the writing, we are witnessing painful demonstrations of what tacit agreements among municipal police forces (and a little FBI persuasion) may accomplish by provoking, selectively eliminating, killing or jailing leaders that groups like the Panthers so desperately need, either to stimulate social action or to spearhead psychological or armed rebellion. Most of us pray, on the other hand, that the United States will be spared the carnage that will occur if the black militants attempt an armed revolution. Prison camps for

[11] Grier and Cobbs, *op. cit.*, p. 206.

[12] See Frazier's books cited above, particularly *Black Bourgeoisie*.

this eventuality have already been built and are maintained by federal authorities.[13]

In their capacity as terrorists, however, the Panthers and their sympathizers have already been selectively effective in bringing about, in communities like Watts, minor social changes (major to their beneficiaries) that might never have occurred had not the pressure of violence induced them. The two problems that attend such selective employment of violence, of course, are its tendency to run wild, and the destruction that it frequently causes the innocent bystander: the young, and the very constituents the militants are attempting to help. Nor does "selective" terror or violence affect much the degree of control "the man" still maintains over black culture.

Black power does, however, promise a certain amount of leverage upon the white establishment. But the power is best understood in psychological and political terms. In both respects, the greatest personal loss the black cause has suffered has been, ironically, the work of black hands: namely, the murder of Malcolm X. Malcolm was more than the charismatic leader. He was one of the few genuinely brilliant, self-taught, pragmatic intellectuals of our time, obsessed, of course, with black rage, but eminently competent, also, to see beyond it into the paranoid diversions both of black politics and the cultural schizophrenia of libertarian whites. (The latter profess to espouse the black cause only as long as it remains a domestic civil rights issue to be solved in court by statute and by benevolence in the social worker's office.) Malcolm knew that the black problem's situation lies in the homes and living rooms of white American families, in white corporate boardrooms, in white executive suites and in all the places that are segregated today—not by statute or economics—but by race psychosis. This knowledge is, of course, shared by other clever blacks who recognize also that this is the essential socio-psychological *fact* that terrorizes the anti-Negro bigot, who is himself aware of it. This accounts for the peculiar attitude of many militant blacks who say they prefer the company of the Georgia redneck to the Urban League, NAACP-oriented white liberal because, in the presence of the true bigot, the black man knows where he stands.[14]

---

[13] Yes, the concentration (or prison) camps are there. See Michael Myerson, "Concentration Camps: Whose Fantasy?" in *Civil Liberties* (Published Bi-Monthly by the American Civil Liberties Union), February, 1969, pp. 8–11. It is difficult to determine exactly for whom they are waiting, but it is generally understood that they are safeguards against an outbreak of racial rebellion, among other possibilities.

[14] John Dollard, *Cast and Class in a Southern Town* (New Haven: Yale University Press, 1937), is still the best study of the social, sexual and historical roots of what is called the "southern mentality" in regard to blacks, but by no means confined to the south. I know of no volume, however, that provides comparable study or analysis of the northern legalists to whom I am constantly exposed and who, on one hand, espouse the doctrine of equality, but, on the other, would not countenance its application to their apartment buildings, neighborhoods, families or personal attitude structures. Symptomatic of schizophrenics, they display one set of attitudes towards

In psychological terms, the new blacks possess sensitive social pressure points that Eldridge Cleaver appears to understand best. They are epitomized by statements such as, "For all these years whites have been taught to believe in the myth they preached, while Negroes have had to face the bitter reality of what America practised . . . When whites are forced to look honestly upon the objective proof of their deeds, the cement of mendacity holding white society together swiftly disintegrates." [15] The mendacity, of course, is the myth of the Constitution and Declaration of Independence, neither of which *ipso facto* have made good their promises to the blacks. Or, when in writing to his lawyer Beverly Axelrod, Cleaver parables their relationship thus: "We (Cleaver and Axelrod) represent historic forces that are coalescing and toward each other" in the union of the black militant and the receptive, humane white woman. "We live," he continues, "in a disoriented, deranged social structure, and we have transcended its barriers in our own ways and have stepped psychologically outside its madness and repressions." [16]

Cleaver is a poor political polemicist and revolutionary pamphleteer, having apparently chosen to write his *agitprop* in the style of Norman Mailer rather than Lenin, du Bois or even the late Earl Browder, any of whom would serve him as better models. But he is an excellent self-taught social psychologist, and, when he writes for himself, a talented and powerful prosodist who shows the rare skill of translating extremely abstract perceptions of social processes into no-nonsense human dynamics. This talent, ironically, imbues Cleaver's vision of the white and black world with considerable potential political power, largely because opinions and actions have first, rarely been moved by blacks into direct political assaults; and, second, he has been sensitive to clear, dramatic and emotional constructions of real social problems from which political solutions are implied. (John A. Stone's nineteenth century play *Metamora*, Edwin Forrest's perennial vehicle about the white man's perfidy towards the Indians and *Uncle Tom's Cabin*, both the book and numerous theatrical versions, are both examples of this sort of literature, their poor literary and dramatic qualities heightening in relief their didactic implications.)

What Cleaver is competent to accomplish beyond the reach of most

---

Negroes among fellow whites, particularly those of their own political orientation, and another in their official capacities as intellectuals, philanthropists and social ameliorists. Their opinions, as espoused, sound fashionably equalitarian, and their behaviors invariably involve supporting high-minded causes, frequently for ego-enhancing purposes. I cannot, of course, make these charges against *all* the civil rightists and other righteously indignant liberals I know. But the lion's share of them, I believe, use their inclinations towards social benevolence to patch deep schisms in their own consciences. A number of such individuals recently surfaced in our intellectual community when news of black anti-Semitism warned them that some of their apprehensions about black attitudes towards *them* just might be true.

[15] Cleaver, *Soul On Ice*, p. 79.

[16] *Ibid.*, pp. 140–141.

other black writers[17] (and what Malcolm X appeared to be preparing for at the time of his death), is a direct and terrifying but irresistible assault upon the collective conscience of the American people, blacks included. If he does not drown his message in the rattle of swords and Maileresque rhetoric, he may yet succeed, if and when he emerges from his present exile.

Roger Burlingame and others have demonstrated [18] a peculiar American phenomenon (sickness and softness to the right wing radical) of oscillation between social abuse and social sensitivity, swings of the pendulum that have increased as our population has grown larger and abuses multiplied. Call it a collective "conscience," "super-ego," "puritan heritage," or simply a "moral sense," but it explains the enormous contradictions (and hypocrisies) in the American tradition towards the minority groups, be they drawn along economic, social or racial lines.

The Marxist sees these contradictions as inevitable class conflicts that synthesize into revolutions. But in most American historical instances they have not, even during the great depression of the 1930's, because the antithesis to social inequity invariably was forceful enough to neutralize the revolutionary threat. Men like Cleaver appear to recognize this, and (despite disclaimers) translate this particular cultural reaction into political language, political action and political alternatives. Their messages produce revulsion, fear, sympathy and self-hatred among their white readers and listeners, as well as a degree of direct antagonism. But moral feelings and

---

[17] Cleaver correctly points to Richard Wright (particularly his character of Bigger Thomas in *Native Son*) as the major black writer to date who has captured the genuine tension between blacks and whites and has placed them in their correct psycho-sexual setting. Playwright Le Roi Jones is more difficult to assess, but his most powerful statements are probably yet to be made. As for James Baldwin, I agree with Cleaver that he speaks more for himself than for blacks in general. And yesterday's writers, like Ralph Ellison and Langston Hughes, were too bemused by their full and wise vision of the curiosities and caprices of life in general to be translated by blacks or by the general public into expositors of politically viable concepts. As for the prose that currently appears in black periodicals, much of it is so imitative of slick white writing as to be indistinguishable from it. The Muslims and Panthers have mastered a crude transliteration of their "cool" argot in their newspapers with more distinctive revolutionary vigor than Cleaver. But I have a feeling that this literature is read mostly by people who already agree with it, and I therefore question its political force—except, of course, the possibility that, because it is blunt and clear, it may produce a negligible backlash among both dissenting blacks and whites.

[18] See Roger Burlingame, *The American Conscience* (New York: Alfred Knopf, 1957). The militant black might scoff at Burlingame's insistence upon the power of moral drives in all American history and see in it the seeds of still more "tokenism." Yet, to date, the truth remains that, despite the extremes of bestiality that the record displays "in critical instants when the extremes of our conduct have brought us to the very verge of moral bankruptcy, the voice has spoken and the American soul has been saved" (p. 405), by a vestige, probably, of the puritan conscience. I think we are entering into (or are in) such a period of redemption at present, and, as usual, we fumble a while before both black and white men take the political steps necessary to diminish the humanistic and materialistic gap that presently exists between them. I think, personally, that the humanitarian one is more important than the materialistic one, but I write as a well-fed white, not as a hungry black.

acts of conscience are generally brewed of just this potent and emotional mix, and require the moralist to swallow his aggressive feelings to make good the dictates of conscience. Consciously or not (and the black writer's emphasis upon sex and profanity indicates that it is well calculated,[19]) in the meeting of morality and politics lies the best potential for black power to produce results.

Black power's bid for activation is therefore most likely to succeed in a political matrix based upon the shrewd psychological estimation of those blacks who recognize that, in moral terms, they have—or will have eventually, with continued pressure—the white man (with the exception of the hard core bigots and anesthetized liberals) exactly where they want him. They are also correct in construing "the man" as the enemy, because *only* such extremist personifications, although not entirely true, are politically viable in the American tradition. Politicians, community leaders and the rank and file blacks and whites must now be, and no doubt will be, pushed into the position where they must make an either/or decision: whether they are with the black man or against him. Unfortunately, the liberal's compromise among the whites must be considered "nays"; so must the positions of such outstanding Negroes as Thurgood Marshall, Roy Wilkins and the black entertainers and athletes who are so beloved by white audiences. In other words, political and psychological revolutions demand the same sacrifices and exacerbation of conflict as military ones if their victories are to be significant.

One important political error might destroy this manifestation of black power. This would be the dilution of the moral clarity of the recourse to white (and black) consciences by means of cross pressures: for instance, the encouragement of anti-Semitism and anti-Semitic propaganda among blacks, or undue emphasis by blacks concerning anti-Negro prejudices among Jews.

The first matter was, sometime ago, most forcibly called to public attention by James Baldwin.[20] Since then, the sociological community has twisted itself into knots using small sample surveys attempting to show that Negroes are no more anti-Semitic than whites in general; and that Jews are

---

19 One of Cleaver's most eloquent statements was addressed to the white élite of Orange County, California and their young, when, in his 1968 campaign for president, Governor Reagan was attempting to prevent Cleaver from lecturing on sociology at the University of California at Berkeley. Said Cleaver, "Who the hell is Mickey Mouse Ronald Reagan to tell you who you can hear, to tell me when I can speak, and to tell the faculty how many lectures of mine they can schedule—to all that I can only say 'Fuck Reagan.'" He received a three-minute ovation from this unlikely audience. Here is a near perfect fusion of morality, political astuteness and scapel language that indicates knowledge of exactly where, and to what, *this particular* audience's conscience could best be exploited. It is a clean affirmation of American idealism, incidentally, the likes of which are not frequently heard these days.

20 See James Baldwin, "Negroes are Anti-Semitic Because they are Anti-White" in *The New York Times Magazine*, April 9, 1967.

no more anti-black than Christians; and that even if this untruth is true, there are good reasons for it that have nothing to do with racial or religious prejudice.[21] Conclusions such as this one emerge: "The matter boils down to this: the kinds of anti-Semitic beliefs that are current in the larger society provide a meaningful and ready-made framework into which Negroes can place their personal experience with Jews."[22]

Sociological sophistry aside, Negro anti-Semitism and Jewish anti-Negro dispositions are probably matters of fact of the kind that cannot be eliminated either by good will or statistics. But the moral issues and the cross-pressures to which they may subject both blacks and whites are essential diversions from the apparent mission of black power in America. By denying their existence (or relevance), white intellectuals are, in fact, helping to create this diversion, just as writers like Baldwin are in publicizing them.

Many, many moral qualifications may be applied to the black argument of class bondage; just as many, many moral qualifications may assault the growing impetus among whites to misunderstand their part in black rage, all with some measure of justice. These are dangerous qualifications which may obscure otherwise clear reactions in the hearts and minds and consciences of countless black and white Americans, in whom the ultimate and non-qualified political decisions and social actions must occur that eventually (and hopefully) will eliminate the anachronisms of the angry black and nervous white, both of whom are unable to see the other as a human being. What irony if the major obstacle to this end is the do-gooder who attempts to qualify the polarity between them which men are presently giving their lives to create.

Black Persuasion

Because this chapter has centered upon beliefs, attitudes, opinions and actions of blacks and whites in regard to the role of the Negro in our culture, we have already discussed in some detail the quality of persuasion emerging from the new black movements. Even in the absence of a master like Malcolm X, much of it is highly effective for its intended audiences. Discounting the sloganistic shortcomings of ambiguous cries like "Black is Beautiful," or trite chestnuts like "Power to the People," the transmutation of "colored people" and "Negroes" in "blacks" has obviously influenced both black and white attitudes and, beyond the semantic dimension, given unity to what was a disparate, confused racial notion. Being black is now a matter of class, which, in itself, is an indictment of the moral integrity of the society that created such a class according to racial factors alone.

Black persuasion has accomplished for opinions at large—again for

[21] See, for instance, Gertrude J. Selznick and Stephen Steinberg, *The Tenacity of Prejudice* (New York: Harper and Row Publ., 1969), pp. 117–131.

[22] *Ibid.*, p. 127.

both blacks and whites—the basic services of solidifying them and creating a psychological crisis whereby white schizophrenia towards blacks (loving and hating) is untenable. And black paranoia has been cruelly exposed, resulting in attempted identity resolutions among blacks that have polarized both attitudes and opinions about such matters as ghetto slums, racial discrimination, social roles and intermarriage. It is at the opinion level, of course, that black persuasion will eventually be most effective among whites. It has, and is, liberating non-prejudiced (or just *slightly* prejudiced) whites by confronting them directly with the question of where they stand: *with* the black man or *against* him. If against, it provides a reasonable avenue of retreat into yesterday's notions of moderate equality, distaste for violence and other respectable stances. But the individual so repelled must still live with his conscience and is therefore free to change his opinions and turn to guilt-assuaging political action.

Those analysts (and plain citizens) who observe that the attitudes of young blacks in general have changed during the past few years are, perhaps, too facile in their analysis of a new tone among people who they have not until now regarded in a class context, and who, a few years ago, were small children whose dispositions were not, in any measure, visible. The new attitude is, with many exceptions, not that of the retreaded old Negro but the visible member of a new class of Americans who has grown to adulthood and for fifteen years has been acutely aware of its place in the "promised land," in Claude Brown's term.[23] The visible manifestation of the old (by now) attitudes of this new class are cosmetic and color distinctiveness carried to extremes, a forcefulness that appears occasionally (in the light of former experiences with Uncle Tom) as arrogance, a penchant for monomania, because *all* issues resolve into class issues and a rhetorical style that resists dialogue and inclines to polemicism. The latter manifestation, no matter how annoying to some, is an inevitable reaction to the barrage of white moral platitudes that have, for a century, been covertly laughed at by blacks. In effect, this black citizen of the new class is himself an instrument of persuasion, and, whatever the outcome of his mission, he has affected his own community and the white world irreversably. The limits of distinct Negro impression upon our culture at large, in other words, now transcend the previous boundaries of the black musical heritage, dance and ethnic humor into many other areas of life-style.

The new black as the *recipient* of persuasion is unquestionably suspicious and often paranoid toward many of the voices that attempt to speak to him. White politicians and business men traditionally hide behind black front-men in appealing to blacks. Nearly all the so-called "black" radio sta-

---

[23] See Claude Brown, *Manchild in the Promised Land* (New York: The New American Library, 1966), for a sensitive account of the origins of the so-called "change" in the black communities through the eyes of a gifted young man raised in New York's Harlem. This volume is as excitingly written as it is accurate.

tions in the USA, for instance, are owned and effectively programmed by whites. But, in this respect, the new blacks are becoming increasingly difficult to deceive, because they are now listening to content and disregarding form. In the long run, however, words have lost their meaning, and only good works, money or results matter. In regard to education, for instance, much of the government's *Headstart*-type of persuasion has fallen upon deaf ears because of the fact that, while "black schooling" may sound fine in theory, the question of where it will lead the black man politically and materially is not answered in explicit terms by the altruist's all-purpose ameliorative, more and better education.

Black private schools in the north and west have done better than these programs, and, at the writing, young blacks seem also to have been strongly influenced by the apparently harmless construction of Black History. (This is surprising, because it belies a new black sophistication, in the face of similar white diversions, from main purposes.) While it is noble for people to feel they have roots, and to pay proper homage to their heroes, Black History *per se* is as relevant to the future of the new blacks as Polish, German or British history is to third generation WASPs. What the black's enthusiasm for the history of black men says to historians in general is that our *white* history books, particularly American history textbooks, have been, and are, selective and incomplete. The problem will not be solved by adding Black History courses to the high school and college curriculum (where they are usually regarded by both blacks and whites as sheer propaganda), but by revising the entire history curriculum to include Black History as well as other lost threads of our past. Paradoxically, white children may need to study Black History today, in the writer's opinion, more than black youngsters in order to face their own futures!

White men have done many things to American Negroes. But whatever else they have given the blacks, including a second-hand class structure, they have taught them the arts of argument and persuasive style. This learning, at present, serves the black man well, both as he influences the attitudes of his own new class and as he speaks to white Americans. The day will probably come, however (as it does for all successful social revolutions) when the rhetoric of agitation will yield to the rhetoric of social progress and organization. Black persuasion will be subject to new ground rules by then, hopefully sooner rather than later.

Conclusion

Complex social dynamics resist easy summation and are open to misinterpretation. The new black phenomenon in the United States is such an issue that involves, today, the change of what was once a race issue into a class problem that will probably be resolved in the way that most class issues are: by revolution, either military, social or political. In present pragmatic terms, the direction most profitably pursued by that percentage of twenty-three million blacks committed to activism is probably political. The outcome of a military rebellion of, at most, eleven per cent of the population of contemporary America is not a pleasant conjecture, unless the blacks are joined by other armed minorities—an unlikely possibility.

Racial persuasion of the type to which many of us have become accustomed is today obsolete, because an ongoing race issue is now a class issue with distinct lines drawn between black and white society within the United States. This has been a desperate move on the part of many Negroes but their only alternative to a century of gradualism in integration and civil rights that has accomplished little in humanistic or economic terms. Old ideas of equality on white terms, brotherhood according to white strictures, and equal opportunity as defined by liberal whites are today meaningless promises to young blacks. On the other hand, to the black middle class, to black matriarchs and black women in the professions, to non-engaged Negroes of the old school, to resident blacks in white enterprises and to Negroes in professional, white-oriented politics, they are satisfactory constructs. But such individuals tend to be middle-aged and are passing from the black scene.

Changes in black life styles, however, display persuasive thrusts, because they are visible in dress and fashion, as well as in intellectual and religious orientations. While many leaders and slogans have also emerged from the new black movement, none is as meaningful as "black power," a phrase that has little genuine economic or military relevance but contains the potential of a psycho-political revolution if met by a receptive social climate. In the latter context, the blacks have in their future a formidable political role to play in the United States, enforced by the psychological power of the activated moral sense of much of the total political community, black and white, that will demand that blacks receive not only civil rights, *de facto* segregation and judicial protection of equal opportunities, but also a good share of the material wealth of the nation and the respect that decent human beings show one another. This includes the right (which must be regarded as natural rather than civil or statutory) to follow personal choices in the selection of sexual partners and/or mates. These simple propositions cut across class lines and include the right to preserve whatever myths *both* blacks and whites hold dear concerning the purity of their blood lines—nonsense, in the author's opinion, but of critical importance to others.

Set in the context of black rage and white liberal schizophrenia, the likelihood of such an outcome to the present tense standoff may seem remote, but voices of extraordinarily persuasive power are heard among the new blacks. And white benevolent dispositions towards the deprived blacks are moving in the direction of a new confrontation in which extreme positions and polar commitments will be demanded. In this setting, black persuasion has been, and will continue to be, a major force—some of it, unfortunately, violent, but probably necessarily violent. The next, and following step will require modifications of persuasive techniques and the arduous but necessary task, by blacks, of achieving (through education or persuasion or both) the diminution to extinction of what is presently their century old, bitterly learned and absolutely justified cynicism in the face of white persuasion.

Chapter 25

LAW AND ORDER

The law is only a memorandum. We are superstitious, and esteem the statute somewhat: so much life as it has in the character of living men is its force. The statute stands there to say, "Yesterday we agreed so and so but how feel ye this article today?" Our statute is a currency which we stamp with our own portrait: it soon becomes unrecognizable, and in the process of time will return to the mint.

Ralph Waldo Emerson

STRANGE THINGS happen to men when they don the jurist's robes. But one of the strangest is the resort by men (who should know better) to the words, "The law is man's most civilized and noblest invention."

Out of their robes, the sages of this brethren will concede that exceptions are admitted, because the law, unfortunately, is neither civilized nor noble in many of its manifestations, although it may be *necessarily* uncivilized and ignoble. The first legal thinker to run upon this truth was Socrates as he sat with his students, waiting for his cup of hemlock. Urged by Crito to escape Athens, the philosopher instead affirmed his decision for death in preference to exile. Having been found guilty of breaking the State's laws—uncivilized, ignoble *and* repellent to *him*—and having been tried and found guilty by its courts, he was logically bound to accept their consequences, no matter how unjust, lest he "make himself ridiculous by escaping out of the city." To Socrates, individual dignity in the face of unjust law was preferable to personal cowardice, rationalization or simply looking ridiculous. Man, he implied, is frequently debased by the unimaginativeness of his law; but so be it, and so much the worse for man. The absence of law, he added, would be a far greater calamity.[1]

As Nietzsche many, many years later was to observe in his *Genealogy of Morals*, the law is a pragmatized version (what we might call today a

[1] See the whole argument in the *Apology* and the dialogue in *Crito* in J. D. Kaplan, *Dialogues of Plato* (New York: Pocket Books, 1951), pp. 5–62, or any other edition of them, sometimes published as *The Trial and Death of Socrates.*

"system" or "program") of society's notion of what *truth* is. When and if men maintain, as they have for short periods of time, that *nothing* is true, freedom in the strictest sense reigns, because it is impossible, under these circumstances, to construct laws. As individuals accept truths, these agreements are subdivided into rules and regulations, institution for safeguarding these rules and regulations, and finally instruments by which transgression of them may be controlled and punished.

The development of these latter structures (in fact, techniques of social order, or technologies of intercourse) reflect the adequacy, wisdom or accuracy of the truths from which they spring. They cannot, therefore, attain nobility or civilization (or anything else) unless they are referred back to the philosophical ideas from which they grew. Contemporary American law rests upon a tradition of British philosophy and eighteenth century rationalist thought. True enough, in this tradition, the magistrate in his robes may strike some impressively noble and civilized poses. But the structure of legal technology itself was well drawn and efficiently applied in the Rome of Nero and Caligula, just as it was in Hitler's Germany, and is today in Mao's China. Nobility and degree of civilization do not refer directly to the structures of legal activity in any of these societies, but rather upon the relevance to man's social needs of their fundamental philosophies—in other words, construction of truths.

The technology of law, however, constitutes one of the most basic man-made structures in any society where an individual and his immediate family are not self-sufficient. In technological cultures, institutions of law are the "big leagues," as Martin Mayer's clever cousin observed upon hearing that Mayer was writing a book of analysis of the American legal profession.[2] Following a nineteenth century tendency, we turn largely today to technicians of law for the determination of those societal matters that we really consider important. Our presidents, governors and other political officials, including representatives in the Senate and Congress, are usually lawyers. The judicial arm of our federal government, in many ways a law-making as well as law-interpreting body, is, quite correctly, confined to professional lawyers, jurists and an occasional law professor. If our captains of industry, finance, philanthropy and education are not themselves lawyers, they are surrounded by legal technicians who fit their activities into legalistic frameworks. Constant tension between the behavioral sciences, medicine and the arts with the structure of law has left its impression on all of these fields of endeavor, just as the law has felt their impress and is, to a degree, an area of substantive concern of each.

In short, in our time and place, the law is *important*. Like many similar organizational structures (education, for one), it is reflective of cultural

[2] See Martin Mayer, *The Lawyers* (New York: Dell Publishing Co., 1967), p. 7. Mayer has odd cousins, and I did not expect to be quoted when I ran into him in midtown New York and asked his plans for future books.

dispositions to as great a degree as it is directive of them. Law, without a myth of consensus behind it, is a laughing matter, impotent and pompous. The infamous 18th Amendment to the United States Constitution, for instance, turned our country into a chaotic nation of lawbreakers, self-poisoned by fusel oil and other impurities in inferior liquor. Many other unpopular statutes, violated frequently intentionally or in ignorance, appear on state and local ledgers and are conveniently forgotten by police and courts—or rarely invoked because they are foolish, or because times or custom have changed since their enactment.[3] Laws that cannot be enforced, particularly those involving personal conduct of individuals and small groups, present other problems. (The present sale and use of marihuana almost wherever one looks is an example.) So do laws that may be enforced, but for which penalties cannot be exacted, the classic statutes being those which make suicide a crime. Punishment for the successful completion of this act is difficult.

To the legal theorist—and many jurists—the law is *completely* reflective of society in that it provides, in its manifold structures, specific required answers to obvious social needs. It is seen by them as a malleable mechanism that somehow scans the cultural processes of society, sets their procedural limits and facilitates their operations. Individuals, in their primary and secondary groups, reach consensus upon morals. Moral agreements lead to the coagulation of ethics. And ethics, finally, crystalize into the law. By numerous devices, the electoral process most obviously, the truth of law is therefore discerned, and the technology of law is modified in response to the need for, and agreement of, majorities concerning the ethical functionalism appropriate to the requirements of society.

This kind of theory, of course, is consonant with democratic governmental idealism. Other visions of society exist, however, but their main difference from democratic tradition lies in the manner in which they locate the *source* of truth. In democracy, the myth obtains that on-going functionalism ("the voice of the people") is the main avenue to truth. In other forms of government, equally as benevolent or moreso, truths may spring from the frontal lobes of philosopher-kings, may be discovered in the talmudic fabric of an entity called "tradition," may be revealed by God to his princes on earth, or flow from *Blut und Bogen* in mystical spurts. In all cases, including democracy, these truths are first, mythical in form and function, and second, require either public assent or force of arms for implementation and maintenance in legal structures. Law, therefore, and its progeny of technologists (law makers, lawyers, judges, policemen and jailers) are guardians of society's fundamental myths—not necessarily myths

[3] In many northern cities, it remains a statutory misdemeanor to spread salt to melt sidewalk snow in the winter, because salt irritated horses' feet in horse-and-buggy days. The statutes, frequently, have not been repealed, but they are non-functional like many other similar laws.

of truth (because the two terms may be incompatible), but *myths of how certain truths are created, the nature of their sources, and how they apply to the dynamics of culture*.

In this process, the juridical community is not, from another view, a passive agent. It is rather an active force of highly committed individuals, not unlike the practicing clergy, who are instrumentalists of accepted ethical and moral truths. They may question the truth itself, as many lawyers and jurists have, and remain true to their commitment. They may even express doubts about its sources and applications, as others have, usually by offering new sources for, and novel applications of, accepted truth. But the juridical figures whom we often deride as "legal minds" and who appear to have accepted a highly circumscribed vision of mortality, cannot, will not, and must not tamper with the myth of *how* truth functions in a societal matrix.[4]

For these reasons, the application of law, including its enforcement, has remained throughout history and in different cultures always and everywhere much the same, even in the remote cultures surrounding Tibet where hereditary chieftains adjudicate disputes *ad hoc*. Procedures, of course, differ, as in the instance of our adversary courtroom system versus the Napoleonic system of France. But the main configurations of the process are similar, and the end in view is identical: the enforcement and protection of societal truth in the affairs of men.

In the *use* of law, however, truth is in a procedural sense invariably irrelevant; and more than one jurist, ensconced in this irony, has been forced to the terrible choice of honoring his blind commitment to myth or to ceasing to be a jurist. Should the truth he is enforcing become intolerable, he may reject it and leave town.[5] But should he question the *need* for

---

[4] Mayer is generally sympathetic towards the legalistic way of looking at life, but clearly indicates in his astute volume that other perspectives are, in the face of certain social problems, more satisfying to him. He is essentially a journalist and prefers, I imagine, the reporter's conceits concerning non-engaged, objective observation, a construction of reality, in its way, as limited as the jurist's. All Mayer knows, however, is *not* "what he reads in the newspapers"—or what his interviews with newsmakers reveal, because he is too sensitive to be so crudely deceived. What he knows is what he, personally, has discovered about the institutions he investigates.

[5] The late Otto Kruger in the film *High Noon*, presented a cameo characterization that is a gem in screen annals. As a judge who had sentenced a presently avenging gunslinger to prison, he is seen packing up his law books, flag, scales of justice and other symbols of law into his saddlebags, preparing to flee the community before the liberated prisoner gets to town. Packing these impedimenta, he tells the sheriff, "I've been a judge before, and I'll be a judge again," but the time has come, he knows, to turn tail and run. He will not desert the myth of law or its structure, merely the consequences of a societal truth he implemented when he sentenced the homicidal, avenging gunslinger. He leaves the sheriff, in the person of the late Gary Cooper, to stand up to the truth, which Cooper, of course, does. Cooper eventually defiles the truth he has defended, at the end of the film, by throwing his badge of office into the dust. This act, a metaphor drawn from Greek tragedy, negates his temporary alliance with the cowardly frontier citizens who left him to face their enemy alone. The symbolism spits

truth, its source, and the necessity for its application, he has left the juridical world and joined those philosophers who cannot function as juridical technologists.

The Persuasion of Law

The law is also, from another perspective, an institution of enormous prestige, given power by the various factions in culture that it is involved in, and to some degree shapes, almost every occurrence of significance in a technological society.

To the average citizen, the law is a given cultural reality that was there before he was born and will survive him after he is gone. It regulates, in various measures, his home life, his working life, his pleasures and his travails. Its minions in uniform are ubiquitous, and its strictures constitute super-ethics that delimit many of his personal inclinations. To the revolutionary, the law is a dinosaur; to the liberal-intellectual, an enormous globe of silly putty; to the conservative, it is the framework and cable structure that supports the suspension bridge of culture over a wild and deadly river in a continual hurricane. To all, it is an integral part of the momentary cultural scene, and an influence, by force or precept, upon their own dispositions and behavior, and upon those of other people. Mediated to society more by means of its guardians than its statutes and professional arbiters, the law influences the life-style of culture on personal, professional and community levels in a host of invisible ways, just as it also influences many beliefs, numerous attitudes, multitudinous opinions, and also circumscribes and directs, in one way or another, nearly all social action, both trivial and important.

The law is not, however, influential as a sheer abstraction. Every aspect of legal technology is personified, mythologized and the source of numerous symbols; in fact, the intensity of emphasis upon symbolic discourse in many cultures is directly reflective of the significance of the structure of law to society. The average American courtroom is as replete with mythic symbolic trappings as the average church. More symbols of cultural magic are usually found in the office of a small town lawyer and/or justice of the peace than in the medicine chest of a Haitian witch doctor; and the former's voodoo works better than the latter's, because it reflects firmer (if not greater) cultural consensus. Persuasion therefore flows *from* people and their symbols and effectively influences other cultural dynamics—all of those dscussed in this Part of the present volume and more.

Because the persuasion of legalism is therefore invariably personal, let us examine, one by one, the classes of people most closely associated with legal technology in the order of their remoteness from the personal perceptions of the average citizen. Each, let us remember, represents a distinctive

---

magnificently in the face of the supposedly civilized truths by which men live, the main point of this superb drama.

portion of legal technology, not its *gestalt*. Attacks about which we read in our newspapers directed at the police, therefore, disruption in courts and rebellions in jail are not themselves assaults on the structure of law in culture. True enough, the attackers think they are hurting the structure, and much of the public, including members of the legal establishment, behave as if they do by mouthing platitudes concerning "respect for law and order." But law and order are not as vulnerable to assault as they may presently seem. To destroy the technostructure of legalism is a multi-faceted and formidable task, better accomplished by destroying its philosophical and statutory end than by undermining the enforcement or judicial parts of it. Even in these former cases, an ameliorative and self-healing process is always at work, and gaps are usually filled.

On the other hand, an assault on the *truth* that justifies the structure of law may be devastating, at least so the successful revolutionary discovers from history. Recent examples of destroyed legal systems tell the story clearly, with results visible today in Cuba, China, Czechoslovakia and the USSR—as they were yesterday in Italy, Germany and other nations, where, for all practical purposes, legal structures (and many policemen, lawyers, judges and jailers) did not change in the course of revolution. But they are now beholden to the enforcement of laws derived from new versions of *truth*. In fact, they are performing much the same kind of tasks they always performed, but in new ontological and epistemological worlds.

Police: All kinds of policemen, from process-servers to directors of enormous agencies, bear the brunt of attitude and opinion-oriented discontents with the law. They—and their traffic signs and "most wanted" posters —are the most immediate symbols of law that most of us encounter in daily life. *En masse*, they represent a bewildering grab-bag of federal state and local statutory law enforcers. And in the modern technological state no method has yet been devised to sort out the limits of their overlapping authority, except the "Rube Goldberg" mechanism of appeal to outside or higher authority. Add to our official policy representing multitudinous government, state and local agencies the hosts of quasi-legal private guardians of property and process, and one realizes the utter futility of assaulting guardians of the law for purposes of destroying the structure of law. Were all of these police forces drawn together for common purposes, they would constitute a civil army of formidable size and strength. Nor is there any intrinsic reason why agencies like the FBI cannot, by mere order, expand and extend their operations into areas at present beyond the hazily enforced interstate delimitations. All matters, of course, may be interpreted, if necessary, as "interstate" in ramification and with minimum sophistry.[6]

---

[6] Nothing officious is intended in comparison, but Hitler's famed *Gestapo* was a national police force, meticulously organized and intentionally operating in constant conflict with other enforcement arms in Nazi Germany. Hitler used the non-totalitarian device of overlapping authority to control his underlings, and was as cautious of the

Many behavioral scientists, with the exception of some sociologists, tend to perceive police as negative psycho-social forces, prohibitive of numerous innate or instinctual expressive forces in man, rather than as *instruments* of legal structure. A photograph of a policeman appears frequently in the Thermatic Apperception Test; and to the psychologist, games theory specialist and social scientist, the policy symbol functions as a super-ego surrogate that *prevents* individuals from doing what they want. They are joined by literary tradition, starting, probably, with *Les Miserables,* winding through *Crime and Punishment* and *The Trial* into Genet's play *The Balcony,* in all of which the policeman, or his image, is regarded as the counterforce to personal freedom. The law, not the policeman, is the actual counterforce, and the social truths behind *it* do unquestionably limit free behavior. But it is the policeman who is often the recipient, both of the individual's psychological reaction and direct political action.

Compare, for instance, political reactions against two Nazis. One, Albert Speer, was a virtual architect of the instrumentalities of provisional truth in Nazi Germany, albeit too sophisticated to share in the concoction of these same truths. He survived the Nuremberg trials to write his autobiography and become a Book Club selection.[7] Adolph Eichmann, on the contrary, was a functionary of the Nazi system: a policeman-clerk whose pride lay in implementing structures to facilitate a cause he apparently did not fully comprehend. His trial was an international occasion of mass vengeance, and he was hung, through complex legal maneuvers, amidst worldwide publicity.[8] Public psychological reaction to Speer, the backstage philosopher, was and is benign; to the functionary policeman, Eichmann, outraged, bitter and redolent with vengeance, as if his death might somehow exculpate mankind for its own blood thirstiness. Like most policemen, Eichmann loved his uniform; while Speer, until the outbreak of World War II (and whenever possible thereafter), preferred to dress in civilian clothes. The difference is critical.

Sociologists, historians, legal thinkers and others tend to reject the powerful psychological man-in-the-street view of the policeman and police power. Policemen are, after all, part of the socio-economic structure of soci-

---

potential revolutionary power of the *Gestapo* as any other bureau he created. The legal aspects of the *Gestapo* are treated in the study by British historian Edward Crankshaw, *Gestapo* (New York: Pyramid Books, 1957).

[7] See Albert Speer, *Inside the Third Reich* (New York: The Macmillan Company, 1970).

[8] See Hannah Arendt, *Eichmann in Jerusalem* (New York: The Viking Press, 1963), for the discussion of what Arendt calls "the banality of evil." Evil policemen are almost invariably banal, and Eichmann was no exception. Speer bares his soul in Albert Speer, *op. cit.*, and demonstrates how persuasive philosophers can be *post hoc.* History is not prepared to tell us whether either man received his share of justice, because both were judged in differential legal structures by different means at different times, and it is too soon after the events in which they were involved to weigh them dispassionately.

ety and as much customers of their own services as dispensers of them. Working policemen claim—and often receive—partial relief from their customer status while in uniform, but a man's police role is less a facet of character than a professional stance as a symbol of authority. By and large, policemen of all kinds leave more of themselves at the station house when they go off duty than physicians or teachers when they go home.

The long view of policemen takes them for what they are: instruments of a system. First, they did not create any part of that system. Second, their options concerning how to administer it are of small consequence, confined to person-to-person decisions in ambiguous situations. Third, they are morally free at any time to stop being policemen, an option not as freely given to individuals whose socio-professional roles have been integrated into their characters and result from years of specialized study. Ironically, therefore, the policeman's familiar explanation, "I was only doing my duty," means both less and more than it says. On one hand, it is a statement of truth and an honest bid for sympathy. But, on the other, it means that a high degree of moral acceptance was involved in assuming the police role and in affirming individual duty.

Eichmann is an excellent example of this ambiguity, drawn to absurd lengths. And, unfortunately, the trigger-happy dispositions of many policemen in our culture lead them to keep the peace by the exercise of arbitrary authority against those who *may break* the law, rather than those who *have broken* it. In this regard, it is the citizen without money for legal defense, the black, the young and the harmless non-conformist who suffers most. Many policemen are quite sophisticated in legal matters and almost presciently sensitive to those members of the population against whom they may exercise arbitrary and unwarranted authority without worrying unduly about reprisals. (A Latin American police chief in one of Graham Greene's novels, if memory serves, distinguishes instinctively between the people he is able with impunity to imprison, torture and kill without worrying about the consequences, and those he cannot. Amusingly, he makes no bones about the difference.)

All the deliberations of the United States Supreme Court, all the *Gideon* or *Miranda* decisions, all the legal thrusts at high levels to protect individuals against false arrests, quick confessions, interrogation without counsel and similar violations of civil rights do not (and probably cannot) change the small, intimate social dynamic between the cop on the corner and the "suspicious character" he brings to the station house for questioning. At present, suspicion and hostility in many localities towards policemen is counterbalanced by increasing police fear of the "suspicious character." This has created a climate wherein false arrests and arbitrary brutality by law enforcers are regarded, unhappily, as a necessary by-product of the slogan "law and order," words frequently used but poorly understood by the people who use them.

The popular view of the policeman's role in our culture is also ambiguous, and is perhaps best seen in the context of the detective story, an ever-popular novel form that offers two views of the policeman, one old and one much newer. The older version runs back to Poe, Collins, Conan Doyle (it is British as well as American) and into the contemporary hands of Rex Stout, Agatha Christie and others. It construes the police as an agency of law that is little more competent to administer legal technology than the man in the street is. Policemen, therefore, keep the peace, but not too well. When the peace is broken, a superman is required, usually a quasi-policeman like Dupin, Holmes, Wolfe or Poirot (but certainly not a cop) to expedite or apply legal procedures. Policemen are average men of average intelligence and skill. They are neither better nor worse than anyone else, nor are their powers extraordinary.

The newer version is derived from detective tales published in the pulp magazine *The Black Mask*,[9] and later in stories and novels of Dashiell Hammett, Raymond Chandler and others. Although the protagonist of these stories is often a private operative, he is essentially a policeman, brighter than the average, but each case (or story) is, for him, just part of the day's job. Hammett's Sam Spade and the Fat Man are prototypes; so is Chandler's Philip Marlowe.[10] The most important aspect of this latter stereotype is that the protagonist policeman does not hesitate, when his own conscience dictates, to step aside from the law and pursue justice directly; that is, to find his own way to social truth. That he is invariably right in his decision is irrelevant to his choice. He is *expected* to act in spite of the law rather than at its behest. He is also bigger than the structure of legality around him and the personal exemplification, not only of what it is but what it *ought to be*. Frequently, he is also uncivil, arrogant, tough, and something, in the patois of the young radicals, of a "pig." But, as W. S. Gilbert observed, "A policeman's lot is not a happy one."

Lawyers:[11] The wide variety of human beings who comprise the legal profession is delineated clearly by Mayer.[12] To say that a man or woman is a lawyer indicates little about him except that he or she is able, probably, to

---

9 For a vintage collection of surprisingly well conceived and written *Black Mask* stories (none of them by Hammett), see the recent collection, Ron Goulart, *The Hardboiled Dicks* (Los Angeles: Shelbourne Press, Inc., 1965).

10 Romanticized to the extreme, this character has traveled in many literary directions, some as absured as Mike Hammer and James Bond, both of whom no longer reflect human stereotypes but personified subcultural attitudes.

11 A statement of personal bias should be entered here, lawyer-like. I am a black sheep in a family of lawyers. My father was a magistrate and lawyer; my brother and most of my other male (and some female) relatives are lawyers. Raised as I was in a household where legalism was one of the main subjects of discourse, I grew up with numerous and deep seated attitudinal biases in regard to the legal mind that so many lawyers (not blood-related, happily) display. The legal mind is merely a narrow mind following a set path in a constricted wind tunnel.

12 See Mayer, *op. cit.*, pp. 15–36.

read. Castro is a lawyer; so were Trotsky and Erle Stanley Gardner. Like most professionals, lawyers these days tend to pursue specialities, although a minority still carry on general practices and some still chase ambulances. The public image of the lawyer as courtroom advocate is, of course, a picture of an exception, not a rule. But so is the image of the lawyer as a scholar, hunched over law books, searching for precedents and humane logic to justify a position in his brief.

Because of their position close to the structure of legal technology—and because they are also technologists within that structure—the professional whom the lawyer most closely resembles is the contemporary theatrical critic. The latter is in the position of publicizing his opinions of what passes for contemporary drama and theatrical production, and most of it, his intelligence tells him, is simply horrible. But so deep is his respect for the drama, and so fearful is he of its fragile state in contemporary culture, that he devises all manner of stratagems, including occasional resort to exaggerations and lies, to elicit public support for the shoddy and ill-conceived shows he must attend and audit. His professional schizophrenia is similar to the lawyer's, demanding, frequently, applications of dubious techniques and means for a larger good and to a salubrious end. The lawyer's concern centers on the structure of the law or legal technology that often may only be maintained at the expense of affirming shaky myths and accepting dubious practices. What neither the dramatic critic nor the lawyer usually realizes, however, is that the structures they are attempting to preserve are *both* crumbling regardless of their efforts and, at the same time, under repair, in much the manner that it is said the human organism replaces itself, cell by cell, every seven or so years. While the forms with which they deal are changing, the technological edifice will still be standing long after they are gone, in all probability.

The public's image of exactly what lawyers *do* is also unclear, but it is almost equally as unclear in the juridical community. Lawyers' main functions are to provide liaison between the culture at large and its regulatory forces, and this service may be accomplished in countless ways. The lawyer, therefore, must face in two directions at the same time, an easy posture for Janus but difficult for a human being. The usual psychological stance of the lawyer is, therefore, equally as dualistic as his occupational stance. On the one hand, he is privy to the world outside the juridical scene and what he believes is *really* going on—in other words, he is party to the countless extra or quasi-legal personal, social, economic and political transactions that are kept at bay from juridical procedures. On the other hand, he is also involved in the technological structure of law as it influences, circumscribes, audits, facilitates and limits these and other transactions. He is, in common terms, concerned with what members and institutions of society *can get away with*, that is, how much freedom they may be permitted without countervailing too harshly social truth. And in this capacity he is capable of a stereopticon picture of societal functions. Because of this vision, and because he often mistakes the structure itself for truth—and personal, social, economic and political activity for process—the lawyer's psychological disposition inclines him to consider himself an "insider," when, in fact, he is in many ways peculiarly and inevitably alienated both from the myths of legalism and the activism of social processes.

Lawyers are supposed to symbolize the common man's access to the functions of law as his requirements demand. In general, the less a citizen knows about this structure, the more important becomes the lawyer to him, especially as an individual's relationships with impersonal institutions impinge upon his welfare. Our prisons are filled with convicts who have absorbed more statutory law and legal precedents than most lawyers learn in a lifetime. And yet this knowledge is useless to most of them, because they are not in the lawyer's position to apply it within the legal structure. To the convict, a lawyer *makes* law, and a judge (or some other arbiter) decides upon its adequacy. And the chronic prisoner or ex-convict may often be easily detected in a crowd by his extraordinary knowledge of the letter of the law.

The lawyer, as juridical middleman, is the symbol (whether he likes it or not) of the *spirit* of the law. He is, in persuasive terms at any rate, the technologist of the myths of legal structure. In this capacity, he is both the hero and villain of the drama of conducting cultural affairs within the limits provided by societal truth. He stands for *freedom* in the sense that he may be able to "spring" a man caught in the structure of legalism. But he also stands for the impressive enactment of those *limits of freedom* that the supposed welfare of society delineates. In these senses, he is indeed an advocate.[13]

The public is generally aware that, in a sense, most lawyers are continually involved in professional gamesmanship. According to legend, attorneys for the prosecution and defense josh together at lunch and tell dirty stories; judges smoke cigars with defense lawyers and prosecutors in their chambers. All the while, under public scrutiny, the participants indulge in legal formalities similar to religious ceremonials. Some of this play-acting is necessary for orderly procedures; much of it is pure psycho-symbolism that generally impresses the actors more than its audiences. The law, however, remains the mythic god-head for the lawyer. His business is not necessarily justice. That is a matter for other participants in the legal structure to deal

[13] There are exceptions. Because they live in a manipulative world, some lawyers are basically dishonest and care neither about the structure of law nor their clients' interests but merely their own. Murray Teigh Bloom, *The Trouble With Lawyers* (New York: Simon and Schuster, 1968), is an accurate exposé of the kind of chicanery some lawyers get away with. But a similar book might easily be written about doctors, engineers, generals or college administrators. It is an entertaining casebook of legal malpractice (with a good deal of justifiable venom directed at surrogate procedures), but hardly descriptive of the legal profession as a whole.

with. For these reasons, the persuasion that lawyers bring to the public as politicians, civic leaders, part-time public relations men, journalists and educators is frequently greeted with glassy stares of skepticism.

Being malleable—and human—lawyers may step out of their fixed roles if and when they step into jurist's gowns or take an oath of office. It is axiomatic that tricky courtroom lawyers become the severest of judges, impatient of tricky courtroom lawyers; the late Samuel J. Leibowitz, attorney and justice respectively, is now a classical example. Within a month of the present writing, the President of the United States, a licensed lawyer in New York State, committed in an extemporaneous interview a legal error so egregious as to cause first-year law students to shudder. He referred in a press interview to an "accused murderer" as a "murderer." (It is hard to believe that the President's error was not intentionally designed to accomplish some esoteric political end.) Lawyers are also prone to involvement in illegalities of the most obvious nature, and frequently get caught in disarming ways, a function, probably, of their own feelings of infallibility or plain dizziness from looking at the world through the barrister's stereoscope.

Courts: That the courtroom is an obsolete cultural convention, and that court procedures as presently conducted cannot satisfy the needs of large, complex industrial cultures is, in non-legal circles today, almost beyond dispute. Nervy defendants—or anyone with a bent towards mischief —can usually so subvert the *individual* trial process so as to make a mockery of the advocacy system. Removing such individuals to padded cells equipped with closed-circuit television sets (to maintain the illusion of an open trial) or binding and gagging them serves their disruptive purposes all the better.

Hamlet moaned about "the law's delay," but Elizabethan justice acted with the dispatch of a jet engine compared to the horse-and-buggy courtroom procedures in our nation to a point beyond farce. Stresses in the cumbersome system probably cause as much social dysfunction as they prevent, some claim, and their argument is dramatized by procedural, court-directed roadblocks thrown into the world of commerce and into the personal lives of victims of this obsolescence. Most dramatically, citizens awaiting criminal trial and unable to raise bail linger—many of them innocently —in jails and houses of detention for months and sometimes years. Riots and rebellions are the result, and cause increased demoralization in an already demoralized arm of the judicial system. Appeals and procedural ploys and counter-ploys complicate the problem.

Courts themselves suffer from a mythic over-exposure that began modestly enough forty years ago in the professional theatre, but today has generated soap-opera stereotypes of behavior mediated to the public by television and films that apparently effects everyone who enters a courtroom. This influence is as great, incidentally, in state as in local courts; only certain federal courtrooms seem spared. Judges, juries, lawyers and on-lookers often appear busier at role-playing than pursuing concrete aims of judicial procedures. Darrow, Fallon, Rogers and few other attorneys were masters of courtroom psychology, but the tradition they represented is today lost in a maze of courtroom heroics and myth. How many readers, familiar with the fiction and non-fiction of the Leopold-Loeb case, for instance, remember—or ever knew—the critical humanitarian issue that Darrow metamorphosed into the point of law that was responsible for sparing the lives of his two defendants? How many would be willing to bet hard cash on their recollection of whether Scopes was acquitted or found guilty? A half-dozen lawyer-performers may be competent today to produce such a virtuoso result as the New Jersey acquittal of Dr. Coppolino[14] or the pyrotechnics that sent Candy Mosler back to her garden apartment, both accomplished with enough *panache* to justify, in a poetic sense only, the probable miscarriages of justice involved.

Great courtroom lawyers are exceptions, available as advocates either for the very rich or the notorious. This fact does not prevent minor league dramatists from transmuting attempts to enforce law into cheap melodrama, a process on view daily in our municipal, juvenile and domestic courts, open to those with stomachs strong enough to audit them. A. N. Whitehead once said, "Where attainable knowledge could have changed the issue, ignorance has the guilt of vice." These are not comfortable words to bring with one into today's court of criminal law, especially as R. Taver's novel, *Anatomy of a Murder*, makes painfully clear, all the more so for having been written by a pseudonymous trial jurist.

Granting that the courts deserve the lion's share of abuse they presently receive from inside and outside legal cognoscenti, solutions of what to do about them have been long in coming and remain vague. Obviously, some combination of computerized information systems, rapid information retrieval, and perhaps, tape or closed-circuit audio and video recording and transcription may (and will eventually) be applied to the numerous processes now reserved for court procedures. Such changes would today be quite feasible were legal minds open to advice from disciplines outside both their hegemony and comprehension.[15] Presently, they are not. Nor will they be soon forthcoming, because of one obvious reason: they must eventually *de-*

[14] See John D. MacDonald, *No Deadly Drug* (New York: Doubleday and Co., 1968), for a well written account of F. Lee Bailey's defense in the first Coppolino trial at the Monmouth County Court House, prior to the latter's conviction in Florida. It is a remarkable story of the search for legal truth in a psychological crazy-house.

[15] I am even fairly certain that, given proper advice, I myself am competent, based upon a reasonable familiarity with the logical limits of contemporary technology, to figure out schemes involving this technology that are able to modify many of our civil and criminal court procedures without violating either the philosophy of American law or the essential functions of our legal structures. But I am not exceptional in this competence, and wiser students of communications would probably achieve the same ends more effectively. Having already discussed this matter with a number of legalists, I am

stroy our present courtroom procedures *as we know them*. Such destruction need not interfere with the competent administration of legal truth: the right to open hearings, fair trial, and the judgment of peers etc. But they will indeed destroy the current symbolic, dramatic mystique of the courtroom as a theatrical-societal temple.

In other words, the conventional roles which participants play in court will be changed, and the present employment of skills as well as the exact forums of expression must be modified.[16] All participants in the present process feel therefore threatened by the prospect of such changes. Because clerks, lawyers, judges, stenographers and others involved do not suffer themselves directly the procedural abuses so noticeable to the rest of us, little sense of urgency impels them to action.

The change, of course, is inevitable, but will result from pressure brought to bear upon the judiciary by the slow erosion of attitudes and opinions regarding the integrity of the legal process—less a dissatisfaction with law than the peculiar way it is handled in our courtrooms and the results achieved therefrom. Court procedures in criminal cases are extremely fragile; it is remarkable that they have lasted in their present form these hundreds of years. In civil matters, they are equally as fragile and sometimes more vulnerable than in criminal matters to subversion by those who believe that bureaucracy and procedural mechanics are depriving them of their rights to due process.

Television and films will continue to bolster the myth of the court as church, but as more and more citizens in opinion-influencing positions feel the strain, pressure and breakdown of the procedures of the juridical and interpretive functions of the courts, the myth will necessarily lose its psychological power. As sad a prospect as it seems, the psychological prestige and power of juridical decisions upon personal and social behavior will henceforth decrease from year to year—a process already noticeable on local, state and federal levels—because personal and social perceptions of the authority of our courts will increasingly be negativised. Judicial decision will become no more valid than the power of the muscles behind them. We shall not have lost faith in the law, but as a people, we shall question profoundly the adequacy of the instruments that interpret it for us.

At this point, jurists will inevitably turn to social psychologists to ask the already answered question, "What went wrong?" Considering the present potentials of what Whitehead called "available knowledge," they may then be intellectually and emotionally ready to learn their first lessons in cultural persuasion.

---

also aware of the degree of intransigence (not to the operational nature of such a change, but to the *idea* of it) that major innovations in courtroom procedures face.

[16] My present freshmen students would express this modification more succinctly by saying, "The bullshit will be eliminated." Unfortunately, it will probably not; but at least it would no longer clog the gears of the judicial mechanism.

Jails and Prisons: Rationales for our present assumptions of penology are many and ancient. Enlightened criticism of these rationales is newer and at its best in Menninger's recent volume,[17] a powerful dissection of modern penal methods. Menninger's viewpoint is psychiatric, but it is likely to have considerable effect in the world of criminology.[18] But this reform will come too late and will probably be too feeble. What our jails and prisons have done to tens of thousands of individuals in terms of ruined lives and injustices cannot be undone.

More important, however, is what our penal institutions have done to the technologies of our legal structure, a more significant and longer-lived issue of which the public remains more or less unaware. Various indices of dead-rot that surface in the press occasionally are dissipated by arguments over such minor issues as capital punishment, a moral problem of delightful complexity and rhetorical potential, but one that, in its widest ramifications, cannot affect directly more than a relative handful of people at the moment, both directly or indirectly. Such red herrings aside, the philosophy of penology by which our society operates today—and its persuasive implications—immediately affects us all, but in indirect ways bereft of the drama of great issues like the right of the state to take a human life.

What is mainly involved in this aspect of our legal structure is the basic psychology of punishment, which is accepted by both legalists and the general public as a *less* complex matter than either the psychology and sociology of crime or the intricacies of legal structure. Today's simplistic notion of punishment is an example of idiotic conventional wisdom at its worst, so patently foolish as not to deserve the epithet "myth." In the first place, when the idea of punishment is detached from its social matrix and associated with the Freudian notion of "thanatos" (as it frequently is in modern as well as pre-Freudian literature and drama), its complexities are immediately apparent. But the major reasons given for modern punitive practices, in their probable order of historical significance, are, 1.) to redress wrongs done to man, the state or our gods; 2.) the removal of the wrong-

[17] Karl Menninger, *The Crime of Punishment* (New York: The Viking Press, 1966), is recommended as a knowing analysis of where penal psychology deviates from social psychology, and why more crime is born in prison than dies there. See also the forcefully written, but less extensive volumes, John B. Martin, *Break Down the Walls* (New York: Ballantine Books, 1953), Abraham S. Blumberg, *Criminal Justice* (Chicago: Quadrangle Books, 1968), and Edward D. Radin, *The Innocents* (New York: William Morrow, 1964). See also, Nathan Leopold, *Life Plus 99 Years,* previously cited, in many ways the most intelligent of them all. Leopold was a "lifer" at Joliet at the time the book was written.

[18] A discussion of prison reform is not complete without noting the dedication of Austin MacCormick and the Osborne Association which has been fighting an uphill battle for years against abuses of our present penal system. MacCormick's devotion to sanity in the administration of punitive institutions over the years is both outstanding and exceptional. He has continued his efforts unabated until the present writing for nearly two generations, in spite of the public apathy he still encounters. See the Osborne Association's yearly *Handbook of American Prisons.*

doer from society for a period of time to deactivate his potential harm; and 3.) the rehabilitation of the wrong-doer into productive citizenship.

Our present plurality of penal systems, to the best of the author's knowledge, does not substantively accomplish *any of these objectives.* This is a point that will usually be granted by those who defend these systems on the premise that they are better than nothing, a difficult comparison to make.

Few prisoners seem to perceive institutionalization as *quid pro quo* punishment. The author has conversed with hundreds of men and women either "doing time" or alumni of various jails and prisons. And each almost invariably claims he is (or was) technically innocent and that others who offended more seriously were treated more fairly in court or had better legal counsel than he did. Some personality types appear even to thrive on the status they achieve (or behavior in which they may indulge) while in prison. And others, presently incarcerated, are so frightened of freedom that they require the highly structured environment of prison to live at peace with themselves. Prisons are ideal places for such individuals, but for the wrong reasons.

As far as redress of wrongs is concerned, it is hard to conceive, except in a fraction of cases, how institutional confinement as currently practiced does more than stimulate a typical prisoner's glands of revenge.

Rehabilitation in prison is so exceptional that it often surprises prison psychologists when it occurs. Most jails are simply zoos, and prisons are crime schools in which both instruction and motivation are far more effective than at our prize universities.[19]

The pathways of legal structure, therefore, lead us finally to a bleak and remote dead end street. If we step aside from the means of the penal system to its ends, the picture is most dismal. The worst part is the self-containment of this final process of punishment: the impression one receives upon entering a Bertillon cell bloc, when the metal door is bolted, that one is insulated absolutely from the normal dynamics of society, including all access to normal conduits of communications. The feeling is justified. For all practical purposes, our prison worlds are as remote from the consciousness of most supposedly enlightened citizens as the labor camps of Siberia. In contexts beyond the limits of this discussion, they *are* in another country where standards, values, morals, ethics and behaviors of both the keepers and the kept are foreign to most of us "outside." For this reason, also, the average convict, innocent or guilty, is correctly aware that

---

[19] The above paragraph is not vapor culled from sociology texts. Avocational interests bring me into frequent contact with numerous former inmates, male and female, of jails and prisons around the world. These conclusions are based upon seven years of discussions with them, as well as with present inmates at local institutions. While my relationship with these populations is non-professional, my outrage at the system in which they are enmeshed is relevant to my professional interest in persuasion.

his true story will never be told, not because he is incompetent to tell it but because society's ears are closed to him.

The worst part of the failure of both our judicial philosophers and technologists to articulate an adequate punitive philosophy is the apparent futility of attempting to do anything about this ungodly appendage to our legal structure. True, many individual prison systems are presently being modified. But modification is not change. What is needed, first, is a sophisticated *raison d'être* for *all* punitive measures dealt out by law; the present ones are crude enough to have been written by a clever ape. Second, the difference between social sickness and crime (or cultural pathology) must be clarified; this necessitates a distinction between treatment (or therapy) and imprisonment. The two are hopelessly muddled today. Third, only pragmatic attacks directed at the causes of crime will, in the long run, salvage the ideal of rehabilitation. We are, therefore, back again at the need for a punitive philosophy and realistic psychology to guide our courts, immersed and distracted as they are in their own problems.

Our punitive procedures today function as cultural persuasion in exactly the same manner that Egyptian slaves were persuaded to their labors by overseer's whips, so little progress has been made in this respect in 3,000 years. If our jails and prisons presently serve a social function, it is because most people, excluding, of course, those most likely to commit crimes, are afraid of them. This is a realistic fear and a viable social control of sorts, but hardly as consonant with our supposedly advanced legal structures as compared with those of primitive societies.

When the Lindbergh law, for instance, made kidnapping a federal offence, kidnapping appeared to decrease. Potential kidnappers, faced with the fear of greater punitive actions than heretofore, were forced to turn their talents to other, and perhaps fouler, crimes. In this vein, an argument may also, of course, be made for capital punishment. But this entire punative premise stands in opposition to the social truth we supposedly prefer in the West, articulated by Fromm[20] (who had experienced the consequences of its abnegation in Germany): that society cannot be held together by fear, but rather by a sense of civil cooperation, which, while neither perfect nor entirely adequate for man as he currently lives, constitutes an ideal to which our structures of law may strive.

Conclusion

The persuasive aspects of law are many, and their description has required a full chapter. Because law functionalizes culturally accepted truth, it is fundamental to effective social intercourse. The wise application of its

---

[20] See Erich Fromm, *Escape From Freedom* (New York: Avon Books, 1965; originally published in 1941), pp. 163–201. Fromm cuts to the heart of the sado-masochistic roots of totalitarian truth and the exploitation of fear as a fundamental societal dynamic of law.

technology is also critical to the welfare of the state and integral as well to its decay or destruction. Because this is not an insular professional matter, the persuasive dynamics of law are the business of the citizenry at large. Like war in the hands of generals, the law is far too important to be left in the hands of jurists or juridical technicians. Although it has survived to the present writing, our legal traditions offer in themselves no promises for the future.

Most critical to their health is the confidence of both the public and jurists in the major myths of legal structure that maintain the application to culture of truth. What society regards as true is not difficult to achieve consensus upon, but its implementation is a more perilous process. Fortunately, the structure of law in a complex society like ours is enormous and intricate, and therefore more or less invulnerable to simple revolutionary upset, even were consensus on truth somehow changed either by force or persuasion. The faces that the main constituents of the legal world present to the public are numerous and changeable, each with its own present institutional vulnerabilities.

We have examined these faces: the images that policemen, lawyers, courtrooms and penal institutions have achieved in our culture, noting the stresses they undergo and problems they face, sometimes at cross-purposes as cultural institutions and/or as parts of the juridical structure. To some degree, all misunderstand their own roles in society. The notion of the legal mind, the policeman as keeper of the peace, the jurist as philosopher of statute, and the prison as the instrument of rehabilitation are common examples of this misunderstanding. To another degree, considerable confusion seems common *within* the world of legal technology itself, including problems of transference of symbolisms and rituals from the past into the modern world, where they are neither relevant nor useful for maintaining the myths of our legal structures.

Our discussion has not included the problem of achieving justice. Functional justice is a main constituent of the legal myth and, *ad astra per aspera,* also the pragmatic ideal to which jurists strive in the knowledge that, although they will never achieve it, a hopeless goal may at least direct one to an operative and productive system. Philosophical justice is a philosophical problem and has little to do with the matters of persuasion raised in this chapter. It is, however, fundamental to the future of *functional* justice, which, in turn, is fundamental to the future of law. It belongs in the dialogue of our times and should be pursued in our schools, on our mass instruments of communication, in our arts and sciences and at the dinner table. We frequently reject confrontation with it today in favor of what we believe to be more profitable discourse. But a people's beliefs, attitudes and opinions that are not grounded in a philosophy of justice are morally barren. And, if this is true, the structure of law in our culture is certainly, at present, moribund but still breathing.

Chapter 26

CENSORSHIP

The truth is what a man or an interest or a nation can get away with. That dependence upon intellectual laissez-faire, more than any other single factor, has destroyed the foundations of our national education, has robbed of their meaning such terms as "reasonableness" and "intelligence" and "devotion to the general welfare." It has made intellectual freedom indistinguishable from intellectual license.

Alexander Meiklejohn

CENSORSHIP is persuasion by restraints upon speech or behavior of certain kinds that often extend far beyond law. It is an inevitable part of the social process, of family life in every culture we know, of education and, as Albig has cleverly demonstrated,[1] apparently a part of the individual's own cognitive processes. Repressions of speech (and thought) begin with auditing process in the mind-lives of each of us, and are affected by cultural controls, group standards, climates of opinion, and finally crystallize formally as organized group censorship and legal impositions against certain specific forms of speech and behavior.[2]

The United States is no exception, although the First Amendment of our Constitution specifically guarantees freedom of speech and the press as conditions for functional democracy. Conditions of social life, however, demand exceptions under law, if the truth the law functionalizes includes equal rights for all and concepts of reasonable fair play. Speech is therefore restricted when it is libelous, when it is dangerous (as in the trite illustration of an idiot yelling "Fire" in a crowded theatre), and in numerous other social situations. Supreme Court Justices delight in reminding us of this truism whenever a decision is rendered on a First Amendment issue. The words, usually phrased gently, repeat the obvious fact that "the unconditional phrasing of the First Amendment was not intended to protect every utterance," or words to that effect.[3]

Some speech, in nations where freedom of speech constitutes a funda-

[1] See William Albig, *Modern Public Opinion* (New York: McGraw-Hill Book Co., 1956), pp. 243–46.

mental guarantee of law, is free; some, necessarily, is not. Censorship occurs when restraints, legal or social or personal, are used to silence that particular kind of speech which is not, *under certain conditions,* free. And in today's world, words are understood not to be the only methods of human discourse or communication. The principle applies by extension to still pictures, and (after many a legal battle) to motion pictures, and, presumably, dance, sculpture, sign language and all other forms of human communication.

Censorship is also a pejorative term that can, with some justice, be applied to most social occasions in which someone is told (or forced) to "shut up"—as in the instance of a teacher quieting a disruptive student, a woman remonstrating a drunken housemaid, a male nurse stuffing cotton into a raving maniac's mouth, or a night-club manager physically silencing a disruptive patron who did not like his floor show—all examples of censorship that are frequently sustained by law. Censorship also occurs when participants in a given occasion agree to abide by their own rules of decorum, as in the case of a lodge meeting or the self-censoring activities of today's comic book industry. In this vein, lawyers scrutinize fiction and non-fiction books before they are published with an eye towards potential libel suits, and publishers, at their advice thereafter, frequently censor their authors. Radio and television continuity acceptance personnel, sensitive to the public's pulse as well as the law, perform much the same function for broadcasters. Movie makers are sensitive to the needs of exhibitors and are often willing to censor films directed at certain publics, if informed that audiences will object to what they say, or for other reasons.

All of this latter type of censorship, and much more, has one element in common. It is not called "censorship" *except by those who oppose it.* To those who accept its logic or need, it is merely considered a function of the operational right of individuals in communication with other people to circumscribe that communication according to its intention and probable results. When this circumscription is viewed with opprobrium, it is given an opprobrious name: "censorship."

Censorship is not unique to advanced cultures or those with legal structures that concern speech. Anthropologists and cultural psychologists have noted taboos in discourse, expressed in much the same form as the examples above, in nearly every society known. No one has yet *proved* that the elimination of censorship from human affairs is impossible; but it has not yet been attempted, even at the sub-cultural level. And the notion of a culture where impositions upon communications are *not* made in primary and secondary groups, as well as the larger social arena, is difficult to enter-

---

[2] *Ibid.*, p. 244.

[3] I have quoted Mr. Justice Brennan in *Roth vs The United States* (1957). This phrase, however, appears in one form or another in most recent opinions the high court has delivered on free speech disputes.

tain. At such bizarre pastimes as "encounter therapy" and psychoanalytical sessions, perhaps, an individual may indeed say anything to another individual that comes into his mind, but even here the clinical climate of the occasion somehow circumscribes both speech and action. And what comes into an individual's mind is delimited, most psychologists agree, by the dynamics of personal censoring mechanisms connected with memory, perception, attention and other factors.

Given censorship as a dynamic of culture—and ridding it of its semantic impedimenta—restraint upon communications seems to respond to a rough relationship to *numbers* in large complex cultures with many conduits of communication. Legal factors aside, the likelihood of the range of censorship of communications will increase as the number of recipients to a source of speech (in its broadest sense) also increases. A man or woman by himself or herself may say anything about anything. With one or two of his peers, he may say *almost* anything, but not quite. Add a few strangers and the breadth of discourse is still more limited. And so on.

This principle applies directly to culture at large. A small group with common interests may, with impunity, discuss matters (like blowing up the White House, for instance) that would be considered dangerous in a larger group. The range of permissible discourse in our time is freer among the relatively small number of live theatregoers and book readers than for the film audiences—excepting patrons of those films for which the potential audience is *decreased* by proscribing the film for one part of its possible audience: children, for instance. Radio and television come into the home and travel instantaneously across the nation to millions of people of all ages and dispositions; their breadth of discourse, especially when children are likely to be watching, narrows accordingly, and the restraint of censorship increases.

Another factor influencing the permissible range of discourse, and likelihood of censorship, is *community of interest.* A group of physicians or psychiatrists may discuss freely and openly a wider range of subjects without fear of restraint than a similarly sized group drawn at random from the general population. Films shown in special theatres for adults only—but, in practice, attended largely by adult male voyeurs—usually avoid the censorship they would receive were they shown in local, neighborhood, family-type theatres. The audience for network television is heterogeneous; the specter of the censor therefore looms large over the shoulder of even those late night interviewers who delight in ribald innuendo. The audience for educational television is so small in many areas as to be virtually non-existent. But those who watch are bound together, it is understood, by common interests. The probability of censorship circumscribing material directed to them is therefore small.[4]

---

[4] When, for some reason, the audience for educational television suddenly grows, censorship problems begin. The first Public Broadcasting Laboratory program on an educa-

In law, these rough principles are utilized as needed. For instance, most of the Supreme Court's recent constructions of obscenity contain, as guidelines for censors, consideration, first, of the probable audience that will be exposed to a communication; second, contemporary community standards; third, motives for dissemination, and other matters, all concerned, in part at least, with the breadth of saturation the speech involved will receive and the communities of interest that it is both intended for and likely to reach.

Lastly, the *focus* of censorship (that is, exactly *what* is censored) is *constantly shifting*, with the result that, in large countries particularly, one receives the illusion that the amount of active censorship occurring, in the short run, is continually decreasing, and, therefore, that freedom of expression in general is increasing. This is an illusion shared, incidentally, as freely by laymen as lawyers, psychologists and historians. From the individual's perspective, what was censored yesterday appears not to be censored today. Female breasts, for instance, were not bared a decade ago in American entertainment films; today they appear to be mandatory costuming (?), even in documentaries. The result is an apparent liberation from a former restraint. Ten years ago, the author probably could not have written the obscenity FUCK on this page without feeling the hot breath of his editor or publisher (as censor) against his neck. (He might have written F____K, and all would have been well.) The fact that the letters UC have been liberated to appear in context above appears to indicate a decrease in censorship in contemporary culture, at least as far as books directed to markets like this one are concerned.

What is *actually* occurring is, however, the all-too-human proclivity for over-generalizing from special instances. In the first place, the right to show a mammary gland in Cinemascope, and the right to say, or print, the venerable word "fuck," constitutes a dubious victory for the cause of free speech. Bursts of enthusiasm or disgust that attend the liberation of such anatomical objects and words are often carried further than their immediate cultural relevance properly demands. Second, because these liberties are granted by law and cultural consensus with fanfare, one frequently does not notice that the tendency to censor still remains; it merely centers now upon new subjects and areas of discourse, as the concept of public welfare is reconstrued in the wake of changing morals, ethics and manners of speech.

Forty-five years ago, for instance, a film maker and exhibitor would have been free to portray Fagin in *Oliver Twist* as the repulsive, dirty, stereotyped Jew we encounter in Dickens' novel. The producers of the re-

tional network contained a bitter play concerning Southern mores, encapsulating in satire a devastating picture of white attitudes towards blacks. Numerous public objections were raised, and censorship was in the wind. When it later became apparent that few people were watching PBL broadcasts, the threat diminished, and in subsequent PBL programs even more controversial issues were openly treated without threats of censorship.

cent musical *Oliver* were not that free in this regard. And such a portrayal would probably have caused picket lines and pressure group censorship in many cities in the United States.[5] The present author may now have a right to use some hitherto suppressed Anglo-Saxon expletives in his exposition here. But should he begin a serious discourse involving terms (and remember that the General Semanticists assure us that "a word is not a thing") as "niggers" (without quote marks) for Negroes, or discussed, quite seriously, the quaint folkways of "dagos," "kikes," "micks," "coons," "yiddles," "frogs," "chinks," "spiks" and company, the publisher of this book (being a gentleman sensitive to the dispositions of his constituency) would probably suggest that the author remove them, and, that if he did not . . . In the 1920's, of course, such words appeared freely (but infrequently) in critical writings of such gentlemen of the arts as George Jean Nathan, Stark Young and others, and were rarely censored. Today they are generally proscribed.

Censorship, in other words, is a mobile, shifting phenomenon that apparently does not decrease much in a given culture, even over long periods of time. It moves from one area of discourse, or one instrument of communication, in devious ways, to another. Behind this observation, of course, remains the fact that *some* ideas therefore always remain continually unpopular, taboo and unfit for open discourse in every culture. But ideas that were taboo yesterday need not be taboo today; and tomorrow will see no sudden revision of this consistency of change in culture. As these changes occur, however, people tend to perceive them (for better or worse) as liberations. Thus freed from old restraints, psychologically, they became quite vulnerable to new restraints upon permissible speech and behavior, because, in effect, their apprehensions of unsuspected restrictions are decreased by their attentions to the novel freedoms they now enjoy.

The tendency to censor, both legally and extra-legally, is one that appears continually to increase as the conduits for the pressures of restraints (by individuals and groups who would guard the public welfare in eliminating what they consider offensive and corruptive communications) also increase apace. Mill noted over a century ago this specific proclivity in civili-

[5] Such portrayals of Jews were common in American films of the 1920's and '30's, and most Jews did not seem to mind them. In fact, many of the film makers were Jewish themselves. *Abie's Irish Rose* (a play riddled with stereotypes unthinkable today) was made into numerous movies, and the first "talkie" (or "semi-talkie"), *The Jazz Singer*, is full of them. In the late 1940's, however, pressure from Jewish organizations forced the "voluntary" censorship of all of the close-ups (and other scenes) in a British film version of *Oliver Twist* with Alec Guinness as Fagin. The full version was shown in Britain, where I viewed it at the time. Guinness' Fagin was a perfect Dickensian Hebrew stereotype, emphasizing every grimy, slimy, Semitic aspect of character in the Jew-baiter's book. The American version of the film was almost unintelligible, bowdlerized as it was. Guinness' magnificent performance was ruined, along with the rest of the drama.

zation that subsequent history has confirmed. But it is invariably ignored in the scramble of liberal delight that follows every new illusory emancipation. Wrote Mill:

> The disposition of mankind, whether as rulers or as fellow citizens, to impose their own opinions and inclinations as a rule of conduct on others, is so energetically supported by some of the best and by some of the worst feelings incident to human nature, that it is hardly ever kept under restraint by anything but want of power; and as the power is not declining, but growing, unless a strong barrier of moral conviction can be raised against the mischief, we must expect, in the present circumstances of the world, to see it increase.[6]

Censorship As Persuasion

The history of censorship has been told well many times, sometimes by "engaged" historians, out to demonstrate that this or that type of censorship is wrong, or that certain topics should or should not be censored in certain ways.[7] There is neither reason nor space here to reprise fully that

---

[6] John Stuart Mill, *On Liberty* (New York: Appleton-Century-Crofts, Inc., 1947), p. 14. The essay was originally published in 1859.

[7] Regardless of their particular orientations, let me recommend (from a hopefully "non-engaged" perspective) the following for their thoroughness in presenting a reasonably long-range perspective of censorship: Morris L. Ernst and Alan U. Schwartz, *Censorship* (New York: The Macmillan Co., 1964), an excellent broadside against censorship of obscenity, set in its historical context and oriented mostly to matters of law. James Jackson Kilpatrick, *The Smut Peddlers* (Garden City, N.Y.: Doubleday and Co., 1960), is less legalistic but more conservative and appreciative of the controversial nature of the problem of censorship. It contains well-rounded pro and con consideration of many aspects of censorship and is a far better volume than its title implies. My personal *variorum* on free speech problems in America is Zachariah Chaffee, *Free Speech in the United States* (Cambridge: Harvard University Press, 1948). The same author's, now unfortunately dated, *Government and Mass Communications* (Chicago: University of Chicago Press, two volumes, 1947), written with both wisdom and style, is a major study of its genre. So, also, is Bryce W. Rucker, *The First Freedom* (Carbondale: Southern Illinois University Press, 1968). Paul Blanshard, *The Right to Read* (Boston: Beacon Press, 1955), contains many excellent historical materials well presented. See also the authoritative essay on religious censorship, often neglected by historians, Normal St. John-Stevas, "The Church and Censorship" in, John Chandos (ed.), *To Deprave and Corrupt* (London: Association Press, 1962). The way the historical pendulum of obscenity censorship has swung is clarified in Alec Craig, *Suppressed Books* (New York: World Publishing Co., 1963). And a highly readable chronicle of Charles Rembar's defenses of such symbols of human freedom as Lady Chatterley, Henry Miller and Fanny Hill is *The End of Obscenity* (New York: Random House, 1968). In his book, Rembar casts himself as the Perry Mason of contemporary free speech in America. He is not. Numerous other attorneys have served this cause both longer and more modestly. A man of no little ego, Rembar tells his anecdotes neatly, especially when they make him look clever, a quality of his character open, I think, to debate. Anne Lyon Haight, *Banned Books* (New York: R. R. Bowker Company, 1955), constitutes merely a list of books that have been censored since antiquity and the reasons why. But, for the perceptive reader, this volume follows the story of censorship as revealingly as a formal history. The larger context of culture in which censorship resides is told in many analyses of Western society, but I

entire history; it is a subject of encyclopedic length and complexity as it occurred in the West alone.

Books, plays, poems and pictures were censored by various authorities in the ancient world for reasons that are modern: corruption, subversion and similar evils. But the immediate tradition of censorship in which we live today dates from the invention of printing. Because religious works were first printed and circulated widely, censorship centered on *blasphemy*, the definition of the term depending upon who was doing the censoring. More than coincidence fuses the dates of the Reformation and the spread of printed books throughout Europe. Censorship illustrates their meeting. The Catholic Church took the historical lead in proscribing corruptive books, as she saw heresies gaining momentum and emerging in society as permanent schisms, resulting in an unwarranted notion, common to the present day, that Catholicism and censorship have a natural affinity for one another. The various Protestant sects in Europe were as zealous in guarding the virtue of their followers by censoring printed heresies as the Catholics, notably in England, where censorship for blasphemy was eventually to merge with censorship of king and state.

As the crime of blasphemy was considered less and less heinous, and/or the Church's grip upon its parishioners became more and more secure (or less and less important), blasphemy, as the main focus of censorship, gave way to the incitement to *sedition*. Churches and states were merging throughout Europe in the seventeenth and eighteenth centuries, and offenses against God might easily be subsumed to offenses against the law of the state. Blasphemy as a focus for censorship decreased to the degree, also, that the persuasive influence of churches has also decreased in the past and present centuries. Sedition, however, remains a sensitive area, as far as censorship is concerned, in every nation in the West including ours, but one to which public attention is infrequently called.

In the United States, subversion, as an *exception* to the Bill of Rights, was affirmed by Congress in the form of the Alien and Sedition laws of 1798, slapped almost immediately in the face of the First Amendment. Designed to protest our new nation from British propaganda (and *their* subversion), the laws were found to be unnecessary, so great was post-revolution American anti-British feeling. Writers and newspaper editors were, nevertheless, jailed and convicted because of them. But they were also unpopular and quietly allowed to expire after two years. They remain the first and last such legislative devices passed by Congress directly censoring subversion in the United States.

Critical to the issue of censorship of subversive communications by state, local and non-governmental bodies, a trend which ebbed and flowed through the nineteenth and into the twentieth century, was the figure of

---

recommend Herbert J. Muller, *Freedom in the Modern World* (New York: Harper and Row, 1963), as particularly relevant.

Supreme Court Justice Oliver Wendell Holmes in decisions and dissents delivered at the turn of the century and the years following.[8] Holmes invariably affirmed the main intent of the First Amendment *in time of peace*. Subversion in time of *war*, however, appeared to him to change the issue. From Holmes' concern emerged the well-known "clear and present danger principle," whereby logic as well as law is called upon to affirm that a government has the right to deny speech intended to destroy its own fundamental institutions when an immediate danger to these institutions is present in that speech—for instance, in time of national emergency. The principle, in the years since it was enunciated, has raised more questions than it has answered.[9] Far from resolved at the writing (because our nation invariably resorts to its shelter when a "clear and present danger" appears in fact or mirage), the principle remains in force at present to the degree that persuasion by censorship in the context of subversion still exists, although the decision of a majority of the Supreme Court concerning the publication of the so-called "Pentagon Papers" vis-a-vis military and diplomatic "security" may portend a sea-change in this custom. The decision, however, was given in haste in the summer of 1971 and will doubtless be reviewed eventually in the light of the "clear and present danger principle" with great care.

The third major focus of censorship was (and is) upon *obscenity*. Often, it serves as a diversion from consideration of other types of censorship, and remains to this day, at the focus of public interest,[10] although, to some, it concerns, essentially, matters of trivia.

The image of the censor most of us hold today, because of his recent preoccupation with obscenity, is that of the neo-puritan, repelled by dirty words, exposure of epidermis, primary and secondary sexual apparatuses,

---

[8] See particularly Holmes' dissent in *Abrams v. the United States* (1919), and his opinion of the court in *Schenk v. the United States* (1919).

[9] Almost every philosopher of free speech in its political contexts in the USA has, since World War I, taken his crack at the "clear and present danger principle," including jurists like Brandeis, who tried to prescribe limits for its application, to philosophers like Chaffee who seem to prefer its Holmesian vagueness. The best discussion of the principle—and the acceptance of a credo of faith concerning the inherent civility of mankind with which I, personally, do not agree—is found in Alexander Meiklejohn, *Free Speech* (New York: Harper and Bros. 1948), pp. 57–91. Meiklejohn brilliantly reviews with care the history and main philosophical elaborations of the principle, through the World War II period, by jurists and students of law, concluding eventually (and in the face of some of his own best arguments) that the principle is essentially destructive to traditional democracy. See also Chaffee, *Free Speech in the United States*, pp. 80–82, for a more objective but less sensitive discussion.

[10] The literature concerning censorship of obscenity is both voluminous and curious. During the 1960's, much of it was merely a cover for publishing so-called "obscene" sections of certain books in pseudo-scholarly contexts. Today, in a book market where pornography in print flows freely, books obviously designed *as* pornography are written *about* censorship, in much the way that pseudo-scientific volumes concerning sexual perversions are actually pornographic documents for those attracted to graphic descriptions of these behaviors.

lurid stories, risqué songs, dirty pictures, lewd photographs and exposure of sensual activities. In sum, he is totally shocked by communications involving most of the activities that most people enjoy most in life. Our stereotype of the contemporary censor is cast in the mold of the one-time President of the New York Society for the Suppression of Vice, Anthony Comstock.[11] His ridiculous, nineteenth-century farce-comedy ghost has influenced the modern construction of the term "censorship" in such a way that some of us do not remember that the word may refer to matters more serious (but not more pleasant) than the descriptive proclivities of certain writers, still and moving photographs of sexual exhibitionists and the apparent desire of the public to make pornographers rich.

Censorship of obscenity originates in English law in the first decade of the eighteenth century. In America, a Philadelphian named Jesse Sharpless was convicted of exhibiting for profit a lewd picture of a woman in 1815.[12] But its recent manifestations are by-products of Victorianism and the results of many factors, including Freudian psychology and a natural attitudinal pendulum swing, among other cultural factors.

It was not until 1868 that the British Justice, the Rt. Honorable Sir Alexander James Edmund Cockburn, centered his legalistic intellect upon a clearly blasphemous and randy booklet entitled *The Confessional Unmasked*, an event of importance in the history of censorship. He also had before him a court decision by one Justice Benjamin Hicklin, setting forth the proposition that a Mr. Henry Scott, who had publicly sold the booklet, had done so with high motives and was therefore not guilty of any crime. As the result of the Queen's appeal in this case, Cockburn rendered a decision in the Queen's Court (overruling Hicklin) that contained a definition —the first in British law—of obscenity. Although many *caveats* have been added to it since, it remains the basis of our present construction of the term.[13]

Justice Cockburn could not, of course, have been aware of the side problems his simple definition was to raise a century later. But, critical to

---

[11] See and enjoy Haywood Broun and Margaret Leech, *Anthony Comstock* (New York: Albert and Charles Boni, 1927), a delightful biography of this colorful figure whose career probably set back his own cause at least a century.

[12] That eternal chestnut, *Fanny Hill, Memoirs of a Woman of Pleasure*, was banned in America in Massachusetts in 1821 for the first time. See Ernst and Schwartz, *op. cit.*, p. 15. She stayed banned in the USA until the 1960's when Mr. Rembar, according to his own account in Rembar, *op. cit.*, rushed about the country setting her free. Of course, thousands (perhaps hundreds of thousands) of copies of this volume had been read by Americans who smuggled them from Europe into their native land. I read *Fanny Hill* for the first (and last) time in the 1930's when I was twelve years old. A high school chum let me savor his copy daily during English period. The rest of the class was reading, I think, *Silas Marner*. I have never, to date, read the complete and unexpurgated *Silas Marner*.

[13] *Regina vs. Hicklin* (1868) and its ramification are amusingly described in Kilpatrick, *op. cit.*, 109–113.

his definition was a *single* notion: that obscene literature (and, by extension, pictures, films, exhibitions and similar phenomena), under certain circumstances, may be understood to "deprave and corrupt" certain individuals. The United States Supreme Court has since further sophisticated this simple notion of depravity and corruption. Most particularly, in the decision in *Roth vs the United States* (1957), the idea was expressed that obscenity might be defined, not entirely in terms of results (depravity and corruption)—which are, after all, often matters of opinion—but, instead, as to whether a communication at hand appeals *solely* "to prurient interests." "Prurience" has to do with itching, and is not the most explicit word the Court might have used. But the Court's intention was quite clear: to exempt from protection of the First Amendment hard-core pornography, dirt for dirt's sake, or whatever one calls it, although defining "hard core pornography" or "dirt" is far more difficult than knowing what they are when you see them or feel their effects below the waist. This the Court, of course, recognized in the choice of the word "prurient."

The ultimate revision of Cockburn's rationale posed two main problems, however. One was that, try as they might, the Justices could not free the concept of obscenity from its previous connection with "depravity and corruption." Qualifications, such as questions concerning who the probable recipient of obscene materials is likely to be and similar necessary considerations, illustrated the Court's obvious concern with corruption. Second, mischief lay in the word "solely." Subsequent interpretations of the "prurient interest" concept have led the Court to indicate that if it is possible to find *any* sort of redeeming virtue in suspected pornography or obscenity, it cannot appeal *solely* to prurient interests. In a society where wide measures of intellectual and moral freedom are permitted, one man's vice is frequently another man's virtue. The reader does not need to stretch his imagination to conceive the rationales for the virtues—logical, psychological and even spiritual—that authorities of various sorts, especially psychologists of the neo-Freudian persuasion, have been able to find for pornography of many kinds, and find quite easily.[14] We shall return below to both of these problems.

---

[14] I have in front of me a book (in modest paperback), Joseph R. Rosenberger, *Bestiality* (Los Angeles: Medco Books, 1968), a supposed "study" of this interesting sexual variation in some detail. Dr. Rosenberger quotes copiously from his "case studies" with such extraordinary detachment that every interviewee recounts his or her sexual adventures in blunt, and apparently unedited, detail. For instance, a prostitute describes minutely, in appropriate Anglo Saxon terms, her techniques for providing party entertainment by masturbating, fellating (actively and passively), copulating and performing analinctus with Count, her collie dog, a sex partner especially trained for such performances. Other equally interesting segments abound. The prurience of this volume is unmistakable, but its social significance is another matter. Supposedly written by a man with a Ph.D. who describes himself as a sexologist (licensed, I wonder?), the volume, I must admit, says *something* about our culture, if only that a good number of people must be curious enough about bizarre sexual contacts with animals to want to read a book about it. Rationales such as this one may be extended *ad absurdum* to include the possible legal protection of such exhibitions as I attended years ago in

All censorship is, in a way, negative persuasion, based crudely upon a premise that what one does *not* see, read, hear or somehow expose oneself to will not hurt one. This proposition is assumptive, but contains considerable common, self-evident wisdom. Granting that *ideas* may corrupt, were one able to single out and control those that are corruptive, men might eventually not know corruption, or so Plato thought in his visions for the *Republic;* and so many continue to think today. By and large, our systems of education and communications industries accept (broadly) this premise. And so does anyone who, in any context, is careful about a suggestion he to their own or someone else's detriment. This is sound behavior, based upon a reasonable assumption that the beliefs, attitudes, opinions and actions of others may be manipulated by suggestions or overt actions. It is logical to believe, therefore, that *withholding* that suggestion or action (particularly when it occurs in symbolic form) will probably prevent that modification of dispositions, if all other factors are under control.

What every adversary of censorship has implicitly denied over the years is that all other factors can possibly be under control, of course, and that selecting suggestions and actions likely to produce unwanted dispositions may be fairly and effectively accomplished without unwanted by-products in the form of severe restraints upon freedom. Idealistic arguments *against* censorship posit, usually, that, in the end, a cultural self-righting process will occur as a natural social eventuality, while good and bad suggestions and actions interact in society. Upon this premise Milton wrote his famous defense of Truth and Falsehood put to "a free and open encounter," stating that truth somehow would inevitably be victorious.[15] Two hundred years later, Mill offered convincing reasons for allowing a free marketplace of ideation: points that centered on the eternal difficulty of determining error, the achievement of justice by debate, and the continual necessity to test error so that truth does not become dogma.[16]

Milton and Mill (and others following them) were practical men as well as idealists, and both recognized the same curious variables which makes, in their own arguments, censorship both unnecessary and necessary at the same time. "I mean not tolerated popery and open superstition," [17] wrote Milton. And Mill begged off his rationale with the qualification that

---

Africa during which a human female copulated publicly with a burro. As interesting (and unforgettable) as the spectacle was, am I to assume that my youthful Candidian presence at the event was an act of social significance? If the answer is "yes," *any* form of human behavior that does not, theoretically, injure someone (I pass over the sensitivities of both the young performer and those of her burro) may by extenuation deserve legal protections. (People may be exploited or debased without being hurt, of course; but this is another matter.) Where, in the other words, do the limits of the operative concept of social value begin and end, and who decides for whom?

[15] John Milton, *Areopagitica* (Appleton-Century-Crofts Inc., 1951), p. 50.

[16] Mill, *op. cit.*, p. 52. Mill's main arguments are briefly summarized here.

[17] Milton, *op. cit.*, p. 52.

"We are not speaking of children or of young people. . . ."[18] Each man feared that falsehood (Milton) and/or error (Mill), if allowed entirely free expression in *certain contexts* to *certain audiences*, just *might* create bad or harmful results.

The same difficulties attend all equally idealistic arguments *in favor of* censorship, the simplest being that the censor figuratively throws the baby out with the bath water, a point well made by Mill's idea that all so-called "error" might contain a "portion of truth." In considering both sides of the ongoing debate, it is notable, however, that society everywhere, formally or informally, appears to favor taking its smallest chances with destiny, that is, encouraging a specified degree of censorship of those communications which may, indeed, deprave and corrupt some segment of the population.

Persuasion by denial of exposure may sound odd, but it is a process often taken for granted when, in the political arena, for instance, the trite claim is entered that the public is the victim of a biased press, and that they are not being given all the facts about a certain issue. A high school biology course that covers its curriculum but says nothing about relevant human sexual behavior may be, in certain instances, another example. So are the sins of omission of important details in contemporary advertising, concerning which consumer groups and Federal agencies often display considerable ire. Because circumstances alone determine the meaning of so much mass communication spread in contemporary culture, what *is not* said or pointed out about a particular matter is as likely to be as important to its audience as is what *is* said, particularly when the intent of that communication is to modify dispositions.

Silence may, at times, therefore, be *most* persuasive. The enforced absense of revolutionary propaganda in a totalitarian state may stifle, for a time at least, the impetus to revolution. Censorship may serve precautionary measures, and, in issues at dispute, what is not said often insulates from guilt or opprobrium those who might say the wrong thing. In certain forms of censorship, this principle is obvious: censorship of letters from front-line soldiers, censorship of information that might create panic or riot, censorship of incomplete news that is likely to be misunderstood and many other instances.

Nearly *all* silence is, however, eventually broken. And, at this point, common sense does *not* serve us well. Almost every sort of communication that people feel they require, they seem competent, somehow, to achieve, even when the weight of law and custom are both imposed against them. Consider, for instance, in the history of the censorship of obscenity and pornography, that every technological instrument of communication yet invented (including television) has been employed *almost immediately at its invention* for the (usually covert) dissemination of pornographic materials. In nations like Germany, during World War II, where press and broadcast-

[18] Mill, *op. cit.*, p. 10.

ing censorship was severe, masses of citizens risked penalties from imprisonment to death in order to listen to enemy broadcasts that, they presumed, told them the truth about the progress of hostilities. Publication in 1971 of the "Pentagon Papers" by *The New York Times* (and other influential newspapers) is a specific application of a general psychological trend that applies to all relevant so-called "secret" documents.

In this regard, the persuasion of censorship seems almost self-defeating, in that it creates the desire for the very forbidden fruit it has grown. True, the individual searching out the fruit knows that it is forbidden, but this knowledge is as likely to accelerate as to discourage him. One must assume that persons so affected have considerable interest in the censored materials and a strong hunch that it exists. Censorship is of little consequence, accordingly, to the apathetic, except to assure the continuation of their apathy—a use to which it has frequently been put in its long history.

Some censorship is directed against exposure to materials that it is generally known *do* exist. Censorship of obscenity is an example, and to the unimaginative, therefore, it seems to serve no purpose, because they suppose that it will somehow be obtained, possibly illegally, by those who want it, and that it is harmless to those who are already familiar with its nature. To a degree they are right, and custom seems increasingly to agree with them. But censorship of the *known* serves a continual cultural function similar to that of the wearing of clothing, protective functions aside. Most wearers of clothes in our society *know* full well what anatomical items are concealed by them, but clothes serve as symbols of societal evaluations tradition has placed upon bodily functions, largely sexual and excretory. Similarly, censorship of the known serves as societal enforcement in the persuasion of cultural taboos, traits, incidentally, of all civilizations. It is never totally effective, because the known is easily communicated to those interested in the enjoyment of breaking taboos. Such individuals replicate the impulse of Dr. Johnson's friend who loved pork so much that he wished he were a Jew and might therefore enjoy the double pleasure of eating pork and committing a sin at the same time.

Censorship of the unknown serves the short-term Platonic function of preventing the immediate occurrence of a presumed evil. This it has accomplished, Milton and Mill notwithstanding, many times in history, but only for brief periods. In the first place, the presumption of the cause of the precise evil in a communication was (and is) frequently incorrect. The evil occurs anyway, but not because of the presumed and censored cause. In the second place, the presumed cause almost invariably leaks somehow, beyond the censor's barrier. And the more apparently potent and dangerous the censored material is, the faster it often escapes its bounds and the wider it is spread. Bad war news, suppressed revolts, subversive doctrines, scandals and similar censor-bait almost invariably find their way to the public despite all counter-measures, usually because releasing such information serves someone's immediate advantage, even that of the mischief-maker.

Contemporary Currents of Censorship

The main question about censorship relevant to the dynamics of persuasion in the West today is, naturally, "Who censors what and why?" The answer is so complex, and so much is censored in our society by so many, that it cannot be answered definitively here. We have noted that trends in censorship change, and that the oscillation of the pendulum is invariably perceived as a liberation from former impositions against free speech. To the conservative, this new period portends dangerous and unwarranted freedoms and the decline of standards. To the liberal, a climate of rationality seems to be increasing in matters of discourse, augering a tendency of men to control sensibly their own destinies. Both viewpoints are distortions of immediate reality. Like generations before us, we are today living through such a period of generally accepted distortions.

Many reasons exist for the present shift in patterns of censorships and taboos, and many rationales are found for them, invariably speculative and probably largely incorrect. The psychological impositions of technology, the popularization of psychology, various currents of inquiry in the field of sociology and changes in patterns of family life are certainly, in some manner, related to them, but, once again, they are lost in muddles of causes and effects.

Obscenity, pornography, profanity and vulgarity are, all in their ways, different issues, but they all share a single historical element in almost every culture where they are found. Being associated with taboos, they are usually relegated to the *private* or personal aspects of living in one or another degree. And so have they been in Western tradition—sometimes, as in Victorian times, so absurdly private and personal as to necessitate a public pretense that neither they, nor any matters pertaining to them, existed at all.[19] Every individual, of course, must indulge daily in numerous behaviors which, if viewed on a wide screen by an audience, would be scatological, profane, vulgar, obscene and possibly pornographic. Sexual intercourse is a frequent manifestation of human behavior that easily becomes blatant pornography when photographed or written about in detail and distributed to voyeurs. Restraints against vulgarity and profanity in speech are often impressed upon groups, but also continually constitute trenchant means of discourse within certain sub-cultures or among peers, usually of the same sex, as those of us who have served in the armed forces have experienced *ad nauseam.*

---

[19] Victorians gave us panties on lamb chops (to spare our sensibilities), as well as lace covers for the legs of chairs and lion's claws to disguise the legs of bathtubs. "Breasts" and "legs" of fowl became "light" and "dark" meat, and so forth. We laugh at these conceits today, but they are merely extenuations of almost universal tenden-

In most traditions, when these special private behaviors are increasingly publicized, they gather social disapproval. The behaviors themselves apparently do not change noticeably, but attitudes towards them do. As these negative attitudes gain currency, they become more and more specified as well, gathering power as discrete opinions that are eventually given legal or extra-legal restraints. Finally, action is the result. Certain of these now public behaviors (or pictures, words and demonstrations) are forced back into the private realm of behavior. This action, of course, is censorship —either legalized or by "gentleman's agreement." The action may also occur by non-legal fiat, for instance when single channels of communication are controlled by a paternal despot, for example, the American broadcasting networks where continuity acceptance departments continually censor material for numerous reasons, as noted previously.

We are, at present, living through a period of decreasing privacy,[20] not the least significant aspects of which have to do with private speech, clothing, excretory functions and sexual behavior. Associated with it is the tendency to eliminate formal and informal restraints formerly associated with these matters. Severed from their historical setting, as they frequently are by certain psychologists and sociologists, exclusive rights to privacy of thought, speech and behavior are ridiculous, as are attempts to censor or control literature or films dealing with them. After all, everybody, including little children, *knows* those nasty Anglo-Saxon words of four letters. Why should we not use them in mixed company or in Congressional debates, for that matter? When bathing costumes cover merely a few inches of mucous membrane, nipples and some pubic hairs, why not dispense with the patent absurdity of two inches of cloth? In a culture in which, among young people primarily, group sexual activities are accepted as norms in *some* measure, why not *every* measure? Why preserve obscenity and pornography restraints upon material in motion pictures and novels? Every adult *knows* what the heroes and heroines of feature films and literature do in private; why not publicize it in Technicolor and purple prose? We live, in short, in an age of publicity and ubiquitous devices for mass communication. Why should we not use them in consonance with a growing social tendency to denigrate both the necessity or desirability of privacy in life and art?

Detached from history, and without recourse to morality, these questions cannot be answered logically, except to accept the demise of privacy and the need to censor matters pertaining to them. Many behavioral scientists (and others), who are frequently aware of the significance of history

---

cies, and no less illogical than the semantic delicacy we employ today to describe an "imbecile," officially recognized by educationists as an "exceptional child" or the euphemism of "insanity" into "mental illness."

20 See Vance Packard, *The Naked Society* (New York: David McKay and Co., 1964), for some deserved righteous indignation concerning an all too apparent trend that has increased considerably since Packard wrote his well documented exposé.

(called pejoratively by them "traditions"), in what they misunderstand to be a scientific style of inquiry, do not wish to make moral judgments. They share exactly these conclusions with other rationalists and latter-day positivists, and are also generally accepted by some of the public, because the auspices of behavioral scientism enhances this viewpoint's persuasive power.

One other factor also confirms this position. It is the unfortunate misunderstanding and vagueness, shared by jurists and academics, concerning the power and ubiquity of taboos in the history of man's cultures. Upon an unmerited premise that obscenity may cause harm (an argument also just as foolishly and frequently resorted to by libertarians and censors), great pains have been taken to show that obscenity and pornography in any form do not cause social or individual dysfunctions. A report of the President's Commission on Obscenity and Pornography[21] recently came quite rationally to this conclusion, and (with a number of dissents from its members) recommends that all legislation forbidding censorship of them be eliminated, except in the case of children. (The latter *caveat* was entered because the Commission's search for corruption had *not* shown that children, specifically, were *not* affected adversely by obscenity and pornography.) The Commission even notes various functional reasons why obscenity and pornography may even be healthy for people, construing "health" in terms of what is currently understood to be desirable personal and sexual behavior.

Upon publication, the Commission's logical inquiry and consistent suggestions were both praised and damned. But its apparent pristine discovery that "depravity and corruption" are will-o'the-wisps was not in the least surprising to those of us who have grown up super-saturated with obscenity and pornography of numerous types, most of it illegal. Were *we* corrupted by it? Did it do *us* harm? The author, for one, believes he was neither hindered nor helped much in his battles with life by it. Nor has he seen many indications, in a quarter of a century of working with children of various ages and sexes, that socially undesirable results inevitably occur when youngsters use foul language and/or look at dirty pictures. Nor does he believe that our society is in danger of falling apart solely because books and pictures of normal and abnormal sex are today apparently both legal and freely available.

The legalists, sociologists and other consultants on the President's Commission, as well as the liberal community of psychologists and sociologists, however, overlook one major consideration in regard to censorship. To the perceptive student of culture, the problems of *harm per se* and *social dysfunction per se* are not necessarily relevant to the issue of whether or not censoring what were once private, but are becoming public affairs is

---

[21] See *The Report of the Commission on Obscenity and Pornography* (New York: Bantam Books, 1970), pp. 7–81, especially. *N.B.* also the assents and dissents of various Commission members on pp. 443–455 and their detailed arguments which follow.

appropriate at a given time. The fundamental issue is one of *individualized morals,* that is, institutionalized *goods* and *bads* that society sanctions either as public matters or reserves for the private realm of life. By dropping sanctions against literature, pictures and films that, to the author, are often stupid, sometimes pleasurable and usually vulgar, the authorities of culture at large are enunciating a clear moral statement (whether they like it or not) in favor of the publications of obscenity and pornography as implicitly *good.* If this is what society wants (and adult human beings with doctoral degrees like Albert Ellis, the Kronhausens, and others certainly want it), well and good. But the maintenance of historical taboos, especially when they relate to individual issues such as intimate, private behaviors, is not something mature legislators overthrow mindlessly, merely because these particular taboos have been scientifically (?) demonstrated to be harmless.

An apt analogy is the eternal problem of prostitution, an ancient and ubiquitous cultural institution. While controlled tests on the matter have, to the best of the writer's knowledge, not been made, the practice of prostitution (given measures to control venereal infection) is probably, by and large, harmless, both to prostitutes and to their customers. In fact, a case may be made *for* prostitution as a variety of therapy for cetrain people in certain ways. (If memory serves well, Philip Wylie once set himself, in an autobiographical novel, to present such a case: and he made it convincingly.) Prostitution is, at present, legal in certain places, and the citizens of those localities seem to survive about as well as residents where prostitution is illegal. Clearly, as in the cases of obscenity and pornography, the impositin of legal prohibitions against whoring is a *moral* choice, based upon the authority of law in relationship to individual behavior, and largely dependent upon tradition, the particular values society wishes to preserve, the examples of decorum it desires to express and its stance in the face of an apparently harmless but, to many, immoral institution.

Cultural relativists avoid these points in regard to patterns of censorship. Nor do they seem cognizant that it is possible that we have come to the end of a trend in regard to obscenity and pornography and will henceforth see reactive forces overswing in a counter-direction. But, in terms of the entire matter of restrained behavior, they are also, often, equally as blind. Delight with insignificant victories of bad writing and masturbatory fantasy (Rembar's beloved *Fanny Hill,* for instance) are diversions, as we have seen, from other changes in the climate of freedom. New impositions on previously open channels of communications are swiftly occurring while many well-meaning libertarians are preoccupied with French postcards.

Privacy extends far beyond matters of sex and profanity, and incursions on freedom, not necessarily confined to censorship, are today moving apace. Political speech, in its broadest sense, seems more constricted by and large today than it did a generation ago, not as much by legal restraints (although numerous and increasing) but by limitations imposed by privately owned communications outlets upon *spokesmen for* unpopular political ideas. There is something to be said for repeated charges that our news reporting establishment tends to reflect discouragingly homogeneous, popular (and usually middle-of-the-road) political sentiments, but this is a minor manifestation of the issue. What about those ideas that are *really* unpopular, that rub even apparently benign politically-oriented liberals the wrong way? Would an anti-Semitic, neo-fascist like Father Coughlin be permitted free access to our nationwide television networks today, as he did on radio in the 1930's? Or just a fascist, anti-Semitic or otherwise? How freely do we at present allow Marxists (who are not necessarily "characters" or "colorful" figures) to present their cases to our people in civil contexts in the national press and over broadcasting channels? When may one find, on commercial television, a program about pollution in which the facts concerning the damage detergents and gasolines cause are phrased in blunt and honest terms? (Never, the writer suspects, as long as soap operas are soapy, and oil corporations sponsor programs). If social and political revolution are indeed in the air, when will our newspapers and news magazines print their rationales without the inevitable "interpretive comment" that makes their copy satisfactory to their advertising departments? (Following revolutionary trends and unconventional political thinking, at present, requires purchasing journals to whom major conduits of distribution are not available and which do not subsist on national advertising.)

Would the brave managers of our educational network assay, presently, a documentary series of programs concerning the history and caprices of the Ford and Carnegie Foundations? Might our TV networks, even now that they are no longer immediately involved with cigarette advertising, screw up courage to present a serious hour's documentation on the *joys* of smoking as articulated in the history of the use of tobacco—or the *evils*—in realistic terms? The writer has yet to read a single reasonable assessment of either the problems of soft drugs (tranquilizers particularly), marijuana or alcohol in a mass magazine that does not somehow bow deeply to both common wisdom and the sensitivities of their readers and advertisers on these issues. He has, however, discussed them in detail with many writers for these periodicals, but what they obviously *know* about the issues rarely appears in print. Nor do their own experiences and those of their families (which often deny contemporary myths and stereotypes) appear in the publications *they themselves write and edit.*

Censorship of many kinds by common consent is accepted as mere "procedure" in the editorial offices and executive suites of our most highly regarded newspapers, news magazines and all broadcasters, even in the managerial echelons of the latters' large local outlets, much less the networks. It operates under the cover of the proprietary rights to freedom of speech by the mass communications establishment, rights exercised with selective, paternal, generally self-serving and periodic obeisances to the obligations they entail, be they statutory or traditional. In essence, these rights to freedom—and, of course, to the selection of who receives them—are not public rights but reside in the hands of a small number of corporate executives whose view of culture is not only bound by ethnocentrism and self-interest, but circumscribed often by personal eccentricities and megalomania (rationalized neatly by questionable scientific data) concerning the desires and needs of the public.

In sum, more people are probably censoring more written and pictorial material more avidly today than any time in our history. Most of it is not accomplished by legal restriction, but it is accomplished within the law. It affirms, in effect the inalienable rights to freedom of speech of a gaggle of corporate directors of our communications' monoliths: the press, film, radio and television. They are free, in the manner oligarchs everywhere are free, to speak as they please, and they please *not* to speak of many things.

The specific obligations of responsibility incurred by those who may speak freely to the masses are entirely clear in our tradition, and have been noted with wisdom and clarity by Hocking[22] in the context of today's communications technology. Self-circumscription in the interest of accuracy, and the interest and rights of the public—even voluntary mandatory censorship under certain conditions—are both moral and ethical necessities in specific critical times for any human being given the public's eyes and ears. And analogous impositions circumscribe interpersonal communications. But censorship exercised exclusively according to clear ethical principles is one kind of restraint. Censorship guided by caprice and personal self-interest is another. Many of today's army of censors are operating in the interests of the small and special constituency they represent, not of the public at large.

Most of us do not notice this practice, however, because we are diverted to a side-show striptease in which the young lady does indeed "take it all off," right to the last stitch. And the gray ghost of Anthony Comstock (now privy to heavenly truths) is unquestionably laughing his ectoplasmic head off at us.

Conclusion

Censorship of one sort or another appears to be a condition under which communications in all cultures operate, most notably those with advanced technologies. To be "for" or "against" censorship is therefore naïve. Considerable evidence indicates that even individual thought is, in a manner of speaking, as circumscribed by psychological impositions, and as continually, as most forms of social discourse. The legal principle that *all* speech in society *cannot* be absolutely free confirms this observation from another perspective.

22 See William Ernest Hocking, *Freedom of the Press* (Chicago: University of Illinois Press, 1947), a thoughtful analysis of the obligations invariably and implicitly assumed by the few who attain the privilege of expressing their ideas to the many.

In our time, however, "censorship" is a pejorative term, and much of it is accomplished under other rubrics, thus making it difficult to observe. Our cultural obsession, at the present moment, is with censorship of obscenity and pornography. But both were late-comers to the censor's eye. During the centuries immediately after its invention, print was censored mostly for blasphemy. Sedition becomes the next focus of censorship and remains an active but unnoticed area of discourse upon which numerous types of restraints are placed today.

A common cultural conceit in liberal democracies is the belief that the amount of censorship at any given time is decreasing and that speech is becoming increasingly free, while quite the opposite situation obtains. This is the case in our society today, because restraints upon censorship of obscene and pornographic materials have, within recent years, decreased dramatically. What is occurring, however, is a shift of censorship along with an apparent shift of cultural taboos. Matters, particularly of a political and socio-cultural nature, that might have been discussed heretofore are often taboo today. But this is little noticed as we exercise our new freedoms to observe our species in the nude, in acts of copulation and practicing vulgarisms one upon the other. Thus liberated, we are now persuaded that we are freer than we were, little noticing enormous measures of control, more extralegal than legal, continually exercised by managers of our instruments of communication on public discourse, even by nine out of ten writers of books and articles *about* communications. The latter find it necessary to echo the views of their corporate patrons and to quiet dissent by means of pseudoscholarly affirmations of the status quo upon which they depend for patronage.

We are presently free from censorship, in other words, as long as we do *not* try to use the instruments of communication in society—largely radio, television, much of the press and films—to say unpopular things, particularly those notions that offend current arbiters of established wisdom, be they corporate magnates, legal solons, academic gurus or other exponents of that mythological *bouillabaise*, the current "best" thinking. But should we wish to express the "worst," we are usually censored, either by denial of access to the public forum directly, or by the man with the blue pencil who is busier today than he ever was.

Part Five

HUMANISTIC PERSUASION

If my hypothesis is correct, the primary function of writing, as a means of communication, is to facilitate the enslavement of other human beings. The use of writing for disinterested ends, and with a view to satisfactions of the mind in the fields either of science or the arts, is a secondary result of its invention—and may even be no more than a way of reinforcing, justifying, or dissimilating its primary function . . . The struggle against illiteracy is indistinguishable, at times, from the increased powers exerted over the individual citizen by central authority. For it is only when everyone can read that Authority can decree that "ignorance of the law is no defense."

Claude Lévi-Strauss

The most remarkable paradox of our time is that, in proportion as the instruments of communication have increased in number and power, communication has steadily declined. Mutual intelligibility is probably a rarer phenomenon now than at any time in human history.

Robert Hutchins

Chapter 27

PERSUASION AND PROPHECY

Human freedom is not a postulate; it is a fact, which is present or absent in degree. In the course of human history, most people have had precious little of it. In the affluent societies of the contemporary world, they have more of it than ever before, but they enjoy it insecurely. It can be frightening. Too few of them have been raised so as to be endowed with inner capacities for freedom—responsiveness as a person to the wishes of the self—that match their widened range of outer responsibility. Free will itself is caused; it is an achievement, not a paradoxical assumption.

M. Brewster Smith

PROPHECY is invariably persuasion.

Merton modestly acknowledges[1] W. I. Thomas as the original author of his concept of the "self-fulfilling prophecy." But Thomas was referring to the psychological truism that man's personal construction of reality is the *only* reality he knows. Merton is concerned with action in a social context, wherein fears (and hopes) are woven variously into the cultural fabric of the apprehended future and accordingly appear in the form of prophetic beliefs, attitudes and opinions of the people who create that future. Self fufilling prophecies, from a sociological orientation, occur in relatively discrete, and on measurable, social occasions. Prophecy at large may influence the destiny of a total culture, but its influence is rarely discrete or measurable, filtered, as it is, from prophet to social field to myth and then into the future.

Prophets of various kinds have walked beside historians since antiquity, and they have always found listeners. When a culture approaches a landmark, an anniversary or a numerical mystical time period, like "the year 2000," prophecy increases, as well as in times of apparent social, political and materialistic high aspiration or apparent novelty. In all probability, no more prophets per thousand people are on the loose in our culture at pres-

[1] See Robert K. Merton, *Social Theory and Social Structure,* pp. 475–490, for the negative face of this famous postulate: that is, of the events that result from fears that are treated as social reality. Self-fulfilling ideation has a positive (although

ent than in other recent periods, but their prophecies are given publicity more freely, because public interest in them runs high.[2]

To construe the avidity of our avid grasp after prophecy as an index of uncertainty about the future is to belabor the obvious. In a personal and cultural sense, Moore, Butler and Bellamy, who lived in eras we sometimes sentimentalize as "secure," probably also perceived their own future prospects with considerable anxiety. And their prophecies had their effect upon their own and others' attitudes, which, in themselves, influenced the future in subtle ways.

The single most influential prophet of our immediate tradition in the West was Jules Verne. Little is especially interesting about his visionary constructions of either science or technology. Verne knew almost nothing about the former and not much more about the latter. Nevertheless, a coherent science-fiction image emerges from his works. He is responsible, among other things, for the notion of Captain Nemo and his "other world," along with other equally imaginary notions that, in large measure and over a long time, helped encourage our technology to dispatch an insulated pair of men to the moon for what were essentially Vernian romantic reasons. By reason of his humor and clever writing, he is also one of the fathers of the notion of controlling by technological means the aspirations of men, popularizing, in his time, crude cybernetic notions in such delightful works as *Around the World In Eighty Days.*

The long history of prophecy has demonstrated clearly two major points: First, the future is unknowable, and the only working generalization one may make about it is that the unexpected and unforeseen are both likely to happen. If one, therefore, considers the predictive consensus of the wisest minds in history, this consensus has been invariably wrong. But, because even the worst fool is correct sometimes in some of his nonsense, a second generalization is also inevitable: *elements* of culture that will be important in the future can and will be predicted accurately by some prophets some of the time. This is the shotgun approach to prophecy that

possibly destructive) face as well, whereby hopes and aspirations—no matter how wild—are concretized in the unfolding of events and creation of myths and illusions.

[2] Assorted prophets have received considerable exposure on television, and countless dreary prophetic articles in periodicals abound these days—roughly one per issue, at least, in family magazines. McLuhan, early in his career, ran out of relevant meaningful observations concerning technology and has been functioning during the last decade mostly as a prophet who, along with Buckminster Fuller and a few others, are as likely to influence currents of behavior in the future as any other seers presently crystal-gazing. In formal literature, current prophetic material is both dense and popular. Much of it is encapsulated in Alvin Toffler, *Future Shock* (New York: Random House, 1970), a breathless assault on the reader by a high-pressure futurist discussed below. See also the far better essays in Irving Falk (ed.), *Prophecy for the Year 2000* (New York: Julian Messner, 1970); Herman Kahn and Anthony J. Weiner, *The Year 2000* (New York: Macmillan Co., 1967); Theodore J. Gordon, *The Future* (New York: St. Martin's Press, 1965); and Daniel Bell (ed.), *Towards the Year 2000* (Boston: Houghton Mifflin, 1968), among others. *Caveat emptor.*

professional fortune tellers often employ, confident that their clients will remember their few correct predictions and forget the wrong ones. Toffler, Kahn and Weiner and others, for instance, cover the waterfront of popular possibilities for social and technological change in culture, and therefore they will be correct, in some measure, about some of the prospects they offer.

With the same breath, therefore, reasonable critics may affirm the wisdom of *both* Huxley in *Brave New World* and of Orwell in 1984 in predicting correctly certain aspects of culture seen in society today, decades after both books were written. In a way, they were both right, although specific projections in the two books are entirely different one from the other, and, taken as wholes—that is, in general theses—both visions of the future (still remote from the present writing) appear, in many ways, to be differently distorted projections of unwarranted apprehensions. In other words, both Huxley and Orwell were poor prophets, although they were lionized in their day, and may be defended at present, as partly correct (which is more or less inevitable) as well as superb story-tellers.

This is also the inevitable fate of Robert Heinlein, Arthur C. Clarke (in fiction and non-fiction), Ray Bradbury and their colleagues as their predictions meet the future, although it is presently—and probably will be—far harder to accuse them of being superb story tellers. They are all shortgun artists, enamoured of a few main thrusts in their work: extra-human worlds, control of time and space or one or another romantic popularizations of ancient philosophical puzzles.

In the case of Toffler, whose recent book has been extremely successful, the situation is somewhat sadder, because, in his simplistic view of history, he is so utterly amazed to discover that nothing is permanent. Having been devastated by this modest and reasonable conclusion (valid under certain circumstances), he urgently postulates the earth-shattering thesis that sometimes change upsets people. So it does, but Toffler (and, one assumes, his wily editors) expands this tiny corner of common wisdom into the alarmingly phrased syndrome he calls "future shock."[3] Having created the disease, Toffler then heroically articulates a cure-all—composed in the monotonous but urgent language of the mass press—with the disarming innocence of a man who interprets every rumble in his own stomach as an earthquake.

(That Toffler is still at it—and successful—is an indication of the immunities we grant prophets. In 1964, he was noisily predicting[4] a cultural renaissance in America and advanced a theory—more elaborate than "future shock"—of an impending diversity of culture via mass communications: that is, greater exposure by more people of various forms of culture,

---

[3] Toffler, *op. cit.*, pp. 295–315.

[4] See Alvin Toffler, *The Culture Consumers* (New York: St. Martin's Press, 1964).

art and education as the result of new technology at hand. While he still appears attracted by this idea,[5] he has apparently not noticed that nearly all types of diversity in mass culture have, in recent years, decreased at the same time that circulation has vastly increased. Giants now dominate the mass culture market, while midgets try to imitate them, yielding far less diversity in television and in the newspaper press, particularly. What Toffler, in this regard, does not seem to have discovered in six or more years is that large circulations and plurality of output do not necessarily create *diversity*. To a World's Fair intelligence like his, long lines of differently packaged breakfast cereals in a supermarket—all containing, more or less, the identical product—is a demonstration of diversity of production and breadth of consumer choice.[6] In fact, it is a manifestation of quite the opposite trend.)

By a converse quirk of fate and logic, the anti-prophet, or what, in one of his sager moods, Toffler calls the Denier,[7] is in as safe a position in his skepticism as the prophet, because he too *must* both be right and wrong in the face of the unknowable. The Denier, however, has less to show than the futurist for his pains of restraint. But no reader will misconstrue history or misjudge the future if he follows Thoreau's dictum, "Let him not quit his opinion that a popgun is a popgun, 'though all the ancient and honorable of the earth affirm it to be the crack of doom."

Historical conservative tendencies, like the inertia of rest, work on the sides of both Denier and futurist, making prediction or nay-saying comparatively safe occupations. Nor have many popular writers recently diminished their popularity by repeating the eternal, stereotyped premises of the futurist: 1.) the future will be vastly different from the past; 2.) the future will be better than the present, but notions of what is "good" and "better" will change; 3.) the present is a period of transition between (something) and (something); 4.) no generation has had the options, challenges and power to change the present that this one has; 5.) rules and guidelines drawn from the past simply do not apply to the present; 6.) doom portends if we do not construct our destiny in a certain (specifically described in a well loop-holed way); 7.) values tomorrow will be radically different from values today.

The professional prophet or futurist enhances the personal feeling of importance of his audience, of course, with his bagful of illusions in much the same way as a high school valedictorian with his cliché about the destiny of the nation residing in the hands of the young—to the historian, as incorrect and mischievous a notion as has ever been compounded by man.

---

[5] See Toffler, *Future Shock*, pp. 132–156. This section may encourage the sensitive reader to doubt the wisdom of the invention of printing.

[6] Consider the basic reasoning involved in *ibid.*, pp. 226–231.

[7] *Ibid.*, pp. 308–315. This concept is one of Toffler's better notions.

The future, in truth, does not reside in anybody's hands, and the best historical evidence indicates that much of it has, at any moment, already been "forged" (if that is the correct word) by people who are dead, buried and rotted. In terms of prophecy, the young are probably best regarded as instruments of the old. They are, however, more likely than the mature to believe the futurist's flattery—in fact, to believe *anything* that expands their delicate egos and makes them feel important.

While the blind adulation of history is just as heinous (if more difficult) an intellectual crime as futurism, common notions about the value of past experience are frequently correct. Machiavelli notes that, in order to foresee the future, we must look backwards, because present problems are invariably similar to past ones. "This arises from the fact," he wrote, "that they are produced by men who ever have been, and ever will be, animated by the same passions, and thus necessarily have the same results." This is one proposition that the futurist denies, because he invariably posits that human nature and motives are continually (or at least *now*) involved in a process of change, although history severely denies this assumption. (Santayana once warned us that to forget the lessons of history is to doom oneself to relive them, an adage more applicable as a psychological generalization than as a historical one.)

In its function as persuasion, however, the myth of futurism is often more influential than either the impetus of the present moment or the record of the past, producing, therefore, strange consequences that require examination.

Futurism and Myth

Oracles, seers, haruspices, soothsayers and other fortune tellers have been, since pre-history, associated with most cultures and have performed many functions besides predicting the future: namely, managing, in their magical ways, the present behaviors of people by means of usually benign but crude attempts at social services, psychosomatic medicine, population control and (sometimes) political analysis. Shakespeare's soothsayers are fairly sophisticated examples of such oracles as socio-political and psychological manipulators; *Caesar* and *Macbeth* come immediately to mind. In more primitive traditions than those of the Elizabethans, functions of the futurist were and are much the same, but the soothsayer is more obviously a spokesman for the gods than for man or his institutions.

Thus, futurism has a long history in myth and one which displays unusual freshness in periodical revivals of the classics. The futurist's means of persuasion is powerful because he asks—and always has asked—absolute acceptance or rejection. The more ambiguous, also, the values of any culture, the more likely is the futurist to give them form and direction, and, sometimes, meaning.

The Greek demi-god Tiresias was the prototypical futurist, although extant myths about him are contradictory. It is significant that Tiresias had lost his sight, blinded, in various legends in different ways, invariably by a woman. He was, thereafter, somehow given second sight, also usually by a female demi-god. The source of this gift accounts for his appearance in various epics and plays as an hermophrodite, set apart from the limited visions, therefore, of both mortal men or women. In certain tales he is nevertheless the father of various daughters, all of whom also become soothsayers. Most important, it is generally agreed that the gift of longevity (about three times the normal life span) was given him, although he died an ironical death—as victim of a catastrophe that he himself had predicted.

The bulk of Tiresias' predictions concerned death and destruction, but they also centered, as do the interests of today's futurist, upon the conflicts between men with enormous forces beyond their control. Oedipus was the cruel victim of his own tragic *past*, the main points of which Tiresias cleverly inverts into predictions of the *future*. And indeed, as various messengers unfold their discoveries on stage, they *are* the future. Fundamentally, Oedipus' *hubris* or pride was a matter beyond his control; the gods had already determined that he kill his father and marry his mother, these critical acts have been completed *before* the play begins. And, as his personal future unfolds on stage, he is warned at every step by Tiresias to inquire no further. But, being a man of pride, Oedipus *does* inquire to his eventual ruin.[8]

The contemporary shotgun futurist operates more in the manner of Tiresias than highly specialized oracles and/or contemporary tea-leaf types like Jeane Dixon, Maurice Woodruff and company. Nor is the modern futurist a Nostradamus who set himself to the construction of long-range generalities that, he claimed, would occur after his death, and constituted more or less inevitable components of history to come. (For this reason, anyone content to achieve lasting fame after his or her demise is free to emulate Nostradamus—if he finds some way of being noticed in a century or two.) Nostradamus' basic predictive focus, however, was identical to Tiresias': the conflict between man and forces beyond his control.

In the contemporary futurist's constructions, "man" is generalized into society at large—as was Oedipus, held to be the cause of the foul sickness in the air of Thebes. And the forces beyond man's (or society's) control are usually myths compounded of the popular admixture of science and technology—neither science nor technology in *fact*, but their collective images. Tiresias invariably predicted doom. Our modern seers indeed offer doom as an alternative to salvation, but tend to elect a cheerier frame of mind. The fundamental sin of *hubris* remains the main contemporary futuristic sub-

[8] For an intelligent discussion of the Oedipus myth as drama, see H.D.F. Kitto, *The Greeks* (New York: Doubleday and Co., 1952). I hesitate to single out any section of this volume as more revealing of Greek futurism than another, but see especially the excellent discussion of Sophocles' *Oedipus the King* on pp. 142–149.

ject, however. Man (or society) is still in conflict with contemporary fates, and, like the Greek heroes, the unwitting author of the vengeance that they portend. Our contemporary problems are not murder and incest (except metaphorically), but rough equivalents, including the violation of countless taboos that result from our guilt in tampering with nature—not, as in Attic myth, with "the infernal machine," as Cocteau calls fate. Pollution problems, traffic deaths, overpopulation, drug addiction, atomic warfare, cigarette-caused cancers, executive coronaries, suicides, homicides, mental illness, urban crime, poisons in our food and the full chronicle of our most powerful mythic contemporary evils (or potential evils) are equivalent to the sins of Oedipus, because they are all perceived by most of us as results (and just retribution) for the *hubris* in the application of our techno-science to God's environment.

To these harsh issues the futurist brings in reality hindsight. The crimes man has committed *have passed:* the atmosphere is *already* contaminated, the atom bomb *has been* set off, children glut continents and people starve *now*. But, in the manner of Tiresias, this history cleverly becomes the future. Futurism is the drama of discovery. It arrives in special issues of magazines, breathless books and pronunciamentos from gurus—all occurring *now* as contemporary events, just as Oedipus' discovery and self-destruction are contemporary events to the spectator at a re-enactment of *Oedipus*.

So the wisdom of the futurist is therefore verified in two ways: First, he identifies and calls attention to specific evils that myth accepts as transgression against nature or fate. Second, he is likely to anticipate (as Tiresias anticipated) the unfolding of relevant predictions on the stage of culture, because he is merely describing the past and waiting for the effects of former events to appear in the present. When they do not appear, as is often the case, he has merely read history poorly and is forgotten. This is the case of most science-fiction writers today (Isaac Asimov excepted) who are not educated in, or familiar with, much history, science, technology, or cultural analysis.

Futurism derives its power solely from its mythic dimensions. Another way of putting this axiom is that futurists do not generally deal in trivia as fortune tellers, for instance, do. Their currency of discourse centers on the important matters of society: the myths that indeed *do* result from man's startling impudence in the face of fate and nature. Science is one such impudence, but not usually startling, because its findings are less mythically powerful than informational and intellectual. Technology *is* a remarkably startling impudence, and for this reason one of the main by-products of its thrust in the past century are the many myths that have been generated about it.[9] They may, of course, be studied modestly and analysed free from

---

[9] See Chapter 5 where these myths are discussed as cultural data of Western society.

their mythic orchestration, as they have been, for instance, in a positive vein by Ferkiss and more negatively by Ellul.[10]

To the futurist, such non-mythic or anti-mythic constructions of technology—the effects of technology described without positive or negative assumptions concerning the results of man's *hubris*—are unrealistic, and, from his viewpoint, mystical in some measure, because he is incapable of understanding them. The futurist *cannot* comprehend that science and technology (and their results) inevitably, and in some measure, fail because of man's halting and sometimes quite feeble efforts to bend nature in the direction that he *thinks* will be a convenience, but often is not.

Thus does McLuhan accuse us of future blindness (looking through a rear-view mirror, he calls it) and, in analogy, he is correct—about *himself* in exaggerating the enormity of change that communications technology will, he predicts, produce in tomorrow's world. What he (like most futurists) is reacting to, in fact, is the immensity of the *hubris* (and its guilt) that technology has *already*, in its random, blundering way, produced in mythically sensitive men. Toffler, on another, less sensitive level of perception, cannot comprehend why we are not rendered breathless at the technological innovations of society of the *past* fifty years: in fact, the "future" period about which he writes. He diagnoses as endemic sickness various misconstructions (felt by most of us) of this rich technological mythology that he, as a layman, has been sold by tunnel-visioned technological specialists. The latter, incidentally, rarely lack *hubris*.

Response chords to the futurist are naturally felt by many, particularly in those who experience guilt in their own dependence upon technology. Some of our affronts to nature are all too obvious. Our awe of new giant aircraft, for instance, is often tempered by fear of it and, to some degree, guilt that we are (perhaps) unworthy of such magnificent transportation. Should a futurist like Toffler be forced regularly to ride the New Haven Railroad at commuter hours from his home in Connecticut to New York City and back, his immense awe at man's conquest of nature might be leavened, but only regarding railroads—not so long ago, myth-generating miracles of major dimensions themselves. Toffler would still stand aghast at the enormity of choices in his Ridgefield supermarket, unless he began, by some miracle, to examine realistically both the cultural and economic deterministic limitations of that choice.

Public response, by and large, to myths (especially technological myths) is usually greatest where and when general ignorance is also greatest. Our awe increases, and myths become most tenable, in matters about which we have little specific knowledge. Note, for instance, how space myths have, in fiction and public discourse, fallen off since the actual mechanics of moon exploration were broadcast so widely. Rocketry, seen as a

10 Both Ferkiss, *Technological Man* and Ellul's *Technological Society* are discussed—with dissents from their conclusions—in the chapter cited above.

not-so-recent offshoot of aviation, and the moon as a mineral heap, are not conducive to myths, although scientists and others have attempted manfully to persuade the public that the Apollo missions have provided important scientific data concerning something-or-other, efforts that diminish once-potent space myths still further.

Laser beams, another not-so-recent technological novelty, are, however, still mythically viable. All of the things that *have been done* with laser light (drilling holes, measuring true distances, keeping bridges straight, producing so-so three dimensional photographs and storing "information") are grist for the mill of the futurist to inflate as expansively as he wishes, and quite safely. When we see, use and adjust our lives to lasers—or discard them—their mythos will accordingly diminish. They will constitute an interesting and clever way of employing part of the light spectrum, in much the way that oxide tape for sound reproduction is today accepted as a mundane cultural artifact. Our living rooms did not become concert-halls, as the futurist predicted when tape-recorders were invented. Nor were most of us eager to preserve on tape the joy of baby's first cry, the thrill of our marriage vows and similar experiences—not because there was anything wrong with tape technology, but because the futurist's myths disappeared along with the joy and thrill of the events we recorded.

We have been treating characteristics of the real world and the real future: one of inevitable personal decay and death and, these days, the birth of a rapid succession of new mythologies. The futurist, of course, is not interested in these real matters. And if there is some way he may promise the myth of eternal life (or, *a la* Huxley, the illusion of it), he certainly will. Worst of all, the futurist literally *cannot* deal with the *one* unpopular (and therefore non-persuasive) fact that his example may, if read well, teach the present moment: that is, the fact that the future remains inevitably problematical.

The Future and Illusion

Future myths are simply descriptions of certain kinds of present dispositions. As we have seen, guilt and fear are among the main dynamics of the mythos of the future. The greatest psychological value of the intelligent oracle, be he Tiresias or Verne, is not that he dulls the edge of a necessarily frightful future, but rather that he exculpates people from the anxiety of the past. Technology has had an ambivalent history. But even in its benign phases, its lethal by-products emerge all too clearly. Prediction of technical wonders-to-come makes up, in some measure, for damage that has already been done, or so we often feel. Fortune tellers know that the anxieties of their clients center largely upon three areas of life. They, therefore, frame their predictions so as to comfort disturbances stemming from these sources. They are first, love; second, money; and third, health. The futurist responds to much the same sort of anxieties, but he is concerned with love, money and health in their larger and mythical, psycho-social manifestations.

Some future myths, of course, are more fully justified by history than others, and center on natural curiosities as to what is likely to become of the human race. The future development, for instance, of modern gadgetry is an interesting, if somewhat unprofitable, game that anyone may play.[11] So is conjecture about the fate of our cities, future food supplies, problems of leisure time and similar subjects—particularly the supposition that technology somehow alters the ontological state of man and will eventually and inevitably also change his methods of perception by chemical and electronic means.[12] The latter topic is, of course, one favorite concern of nearly all futurists, and an extremely antiquated one (found in More's *Utopia* and Plato's *Republic*): a vision that the mind of man will, like the rest of nature to which he is spuriously compared, yield to the same sort of manipulation as rivers, soya beans, atoms and nucleic acids in order to generate, through some form of evolution or another,[13] (or by biological, chemical and/or, electronic conrol) a new *Homo modernus*.

Such visions obey the general rules of all futuristic thinking, in that they are essentially forms of regressive exculpation and invariably infantile in their premises. They sound a bit like genuine philosophy. But they have, in fact, moved not a jot beyond the textbook puzzles of Descartes and Bishop Berkeley and are anchored firmly in eighteenth century rationalism. They are not philsosophical; they are entirely illusions, centering basically upon cultural and psychological misconstructions of the relationship of men to society and, therefore, to our own beliefs, attitudes and opinions.

These illusions of mind take many forms (including re-definitions of the word "mind" itself), but one common example, accepted as a futuristic truth by academicians, librarians, statesmen *and* futurists should serve as a paradigm for other instances in which common wisdom has opted for bogus philosophy, dubious myth and clever illusion.

---

[11] When I was a child, I remember adults (including some scientists and technicians) predicting with great precision prophecies concerning what tomorrow's automobiles would be like. I cannot remember anyone who predicted that the "car of tomorrow" would be, substantially, almost identical to contemporary automobiles (except for automatic shifts and power features), although more expensive, more shoddily built, more difficult to repair, and, in many instances, uglier.

[12] This kind of nonsense is silenced most effectively by the one physiologist who has, to date, in fact achieved the greatest degree of sophistication in his experiments, having implanted electrodes in the brains of apes and men. See Delgado, *Physical Control of the Mind*, pp. 231–262, in which science-fiction implications of the author's fascinating work are treated to a well-earned debunking.

[13] The biological limits of this kind of prediction are well spelled out in P. B. Medawar, *The Future of Man* (New York: Mentor Books, 1959), who foresees a Lamarekian-style evolution possible for the human organism, but extremely limited in its capacity to create new men.

Let us take up the well-known issue of the so-called *knowledge explosion.*

Problems posed by the supposed recent increase in human knowledge (rarely defined) during the past century appears to be such a self-evident proposition that they are rarely, if ever, questioned. These propositions are based upon a reasonable premise: that we know more about more things today than ever before, and it is therefore nearly impossible to move beyond one's specialism in one of thousands of so-called "natural divisions" of knowledge. To integrate, or handle, discrete parts of this mass of knowledge, sophisticated instruments of rapid access like computers are necessary to find what one is looking for. But, because of the plethora of exploded information, it is also difficult, under many circumstances, even to know the very options that one may take within this mass of data. In other words, it is near-impossible for an individual to know what information he is searching out, so explosive has been our genius for collecting important material.

This viewpoint is based upon common sense and common experience, and, in some measure, it is the truth, but neither a truth of explosive nor overwhelming dimensions. It depends for its apparent validity upon a "Sears-Roebuck catalogue" conception of knowledge that, by analogy, fills a single catalogue up with more and more choices, as more items are offered for sale. Print gets smaller, and one catalogue spawns another, and another, and another, and so forth. Because we appear to know today so much more than ever before, the Sears-Roebuck mentality interpets knowledge, therefore, as somehow stored in discrete catalogues, each titled according to its proper subject and piled ever higher and wider.

To deny the Sears-Roebuck analogy completely is, of course, absurd. True enough, we *do* know more about more *things* today than we did one hundred years ago, but not tremendously more, as much as this observation may injure our hard-earned vanity. What we have accomplished, thanks to modern technology, is to have stored more *data* than formerly—an enormous amount, perhaps. But *knowledge* is one thing and *data* are another. What, we may correctly ask, *are* these data and how do they relate to what we know?

In the first place, the amount of present duplication of data is unbelievable for many practical reasons that are relatively simple to comprehend. Far more difficult to discern is the way in which data have duplicated as the results of conventions of thought that have created knowledge specialties and knowledge specialists. Most subject matter specialties were invented long before their subject matters were clearly defined and delimited —one reason, the author suspects, why most discrete disciplines, as we know and teach them today, are neither hazy or arbitrary, but merely insane. Like most other culturally sanctioned psychotic social and intellectual institutions, however, the issue of subject matter specialties does not permit much argument. In other words, enormous amounts of data labeled "history," "sociology," "biology" and "physics," are entered again and again within our discrete catalogues and among them, sorting away the same "knowledge" under different categories with elegant precision.

One flagrant example is sufficient to illustrate the point. The "nature-nurture" controversy in an old cultural problem that asks a comparatively simple question, "What components of human behavior are inherited, and what parts are given by culture, and, if the two intermix, how, when and where does the combination generally occur?" Some excellent and brilliant answers—perhaps as many as twenty that might fill a book this size—have been given, with any degree of sense, to this problem at this present point in our ignorance. Armies, however, of historians, psychologists, philosophers, social scientists, biologists, sociologists and numerous other specialists have taken off in countless directions in pursuit of the answers to this question, mostly within the gentile heuristic traditions of their specific disciplines. And the heat, light and (mostly) data that have resulted from these explorations has been immense. In general, the intelligent and honest findings of these specialists confirm one another, a pleasant serendipity. But they also illustrate enormities of waste, duplication, conceit and, inevitably, ignorance of what is going on, or is known, outside one's own field of specialism.

Do the voluminous catalogues of data, theories, conclusions, analyses etc., pertaining to this issue and piled up as, in fact, symbolic sacrifices to the myth of specialty, illustrate an expansion or portend an explosion of knowledge? Hardly. Knowledge, it is true, about nature and nurture has grown slowly and modestly, impeded, in fact, not by an explosion of knowledge, but by the blockage of data that over-specialization has created.[14] The application of computer technology to this problem does not change it fundamentally. The most sophisticated access system used in handling it merely substitutes dynamic and busy intellectual back-ups and blockages for static ones.

---

[14] Please do not regard these paragraphs as a polemic against specialty. Certain people do certain things better than they do other things. But specialty carried to extremes —as it has been for years in our culture—is both foolish and dangerous, as super-specialist trends in both medicine and dentistry today clearly illustrate. Whitehead presents a vision of education (and an attendant heurism) that allows for specialty, at the same time stressing the need for understanding of many types of significant matters in breadth, thereby creating a contradiction, in both education and culture at large, that may only be handled by accepting the concept of the general-specialist or specialized-generalist. See *The Aims of Education*, pp. 21–24. Whitehead himself was, by specialty, a mathematician, and, were he a young scholar at work in our country today, chances are he would be filling our catalogues with mathematical concepts already utilized in other disciplines. Living as he did in early twentieth century Britain (where contradictions were considered less sinful than in the United States), he was free to apply his giant intellect to numerous subjects with equal agility.

In addition to duplication, for many reasons (less heuristic than pig-headed), much of the data in our extant catalogues is incorrect, obsolete, irrelevant, incomplete, incompetent and transient in interest, even to specialists in blinders. How much? Perhaps half; perhaps more—most of it with one or another imprimatur of intellectual respectability upon it. While the recent trend to boil down knowledge into summaries and develop sophisticated categories for it may, in slight measure, help to eliminate some duplication, it cannot express relative values in the remaining data, because the articulation of value requires comparative judgment. Without the free application of value judgments, the problem of worthless data becomes, therefore, the agent of its own metastasis.

True enough, recent forays into art, science and technology have left us with a number of important and valuable generalizations that constitute almost a skeleton key to this knowledge dump (a more accurate term than "explosion"), but even here a problem arises. Generalizations are of greatest use to generalists; specialists are frequently annoyed by them and, outside of those that apply in mechanical fashion to their specialty, are usually incompetent either to appreciate or understand them. This occurs because the true specialist, whose expertise has been limited, not by nature or epistemology but by treaty and fiat, is, in the words (previously quoted in this volume) or Ortega y Gasset, a "learned ignoramus." And ability to handle or apply even this skeleton key (with its relatively modest offerings) is severely limited.

Most university faculties are largely collections of "learned ignoramuses," or at least *good* universities are. Bad universities are simply made up of "specialized ignoramuses," whose specialties may or may not involve some learning. This situation is not necessarily a poor reflection of the individuals involved, who, in their way, are some of the most well-meaning idealists in our culture. It is rather the organization of their schools and institutions, with their disconnected diversions and competitive departments, that is one major factor destroying higher education today. It is, whether the offending parties know it or not, one of the main causes for and focal points of student rebellions and demands for *relevance*. In fact, academic university structure is presently a monument to the illusion of the knowledge explosion, the tragedy of over-specialization and the futuristic canard that *man*, who brought forth so much magnificent scientific and technological truth, is competent to manage it in *godly* fashion. *Vanitas vanitatum, omnia vanitas.*

Hence, our current attempts at educational systems and strategies, information access devices, computerized instruction and so forth are all built upon illusion at worst, or pathetic attempts to ameliorate a hopelessly idiotic logjam of data at best. All intellectual life is therefore increasingly less and less "relevant," as students use the term. ("Disconnected" is a better word). The sustenance of two futuristic illusions are, therefore, necessary for this tragedy: first, the information explosion, and, second, "the man of tomorrow" who will be all brain, no brawn.

This is but the story in outline of but *one* such illusion and its influence upon contemporary culture. There exist countless others.

Prophecy and Purpose

While the following may be, in some ways, too facile an observation, the realistic social function of prophecy—the ends to which most professional futurists are unwitting dupes—is the constriction of freedom and free choice in the present. In this sense, prophecy always has been, and will continue to be, doctrinaire contemporary persuasion of the strongest kind, sometimes on behalf of the status quo, and sometimes for carefully manipulated and directed change. It matters little whether the prophecy is positive or negative. Its degree of understood certainty is its major significant factor. And the better a futurist can sell his apparent vision, the more likely he is to exert this persuasion.

Futurist persuasion provides absolutely certain persuasion, naturally, when dealing with certainties. To predict to an agrarian peasant that his progeny will be raised in the same life-style as he has been, and that they will be subject to the same deterministic forces as he has, must serve as a social control which restricts whatever small options the peasant may actually have over his children's future. To predict that his children will be liberated from peasantry, spearhead a revolution or see great changes in their lives may be unrealistic, but the moment is present, at least, invested with a modicum of possibility for the action of free will. In both instances, because all prophecy involves both the nature and direction of change, opportunities for transcending the limits of prophecy are eliminated.

Modern prophets, for instance, keep producing images of cities (images usually of the most unattractive aspects of urban life) which stress novelty, technology, destruction of old neighborhoods, specialism and other features that, Jane Jacobs excepted,[15] portend a vision of stainless steel, iron and glass monoliths for the future. These fantasies are the models by which we have come to regard "ideal" cities. Our freedom to make other choices, and to conceive other options, are thus eliminated. Were we, for

---

[15] See Jane Jacobs, *The Economy of Cities* (New York: Random House, 1969). Jacobs is not a futurist, and is therefore one of the few urban experts who is free to delineate the wide and exciting possibilities for variations in city structure possible in the years to come. Like the author, she prefers the potentials of urban living to the suburban, exurban or rustic life. But, also like the author, she is the victim of futuristic visionaries who regard city living as essentially obsolete. Old cities (and old sections of others) are entirely viable, and there exists no economic, technical, stylistic or functional imperatives that command cities to give up old patterns of residence and work to accept new ones. Numerous cities have been destroyed as nice places to live and work in, in large measure by urban planners and architects who reside in dismal exurbs or remote retreats, and *hate* city life. Their futuristic visions, therefore, tend to turn cities into hateful, cruel, and difficult places in which to live.

instance, to attempt to replicate functionally in tomorrow's cities the pace, charm and life styles of *yesterday's* Boston, New Orleans or Baltimore, we would be considered either hopelessly out of step with progress or deluded. There are no good reasons, however, why our cities of tomorrow must be accommodated to the futurists' mold, serving instead, let us imagine, as ideal places for living and raising children, except for the prophets' generally accepted prediction that this state of affairs *cannot be*. In spite of the large measure of choice we have in this matter, we are not generally aware of our options and therefore continue in a path that we believe is unavoidable: in the case of cities, rendering them increasingly more unhabitable than they were. Planning for habitation is just as feasible as planning for non-habitation, but we are unable to believe it. And, if the truth were told, most city planners are simply incompetent to achieve this end and unwilling to believe, as Jacobs has shown, that a study of yesterday's cities provides fine examples of how tomorrow's ought to be built.

It may be impossible to calculate, at this point in time, to what degree prophets and futurists will determine the main courses of other technology by means of their present persuasion. Putting economic motives aside (which may often be bent to popular demand), yesterday's futurists gave us one of our most frustrating and disordered aspects of today's technological cultures: our automobile and highway transportation system that doomed short line railroads, monorails and other forms of non-automotive surface transportation, at the cost of traffic jams, multiple accidents, bad smells, investments in cars and other unnecessary hazards, most particularly the diesel trailer-truck, that modern stegosaurus. Holland, France, Japan and various other contemporary cultures did not opt for this technological prediction, and therefore are not saddled today with investments in highways and automobiles to the degree that it is no longer feasible for them to develop alternate forms of surface transportation. We did; and, by virtue of accepting one particular prophecy, excluded other possibilities now open to other nations.[16]

More important at present than either cities or methods of transportation is the image of man himself as seen by futurists. There exists little unanimity on this matter, except, perhaps, that science-fiction writers tend to portray the man of tomorrow (really some men of today) as more inclined to express individuality and self-will than do serious, non-fiction futurists. But there are many exceptions, particularly the late Norbert

[16] I have most vivid memories of the New York World's Fair of 1939 where, at the extremely popular General Motors exhibit and at the less crowded Ford Pavilion, highly specific visions of our highway system of the future were shown. Not so remarkably, these prophecies were almost completely accurate, made as they were by the prophets who would design these very systems. The deck, in other words, was stacked, a fact which I did not know then! What was *not* clarified at these exhibits, of course, were the options we would have necessarily to discard in order to achieve these prophecies, or what expenses to the population they would, in various ways, exact.

Weiner, a thinker history may treat as one of few prophetic realists in a world that did not listen to his quiet humanism.

The vision of the man of tomorrow is probably more central to contemporary persuasion than most futurists are competent to imagine. We shall, of course, be the manner of men we are expected to be if we believe that we have no choice but to let nature (meaning other men) take its course. All too often, it seems to the writer, the direction of this vision is quite clear: Man is regarded as an object of manipulation whose way of living, values, choices and goals are determined solely *by what technology will let him be.* Built into this assumption is the notion that scientific and technical discovery will somehow create by themselves both limitations and imperatives to which man must adjust or perish.

Too rarely is the opposite view—the logical truth of the matter—voiced, even in tentative terms—namely, that science and technology are servants of man. And men may decide, as they have decided throughout history, how, when and where these servants may be asked to perform. Such a banal vision is, of course, uninteresting to the futurist, because it places man, that greasy, unpredictable and ignorant mammal, in the position of power where he would rather see whirling instruments with flashing lights or mechanistic and carefully programmed input and output systems in operation. Because man may soon invent reliable chemical or electric methods of thought control, however, he does *not* need to use them, except when and where and how he wants to. Nor must he, of necessity, control the sources of life just because he understands eventually the bio-chemical structure of his own germ plasm.

In our time, we *have been* wise enough to limit, if not delimit entirely, our militaristic impulses to use poison gas and bacteriological weapons in recent wars. And we have *not* thrown hydrogen bombs at one another, although a few sages (including Bertrand Russell) were unable to believe that we could not, simply because they thought that, in some mysterious way, technology *demanded* that we must. In fact, technology demands *nothing* of us, neither to be used nor neglected, unless one is convinced that man is an instinctual servant of his own devices, and that the human race is a collective incarnation of a Dr. Frankenstein whose will and power must eventually be vanquished by his monster.[17]

This is almost exactly the contemporary futurist's view of man: the victim of the environment he has created and will be in the last analysis, unable to control in the future. Obviously, such a view is nonsense. Perhaps

---

[17] This is the general argument, and hence the title, of Herbert J. Muller, *The Children of Frankenstein* (Bloomington, Indiana: Indiana University Press, 1970), a generally knowing and sympathetic study of our main contemporary problems. Despite its dramatic title, the volume is optimistic enough to be accepted by American readers. The historical bases of its contemporary analysis are particularly impressive.

man cannot control the results of his *past* technological enterprises; what is done is done, and he must suffer the consequences. But the very opposite of the futurist's view regarding the future obtains in truth. Man is also entirely competent and free *not* to utilize *any* aspect of technology present or technology future he chooses. In theory and fact, he can turn off the current and live without electricity if he finds it necessary. He can abandon his automobile and highways and learn again to walk. He is free to construct any sort of city he wishes from a modern version of Renaissance Florence to a Shanghai-on-the-Hudson, *if he wants to.*

This insight is as staggering to most people as it is ridiculous to the futurist. And most statements are indeed staggering when they present people with a flat proposition illustrating the tremendous measure of free will available for them to exercise. In their reactive spasm, they usually attempt every stratagem to escape from the exercise of so much freedom! This reaction is the topic of much contemporary social analysis, from the philosophy of Sartre to the psychology of Fromm. From the perspective of persuasion, it encourages people to flee from freedom and accept those well defined, formal definitions of the future that are suggested to them, often by fools.

Our choice has been spelled out clearly by London, at least insofar as the two major models of tomorrow's man are concerned: man the machine versus man the humanist. Man the machine is controlled by technology; and man the humanist relegates technology to the sub-category of a means to establish a decent life. London expresses faith in a compromise, but no such humane settlement may be open to us. "Tomorrow's myth of human nature," writes he, "probably must be that of the 'aware machine' because it is more acceptable in a scientific age where will can be controlled than is the dualistic notion of an inviolable core of self in man" [18] (the latter being the humanistic myth). London's synthesis is high-minded, but he misses the tendency towards simplism that futuristic persuasion induces. May a machine ever possibly be *aware*—meaning capable of an ethical, moral, creative and loving sense of being?

This question cannot presently be answered. And the distance between man as a machine and man as an "inviolable core of self" sub-divides into many stops on the scale between them. These two images, like most myths, tend to polarize, however, because the futurist keeps his eyes on gadgets, systems, models and techniques—not on the joy of life, the fulfillment of love or the invigoration of fellowship. As far as he is concerned, these latter factors may one day be simulated as results of the application of mechanisms to social fields. And, if they cannot be achieved the way London hopes (or only by means of "benevolent" psycho-chemical control), so

[18] See Perry London, *Behavior Control,* pp. 182–224.

much the worse for sentiment. But life will continue, and society will carry on. To the humanist, on the other hand, these factors are critical to both, and non-being or death are preferable to existence without them.

The ledger is not closed for the humanistic possibilities of tomorrow, however, because there is always a chance (apparent in history) that man will reject the images that the futurist holds out for him. The best protection against the persuasion of futurism is first, an open mind and second, the adventurous apprehension that the unexpected *will* indeed occur. No cultural optimist (or mechanist) himself, Heilbroner writes:

> As long as there is still visible in American society a continuing evidence of new thought and dissent, a self control with respect to the use of political power, and above all, a nagging awareness that all is not right, it would be arrogant and unjust to shrug away our future as a hopeless cause. There are, after all, great traditions of responsibility and social flexibility in America. In them there may yet reside the impetus to seize the historic possibilities before us, and to make those changes which may be necessary if the forces of history are not to sweep over us in an uncontrolled and destructive fashion. But it is useless to hope that this will happen so long as we persist in believing that in the future toward which we are blindly careering everything is 'possible' or that we can escape the ultimate responsibility of defining our limits of possibility for ourselves.[19]

Man the machine may neither rise to such heights nor assume such responsibilities. Human beings *may*, if they are allowed to believe they *can*.

Conclusion

Prophecy is an ancient art, but it has always functioned in similar ways in most cultures. It selects from the past various elements, provides for them an aura of myth, and, accordingly, persuades their acceptance in the future. Thus is prophecy a facilitating social agency of the moment and the status quo. Futurists, however, deal usually with large numbers of general propositions, many of which are lost or forgotten on their trips into destiny, and a selective process occurs in extenuating certain myths and terminating others. It is therefore difficult for the futurist to be excessively incorrect in his predictions, just as it is difficult for a fortune teller to give bad advice to a client, as long as both, by means of various clues, know something about the pasts of their subjects.

Scoffers or Deniers possess the same advantages as futurists, and history usually passes along more than a few dissenters to futurism as "minds in advance of their own times." At the moment of their activity, however, futurists enhance the vanity of their constituency; Deniers denigrate it, and, therefore, society usually prefers the former to the latter.

Futurists are myth makers, and their self-fulfilling prophecies are actu-

---

[19] Robert L. Heilbroner, *The Future as History* (New York: Harper and Bros., 1960), pp. 189–190.

ally social dramatizations of those myths, not unlike the device of the Ancient Greek theatre wherein a chorus, or old Tiresias, would herald or predict action to come. The major theme of futurism is today also much the same as it was in ancient times: the sin of *hubris*, construed presently as the punishments that result from man's pride and arrogance in interfering with and controlling forces of nature. Guilt resulting from this supposed sin runs deep and wide and renders the public vulnerable to assurances which diminishes it, usually one important function of the futurist.

Futurism is based upon myths that are common knowledge, especially myths that seem to distinguish contemporary society from other times and places. Like most myths, they are based upon morsels of truth, but also like most myths, this truth is expanded to fantastic proportions. The present knowledge explosion is one example. But others abound and, in our society, are invariably related to technology.

In the end, futurism tends to create an image of man subservient either to nature or the various instruments he has created to control nature. This image is mechanistic and self-defeating; the only palliative the prophet brings to it is the concept that the mind of man will itself adapt to the species' future, and values will change, so that the mechanization of human nature will eventually constitute a force for social good. The palliative—usually called "education for the future"—is obviously absurd on its face. The alternative to man the machine is the humanistic ideal of the human being who is not fearful of exercising self-will in the face of supposedly determinisitc forces. He recognizes that both science and technology are devices of his own creation. And he is competent to start, stop or direct them according to his conscience and wisdom—if he chooses.

Chapter 28

PERSUASION AND SURVIVAL

What we cannot think, we cannot think: we cannot therefore say what we cannot think.

Ludwig Wittgenstein

Futurism as persuasion, especially when it centers upon technology, sustains and generates myths that tend to limit the exercise of free will and constrict the choices that men might make in determining the directions of their own futures.

This notion, central to the previous chapter, is by no means unanimously accepted by social and behavioral scientists or students of philosophy. It is closely associated with the pessimistic ideas of a few of them. It is denied by optimists who construe technology as a mere culture trait that opens new options for us to *become* new types of men—not necessarily just to do new things, the obvious result of all inventions. Nor is there a shortage of optimists. Most technological specialists—and others—are in love with their specialties, and are convinced that *its* specific liberation will provide the setting for a better world. Specialists in the arts and skills of managing instruments of mass communication are usually perfect—but somewhat grotesque—examples of this genre, along with educational technologists, behavioral psychologists and others. The famous "common man" is also an optimist, but one of a different sort, basing his faith in the psychologically plural possibilities of the future. He is like Thornton Wilder's Mr. Antrobus, convinced that human beings have, and will always, manage to progress to the next higher rung of culture's ladder by the "skin of their teeth."

If such persuasion as discussed in Chapter 27 does indeed constrict free will (this author's contention), *must all persuasion?*

At this point, common wisdom might, in spite of a lack of consistency and logic, reverse itself sharply, especially if the presently pejorative term "propaganda" were substituted for "persuasion." General agreement would probably obtain in the affirmative, possibly a wise response—but for the wrong reasons. One is the widespread assumption that all persuasion works, or accomplishes something. We have seen that much of it does not. Another is the general confusion about the effects of persuasion upon dispositions, and the usually misunderstood differentiation of dispositions into constellations of beliefs, attitudes and opinions. A third is that many sorts of simplistic and incorrect conclusions are frequently drawn by intelligent people regarding the relations between dispositions and actions, and vice-versa, a complicated matter that we have considered in some detail. Fourth, it is beyond the comprehension of many that people may be persuaded to give up certain restrictions upon their freedom in order to seek out further independence of thought and behavior. Our study of persuasion has shown that, at times, this is the case.

If the pages that precede this one illustrate one point, it is, (hopefully) that naïve, dichotomous thinking which places "persuasion" on one side of a psychological axis and "free will" on another is hopelessly irrelevant to what history shows and contemporary analysis demonstrates. Such interpretations of the role of persuasion in culture merely increase the vulnerability of individuals who live in that culture to the kind of manipulation that indeed *does* limit free choice, and is itself an instrument of persuasion spread as myth. When it is advanced (even in such negative and positive propositions as "propaganda" versus "the right to think for yourself"), the position is indicative of a paucity of sophistication in the sayer. Even at a superficial level, the statement is ridiculous. In its deeper logical and psychological contexts, it may be dangerous—and sometimes tragic. Yet, it is frequently heard as a part of our common wisdom—on political platforms, at universities and in day-to-day discourse.

One gains free will, free thought and freedom of behavior and expression only superficially from the absence of restraints. And the absence of the restraint of persuasions is one of the most puny of all liberties on the roster of our freedoms. At any rate, it is merely *one* of the "freedoms from," never essential or fundamentally germane to how liberty is *exercised* by society. The *use* of freedom depends upon the constituent elements of culture that are available, at a given time, for its inventive *use*. This is "freedom for," and upon its nature depends most critically how, when or where a person may exercise free will. To free a moron to speculate upon the various laws of thermodynamics is as foolish as thrusting pornographic photographs into the hands of a eunuch. Prior restraints are exercised against both, limiting their freedom. In the first case, the moron cannot be free to apply theoretical principles to nature. And, in the second, the eunuch is not competent to drool properly over the lascivious. Neither is able, nor will ever be equipped to exercise his free will. These liberties granted both are therefore rhetorical.

Much discussion about free will today, involving persuasion, manipulation and (God save the word) propaganda, concerns just such constricted classes of freedom. Having been freed of unfashionable cultural guidelines, myths, arbitrary morals, unscientific ethics, arbitrary manners, unrealistic goals and other societal persuasion by our apostles of progress, we have been left free merely to wander in a fog. We have been liberated from the conceits of our past but have been given no new directives in their place for the future. And even granting that we may somehow formulate these directives for ourselves, we have not been properly trained to follow them. In other words, we are like the passengers on a ship that is out of control; but this does not make any difference, simply because the vessel is not really headed anywhere, anyway.

The author believes that *this* is *the* essential contemporary sickness. Various symptoms of alienation, anomie and their variations are but different psychological perspectives of the same problem. So are their subproblems that reach intimate places in our daily lives, discussed in the past chapters: disaffected young people, sexual confusions, infelicitous drug use, campus riots, gratuitous urban violence, minority group frustrations, female identity confusion and the entire roster of mysteries that have been treated, perhaps at times, all too ruthlessly in this book. They are all manifestations of our liberation from obsolete bondages and the resultant exercise, therefore, of free will: the widest exercise of personal freedom given any people in history for the longest times of their lives—a veritable societal glut of free will—in the patent absence of either sufficient skills or opportunities to exercise that freedom to construct for each of us a good life in a livable culture.

At the same time, however, we have observed other forces at work as well. Man may no more live in in the absence of the persuasion of his myths than without air and water. What has occurred today, it seems, is that idealistic and formless libertarian myths have replaced former, less idealistic but specific mythic restraints. A modern and mystical cult of personal and individual transcendental freedom is, therefore, rapidly taking the place of the latter myths. Viewed from older perspectives, it constitutes neither more or less than institutionalized, culturally sanctioned apathy: the moron reading Einstein; the eunuch looking at dirty pictures—or, more concretely, the mindless adulation of youth, psychedelic mystiques, bogus "oriental" detachment, naïve revolutionary dreams and meaningless protests and riots in the name of peace and progress. All of these culture traits (or societal problems) relate to the new persuasion *that free will is, by itself, an end in life and not a means to something else.*

This phenomenon has not risen entirely in negative contexts. It shows, surprisingly, compatibility in many ways with current trends in psychology, industry and education, where we find content sacrificed to method and substantive objectives sacrificed to pseudo-social graces like the "arts" of communicating and loving. When a scientific logos has "gone loco," in the words of Braden, pursuing, as it does today, the complex construction of behavioral learning systems and human engineering schemes that literally lead nowhere but back one's own personal freedom—to divine, for instance, in the thinking of one such engineer, a "universal consciousness"—we are standing at the brink of rationalized chaos. Human systems engineering (even the kind that supposedly "works"), from a philosophical view, manifests all of the clinical symptoms of psychosis. And when the precise instrumentation of science is employed to this endless end, one detects the smell of *paranoid* psychosis. The equivalent tendency in technology, the perfection of instruments to conquer nature simply because one is *free* to conquer it (Everest is *there!*), describes a slightly more benign social schizophrenia. And, and when one recognizes that the most astute minds of our time are engaged in perfecting tautologies like these, and that the persuasive drift of culture now exalts apostles of free will as an end rather than as a means at the highest levels of sanctioned intellectual endeavor—and that such creatures are "at large," as Braden notes[1]—one wonders whether he has wasted his money buying life insurance.

On the personal level, the grand tautology is apparent everywhere, and, as Ruesch notes,[2] continually and necessarily drawn to the attention of psychiatry. Whenever culture may offer the individual *no more* than assurance that he is free, and that he may, if he wishes, pursue with immense and idiotic glee patently meaningless illusions of success, popularity, longevity, technological supremacy and immunity from personal death, the victim naturally produces wild symptoms of insecurity, and sometimes, when exogenic forces have shattered particularly significant individual illusions, extremely dangerous ones. Ruesch recognizes that all the humane therapist may accomplish in such instances is to confirm the basic persuasion of myth in the hopes of reducing subjective insecurity, or to attempt to help the individual (now a patient) "to relinquish the idea of security altogether . . . , (to recognize) that he has reached bottom . . . , and learn to enjoy life as it is." [3]

The therapist must, unhappily, accept man and culture as they are. Ruesch's solution to this existential problem on the therapeutic level satisfies adequately the obligations of a physician towards his patient. He offers a particularly significant set of options, because they delimit the possibilities for a solution of the same problem in a social context with simplicity and clarity: we must either believe the anchorless mythos of culture and accept our dose of persuasion happily, or stop playing the game (if we know it is a

[1] See William Braden, *The Age of Aquarius*, pp. 188–89.

[2] Jurgen Ruesch, *Therapeutic Communication*, pp. 111–112.

[3] *Ibid.*, p. 112.

game) and live each day as if it were the only one we have. Of the two solutions, the second seems preferable for men and women of sensitivity.

Neither solution is acceptable to the social critic whose main concern at present is not personal survival but reasons why culture today displays the same sort of symptoms that mental patients do.

One contributing factor is the myth of science as the only real arbiter of truth, and that depends upon a construction of the scientific method which pretends, in the words of P. B. Medawar, "that your mind is a virgin receptacle, an empty vessel, for information which floods into it from the external world for no reason which you yourself have revealed." Medawar notes that science in fact requires no such assumption, merely science in myth and in fantasy.[4] Another factor derives from myth that technology must somehow—and blindly—"handle" every existential dysfunction man knows, including the problem of death. (Thanatology is one of our newest "sciences.") Another is the grand cultural fallacy that schooling is the same as education, and that most, if not all, dysfunctions (moral problems, in great part) may be cured by granting diplomas and degrees to all who want them and by coaxing better communication between men. Many pages might be filled with numerous other mighty myths of our time which we were easily persuaded to believe, because our egos have been built upon them.

The most devilish and deadly aspect of culture today, in the author's opinion (and the myth upon which our culture pivots) is the cold lie that every problem must have a solution. Here is cultural persuasion that, on the wings of science, technology and education has been bred into the young, and, while it offers vigor to the life-style of many of our people for short periods of time, must invariably lead one to alienation from the realities of life. An individual discovers wisdom (and avoids alienation) in the achievement of the profound feeling and certain knowledge that everything is *not* possible, that the ideal of a happy ending is a delusion (simply because nothing ends except with death) and that there is, perhaps, no cure for the common cold.

The main error of most of the great determinisms of history has been their gnostic path of tracing abuses in society to self-evident correctable über-causes (or dynamics) which, if managed wisely, might expunge evil, eliminate poverty, sickness and crime and, given time and good weather, eventually perfect the cultural order. Should we elect today to follow any of these courses, as many urge, we shall follow a path to oblivion, just as surely as other civilizations, in search of the philosopher's stone, have likewise been benumbed by the worship of their imaginary virtues and fallen into utter disaster. Whatever else He may be, God is surely an ironist, because invariably, when man appears about to emerge into a golden age of perfection, he is rewarded for his accomplishments by a long period of abject misery and cultural stasis.

---

[4] Quoted in Rudolph Arnheim, *Visual Thinking* (Berkeley and Los Angeles: University of California Press, 1969), pp. 162–163.

The Reformation provided our society the most viable myths that Western man has so far achieved. In cultural terms, it respected as given the imperfection of the human mechanism and mortal mind and asked from both measures of social control and restraint in aspiration and action, in order that the greatest quantum of bliss might be achieved in an after-life. Men were thereby freed to behave on earth like men, to sin if properly contrite, to achieve happiness if possible, but invariably on a contingent basis and at the whim of God. They were also accountable, at the summing up, for the total record of their various uses of life.

Progress destroyed this myth and naturally destroyed the God of the Reformation at the same time. As noted previously, today we escaped into freedom in order to pursue perfection by means of science, technology, education and political democracy, and to construct countless determinisms that still promise perfection as the by-product of the application of human intelligence to solving (when all is said and done) the not too complicated dysfunctions of our culture. How great is our will to believe that the same intelligence that is able to solve the riddles of nucleic acids and laser lights is obviously competent to redefine seven deadly sins into workable, objective, "social projects" and to assign efficient "task forces" to their analysis, description and, of course, solution! Many monuments to this illusion abound, and some of them have been discussed at length in this book.

The ultimate persuasive myth, therefore, is that man—given the exercise of free will—is not only competent, but *inexorably bound*, to control his own ontological universe and subsequently manage his own destiny. Here we have not only a myth, but an illusion. Not only an illusion, but a delusion. Not only a delusion, but also a weapon of destruction, as powerful as any that technology has produced. Here is the fount of human false pride, arrogance, stupidity, ethnocentricism and tunnel vision. Here is insanity, springing from premises that cannot be uncovered in the study of history or from any known science or art. And yet it is pursued avidly by the man in Le Bon's "crowd," the professor, the writer and the foundation pundit, because its appeal is universal. This pursuit has accordingly led to the devaluation of much that history, science and art have shown they *cannot* accomplish, as encodified in the *moral* heritage of our culture that contemporary life is rapidly tearing to shreds.

Conclusion

Thus, the conclusion to this inquiry: Persuasion may destroy us, so long as we continue to believe we are not persuasible. Propaganda will quench our chances for survival, as long as we believe what it tells us about our powers of survival. The major persuasive threat facing us is not the manipulation of the Devil, be he a Communist, Socialist, Fascist or Capitalist Devil—or just plain old Lucifer. The Devil, the author believes (after consultation), is a gentleman who allows his opponents to fight their battles with him in open combat. Evil is conquerable when its source is obvious. When it is generated by those who believe they serve an angelic purpose, however, few defenses exist against it.

That persuasion against which we must resist is, therefore, the very persuasion we generate in ourselves, not that we see on television or billboards: the persuasion of vanity that would recreate all mankind in our own images of perfection. Sad to state, concentration camps, nuclear bombs and endless warfare are but a few *recent* sacrifices offered by man attempting to master his own grand destiny. Add to them every increasingly destructive social catastrophe in the contemporary textbook, and include also all of those, inevitably and progressively worse and worse, that we shall learn of tomorrow.

Nor does a simple solution lie at hand to the problems we have inflicted upon ourselves in this era of heroic self-deception. Society is *not* a patient on the psychiatrist's couch, and self-insight cannot occur in those who do not hear their own heartbeats or feel themselves breathe.

If we are to survive, we shall survive as we came into the world—alone. There is no collective solution to the agglomerative powers of mythic persuasion. Resistance and insight are individual matters, neither acceptably studied in school as we know them nor amenable to the razzle-dazzle thrust of mass communications. In time—and as individuals—some of us may learn to believe in our hearts that everything cannot be solved, that the measure of a good life is achieved by ongoing reference to ideals and moral perfection, and that, in the long run, as Keynes said, we are, indeed, all dead.

What *is* possible for us and our culture, however, is to accept the existential viability of the moment and hope (or pray) for a *possible* tomorrow: not necessarily better, cleaner or richer than today, but, at least, fit to live in no matter how it will have changed. Taken a day at a time, and bereft of grand myths for the transmorphology of men into gods, that future is possible. All other alternatives seem to lead to what we know we are now competent to achieve expertly: total, or near-total, destruction. And nothing will stop us, if we have, as many believe, already chosen from among our alternatives.

We shall also have to make peace with all of our myths and accept, as cultural persuasion (but not as truth), the numberless conceits upon which we hang our self-images today. For, if there is a central art to understanding persuasion in theory and practice, it is a constant awareness that, in the profundities of the wise, the powerful and the mighty, one discovers, usually, *less* than meets the eye; that man is forever insulated from reality, at various distances and according to his needs, by his myths, dreams and illusions. Understanding persuasion requires the ruthless twist of Occam's razor, even into one's self, until one slices to the moral fundaments of the world, and eventually achieves a glimpse of the bony, feeble structure of culture—society and self out of costume, its participants bereft, at last, of their inhumane vanity.

SELECTED BIBLIOGRAPHY

The following books have been selected from those noted in this volume and from others of more than passing relevance to the subject of persuasion. An attempt has been made below to cover the topic in its many manifestations from the best and clearest sources currently available; many excellent and interesting books are therefore *not* listed. But the author has attempted to be mindful of the student reader's needs (especially) to be spared the frustrations of duplications of data, viewpoints, theories and repeated case studies. A few citations have been selected from somewhat dated materials (most of them written between World Wars I and II) that are listed and annotated in Laswell, *et al.*, *Propaganda and Promotional Activities*, as well as a small number of classics like Le Bon's *The Crowd* and Machiavelli's *The Prince*. In the interest of brevity, however, familiar classical documents on persuasion that are freely available in paperback (Aristotle, Plato, Cicero and Elizabethan dramatists, for instance) are not included but are cited in footnotes where they appear in the text.

Albig, William, *Modern Public Opinion*. New York: McGraw-Hill, 1956.
Allport, Gordon, *Becoming*. New Haven: Yale University Press, 1955.
Amscombe, G. E. M., *Intention*. Oxford: Basil Blackwell, 1958.
Arendt, Hannah, *Eichmann in Jerusalem*. New York: Viking, 1963.
———, *The Human Condition*. New York: Doubleday, 1959.

Arnheim, Rudolph, *Visual Thinking*. Berkeley and Los Angeles: University of California Press, 1969.

Barrett, William, *Irrational Man*. New York: Doubleday, 1958.

Berelson, Bernard, *Content Analysis in Communication Research*. Glencoe, Ill.: Free Press, 1952.

———, and Gary Steiner, *Human Behavior*. New York: Harcourt, Brace and World, 1964.

———, and Morris Janowitz (eds.), *Reader in Public Opinion and Communication*,. Second edition. New York: Free Press, 1966.

Berle, Adolph A., *Power*. New York: Harcourt, Brace and World, 1969.

Berlo, David K., *The Process of Communication*. New York: Holt, Rinehart and Winston, 1961.

Boorstein, Daniel J., *The Image*. New York: Harpers, 1961.

Braden, William, *The Age of Aquarius*. Chicago: Quadrangle Books, 1970.

Brinton, Crane, *A History of Western Morals*. New York: Harcourt, Brace, 1959.

Brown, Claude, *Manchild in the Promised Land*. New York: New American Library, 1966.

Brown, J. A. C., *The Techniques of Persuasion*. Baltimore: Penguin Books, 1963.

Burke, Kenneth, *Language as Symbolic Action*. Berkeley and Los Angeles: University of California Press, 1966.

Burlingame, Roger, *The American Conscience*. New York: Alfred A. Knopf, 1957.

Cantril, Hadley, *The Psychology of Social Movements*. New York: John Wiley, 1941.

Cassirer, Ernst, *The Myth of the State*. New York: Doubleday, 1955.

Casty, Allan (ed.), *Mass Media and Mass Man*. New York: Holt, Rinehart and Winston, 1968.

Chandos, John (ed.), *To Deprave and Corrupt*. London: Association Press, 1962.

Chafee, Zechariah, *Free Speech in the United States*. Cambridge: Harvard University Press, 1948.

———, *Government and Mass Communications*. Chicago: University of Chicago Press, 1947.

Christenson, Reo M. and Robert O. McWilliams (eds.), *Voices of the People*, First edition. New York: McGraw-Hill, 1962.

Choukas, Michael, *Propaganda Comes of Age*. Washington, D.C.: Public Affairs Press, 1965.

Cleaver, Eldridge, *Soul on Ice*. New York: Dell, 1970.

Clews, John C., *Communist Propaganda Techniques*. New York: Frederick A. Prager, 1964.

Cooley, Charles Horton, *Human Nature and the Social Order*. New York: Scribners, 1902.

Craik, Kenneth, *The Nature of Explanation*. Cambridge: University Press, 1967.

Cremin, Lawrence, *The Genius of American Education*. Pittsburgh: University of Pittsburgh Press, 1965.

Cressy, Donald R. and David A. Ward (eds.), *Delinquency, Crime, and Social Process*. New York: Harper and Row, 1969.

Daugherty, William E. and Morris Janowitz (eds.), *A Psychological Warfare Casebook*. Baltimore: Johns Hopkins Press, 1958.

Delgado, M. R. José, *Physical Control of the Mind*. New York: Harper and Row, 1969.

De Rougement, Dennis, *Love Declared*. New York: Pantheon Books, 1963.

Dingwell, Eric John, *The American Woman*. New York: New American Library, 1958.

Dorfles, Gillo, *Kitsch, The World of Bad Taste*. New York: Simon and Schuster, 1968.

Egner, Robert E. and Lester E. Denonn, *The Basic Writings of Bertrand Russell*. New York: Simon and Schuster, 1961.

Ellul, Jacques, *Propaganda*. New York: Alfred A. Knopf, 1965.
———, *The Technological Society*. New York: Alfred A. Knopf, 1965.
Emery, Edwin and Henry Ladd Smith, *The Press and America*. New York: Prentice-Hall, 1954.
Emery, Walter B., *National and International Systems of Broadcasting*. East Lansing: Michigan State University Press, 1969.
Erikson, Erik H., *Youth and Crisis*. New York: Norton, 1968.
Ernst, Morris L. and Alan U. Schwartz, *Censorship*. New York: Macmillan, 1964.
Ferkiss, Victor C., *Technological Man*. New York: George Braziller, 1969.
Festinger, Leon, *A Theory of Cognitive Dissonance*. Evanston, Ill.: Row, Peterson, 1957.
Fischer, Heinz-Dietrich and John Merrill (eds.), *International Communication*. New York: Hastings House, 1970.
Flavell, John H., *The Developmental Psychology of Jean Piaget*. Princeton: D. Van Nostrand, 1963.
Frazier, E. Franklin, *Black Bourgeoise*. Glencoe, Ill.: Free Press, 1957.
Freud, Sigmund, *Civilization and Its Discontents*. New York: Doubleday, n.d.
———, *The Future of An Illusion*. New York: Doubleday, 1957.
———, *Group Psychology and the Analysis of the Ego*. New York: Bantam Books, 1965.
Friedan, Betty, *The Feminine Mystique*. New York: Norton, 1963.
Friedenberg, Edgar Z., *Coming of Age in America*. New York: Random House, 1965.
Fromm, Eric, *Escape From Freedom*. New York: Avon Books, 1965.
———, *The Sane Society*. New York: Rinehart, 1955.
Galbraith, J. K., *The New Industrial State*. Boston: Houghton-Mifflin, 1967.
Ginsberg, Herbert and Sylvia Opper, *Piaget's Theory of Intellectual Development*. Englewood Cliffs, N.J.: Prentiss-Hall, 1969.
Goffman, Erving, *The Presentation of Self in Everyday Life*. New York: Doubleday, 1959.
———, *Stigma*. Englewood Cliffs, N.J.: Prentice-Hall, 1963.
Gordon, George N., *The Languages of Communication*. New York: Hastings House, 1969.
———, Irving A. Falk and William Hodapp, *The Idea Invaders*, New York: Hastings House, 1963.
Gottschalk, Louis. *Understanding History*. New York: Alfred A. Knopf, 1964.
Grier, William H. and Price M. Cobbs, *Black Rage*. New York: Basic Books, 1968.
Haley, Alex, *The Autobiography of Malcolm X*. New York: Grove, 1965.
Hall, Edward T., *The Hidden Dimension*. New York: Doubleday, 1969.
———, *The Silent Language*. Greenwich, Conn.: Fawcett Publications, 1959.
Heilbroner, Robert L., *The Future of History*. New York: Harpers, 1960.
———, *The Worldly Philosophers*. New York: Time Inc., 1961.
Hitler, Adolf, *Mein Kampf*. Boston: Houghton-Mifflin, 1933.
Hovland, Carl, *et al.*, *Communication and Persuasion*. New Haven: Yale University Press, 1953.
———, *Personality and Persuasibility*. New Haven: Yale University Press, 1959.
Huizinga, Johan, *Homo Ludens, A Study of the Play Element in Culture*. Boston: Beacon, 1955.
Hunter, Edward, *Brainwashing*. New York: Pyramid Books, 1958.
Inkeles, Alex, *Public Opinion in Soviet Russia*. Cambridge: Harvard University Press, 1958.
Huxley, Aldous, *Brave New World Revisited*. New York: Harpers, 1958.
Jacobs, Jane, *The Economy of Cities*. New York: Random House, 1969.
Jacobs, Norman (ed.), *Culture for the Millions?* Princeton, N.J.: D. Van Nostrand, 1961.

Jencks, Christopher and David Riesman, *The Academic Revolution.* New York: Doubleday, 1968.

Kahler, Erich, *Man the Measure.* New York: George Braziller, 1956.

Kaplan, Michael (ed.), *Essential Works of Pavlov.* New York: Bantam Books, 1966.

Katz, Daniel, *et al.* (ed.), *Public Opinion and Propaganda.* New York: Dryden, 1954.

Kerlinger, Fred, *Foundations of Behavioral Research.* New York: Holt, Rinehart and Winston, 1966.

Koester, Arthur, *The Ghost in the Machine.* New York: Macmillan, 1967.

Kiesler, Charles A., Barry E. Collins and Norman Miller, *Attitude Change.* New York: John Wiley, 1969.

Kilpatrick, James J., *The Smut Peddlers.* New York: Doubleday, 1960.

Kronhausen, Eberhard and Phyllis, *Pornography and the Law.* New York: Ballantine Books, 1959.

Krutch, Joseph W., *Human Nature and the Human Condition.* New York: Random House, 1959.

Laing, R. D., *The Divided Self.* New York: Pantheon Books, 1960.

———, *Self and Others.* New York: Pantheon Books, 1969.

Lang, Curt and Gladys, *Collective Dynamics.* New York: Thomas Y. Crowell, 1961.

———, *Politics and Television.* Chicago: Quadrangle Books, 1968.

Langer, Susanne K., *Mind: An Essay on Human Feeling,* Volume 1. Baltimore: Johns Hopkins Press, 1967.

———, *Philosophy in a New Key.* New York: New American Library, 1946.

La Piere, Richard, *The Freudian Ethic.* New York: Duell, Sloan and Pearce, 1959.

Larsen, Otto, N. (ed.), *Violence and the Mass Media.* New York: Harper and Row, 1968.

Laswell, Harold, *Propaganda and Promotional Activities.* Chicago: University of Chicago Press, 1969.

———, *Psychopathology and Politics.* Chicago: University of Chicago Press, 1930.

Le Bon, Gustave, *The Crowd.* New York: Viking, 1960.

Lee, John (ed.), *Diplomatic Persuaders.* New York: John Wiley, 1968.

Leopold, Nathan, *Life Plus 99 Years.* New York: Popular Library, 1958.

Lévi-Strauss, Claude, *Structural Anthropology.* New York: Doubleday, 1967.

Lippmann, Walter, *Public Opinion.* New York: Penguin Books, 1946.

London, Perry, *Behavior Control.* New York: Harpers, 1969.

Lerner, Max, *America as a Civilization.* New York: Simon and Schuster, 1957.

Lindner, Robert, *Must You Conform?* New York: Rinehart, 1956.

Lynes, Russell, *The Tastemakers.* New York: Harpers, 1955.

Machiavelli, Niccolo, *The Prince.* New York: New American Library, 1961.

MacNeil, Robert, *The People Machine.* New York: Harper and Row, 1968.

Marcus, Steven, *The Other Victorians.* New York: Basic Books, 1966.

Marcuse, Herbert, *One Dimensional Man.* Boston: Beacon, 1964.

Matson, Floyd W. and Ashley Montagu, *The Human Dialogue.* New York: Free Press, 1967.

May, Rollo, *Love and Death.* New York: Norton, 1969.

Mayer, Martin, *The Lawyers.* New York: Dell, 1967.

———, *Madison Avenue, USA.* New York: Harpers, 1958.

McGuiness, Joe, *The Selling of a President.* New York: Trident, 1969.

McLuhan, Marshall, *Understanding Media.* New York: McGraw-Hill, 1964.

Mead, Margaret, *Culture and Commitment.* New York: Doubleday, 1970.

Medawar, P. B., *The Future of Man.* New York: New American Library, 1957.

Meerloo, Joost, *The Rape of the Mind.* New York: World Publishing, 1956.

Mehrabian, Albert, *An Analysis of Personality Theories.* Englewood Cliffs, N.J.: Prentice-Hall, 1968.

Menninger, Carl, *The Crime of Punishment*. New York: Viking, 1966.
Merton, Robert, *Mass Persuasion*. New York: Harpers, 1946.
———, *Social Theory and Social Structure*, Enlarged edition. New York: Free Press, 1968.
Millet, Kate, *Sexual Politics*. New York: Doubleday, 1970.
Mills, C. Wright (ed.), *Images of Man*. New York: George Braziller, 1960.
———, *The Power Elite*. New York: Oxford, 1956.
Myrdal, Gunnar, *An American Dilemma*. New York: Harpers, 1944.
Ogden, C. K. and I. A. Richards, *The Meaning of Meaning*. New York: Harcourt, Brace, 1953.
Olson, Philip, *America as a Mass Society*. Glencoe, Ill.: Free Press, 1963.
Ortega y Gasset, José, *The Revolt of the Masses*. New York: Norton, 1932.
Packard, Vance, *The Hidden Persuaders*. New York: David McKay, 1957.
Parrington, Vernon L., *Main Currents in American Thought*. New York: Harcourt, Brace, 1930.
Piaget, Jean and Barbel Inhelder, *The Psychology of the Child*. New York: Basic Books, 1969.
Pierce, J. R., *Symbols, Signals and Noise*. New York: Harper and Row, 1961.
Plog, Stanley and Robert B. Edgarton (eds.), *Changing Perspectives in Mental Illness*. New York: Holt, Rinehart and Winston, 1969.
Qualter, Terence H., *Propaganda and Psychological Warfare*. New York: Random House, 1962.
Rapoport, Anatol, *Strategy and Conscience*. New York: Harper and Row, 1964.
Rembar, Charles, *The End of Obscenity*. New York: Random House, 1968.
Richards, I. A., *Practical Criticism*. New York: Harcourt Brace, 1954.
———, *Principles of Literary Criticism*. New York: Harcourt, Brace, 1947.
Robinson, Paul A., *The Freudian Left*. New York: Harper and Row, 1969.
Rogers, Lindsay, *The Pollsters*. New York: Alfred A. Knopf, 1949.
Rossiter, Clinton and James Lare (eds.), *The Essential Lippmann*. New York: Random House, 1963.
Ruesch, Jurgen, *Therapeutic Communication*. New York: Norton, 1961.
Sargant, William, *Battle for the Mind*. New York: Doubleday, 1957.
Schwebel, Milton, *Who Can Be Educated?* New York: Grove, 1938.
Shibutani, Tamotsu, *Improvised News*. New York: Bobbs-Merrill, 1966.
Siepmann, Charles A., *Radio, Television and Society*. New York: Oxford, 1950.
Skinner, B. F., *Science and Human Behavior*. New York: Macmillan, 1953.
Small, William, *To Kill a Messenger*. New York: Hastings House, 1970.
Smith, Alfred G. (ed.), *Communication and Culture*. New York: Holt, Rinehart and Winston, 1966.
Smith, M. Brewster, *Social Psychology and Human Values*. Chicago: Aldine, 1969.
———, Jerome S. Bruner and Robert W. White, *Opinions and Personality*. New York: John Wiley, 1956.
Sopkin, Charles, *Seven Glorious Days, Seven Fun Filled Nights*. New York: Simon and Schuster, 1968.
Staats, Arthur W., *Learning, Language and Cognition*. New York: Holt, Rinehart and Winston, 1968.
Stalin, Josif V., *Leninism*. New York: International Publishers, 1928.
Stein, M. R., J. Vidich and D. M. White, *Identity and Anxiety*. Glencoe, Ill.: Free Press, 1960.
Steiner, George, *Language and Silence*. New York: Atheneum, 1967.
Stephenson, William, *The Play Theory of Mass Communications*. Chicago: University of Chicago Press, 1967.
Storr, Anthony, *Human Aggression*. New York: Atheneum, 1968.

Swartz, Robert J. (ed.), *Perceiving, Sensing and Knowing.* New York: Doubleday, 1965.

Tarde, Gabriel, *On Communication and Social Influence.* Chicago: University of Chicago Press, 1969.

Tiger, Lionel, *Men in Groups.* New York: Random House, 1969.

Tillich, Paul, *The Courage To Be.* New Haven: Yale University Press, 1952.

Toch, Hans, *Violent Men.* Chicago: Aldine, 1969.

Toole, K. Ross, *An Angry Man Talks Up to Youth.* New York: Award Books, 1970.

Toffler, Alvin, *Future Shock.* New York: Random House, 1970.

Van Den Haag, Ernst, *Passion and Social Constraint.* New York: Stein and Day, 1963.

Vetter, Harold, *Language, Behavior and Psychopathology.* Chicago: Rand McNally, 1970.

Viereck, Peter, *Metapolitics.* New York: Capricorn Books, 1961.

Von Bertalanfy, Ludwig, *General Systems Theory.* New York: George Braziller, 1968.

Watzlawick, Paul, Janet H. Beavin and Don D. Jackson, *Pragmatics of Human Communication.* New York: Norton, 1967.

Warnock, G. S., *English Philosophy Since 1900.* London: Oxford University Press, 1958.

Whale, John. *The Half Shut Eye.* New York: Macmillan-St. Martin's, 1969.

Wiener, Norbert. *Cybernetics.* Cambridge: The MIT Press, 1965.

Whitehead, A. N., *The Aims of Education.* New York: New American Library, 1949.

———, *Science and the Modern World.* New York: New American Library, 1953.

———, *Symbolism.* New York: Macmillan, 1958.

Widmer, Kingsley and Eleanor, *Literary Censorship.* San Francisco: Wadsworth, 1961.

White, David Manning and Richard Averson (eds.), *Sight, Sound and Society.* Boston: Beacon, 1968.

Zimbardo, Philip and Ebbe B. Ebbesen, *Influencing Attitudes and Changing Behavior.* Reading, Mass.: Addison-Wesley, 1969.

INDEX